AMERICAN

BUSINESS

and

ITS

ENVIRONMENT

SCOTT D. WALTON

College of Business Administration
University of Washington

AMERICAN
BUSINESS
and
ITS
ENVIRONMENT

THE MACMILLAN COMPANY, New York   COLLIER-MACMILLAN LIMITED, London

First Printing

Library of Congress catalog card number:
66-14694

THE MACMILLAN COMPANY, NEW YORK
COLLIER-MACMILLAN CANADA, LTD.,
TORONTO, ONTARIO

Printed in the United States of America

To **Kathleen** and
Nan
Sally
David
Randy
Susan

Preface

Recent investigations of the education of American businessmen have stressed the importance of the market and nonmarket environment of the business enterprise.[1] As a result of these investigations many schools have laid greater stress upon students' understanding of the surroundings of the business firm, including the requirement that students take business environment courses. Unfortunately, few textbooks have been available for instructors in those courses. This book is intended to pro-

[1] Robert A. Gordon and James E. Howell, *Higher Education for Business* (New York: Columbia University Press, 1959), pp. 64–66.

Frank C. Pierson *et al.*, *The Education of American Businessmen* (New York: McGraw-Hill Book Company, Inc., 1959), pp. 89–93.

vide an integrated way of looking at the external influences on business, to set forth some facts concerning those surroundings, and to examine the ways in which the environment has influenced business decisions and the results of business operations. Also, an examination is made of the ways in which businessmen have, and should, come to terms with their environment.

To present an integrated treatment of business and its environment, a number of steps are taken. A fundamental theory of business behavior is set forth, emphasizing the influence of environment upon decisions and results of business operations. Based on that theory, a model of the environment of a firm is established, giving structure to the book. In this structure, the economic, social, and political environments of a typical business firm are given positions of greatest importance.

Little emphasis is given to the physical, scientific, and technological environments. These surroundings are quite specific to a firm and, as a result, difficult to generalize about. Too, business has gained great conquests over the physical world—it is the economic, social, and political environments that presently pose the greater problems. To fill in the basic structure, the literature of the social and behavioral sciences has been drawn upon. In addition, business periodicals and other journals containing data on business and its environment have been investigated. From this vast quantity of data, certain concepts and conclusions have been selected for incorporation into the text. To illustrate key concepts and findings, some articles or excerpts from books have been appended to most chapters as readings. The conclusions contained in these readings are not necessarily to be regarded as scientific truths but rather as important points of view, since divergent points of view must be recognized and understood when they are held by influential individuals and groups.

A number of pitfalls inevitably confront those who attempt to synthesize the insights of workers in a number of specialized scholarly fields. Will Durant, in his first preface to the many-volumed *The Story of Civilization,* wrote: "The probability of error increases with the scope of the undertaking and any man who sells his soul to synthesis will be a tragic target for myriad merry darts of specialist critique." Some of my colleagues in the College of Business Administration at the University of Washington have made merry with my manuscript, but also have been of assistance in ridding it of some fundamental errors. Especially helpful have been Professors Edward J. Chambers, Leonard Goldberg, Dwight E. Robinson, and Bayard O. Wheeler, who read various portions of the original draft and made valuable suggestions for its improvement. Acknowledgment is also due Dean Richard W. Lindholm of the University of Oregon's School of Business Administration for the role he played in the introduction of business environment as an undergraduate course at that school and for the encouragement given the author to write a textbook for such courses. The assistance of those whose writings were especially valuable in putting flesh on the bare bones of the skeleton is acknowledged elsewhere, and—as is customary and proper —upon the author must fall the blame for all errors that may still be discovered in this work.

S. D. W.
Seattle, Washington

Contents

PART **I**   **Business and Its Economic Environment**   1

1. AMERICAN BUSINESS AND ITS ENVIRONMENT   3
Views of Business Behavior / The Nature of American
Business / The Nature of the Environment of Business
/ Coming to Terms with the Environment of Business

2. THE DEVELOPMENT OF AMERICAN BUSINESS   17

The Nature of Human Wants / The Satisfaction of Human Wants / The Development of Exchange / The Development of Business / The Development of American
Business // *Reading: The Founding of the English Colonies*

xi

3. THE BUSINESS FIRM   39

Families, Clans, and Tribes / Cooperative Associations
/ Governmental Enterprise / The Modern Business Firm
// Appendix: Functional Organization Chart // *Reading:
Standard Oil Company (New Jersey)*

4. AMERICAN INDUSTRIES   65

The Development of American Industries / Classifications
of American Industries // Appendix: Standard Industrial
Classification // *Reading: The Petroleum Industry*

5. THE AMERICAN ECONOMIC AND BUSINESS SYSTEM   83

The American Economic System / The American Business System / The Structure of the American Economy
// *Reading: Can Anyone Explain Capitalism?*

6. OTHER ECONOMIC SYSTEMS   102

Pre-Industrial Economies / Socialism / Cooperativism
/ Fascism / The Significance of Other Economic Systems
// *Reading: The Communist Manifesto*

7. AMERICAN PRODUCT MARKETS   120

Markets / Product Markets / Theories of Markets / History of Markets // *Reading: Markets for Petroleum Products*

8. PRODUCTIVE RESOURCES AND THEIR MARKETS   139

Productive Resources / Conclusions // *Reading: Standard Oil and the Crude Oil Market*

9. FOREIGN AND WORLD MARKETS   157

The Development of Overseas Markets for American
Products / The Historical Importance of Foreign Productive Resources / Present Importance of Foreign
and World Markets / Foreign Markets / World Markets
/ The Importance of Certain Foreign Markets / Conclusions // *Reading: America Becomes a Trader*

10. THE DYNAMIC NATURE OF MARKETS   177

Changes in Total Sales by Business / The Nature of Market Changes / Causes of Market Changes / Coming to Terms with a Changing Economic Environment // *Appendix: Historical Charts*

11. THE ECONOMIC RESPONSIBILITIES OF BUSINESS 201

Profit-Making the Basic Responsibility / Responsibilities Toward Others in the Markets / Responsibilities for Preserving Free Market Institutions / Responsibility for Preserving Economic Stability / Responsibility for Preserving High Output and Employment / Responsibility for Preserving a Growing Economy / Responsibility for Beating the Communists on the Economic Front / Responsibility for Solving the Balance-of-Payments Problem / What *Are* the Economic Responsibilities of Business? // *Reading: The American Economy: Is It Growing Fast Enough?*

PART **II** The Social Environment of Business 219

12. AMERICAN SOCIETY FROM THE BUSINESSMAN'S PERSPECTIVE 221

The Nature of American Society / Individuals and Groups in the Business Environment / The Firm's Relations with Society / Coming to Terms with the Social Environment / Kinds of Social Action / Conclusions // *Readings: Various Views of the Nature of Society*

13. CUSTOMERS 242

Domestic Consumers / Business Customers / Governments as Buyers // *Reading: U.S. Business' Most Skeptical Customer*

14. SUPPLIERS OF LABOR AND SERVICES 262

What Workers Want / Employee Organizations / The History of Unions in America // *Reading: The Future of American Unionism*

15. SUPPLIERS OF MONEY 284

Creditors / Owners // *Reading: Shareholders at Their Annual Meeting*

16. SUPPLIERS OF MATERIALS   303

Raw Materials Suppliers / Suppliers of Parts for Assembly / Suppliers of Goods for Resale // *Reading: The Platform of the Populists*

17. COMPETITORS AND COOPERATORS   319

Private Firms as Competitors / Cooperatives as Competitors / Governments as Competitors / Foreign Competition / The Nature of Competition / Cooperation Among Competitors / Trade Associations / Employers' Associations // *Reading: Trade Association Activity*

18. GENERAL BUSINESS ORGANIZATIONS   339

Chambers of Commerce / Manufacturers' Associations / Other Associations of Businessmen // *Readings: Objectives and Activities of General Business Organizations*

19. BUSINESS AND THE COMMUNITY   355

The Nature of the Community / Civic, Health and Welfare Organizations / Educational Organizations / Religious and Moral Organizations / Recreational Groups // *Reading: The Minister Guides the Manager Toward More Effective Community Action*

20. THE IMAGE OF BUSINESS   377

The Public's Opinion of Business / The Problems of Polls / Bases of Opinion / Changing Unfavorable Public Opinion // *Reading: How High School Students Feel About Business*

21. CREATORS OF THE BUSINESS IMAGE   394

Intellectuals / Schools and Scholars / Writers / Cartoonists / Unions and Government / Business as a Creator of the Image // *Reading: A Profit Should Not Be Without Honor*

22. THE SOCIAL RESPONSIBILITIES OF BUSINESS   412

Business Ethics / The Difficulty of "Responsible" Business Behavior / The Public Relations Movement // *Reading: Have Corporations a Higher Duty Than Profits?*

PART **III** **The Political Environment of Business**   433

23. THE POLITICAL ENVIRONMENT OF BUSINESS   435

Government Relations with Business / Government Relations Are Social Relations / Government Officials / Nonofficial Individuals and Groups / Theories of Politics // *Reading: The Political Process*

24. BUSINESS AND THE U.S. CONSTITUTION   453

Origin of the Constitution of the United States / The Implementation of the Constitution / The Development of the Constitution // *Reading: Excerpts from the Constitution*

25. LAW AND THE AMERICAN BUSINESS FIRM   472

Classes of Laws / Governmental Laws // *Reading: The Standard Oil Case of 1911*

26. BUSINESS AND THE FEDERAL GOVERNMENT   490

Development of the Federal Government's Power / Development of the Federal Bureaucracy // *Reading: Independent Regulatory Commissions*

27. STATES, LOCAL GOVERNMENTS AND BUSINESS   507

Powers of State Governments / State Agencies and Officials / Local Governments and Business // *Reading: Cases on Constitutional Law and the Powers of States*

28. BUSINESS, FOREIGN AND INTERNATIONAL GOVERNMENTS   531

Foreign Government and American Business / International Government and Business / Conclusions // *Reading: Europe Super-State*

29. THE ADMINISTRATIVE PROCESS AND BUSINESS   550

Administrative Rule-Making / Administrative Investigation and Decision-Making / Administrative Sanctions

/ Courts and the Administrative Process / Business and the Administrative Process // *Reading: The Not-So-Long Arm of the Law*

30. BUSINESS AND THE COURTS   570

American Courts / Civil Court Procedures / The Businessman and the Courts // *Reading: Enforcement of Fair Trade Contracts*

31. LEGISLATURES AND THE LEGISLATIVE PROCESS   589

American Legislatures / Lobbying and Lobbyists / The Legislative Process / Business and the Legislative Process // *Reading: Report of the House Select Committee on Lobbying Activities*

32. THE POLITICAL RESPONSIBILITIES OF BUSINESS   611

Political Activity of Business / The Political Responsibility of Business / What *Are* the Political Responsibilities of Business? // *Reading: Corporations Make Politics Their Business*

PART **IV** Business and Its Environment in the Future   631

33. THE FUTURE   633

Business in the Future / The Future Economic Environment / Future American Society / Future Political Environment / The Favorable Future

INDEX   647

AMERICAN

BUSINESS

and

ITS

ENVIRONMENT

Every business firm is the fo-cus of a complex of relation-ships. It has lines which run to a number of suppliers of ma-terials, to subcontractors, to employees, to financial backers (both lenders and equity hold-ers), to customers, to compet-itors, to governmental agents. This web of relationships is largely of the firm's own weav-ing. While it is entangled in certain of these ties whether it wishes or not (as, for example, to government inspectors or regulatory agencies, or to unions chosen by a majority of its em-ployees), on the whole it has fashioned its own web like some master spider.

NEIL W. CHAMBERLAIN

PART I

Business and Its Economic Environment

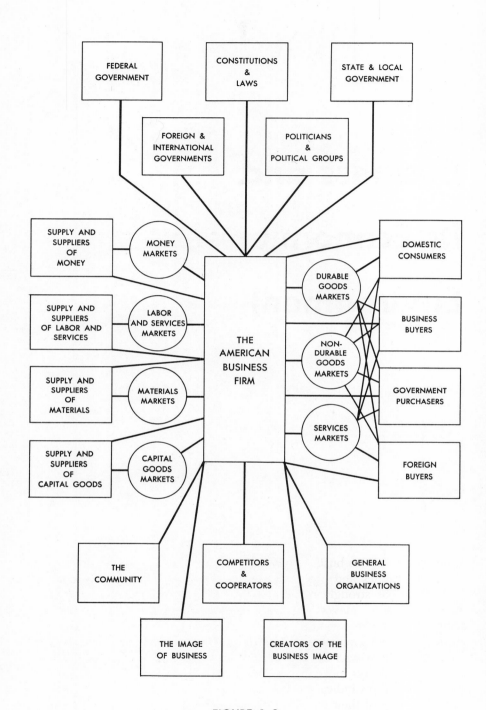

FIGURE 1-1.

CHAPTER 1

AMERICAN
BUSINESS
AND ITS
ENVIRONMENT

When the American businessman, in his day-to-day operations, deals with the opportunities and problems confronting him, he is usually dealing with situations strongly influenced by forces outside his business firm. The decisions he makes and the actions he takes are in large part attempts to come to favorable terms with such environmental influences. Businessmen who properly adjust to and control their environment are successful; those who do not, or cannot, fail. The behavior of business firms is not always looked at in this way, but studies of successful and unsuccessful firms indicate the importance to businessmen of understanding the nature of their environment and of coming to proper terms with it. In this chapter we shall look briefly at some views concerning business behavior, at the essential nature of business, at the nature of the environment of business, and at the general ways in which businessmen should and must come to terms with their surroundings.

VIEWS OF BUSINESS BEHAVIOR

There are a large number of widely held and frequently conflicting views on how businessmen make decisions. Some depictions of business operations do not provide a clear picture of the degree to which businessmen do, and must, take into account relationships with their surroundings when conducting the affairs of an enterprise. Such views are usually promoted by those who examine business from the outside, without any real insight into the way in which business is conducted. Those careful students of business—such as business historians—who have had the opportunity of examining business from the inside, and some businessmen themselves, have developed other ways of looking at business that stress the importance of the environment of business.

The Popular View

A quite popular and quite uninformed view of the businessman, especially if he is or has been the head of a large enterprise, is that he is a "captain of industry," "master of finance," or, in less complimentary terms, a "robber baron." This characterization of the businessman has been made popular by some journalists, writers of fiction, and even by some historians (a widely known, if not widely read, history of the activities of businessmen was entitled *The Robber Barons*).[1] Whatever truth there might have been at one time in such descriptions of businessmen, they have little validity in the middle of the twentieth century. Unfortunately for present-day business, these images persist in the public mind and there is little genuine understanding on the part of most of the American public of how American business operates. It is frequently surprising to those scholars who have carried on research within the offices of large corporations to note the great sensitivity of the top executives to public opinion, no matter how little influence the persons holding such opinions may have. The image of the dictatorial ruler of business making decisions without any regard to their consequences for persons inside or outside the business is one which should not be given much serious attention, despite its widespread appearance in works of fiction and elsewhere.

[1] Matthew Josephson, *The Robber Barons: The Great American Capitalists, 1861–1901* (New York: Harcourt, Brace, 1934).

The Economist's View

It is hardly fair to ascribe one view of the decision-making process to all economists, since there actually exists considerable difference of opinion among them about how businessmen act. (Someone once said that when five economists discuss a particular issue, they will hold at least six different opinions on it.) However, a basic assumption usually made in the traditional economic theory of the business firm is that businessmen will set that price and/or produce that quantity that will maximize their profit from the sale of a certain product. This profit-maximizing assumption is employed in almost all of the traditional economist's examination of various business operations. This assumption conjures up the picture of the coldly calculating capitalist looking for the "right combination" that will yield him the highest possible profit without regard for the effects of his actions on customers, employees, unions, competitors, or the government. Although some advanced economic theory relaxes somewhat this assumption concerning profit-maximization, the net effect of this theory of the firm remains as an image of businessmen scrambling for as much money as possible, heedless of the consequences for others.

Not all economists accept the profit-maximizing view of the businessman. A recent investigation of the economic theory of the firm led a distinguished economist to question and discard that view. Instead he suggested that the decision-maker in business attempts to maximize a "preference function" that includes profit as one of many related goals sought by the businessman. Also, he pointed out that there are a number of influences on such decisions other than market influences: "It is a major thesis of this essay that the preference function maximized by the peak coordinator is itself a resultant of the influences which are exerted upon the firm." [2] The external influences that he felt warranted recognition were those of the government, suppliers (including suppliers of money and labor), the customers of the firm, and competitors.

Other economists, in this case writing about the education of businessmen, have noted the importance of external influences on the operations of business: "The business firm, like any organization, operates within a set of environmental influences. There is continuing interaction between the firm and various parts of its environment...." [3] A well-informed businessman, they conclude, requires some knowledge of both his market and nonmarket environment. In the nonmarket environment, they include

[2] Andreas G. Papandreou, "Problems in the Theory of the Firm," in Bernard F. Haley (ed.), *A Survey of Contempory Economics,* Vol. II, (Homewood, Ill.: Irwin, 1952), p. 211.

[3] Robert A. Gordon and James E. Howell, *Higher Education for Business* (New York: Columbia U.P., 1959), p. 64.

such elements as the climate of public opinion toward business, the pressures of private groups, the legal and political framework, international developments, and "the larger economic forces." The market environment, according to Gordon and Howell, includes the markets in which the businessman buys his inputs of human, financial, and physical resources as well as those in which he sells his output.

These newer developments in economics are encouraging, although, unfortunately, there is yet no well-developed and generally accepted theory of the firm that reflects this recognition by some economists of the complex forces affecting the behavior of business. In order to make theory manageable, many economists adhere to the profit-maximizing assumption, unrealistic as it is.

The Business Historian's View

Some scholarly historians have been able to study the records of certain business organizations in great detail. The conclusions they have drawn about businessmen who have existed in the public mind (and in some histories) as "ruthless monopolists" reveal that even such powerful figures on the business scene were sensitive to and influenced by external forces. A study of the Standard Oil "monopoly" (almost 90 per cent of the refining capacity in the U.S. was once under its control) prior to its dissolution in 1911 showed that

> the behavior of John D. Rockefeller and his associates, large and small, seemed to us to be most realistically presented as a result of decisions made in response to prods and pressures. Among the influencing factors were habit, inertia, pride, desire for profit and prestige, normal human reactions to the novel and the disproportionately powerful, new economic developments, modifications in public beliefs and concepts, and the political and legal climate arising from the convictions, reasonable and unreasonable, of an electorate swayed by the politicians and the press.[4]

Books in business history have emphasized that successful businessmen and business firms of the past were those able to come to terms with changing economic, social, and political environments. Business historians, also, have noted that the external conditions confronting firms have become increasingly important as firms have grown in size and as our nation has matured; this is especially true of those large firms that have become more and more the objects of social and political action.

[4] Ralph W. Hidy and Muriel E. Hidy, *Pioneering in Big Business, 1882–1911* (History of Standard Oil Company (New Jersey), Vol. I), (New York: Harper & Row, 1955), p. xxviii.

Views of Other Social Scientists

Other than economists and historians, it has been mainly the political scientists and sociologists who have employed the methods of social science in examining business. The role of the businessman in the political process has been the central concern of the political scientists, many of whom feel that business interest groups have played a disproportionate role in shaping public policy and that such activity by these "special interests" is contrary to the democratic ideal, and possibly to the "public interest." Sociologists have examined the social origins of business leaders and the place of such businessmen in American society (with a few being concerned about the development of a "power elite" composed principally of businessmen). Later in this book we shall deal in some detail with the views of specific sociologists and political scientists, but for the present it is sufficient to say that many of them regard businessmen with some suspicion, suspecting them of actions contrary to the ideals of political and social democracy.

Views of Behavioral Scientists

Some sociologists have also been concerned with the explanation of the behavior of individuals and groups in business firms. In this, they have been joined by psychologists. Although anthropologists also are classed as behavioral scientists, as yet they have not concerned themselves to any great extent with studies of American business. When psychologists and sociologists have conducted examinations of specific business firms, their findings have reflected the complex and diverse nature of those business organizations. Indeed their greatest contribution may lie in their finding that businessmen are motivated toward a large variety of objectives, and that the relative values of those goals are constantly changing. The significance of this finding for understanding business behavior lies in its implication that we ought not to ascribe one unchanging objective to businessmen. Generally speaking, behavioral scientists are more concerned with interpersonal and intergroup relations within business firms than they are with the relations of businessmen with outsiders (although an exception should be made for those sociologists concerned with union-management relations). They have also concerned themselves, however, with the formation of attitudes and goals and have studied segments of society important to business. We shall, therefore, draw upon their concepts and findings throughout this volume.

Views of Administrative Scientists

Public administration has been an object of investigation for centuries, but the scientific study of business administration is of relatively recent origin. Although some of the findings of students of public administration have relevance for those attempting to understand business, there are some significant differences between the operations of public and private organizations. The books and articles on the behavior of business units written by administrative scientists support the conclusion drawn from the findings of behavioral science—firms are complex, with a variety of goals possessing varying importance at different times. They have also pointed out the existence of various external influences upon decisions made in the firm and upon the results of operations of the enterprise.

The Businessman's View

Businessmen themselves, of course, have long been aware of the need to come to some proper terms with their market and nonmarket environments. In the past and at the present time, the market conditions confronting the firm are of prime importance. However, the growing significance of certain social groups and of political pressures has led some large corporations to set up special units in their organization to deal with problems generated in the social and political environments. There are, for example, departments of Public Relations, Customer Relations, Dealer Relations, Stockholder Relations, Industrial or Union Relations, Community Relations, and Government Relations. Smaller firms have also recognized the need for dealing with many different aspects of their surroundings, even though their relatively simple organizational structures may not reflect the importance of this need, since each of the managers of a small firm performs many different duties.

In their public statements, the more articulate of business spokesmen have testified to the need for taking into account individuals and groups outside the firm. Frank Abrams, Chairman of the Board of Directors, Standard Oil Company (New Jersey)—one of the successor companies of the old combine—has shown that the company learned lessons from its hard experience by stating that it is necessary to "conduct the affairs of an enterprise in such a way as to maintain an equitable and working balance among the claims of the various directly interested groups— stockholders, employees, customers, and the public at large." [5] A president of the New Jersey Bell Telephone Company wrote a highly regarded

[5] Quoted in "Have Corporations a Higher Duty Than Profits?", *Fortune* (August, 1960), p. 108.

book in which he discussed the decision-making function of an executive. In it he declared: "The function of decision is to regulate the relations between these two parts [the purpose of the organization and the external forces of the moment]. This regulation is accomplished either by changing the purpose or by changing the remainder of the environment." [6]

Thus some economists, business historians, behavioral scientists, administrative scientists, and businessmen have pointed out, in a general way, how business decisions are and must be made, stressing strongly that taking into account various environmental factors is important and that successful business performance requires coming to favorable terms with the environment. The environment of a particular firm is quite specific to it, but there are certain general statements that can be made about the surroundings of business that are helpful in understanding the nature of the more important external influences and, therefore, in taking effective action with respect to those forces. The businessman, of course, has considerable knowledge of American business, and especially of his particular firm and industry. For the student of business, however, it might be well to examine briefly the nature of American business before studying its environment.

THE NATURE OF AMERICAN BUSINESS

It should not be surprising to learn that the term *business* can mean a large number of things. All of us use the word in a variety of ways. The Oxford English Dictionary—the largest dictionary of the English language—has several pages of different meanings. Not all definitions are relevant to our discussion, but a review of those having relevance is necessary before we can intelligently proceed.

The Activity of Business

Frequently the term *business* is used to denote the activity of business units. This activity involves acquiring productive resources, combining them into some useful product (either a good or a service), and selling the product in markets, usually for the profit of the owner(s) of the business. This general activity is frequently broken down into specialized functions within the business unit (of which, more later), but the performance of one of those specific functions is not business activity: all three of the elements indicated above—acquiring inputs, making a prod-

[6] Chester I. Barnard, *The Functions of the Executive* (Cambridge, Mass.: Harvard U.P., 1938), p. 195.

uct, and selling it in the expectation of profit—are essential parts of business activity. We have pointed out that "business units" conduct these actions; examination reveals a variety of units conducting business.

Kinds of Business Units

Businessmen, business establishments, business firms, and industries—all are said to conduct business activity. Obviously it is only businessmen who act. Within firms, establishments, and industries, businessmen are making decisions and taking other actions. However, rather strangely, we tend to regard the firm rather than the businessman as being the basic business unit. Later on, we shall see how the behavior of a firm depends upon the actions of those within it and some individuals and groups external to the firm, but for the present we might try to resolve this seeming inconsistency by stating that when we talk about the behavior of a firm, it is a convenient way of referring to the behavior of those businessmen within a firm.

There is a great variety of businessmen. Those who are owners as well as managers are sometimes called "entrepreneurs" (although some feel that the owner-manager does not deserve this title unless he is also an "innovator"). Some businessmen are "professional managers." Although they may be the heads of firms, they may own no share in the business and receive salaries for managing the activity of the enterprises. In large corporations, there may be several managerial levels in the organizational structure, and all of these managers are sometimes regarded as businessmen. Distinctions are frequently drawn among businessmen, professional men, and farmers. However, farmers and professional men (such as dentists) are usually owner-managers or paid managers of enterprises conducting business activity as we have defined it here and therefore fall under our heading of businessmen.

Some writers feel that the business establishment, rather than the firm, should be regarded as the basic business unit. An establishment is a business unit at one location: it may be a firm, but it may be just a part of a firm. For example, the Chevrolet Division of General Motors has a number of assembly plants throughout the nation; each plant is a business establishment and is frequently regarded as being the basic business unit, since it performs all of the elements of business activity. Also, as we shall see in the chapter dealing with American industries, an industry is properly regarded as being made up of establishments rather than of firms. For some purposes, the industry—conceived of as being all the establishments or firms producing essentially the same product and selling in the same market—is regarded as the basic business unit. We shall, however, focus on the firm rather than on either the establishment or the industry.

The Business System

Writers and speakers frequently refer to the "American Business System." Unfortunately, this phrase also means a variety of things. Businessmen, establishments, firms, and industries are not independent of one another. They are interdependent and systematically related. Only a few conceive of the business system as being a system of interrelated businessmen: more commonly, the phrase refers to the systematic relationships among firms, establishments, or industries. There is another meaning, however, that the phrase is perhaps most often intended to convey. The "business system" can also be conceived as a system of interrelated institutions (defined as established ways of thinking and doing). One of the institutions said to be characteristic of the American business system is "private property"—key legal principles upholding the right of persons to own, to use, and to dispose of things. Although this is not an unrestricted right, still it gives managers of business firms considerable freedom to acquire productive resources, to use them to produce whatever they wish, and to dispose of the products through sale. An understanding of the "American business system" is so important to an understanding of business that a later chapter will be devoted to this subject.

Since there are so many possible meanings attached to the term *business*, we shall try to avoid using it except where it makes little difference. Instead, the terms *entrepreneur, professional manager, firm, establishment, system of firms, system of industries,* and *system of institutions* will be employed in the interests of precision. Here we are only briefly defining the subject. Succeeding chapters will contain more detailed examinations of business.

THE NATURE OF THE ENVIRONMENT OF BUSINESS

In order to study the surroundings of the business firm in scientific fashion we shall need to specify clearly what we mean by *environment*. A dictionary definition of *environment* is: "Surroundings; the aggregate of all the external conditions and influences affecting the life and development of an organism." [7] It serves our purpose to modify this to read: "Business Environment—all of the external conditions and influences

[7] *Webster's Collegiate Dictionary*, Fifth Ed. (Springfield, Mass.: G. & C. Merriam, 1946), p. 334.

affecting the life and development of a business firm." We cannot, of course, deal with all of the external influences individually, since they are countless. Some sort of classification is necessary to bring some order out of the seeming chaos. Although it is possible to classify the surroundings of business in a number of ways, we shall restrict our study to three major classes of influences external to the firm: the economic, the social, and the political environments. Too, we cannot and shall not exhaustively study these areas, but only those aspects of them that have some enduring importance to the business manager.

The Economic Environment of Business

Although the economic dealings of businessmen are in fact with individuals and groups, it is frequently useful to think of business firms as buying and selling in markets. These markets can be classified in many ways. Sometimes it helps to regard them in terms of their geographical nature—that is, we can think of markets as being local, regional, national, foreign, international, or world markets. Other times it is useful to break down the markets in which businessmen buy goods and services into raw materials markets, money markets, labor markets, and capital goods markets. Another classification based on the nature of what is being exchanged in the market is one separating markets into durable goods markets, semidurable goods markets, nondurable goods markets, and service markets. We sometimes define the markets in which businessmen sell as consumers goods markets or producers goods markets, a classification based on the nature of the purchaser. No matter how markets are classified, it is clear that the businessman is "surrounded" by a vast number of them and that market conditions are of major importance to him.

Since markets play such an important role in influencing American business, our economic system is frequently referred to as a "market economy" with certain well-defined institutions governing the operations of that system. Not all economic systems throughout the world are like ours, and since many American businessmen are subject to the influence of these other systems and since these other ways of conducting economic activity are sometimes regarded as substitutes or competitors, they are of considerable importance to business firms in the United States. The markets in which firms buy and sell are highly dynamic and interdependent, and fluctuations in one major market can have a substantial effect on the entire economy. It should be apparent at this point that the effective operation of a business enterprise requires some knowledge of the nature of markets in which businessmen deal, the interrelationships among those markets, economic institutions and systems, and economic fluctuations in order that the firm might come to appropriate terms with the economic environment. All of these will be discussed in some considerable detail in succeeding chapters.

The Social Environment of Business

In this broad area of his surroundings, the businessman finds—among other things—individuals, groups, social attitudes, social institutions, and social systems. Viewing the operations of business realistically, we recognize that the business firm is not confronted by society as a whole but by certain individuals and groups holding certain opinions of the firm and having different and frequently conflicting interests and being capable of instituting various influences upon the decisions and operations of the firm.

The way in which a certain class of individuals and groups in the social environment of business thinks and behaves is a product of many things. The existence of certain prevailing social attitudes toward business generally influences opinion concerning a specific firm. The ways in which members of a firm conduct themselves also affect public opinion. Since public opinion, when made effective through social action, is of great importance to a firm, the nature and the forming of opinion toward American business will be discussed in detail later. The problem confronting firms faced with hostile "publics" and unfriendly public opinion is how to make appropriate adjustments to the views of society, or, when the views of the public are in error, how to bring about some change in public opinion.

Every society has certain traditional ways of thinking and behaving—institutions—that fashion the ways in which business can be conducted. Beyond economic institutions, there are certain social and political institutions that shape the social and political system of the United States. These systems provide a framework within which manufacturers, merchants, and other men of business must operate, although they may be able to influence institutions and, therefore, systems.

In discussing the social environment of business, we shall place chief emphasis on the groups confronting business. Groups, especially when organized for action, are normally more influential than individuals. Ours is an "associational" society and individuals have found that when they associate with others having the same or similar interests, much greater influence can be brought to bear. Labor unions provide good examples of effective association on the part of individuals whose influence has been slight when they have not been organized into groups. [There are a number of business associations other than business firms, such as trade associations and chambers of commerce, since businessmen have also long appreciated the value of organized activity.] In examining the various groups of importance to business, in addition to their structure we shall look at what they want in their relations with business, what resources they possess with which to attempt to gain their goals, what lines of action they take in their relations with business, and what the businessman has done and should do in dealing with such groups.

Our classification of society will not embrace all individuals and groups in America, but those of special relevance to business will be studied. We have noted that businessmen deal with certain individuals and groups in markets. Various classes of customers relate in different ways. Suppliers of raw materials, money, labor, and capital goods differ in the ways in which they attempt to influence a firm. Most firms have competitors in the markets, and while competitors sometimes cooperate with a firm, they frequently compete fiercely, and even unfairly. Normally firms within an industry selling in the same market will organize a "trade association" that sometimes attempts to influence a firm to take action "for the common good" that the individual firm may be reluctant to take.

A listing of the categories of individuals and groups with whom businessmen have relations in their market activities does not, of course, exhaust the list of social classes with whom firms deal. In addition, there are a vast number of government groups; these will be dealt with under the political environment because of their great importance and special nature. Firms in other industries and their trade associations sometimes have an impact on the operations of a firm even though they are not operating in the same markets. General business organizations, such as chambers of commerce, also have some influence. Beyond business groups, we find community groups that make certain demands upon business firms. There are some individuals who, while having no direct relationships with a firm, may have some influence on public opinion toward business generally or an industry or firm specifically. Journalists, scholars, ministers, and others come under this heading. Although this listing, too, is not exhaustive, we may have reached the "point of diminishing returns" in our classification of society as it relates to business, and hence our discussion of the social environment of business will be confined to the classes of individuals and groups mentioned under this heading.

The Political Environment of Business

American businessmen have a host of relationships with government agencies and officials who operate at many different governmental levels and confront the businessman with countless rules and regulations. These agents of local, state, national, and international governments are mainly engaged in administering laws passed by legislative bodies, although there are some legal rules formulated by judges and executive orders that also determine what government administrators are to do. American legislatures operate under written constitutions or charters; these contain basic laws of greater permanence than statutes.

The legal and governmental framework within which businessmen operate is politically determined. In the United States, government officials and agencies, legislative bodies, laws and constitutions are all products of, and involved in, political processes—the administrative process, the legislative process, the judicial process, and the elective process. Businessmen, if they are to secure their objectives, should be sufficiently aware of the realities of the political and governmental process—to understand the relationship between politics and government and between government and business. Since businessmen, willingly or unwillingly, consciously or unconsciously, affect and are in turn affected by government policy and action, they should concern themselves with their proper role in the political process. Since the birth of our nation, businessmen have been politically active and because group action is more effective than individual action, businessmen have been inclined to take political action through business associations of various kinds and through political parties. In studying the political environment, we shall examine some of the major official and nonofficial groups who play important roles in the various political processes.

COMING TO TERMS WITH THE ENVIRONMENT OF BUSINESS

The environment of each firm is unique. Although it may be possible to identify certain categories of external elements and to show how some firms have been influenced by, and have influenced, their surroundings, each firm must determine which aspects of its total environment require action. What the businessman can do with respect to his environment is well stated in an ancient prayer: "Grant us the courage to change that which can and should be changed, grant us the serenity to accept that which cannot be changed, and grant us the wisdom to distinguish between them." There are external conditions over which the firm has no control. This does not mean that no action will be taken in those circumstances, but rather that whatever action is taken will be in the nature of adjustments to the unchangeable influences. On the other hand, there are some influences in the environment of a particular firm that can and should be changed. Unless it requires an undue amount of effort and is too great a drain on the resources of the business, effective action can be taken. Finally, whether or not external conditions can be changed is a matter of judgment on the part of the businessman; one characteristic of the successful business firm is good judgment in this area. Maintaining some sort of dynamic equilibrium with its environment permits the firm to survive, grow, prosper, and achieve whatever other objectives it might have.

In the following chapters, we shall examine in considerable detail the more important aspects of American business and its environment. The preceding discussion has set forth the basic approach we shall take in the more intensive study and provides a framework for the details of the nature of business and its surroundings. Included at the end of most chapters will be one or more readings dealing with some topic of that portion of the book. These readings have been selected for their interest and significance and as possible points of departure for class discussion. The opinions of the writers should not be regarded as "gospel truth," but rather as the considered views of persons interested in business, economics, society, and politics. The readings will not only present opinions, but will frequently be selected to illustrate something of American business and its environment.

SUGGESTED READINGS

Brady, Robert A., *Business as a System of Power* (New York: Columbia U.P., 1943). Written at a time when the world was at war, this book by a social scientist views with alarm the rise of "big business" to positions of power in Nazi Germany, Fascist Italy, Imperial Japan, and the United States. It has been said that "he [the author] seems to have been so anxious to prove that the United States was well on the way to Fascism that his treatment of the evidence is uncritical and at times even highly dubious."

Gordon, Robert A., *Business Leadership in the Large Corporation*. (Berkeley: U. of Calif., 1961). Originally published in 1945, this book by an economist has become a classic. Gordon has been a pioneer in developing a theory of decision-making that reflects the influence of environmental forces.

Simon, Herbert A., *Administrative Behavior* (New York: Macmillan, 1958). This administrative scientist concludes that business firms pursue a number of goals, and not just profits. Also, he observes that businessmen "satisfice" rather than attempt to maximize the attainment of any goal: "Administrative theory is peculiarly the theory . . . of the behavior of human beings who *satisfice* because they have not the wits to *maximize*."

CHAPTER 2

THE DEVELOPMENT
OF
AMERICAN
BUSINESS

How did business begin in America? How has it grown? The past illuminates the present, and by reviewing the origin and development of business in what is now the United States of America, we arrive at a better understanding of our present business system. Business, of course, did not originate in America; and economic activity has been and is conducted in ways other than through the private enterprise of firms. Therefore we should also look at the way in which business activity has grown and largely replaced other kinds of economic activity in satisfying the needs and wants of humans.

THE NATURE OF HUMAN WANTS

Humans have many wants. Economists have traditionally regarded the wants of human beings as having no limit; although this is an exaggeration, it is certainly true that almost all of us have more objectives that we want to reach than is possible with the limited resources available to us. Human wants are in large measure based on biological and psychological needs, but many are also the result of living in a certain culture. What college students want, for example, is strongly influenced by the prevailing ways of doing things at their colleges, and in the other "subcultures" in which they live. Whatever the source of the wants, their existence leads to economic activity. Decisions have to be made by someone on which wants to satisfy, the amount of scarce resources that will be used to satisfy certain wants, and how the resources will be managed in creating satisfactions.

THE SATISFACTION OF HUMAN WANTS

Human wants can be satisfied in many ways, with business activity developing as the major means of doing so. Basically, persons can satisfy their wants by taking goods abundantly provided by nature, by producing want-satisfying goods and services for themselves, or by inducing others to provide them with useful things.

In part, humans can satisfy their cravings by consuming goods so abundantly provided by nature that they are called "free goods" by economists—air and sunlight being prime examples of abundant natural resources freely taken to satisfy our wants for oxygen, heat and light. Our consumption of these useful things is normally automatic and unconscious, and economic activity is not involved (it not being necessary to decide whether or not to satisfy these wants or to make decisions concerning how scarce resources should be employed in doing so). Of course, if a person desires cool and pure air rather than the type of air he is currently breathing, or if he desires Florida sunshine instead of Minnesota sunshine during the winter, then the production, distribution, and consumption of these relatively scarce commodities become part of economic and business activity.

Beyond consuming free goods, we can satisfy some of our wants by "do-it-yourself" means. In simpler societies, the bulk of the desires of people are satisfied directly by their own activity. The classic example of the "do-it-yourselfer" is Robinson Crusoe, that fictional character who was cast away on an island. Until he found his man, Friday, he was obliged to provide food, shelter, and clothing for himself through his own efforts, using those natural resources available to him and some things salvaged from shipwrecks. It is not necessary to go to fiction for examples; on the American frontier, pioneer families secured gratification of their wants directly through their own efforts, securing only a few things of value through trade with neighbors, Indians, peddlers, and distant trading posts. Even at present, some Americans exist in this fashion, although the bulk of us engage in "do-it-yourself" projects only a small proportion of the time, and then partly because of the satisfaction derived from creative activity.

Throughout recorded history, people have induced others, through one means or another, to provide useful things. For many centuries, large numbers of persons were enslaved by dominant social groups and performed productive services chiefly because they feared to displease their masters. Also, in some societies having quite rigid class structures, the position of a person was fixed by the circumstances of his birth and he performed, as a matter of custom, the duties associated with that position. Although the condition of most of these persons was not that of slavery, still they feared to try to rise above their position because of the various social sanctions which might be imposed.

Affection, as well as fear, has also been employed to induce persons to produce valuable things for others. This has its roots in the family, wherein the members do things for one another out of love. This feeling of affection has been extended to the clan—the kinship group—and even to larger groups. A number of "utopian" communities have been established in many parts of the world—including the United States—in which the members have produced goods and services for common use out of affection for their fellows. Duty, of course, has been a companion of affection in motivating such economic activity.

In the modern world the main inducement to get others to provide useful things, however, is the appeal to a person's desire to secure things of value through exchange. Fear, custom, duty, and affection have only limited power to induce others to part with their goods nowadays, and the development of business is closely interwoven with the growth of exchange.

THE DEVELOPMENT OF EXCHANGE

Exchange apparently goes back to the most primitive civilizations. The earliest humans were much like the lower animals in satisfying their wants. They hunted, fished, and gathered berries and other vegetation for food without tools or weapons; they were collectors, appropriating what they needed from their natural surroundings. Since the physical environment of various tribes differed, they tended to collect different things, and sometimes members of a tribe would specialize in the collecting of one commodity that they would exchange with a neighboring tribe specializing in the collection of something else. Exchange also developed within the tribes, since there was some specialization in the processing and manufacturing of the things gathered. Much of what was acquired and produced was for common consumption, however, and exchange within the tribe was quite limited.

The cultural nomadic economy followed the collectional economy. Collectors began to cultivate animals and plants rather than rely solely on the gifts of nature. To find better pastures and better lands for cultivation, tribes continued their nomadic ways. Migration brought contacts with other peoples, and trade took place, with the nomads trading surplus animal products for other goods. It should be pointed out that this was essentially an exchange of group property for goods to be shared by the tribe. There was little individual property, and the ownership of land, herds, and flocks was vested in the family, clan, or tribe, not in individuals.

Eventually the cultural nomads settled upon the soil, and the settled village economy developed. With settlement, individual ownership of animals, lands, and crops developed. Manufacturing increased, and the specialization of production extended beyond anything known theretofore. As the institution of private property developed, exchange increased within the village. Exchange among villages also developed, providing opportunities for men to specialize as traders.

Markets appeared in the villages and became permanent institutions. However, there were no specialized middlemen in these markets, and peasants traded directly with one another on a barter basis, without a medium of exchange. Eventually specialized traders came into existence in the villages, trading at their houses rather than in the marketplace—although they sometimes dealt in the local market or in the markets of other villages. The growth of trade changed villages into market towns and towns into metropolitan centers—and modern business was born.

THE DEVELOPMENT OF BUSINESS

As towns grew out of villages and as markets grew larger, private businessmen appeared. They were distinguished from previously existing producers by their employment of productive resources in a process that led to the sale of goods and services in the market for material gain. This was their primary occupation, whereas earlier sellers had been concerned with the disposal of surplus goods. The relatively large number of trans-actions engaged in was also a distinguishing feature.

The earliest businessmen carried on their rather small enterprises as individual shopkeepers, storekeepers, and traveling merchants. Shop-keepers were distinguished from the other classes of these "petty cap-italists" by engaging in the production as well as the exchange of certain goods. Blacksmiths and shoemakers were among the first shopkeepers to appear. The earliest stores were general stores, and the storekeeper relied heavily on the traveling merchant for inventory. The traveling merchant carried on trade between towns, and provided the shopkeepers with raw materials as well as sold goods to storekeepers at wholesale. Without the trade between towns, there would have been only a local exchange of goods for goods between producers, and little business activity. The traveling merchants brought in essential commodities, taking in return the valuable products of the district. This was essentially an exchange of goods for goods. Although the exchanges probably took place in terms of money, little money changed hands in these early business transactions.

Shopkeepers and storekeepers relied mainly on three types of trade. The oldest and most basic exchange was with persons in the countryside, with trade between townsmen being of secondary importance. Trade with other towns was limited and dependent on the traveling merchant. With-out an increase in the size of the market, business necessarily remained small. Because, without improvements in transportation, trade with the countryside was limited, business grew mainly as a result of the growth of towns and the increase of trade with other areas. When this happened, the general store was replaced by more specialized stores and the number and kinds of shopkeepers increased. As the market in which farmers from the countryside sold their surplus grew, they tended to become more specialized in their production and to produce for specific markets.

During the early stages of the development of business, a fourth type of small businessman was active. This was the peddler, who traveled about with his pack upon his back—although he sometimes went by horseback, cart, wagon, or boat. He sold his goods at retail in the country, securing his inventory from shopkeepers, storekeepers, traveling mer-chants, and from his rural customers, who bartered handmade products for peddlers' goods. The market was not a large one, and to some degree the peddler was in competition with businessmen in the town. Those who attained some business success in this enterprise normally graduated to the ranks of storekeeper or traveling merchant.

A kind of "big businessman" developed relatively early in the history of business—the landlord. In many parts of the world, large estates of land were acquired by "lords." Although the lords, or their agents, grew agricultural commodities on portions of their estates, they relied mainly on rents received from tenants for their income. These rental payments took the form of services, money, and commodities. Eventually large markets for agricultural products developed, and the estates were run in a businesslike fashion; but in great measure the lords preferred to hunt, battle for the spoils of war, and to engage in chivalrous and romantic escapades rather than to conduct business enterprises. Their agents and servants—including collectors, bookkeepers, auditors, and treasurers— performed certain business functions, but the lords themselves rarely gave themselves wholeheartedly to the conduct of business. As a consequence, the "mercantile capitalist" has been regarded as the first true type of big businessman.

The mercantile capitalist or "sedentary merchant" had a "seat of operations" in the town or city in which he conducted his wholesale and retail activity. Although he performed the function of a traveling merchant in importing and exporting goods, he did not travel himself, leaving this to his agents and partners. Instead, he stayed in his "accounting house," administering his business from it in addition to "counting out his money." He was the complete businessman, performing almost all of the business functions. In addition to importing, exporting, wholesaling and retailing, he was engaged in transportation, communications, banking, insurance, warehousing, and the promotion of production.

Frequently, to secure new markets as well as new sources of supply, he supported exploration and colonization. In his office, he employed accountants, cashiers, and clerks. Small businessmen remained on the scene —still having a role to play—but the big merchant occupied the center of the stage. In different countries, this phase in business development lasted for varying periods of time, but as markets grew larger and the conduct of business became more complex, businessmen tended to specialize in one of the many functions performed by the mercantile capitalist. Thus began modern business, with business firms specializing in production, transportation, importing and exporting, wholesaling, retailing, warehousing, communications, finance, or insurance.

There have been some new classes of businessmen appearing since the rise of the industrial capitalist—as the businessman specializing in one industry was called. One of these classes was that of the "financial capitalists," who were something more than specialists in commercial banking, investment banking, and other types of financial enterprise. In order to protect their reputations, securities, investments, and loans, they exercised considerable control over other firms and industries. To bring order out of chaotic competition in some industries, they created giant combinations whose policies they were able to influence. In America, for example, U.S. Steel was organized in 1901 by J. Pierpont Morgan and his financial associates to stabilize production, prices, and profits in the steel industry. Through such combinations, and through influence obtained as a consequence of making loans or holding the securities of companies, such financiers were the dominant businessmen in the first three decades of this century, according to some business historians.

After the Wall Street Crash of 1929 and the subsequent decline of the importance of the financial capitalist, the managerial class achieved an important—even dominant—position in American business. It has been pointed out by a number of writers that the owner-manager is disappearing in large enterprises, being replaced by managers having little or no ownership interest in the business. This development began prior to the 1930's, but became increasingly evident as financiers were reduced to a relatively minor role in influencing business decisions. Ownership in many large corporations is widely held, with no owner being in a position to line up a majority of shares to support his candidates for board membership or to advance his policies at stockholders' meetings. In such cases, the managers have been able to get their nominees for the board of directors—very frequently themselves—and their policies adopted by shareholders and thereby to perpetuate their control over the corporation.

On the present business scene we see almost all of the classes of businessmen mentioned. The sole exception is the mercantile capitalist, who has been displaced by industrial specialists who can perform each of the mercantile capitalist's functions more satisfactorily than he could. (Perhaps this may change. A number of large, diversified firms are appearing on the business scene, and we may again see some firms performing many, if not all, of the functions performed by this early arrival in the development of big business.) Of petty capitalists (small businessmen) we have millions; there are still many industrial capitalists to be found; and, perhaps, financial capitalism is not dead (although it may be underground). Certainly, professional managers abound. Statistics on the relative proportions of different classes of businessmen are, unfortunately, unavailable, although we shall later examine the quantitative relationships among individual proprietorships, partnerships, and corporations.

In the history of American business, these various kinds of businessmen have appeared pretty much in the order in which we have discussed them. However, there are other significant ways of examining business development in the U.S. For a more complete comprehension of the nature of American business a brief examination of other aspects of the growth of the United States as the premier business nation is in order.

THE DEVELOPMENT OF AMERICAN BUSINESS

Business in that part of America which is now the United States did not always develop according to the general pattern described above.

Native Americans did not get much beyond the collectional and cultural nomadic economies, and business did not begin until the white man came, planting the economic institutions of Great Britain and European countries on this continent in addition to their flags. Attempts were made to shorten the process of economic development through the establishment of towns with strong commercial ties to the colonizing country in which there existed great metropolitan centers with their large markets and enterprising mercantile capitalists.

Business in Colonial America

The colonies on the eastern shore of North America were products of business ventures. Jamestown, Virginia—the first permanent colony—was founded by the "Virginia Company of London" in 1607 in order to secure whatever profit there might be realized from trade in the products of the colony. The Plymouth Company (another English company organized under the Virginia Charter of 1606) was unsuccessful in colonizing Maine in 1607 and, after reorganization into the Council for New England, made grants of land to several groups settling on Massachusetts Bay. One of these—the Pilgrims—financed their enterprise by establishing a joint stock company, selling shares to English merchants after each emigrant received a share. Dutchmen, acting through the United New Netherlands Company and its successor, the Dutch West India Company, colonized New York. The colonies were quite unsuccessful as business enterprises; the trading companies lost control of them, and the lands passed into the hands of the English crown (the New Netherlands being seized by English armed forces in 1664).

The proprietary colonies were also business enterprises of a sort. To reward or repay various individuals, the English kings granted land on a large scale in North America. Those holding grants—men such as William Penn and Lord Baltimore—hoped to profit from trade as well as to secure income from rentals or sale of lands. Not many of the proprietors were successful, those in the middle colonies of Pennsylvania, Maryland, and Delaware being the exceptions.

Although the trading companies and proprietors did business on a grand scale, most American enterprises in the early colonial period were small. Colonial markets were limited in size, and difficulties in transportation—and the resulting high cost of moving goods to widely scattered markets—kept down the size of firms producing for domestic consumption. The extractive industries—agriculture, logging, fishing, hunting, and some iron mining—were the major industries in this period. Much of the farming was for the subsistence of the individuals and families engaging in it, although some crops were produced for domestic and foreign markets. In the middle and southern colonies, indigo, tobacco, and the cereal grains—rice, corn, and wheat—become commercially important, especially in the export trade.

Extractive industry gave rise to manufacture by colonial businessmen. The bulk of manufacturing took place in households, with the rest occurring in the shops of craftsmen. Many manufactured goods were produced in the households of farmers, who used raw materials stemming from the extractive industries of logging, hunting, and trapping in which they engaged in some of their spare time. The cutting down of standing timber gave rise to the ship-building industry in the northern colonies, while in the South, shingles and naval stores—tar, turpentine, rosin, and so on—were produced. In New England, the large catches of whale and cod led to substantial export of whale oil and dried or salted fish. The production of iron products grew to substantial proportions in the middle colonies in the later colonial period, having been encouraged by the English from the first, and some partnerships were formed to conduct the operations of the larger concerns.

Production for the market, whether on a small scale or large, led to specialization in trade. True, the craftsman and household producer tended to sell his own products in local markets. Retail traders, however, selling imports were scattered throughout the colonies, and in the large seaports an appreciable wholesale trade developed. Toward the end of the colonial period, great merchants—such as John Hancock and Robert Morris—gathered together colonial products for export and imported products for sale at wholesale and retail. The firms of the merchant traders were the largest enterprises of the time, and they performed the business functions of importing, exporting, transporting, warehousing, wholesaling, retailing, financing, and insuring. Since large investments were required to finance ships and goods, partnerships were frequently formed.

On the eve of the American Revolution, there was considerable business activity in the colonies, but the restraints placed by the British on colonial businessmen led many of them to support the revolutionary cause. In line with their economic policies of "mercantilism," both Crown and Parliament worked to control the development of American enterprise. Many times, business was fostered—the production of ships, naval stores, and certain crops, for example, was promoted by the English government. On the other hand, many restrictions on manufacturing and trade were established. Some businessmen, such as Hancock, were openly defiant of these regulations and supported those political elements in the colonies that were proposing revolution.

Business in the New Nation

The Revolutionary War had an important impact on American business. Seaport cities were either held or blockaded by the British, thereby cutting off the business of those large merchants rebelling against the Crown. Many merchants, however, grew rich through supplying the needs of the British armed forces. Fishing, whaling, and shipping came almost to a standstill, as did the construction of ships. Some manufacturing for American war needs was stimulated, especially the production of gunpowder, guns, iron, and cloth. Business did not grow and prosper in the same degree as it has grown in more recent wars because of some indecision about which markets to produce for and sell in, the lack of sound currency issues by the revolutionary governments, and the generally confused economic and governmental situation.

The coming of peace did not immediately bring about a more stable situation. Relationships among state governments and the power of the federal government were unsettled issues. Some states passed legislation that was unfavorable to certain business groups, including laws restraining interstate commerce. Foreign manufactures began to flood American markets, with consequent difficulties for those producers who had got a start during the war when imports were shut off. Foreign markets did not develop as American businessmen had hoped. Some of these problems were resolved by the adoption of the new Constitution in 1789 and by the acts of the Federalists, a political group friendly to business that held political power from the adoption of the new Constitution to the inauguration of Thomas Jefferson in 1801.

Jeffersonian foreign policies were to transform the nature of American business. The purchase of the Louisiana Territory (1803) from Napoleon was to change from emphasis on foreign markets to emphasis on the interior. Acts restraining foreign trade were passed by Congress, beginning in 1807 and lasting until the end of the War of 1812. Consequently American overseas trade and shipping declined greatly, after American merchants had developed these business activities to a place second only to Great Britain. Manufacturing, which had been largely on a small scale for domestic markets, received great impetus from the falling off of foreign trade. Banks—which had been nonexistent as separate enterprises prior to the Revolution and which had been confined to a few banks on the seaboard during the late eighteenth century—boomed in numbers, although their quality was not equal to their quantity. Their increase was largely a consequence of Jeffersonian suspicion of the "monopoly power" of the large Eastern banks, and the need for convenient banking facilities in the interior.

After the War of 1812, business activity continued to be more concerned with domestic markets. Additional territory was acquired until by
the eve of the Civil War the area from which forty-eight states were to
be made had been secured. Villages, towns, and great metropolitan centers such as St. Louis, Cincinnati, and Chicago sprang up in this interior;
new markets were created, and business expanded greatly. Commercial
agriculture was the dominant and most rapidly growing economic activity, but it carried along with it canals, steamboats, railroads, banking,
trade, and manufacturing.

By 1860, the United States was a major business nation. It led the world
in the production of farm implements, and the processing of agricultural
products was big business. The demand for railroads and steamboats had
created an opportunity for the vast expansion of iron and steel and
machinery industries. "King Cotton" reigned in the South, providing raw
material for a rapidly expanding textile industry in the United States.
Canals and their canal boats connected widespread markets, a development enhanced by river boats. Railroad mileage increased from about
3,000 to approximately 30,000 between 1830 and 1860. Banks to serve
agricultural areas sprang up where wildcats still snarled, thereby earning
the name "wildcat banks." To concentrate agricultural products for shipment to market, trading centers developed. Some of these urban areas
became metropolitan centers in which wholesaling of goods to retailers in
the agricultural regions took place. The factory system started in the
textile industry and spread to others. With the growth of large-scale
enterprise, the corporate form of doing business was more and more
widely adopted, and by the time of the Civil War some iron and steel
corporations had capital stocks in excess of one million dollars.

Among service industries, change was seen in the variety as well as the
size of firms. Life insurance companies, savings banks, investment banks,
and trust companies joined commercial banks in the ranks of financial
institutions. The production and sale of gas was added to the sale of
water in the utilities field.

Although great changes were still to come, the years from 1816 to 1860
saw American businessmen creating a modern industrial nation, in many
respects second only to England. Business had come of age, possessing
most of the characteristics that mark it today.

The Growth of the Giants, 1860–1929

Although new industries were to rise and there was to be a change in
the relative importance of different kinds of business, perhaps the outstanding change in business in the years since the Civil War has been in
the size of firms. This growth was not so much the result of increased

sales in product markets, but more the result of the joining together by various devices of related and unrelated firms into large combinations.

INDUSTRIAL CHANGES.   Colonel Drake drilled the first oil well in 1859, giving impetus to a new manufacturing industry—oil refining. Although at first the industry produced chiefly illuminants and lubricants, the development of the gasoline engine and its use in propelling automobiles created a new market for refinery products and elevated petroleum refining to fifth place among American industries by 1929. The rise of the motor vehicle industry, stimulated by the use of the gas engine, was even more dramatic. From the few small firms existing in 1900, the industry catapulted to first place by the end of the twenties.

The "motorization of the United States" was accomplished by the electric motor as well as by the gasoline engine. Electrical energy was used more and more to power machinery of various kinds—even automobiles. So widespread was the adoption of electric machinery that in 1929 it ranked sixth in American industry.

Other industries rose as well. Stimulated by the demands of the federal government during the Civil War and being able to ship to more widespread markets after the refrigerated railroad car was developed, meat packing rose in prominence. In 1914, it was the number one industry, although it was to fall to second place behind motor vehicles by 1929. Department stores began to displace specialty shops in the 1860's, and by 1929 the biggest retailers were those departmentalized stores conducting a mail order business in addition to selling goods over the counter. World War I stimulated chemical manufacturing in the United States, and this too rose to a significant position.

THE COMBINATION MOVEMENT.   Wartime taxation and the needs of the federal government during the Civil War favored the large firm, and the process of consolidation of small firms into one giant firm had its beginning during this period. The successful prosecuting of the war required rapid movement of men and materials. Many smaller railroad companies were consolidated into a large "system" in order to eliminate the frequent transferring of freight necessitated by each railroad having different-gauge tracks and different types of rolling stock. Some of the great systems set up were the Pennsylvania, Lehigh and Erie. Western Union acquired the American Telegraph Co. and the U.S. Telegraph Co. during the Civil War, and provided telegraph service by one company throughout the states of the Union.

The corporate form of doing business, being gradually adopted prior to the Civil War, was the main instrument in creating the giant firms that came to dominate the business scene. Relatively small firms could exist as individual proprietorships or partnerships, but when technology or the market situation dictated large-size enterprise, the corporation was the best means for securing sufficient capital and enough market power. After the laws of states permitted it, one corporation could acquire sufficient voting stock of a number of other corporations in a certain industry to give it effective control over them by holding and voting those shares of stock. Such "holding companies" have become the giant firms of modern business, with few exceptions. The two largest manufacturing companies at present—General Motors and Standard Oil of New Jersey— are combinations in which holding companies have played an important role.

Chain stores were part and parcel of the combination movement, since many branches were acquired through purchase or other means. The Great Atlantic & Pacific Tea Co. was founded in 1858 and by 1930 had about 1600 branches and sold more than one billion dollars of goods annually. Other chain stores in other fields—Woolworth, Kresge, United Cigar Stores—followed. Montgomery Ward & Co. and Sears, Roebuck & Co. also grew to giant proportions. Chain stores now sell about one fourth of all goods sold at retail.

The chief impetus to the combination movement was the worsening market situation confronting many industries after the Civil War. The expansion of production by business firms in the postwar period coexisted with a market situation wherein there was not sufficient demand to clear the product markets of goods at wartime prices. Attempts to sell all that could be produced by cutting prices brought product prices to unprofitable levels. Although some attempts were made to reduce costs, the major focus was on restoring prices to satisfactory levels. After voluntary agreements by the firms in an industry failed to have any long-term beneficial effects on production and price, other devices were employed. One of these was the trust—which has given us the inappropriately named "antitrust" laws. The major stockholders in the cooperating firms in an industry would turn over their shares of stock to a group of trustees in exchange for trust certificates. Such trustees could then control the affairs of the corporations whose stock they held, insuring their cooperation in production and pricing policies. After "antitrust" laws were passed (they were aimed at many forms of combination), trusts disappeared as combination devices, but holding companies took their place.

In some industries, combinations through trusts, holding companies, or purchase of one company by another was not practical. Trade associations—an organization of most or all of the firms in an industry—were widely adopted as a means of bringing about some stability to the industry through cooperative action on prices, output, and other matters of common interest. Their growth and continuance testifies to their value to their members, although they suffer from being voluntary associations in which member firms need not adopt policies calculated to benefit the membership generally. By 1929, there were some 12,000 such associations in the United States.

Business Since 1930

Since 1930, business has not changed radically. There has been growth, of course, with important new firms and industries arriving on the business scene. However, the trends established prior to the "depression decade" have continued. Big business has grown bigger, partly due to combinations of firms. Many industries have come to be dominated by a few firms, but this had been developing since earlier in the century. These large firms were seen to be more under the control of their managers than of their owners; however, this too had been in the making for some time.

Among major divisions of American industry, manufacturing continues to be foremost, having surpassed agriculture in the years after the Civil War. There have been many fast-growing manufacturing industries: the drug industry, given new life by the discovery of antibiotics; the "aerospace" industry, spurred on by "hot" and "cold" wars and by the "race into space"; the electronics industry, with television primarily responsible for its rapid expansion; and the electric appliance industry, made prosperous by the widespread adoption of electrical products for the household. Other manufacturing industries seeing substantial growth have been the chemical industry—especially since the development of synthetic fibers—and the light metals industry as aluminum and magnesium have found more and more applications. Some manufacturing industries—older ones such as the cotton textile industry—continued to suffer from what appears to be chronic illness and it is suspected that many of the older industries will continue to decline.

Big firms continue to dominate American business. Every year, a slightly larger percentage of the total sales of business is made by giant firms. This change is not as rapid as it was during the period from 1860 to 1929 and it is quite likely that the proportions of business going to large, middle-sized, and small firms will stabilize in the near future. Small firms continue to be formed—some grow, but most die in a relatively short time. However, the proportion of small firms to large firms is fairly constant and it appears that there will continue to be, in the foreseeable future, considerable room for small business in the American economy.

The dominance of many industries by a few large firms has become a recognized and accepted fact of business life in the United States. At one time, the issue of "monopoly"—the domination of an industry by one large firm—was an important political and economic question. Considerably less concern has been shown over the question of oligopoly raised by the emergence of a few large firms in so many American industries. There is a widespread belief that "competition among the few"—as in the automobile industry—will work out satisfactorily. This oligopolistic situation has developed in large measure from continuing combinations of business firms, although a few firms, such as the Ford Motor Co., have achieved their size through "natural" growth.

One result of combination has been the rise to top positions of managers who are not major owners of the firms. Only in rare circumstances do the majority owners of giant firms manage them. Normally, the top management has acquired control of the operations of the firm they manage and is able to get the owners—none of whom owns a major part of the corporate stock—to support it. Although this development has been a matter of concern only in recent decades, it has been under way since the latter part of the previous century.

In the foregoing, we have briefly sketched the development of American business. The student of business is, perhaps, more interested in the current scene. What does American business look like now? What are some of its more permanent characteristics? In the following chapters, we shall examine in some detail the nature of firms, the industries of which they are part, and the American economic system in which they function. Then, after comparing the U.S. business system with some other economic systems—such as that of the U.S.S.R.—we shall be ready to take a look at the environment in which American business firms operate.

READING: The Founding of the English Colonies

[*Among the most interesting documents of American business history are the charters granted English corporations to found colonies in "Virginia" and the agreements between colonists and those financing them. Although the English crown laid claim to substantial territory in the New World, it was unwilling to bear the expense of founding colonies. Initially, it granted charters to joint-stock companies of the type which had already been conducting trade in other parts of the world. The Virginia Charter of 1606 gave rights to two companies to make settlements along the seaboard of what is now the United States (with the exception of Florida, which was claimed by Spain). Although the Plymouth Company attempted a settlement in Maine, the first permanent colony was established on the James River in 1607. In 1609, King James expanded the rights of the London Company (which had founded the colony at Jamestown), increasing its territory among other objects desired by the owners of that company.*

Before the King of England revoked the charters in 1624, the Pilgrims estab-

*lished a second permanent colony. This band of "Separatists" had negotiated
with the Virginia Council for the right to found a settlement, and the London
Company eventually granted a charter giving the group authority to found a
plantation. However, the company would not finance the attempt at settlement,
and the religious group was obliged to seek assistance from others. Seventy London merchants were found to be willing to enter into an agreement to form a
joint-stock company and to purchase shares at a price of £10 per share. This
agreement is also included in the following readings.]*

First Charter of Virginia°—April 10, 1606

I, JAMES, by the Grace of God, King of *England, Scotland, France,* and *Ireland,* Defender of the Faith, &c. Whereas our loving and well-disposed Subjects,
Sir *Thomas Gates,* and Sir *George Somers,* Knights, Richard Hackluit, Clerk,
Prebendary of Westminster, and Edward-Maria Wingfield, Thomas Hanham,
and Ralegh Gilbert, Esqrs. William Parker, and George Popham, Gentlemen, and
divers others of our loving Subjects, have been humble Suitors unto us, that We
would vouchsafe unto them our Licence, to make Habitation, Plantation, and to
deduce a Colony of sundry of our People into that Part of America, commonly
called Virginia, and other Parts and Territories in America, either appertaining
unto us, or which are not now actually possessed by any Christian Prince or
People, situate, lying, and being all along the Sea Coasts, between four and
thirty Degrees of Northerly Latitude from the Equinoctial Line, and five and
forty Degrees of the same Latitude, and in the main Land between the same four
and thirty and five and forty Degrees, and the Islands thereunto adjacent, or
within one hundred Miles of the Coast thereof;

And to that End, and for the more speedy Accomplishment of their said intended Plantation and Habitation there, are desirous to divide themselves into
two several Colonies and Companies; The one consisting of certain Knights,
Gentlemen, Merchants, and other Adventurers, of our City of London and elsewhere, which are, and from time to time shall be, joined unto them, which do
desire to begin their Plantation and Habitation in some fit and convenient Place,
between four and thirty and one and forty Degrees of the said Latitude alongst
the Coasts of Virginia and Coasts of America aforesaid; And the other consisting
of sundry Knights, Gentlemen, Merchants and other Adventurers, of our Cities
of Bristol and Exeter, and of our Town of Plimouth, and of other Places, which do
join themselves unto that Colony, which do desire to begin their Plantation and
Habitation in some fit and convenient Place, between eight and thirty Degrees
and five and forty Degrees of the said Latitude, all alongst the said Coast of
Virginia and America, as that Coast lyeth:

We, greatly commending, and graciously accepting of, their Desires for the
Furtherance of so noble a Work, which may, by the Providence of Almighty
God, hereafter tend to the Glory of his Divine Majesty, in propagating of Chris-
tian Religion to such People, as yet live in Darkness and miserable Ignorance of
the true Knowledge and Worship of God, and may in time bring the Infidels and
Savages, living in those Parts, to human Civility, and to a settled and quiet Gov·

° From: Poore, ed., *The Federal and State Constitutions,* Part II, pp. 1889 ff.

ernment; Do, by these our Letters Patents, graciously accept of, and agree to, their humble and well-intended Desires;

And do therefore, for Us our Heirs, and Successors, Grant and agree, that the said Sir Thomas Gates, Sir George Somers, Richard Hackluit and Edward-Maria Wingfield, Adventurers of and for our City of London, and all such others, as are, or shall be joined unto them of that Colony, shall be called the first Colony; And they shall and may begin their said first Plantation and Habitation, at any Place upon the said Coast of Virginia or America, where they shall think fit and convenient, between the said four and thirty and one and forty Degrees of the said Latitude; And that they shall have all the Lands, . . . from the said first Seat of their Plantation and Habitation by the Space of fifty Miles of English Statute Measure, all along the said Coast of Virginia and America, towards the West and Southwest, as the Coast lyeth, . . . And also all the Lands . . . from the said Place of their first Plantation and Habitation for the space of fifty like English Miles, all alongst the said Coast of Virginia and America, towards the East and Northeast, or towards the North, as the Coast lyeth, . . . And also all the Lands . . . from the same fifty Miles every way on the Sea Coast, directly into the main Land by the Space of one hundred like English Miles; . . .

And we do likewise . . . Grant and agree, that the said Thomas Hanham, and Ralegh Gilbert, William Parker, and George Popham, and all others of the Town of Plimouth in the County of Devon, or elsewhere, which are, or shall be, joined unto them of that Colony, shall be called the second Colony; And that they shall and may begin their said Plantation and Seat of their first Abode and Habitation, at any Place upon the said Coast of Virginia and America, where they shall think fit and convenient, between eight and thirty Degrees of the said Latitude, and five and forty Degrees of the same Latitude; And that they shall have all the Lands . . . from the first Seat of their Plantation and Habitation by the Space of fifty like English Miles, as is aforesaid, all alongst the said Coast of Virginia and America, towards the South, . . . And also all the Lands . . . from the said Place of their first Plantation and Habitation for the Space of fifty like Miles, all alongst the said Coast of Virginia and America, towards the East and Northeast, . . . And also all the Lands . . . from the same fifty Miles every way on the Sea Coast, directly into the main Land, by the Space of one hundred like English Miles. . . .

Provided always, and our Will and Pleasure herein is, that the Plantation and Habitation of such of the said Colonies, as shall last plant themselves, as aforesaid, shall not be made within one hundred like English Miles of the other of them, that first began to make their Plantation, as aforesaid.

And we do also ordain . . . that each of the said Colonies shall have a Council, which shall govern and order all Matters and Causes, which shall arise, grow, or happen, to or within the same several Colonies, according to such Laws, Ordinances, and Instruction, as shall be, in that behalf, given and signed with Our Hand or Sign Manual, and pass under the Privy Seal of our Realm of England; Each of which Councils shall consist of thirteen Persons, to be ordained, made, and removed, from time to time, according as shall be directed and comprised in the same instructions. . . .

And that also there shall be a Council established here in England, which shall, in like Manner, consist of thirteen Persons, to be, for that Purpose, appointed by Us, . . . which shall be called our Council of Virginia; And shall, from time to time, have the superior Managing and Direction, only of and for all Matters, that shall or may concern the Government, as well of the said several Colonies, as of and for any other Part or Place, within the aforesaid Precincts of four and thirty and five and forty Degrees, above mentioned. . . .

And moreover, we do Grant . . . that the said several Councils, of and for the said several Colonies, shall and lawfully may, by Virtue hereof, from time to time, without any Interruption of Us . . . , give and take Order, to dig, mine, and search for all Manner of Mines of Gold, Silver, and Copper, as well within any part of their said several Colonies, as for the said main Lands on the Backside of the same Colonies. . . . Yielding therefore, to Us . . . the fifth Part only of all the same Gold and Silver, and the fifteenth Part of all the same Copper, so to be gotten or had. . . .

Giving and granting, by these Presents, unto the said Sir Thomas Gates . . . and their Associates of the said first Colony, and unto the said Thomas Hanham . . . and their Associates of the said second Colony . . . Power and Authority to take and surprise, by all Ways and Means whatsoever, all and every Person and Persons, with their Ships, Vessels, Goods, and other Furniture, which shall be found trafficking, into any Harbour or Harbours, Creek or Creeks, or Place, within the Limits or Precincts of the said several Colonies and Plantations, not being of the same Colony, until such time, as they, being of any Realms or Dominions under our Obedience, shall pay, or agree to pay, to the Hands of the Treasurer of the Colony, within whose Limits and Precincts they shall so traffick, two and a half upon every Hundred, of any thing, so by them trafficked, bought, or sold; And being Strangers, and not Subjects under our Obeysance, until they shall pay five upon every Hundred, of such Wares and Merchandises, as they shall traffick, buy, or sell, within the Precincts of the said several Colonies, wherein they shall so traffick, buy, or sell, as aforesaid; Which Sums of Money, or Benefit, as aforesaid, for and during the Space of one and twenty Years, next ensuing the Date hereof, shall be wholly emploied to the Use, Benefit, and Behoof of the said several Plantations, where such Traffick shall be made; And after the said one and twenty Years ended, the same shall be taken to the Use of Us. . . .

Also we do . . . Declare . . . that all and every the Persons, being our Subjects, which shall dwell and inhabit within every or any of the said several Colonies and Plantations, and every of their children, which shall happen to be born within any of the Limits and Precincts of the said several Colonies and Plantations, shall Have and enjoy all Liberties, Franchises, and Immunities, within any of our other Dominions, to all Intents and Purposes, as if they had been abiding and born, within this our Realm of England, or any other of our said Dominions. . . .

And finally, we do . . . Grant and agree, to and with the said Sir Thomas Gates . . . and all others of the said first Colony, that We . . . , upon Petition in that Behalf to be made, shall, . . . Give and Grant unto such Persons, their Heirs, and Assigns, as the Council of that Colony, or the most Part of them, shall, for that Purpose nominate and assign, all the Lands, Tenements, and Hereditaments, which shall be within the Precincts limited for that Colony, as is aforesaid, To Be Holden of Us, our Heirs, and Successors, as of our Manor at East-Greenwich in the County of Kent, in free and common Soccage only, and not in Capite: . . .

Second Charter of Virginia °—May 23, 1609

[*After reciting the grant of 1606, the charter continues.*]

Now, forasmuch as divers and sundry of our loving Subjects, as well Adventurers, as Planters, of the said first Colony . . . have of late been humble Suitors unto Us, that . . . We would be pleased to grant them a further Enlargement and Explanation of the said Grant, Privileges, and Liberties, and that such Counsellors, and other Officers, may be appointed amongst them, to manage and direct their affairs, as are willing and ready to adventure with them, as also whose Dwellings are not so far remote from the City of *London,* but that they may, at convenient Times, be ready at Hand, to give their Advice and Assistance, upon all occasions requisite.

We . . . do . . . Give, Grant, and Confirm, to our trusty and well-beloved Subjects, . . . , and to such, and so many, as they do, or shall hereafter, admit to be joined with them, in form hereafter in these presents expressed, whether they go in their Persons, to be Planters there in the said Plantation, or whether they go not, but adventure their monies, goods, or Chattels, that they shall be one Body or Commonalty, and that they, and their Successors shall be known, called, and incorporated by the Name of, *The Treasurer and Company of Adventurers and Planters of the City of London for the first Colony in Virginia.* . . .

And we do also . . . give, grant and confirm, unto the said Treasurer and Company, and their Successors, under the Reservations, Limitations, and Declarations, hereafter expressed, all those Lands, Countries, and Territories, situate, lying, and being, in that Part of *America* called *Virginia* from the Point of Land, called Cape or *Point Comfort,* all along the Sea Coast, to the Northward two hundred Miles, and from the said Point of *Cape Comfort,* all along the Sea Coast, to the Southward two hundred Miles, and all that Space and Circuit of Land, lying from the Sea Coast of the Precinct aforesaid, up into the Land, throughout from Sea to Sea, West, and Northwest; . . .

And forasmuch, as the good and prosperous Success of the said Plantation cannot but chiefly depend, next under the Blessing of God, and the Support of our Royal Authority, upon the provident and good Direction of the whole Enterprize, by a careful and understanding Council, and that it is not convenient, that all the Adventurers shall be so often drawn to meet and assemble, as shall be requisite for them to have Meetings and Conference about the Affairs thereof; Therefore we Do Ordain, establish, and confirm, that there shall be perpetually one Council here resident, according to the Tenour of our former Letters-patents. . . .

And further . . . we do . . . Give and Grant full Power and authority to our said Council, here resident, . . . to nominate, make, constitute, ordain, and confirm, by such Name or Names, Stile or Stiles, as to them shall seem good, and likewise to revoke, discharge, change, and alter, as well all and singular Governors, Officers, and Ministers, which already have been made, as also which hereafter

° *From:* Poore, ed., *The Federal and State Constitutions,* Part II, pp. 1893 ff.

shall be by them thought fit and needful to be made or used, for the Government of the said Colony and Plantation: And also to make, ordain, and establish all Manner of Orders, Laws, Directions, Instructions, Forms and Ceremonies of Government and Magistracy, fit and necessary, for and concerning the Government of the said Colony and Plantation; And the same, at all times hereafter, to abrogate, revoke, or change, . . . as they, in their good Discretion, shall think to be fittest for the Good of the Adventurers and inhabitants there. . . .

And we do further . . . Ordain and establish, that the said Treasurer and Council here resident, and their Successors, or any four of them, being assembled (the Treasurer being one) shall, from time to time, have full Power and Authority, to admit and receive any other Person into their Company, Corporation, and Freedom; And further, in a General Assembly of the Adventurers, with the Consent of the greater Part, upon good Cause, to disfranchise and put out any Person or Persons, out of the said Freedom of Company. . . .

Also we do . . . Declare . . . that all and every the Persons being our Subjects, which shall go and inhabit within the said Colony and Plantation, and every their Children and Posterity; which shall happen to be born within any of the Limits thereof, shall Have and Enjoy all Liberties, Franchizes, and Immunities of Free Denizens and natural Subjects within any of our other Dominions to all Interests and Purposes, as if they had been abiding and born within this our realm of *England*. . . .

And forasmuch, as it shall be necessary for all such our loving Subjects, as shall inhabit within the said Precincts of *Virginia*, aforesaid, to determine to live together, in the Fear and true Worship of Almighty God, Christian Peace, and civil Quietness, each with other, whereby every one may, with more Safety, Pleasure, and Profit, enjoy that whereunto they shall attain with great Pain and Peril; We . . . do Give and Grant unto the said Treasurer and Company, . . . and to such Governors, Officers, and Ministers, as shall be, by our said Council, constituted and appointed, . . . that they shall and may, from time to time for ever hereafter, within the said Precincts of Virginia, . . . have full and absolute Power and Authority, to correct, punish, pardon, govern, and rule, all such the Subjects of Us . . . as shall, from time to time, adventure themselves in any Voyage thither, or that shall, at any time hereafter, inhabit in the Precincts and Territories of the said Colony, . . .

And further . . . in all Questions and Doubts that shall arise upon any Difficulty of Construction or Interpretation of Anything contained either in this, or in our former Letters-patents, the same shall be . . . interpreted in most ample and beneficial manner for the said Treasurer and Company . . .

And lastly, because the principal Effect, which we can desire or expect of this Action, is the Conversion and Reduction of the People in those Parts into the true Worship of God and Christian Religion in which Respect we should be loath, that any Person should be permitted to pass, that we suspected to affect the Superstitions of the Church of *Rome*, we do hereby Declare that it is our Will and Pleasure, that none be permitted to pass in any Voyage, from time to time to be made into the said Country, but such, as first shall have taken the Oath of Supremacy; . . .

Articles of Agreement of Plymouth Plantation.°

1. The Adventurers and Planters do agree that every person that goeth, being sixteen years old and upwards, be rated at ten pounds, and that ten pounds be accounted a single share.

2. That he [who] goeth in person, and furnisheth himself out with ten pounds, either in money or other provisions, be accounted as having twenty pounds in stock, and in the division shall receive a double share.

3. The persons transported, and the Adventurers, shall continue their joint stock and partnership the space of seven years, except some unexpected impediments do cause the whole company to agree otherwise; during which time all profits and benefits that are gotten by trade, traffic, trucking, working, fishing, or any other means, of any other person or persons, shall remain still in the common stock until the division.

4. That at their coming there, they shall choose out such a number of fit persons as may furnish their ships and boats for fishing upon the sea; employing the rest in their several faculties upon the land, as building houses, tilling and planting the ground, and making such commodities as shall be most useful for the Colony.

5. That at the end of the seven years, the capital and the profits, namely, the houses, lands, goods, and chattels, be equally divided among the Adventurers.

6. Whoever cometh to the Colony hereafter, or putteth anything into stock, shall, at the end of the seven years, be allowed proportionally, to the time of his so doing.

7. He that shall carry his wife, or children, or servants, shall be allowed for every person now aged sixteen years and upwards, a single share in the division; or if he provide them with necessaries, a double share; or if they be between ten years old and sixteen, then two of them to be reckoned a person, both in transportation and division.

8. That such children as now go, and are under the age of ten years have no other share in the division than fifty acres of unmanured land.

9. That such persons as die before the seven years be expired, their executors to have their parts or share at the division, proportionately to the time of their life in the Colony.

10. That all such persons as are of the Colony to have meat, drink, apparel, and all provisions, out of the common stock, and goods of said Colony.

SUGGESTED READINGS

Cochran, Thomas C., *The American Business System* (Cambridge, Mass.: Harvard U.P., 1957). Subtitled "A Historical Perspective, 1900–1955," this readable volume by a master historian traces the important changes in business and its environment during the first half of this century.

° *From:* William Bradford, *History of Plymouth Plantation* (Commonwealth of Massachusetts edition), pp. 56–58.

————, *Basic History of American Business* (Princeton, N.J.: Van Nostrand, 1959). A brief (one hundred pages of text) history of American Business from the planting of the colonies to the present. Readings of approximately eighty pages make up the balance of this valuable little volume.

Gras, N.S.B., *Business and Capitalism* (New York: F. S. Crofts & Co., 1939). An introduction to business history by a pioneer business historian, mainly concerned with the evolving stages of capitalism.

Heilbroner, Robert L., *The Making of Economic Society* (Englewood Cliffs, N.J.: Prentice-Hall, 1962). A highly readable volume combining economic thought with economic and business history.

CHAPTER 3

THE BUSINESS FIRM

Economic enterprises can take and have taken a number of forms, among which private business enterprise is a relatively recent development. First came the family, the clan, and the tribe as economic units producing and distributing goods and services. Next came cooperative associations in which certain kinds of workers banded together to achieve common economic objectives. Government enterprise was also an early development. Out of the family, operating as an economic unit, came the family partnership, which was followed by the "occasional partnership" of producers who traded only on occasion. These associations were the first organizations to have the transaction of business as their main objective;

since then, the rapid expansion of kinds and numbers of business firms has led to a situation in which economic activity in most of the highly developed societies of today is conducted mainly by private business enterprise.

FAMILIES, CLANS, AND TRIBES

The kinship organizations of family, clan, and tribe were not instituted primarily for economic purposes. However, they did need to provide for their material requirements in some fashion and in order to do so, they engaged in productive activity. When they had, due to chance, occasional surpluses, it is likely that they exchanged them for other goods or for services. At a certain stage, surpluses were produced for the purpose of exchange, and regular markets sprang up. Whether such organisms should be called enterprises is doubtful; hence, the term *semi-enterprises* has been attached to them, because they produced partly for their own needs and partly for the market.

Household Enterprises

In ancient Greece and Rome, household economies began the transformation into large-scale business enterprises. The *oikos*—as the aristocratic household of Greece was called—has given us the word "economics," which comes from *oikonomika,* meaning "household management." In Rome, particularly, the households became large enterprises. This was possible because of slavery, with large groups of slaves being incorporated into the *familia.* Such households were engaged in a large number of agricultural, industrial, and commercial enterprises, but yet were not mainly business enterprises.

Individual Private Enterprise

As social organization changed, the tendency was toward individual enterprise. The decline of the clan and tribe in importance and the resultant elevation of the family as the primary social group placed the family head in a position where he was obliged to provide for the material well-being of his immediate blood relations. Although he joined others in cooperative ventures and was, at a later date, to become involved in family partnerships, he was, in large measure, thrown upon his own resources and therefore had to find some kind of productive occupation. Many became artisans, selling what they were best able to produce. Some became merchants, but were unlike the modern commercial trader. They were not strongly motivated by the prospect of making large profits from trade but, rather, worked toward the objective of earning a living for themselves and their families.

Partnerships

The family partnership did not reach its fullest flower until the late Middle Ages and early modern period. The origin of such enterprises lay in the continuation, as a unit, of the individual business of a father by his sons after his death. Some of the most important commercial, industrial, financial, and shipping enterprises were conducted in this fashion.

From the family partnership to similar organizations of men not related by blood or marriage was a short step. Some family partnerships took in relatives outside the immediate family and even some befriended strangers. As "strangers" began to form partnerships, contractual ties rather than family ties became more important, and business activity became the main function of these first "pure" business organizations.

COOPERATIVE ASSOCIATIONS

The conscious establishment of cooperatives to carry on economic activity also reflected the passing away of the clan and tribe as significant economic units. Communal cooperation for various purposes had existed among kinship groups beyond the immediate family until such groups were transformed into local communities and the family became the major social group. In some circumstances—clearing fields, felling trees, building roads, constructing dams, handling disaster situations—communal cooperation continued. However, in fishing, shipping, and in almost all types of industry—agriculture and trade being the major exceptions—cooperative associations of male workers emerged as major economic units. These groups were scarcely business enterprises, since they were not united on the basis of contract so much as on tradition and ceremony. Fraternal bonds were established among the members, and proceeds were shared from whatever undertaking was under way. However, there was no common sale of products; each member sold and bartered goods as an individual.

GOVERNMENTAL ENTERPRISE

States have organized economic activity from ancient times. Royal families governed most of the emerging states—which developed from the tribes and tribal leagues—and much productive activity by governments consequently partook of a family flavor. Royal ships, constructed with tax funds, proved themselves superior in both construction and operation to those of the cooperative associations, and government enterprise therefore replaced cooperation in shipbuilding and shipping. Economic activity carried on by government still plays an important role in many nations, and even predominates in some. In other chapters we shall deal in greater detail with government enterprise at home and abroad.

THE MODERN BUSINESS FIRM

The basic producing unit in the American economy is the business enterprise or firm. Firms take many forms, but essentially they exist as sole proprietorships, partnerships, or corporations. Throughout this book we shall regard the firm as the focus of environmental forces. But, as we have noted, the firm does not merely move in the direction in which it is pushed; it has goals of its own which it tries to reach. What are the objectives of the firm? Observers differ in their conclusions, and some different views merit examination. There is greater agreement on what functions business firms perform; hence, a study of these functions and their effect on the structure of firms gives a clearer picture of what is meant when we refer to "the firm."

The Essential Nature of the Firm

We have indicated that a number of different types of producing units can exist. Producing units are those entities that acquire productive resources—raw materials, capital goods, and labor—and use them to create something useful to someone. What distinguishes business enterprises from other kinds of producing units is that firms are privately owned entities that produce goods and/or services for sale in product markets for economic gain. Individuals and families engaging in "do-it-yourself" productive activity are not producing for markets. Some cooperative organizations aim at economic gain for their members, but do not sell in product markets; those "co-ops" that do are really business firms. Government enterprises, although they may sell goods and services in the markets, are publicly owned and normally are not operated for material gain through exchange. The distinguishing features of the firm as a separate kind of producing unit, then, are (1) private ownership; (2) production for sale in markets; and (3) the objective of economic gain from such sale.

Objectives of Firms

Having briefly examined what firms do, we come to the question that logically follows: Why do firms do what they do? Many answers have been given to this question. This is understandable, because the objectives of the firm depend largely on the motives of the managers of business firms, with sometimes quite strikingly different motives. Perhaps the most frequent answer given is the "profit motive." Although there is considerable truth to the contention that profit motivation is the answer, it does not adequately explain managerial behavior because it does not take into account the difference in kinds of firms and the many motives of managers. In the following sections, we shall examine some current notions of managerial motivation and indicate the view that will be adopted throughout this volume.

THE PROFIT MOTIVE. A prevalent view represents the manager of a firm as motivated by the prospects of making profits by selling goods or services in product markets for more than the costs incurred in the resource markets and in production operations. When we consider the merchant or shopkeeper of the early days of business, it seems quite obvious that the motive of each was profit or material gain in the sense it is used here (the excess of income over outgo). However, as business has become more complex—especially with the rise of corporations in which the managers are not the owners—the motives of management have become mixed. Job security or managerial income or prestige or a host of other things may be more important to such managers than making profits for the owners. Profits are still sought by these salaried employees of the corporation, but perhaps they are sought more to keep dissident stockholders or creditors from seeking a change in the management or to secure the prestige and increased income that comes from running a profitable operation. Some students of business have gone so far as to suggest that profit is a survival condition rather than a goal of business, and that survival and growth are central goals.

MANAGERIAL MOTIVATION. Our definition of the firm—which states that business enterprises are privately owned producing units selling in product markets for economic gain—gives us a clue to the motives of managers. "Economic gain" as used in this definition is something more than profit. Economists speak of "utility" (defined as useful things) as being those useful things that individuals want to gain, and there are many things—both tangible and intangible—that are useful in gaining whatever ultimate objectives humans have. The economic gain that owners may wish to realize from the operations of the enterprise may not be the same as that which the manager wants when the owners are not the managers, as is true in many corporations. Also, the gain desired by owners may consist of something in addition to profits. Even where the owners and the managers are the same—as in the proprietorship and the partnership—the sole owner or partner is a complex human with many motives, and there are things other than profit useful to him in gaining what he values.

One answer to the question of what motivates firms might be that they are motivated by whatever motivates their managers. In firms whose owners are the managers, profit will be a somewhat stronger motive than those whose owners neither manage nor exercise close control over operations. Earlier we quoted Professor Papandreou as saying that the "peak coordinator"—the top manager—attempts to maximize his "preference function." This means that such managers have a number of things they value and that the decisions they make will not be concerned with just one object—such as profit—but will try to strike some balance among sometimes conflicting and competing goals so that the total satisfaction or "utility" secured from attaining those various objectives in varying degrees will be a maximum. Certainly this view seems more realistic, and though profit has been and remains a powerful—perhaps the strongest— motive, it should not be regarded as the only one.

In relatively large organizations, however, "peak coordinators" must concern themselves with the objectives of important members of their firm when deciding what objectives the firm should pursue. In planning policies and programs for the future, these coordinators must make some decision on the objectives to be sought because intelligent planning requires some goals to be gained. It may well be that in a large corporation, for example, the vice-presidents of finance, sales, and production—all differ on the output the company should produce and sell in the forthcoming planning period, and on the price the company should charge for the product. The top manager may conceive of his function as coordinator of the internal bargaining among these members of his organization in such a way as to satisfy them sufficiently to keep them attached to the organization. Or he may consider it his function to settle the disagreement by making the "right decision." In this latter circumstance, he will of course be influenced by the information and arguments his three subordinates have provided, so that in either case we can properly consider the final decision on what objectives the firm should pursue to be influenced by various members of the organization, and not dependent upon the motivations of the top manager alone.

This is, however, not an end to the matter of what causes firms to pursue certain objectives. Individuals and groups outside the firm also bring influence to bear on the top manager. In the first chapter, we discussed the various classes of individuals and groups in the social environment of a firm that are able and sometimes willing to bring pressure on a firm, including pressure to pursue certain objects. The decision, then, that the top manager of a firm reaches on what goals the firm should try to gain reflects not only his motives, but also the motives and influence of individuals and groups *inside and outside* the firm.

Goal Attainment by Firms

Managers and firms, as is true of other individuals and groups, do not always secure the objectives for which they are striving. Although they might make decisions that will "maximize their preference functions" and take action to gain that goal, they frequently fall short. What a firm winds up doing may not be what it intended to do at all. This is true because it is involved in a number of relationships with other individuals and groups who may be striving for objectives, the attainment of which is in some way inconsistent with those of the firm, and because these other parties have various resources with which to secure their objectives and to frustrate management in the attainment of its goals. (There is a general social principle I have immodestly called "Walton's Law" which states: "The results of any social interaction depend on the objectives and resources of the parties and on the way in which the resources are managed." This "law" explains why—when the objectives of the firm and other parties are incompatible and when other parties to social interactions involving the firm have some resources they are willing to commit to the attainment of their objectives—the firm is unable always to gain what it wants.) Viewing business behavior in this way makes it possible to explain why the results of business action are what they are and even may make it possible to predict what will happen in the future.

A Theory of the Firm

It is possible to develop a fundamental theory of the behavior of the firm by looking at the firm pursuing its objectives with certain resources in an environment composed, in part, of other individuals and groups pursuing their objectives with their resources. Professor Papandreou has pointed the way by stating, with reference to government: "It may be hypothesized . . . that its behavior is a vector of this multitude of influences and forces exercised upon it." [1] There is sufficient similarity between the operation of governmental units and business firms to warrant

[1] *op. cit.*, p. 203.

a rephrasing of this proposition to state: "The behavior of a firm is a vector of the influences exercised upon it and exerted by it."

The idea of "a vector" is a quite useful one, but it is not familiar to most students of business; it is used mainly by mathematicians and physicists. In physics, it is employed to explain the movement of objects in space. The movement of an object from one point to another is regarded as the vector or resultant of "the parallelogram of forces." For example, the movement of an object from point A to point B in Figure 3–1 is a result of the two forces, C and D. The direction in which each force is pulling the object is indicated by the direction in which the arrow C or D is pointing, and the amount of influence exerted by each force is indicated by the length of each arrow. The result of the application of these two forces is to move the object in yet another direction, the distance of its movement and direction being determined by the direction and magnitude of each of the forces applied.

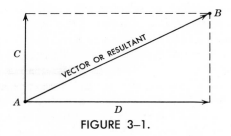

FIGURE 3–1.

Each force acting upon an object in physical space will not, of course, be either perfectly horizontal or vertical; however, each force can be resolved into vertical and horizontal components. For example, the force E in Figure 3–2 can be regarded as being composed of component forces F and G.

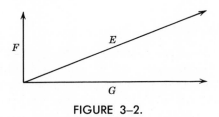

FIGURE 3–2.

So to determine the effect, using graphs, of a number of forces influencing an object to move in a variety of directions, the horizontal and vertical components of all of them can be determined (which may reinforce one another or act as counterforces), and added up algebraically, the actual movement of the object being forecast or explained.

In the physical world and in the world of business, there are frequently more than two forces having some influence upon physical objects, business objectives, and the outcome of business operations. Figure 3–3 shows how four forces might influence an object. In the first illustration [part (1)] they are shown as pushing the object; in the second [part (2)], as pulling it.

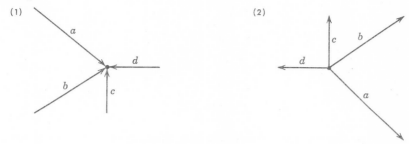

FIGURE 3–3.

As can be seen, the amount and direction of the various influences are the same, regardless of whether we regard them as pushing or pulling the object, and the resultant will therefore be the same. For convenience of analysis, we shall regard all forces as pulling forces, although "push" as well as "pull" counts in the business world.

When a number of forces act upon an object, the net effect of their influence can be determined graphically in a number of ways. The vertical and horizontal components of each force can be determined, the "net" horizontal and vertical forces computed, and the resultant of these established, as in Figure 3–4.

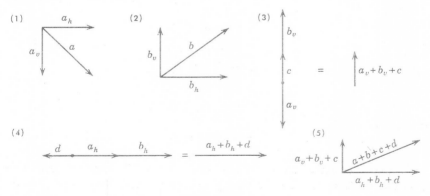

FIGURE 3–4.

A short-cut yielding the same result may be employed, requiring the use of only one graph. This is done by regarding each force as following upon the heels of the other, rather than all acting upon the object at the same time. So when force *a* is followed by force *b*, and so on, our graph looks as shown in Figure 3–5.

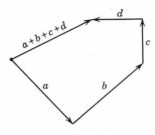

FIGURE 3–5.

We shall use this means of illustrating the influence of a number of forces in the following analysis of the behavior of a firm.

We can make use of vector analysis either to forecast or to explain the behavior of the firm. Our greatest concern here is to explain why the firm pursues certain objectives and why the outcome of its operations is what it is. It is useful and realistic to conceive of the objectives that firms pursue as being influenced by internal and external forces. As we indicated earlier, the vice-presidents of a large corporation may all have some influence to bring to bear on the determination of price and output objectives by the president. In the kind of price-and-output graph traditionally used by economists, the resultant of these influences can be determined, as in Figure 3–6.

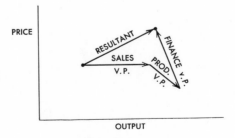

FIGURE 3–6.

However, we have not yet taken into account the external influences upon the decision. It may be that pressures exerted by a union, by the bank, by government agencies, and by the trade association will force some modification of the decision the company will make in the absence of external influences. The leader of a union of the firm's employees may publicly call for a reduced price and expanded output, implying that the union will take some unspecified action if the company doesn't do so. An officer of the bank from which the firm has received a substantial loan and from which it wishes to continue to borrow may suggest that an increase in price and added output will improve the company's position with the bank as well as the firm's own profits. Some government officials may suggest that the price is too high, that the company has too large a share of the market, and that some action may be taken if the firm doesn't amend its price and production policies accordingly. Finally the trade association in the industry of which the firm is a member may let it be known that the "good of the industry" requires each company to cut back its output and at the same time raise its prices. Our graph (Figure 3–7) will now incorporate these external influences, with the resultant decision stemming from internal forces.

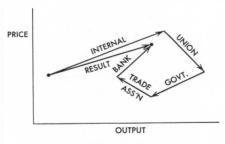

FIGURE 3–7.

As we have indicated, it is quite unlikely that the firm will gain the objective determined by internal and external influences because some external forces that have no role or disproportionate roles in determining objectives have some impact on the price and output actually realized. These forces may stem from the action of materials suppliers, who may unexpectedly raise prices or cut shipments; from the action of competitors, who have cut prices and raised output beyond the expectations of the firm; and from the action of customers, who do not buy the quantities forecast. On a graph, these influences would affect the actual price received and the actual output sold, as shown in Figure 3–8.

Although the three graphs show both the decision and the result of operations being determined precisely as a consequence of internal and external forces, the analysis of such forces in the real world cannot be performed with such precision. It is obvious that in order to determine with pinpoint accuracy the resulting decisions and results of operations, it would be necessary to be able to determine the exact direction and magnitude of the internal and external forces. No precise means of measurement exists for doing so. However, estimates of the direction and amount of influence of internal and external forces are made—either

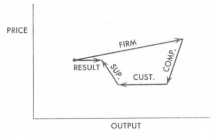

FIGURE 3–8.

consciously or subconsciously—by those responsible for making the final decisions on objectives. That they do not always reach their objectives may be explained by poor estimates on the part of the decision-makers or by the development of unforeseeable influences. At any rate, in order to understand why firms behave as they do, this relatively simple theory provides a useful explanation; therefore, throughout the remainder of this work we shall be concerned with the direction and amount of influence exerted upon firms by various individuals and groups.

There are many examples of firms behaving in ways that may not be closely related to their basic functions of producing and selling for economic gain because of the influences exerted upon it. They pay business taxes, not because they wish to, but because governments force them to do so. Business firms are frequently reluctant to enter into costly agreements with labor unions, but do so because of the pressure that unions, and sometimes governments, exert. Costly public relations programs may be entered into because the management feels the influence of unfavorable public opinion. Market forces may cause firms to sell goods at different prices and in different quantities than they intend. Important suppliers and customers sometimes exert influence outside the markets. Competitors and trade associations bring pressures to bear that force changes in the behavior of businesses. Firms in other industries and general business organizations have, on occasion, an interest in what action a firm takes and attempt to influence it into going in what they regard as the proper direction. Community groups may want certain things and pressure firms to contribute to their objectives. It may be apparent that the influences we have been discussing are those stemming from the economic, social, and political environment of the firm. In our diagram (Figure 1–1), we see not only lines of relationship but also lines of influence. Many of the following chapters will deal more fully with the nature of these different sectors in the environment of business, the relationships they have with business, and the kinds of influence that are brought to bear on the firm.

It should be clearly understood that the behavior of the firm does not depend solely upon the influences exerted upon it. The firm exerts influence. It is not powerless to resist what it regards as undesirable pressures. However, it rarely succeeds in altogether countering such influences and the result is that the firm rarely reaches its intended goal. The degree to which a business enterprise gains its objectives depends, then, not only on its resources and the way in which they are managed but also on the objectives and resources of the parties with whom the firm comes into contact, and the ways in which those individuals and groups manage their resources.[1]

Forms of Firms

The individual proprietorship—in which one person owns and manages a business—is historically the oldest type of business firm. At one time, it also accounted for the bulk of business done, as there was no need for a more highly developed business form. However, as business opportunities grew, requiring more money, goods, time, or talent than an individual possessed or was willing to put into a single venture, partnerships were formed. Sole proprietorships, however, have not passed from the business scene. In every major division of industry, more businesses are owned and operated by one person than by either partnerships or corporations. Out of some 11 million firms in the United States, about 9 million are proprietorships.[2] Though numerous, these businesses tend to be small, and the bulk of sales in the markets are made by other kinds of firms.

[1] For example, the behavior of the United States Steel Corporation in setting the price of steel in 1962 clearly illustrated how the firm's actions were the result not only of what it wished to do, but of influence exercised by the economic situation, the steelworkers' union. other members of the steel industry and the Kennedy Administration. Grant McConnell's *Steel and the Presidency—1962* (New York: Norton, 1963) is an absorbing study of the steel price crisis of April 1962.

[2] This figure may seem rather large, especially when compared with statistics on business population as reported in the Department of Commerce's *Survey of Current Business,* which currently (1965) shows the number of firms at about 5 million. However, this reported figure on business population does *not* include commercial farms or professions, rather surprisingly because the Office of Business Economics in the Commerce Department elsewhere defines business as including "all private enterprises organized for profit, both corporate and noncorporate, including farm operators, independent professional practitioners, and lessors of real property." The figure 11 million is taken from a study by the Internal Revenue Service of income tax returns.

Partnerships—in which a relatively small group owns and manages the firm—have a number of disadvantages, along with their advantages. Among these disadvantages are (1) a relatively short life: the demise of a partner leads to the death of the partnership, although the firm might be continued in altered form under a new partnership agreement. (2) Unless special arrangements are made, any one partner can bind the entire firm to agreements he has made in the name of the partnership— contracts that may be ill-advised. This is especially important because the members of a partnership are liable to the extent of their personal wealth for debts of the firm. (3) As business opportunities requiring large amounts of capital develop, it is difficult to find a few sound men with sufficient funds to finance the large partnerships that would be required to take advantage of the developments. In their search for a solution to these problems, businessmen have found the device of the corporation most suitable.

As in the case of the proprietorship, there are still many business ventures for which the partnership is quite suitable—although in some instances professional men such as doctors and lawyers are prohibited by law from operating as corporations and must choose either the sole proprietorship or partnership. For whatever reason the partnership form is selected, there are about as many partnerships as there are corporations (approximately one million of each) among American business firms, although the sales of corporations far overshadow those of partnerships.

In between the partnership and corporation, there exists—although not in any great degree at present—the joint-stock company. Historically, it appeared on the scene somewhat prior to the corporation as a device to solve some of the problems involved in organizing and operating a large enterprise as a partnership. A capital stock was established and shares in it were sold to various investors or exchanged for goods or services. Rather than each shareholder having a voice in management, a governing body was elected to conduct operations. These joint-stock companies did not have corporate existence—that is, they did not have legal authority to operate as a unit with the liability of the shareholders limited to the extent of their investment. In the colonial period some joint-stock companies were established, but it was not until after the American Revolution that corporations made any widespread appearance in that part of North America that is now the United States.

The corporation is, in some respects, a relative of the individual proprietorship as well as kin to the joint-stock company. Whereas the proprietor is a living flesh-and-blood person, the corporation is an artificial person, created by the law and capable of having perpetual life. It has the advantages of the proprietorship in that it acts as a single person, and in most American corporations, only one person—the president—has the authority to manage the affairs of the enterprise, although he may delegate this authority to others or exercise it jointly with other corporate officers. Not only are some of the virtues of the proprietorship regained through the medium of the corporate form, but some of the disadvantages of the partnership are overcome. The issuance of shares in the capital stock of the corporation makes it possible to secure large amounts of money from many persons who might, individually, possess only modest sums. Laws have been secured protecting these investors from losing anything more than the value of the shares they had subscribed for and/ or purchased. The long, sometimes perpetual, life granted corporations by the states chartering them has solved the problem of disruption of the enterprise because of the death of an important partner or of the sole proprietor.

Because of its many advantages, it is little wonder that the corporate form has come to dominate the American business scene. Corporations do about three times as much business as do partnerships and proprietorships combined. This is a consequence of the larger size of the average corporation as compared to that of the other types of firms and we have come to equate big business with corporations.

Without a doubt, American firms have been getting bigger. A century ago there were few firms with a capital of more than a million dollars. The turn of the century saw the United States Steel Corporation created —-the nation's first billion dollar corporation. Since then, a number of other firms have joined United States Steel in the billion dollar class and there are now a host of giant corporations. This development sometimes gives the impression that small business is fading away and that its days are numbered. Such an impression is false. Employing a commonly used measure of the size of firms—the number of employees—experience since World War II indicates that both small and medium-sized business have been increasing at a faster rate than has big business. Small firms—having fewer than 100 employees—have become a larger percentage of the total population of enterprises, and the percentage of the middle-sized—having from 100 to 499 employees—has declined, although not as much as that of the big businesses. Of the more than 3 million firms in the nation reporting to the Social Security Administration over one-half have no more than 3 employees. So although the number of big and medium-sized firms is increasing, this increase is not as rapid as that of the small firm.

At times it may seem that corporations will replace other forms of firms because they are granted perpetual life. Corporations, too, are mortal. The perpetual life which most state-issued charters grant to corporations is very frequently not realized in practice. As with other forms of firms, it is necessary to remain profitable, or at least solvent, in order to remain in business. The average life of any business firm is short—in all industries, only about 20 per cent of new firms live to be ten years old. The corporation is no exception to the rule that most enterprises are short-lived, although the mortality rate is greater among the small corporations than among the large.

Functions of Firms

Regardless of their legal form or size, all firms perform certain basic business functions. All are engaged in employing productive resources in producing goods and/or services for sale in a market. These basic functions of the firm may be supported by others, such as financial, accounting, personnel, purchasing, and public relations. Not all firms provide for these supporting roles in the same way, with the small firm frequently employing outside assistance for this work. Large corporations usually have one or more employees handling these varied functions within the firm, with the chief executive acting as a "peak coordinator"—coordinating the functions and activities of the other members of the firm.

PRODUCTION. Production is used here in a broad sense—the employment of productive resources in producing goods and/or services. We tend to think of production almost solely in connection with extractive and manufacturing firms, but business enterprises in the service industries are also producing things of value, although intangible. In the manufacturing industries we are accustomed to seeing production managers in charge of this function. They have counterparts, however, in the transportation and other industries who are referred to as operations managers. It is the job of the production and operations managers—or whatever their counterparts in various industries are called—to see to it that men, materials, and machines function to create the kind of utility the firm is established to produce.

MARKETING. The other basic function of business firms is marketing —getting the product into the hands of those who will use it. Manufacturing and extractive firms usually have a sales manager who is basically charged with the proper performance of this function. Other firms, such as railroad companies, have traffic managers who have essentially the same duties and responsibilities. These business managers conduct their operations through a sales force, dealers and distributors, and/or advertising. In most cases, salesmen, whatever they may be called, contact prospective purchasers of the good or service and attempt to secure the agreement of the prospect to buy. This may involve calling on dealers and/or distributors who in turn sell in the ultimate market, or deal directly with the ultimate user. To stimulate inquiries and sales, many firms also engage in one or more types of advertising. In large corporations, managers might be in charge of these various subfunctions. In small firms, one man might perform all of these marketing duties in addition to discharging other responsibilities.

SUPPORTING FUNCTIONS. In order to produce and market products, it is necessary to acquire productive resources. This need and the needs to maintain some accurate record of and control over the operations of the enterprise and to come to terms with external influences on the firm require firms to perform the functions of purchasing, personnel administration, financial management, accounting, and public relations.

Before any firm can conduct operations, it requires financial resources. In order to continue to exist, it must maintain a sound financial position. This requirement gives rise to the function of financial management. The chief financial manager of a firm, whatever his title, must secure funds initially and see to it that the firm continues to have enough, but not too much, money on hand to finance its operations. The funds are usually secured from both owners and creditors, and the financial manager deals with both groups, attempting to strike the right balance between ownership money and borrowings.

After a new firm has secured financial resources, its next step is normally to acquire certain physical resources—plant, equipment, raw materials, and supplies. Although many firms have a person with the title of purchasing agent, the duties of that position are usually limited to the purchase of supplies and less expensive equipment. When buildings and other constructions are acquired, and when expensive equipment is bought, the decisions are typically made by the top management of the firm.

Human resources as well are required, and the function of personnel management has developed to "build and maintain work groups." In the one-person firm, this function is not performed, but whenever employees are involved in operations, it is necessary to hire, train, pay, and supervise workers. This function is performed regardless of whether or not there is a formally designated "personnel manager." Large firms tend to place some of the subfunctions in the hands of professional personnel people, but persons in managerial and supervisory capacities are still obliged to perform the more important duties.

Although the top manager of a firm has some "feel" for the way in which the affairs of the enterprise are going, a better way of determining the results of operations and of controlling them is through securing some numerical measurements. Accounting was originally developed for this purpose, although modern accountants perform other important duties as well, including determining what the prospective results of certain courses of action will be. As numerical data have become more important to businessmen, statisticians have been added to the accounting staff to supply different kinds of information. Again, this is a functional area that is integrated into the operations of a large firm, while smaller firms frequently go outside for bookkeeping, accounting, and statistical services. In many cases, reports must be made to outside parties, such as owners, creditors, and governmental agencies, and this obligation has also tended to make the accounting function of greater importance.

Although a businessman may have no employees within his firm, he always has dealings with individuals and groups outside the enterprise. The list is large. He always has dealings with customers, and normally has relations with suppliers. While he may have no outside owners, there are usually some creditors to deal with. He may have officers of an employees' union to contend with. Frequently he is in contact with other firms in the same industry—either as competitors or in a cooperative relationship. Nor are outside contacts restricted to those with whom he has some business dealings. There are the ever-present governmental agencies, along with service clubs, business associations, charitable organizations, and a number of other individuals and groups attempting to influence his firm. The way in which he comes to terms with such influential parties is usually referred to as "public relations."

There has developed, as for most business functions, a specialized area in which the practitioners are called "public relations men." The term is not very descriptive. Actually, public relations men are mostly public information men whose duties chiefly involve securing favorable publicity for the firm. Some large firms have broadened the concept of the function to include such things as customer relations, owner relations, dealer relations, community relations, stockholder relations, and so on. However, this is exceptional and the public relations man still plays a limited role in the public relations field. As is true of most business functions, it is something that must be performed whether or not any individual or group is given a public relations title or the duties that go along with it. Many top managers have found that this is a function they cannot delegate entirely to others and have therefore discharged these responsibilities along with others. Also, other departments, such as the legal department, have duties arising out of the relations of the firm with outsiders, and the importance of the public relations function is not always clearly reflected by the existence or nonexistence of a public relations department.

Regardless of how important certain supporting functions may be, they are still subordinate to those of production and marketing; and of the two, marketing is primary. Many a firm has done a good job of production, but has not met the requirements of the market and has, consequently, failed. Knowledge of, influence on, and adjustment to the present and potential market for the product is essential.

Each firm is part of an industry. Although a complete examination of American business would require studying each firm, this would be a never-ending task, as new firms are continually coming into existence. It is possible, however, to secure a fairly comprehensive view of business in the United States by examining its industrial structure. The industry of which a firm is a member is a part of the environment of that enterprise, as are other industries in the American economy. To secure some clearer notion of the nature of American business and of the environment of the firm, we shall next study American industries.

APPENDIX: Functional Organization Chart

On page 58 is an organization chart of a refining company showing the functional organization characteristic of the structure of most large firms. You will note that this is not a chart of the Standard Oil Company (New Jersey). Jersey Standard nowadays is a holding company not directly involved in the production and sale of refinery products. Atlantic Refining was a member of the Standard Oil combine before 1911, a wholly owned subsidiary of the parent company, Standard Oil of New Jersey. Since its forced separation from its parent, it has been operating as a producer, refiner, transporter, and marketer. The organization chart (Figure 3–9) illustrates these basic functions and the various supporting functions conducted at the time the chart was drawn.

READING: Standard Oil Company (New Jersey) *

At the present time, the Standard Oil Company of New Jersey is the largest oil company in the world and rivals General Motors for the position of the largest manufacturing firm. No firm has had as much written about it as has Jersey Standard, nor has any industry been so much the object of scholarly and other investigation as has the oil industry. The early history of Standard Oil (including the New Jersey company) illustrates very clearly what can happen to a firm which makes an effective adjustment to its economic environment but fails to adapt itself to its social and political surroundings. Throughout this volume, therefore, we shall employ illustrations from the experience of this firm and industry. A quick sketch of the firm and its surroundings will outline the picture of which details will be studied.

° The material for this original reading is taken principally from Ralph W. Hidy and Muriel E. Hidy, *Pioneering in Big Business, 1882–1911* [History of Standard Oil Company (New Jersey)] (New York: Harper & Row, 1955).

ATLANTIC REFINING COMPANY

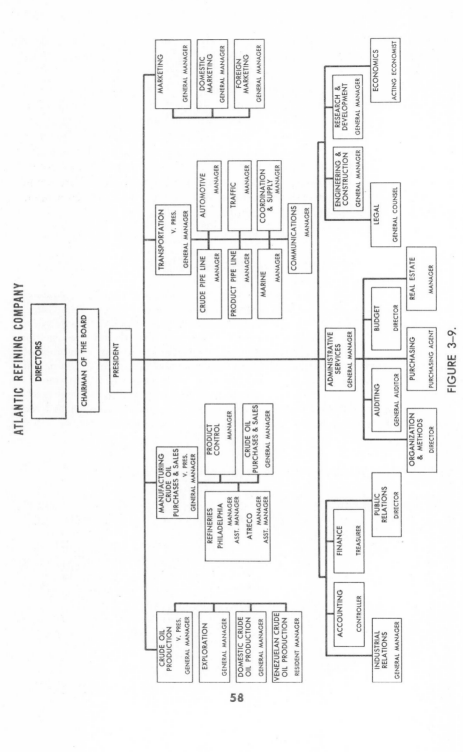

FIGURE 3-9.

The Firm. Jersey Standard was not the first Standard Oil Company. It was preceded by other companies and alliances, beginning with a partnership among John D. Rockefeller, Maurice B. Clark (Rockefeller's partner in a Cleveland mercantile commission firm), two of Clark's brothers, and Samuel Andrews (the only one with experience in refining). The partners established a refinery— the Excelsior Works—in 1863, and added a second kerosene-manufacturing unit—the Standard—a few years later, after the interest of the Clarks had been purchased by Rockefeller and Andrews, and after William Rockefeller had been brought into the partnership. In 1870, the Standard Oil Company (Ohio) was organized by the Rockefellers and their associates as a million dollar corporation, possessing the largest refining capacity of any firm in the world.

Depressed economic conditions led to the creation of the Standard Oil Alliance in the 1870's. Rockefeller and his associates concluded that stable and secure earnings for themselves and others in the industry would be best assured by the formation of an association of stockholders of the refining companies in the Eastern part of the United States (this being a period when corporations had only a few large owners of their stocks). Some producing companies (in the language of the industry, only those extracting crude oil from below the earth's surface are called "producers"), pipeline firms—which gathered crude oil from the producing fields for the refineries, and some marketing organizations were brought into the Alliance in addition to other refineries. This Alliance had a very "loose" nature, being a community of interest of more than forty owners (although the shares of all participants in firms outside of the state of Ohio were held—and voted—for the common body of owners by a few individuals acting as trustees).

Difficulties in managing the Alliance and adverse corporation tax laws led to the birth of the Standard Oil Trust and Jersey Standard in 1882. The Trust Agreement adopted early that year provided for the organization of a New Jersey corporation to own and operate Ohio Standard's transportation, storing, and manufacturing facilities in the seaboard state. Jersey Standard occupied this position as a state unit in a combination controlled by the Trustees until 1892 when the Ohio Supreme Court held that Ohio Standard could not, under the corporate laws of that state, turn over control of its stock to the Trustees.

The Ohio judicial decision compelled a reorganization of the combination, resulting in an expanded role for Jersey Standard. Under a changed corporate charter (and the favorable corporation laws of its home state), the New Jersey company acquired additional operating functions and, more importantly, became a holding company exchanging some of its shares for controlling interests in other units of the Trust. By the turn of the century, Jersey Standard was the major instrument for controlling units of the combination—a position it held until the United States Supreme Court ordered it to divest itself of most of its holdings in a decision handed down in 1911.

Jersey Standard survived the adverse decision and, as has been indicated, has grown to a position of great prominence in modern business. In the experience of its predecessor companies and in its own history prior to 1911, however, we can see much of significance.

The Industry. The nature of the petroleum industry is quite complex as a consequence of the many functions performed. Crude oil must be extracted from its natural location (the "production" process), stored, sold to refiners, transported to refineries, manufactured into refined products, sold to wholesalers, retailers and ultimate users, and transported to them. Initially, firms tended to specialize in each of these functions and, therefore, a number of industries were involved in the process of getting the oil out of the ground and into the hands of the final user in some useful form. However, "vertical" integration began to take place quite early in the history of the industry, with refiners beginning to engage in production, transportation, and marketing in addition to "manufacturing" crude into various petroleum products. (The "major" firms in the industry today are almost completely integrated, doing everything but selling refinery products at retail.) In its early days, Standard Oil engaged only in refining, gradually taking on the transporting function through building and acquiring pipelines and water-borne carriers, getting into "production" through the search for oil fields and drilling for the raw material, taking over the wholesaling function, and so on. The other firms in the industry developed in much the same way, although a few still perform only one or a few of the functions, and so now the industry contains firms in various degrees of integration.

Product Markets. To succeed in business, Standard Oil had to understand the nature of potential markets for its products, adjust itself to existing markets and create new and expanded demands. Fortunately for refiners, ready markets existed for illuminants and lubricants from the beginning. Whale and other oils had been used in lamps as sources of light for centuries, and the rapid growth of mechanization in the nineteenth century required large quantities of oils and greases—a need which had been filled by lubricants derived from vegetables and animals. The various products of Standard Oil refineries were able to compete favorably in these markets, and in large measure displaced the traditional products. It should be pointed out that gas and—more importantly— electricity were also strong competitors as sources of light, with the latter eventually driving the others from the field.

Petroleum products were also sold as sources of energy. Fuel oil, and the diesel oil and gasoline for the automobiles and trucks expanding rapidly in number after 1900, were sold partly in existing and partly in new markets. Although some fuel oil was sold as an energy source prior to 1911, it had little success in displacing coal in this period, its use growing slowly relative to the older fuel. However, greater success was met with in providing a source of power for self-propelled vehicles, although this market was relatively small until after the dissolution of Standard Oil.

Standard Oil's success in adjusting to American product markets was undisputed, but it was less successful abroad. There it met with different requirements of consumers, adverse governmental action, strong competitors refining the petroleum indigenous to their countries, and the Nobels, Rothschilds and others who were pushing the products of Russian crude in all of the markets of Europe and Asia. In the United States, Standard controlled over 80 per cent of the refining capacity and was the dominant seller in domestic markets. Overseas, it had to settle for a minor role.

Productive Resource Markets. The major input of refineries is, of course, crude oil. For some time Standard Oil held back from engaging in crude oil production, preferring to purchase crude from the many small producers whose competition kept them in economic difficulties and the price of their product low. In the early years, there existed an oil exchange on which were traded certificates representing stored crude oil. Initially, Standard paid the price established by trading on the exchange; later, it produced part of its own crude oil requirements and posted the price it would pay producers for the balance of its needs.

Little information exists about the nature of the "labor markets" Standard Oil bought in, and it was financially successful enough to avoid having to enter the money markets for funds. Although labor and money markets are important to any firm, there is little indication that their nature posed substantial problems to the managers of Standard.

The Dynamic Nature of Markets. Among the adjustments required by Standard was the adaptation to constantly changing product and resource markets. Although there was overall a constant expansion in demand for refinery products, some short-term fluctuations posed great problems for Standard. In the early years, new crude oil pools came and went with great rapidity. This was reflected in wide fluctuations in crude production and in the price of the basic resource. Kerosene prices fluctuated with the price of crude, and local price wars aggravated the problem. General depressions of business in the 1870's, 1880's, and 1890's made for further uncertainty, as did seasonal fluctuations in demand. Producers and refiners failed by the score. The alliance of refiners into the Standard Oil combination was, at least in part, a means of dealing with the violent market changes which were responsible for the high mortality rate in the industry.

Customers. Very few of the Standard Oil combination's sales were to the ultimate consumers of its products. Its customers were wholesalers or retailers, of which the former were in a position to have greater influence on the firm's policies and operations. In the early 1880's, most of Standard Oil's sales were to wholesalers not in the combination. Some of these were poor administrators and slow to adopt new distribution methods (which had an adverse impact on Standard's share of the market); others mixed the refinery product with less costly oils, thereby giving the consumer some doubt about the quality of the combination's kerosene; and some failed to pass on special reductions in price to the retailer, frustrating the refiners in the attainment of their object of increasing sales volume. One big railroad customer, annoyed at losing some shipments of Standard products to a competitor, stopped buying from a Standard Oil affiliate —apparently in an attempt to force a change in the company's policy with respect to freight shipment.

Suppliers of Labor and Services.   In the company's vast operations, it dealt
with many classes of employees—although it was reluctant to enter into formal
relations with their unions. There were only a very few strikes prior to 1911,
usually restricted to small groups of workers. A strike of boilermakers at one
Standard plant in 1903 involved a demand for recognition of the Brotherhood
of Boilermakers, a demand which the company was unwilling to grant.

Standard Oil was a large purchaser of transportation services, which usually
put it in a position to ask and receive special concessions. However, after the
group had constructed its own pipelines, railroads were given payments to
compensate them for the loss of traffic. This was not philanthropy on the part
of Standard, but a recognition that the good-will of the railroads was required
to promote other objects of the vast enterprise.

Suppliers of Money.   Throughout its history, Jersey Standard has been in a
strong financial position and has rarely been required to go outside of the firm
for funds. Consequently—other than the influence that the original owner-
managers had over the operations of the firm—the company has apparently not
been the object of strong influence of lenders and other "outside" suppliers of
money.

Suppliers of Raw Materials.   Those supplying crude oil to the Standard
refineries prior to 1911 were frequently unwilling to content themselves with
either selling or refusing to sell at the market price (or at the price bid by buyers
for the combine). They formed associations to curtail production, to fight the
Standard Oil "monopoly," and to conduct negotiations with Standard to cooperatively solve the problems of the producers. Frequently, they took legal and
political action to gain their objects of higher prices and greater volume.

Competitors.   Those firms competing with Standard refineries prior to 1911
also were rarely content with individual economic action in the product and
crude oil markets. The combination itself was the result of agreements among
some American refiners to do something about economic conditions confronting
them, as were organizations such as the Central Refiners' Association of which
Standard was a member. Agreements were also reached with foreign competitors, although the latter sometimes employed their political influence to keep
Standard out of their markets. Some domestic competitors not involved in
agreements with Standard attacked the giant firm in advertisements, pamphlets
and in the courts.

The Image of Standard Oil and Its Creators.   By the time of the dissolution
of the Standard Oil combine, a very clear and very unfavorable image of it had
developed. It was regarded as a monopoly controlled by "evasive arrogant men
grown rich and powerful on railroad rebates, while buying out little businessmen
by the dozens."

This poor opinion of Standard was in part the product of its own behavior, but
others were also influential in shaping the image. Adverse histories of the firm

appeared in books and magazines. Newspapers and ministers fumed over the "immoral" actions of the organization. Reports of government agencies investigating charges against the company helped to darken the shady side of the picture.

Although the company countered by publishing its own history in 1888, by having speeches and investigations made in its behalf, by advertising, by influencing editorial opinion and by presenting its point of view before investigative bodies, this apparently had little impact on public opinion and was characterized as being "too little and too late."

Laws Affecting Standard Oil. Although the company was eventually to be broken up under the Sherman Antitrust Act and was prosecuted under state as well as federal law, not all the laws affecting it were adverse. Laws governing the extraction of crude oil led producers to drill and pump as quickly as possible, providing an ample supply of the raw material at low prices. Corporation laws in the various states made possible the growth of the large combine—this was especially true of the New Jersey legislation of 1889 permitting its corporations to hold the stock of other corporations, which made it legally possible for Jersey Standard to become a holding company.

Some laws adversely affected the firm's operations, however. The Interstate Commerce Act of 1887 and its amendments controlled the company's pipeline-operations and its relations with railroads. State and federal antitrust legislation opened the company to attack by private persons as well as by governments. Foreign governments passed tariff and other laws restricting the entry of Standard into foreign markets.

Governments Affecting Standard. It should be quite apparent by now that state, federal, and foreign government agencies and official exerted great influence on Standard's decisions and the results of its operations. Whether administrative, judicial, or legislative actions were involved, governments influenced the company both favorably and unfavorably. In attempting to influence elections, legislatures, administrators, and judicial decision, Standard Oil met with some early success; but in the end it was government action which killed the combine, leaving a weakened Jersey Standard to adjust to a new environment.

SUGGESTED READINGS

[*There are a number of books that deal with the functions of business in great detail. Characteristically, one or more chapters are devoted to each of the following: production, marketing, business finance, personnel management, business organization, and administration. Two of the best recent publications of this sort are listed.*]

Hart, Donald J., *Business in a Dynamic Society* (New York: Macmillan, 1963). This volume goes beyond the examination of business functions, investigating (among other topics) the roots of the business environment and the consequences of social, economic, and technological change.

Wheeler, Bayard O., *Business: An Introductory Analysis* (New York: Harper & Row, 1962). In addition to more traditional topics, this work concerns itself with the business system and the environment of business.

CHAPTER 4

AMERICAN
INDUSTRIES

American business has grown from a few shops and stores producing and selling a small variety of goods to a system in which millions of firms in thousands of industries are engaged in selling goods and services in many markets. Many attempts have been made to classify business firms according to the nature of the Industry they are in. Statisticians collect data on the output and other important characteristics of industry. Other economists classify industries according to the degree of competition or concentration. Still others have developed tables showing the interdependence of industries. The findings of these scholars and others—including historians—give us a view of American industry as it exists today.

THE DEVELOPMENT OF AMERICAN INDUSTRIES

Business firms produce goods and services for sale in markets by acquiring productive resources, combining them and making their product available to the purchaser. In an earlier day, almost all of the steps in this process were performed by producers who would secure raw materials, combine their labor with them through the use of simple capital equipment, and then sell the product in their own shop or in the market. Consequently, the number of industries was small. As markets grew, it became profitable to specialize in just one of the steps in the business process; where *one* industry had previously existed, a number of them took its place. In the production and distribution of furniture, for example, the industries of logging, lumbering, transportation, manufacturing, financing, wholesaling, and retailing became involved in getting a piece of furniture into the consumer's hands, whereas colonial furniture makers had performed all of these functions.

Changes in the nature of American industry have resulted in an industrial structure in which manufacturing now contributes the largest amount to national income. The pre-eminence of manufacturing in our nation and of American manufactures in the world is a development of the past century and a half. Although manufacturing grew greatly after the War of 1812, prior to the Civil War we ranked behind England and were rivaled by France and Germany for second place as a manufacturing nation. Also, the value of agricultural production was still much greater than that of manufacturing on the eve of the contest between the North and the South.

The relatively late emergence of the United States as a manufacturing nation had its roots in its colonial beginnings and the conditions confronting early American businessmen. England did not wish manufactures to develop in the colonies that would compete with the goods of English businessmen, and took measures to restrict colonial production of certain commodities—although she also took measures to promote the manufacture of such things as ships that could not be produced very economically in the mother country. For the most part, however, England wished the production of plantation staples—tobacco, rice, indigo, and cotton—and the products of the fisheries and forests. Even after the Revolutionary War, American trade was still chiefly with England, and her policies continued to restrain the purchase of manufactured goods from the United States. Further, British goods were cheaper in the American markets than was domestic production. Among domestic factors limiting the growth of manufacturing were the lack of large markets for manufactured products and the lack of transportation facilities to make it inexpensive to sell in widely scattered markets.

After the War of 1812, American business turned its attention to the development of domestic markets and to producing for those markets. The digging of canals, the use of steam power on riverboats, the rise of railroads—all served to link large areas of the United States together economically. Now that it was possible to distribute goods inexpensively to various parts of the nation, large-scale manufacturing grew to serve customers in widespread markets. Recognizing that profit would result from specialization in one or a few of the business functions, businessmen no longer attempted—as had the mercantile capitalists of New England and the Middle Atlantic states—to perform the bulk of the various business functions and the specialized businessman emerged, creating new industries. Specialization in transportation and distribution created the shipping industry, the railroad industry, and the wholesale industry and caused retailers to specialize in the sale of certain classes of goods rather than operating general stores.

Conditions during the last four decades of the nineteenth century were conducive to the further development of manufacturing and consequent change in our industrial structure. Railroad networks were further expanded, population increased, and markets grew. Governmental policies favorable to the growth of manufactures were adopted during the Civil War and in succeeding years. This was the age of "triumphant American capitalism," and the triumph was most noteworthy in the field of manufacturing. By the end of the 1890's we had surpassed England in total value of manufactured products, and manufacturing production exceeded that of American agriculture. The twentieth century has seen the rise of new industries—including many new manufacturing industries as a consequence of scientific discoveries and technological developments—but the revolutionary changes in the structure of American industry had already been made.

CLASSIFICATIONS OF AMERICAN INDUSTRIES

An industry is composed of those firms or establishments producing essentially the same product. In our highly developed business system, there are a great number of industries; these can best be studied through some sort of classification scheme. A quite fundamental breakdown of American business is into extractive, manufacturing, distributive, and service industries. Extractive industries are engaged in extracting natural resources from their location in nature. Agriculture, commercial fishing, forestry, and mining are the major kinds of extractive industry. Normally, freshly extracted natural resources are not ready for ultimate use in their raw state and require manufacturing processes to be put into usable condition. Manufacturers process raw material, fabricate it into various forms, and assemble parts into final products. These final products are usually transported to product markets, where wholesalers and/or retailers distribute them to the consumer if the manufacturer does not sell directly to the ultimate purchaser. Many firms are in industries that do not sell physical products at all, but are engaged in the production and sale of services. Firms selling financial, insurance, real estate, and communications services are only part of the great number of growing service industries. (Figure 4–1 shows this basic division.)

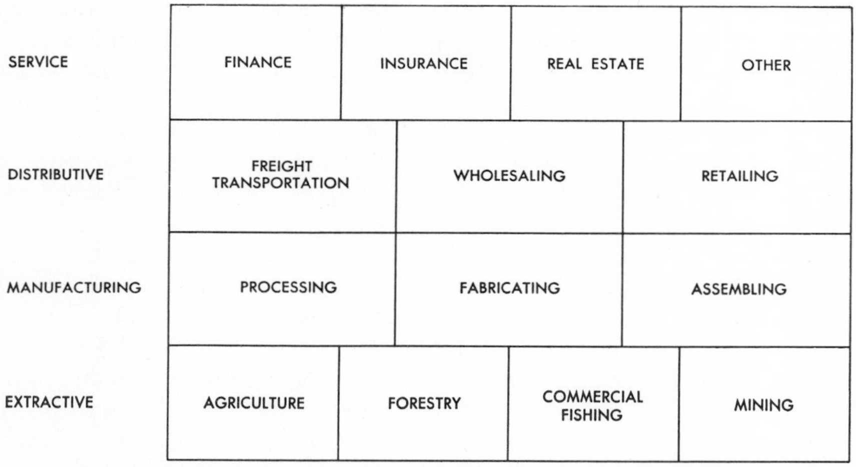

SERVICE	FINANCE	INSURANCE	REAL ESTATE	OTHER
DISTRIBUTIVE	FREIGHT TRANSPORTATION	WHOLESALING		RETAILING
MANUFACTURING	PROCESSING	FABRICATING		ASSEMBLING
EXTRACTIVE	AGRICULTURE	FORESTRY	COMMERCIAL FISHING	MINING

FIGURE 4–1. The Industrial Structure of American Business.

Within each major division of industries, there are many groups of related industries. Mining, for example, can be broken down into metal mining, mining of nonmetallic materials, anthracite mining, bituminous coal mining, and the production of crude petroleum and natural gas. Some of these groups can be further subclassified into industries. Metal mining includes the iron-mining industry, copper-mining industry, and others. (*See* Figures 4–2 and 4–3.)

An industry is sometimes regarded as being composed of those firms producing the same or similar products. Unfortunately, while this is true for many cases, it is not true for all. When specialized business units were small, they fit quite well into just one industrial classification. However, when they began to combine with other firms, classifying a business firm according to the industry it operated in became more difficult. Horizontal combination—a combination of firms in the same industry—did not create a problem, of course, but vertical combination—a combination of firms producing goods or rendering services used by others in the combine—did. For example, the United States Steel Corporation—the first billion

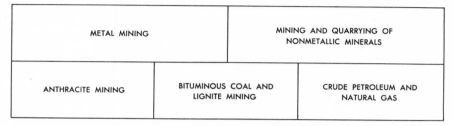

METAL MINING		MINING AND QUARRYING OF NONMETALLIC MINERALS	
ANTHRACITE MINING	BITUMINOUS COAL AND LIGNITE MINING	CRUDE PETROLEUM AND NATURAL GAS	

FIGURE 4–2.   The Structure of Mining Industries Division.

IRON ORES	COPPER ORES	LEAD AND ZINC ORES	GOLD AND SILVER ORES
BAUXITE AND OTHER ALUMINUM ORES	FERROALLOY ORES	MISCELLANEOUS METAL ORES	METAL MINING SERVICES

FIGURE 4–3.   The Structure of the Metal Mining Group.

dollar combine—included mining companies, railroad companies, shipping companies, basic iron and steel manufacturers, iron and steel fabricators, assemblers and constructors of iron and steel products, sales companies, and others. U.S. Steel fits into a number of industrial classifications, and it is not proper therefore to regard the entire firm as falling into the steel manufacturing category. A tendency in business firms toward diversification of products by producing quite different and unrelated products has further complicated the task of industrial classification. General Motors produces—in addition to cars, buses, and trucks—electrical appliances and equipment, diesel locomotives and engines, aircraft engines and earth-moving equipment. In order to fit the operations of firms such as U.S. Steel and General Motors into the standard industrial classification, it has been necessary to define "industry" in terms of something other than firms.

Government Classifications of Industries

In conducting censuses of business, the U.S. Bureau of the Census has adopted the "establishment" rather than the firm as the basic unit of industry classification. An industry is defined as a group of establishments primarily engaged in the same line or similar lines of economic activity. The Standard Industrial Classification Manual then goes on to define an establishment as ". . . a single physical location where business is conducted or where services or industrial operations are performed; for example, a factory, mill, store, mine or farm. . . . An establishment is not necessarily identical with the business concern or firm which may consist of one or more establishments." [1] Establishments are economic units, carrying on a distinctive economic activity at a specific physical location, reporting as units and managed as units. The use of the establishment as the basic reporting unit for census purposes means that data concerning industries are much more accurate than if a decision had to be made to put a firm producing many diverse products into one specific industrial class. (Figures 4–1 through 4–3 are based on the classifications in the *Standard Industrial Classification Manual*. The appendix to this chapter shows in greater detail the basic divisions and major groups of American industries according to this government classification.)

The U.S. Department of Commerce has adopted a classification of industries whose major divisions are very similar to those of the Bureau of the Budget. The Commerce Department employs its classification scheme in reporting information in its monthly publication, *Survey of Current Business*. In the July issue (the "National Income" number) is reported the contributions of major divisions of American industries to the nation's income during the preceding calendar year—that is, the contributions of various classes of industries to wages, rents, interest, and profits received during that year are shown. This breakdown gives us some idea of the relative importance of major industry divisions. Table 4–1 shows the contributions to national income by industry for a recent year.

Economists' Classifications of Industry

Economists who make a study of the structure of American industry go beyond an examination of the relative importance of various industries in terms of contribution to total output. Some have employed a classification of industries similar to government classifications to show, through input-output tables, the relationships among the various indus-

[1] Bureau of the Budget, *Standard Industrial Classification Manual*, Vol. I, Manufacturing Industries, (Washington, D.C.: Government Printing Office, 1945), p. 1.

trial groups. Frequently, however, economists have adopted other classifications of industry. One popular categorization classifies industries according to the type of "utility" they create. Others have looked at industries in terms of the number of firms in the industry and have developed a classification of American industry accordingly.

Table 4–1. *Contributions to National Income by Industry* (1964)

Industry	Dollar Contribution (millions)	Percentage Contribution
All Industries	$514,400	100.0%
Agriculture, Forestry, Fisheries	17,600	3.4
Mining	6,200	1.2
Manufacturing	154,700	30.1
Contract Construction	26,200	5.1
Transportation	21,000	4.1
Wholesale and Retail Trade	78,100	15.2
Finance, Insurance and Real Estate	57,000	11.1
Communications and Public Utilities	21,400	4.2
Services	58,000	11.3
Government and Government Enterprises	70,000	13.6

SOURCE: Office of Business Economics, U.S. Department of Commerce, *Survey of Current Business*, Vol. 45, No. 8 (August 1965), p. 45. Adding up the percentage contributions of the various industries shows that the total falls short of 100.0%. This is the result of excluding the contribution of the "rest of the world," a classification used to show pay received of permanent U.S. residents employed by foreign governments and international organizations, the net inflow from abroad of dividends and branch profits, and net interest paid into the United States.

INTERINDUSTRY RELATIONSHIPS. Input-output tables show the interindustry relationships existing in the American economy. (*See* Table 4–2.) Industries are looked at as being completely interdependent, so that any change in one industry will have some impact on all others. According to the designer of this particular analysis:

> The principle of this method of statistical description is rather simple. Each "industry" (including households) is treated as a single accounting entity ... with sales entered on one side of its trading account and purchases on the other ... the sales of one industry are the purchases of another. Entering the sales and purchase accounts of all the separate industries in one large table we get a comprehensive view of the structure of the national economy as a whole.[2]

An analysis of industry of this type has special value in estimating the impact on various industries of such things as expenditures for defense production during periods of national emergency. Although they are useful for many things, such tables are rather complex, and more elementary

[2] Wassily Leontief, *The Structure of the American Economy, 1919–1939* (New York: Oxford U.P., 1951), p. 4.

Table 4–2. Interindustry Transactions Among U.S. Industries, 1958

(in millions of dollars)

	Agriculture, forestry, and fisheries	Mining	Contract construction	Manufacturing	Transportation	Wholesale and retail trade	Finance, insurance, and real estate	Communications and public utilities	Services	Government enterprises	Total Interindustry Sales
Agriculture, forestry, and fisheries	15,578	—		25,075	37	153	2,173	—	24	625	43,902
Mining	103	1,129	237	13,346	29	8	156	1,715	41	148	17,431
Contract construction	613	10	756	751	1,249	775	6,019	852	971	1,206	12,454
Manufacturing	6,108	1,456	26,528	134,645	3,228	4,489	1,833	959	17,565	495	197,306
Transportation	848	522	2,105	9,770	2,107	396	624	391	422	801	17,986
Wholesale and retail trade	1,993	368	6,341	12,133	1,004	1,582	1,324	307	2,115	104	27,271
Finance, insurance, and real estate	2,677	1,802	729	4,918	1,725	6,628	10,779	463	4,723	162	34,606
Communications and public utilities	399	265	301	4,453	418	2,928	1,022	3,638	3,583	485	17,492
Services	1,214	424	2,968	8,764	1,375	5,997	3,041	823	5,175	173	29,954
Government enterprises	10	12	15	632	794	1,338	1,084	2,989	748	11	7,633
Total Interindustry Purchases	29,543	5,988	39,988	214,487	11,966	24,294	28,055	12,137	35,367	4,210	406,035

SOURCE: Office of Business Economics, Department of Commerce, *Survey of Current Business* (Washington, D.C.: U.S. Government Printing Office) September, 1965, pp. 33–39.
NOTE: The rows show the sales of one industry division to all industry divisions; the columns show the purchases of one industry division from all industry divisions.

classifications (used for different purposes) have been employed by other economists studying the structure of American industry.

INDUSTRIES CLASSIFIED BY TYPE OF UTILITY CREATED. Earlier we noted that the object of business and other economic activity was to satisfy wants. Things have "utility" when they have want-satisfying power. There are, essentially, five kinds of utility created by economic activity: place, form, time, possession, and service. Each industry creates one or more of these kinds of utility. Place utility is created by transporting things from one place to another. The transportation industries are obvious examples of industries creating place utility, although the extractive industries of agriculture, forestry, fishing, and mining also are basically involved in the creation of place utility. When the form of something is changed into something more useful, or when something is combined with other things into useful objects, form utility is created. Manufacturing industries provide the best illustrations of this process. Wholesalers, retailers, and other sellers usually create time utility by holding goods until they are wanted as well as create possession utility by transferring title and physical custody of goods to others. The many service industries create "service" utility, although we should point out that wholesaling, retailing, and transporting industries are also selling services.

INDUSTRIES CLASSIFIED BY NUMBER OF FIRMS. Since all industries contain a determinable number of firms, and since this has some significance for the way in which the industry performs, a classification has been developed on this basis as follows:

Number of Firms in Industry	Industry Type
One	Monopoly
Two	Duopoly
"A Few"	Oligopoly
"Many"	Competitive

The root "poly" used in this classification means "seller" or "sellers," and so monopoly means "one seller"; duopoly, "two sellers"; and oligopoly, "a few sellers." Therefore, a monopolistic industry is characterized by one firm—or one seller—and so on.

Before we examine these industry types in some detail, it is necessary to make a distinction between "industry" and "market." What is meant by a market is the area within which sellers, as well as buyers, find it desirable to carry on trade. It is possible, therefore, that there might be many firms (sellers) in a certain industry, but that only one, two, or a few of them find it desirable to sell in a particular market. That is, we might have a "competitive" industry but a "monopolistic" market in certain cases. Also, there are situations in which one firm may be, for all practical purposes, the only one in American industry, but may not have a monopoly in American markets owing to the presence of foreign firms selling in that market. The structure of American markets, as opposed to that of American industry, will be taken up in a later discussion.

Although many industry studies have been made since the 1930's, we do not yet have a complete catalog of all industries as fitting into certain categories, but we can find numerous examples to illustrate each.

For some fifty years, the production of primary aluminum in the United States was a monopoly of the Aluminum Company of America; it serves as a classic example of a monopolistic industry. After World War II, under pressure from the federal government, some of the facilities which Alcoa operated for the government were sold to the Kaiser and Reynolds aluminum companies and the structure of the industry changed from that of monopoly to oligopoly.

Duopoly is said to be the proper classification of the metal container industry. For a few years at the beginning of the century the American Can Company produced nearly the total output of this industry, but was soon challenged by the Continental Can Company. Although there are other companies in the industry, American and Continental currently produce about 75 per cent of the total production of metal containers, leading to the classification of the industry as a duopoly.

If we are to take a look at an American industry and classify it by counting the number of firms in it, we would find few, if any, pure cases of monopoly or duopoly. There are almost always a few small producers who do not produce for the market or who account for only a small share of the total sales. In the aluminum industry and the metal container industry, such companies exist but are not taken account, since they are of negligible importance as compared to the dominant firm or firms in the industry. However, in most manufacturing industries in America there are a few firms that are dominant, and duopoly and monopoly are the exception. These industries, referred to as oligopolistic, are well known to most of us. There is the "Big Three" of the automobile industry as well as the "Big Five" of the motion pictures. The steel, petroleum, and chemical industries furnish further examples.

Finally there are those industries called "competitive." These are industries in which there are so many firms that the action of any one of them is of no consequence to any other. This is not true of the oligopolistic industry in which the behavior of any one of the firms will almost always bring about some change in the activities of one or more of the others. Relative ease of entry has always been a mark of the competitive industry, and we tend to see small businesses making up the competitive industries of America. Agriculture has long been regarded as competitive. There are a large number of farms in America, although some students of agriculture contend that the farmers have been able to secure the results of monopoly through political action rather than through industrial organization. In various fields of retailing we also see a large number of firms, although it should be again pointed out that each might have a partial monopoly in a given market even though there are a host of firms in America.

Economists who view industries in the light of the number of business firms contained in each are chiefly concerned with the implications for public policy of such analysis. For the businessman, there may be some value in viewing his industry in this way, since he may thereby gain some understanding of what the likely consequences of certain actions on his part might be, or how he should respond to the actions of others in his industry. However, since the businessman is more concerned with the market situation confronting him—including the number of other firms selling or buying in that market—that number is of greater importance to him than the number in the industry.

Other Classifications of Industries

Government statistics and business publications sometimes refer to manufacturing industries according to the classes of buyers of the output of manufacturers and by the durability of the products. Those industries selling goods to other producers to be used in further production are, quite logically, referred to as "producers' goods industries." When the output of an industry is sold to ultimate consumers, the firms or establishments are in a "consumers' goods industry." Since goods vary in durability, we also have the "durable goods industries" and the "nondurable goods industries." Frequently, these two classifications are put together and reference is made to "producers' durables," "producers' nondurables," and so on. Such classifications have value for the student of industry because the sales of all industries in a particular class seem to fluctuate in approximately the same amount and direction as time passes.

There are, of course, other possible classifications of American industries. However, the above seem to be those which are most useful to businessmen or those to which they are most likely to see reference. Each industry has its own characteristics, but through classifying industries as we have, some basic knowledge of the nature of American business and its structure can be secured.

The great growth of American business since colonial times has been influenced by a number of factors. Technological changes, the opening up of the interior, historical and geographical accidents, and many other influences account, in various degree, for the development of industry in the United States. One very important set of influences—some say the most important—has been the existence of certain economic institutions that have permitted and promoted business to grow as it has. To an investigation of these institutions of our capitalistic economic system we shall next turn.

APPENDIX: Standard Industrial Classification

Division A.—Agriculture, forestry, and fisheries:
    Major Group 01.   Commercial farms
    Major Group 02.   Noncommercial farms
    Major Group 07.   Agricultural services and hunting and trapping
    Major Group 08.   Forestry
    Major Group 09.   Fisheries

Division B.—Mining:
    Major Group 10.   Metal mining
    Major Group 11.   Anthracite mining
    Major Group 12.   Bituminous coal and lignite mining
    Major Group 13.   Crude petroleum and natural gas
    Major Group 14.   Mining and quarrying of nonmetallic minerals, except fuels

Division C.—Contract construction:
    Major Group 15.   Building construction—general contractors
    Major Group 16.   Construction other than building construction—general contractors
    Major Group 17.   Construction—special trade contractors

Division D.—Manufacturing:
    Major Group 19.   Ordnance and accessories
    Major Group 20.   Food and kindred products
    Major Group 21.   Tobacco manufactures
    Major Group 22.   Textile mill products
    Major Group 23.   Apparel and other finished products made from fabrics and similar materials
    Major Group 24.   Lumber and wood products, except furniture
    Major Group 25.   Furniture and fixtures
    Major Group 26.   Paper and allied products
    Major Group 27.   Printing, publishing, and allied industries
    Major Group 28.   Chemicals and allied products
    Major Group 29.   Petroleum refining and related industries
    Major Group 30.   Rubber and miscellaneous plastics products

Major Group 31.   Leather and leather products
Major Group 32.   Stone, clay, and glass products
Major Group 33.   Primary metal industries
Major Group 34.   Fabricated metal products, except ordnance, machinery, and transportation equipment
Major Group 35.   Machinery, except electrical
Major Group 36.   Electrical machinery, equipment, and supplies
Major Group 37.   Transportation equipment
Major Group 38.   Professional, scientific, and controlling instruments; photographic and optical goods; watches and clocks
Major Group 39.   Miscellaneous manufacturing industries

Division E.—Transportation, communication, electric, gas and sanitary services:
Major Group 40.   Railroad transportation
Major Group 41.   Local and suburban transit and interurban passenger transportation
Major Group 42.   Motor freight transportation and warehousing
Major Group 44.   Water transportation
Major Group 45.   Transportation by air
Major Group 46.   Pipeline transportation
Major Group 47.   Transportation services
Major Group 48.   Communication
Major Group 49.   Electric, gas, and sanitary services

Division F.—Wholesale and retail trade:
Major Group 50.   Wholesale trade
Major Group 52.   Retail trade—building materials, hardware and farm equipment
Major Group 53.   Retail trade—general merchandise
Major Group 54.   Retail trade—food
Major Group 55.   Automotive dealers and gasoline service stations
Major Group 56.   Retail trade—apparel and accessories
Major Group 57.   Retail trade—furniture, home furnishings and equipment
Major Group 58.   Retail trade—eating and drinking places
Major Group 59.   Retail trade—miscellaneous retail stores

Division G.—Finance, insurance, and real estate:
Major Group 60.   Banking
Major Group 61.   Credit agencies other than banks
Major Group 62.   Security and commodity brokers, dealers, exchanges, and services
Major Group 63.   Insurance carriers
Major Group 64.   Insurance agents, brokers, and service
Major Group 65.   Real estate
Major Group 66.   Combinations of real estate, insurance, loans, law offices
Major Group 67.   Holding and other investment companies

Division H.—Services:
   Major Group 70. Hotels, rooming houses, camps, and other lodging places
   Major Group 72. Personal services
   Major Group 73. Miscellaneous business services
   Major Group 75. Automobile repair, automobile services, and garages
   Major Group 76. Miscellaneous repair services
   Major Group 78. Motion pictures
   Major Group 79. Amusement and recreation services, except motion pictures
   Major Group 80. Medical and other health services
   Major Group 81. Legal services
   Major Group 82. Educational services
   Major Group 84. Museums, art galleries, botanical and zoological gardens
   Major Group 86. Non profit membership organizations
   Major Group 88. Private households
   Major Group 89. Miscellaneous services

Division I.—Government:
   Major Group 91. Federal government
   Major Group 92. State government
   Major Group 93. Local government
   Major Group 94. International government

Division J.—Nonclassifiable establishments
   Major Group 99. Nonclassifiable establishments

READING: The Petroleum Industry * by Joel B. Dirlam

Petroleum in the U.S. Economy. The petroleum industry includes the production of crude oil and natural gas, their transport and refining, and the distribution of petroleum products to the consumer. Changes in technology blur the outlines of the industry as it becomes economically feasible to extract petroleum or its products from oil shale, gilsonite or tar sands, or to manufacture organic chemicals and plastics from petroleum. Petrochemicals, which account for about one-quarter of the total value of chemicals, are manufactured by oil companies, while chemical companies use natural gas and refinery products as raw materials.

Nevertheless, until the two industries effect managerial symbiosis, it is useful to speak of an oil company entering the chemical business, when Standard Oil (N.J.) produces plastics, or a chemical company moving into petroleum when Monsanto acquires Lion Oil. The technologies and, more important, the economic characteristics and behavior of the two industries are still distinct.

Petroleum has been a growth industry. A decline in demand for one product has more than replaced by increases in demand for others. Petroleum refining has been sufficiently flexible, and petroleum engineers sufficiently ingenious, to per-

* Reprinted with permission of The Macmillan Company from *The Structure of American Industry,* by Walter Adams (ed.) Third Edition © The Macmillan Company, 1961, pp. 277–281.

mit the industry to be as powerful in the jet age as it was when it supplied oil for the lamps of China. From the end of World War I through 1956, the U.S. demand for petroleum grew at an annual rate of approximately 6 per cent, far exceeding the rise in Gross National Product. Dieselization of the railroads, mechanization on the farm, and the substitution of oil and natural gas home heating for coal have all contributed to the growth of the oil industry. But it has been the demand for gasoline as motor fuel that has contributed most. Until recently a U.S. phenomenon, it appears that the rush of mankind to self-propelled, wheeled vehicles has just begun. In a global context, petroleum demand may be expected to repeat, on a larger scale, U.S. experience.

Together, natural gas and petroleum products have accounted for about 65 per cent of the energy consumed in the U.S. in recent years.[1] This dominance is a result partly of superior efficiency—as in the diesel locomotive—partly of convenience, as in home heating where both fuel oil and natural gas are attractive. Most important, there is no substitute for gasoline.

Compared with the other American industries, the petroleum industry is of gigantic size. Its capital expenditures have made up about one-sixth of annual Gross Private Domestic Investment. Of the twenty-four manufacturing corporations with assets in excess of one billion dollars at the end of 1957, ten were oil companies.[2] The assets of the three largest oil concerns—Jersey Standard, Gulf, and Socony Mobil—were about four billion dollars in excess of the assets of the automobile companies represented, and $7.6 billion more than steel assets.

Continuing Problems of the Oil Industry. Two problem areas have plagued the oil industry since its inception. The first has been the necessity for arriving at and living with a competitive code, formal or informal, that would be compatible with the industry's economic peculiarities: A high proportion of fixed costs has made the industry especially sensitive to price-cutting. In spite of economies of scale in marketing and refining, niches provided for newcomers in a rapidly growing market have made it impossible for the large oil companies to duplicate the price stability of steel, automobiles, or aluminum. The bounty of nature in making crude oil available has created the second major problem.

The Standard Oil Trust. Shortly after "Colonel" Drake's well was spudded in at Titusville, Pennsylvania in August 1858, there were local squabbles between teamsters and pipelines. They were soon dwarfed by pitched battles between the Standard Oil Trust and independent producers and refiners. For almost thirty years after 1883 (when it gobbled up the last independent pipeline) the Standard Oil monopoly bought, transported, refined, and marketed some 90 per cent of U.S. petroleum.

Although managerial efficiency and economies of large-scale operation played a large part in its success, Standard's domination of the oil industry was abetted by unfair competition. It tried successfully to prevent independent pipelines

---

[1] U.S. Bureau of Mines, *Annual Petroleum Statement No. 434* (November 14, 1958), p. 18.
[2] *First National City Bank Monthly Letter* (September 1958), p. 105.

from reaching markets or oil fields; it used its monopoly of crude pipelines and its domination of Eastern railroads to make crude oil prohibitively expensive to independent refiners; by threat of withdrawing its business, Standard not only got secret concessions on railroad rates but rebates on its competitors' shipments of oil; and, by the use of predatory local price-cutting, bogus independents and "fighting brands" the trust denied independent refiners and marketers access to the consumers.[3]

The customers and remaining competitors of Standard Oil called on the U.S. government, after extensive private and state litigation had proved unavailing, to redress the balance of power. In a landmark decision, the Supreme Court in 1911 ordered the dissolution of Standard Oil. It held that Standard's habitual competitive methods were unreasonable restraints of trade and embodied a successful attempt to monopolize. The dissolution decree could not immediately turn old business associates into aggressive competitors. For a while the marketing companies kept scrupulously within their historic boundaries; refiners refrained from marketing, marketers did not refine. As time passed, the barriers were breached. Independents had appeared, sparked by new crude oil discovered in Texas and California. Fed by the accelerating increase in demand for petroleum products, particularly motor fuel, they grew powerful. The old Standard Oil companies began to invade each other's marketing territories. They also integrated backward to crude oil production and forward to marketing.

As a consequence of these changes, the share of the gasoline market accounted for by members of the old Standard Oil empire has dropped, in their respective original territories, to about 20 per cent. On the other hand, backward integration has made them more significant in crude oil production, a field that John D. Rockefeller had regarded as too risky for heavy commitment of funds. And these Standard companies have remained the price leaders, or "reference sellers," in their respective territories, in quoting the key tank wagon gasoline price, even though some newcomers, such as Gulf and Texaco, are among the giants of the industry.

Controlling the Flood of Crude. During the twenties the industry was moderately prosperous but the collapse of 1929 brought serious trouble. Not only was there a sharp drop in the price of crude oil because of slackened demand, but the supply was increased with the discovery of new reserves, notably the gigantic East Texas field in 1930. The interests of some wildcatters and mavericks in unchecked production were ranged against the more conservative elements in the industry. It was not until 1933 that, after bitter legislative and court battles and several declarations of martial law, the Texas and Oklahoma legislatures were conceded the power to limit the flow of oil. But this was ineffective without Federal checks on interstate shipments of "hot oil," provided first through NRA, and then, after the demise of NRA, by the Connally Act. Under NRA, the industry attempted, with indifferent success other than in the oil fields, to check price-cutting.[4]

[3] H. R. Seager and C. A. Gulick, Jr., *Trust and Corporation Problems* (New York: Harper, 1929), Chap. VIII.
[4] See M. W. Watkins, *Oil: Conservation or Stabilization* (New York: Harper, 1937).

Large integrated refiners in the Middle West, with the blessing of Secretary of the Interior Ickes, tried to support the market for gasoline by absorbing the output of small independents refining East Texas or other cheap crude. The majors selected one or more independents as "dancing partners." After a mammoth trial (requiring the enlargement of the courtroom at Madison, Wisconsin) the Department of Justice obtained Supreme Court condemnation of the "dancing partner" program.[5]

A new threat to price stability and the profits of domestic producers was offered by rising imports of crude and products after 1950. The oil industry is not united in its attitude toward imports. Some refiners would like to be able to buy unlimited quantities of Middle East crude oil at favorable prices. Wholesalers on the East Coast would like to see cheaper import of both crude and products. Companies like Gulf or Standard Oil (New Jersey) with heavy investments in Arabian production properties do not look favorably on import quotas. The so-called "independent producers" whose profits depend on U.S. production, however, are in favor of import restrictions. Politically powerful in the south and west, they have been able to call the tune on import policy. They have found an ally in the bituminous coal industry which, on most issues, does not see eye-to-eye with petroleum.

Technological Developments. The petroleum industry has experienced a rapid pace of innovation, especially in refining. What is sometimes called "the octane race" has forced refiners continuously to redesign their equipment in an effort to produce the gasoline needed for engines with ever-higher compression ratios. Many refining processes are available, which may be used in a variety of combinations. The design of a refinery will normally depend on its legacy of equipment from the past, the type of crude it expects to process, the proportion of residual fuel oil or coke believed profitable, and the grade of gasoline desired. The leading process for getting high octane gasolines is catalytic reforming,[6] commercially developed about 1950, but other techniques are available.

Improvements in transportation have taken the form of larger pipelines and tankers, and increased use of barges. Some tankers exceed 100,000 tons dead weight, carry enough crude to take care of one-seventh of the U.S. daily consumption and attain ocean liner speeds. Oil production has made rapid progress. Holes have been drilled ever deeper; in 1958, the 25,000 foot mark was exceeded for the first time. Only improved pipe and rigs permitted the achievement of this depth. At the same time, drilling and well completion has become commonplace in the Gulf of Mexico, ten miles off the coasts of Louisiana and Texas. The industry foresees, not far in the future, exploratory drilling on the Atlantic Coast, from Connecticut to Florida. On the horizon or already in operation are such advances as liquefied transport of natural gas by insulated tanker, subsurface combustion of shale oil, and wholly automatic refinery operation.

These changes have two aspects. On the one hand, they tend to reduce costs.

[5] Socony-Vacuum Company v. U.S., 310 U.S. 150 (1940).

[6] In catalytic reforming, gasoline that has already been "cracked"—that is, produced by distilling crude under heat and pressure usually in the presence of a metallic catalyst —is further processed by adding light fractions.

It is cheaper to transport crude oil in the largest tankers or pipelines. The bigger refineries achieve somewhat lower refining costs. Offshore oil is often cheaper over the life of the field because huge reserves are discovered at relatively low cost per barrel. Yet the improved techniques require larger and larger investments. According to some oil company executives, roughly $240,000,000 must be invested in refinery facilities to reach the optimum size, where unit costs will be at a minimum.[7] Giant tankers can cost $20,000,000 apiece.[8]

SUGGESTED READINGS

Adams, Walter (ed.), *The Structure of American Industry: Some Case Studies*, 3rd ed. (New York: Macmillan, 1961). This is a volume employing case studies of industries to show, in part, various kinds of industrial structures in terms of the number of important firms in the industry. The results of various industrial structures are examined for implications with regard to proper public policy toward competition and monopoly. A portion of the case study of the petroleum industry was used as a reading at the end of this chapter.

Bain, Joe S., *Industrial Organization* (New York: Wiley, 1959). The author adopts essentially an external and "behavioristic" approach to the subject, concerning himself with the environmental settings within which business enterprises operate and how they behave in these settings as producers, sellers, and buyers. Major emphasis is given to the relative incidence of competitive and monopolistic tendencies in various industries or markets.

[7] J. S. Bain, *Barriers to New Competition* (Cambridge: Harvard U. P., 1956), p. 158. This estimate appears to be excessive, judging from the success of many small refineries, such as Aurora in Michigan, Northwest in Minnesota, and Frontier in Wyoming.
[8] *Petroleum Week* (November 7, 1958), p. 68.

CHAPTER 5

THE AMERICAN ECONOMIC AND BUSINESS SYSTEM

The way in which Americans conduct economic activity is unique, although it bears a resemblance to other "capitalistic" economies. To gain a full understanding of the nature of American business, it is necessary to have some knowledge of those elements which, when combined, make our economic system unique. Although a "system" is any assemblage of objects united by some form of regular interaction or interdependence, references to our economic system most frequently concern themselves with the "institutions" of the capitalistic system. In large measure, these institutional influences upon the way in which business is conducted in America are a legacy from England and other European nations. However, businessmen have themselves instituted certain ways of conducting business in America in order to come to terms with different and changing circumstances.

There are ways of dealing with the American economic and business systems other than regarding them as being systems of interrelated institutions. The economic system might be regarded as being a system of interrelated producing and consuming units (in which case, the business system would be part of the economic system). Thus, before proceeding to an examination of the business system, an examination of the American economic system is in order.

THE AMERICAN ECONOMIC SYSTEM

Any economic system is normally regarded as possessing certain interrelated institutions. Every society develops institutions—customary ways of thinking and acting—to enable it to deal with problems confronting it. These problems may take the form of providing for the "propagation and preservation of the species," and the custom of marriage has been widely instituted to provide a solution. There is a saying, popular among bachelors, that "Marriage is an institution, but who wants to be in an institution!" This confuses, deliberately, two meanings of the term, and when the word "institution" is employed in the following discussion, it will be used solely to refer to customary ways of thought and behavior.

Social institutions are instituted by someone or some group in a society. They are not instituted by "society as a whole" except, perhaps, in very small and simple societies in which all the members join in making the decision to institute certain practices. In American society, we note a number of institutions that have been developed by businessmen in order to come to favorable terms with their environment. The business corporation is an example of such an institution: earlier we saw that problems associated with proprietorships and partnerships led businessmen to organize new forms of firms—including the corporate form—to surmount those difficulties. Since situations change, institutions change. However, there are some relatively stable and basic institutions of the American system that provide the essential ingredients of our economy.

American Economic Institutions

Our economic system has been given a number of names by various speakers and writers. It has been most frequently referred to as "the capitalistic system," "the free market system," "the private enterprise system," or "the free enterprise system." Regardless of the term employed to denominate the system as a whole, there is general agreement on the institutions that make up that system. The mainspring of our economic system is "private property." This, along with economic motivation, free markets, and freedom of enterprise, has aided in making American business the most productive in the world, with shares in that production distributed so as to provide the average American with the highest material level of living known. A word of warning should be inserted here: These terms are not perfectly descriptive of the institutions they refer to. Private property rights are not absolute rights, nor is there perfect freedom of enterprise or markets. Neither is all American enterprise private.

There is a problem that recurs in discussions of American economic institutions. Some treatments of such institutions are theoretical, some are ideological, some are descriptive and some—such as the following treatment—are some combination of the three. Theoretical treatments of economic institutions stem from theoretical economists, who try to abstract from the real world certain essential characteristics of the economic system. Unfortunately, they have set forth in many cases the characteristics of an ideal economic system—such as one in which perfect competition would prevail—and they dwell on the institutions of such a system rather than on those of the existing economic system. The same terms employed by the economists are frequently used by those extolling the "American way of life" for propaganda purposes—that is, they become part of ideology (which may be defined as any set of ideas that are characteristic of a group, class, or nation that relates certain of their alleged attributes to some commonly esteemed values in such a way as to bestow honorific status upon them and their institutions and to provide the basis for invidious comparisons with other groups, classes, or nations). Finally the terms employed in theory and ideology are also used to describe the existing institutions of our economy. The only solution, apparently, is to make it quite clear which way the terms are being used. In the following, we shall try to show when theory and ideology do not accord with practice.

PRIVATE PROPERTY. "Private property" has two meanings. The one most commonly employed refers to tangible things—for example, "Get your hands off my private property!" In dealing with private property as an institution, however, we are concerned with the legal right to acquire, to use, and to dispose of things, either tangible or intangible. It is this right of ownership, instituted by man and protected by law, that makes it possible and profitable for businessmen to acquire things and to sell them gainfully. As has been mentioned, this right is not absolute: it is not possible to secure legal title to certain things, and there may be legal restrictions on the use and disposition of tangibles and intangibles, but there is a large measure of freedom to do so.

Private property rights are important in many areas of our economic and business system. Productive resources are owned by individuals— singly or collectively—and firms acquire those resources through purchase in resource markets when they do not own them. The right to own and dispose of things permits resource owners to sell in resource markets; the right of individuals to acquire and own things permits businessmen to purchase productive resources and use them in producing goods and services. These rights also permit businessmen to sell finished products in the product markets to individuals and groups having the right to acquire, own, and use those products. In short, property rights are fundamental to private enterprise. Businessmen may—through contracts based on private property rights—enter into almost any kind of productive activity they choose in order to secure economic gain from selling goods and services at prices that more than cover the costs of acquisition and production. This leads us to another most important institution of the capitalistic system—economic motivation.

ECONOMIC MOTIVATION. The influences that move people to behave in certain ways are very complex, and economic motivation is only one of a host of motivational forces. However, economic motivation—the desire to gain goods and services—plays an important role in our modern business society and is properly regarded as a central institution of the capitalistic system. Businessmen, whatever their other motives, are strongly moved in conducting their affairs by the possibility of gaining profits from business operations. Although some satisfaction springs from acquiring money itself, the greater influence stems from the power to secure goods and services that gaining money brings. Economic motives on the part of both suppliers and customers supplement those of the businessman, so that we customarily expect, and accept, situations in which the desire for material gain provides the motivating force for economic activity.

The profit motive distinguishes private enterprise from other kinds of productive activity. Households, nonprofit organizations, and governments may produce goods and services, as we have noted. However, their main objective in doing so is not to secure profit. The businessman *does* have profit as a main objective to guide much of his activity. To permit private property and economic motivation to achieve their greatest potential in guiding business activity, "free markets" have been instituted.

FREE MARKETS. The existence of resource and product markets has promoted the development of business enterprise, especially when those markets have been free of governmental and other restraints. "Perfectly free markets" are characterized by (1) freedom of entry into and exit from the markets for both buyers and sellers; (2) freedom from restrictions on price movements or quantities bought and sold; (3) freedom from restrictions on competition among buyers or sellers. In such markets, businessmen can buy and sell as they wish, without hindrance, employing whatever competitive practices they like. They are free to sell at prices as high or as low as they choose, without restraint by governments or others, with market forces the governing influence. In their pursuit of profits, businessmen engage in those productive activities that market conditions make profitable, and total production is at its highest level. This is the theory, anyhow, although in practice we see very few markets, if any, that are perfectly free. Throughout the long history of business, there was until fairly recently a trend toward greater freedom from restrictions on markets. This trend, however, has been reversed in the past century or so, with greater restraints being placed on market behavior by governmental agencies and others, including businessmen themselves.

INDIVIDUAL FREEDOM. The large measure of individual freedom existing in American society has also facilitated the development of the present high level of economic and business activity. Individuals are relatively free to engage in whatever occupation they choose. Those with especially strong economic motivations may enter the business world, and as businessmen, attempt to secure whatever gain is possible. They are free to associate with others in business, either as partners or in corporations. There are, of course, some occupations in which persons may not legally engage and there are certain requirements to be met before businessmen may legally associate for the conduct of their affairs. Still, absolute freedom of any kind rarely exists, and Americans enjoy a relatively large measure of the freedom to do as they wish.

The Development of American Economic Institutions

These institutions, under which businessmen in America have operated for many years and whose virtue they proclaim, have not always existed in their present form. Americans inherited some of them from England while they were still in a colonial status, although there have been important changes since that time. When the Virginia Company established the colony at Jamestown, private property rights and economic motivation were firmly rooted in English life, with individual freedom being rapidly expanded. Despite the provisions of the Virginia Charter, the colonists did not have all the privileges of English businessmen, and in England—as well as in the colonies—free markets did not always exist.

American businessmen of the colonial period had to contend with a market situation dominated by the mercantilistic policies of England. To promote the interests of English merchants, as well as those of the British government, colonists were prohibited from producing certain articles, they were excluded from selling in certain markets, and they were obliged to purchase in England or English colonies. Although these prohibitions and restrictions were difficult to enforce and were widely evaded by colonial businessmen, they still prevented the operation of free markets and dealing therein by Americans.

Not only were there restrictions on entry into certain markets and upon competition, there were also controls placed over price movements in some of the markets in which the earliest American businessmen dealt. This was especially true in the Massachusetts Bay Colony, where religious leaders were successful in temporarily establishing market institutions more characteristic of the feudal period. An important part of these religious doctrines was the "just price." Although in medieval times this price was that which would just permit a man to support himself in his existing station in life, by the colonial period this had been transformed by the Puritans to be a price only slightly above cost, so that one man might not take advantage of another's ignorance or necessity. As the influence of religion declined, and as religious leaders changed their doctrines, it became acceptable—and eventually customary—for businessmen to charge whatever price they chose, including a price as high as the market would bear. Not until relatively recent years have price controls been again instituted, and then only in periods of emergency brought on by wars. Businessmen have, of course, attempted to restrict price movements for their own advantage, but are relatively free of external controls over market prices.

The Development of American Business Institutions

Businessmen are not a group apart from society; on the contrary, American society is essentially a business society, and business has been responsible for the development of many social institutions. The economic institutions of our capitalistic system are what they are chiefly because businessmen of the past pressed for their establishment. Men of business had much to gain from the institutions of private property, economic motivation, free markets, and individual freedom, and lent their support to their attainment.

More than this, they were responsible for the development of business institutions—customary ways of business thought and behavior. Recurring problems confronting business were dealt with in ways that became established; in this fashion, business institutions were born.

THE BUSINESS CORPORATION. A major development was that of the business corporation. At one time, men conducted business solely as individuals or in partnership with others. As the need for greater amounts of capital to conduct business operations grew, unincorporated joint stock associations developed. Up to this point, American experience and English experience were similar. Shortly after the Revolutionary War, however, adoption of the corporate form of doing business became fairly common among Americans while it developed more slowly abroad. This stemmed chiefly from the fact that few Americans had large amounts of capital to invest in business, but this was not true in England. With this problem confronting them, American businessmen employed with increasing frequency the device of the corporation which enabled them to sell shares in a business firm to many investors of modest means. This way of organizing business has become so firmly entrenched in America that the bulk of business is conducted by corporations.

The development of the corporate form of doing business in America has brought a number of other developments along with it. Among these are corporation law and corporation lawyers, both giving powerful assistance to this mode of business conduct. Perhaps the most outstanding development has been the holding company, which developed under laws permitting corporations to hold the stock of other corporations. This reached its greatest prominence during the 1920's, when corporations were piled on top of corporations with as many as ten layers in the structure of some holding company "empires." Although there was some change in this situation after the stock market crash of 1929 and the passage of restrictive legislation in the New Deal period, holding companies still exist today providing a means for one firm to control the activities of a number of subsidiary corporations. A prime example is the United States Steel Corporation, which conducts its affairs through subsidiaries engaged in mining, railroading, shipping, and selling, as well as in the manufacture of steel and steel products. Not all holding companies control corporations engaged in related operations; they may be holding the stock of unrelated enterprises for investment purposes.

THE DEVELOPMENT OF CURRENCY AND CREDIT. To facilitate exchange in markets, mediums of exchange have been developed, and businessmen have played a prominent role in their institution. The basic difficulty involved in barter is fairly obvious: anyone wishing to exchange something must find someone wishing to make an even exchange. To surmount this difficulty, early traders used commodities that were desired and acceptable—such as grain and cattle—as mediums of exchange. Gold and silver were also used and rapidly became the most common mediums of exchange and were eventually coined into money. The creation of coins has been basically a function of governments, but businessmen have created paper currency and credit to make exchange easier; at the present time credit created by business firms is involved in financing the vast bulk of transactions in American markets.

The early English colonists in North America lacked coins. In all of the colonies, both powder and bullets were legal tender for the payment of debts incurred in exchange. In the southern colonies, especially in Virginia, tobacco also took the place of coins. Early New Englanders frequently used grain, fish, and furs as mediums of exchange as well as the wampum of the Indians as money. Eventually colonial governments began to mint coins and create paper money. The role played by businessmen in the creation of currency and credit during the colonial period seems to have been limited to extending credit to buyers.

Business-issued Currency. Since the colonial period, businessmen have been much more active in providing mediums of exchange. The first bank—the privately owned Bank of North America—was instituted in 1781 and began to extend credit and to circulate bank notes. It was followed by many other banks that issued notes promising to pay legal money in exchange for the notes when presented to the issuing bank. Up to the Civil War, many state-chartered banks with note-issuing privileges were created; these business-issued notes were an important part of our currency. During periods in our nation's history when coins were scarce—for example, during the 1830's and also during the Civil War—business firms also issued coins or tokens of silver, copper, or brass which they would redeem in lawful money upon presentation.

Since the Civil War, issuance of notes and coins by private firms for use as currency has declined. The notes of state banks were taxed out of existence beginning in 1865, and since 1933 national banks have ceased issuing bank notes. This does not mean that the role of private firms in creating mediums of exchange has lost its importance. Their expanded creation of credit, and deposits on which checks may be drawn, has much more than offset the gradual disappearance of privately issued currency.

The Development of Business Credit. Although loans had been made prior to the establishment of the new nation, bank credit and installment credit were unknown, for there were no banks or finance companies in the colonial period. After the Revolutionary War began, banks began to develop and have grown to such a position of importance that the bulk of commercial transactions is carried on through checks drawn on banks rather than with currency. Installment credit in the period following World War I made it possible for consumers of modest means to engage in mass purchases of automobiles and household appliances. The fact that so many Americans now are purchasing houses, as well as automobiles and other durable consumers' goods, on the installment plan, never being out of debt, has led to the suggestion that the institution of private property is changing, with the typical American consumer no longer owning property in the traditional sense of the term. Instead it is suggested that he is purchasing services rather than goods, with very few ever securing clear title to the things they are presumably purchasing.

THE ONE-PRICE SYSTEM. Yet another important custom instituted by American businessmen is the "one-price system." Until the middle of the nineteenth century, it was customary for buyer and seller to haggle over prices, with the result depending upon their respective bargaining power. This haggling inhibited exchange. As department stores developed, they began to establish single prices for specific classes of goods and to advertise them at this price. As this method of price setting became more widespread, it enabled both buyer and seller to make better decisions because greater certainty had come to the marketplace. There are, of course, "discounts" and "shading" with respect to list prices in a number of markets at the present time, but even so, great progress has been made toward selling at the same price to all buyers purchasing under similar conditions.

THE AMERICAN BUSINESS SYSTEM

In the preceding discussion, we have been dealing with some important institutions of American business. What this implies is that we could define the American business system in terms of its characteristic institutions. There is such a variety of them that we could not begin to do them justice, so we shall merely mention this possibility without going into detail. As we pointed out at the beginning of this chapter, we could also conceive of the business system as a system of firms or a system of industries; a brief exploration of these conceptions may yield a useful insight into the nature of American business.

Business as a System of Firms

We have been viewing the firm as the center of a "web of relationships" that ties it to customers, suppliers, competitors, government, and so on. Some of these are business firms, and if we were to regard the entire business system as a system of firms we would conceive of it as being a number of intertwined webs, with a firm at the center of each. A leading exponent of this view has stated:

Perhaps a more appropriate pictorial analogy than the spider's web is a windowpane which a winter's frost has overnight covered with a pattern of stars, each one with a nucleus from which glistening lines radiate until they interlace with other lines which run into other nuclei, the whole forming a complicated mosaic. Each of the nuclei is an economic unit—a business firm, a household, or a government—with lines of relationship connecting it to a large number of other economic units, in a tangle of alliances which is far too complex actually to identify even for the smallest of units. The whole fascinating and infinitely intricate design constitutes the economy.[1]

As Chamberlain notes, the relationships even of one firm are far too complex to identify in practice and it would be a never-ending task to attempt to identify all of the interrelationships among the 11 million firms comprising American business. Nevertheless, systematic relationships do exist, even though they cannot be perceived in their entirety.

Business as a System of Industries

Success has been attained in analyzing the American business system as being composed of a system of industries. In Chapter 4, "American Industries," we mentioned the interindustry (or input-output) analysis of Professor Leontief. The input-output charts developed by him and by others employing similar analytical methods are pictures of the relationships among industries and other sectors of the economy. Actually such tables show relationships among industry groups rather than among individual industries (which number in the thousands). Even so, relations among major industry groups are shown, and if the mind can comprehend the entire chart, the American economy in terms of relationships among industries and consuming sectors is seen.

THE STRUCTURE OF THE AMERICAN ECONOMY

In the preceding discussion, we have discussed both the economic system and the business system. It should be emphasized that the two are not identical. The economic system involves all producing, distributing, and consuming units in America; the business system includes only some of them. That is, a considerable amount of production, distribution, and consumption in the United States takes place outside of business. Table 5–1 shows the contributions of the various producing sectors of the economy to national income.

[1] Neil W. Chamberlain, *The Firm: Micro-Economic Planning and Action* (New York: McGraw-Hill, 1962), pp. 7–8.

Table 5–1.   *Contributions to National Income by Origin* (1963)

	Dollar Contribution (millions)	Percentage Contribution
National Income	$478,500	100.0%
Income originating in business	393,600	82.3
Income originating in general government	58,200	12.2
Income originating in households and institutions	23,500	4.9
Income originating in the "rest of the world"	3,200	0.6

SOURCE: Office of Business Economics, U.S. Department of Commerce, *Survey of Current Business,* Vol. 44, No. 7 (July 1964), p. 13.

Governments, nonprofit organizations, and households engage in considerably more economic activity than some business statistics reveal. For example, the Department of Commerce (which publishes the *Survey of Current Business*) states:

> The business sector is defined broadly to include all organizations which produce goods and services for sale at a price intended at least to approximate costs of production. In the main, it covers all private enterprises organized for profit, both corporate and noncorporate, including farm operators, independent professional practitioners and lessors of real property. Mutual financial institutions, cooperatives and nonprofit organizations serving business are also included, as well as government enterprises. Owner-occupied houses and building used by nonprofit institutions serving individuals are considered to be business establishments selling their current services to their owners.[2]

Although we are willing to go along with part of this definition, we should raise a question (or at least an eyebrow) when cooperative and nonprofit organizations are included (not to mention owner-occupied houses). The U.S. Department of Commerce rationalizes this strange definition in the following way:

> The business sector covers a wide variety of organizations and for some purposes it might be desirable to distinguish among them. . . . To regard the business system as an entity is sufficient for many purposes, and the statistical information for establishing further sectors within it either is unavailable or could be assembled and utilized only at the expense of disproportionate effort.[3]

Although we can understand why the definition is used, we should recognize that its use greatly overstates the contribution of the business sector to the gross national product.

[2] Office of Business Economics, U.S. Department of Commerce, *National Income, 1954* (Washington, D.C.: Government Printing Office, 1954), p. 40.
[3] *Op. cit.*, p. 40.

Not all government action is government enterprise. A distinction is made between government enterprises and general government activities. Government enterprises are those agencies of government whose operating costs are at least to a substantial extent covered by the sale of goods and services, in contrast to the general activities of government that are financed mainly by tax receipts and the sale of bonds. That is, government enterprises are engaged in what are essentially commercial operations—producing and selling goods and services. The sale of services is more important than that of goods; the U.S. Post Office is a prime example of government enterprise. There are some governmental agencies—such as state universities and state parks—that charge admission fees, but since these fees cover only a nominal part of their operating costs, they are classed as general government activities rather than as government enterprises. To secure a comprehensive view of the goods and services produced and distributed by the government, we should add general government activities to the output of government enterprises.

Published figures of gross national product are misleading to those who wish to understand the relative output of business, government, nonprofit, nongovernmental organizations, and individuals for other reasons as well. Illegal transactions are traditionally excluded. The value of goods and services produced by those who engage in illegal enterprises would be quite difficult to determine, since those engaged in such activity would not be very likely to inform government agents that they were involved in such enterprise or what their sales were. No estimates are available, so we can only speculate on the output of illegal enterprise. A more fundamental objection to the use of national income data to measure the value of output of various kinds of enterprise is that "do-it-yourself" productive activity is ignored.

In defining national output, the basic criterion for determining whether or not an activity constitutes "economic production" is whether it is reflected in sales and purchase transactions in the markets. For example, the production of radio sets by a firm has its counterpart in the hobbies of amateur radio operators, shaves by barbers are similar to self-administered ones, and the educational services of music teachers are often substituted for with instruction by parents. In spite of these resemblances (and in spite of the fact that in each case essentially the same good or service is being produced), "do-it-yourself" productive activity is not included in national income accounts. Some economists have felt that they should be included; one economist has estimated that we may be understating the total value of final products (gross national product) by as much as 20 per cent a year.

Despite the difficulty of securing proper estimates and despite the definitions of the Office of Business Economics, it should be quite obvious that important contributions to the total production of final goods and services come from government, nonprofit organizations, and individuals as well as from business. We call the American economy a "capitalistic" or "business" system because most of the production does come from business firms. It has been more appropriately called a "mixed economy," but unfortunately we do not know the proportions of various kinds of producing units in the mixture.

We might say, with confidence, that every economy in the world is a mixed economy. However, the proportions vary; in some industrial nations the government is the major producer, and in others cooperative enterprise is much more important than in the U.S. The examination of other economic systems gives us an important understanding of part of the environment of American business as well as shows us alternative ways in which economic activity may be conducted.

READING: Can Anyone Explain Capitalism *
by R. Joseph Monsen, Jr.

Schools in this country are making increasing efforts to explain American capitalism and our economic system within the classrooms. In most plans to develop a program that will explain our economic system to students, however, two crucial factors are overlooked: the bias of those developing such material and the attitude of the teacher toward capitalism. These factors will necessarily color any explanation the student receives. It may be argued that this is true of all education. I would agree. But in the case of capitalism the problem is considerably more involved and controversial than in most. For even if capitalism is defined quite neutrally as a system in which private ownership operates in a market environment for profit-making, the critical role of government remains to be interpreted. Yet in the United States today no issue is more hotly debated than the extent to which government should participate in economic affairs. There is little doubt that the role of government as perceived by J. K. Galbraith or by Arthur Schlesinger, Jr., is considerably larger than that accepted by Barry Goldwater, William Buckley, or the National Association of Manufacturers.

This difference of opinion concerning the role of government brings us to the central point of this article: that in the United States today at least five major versions of capitalism can be found. The role of government in these versions is a major characteristic.

These separate versions of capitalism may, in fact, be considered as separate ideologies—ideologies because they present explanations or rationalizations that are used by groups to justify their own positions. Economic ideologies, like reli-

---

° From the *Saturday Review*, December 14, 1963. Reproduced with permission of the author and publisher. This reading illustrates the difficulty confronting anyone attempting to define capitalism in terms of its characteristic institutions.

gious dogmas, have their "true believers" as well as those adherents who espouse them for more practical ends.

To understand our economy today one must have some idea of what our major ideologies about capitalism are and who espouses them. Congressional debates and public argument in the press on major issues become much easier to follow once the positions of various groups are linked to their ideologies. We frequently hear that we have no economic ideology in the country, or that we have finally reached, as Daniel Bell entitled his book, *The End of Ideology*. Nothing could be further from the truth. Even though Marxian and collectivist ideologies are not significant in the mainstream of American thought today, to argue that we have no other economic ideologies is extremely naïve.

The Classical Ideology. Of the ideologies of American capitalism prominently in print today, the oldest is what has been called the classical ideology of capitalism. It is disseminated in the United States largely by the National Association of Manufacturers, the Foundation for Economic Education, the Committee for Constitutional Government, the United States Chamber of Commerce, and the American Enterprise Association, to name only some of the better-known organizations. While at times these groups may vary, through their many publications they present the major interpretation of this most traditional version of the American capitalist ideology. The importance of this ideology in business circles is indicated by a report estimating that out of more than $32,000,000 spent by corporations to influence legislation, some $27,000,000 was in the form of donations for use by the organizations disseminating the classical ideology.

The essence of the classical ideology is its concept of individually owned private property in a decentralized market operated by the forces of supply and demand in the quest for profit. The official stand of the NAM concerning the role of government in the economy is that the solutions to the basic economic problems of what, how, for whom, and at what price goods should be produced must be left to the voluntary adjustments of a free market rather than to the central authority of government. While this view does not demand that there be no government regulation, it does argue that because of the effectiveness of competition as a regulatory device, government intervention and regulation of the market are seldom needed.

The Managerial Ideology. If the classical ideology had been more flexible in accepting a somewhat greater economic role for government, as well as in allowing the use of deficit spending under certain circumstances, its main rival as a business creed, known increasingly as the managerial ideology, would probably never have developed. The managerial ideology had its birth with the formation of the Committee for Economic Development in 1942. Since that time, this ideology has been vigorously disseminated by the CED and such business magazines as *Fortune*.

Politically, the managerial ideology received its greatest patronage during the Eisenhower Administration. For there was, as *Business Week* observed, "a marked similarity between the CED and the new Administration (Eisenhower's) that involved more than the names of men. Both represent the views of a forward-looking businessman, a sort of progressive conservative."

The managerial ideology of capitalism takes its name from the increasing control by professional management of the large corporation. While the managerial ideology is a reaction to the traditional classical creed, there are great similarities between them. The issues in which similarities occur, however, are usually those about which the managerial ideology is silent. The managerial ideology points largely to the basic changes that have occurred within the economy in the past few decades. It attempts to portray the manager of the large corporation as a trustee for the worker, consumer, and owner.

The dispute over the proper function of government not only partially caused the development of the managerial ideology but indeed remains one of the principal differences between it and the classical ideology. The managerialists accept a considerably greater role for government than the traditionalists will approve.

The managerial ideology's acceptance of a larger role for government is considerably more realistic today than the classical ideology's on this issue. In this regard, the classical ideology is less descriptive and more normative than the managerial creed, for it must argue that it represents the way things "ought" to be, not necessarily the way they are. The managerial ideology deemphasizes the traditional forces of supply and demand as the determinants of prices and accepts a governmental role deeply involved in business affairs, attempting to face what it feels are the realities of modern capitalism. To a large degree, the managerial ideology of capitalism is successful in that it provides arguments in currently accepted terms.

The Ideology of Countervailing Power.   Since its election in 1960 the Kennedy Administration has on a number of occasions used a sort of semiofficial ideology attributed to the well-known Harvard economist and former Ambassador to India, John Kenneth Galbraith. With the publication in 1952 of his book, *American Capitalism: The Concept of Countervailing Power,* Professor Galbraith set forth the main themes of this ideology. Since then, we have seen the term "countervailing power" spread until today it is hard to find any discussion about American capitalism that does not make some reference to it. In fact, Galbraith is now probably the most widely known economist in this country. While countervailing power cannot be considered as full-blown an ideology as the classical ideology, it has nonetheless become one of the most popular explanations of modern American capitalism.

What is the concept of countervailing power upon which the ideology is based? Most succinctly, it is "the neutralization of one position of power by another." For Galbraith argues that "private economic power begets the countervailing power of those who are subject to it." The development of strong unions, then, in this argument, was inevitable in America to neutralize or balance the power of large companies. While this may not be historically correct, the thesis is that as one group develops in power, others arise to offset its power and prevent their own exploitation. By this reasoning, the strongest unions should develop in those industries where the strongest corporations exist.

The role of government in this interpretation is to assist the development of checks and balances of power. Thus, under this view, the concept of competition as the autonomous regulator of economic activity has been superseded. The potential role of government is, therefore, perhaps greater under the ideology of countervailing power than in any of the other major ideologies of modern American capitalism. In this sense, it may be expected to gain more supporters from among politically liberal citizens than from among conservatives, who are more apt to endorse the classical ideology.

While the countervailing power thesis as an economic theory has been subject to much criticism, as an ideological explanation of modern American capitalism it has become internationally known and suggests the basic flavor of modern American capitalism abroad perhaps more than any other capitalist ideology. Whether countervailing power as an ideology will develop independently or will merely be appended to one of the others, only time will tell. The concept of countervailing power appears, in the last analysis, to be far more adaptable as an ideology for the defense of American capitalism than as an economic theory to explain it; this feature, I might add, it shares with the other major ideologies of capitalism.

The Ideology of People's Capitalism.   The label "people's capitalism" has become increasingly fashionable as a title for the contemporary American economic system. The United States Information Agency, which at one time made use of the slogan, admitted quite frankly that "this type of terminology is designed as an eye-catcher, as a thought-provoker. The aim is to suggest at the outset that the American system is a far cry from nineteenth-century stereotypes of capitalism."

The central focus of the ideology of people's capitalism is the widening of both equity ownership and decision-making power among the populace. To its supporters, people's capitalism in America today is distinguished more by its emphasis on this system of property diffusion than by its present structure.

The origin of the term "people's capitalism" is alleged to have been developed in 1956 by the American Advertising Council for the USIA, which used the concept abroad. General Electric and Standard Oil of New Jersey have used the phrase in their ads in this country. Business economists such as Marcus Nadler and corporation executives such as Roger Blough of U.S. Steel have publicly used the term often. As Victor Perlo noted in the scholarly *American Economic Review*, "Future editions of economic texts can hardly fail to discuss the theory—or slogan—of people's capitalism."

The New York Stock Exchange's president, Keith Funston, has vigorously promoted the thesis that America is becoming a people's capitalism. In an issue of IBM's magazine *Think*, Mr. Funston says, "If stock distribution gets wide enough, it will bring capitalism to the ultimate goals of socialism, the people owning the instruments of production, but without sacrificing the incentive system of capitalism. I'm not predicting this will happen in a specific period of time, but we are heading along the lines of a people's capitalism and a stronger democracy." While the short-range goal of greater stock or equity distribution is quite understandable as an aim of the New York Stock Exchange, one wonders whether its members would really desire the long-range achievement of "the ultimate goals of socialism."

Such an atmosphere of conviction and debate in statements about people's capitalism is common. Similarly, contradiction among its various expositors is not unusual. It is possible to find advocates of people's capitalism who infer that the role of government should be broad and active to insure a rapid widening in equity ownership within the country; and those, too, who feel that government should not play anything but a limited role within the economy. Besides lack of consensus on the role of government, problems involved in the responsibility of professional management are not solved by the ideology.

The most important challenge to the ideology itself, however, comes from those, such as Perlo, who question whether there has been any significant increase, in recent decades, in the relative diffusion of ownership and decision-making in the U.S.

Incomplete as the concept may be for a full explanation of modern American capitalism, there is little doubt that the ideology of people's capitalism is widely used as a defense, justification, and explanation of our contemporary economic system both at home and abroad. As such, it is one of the primary American capitalist ideologies.

The Export Ideology. A synthesis of the major American capitalist ideologies, as described by USIA, has been called enterprise democracy. This ideology, perhaps best thought of as our "export" ideology, has been developed over several Administrations. In his book *What We Are For,* Arthur Larson, former head of the USIA under President Eisenhower, has given one of the few explanations specifically intended for home use of what our "export" ideology is.

The argument of enterprise democracy is that class conflict cannot explain American history. Rather, the practice of cooperation between business, labor, and government—out of the necessity of mutual self-interest—explains the American system. Hence, while the traditional competitive spirit in America is cited as important for the development of an industrial economy, alongside competitiveness, modifying it, is the "strong strain of cooperation." The feature that distinguishes modern enterprise democracy from laissez-faire capitalism is the recognition of necessary cooperation and mutual interest among society's basic groups; this includes recognition of government's positive duty to act when necessary for the varying needs of society's members. Government is different, however, from the other countervailing groups in the economy: "Its power over our freedoms, our fortunes, and our lives can be ultimate and absolute. Every other power in our society is secondary. The power of government is final. That is why we instinctively resist its increase."

The key to enterprise democracy is the role assigned to government. Sometimes called by the USIA "the Lincoln Formula," this ideology proclaims that the function of government is to do only that which needs to be done and cannot be done so well privately.

From this thesis, three corollaries are developed: (1) that more than one group should exist to act for the needs of the community; (2) that the major groups in modern industrial society do not basically conflict but rather mutually support one another (i.e., business, labor, and government); and (3) that private methods are always inherently preferable to government action. This, then, means a preference for as little governmental action "as possible." The phrase "as possible" is, of course, elastic and vague.

Other concepts that the ideology of enterprise democracy emphasizes are freedom, property, justice, individuality, group allegiance, and religion. The traditional criticisms of capitalism—competitiveness, class conflict, and inequality of income distribution—are, needless to say, not emphasized.

Essentially, enterprise democracy represents a composite or compromise ideology that, the USIA hopes, will receive a minimum of domestic criticism to let it function abroad as representative of American capitalism. But no term has been made official. Rather, local USIA officers are allowed to describe the American economic system in any terms they feel are appropriate. The basic ideology called enterprise democracy by Larson has not, however, been repudiated by the USIA or the Administration.

The main purpose of the ideology is to produce something that both the two main political parties and the other major groups in this country can agree upon for use in portraying the United States to the world. Its basic outline, therefore, cannot be thought of as inherently Democratic or Republican. If such an identification should occur, enterprise democracy as an export ideology would lose its usefulness as a propaganda instrument.

Like the classical and managerial ideologies, enterprise democracy is backed by an organized group. The main difference is that its support comes from an agency of the government—the USIA which functions abroad as our propaganda instrument. The operation of the USIA is of tremendous scope but, even so, it is not always a match in size or strength for its Communist counterparts. Through the Voice of America, newspapers, magazines, cultural, educational, and scientific exhibits, motion pictures, and libraries, the USIA attempts to project America's image abroad. This may also explain why the enterprise democracy ideology is better known abroad than at home.

The ideology's adherence to reality is a matter of opinion. Since it offers no body of economic theory, as does the classical ideology of capitalism, the way in which the various groups work out their mutual interests is left quite vague. One must assume the presence of countervailing power, a vague answer in itself. What will prevent the government from going beyond the constraints set up by the concept of limited government is indefinite. One assumes that political pressures and traditions are the constraints.

This short perusal of the various ideologies found within contemporary America suggests reasons why we commonly have difficulty defining our economic system and specifying what the role of government should be. Without some knowledge, however, of the prevalent ideologies of capitalism in our country, it is doubtful that the basic issues and arguments within our economy can be brought clearly into the open, as they must.

Meanwhile, it may be worthwhile to remember that American capitalism is, in one way at least, a little like electricity: Nobody knows exactly what it is, but it works—and works well.

SUGGESTED READINGS

Galbraith, John Kenneth, *American Capitalism, The Concept of Counter-vailing Power* (Boston: Houghton, 1956). A statement of the essential nature of our economy by a Harvard economist, critically examining some traditional views of capitalism.

Monsen, R. Joseph, Jr., *Modern American Capitalism* (Boston: Houghton, 1963). A definitive statement of the predominant ideologies of capitalism in American life, and of their importance.

Weiler, E. T., and William H. Martin, *The American Economic System* (New York: Macmillan, 1962). An analytical approach to the structure of the American economy, emphasizing the role of business, agriculture, labor, households, and government.

CHAPTER 6

OTHER
ECONOMIC
SYSTEMS

In discussing any economic system, it is necessary to distinguish between systems of economic thought and systems of economic institutions. In a number of countries, certain ways of conducting economic activity have developed as a consequence of putting into practice certain ideas about how economic activity should be conducted (although we might note some instances where highly structured economic theories followed rather than preceded the adoption of certain institutions). For example, the establishment of socialistic institutions in a nation might be the result of the acceptance of socialist economic thought by those in a position to influence policy and practice. However, what we tend to see in almost any economic system is a substantial difference between theory and practice; accordingly, we shall make a distinction between them. Systems of economic thought and practice may be classified according to their historical development—that is, as pre-industrial, capitalistic, socialistic, communistic, and fascistic.

As societies have industrialized, they have also developed strong governments. In some cases, businessmen have pressed for stronger government in order that their interests might be promoted by it; in others, strong governments have been established in order to force industrialization. In both cases, we note the political basis of economic institutions in industrialized societies. Consequently, when we examine socialism and fascism, we shall see not only the economic institutions, but also the political foundation upon which such institutions rest. Socialism sometimes develops where autocratic political institutions prevail, but sometimes where democracy exists—that is, we sometimes distinguish between democratic socialism and autocratic socialism. In our illustrations of various economic systems, we shall employ the Soviet Union as an example of autocratic or "totalitarian" socialism, Great Britain as an example of "democratic" socialism, and Nazi Germany as an illustration of fascism, or "autocratic" capitalism.

PRE-INDUSTRIAL ECONOMIES

Every modern industrial society that has gone through a capitalistic stage has also had a pre-industrial era. Furthermore, there are still places in the world where social groups conduct economic activity on a pre-business basis and where capitalism is just beginning to make inroads into the institutions of the people. Some Americans seek to do business with these societies; hence, an understanding of and respect for their institutions is essential to the establishment of enduring commercial relations. The economic systems of these societies can be regarded as collectional economies, cultural nomadic economies, and settled village economies. These we discussed in Chapter 2, here we shall mention only some of the economic institutions established after wandering tribes settled in villages.

The Settled Village Economy

When the tribes ceased to wander, they still engaged in animal husbandry and sometimes sent the flocks and herds of the village to the highlands during the summer. Plant cultivation was engaged in more intensively than was possible for the nomads. With the tilling of the soil as the dominant form of economic activity, different institutions appeared in these societies. These differed from place to place, and from time to time, but those of feudal society in medieval England and Europe are illustrative.

Among the institutions developed by these villagers was that of establishing individual ownership of the fields used for pasture, meadow, or cultivation. Initially, some property was held by families, and some came under co-ownership. The tendency was toward ownership by individuals or families of definite pieces of property, a custom which underlies the presently highly developed institution of private property. Provisions were also made for the inheritance of land, and local courts were established to enforce the existing customs of the village and to create laws where new situations arose. Although land was owned by individual persons or families, there still tended to be considerable cooperation in the production process, with little reliance on specialization of effort and exchange of surplus products. Religion played an important role in the development of economic institutions in this stage, with religious beliefs and fear of spiritual authorities providing strong motives for behaving in an approved manner. Although initially free, the villagers were sometimes subjugated by conquerors or gave up their freedom to a lord who could provide them with military security. Those performing different functions acquired different degrees of status in such societies, and eventually social status came to determine economic behavior. Individuals engaged in certain kinds of economic activity according to their status, and not as a consequence of contracts freely entered into. Markets were not well developed, and where they did exist many restraints were placed on their free operation.

There are still a large number of pre-industrial economies in the world today. "Awakening nations" in Asia and Africa are examples of social groups hastening to industrialize their economies. Their importance to American business at the present time is perhaps less economic than political. In the past, the institutions of pre-industrial societies were swept away by capitalism. Nowadays, communism is challenging capitalism in the industrialization of primitive societies and is also engaged in a world movement to sweep away the fundamental institutions of capitalism itself.

SOCIALISM

In contrast with some earlier economic thought that developed after certain institutions were well established and served to rationalize them, socialist thought developed before any large socialistic societies were created. The socialists—of whom there are many kinds—are critics of capitalism, and propose to do away with the "evils of capitalism" by instituting new ways of conducting economic activity. Although there is some diversity in these proposals, there is a central core of institutions advocated by most socialist thinkers: the ownership of productive property by society as a whole, operation and control of production and distribution by the government, and guidance of economic activity by central plans.

Such socialists do not propose the abolition of all private property, but only private property that is involved in production and distribution. All natural resources are to be the property of the state, along with the capital equipment used in manufacturing, transporting, and distributing products. Individuals retain property rights in their income from their labor (but lose all right to income from rents, interest, and profits, since they will no longer be permitted to own land or capital from which such income would accrue). There is also, in socialist theory, to be property rights in personal savings, dwellings, household and personal articles.

Although productive property other than labor belongs to society at large, it is the state which acquires it, uses it, and decides upon the disposition of products, giving it much of what property rights are. Government control of socially owned land, factories, and other capital takes place under central plans developed by bureaucrats. Decisions on what to produce are made by public managers guided by plans, rather than by private managers guided by the market. Free markets do not exist in any significant degree, with government controls set up over prices and quantities sold in the major markets.

With the lack of free markets comes a restriction on the economic freedom of individuals. They are not free to establish a business and enter markets that market conditions indicate might be profitable. The economic freedom that exists is freedom to engage in an occupation of a person's choice, although this too is restricted somewhat by the need of the state for certain classes of workers (a restriction which operates under capitalistic systems as well). Also, there is some freedom of choice in consumption. Socialists suggest that the loss of some economic freedom is more than compensated for by freeing workers from the domination of the capitalist class.

Some socialist thinkers, such as Karl Marx, have envisioned a society developing after a socialistic stage in which communistic institutions will prevail. They state that government is essential only to permit one economic class to exploit another; specifically, it permits—in capitalistic societies—the capitalist to exploit the worker. After socialism has developed to the point where there no longer is a capitalist class, so their argument goes, there will no longer be any class conflict and therefore no need for government. The "state will wither away" and new institutions prevail. Productive property will be held in common, and production will take place as a result of a feeling of altruism rather than for economic gain. The social product will be shared among members of the community according to their needs, rather than according to individual purchasing power or the contribution to output made by persons. Exchange as such will not take place, either in marketplaces or through barter, since all may satisfy themselves at the communal storehouse. A large measure of individual freedom would prevail, for there would no longer be any coercive class or state.

This is quite a visionary view of the prospects of economic development, and seems quite unlikely of realization. Other dreamers have shared this vision and have gone much further than the Communists in attempting to establish such communities. In the past these settlements have been set up on a small scale in various places, including the United States, and have almost uniformly failed. The failure of such attempts seems almost inevitable, since the nature of such experiments seems inconsistent with the nature of man. The world is moving away from rather than toward communism; the threat to the capitalists comes from the socialists, and to a lesser degree, from the fascists.

Socialism in the Soviet Union

Although the leaders of the Soviet Union are referred to as Communists, the economy itself is socialist—as the name Union of Soviet Socialist Republics indicates. This is the most completely socialized nation in the world, with almost total ownership of land and capital by the state. Individuals cannot, generally, establish and operate businesses of their own. Economic planning by the central government determines what will be produced and sold, with the prices to be charged also set by the planners. In the past, decisions have been made to emphasize the production of capital and military goods at the expense of production of consumer goods, and the prices of articles sold for consumption have been placed high in relation to wages to permit productive resources to fill those other needs.

Economic motivation has been retained in the Soviet Union in modified form. Although productive activity does not depend on the drive of businessmen for economic gain, substantial differentials in wages and salaries are paid to guide persons into desired occupations and to move them to work harder in the positions they occupy. Piecework wages are paid wherever possible in productive occupations to stimulate greater production. Much is also made of public honors and devotion to the cause of socialism to stimulate productive effort.

There have been some interesting changes in the ways in which economic activity has been conducted in the Soviet Union since the revolution of 1917. From 1918 to 1921, the economy operated under what is now called War Communism. Agricultural property of the large landed estates was seized and handed over to the peasants, who were permitted to engage in agriculture much as they pleased. Russian manufacturing enterprises (other than some very small ones) were nationalized and the government began the production of goods, with elected councils of workers participating in the management of the enterprises. Market transactions in the products of industry were discontinued, all goods were turned over to the central authorities to be distributed by them and wages were received in commodities, with the government also providing many services without charge. War Communism worked so poorly that the central government introduced a New Economic Policy in 1921.

The New Economic Policy was in operation until 1927. Under this policy, the government turned over many economic functions to private enterprise, although retaining operation and control of large-scale industry, transportation, banking, and foreign trade. Beginning in 1921, the bulk of the small-scale manufacturing enterprises were either returned to their owners for operation or leased to individuals or cooperatives. By 1923, almost 90 per cent of manufacturing enterprises were back in the hands of private owners, with cooperatives operating 3 per cent and the government the balance (these figures are somewhat misleading, since the government retained the big enterprises and employed almost 85 per cent of the industrial labor force). Markets were again used to allocate productive resources and finished goods, with workers and other producers being paid in money. Some revival took place in agriculture, but not as much as was hoped, since some restrictions continued to be placed on private enterprise. Private trade grew rapidly—during War Communism, all private trade had been abolished by decree and the distribution of goods was conducted through consumer cooperatives and government distribution centers. Shortly after the adoption of the new policy, private traders accounted for about three fourths of retail trade, although the government continued to promote cooperative stores and state stores.

Since 1928, the government of the Soviet Union has been attempting to socialize the economy, with a consequent decline in private enterprise. This has been done through a series of "Five-Year Plans." Russian agriculture was "collectivized," state farms were established, and the ownership of land by individual peasants dwindled to almost nothing. A state farm is a kind of agricultural "factory" owned and operated by the state, employing wage workers; whereas on the collective farms the members of the collective share in the remainder of the income of the farm after the government has taken its share and has collected for the use of the land and equipment. The bulk of agriculture now is conducted by the collective farms, which are cooperative enterprises of a kind, and state farms cultivate less than 10 per cent of the arable land in the Soviet Union. The private industrial enterprises that had existed under the New Economic Policy have again been taken over by the government, and most industrial production is now under government ownership and operation. Some producers' cooperatives, however, produce a variety of consumers' goods, and even some products of individual enterprise are created from raw materials they themselves have acquired. Private banking, which had been permitted after 1921, was again eliminated and the State Bank now monopolizes such activity. In 1929, private retail trade (other than that conducted by cooperatives) was again abolished, and in 1935 cooperatives were barred from competing with government stores in the cities and larger towns. Cooperative stores still exist, but the bulk of retail trade is now in the hands of the government, with the balance being conducted by cooperatives and in farmers' markets.

Socialism in Great Britain

Actually it considerably overstates the situation to characterize the economic institutions of Great Britain as socialistic. Rather, the British economy can be more aptly characterized as one of "modified capitalism." Capitalistic institutions prevail, modified by the nationalization of some industries and by the development of cooperatives as an important economic force. The reason the economy has sometimes been referred to as "socialistic" is because the Labor Party (which is an amalgam of socialists and trade unionists) has on occasion held political power in England and has been able to attain some objectives of the socialists. However, their power and their objectives have not been as extreme as those of the Communist Party in the Soviet Union and, consequently, no radical or dramatic changes have taken place in the economic institutions of England. There have been some gradual changes, however, which are of interest since—if Great Britain is an example of "decaying capitalism"— they may foreshadow developments in the United States.

As has been indicated, the changes from a capitalistic system in England have occurred in two ways: Some industries have been nationalized, and cooperatives have risen to a position of importance in the economy. Much has been made of nationalization of British industry since the Labor Party came to power at the end of World War II. However, a large number of industries were nationalized one by one by a variety of governments and over a long period of time. In the nineteenth century, the Post Office took over the telegraph industry (1870) and the telephone industry (1880). As in the United States, the national government operates ordnance plants and naval shipyards (called the Royal Ordnance Factories and the Admiralty Dockyards in Britain). After the development of commercial radio broadcasting, it was taken over by the British Broadcasting Corporation (BBC) in 1927. Some commercial air transportation was nationalized in 1940, with international air transport put under the British Overseas Airways Corporation (BOAC).

After the Labor Party came to power in 1945, a number of other industries were nationalized. In 1946, the Bank of England (which had long served as the "central bank") was brought under government ownership. Also in that year, the British European Airways Corporation (BEAC) was created to own and operate airlines serving Britain and Europe (with BOAC continuing to own and operate long-distance air transport). In 1947, a National Coal Board was created to own and operate British coal mines and auxiliary industries. Additional transportation industries were nationalized in 1948 when railroads, long-distance trucking and some local transportation enterprises were brought under government ownership and operated by the British Transportation Commission. Also in 1948, the generation and distribution of electricity was nationalized, with the British Electricity Authority and Area Electricity Boards being responsible for these operations. The next year, the British Gas Council and Area Gas Boards were established to own and operate the nationalized manufacture and distribution of gas. Finally, in 1951, the Iron and Steel Corporation was established to acquire the securities of some 80 steel companies and operate that industry. Thus, between 1946 and 1951, the Labor Governments were able to nationalize eight major industries.

Although the Labor Party was instrumental in nationalizing a number of industries after World War II, they were not always opposed by the Conservative Party (which presumably represents the "capitalists" of Great Britain). In point of fact, most of the newly nationalized industries had been recommended for nationalization by fact-finding boards dominated by Conservatives; this was true of the Bank of England, the coal industry, the electric industry, and the gas industry. The Conservatives did oppose some nationalization, and after regaining political power in the 1950's, proceeded to denationalize the steel industry and caused some of the long-haul trucks to be sold to private bidders. The Labor Party has pledged itself to "re-nationalize" steel if and when it is returned to political power. Since the Labor Party does have a socialist program, it proposes to nationalize those industries necessary to carry out its objectives, and it is likely that additional nationalization will take place in

Great Britain. It is also probable, however, that this will occur only in certain basic industries and that a large part of British economic activity will be conducted by private business and by cooperatives.

COOPERATIVISM

Although there are many cooperatives in the United States, there are relatively more in a number of foreign countries. Also, the modern "cooperative movement" had its origins overseas—in England and on the continent of Europe. In part, cooperation has developed abroad as a practical means of solving certain economic problems; however, there is also a philosophy of cooperation that has its "true believers." Cooperativism envisions a society in which the profit motive is replaced, and production is for use rather than for profit. Although in its early days it was regarded chiefly as a substitute for capitalism (and became an important doctrine at about the same time that socialism did), nowadays some view it as a "middle way" between capitalism and socialism. The distinction being made is that cooperation is private enterprise rather than government enterprise, although cooperative economic activity is not undertaken with profit in mind but with a view to doing something useful for the members of the co-op. England and Sweden are two countries in which the cooperative movement has become quite important, partly because of the existence of earnest believers in the cooperative way of life.

Cooperativism in England

England is the birthplace of the modern retail cooperative. In the textile town of Rochdale, factory workers—mainly weavers—founded the first successful retail cooperative store. The essential principles guiding the enterprise were (1) sell at prevailing prices; (2) sell for cash only; (3) pay only a fixed return on invested capital; and (4) divide the remaining income among purchasers according to the percentage that their patronage is of total sales. Others, adopting the "Rochdale principles," were formed elsewhere and soon these retail units established a wholesale cooperative. By the end of the nineteenth century, cooperatives were making 6 per cent of all retail sales. Since that time, they have expanded their share to about 12 per cent; however, there is no apparent indication that it will increase to much more than that. For various reasons, England still remains a nation of small shopkeepers; other European nations have developed the cooperative method of economic enterprise to a much greater degree than has England.

Cooperativism in Sweden

Sweden is one of the countries that have developed cooperative enterprise to the point where it is a very important part of the economic system. It has even been suggested that the Scandinavian nation has adopted "cooperativism" as a "middle way." However, there is no Cooperative Party seeking to "cooperativize" the economy through political means. Cooperatives in Sweden have had a pragmatic rather than an ideological origin. It was the high prices and poor quality of the products of private business that started the cooperative movement in this country rather than an ideological commitment to "cooperativism" as a way of life. To protect the interests of consumers, retail and wholesale cooperatives were established and have grown to the point where about one third of the retail (and more than one tenth of the wholesale) grocery trade is conducted by such organizations. In addition to these, some manufacturing enterprises have been established to reduce the prices charged by businessmen manufacturing certain products.

The objective of cooperative action in Sweden, then, has been to reduce prices to the consumer. To do this, Swedish cooperatives have not adopted the methods of English consumer co-ops, that is, selling at market prices and giving member-patrons a rebate on their purchases. Instead, they have made a forthright attack on high prices through selling at lower prices than those prevailing before the organization of the cooperatives. It may be owing to this policy that such organizations have gained a much larger share of the retail market than have their counterparts in England and the U.S. Where they have been unable to reduce the retail price because of the monopolistic practices of "profit-hungry" manufacturers, they have frequently gone into manufacturing the products in question in order to break the monopoly power of the "trust" governing the manufacture of a particular product.

Unlike Americans, Swedes have not believed in the effectiveness of antitrust legislation to curb the "excesses of monopoly" and hence such laws do not appear on their statute books. However, the Swedish government combats monopoly in a different way. It has established government enterprises that compete with business firms and provide "yardsticks" by which the performance of private business enterprise can be measured. Despite the presence of considerable government and cooperative enterprise, the Swedish economy remains essentially "capitalistic," with business making the greatest contribution to the gross national product in Sweden.

FASCISM

Fascism, as compared with socialism, has no substantial body of economic ideas. It did not develop as a challenge to capitalism, but rather promised to save capitalist societies from socialism and communism. Fascist nations, such as Germany and Italy in the years preceding and during World War II, permitted (at least in theory) capitalist institutions to continue. The stress, instead, was on the attainment of certain national goals by the exercise of some control over business. Although much was made, in public statements, of such institutions as economic motivation, private property, and freedom of enterprise, in practice there were severe limitations on these. Occasionally, private wealth was appropriated by the government, and the uses to which private productive resources could be put were limited. Controls over prices and wages hampered the operation of free markets. Economic motivation did not play the role that it might have, as restrictions were placed on the use of profits and on the occupations that persons could engage in. Also, some central economic plans were made by government planners. In short, fascism was a substantially modified form of capitalism that may have had some advantages for the fascist government, but that also hampered the development of business.

Somewhat ironically, fascism in Nazi Germany was called National Socialism. In its early years, the Nazi party did stand for some socialistic measures, although nationalism soon came to prevail. The goal of the economic system was declared to be to enhance the power and prestige of the nation, and by the end of the period of Nazi control of the economy, the Nazis were blaming Communism, Bolshevism, class war, trade union activities, and other factors normally associated with socialism for the problems of Germany. Throughout their history, the Nazis warred with the Social Democratic Party (a traditional socialist organization). Since it was not a socialist party in the sense that the term is normally used, there was little nationalization of industry during the period the Nazis were in control of the economy. Instead, the party courted big business, although subjecting it to numerous controls. Such a system of private ownership but national control has been referred to by one historian as "national capitalism" and seems to be as good a descriptive term as any of the German economy under the Nazis. Since World War II, the Nazis have been out of political power, and the economy has returned to a more traditional kind of capitalism, with both ownership and control in private hands.

There are, at present, no major industrial nations to which the term "fascism" applies. Some Latin American economies might come under this heading; Argentina under Peron was regarded by some as being "fascistic." It may be that at some time in the future the threat of Communism or of a major depression or of war will cause a capitalistic nation to adopt an autocratic form of government, but at present fascism is not very pervasive.

THE SIGNIFICANCE OF OTHER ECONOMIC SYSTEMS

This brief examination of other systems of economic thought and practice yields some generalizations that may be of value. In the first place, it does not appear that "isms" are as important as they are sometimes said to be. That is, there seems to be a tendency for the practical to rule over the ideological. The only major industrial nation in which economic doctrine has held sway over economic structure is the Soviet Union (and then only briefly, during the period of "War Communism"). Secondly, there are a number of similarities as well as differences among the institutions of various economies. Even in the Soviet Union, the price system is employed to a certain degree to allocate labor resources among alternative occupations and in the distribution of consumers' goods (although the prices are in most cases set by the government). It may well be that such similarities will increase rather than decrease, since each economy is confronted with essentially the same problems, and when certain means are found to be effective and efficient in solving them, it is likely that they will be adopted in a variety of economic systems.

READING: The Communist Manifesto, by Karl Marx and Friedrich Engels

[*In 1848, Karl Marx and Friedrich Engels wrote one of the most interesting documents concerning economic systems,* The Manifesto of the Communist Party. *Marx is generally regarded as the founder of modern socialism and Communism. An economist and political philosopher, he wrote a number of works setting forth the reasons why he felt a fundamental change in society was called for. Nowhere else are they set forth so briefly and compellingly.*]

A specter is haunting Europe—the specter of Communism. All the powers of old Europe have entered into a holy alliance to exorcise this specter: Pope and Tsar, Metternich and Guizot, French Radicals and German police-spies.

Where is the party in opposition that has not been decried as communistic by its opponents in power? Where is the Opposition that has not hurled back the branding reproach of Communism, against the more advanced opposition parties, as well as against its reactionary adversaries?

Two things result from this fact:

1. Communism is already acknowledged by all European powers to be itself a power.

2. It is high time that Communists should openly, in the face of the whole world, publish their views, their aims, their tendencies, and meet this nursery tale of the specter of Communism with a manifesto of the party itself.

I: Bourgeois and Proletarians.   The history of all hitherto existing society is the history of class struggles.

Freeman and slave, patrician and plebeian, lord and serf, guild-master and journeyman, in a word, oppressor and oppressed, stood in constant opposition to one another, carried on an uninterrupted, now hidden, now open fight, a fight that each time ended, either in a revolutionary reconstitution of society at large, or in the common ruin of the contending classes.

In the earlier epochs of history, we find almost everywhere a complicated arrangement of society into various orders, a manifold gradation of social rank. In ancient Rome we have patricians, knights, plebeians, slaves; in the Middle Ages, feudal lords, vassals, guild-masters, journeymen, apprentices, serfs; in almost all of these classes, again, subordinate gradations.

The modern bourgeois society that has sprouted from the ruins of feudal society has not done away with class antagonisms. It has but established new classes, new conditions of oppression, new forms of struggle in place of the old ones.

Our epoch, the epoch of the bourgeoisie, possesses, however, this distinctive feature: it has simplified the class antagonisms. Society as a whole is more and more splitting up into two great hostile camps, into two great classes directly facing each other—bourgeoisie and proletariat.

The bourgeoisie, during its rule of scarce one hundred years, has created more massive and more colossal productive forces than have all preceding generations together. Subjection of nature's forces to man, machinery, application of chemistry to industry and agriculture, steam navigation, railways, electric telegraphs, clearing of whole continents for cultivation, canalization of rivers, whole populations conjured out of the ground—what earlier century had even a presentiment that such productive forces slumbered in the lap of social labor?

We see then: the means of production and of exchange, on whose foundation the bourgeoisie built itself up, were generated in feudal society. At a certain stage in the development of these means of production and of exchange, the conditions under which feudal society produced and exchanged, the feudal organization of agriculture and manufacturing industry, in one word, the feudal relations of property became no longer compatible with the already developed productive forces; they became so many fetters. They had to be burst asunder.

Into their place stepped free competition, accompanied by a social and political constitution adapted to it, and by the economical and political sway of the bourgeois class.

A similar movement is going on before our own eyes. Modern bourgeois society with its relation of production, of exchange and of property, a society that has conjured up such gigantic means of production and of exchange, is like the sorcerer who is no longer able to control the powers of the nether world whom he has called up by his spells. For many a decade past the history of industry and commerce is but the history of the revolt of modern productive forces against modern conditions of production, against the property relations that are the conditions for the existence of the bourgeoisie and of its rule. It is enough to mention the commercial crises that by their periodical return put the existence of the entire bourgeois society on its trial, each time more threateningly. In these crises a great part not only of the existing products, but also of the previously created productive forces, are periodically destroyed. In these crises there breaks out an epidemic that, in all earlier epochs, would have seemed an absurdity— the epidemic of over-production. Society suddenly finds itself put back into a state of monetary barbarism; it appears as if a famine, a universal war of devastation, had cut off the supply of every means of subsistence; industry and commerce seem to be destroyed. And why? Because there is too much civilization, too much means of subsistence, too much industry, too much commerce. The productive forces at the disposal of society no longer tend to further the development of the conditions of bourgeois property; on the contrary, they have become too powerful for these conditions, by which they are fettered, and so soon as they overcome these fetters, they bring disorder into the whole of bourgeois society, endanger the existence of bourgeois property. The conditions of bourgeois society are too narrow to comprise the wealth created by them. And how does the bourgeoisie get over these crises? On the one hand by enforced destruction of a mass of productive forces; on the other by the conquest of new markets, and by the more thorough exploitation of the old ones. That is to say, by paving the way for more extensive and more destructive crises, and by diminishing the means whereby crises are prevented.

The weapons with which the bourgeoisie felled feudalism to the ground are now turned against the bourgeoisie itself.

But not only has the bourgeoisie forged the weapons that bring death to itself; it has also called into existence the men who are to wield those weapons— the modern working class—the proletarians.

In proportion as the bourgeoisie, i.e., capital, is developed, in the same proportion is the proletariat, the modern working class, developed—a class of laborers, who live only so long as they find work, and who find work only so long as their labor increases capital. These laborers, who must sell themselves piecemeal, are a commodity, like every other article of commerce, and are consequently exposed to all the vicissitudes of competition, to all the fluctuations of the market.

Owing to the extensive use of machinery and to division of labor, the work of the proletarians has lost all individual character, and, consequently all charm for the workman. He becomes an appendage of the machine, and it is only the most simple, most monotonous, and most easily acquired knack, that is required of him. Hence, the cost of production of a workman is restricted, almost entirely, to the means of subsistence that he requires for his maintenance, and for the propagation of his race. But the price of a commodity, and therefore, also of labor, is equal to its cost of production. In proportion, therefore, as the repulsiveness of the work increases, the wage decreases. Nay, more, in proportion as the use of machinery and division of labor increases, in the same proportion the burden of toil also increases, whether by prolongation of the working hours, by increase of the work exacted in a given time, or by increased speed of the machinery, etc.

Modern industry has converted the little workshop of the patriarchal master into the great factory of the industrial capitalist. Masses of laborers, crowded into the factory, are organized like soldiers. As privates of the industrial army they are placed under the command of a perfect hierarchy of officers and sergeants. Not only are they slaves of the bourgeois class, and of the bourgeois state; they are daily and hourly enslaved by the machine, by the overlooker, and, above all by the individual bourgeois manufacturer himself. The more openly this despotism proclaims gain to be its end and aim, the more petty, the more hateful and the more embittering it is.

The less the skill and exertion of strength implied in manual labor, in other words, the more modern industry becomes developed, the more is the labor of men superseded by that of women. Differences of age and sex have no longer any distinctive social validity for the working class. All are instruments of labor, more or less expensive to use, according to their age and sex.

No sooner is the exploitation of the laborer by the manufacturer so far at an end that he receives his wages in cash than he is set upon by the other portions of the bourgeoisie, the landlord, the shopkeeper, the pawnbroker, etc.

The lower strata of the middle class—the small tradespeople, shopkeepers, and retired tradesmen generally, the handicraftsmen and peasants—all these sink gradually into the proletariat, partly because their diminutive capital does not suffice for the scale on which modern industry is carried on, and is swamped in the competition with the large capitalists, partly because their specialized skill is rendered worthless by new methods of production. Thus the proletariat is recruited from all classes of the population.

Hitherto, every form of society has been based, as we have already seen, on the antagonism of oppressing and oppressed classes. But in order to oppress a class, certain conditions must be assured to it under which it can, at least, continue its slavish existence. The serf, in the period of serfdom, raised himself to membership in the commune, just as the petty bourgeois, under the yoke of feudal absolutism, managed to develop into a bourgeois. The modern laborer, on the contrary, instead of rising with the progress of industry, sinks deeper and deeper below the conditions of existence of his own class. He becomes a pauper, and pauperism develops more rapidly than population and wealth. And here it becomes evident that the bourgeoisie is unfit any longer to be the ruling class in society and to impose its conditions of existence upon society as an overriding law. It is unfit to rule because it is incompetent to assure an existence to its slave within his slavery, because it cannot help letting him sink into such a state, that it has to feed him, instead of being fed by him. Society can no longer live under this bourgeoisie; in other words, its existence is no longer compatible with society.

The essential condition for the existence and for the sway of the bourgeois class is the formation and augmentation of capital; the condition for capital is wage labor. Wage labor rests exclusively on competition between the laborers. The advance of industry, whose involuntary promoter is the bourgeoisie, replaces the isolation of the laborers, due to competition, by their revolutionary combination, due to association. The development of modern industry, therefore, cuts from under its feet the very foundation on which the bourgeoisie produces and appropriates products. What the bourgeoisie therefore produces, above all, are its own grave-diggers. Its fall and the victory of the proletariat are equally inevitable.

II: Proletarians and Communists. In what relation do the Communists stand to the proletarians as a whole?

The Communists do not form a separate party opposed to other working class parties.

They have no interests separate and apart from those of the proletariat as a whole.

They do not set up any sectarian principles of their own, by which to shape and mold the proletarian movement.

The Communists are distinguished from other working-class parties by this only: (1) In the national struggles of the proletarians of the different countries, they point out and bring to the front the common interests of the entire proletariat, independently of all nationality. (2) In the various stages of development which the struggle of the working class against the bourgeoisie has to pass through, they always and everywhere represent the interests of the movement as a whole.

The Communists, therefore, are on the one hand, practically, the most advanced and resolute section of the working-class parties of every country, that section which pushes forward all others; on the other hand, theoretically, they have over the great mass of the proletariat the advantage of clearly understanding the line of march, the conditions, and the ultimate general results of the proletarian movement.

The immediate aim of the Communists is the same as that of all the other proletarian parties: formation of the proletariat into a class, overthrow of the bourgeois supremacy, conquest of political power by the proletariat.

The theoretical conclusions of the Communists are in no way based on ideas or principles that have been invented, or discovered, by this or that would-be universal reformer.

They merely express, in general terms, actual relations springing from an existing class struggle, from a historical movement going on under our very eyes. The abolition of existing property relations is not at all a distinctive feature of Communism.

All property relations in the past have continually been subject to historical change consequent upon the change in historical conditions.

The French Revolution, for example, abolished feudal property in favor of bourgeois property.

The distinguishing feature of Communism is not the abolition of property generally but the abolition of bourgeois property. But modern bourgeois private property is the final and most complete expression of the system of producing and appropriating products that is based on class antagonisms, on the exploitation of the many by the few.

In this sense, the theory of the Communists may be summed up in the single sentence: Abolition of private property.

We have seen above that the first step in the revolution by the working class is to raise the proletariat to the position of ruling class, to win the battle of democracy.

The proletariat will use its political supremacy to wrest, by degrees, all capital from the bourgeoisie, to centralize all instruments of production in the hands of the state, i.e., of the proletariat organized as the ruling class; and to increase the total of productive forces as rapidly as possible.

Of course, in the beginning, this cannot be effected except by means of despotic inroads on the rights of property, and on the conditions of bourgeois production; by means of measures, therefore, which appear economically insufficient and untenable, but which, in the course of the movement, outstrip themselves, necessitate further inroads upon the old social order, and are unavoidable as a means of entirely revolutionizing the mode of production.

These measures will, of course, be different in different countries.

Nevertheless, in the most advanced countries, the following will be pretty generally applicable:

1. Abolition of property in land and application of all rents of land to public purposes.

2. A heavy progressive or graduated income tax.

3. Abolition of all right of inheritance.

4. Confiscation of the property of all emigrants and rebels.

5. Centralization of credit in the hands of the state, by means of a national bank with state capital and an exclusive monopoly.

6. Centralization of the means of communication and transport in the hands of the state.

7. Extension of factories and instruments of production owned by the state; the bringing into cultivation of waste lands, and the improvement of the soil generally in accordance with a common plan.

8. Equal obligation of all to work. Establishment of industrial armies, especially for agriculture.

9. Combination of agriculture with manufacturing industries; gradual abolition of the distinction between town and country, by a more equal distribution of the population over the country.

10. Free education for all children in public schools. Abolition of children's factory labor in its present form. Combination of education with industrial production, etc.

When, in the course of development, class distinctions have disappeared, and all production has been concentrated in the hands of a vast association of the whole nation, the public power will lose its political character. Political power, properly so called, is merely the organized power of one class for oppressing another. If the proletariat during its contest with the bourgeoisie is compelled, by the force of circumstances, to organize itself as a class; if, by means of a revolution, it makes itself the ruling class, and, as such, sweeps away by force the old conditions of production, then it will, along with these conditions, have swept away the conditions for the existence of class antagonisms and of classes generally, and will thereby have abolished its own supremacy as a class.

In place of the old bourgeois society, with its classes and class antagonisms, we shall have an association in which the free development of each is the condition for the free development of all.

Position of the Communist in Relation to Various Existing Opposition Parties. In short, the Communists everywhere support every revolutionary movement against the existing social and political order of things.

In all these movements they bring to the front, as the leading question in each, the property question, no matter what its degree of development at the time.

Finally, they labor everywhere for the union and agreement of the democratic parties of all countries.

The Communists disdain to conceal their views and aims. They openly declare that their ends can be attained only by the forcible overthrow of all existing social conditions. Let the ruling class tremble at a Communist revolution. The proletarians have nothing to lose but their chains. They have a world to win.

Working men of all countries, unite!

SUGGESTED READINGS

Blodgett, Ralph H., and Donald H. Kemmerer, *Comparative Economic Development* (New York: McGraw-Hill, 1956). The authors describe and compare what they regard as the four basic types of economy: capitalism, exemplified by the U.S.; the welfare state, Great Britain; totalitarian socialism, Soviet Russia; and, fascism, as it existed in Nazi Germany.

Burns, Arthur R., *Comparative Economic Organization* (Englewood Cliffs, N.J.: Prentice-Hall, 1955). An analysis of the economic operation of societies past and present in terms of their resources and organization.

Childs, Marquis W., *Sweden: The Middle Way* (New Haven: Yale, 1947). A study of "the story of a constructive compromise between socialism and capitalism."

Loucks, William N., *Comparative Economic Systems* (New York: Harper & Row, 1961). In addition to treatments of the major industrial nations, the author discusses India, Yugoslavia, and Communist China.

CHAPTER 7

AMERICAN
PRODUCT
MARKETS

American business firms sell their products to various classes of customers. These sales involve a direct relationship between buyer and seller, but it is sometimes helpful to think of the seller—the business firm—as selling in a market rather than as selling to some individual or group. As classes of customers and products differ quite widely, and as a large population is spread over a vast area, the American economy contains a number of markets for the products of firms and industries. Foreign purchasers of American products sometimes buy in markets outside the geographical limits of the United States, in addition to their purchases in American markets. These foreign, international, and world markets are of such importance and complexity, however, that they will be dealt with in a separate chapter; our concern here will be chiefly with product markets in America.

MARKETS

In discussing markets, difficulty is sometimes encountered because the term *market* has a number of different meanings. Sometimes it refers to a specific place—one definition being: "A place where merchandise is exposed for sale; specifically, an open space or a large building in a town or city, generally with stalls or designated positions occupied by different dealers." There are a number of such marketplaces in America—produce markets, livestock markets, grain exchanges, stock exchanges, and so on. However, services as well as goods are sold, and many firms do not sell in just one place. If we are to regard them as selling in markets, another definition must be employed. A market, then, can also be "the area in which buyers and sellers can conveniently arrange to exchange." If we think of markets in this way, we can see how it is possible to have regional, national, international, and world markets for products so long as the buyer and seller can readily arrange to sell and purchase in these areas. In the following discussion, we shall be employing both definitions.

Local Markets

Local markets exist both as places and areas. There are places in almost any American city of any size where the sellers of certain products congregate to sell their wares to those "in the market" for a particular class of goods or services. Most sellers in a specific locality, even though selling goods only in their own establishment, think of the market for their products as consisting of something more than just the buyers in the place at the time. They conceive of their market as being composed of all the people in the area who can more conveniently purchase in that locality than in some other. For example, the manager of a department store regards his "trading area" as the territory surrounding the city or town in which the store is located from which persons prefer to come to his store to buy rather than go to a department store in some other town or city.

Regional Markets

Regional markets are larger than local markets and are areas rather than places. Where local markets surround a single town or city, a regional market includes a number of localities. A number of counties or states are frequently contained in a regional market, although economic rather than political boundaries mark off the limits. Wholesalers tend to sell in regional markets, while retailers normally sell in local markets (although there are some retailers—such as Sears, Roebuck & Co. and Montgomery Ward & Co.—that sell by mail order in a region, but these are exceptions to the general rule). The sellers of producers' goods and services, also, tend to market their products in regions. Those who provide certain services to consumers—such as public utility and transportation companies—frequently do so in a region rather than in just a locality.

National Markets

Some selling takes place on a national scale rather than on a local or regional level. It is important to take into account the characteristics of a market when we speak of national markets, since some things are sold throughout a nation, but not on national markets. Automobiles provide a good illustration. General Motors sells its cars throughout America, but there is no national market for these products. Buyers cannot conveniently go anywhere in the United States to buy a new car, and so the markets for new automobiles tend to be local and regional (since some buyers will go to a number of different localities in trying to find a "good buy," and since some dealers have territories including a number of towns). Products sold on national markets carry the same price tag to all buyers in the nation, and therefore when we see the same product sold for different prices in various regions of the United States we recognize that regional markets exist rather than does a national market. An example of a national market is the market for corporate securities. Through their brokers, people throughout the United States can conveniently buy or sell securities of large American corporations that have issued bonds or stock for sale to the public. All can buy or sell at the same market price; thus the conditions for a national market are fulfilled.

Some products are sold outside the geographical limits of the United States. They may be sold in local, regional, or national markets of foreign countries or in international or world markets. American business firms also buy in these markets beyond our political boundaries and what they can sell is closely related to how much is purchased. Since such trade is very complex and important, this topic will be taken up separately.

PRODUCT MARKETS

Business firms produce goods and/or services and sell them to individuals, nonprofit organizations, other business firms, and governments inside and outside the United States. These customers can usefully be regarded as buying in product markets—normally classified as durable goods markets, nondurable goods markets, and service markets. No one of these markets can be associated with any one class of buyer, since almost all buyers make purchases in more than one of these broad types of markets (*see* Figure 1–1). An examination of such product markets gives us some idea of their nature and of their importance to American business.

Available data do not permit us to indicate how much particular firms or particular industries sell in various product markets. This problem may be resolved by regarding all the producing units of our economy as one giant firm. Such a view overemphasizes the importance of business, of course, since some products are produced by government, cooperatives, and other nonprofit organizations. However, this is offset to a certain extent by the fact that gross national product—the value of final products produced within the nation during a year—does not include sales (including sales by business) of intermediate products which go into the final product. Table 7–1 shows how much of the final output of "The American Business Firm" was sold in different product markets during a recent year.

Table 7–1. Gross Sales of Final Products by Purchaser and by Type of Product, 1964

	Billions
Gross national product	$628.7
By Purchaser	
Consumer purchases	398.9
Business fixed investment	60.5
Change in business inventories	4.8
Residential construction	27.5
Net exports (Total exports were $37.0 billion)	8.6
Federal government	65.3
State and local government	63.1
By Type of product	
Nondurable goods	190.0
Durable goods	126.1
Construction	68.6
Services	244.0

Source: Office of Business Economics, U.S. Department of Commerce, *Survey of Current Business,* Vol. 45, No. 8 (August 1965), pp. 3 and 4.

Sales of Durable Goods

Individuals, nonprofit organizations, business firms, and governments—all require structures of some kind to enable them to conduct their activities as well as some equipment to facilitate their operations. Both structures and equipment are durable in the sense that they can be used over and over again before finally wearing out. In examining the sales of final products by business (and other producing units) during the year 1964, we note that sales of durable goods amounted to $126 billion out of a total of approximately $630 billion (or about 20 per cent). This information is reported in such a manner that this durable goods figure does not include new construction, which in 1964 amounted to some $69 billion. Construction and durable goods (which covers only those durable products that are movable), together accounted for $195 billion or 31 per cent of the total final products sold.

Sales of Nondurable Goods

Nondurables—commodities that can be used only once or a few times before losing their value—are also of great importance to all classes of purchasers. This importance is indicated by the sale of $190 billion of nondurable goods during 1964—30 per cent of the total sales of final products.

Sales of Services

Services sold to individuals, nonprofit institutions, business firms, and government agencies are a large and growing part of the total sales of products. During 1964, these sales amounted to $244 billion—39 per cent of the total final sales. It should be noted that this figure includes government services, and business firms do not really sell as many services as might appear to be true at first glance. Purchasers of government services usually "pay" for them through taxes, although some services provided by governments are paid for directly by the user of the service.

Buyers in Product Markets

We have already indicated that there are four major classes of customers for the products of American business firms—individuals, nonprofit institutions, other business firms, and governments. It is difficult to secure data on nonprofit organizations alone, and therefore they are sometimes lumped in with individuals and sometimes with business firms and never appear separately in the national product accounts published by the U.S. Department of Commerce. Neither do the total sales to business firms appear. Also, sales to foreign buyers are dealt with separately in these accounts. Hence, we shall rearrange our classifications of buyers and markets so as to deal with personal consumption expenditures, "gross private domestic investment," government purchases of goods and services, and foreign purchases.

Purchases by Consumers. Sales for personal consumption loom largest in the sales of final products, although this figure is somewhat inflated by what is included under that heading. According to the Department of Commerce, "Personal Consumption Expenditures" consists of the market value of purchases of goods and services by individuals and non-profit institutions (and the value of food, clothing, housing, and financial services received by them as income in kind). This figure also includes the rental value of owner-occupied houses, but does not include purchases of dwellings, which come under another heading.

Some measure of the importance to business today of the individual consumer is secured by looking at present-day personal consumption expenditures. During 1964, individuals and institutions purchased $399 billion of the total final sales of the American economy. This accounted for 63 per cent of the value of finished goods sold. Of this figure, durable goods accounted for $59 billion (9 per cent of all final sales and 15 per cent of personal consumption expenditures); nondurable goods purchased amounted to $177.5 billion (28 per cent of all final sales and 44 per cent of personal consumption expenditures); and services sold were in the amount of $162.5 billion (26 per cent of all final sales and 41 per cent of personal consumption expenditures). If we were to add the value of residential construction (which is sold mainly to individuals) to consumer expenditures on other goods and services, the total amount of spending by consumers would amount to $426.5 billion, or 68 per cent of the total final sales of the American economy. Whether we use the 63 or 68 per cent figure, it is quite obvious that personal consumption expenditures are of major importance to those business firms turning out final products, with consumers buying roughly two thirds of the goods and services purchased by final users. Table 7–2 shows the nature of personal consumption expenditures during recent years.

Purchases by Business. Many business firms buy products from other business firms. These purchases consist of raw materials, supplies and equipment, construction, and a variety of services. It is difficult to measure how much of the sales of firms in certain industries—such as the automobile industry—wind up in the hands of individuals, institutions, business firms, and governments. Also true is the fact that there is a large amount of selling done between firms in the successive stages of the production and distribution process—extractive firms sell to manufacturers, manufacturers sell to wholesalers, wholesalers sell to retailers. If the value of all of these sales were totaled up, we would get a figure in excess of the retail price of the final product. Therefore, when the Department of Commerce concerns itself with the total value of final products (gross national product), it ignores these interindustry sales and concerns itself only with the sales of finished goods, thereby providing us with some idea of how much of these products business firms buy for their own use and not for processing and/or resale.

Table 7–2.   *Personal Consumption Expenditures by Major Type*

(Billions of Dollars)

	1962	1963	1964
Goods and services, total	**356.8**	**375.0**	**399.3**
Durable goods, total	**48.4**	**52.1**	**57.0**
Automobiles and parts	20.6	22.7	24.2
Furniture and household equipment	20.2	21.4	24.0
Other	7.6	8.0	8.8
Nondurable goods, total	**162.0**	**167.5**	**177.3**
Food and beverages	84.6	87.1	91.7
Clothing and shoes	29.9	30.7	33.4
Gasoline and oil	12.3	12.8	13.5
Other	35.2	36.9	38.7
Services, total	**146.4**	**155.3**	**165.1**
Housing	46.5	48.9	51.5
Household operation	21.6	22.7	24.4
Transportation	11.3	11.7	12.2
Other	67.0	72.0	77.1

SOURCE: Office of Business Economics, U.S. Department of Commerce, *Survey of Current Business,* Vol. 45, No. 7 (July 1965), p. 4.

Final products bought by business firms—on which data *are* available —are durable equipment, new construction, and goods added to inventories. Information is not readily available on the amount of services purchased by firms. During 1964, new construction purchased by business and private nonprofit organizations totaled $21 billion, or 3 per cent of the value of final products. Durable equipment was purchased by producers in the amount of $39.4 billion, or 6 per cent of total final sales. Business firms sometimes add to their inventories to enable them to conduct a greater volume of business, although they sometimes invest "involuntarily" in goods because they are not able to sell as much of their inventory as they thought they would. In 1964, almost $5 billion worth of goods were added to business inventories, accounting for almost 1 per cent of the value of final products.

PURCHASES BY GOVERNMENT. Federal, state, and local governments are increasingly important purchasers from business firms. Total purchases by American governmental bodies during 1964 were $128.5 billion, 20 per cent of all final goods purchased. The expenditures of the federal government were only slightly greater than those of the state and local governments—$65 billion as compared to $63 billion. (Much of the payments by all classes of governments is for the purpose of compensating employees, and their purchases from business are not nearly as much as their total expenditures of $185.5 billion might indicate.) Of the federal purchases of $65 billion, almost $50 billion was for national defense (that is, about 77 per cent of federal government spending was defense spending).

FOREIGN BUYERS.   Individuals, institutions, firms, and governments outside of the United States are important buyers of American products. In 1964 they bought $37 billion of goods and services from American producers. Although this amounts to only about 6 per cent of the total final sales, it has importance beyond this, as we shall see in Chapter 9.

THEORIES OF MARKETS

Since there are such a large number and great variety of product markets in the American economy, it is impossible to deal with all of them individually in order to gain a general view of their nature. We have dealt with them collectively in the preceding section, and it would be possible to classify them in yet other ways and through the use of statistical data to acquire some understanding of the importance of certain product markets in the United States. However, we might look at markets in the abstract as well as in the aggregate and thereby enhance our understanding.

Traditional Economic Theory

Economists have long studied markets and have attempted to abstract from their study those essential characteristics from which a theory of markets might be developed. Some economists see markets as solving the problems of "What, How, and For Whom"—that is, every economic system must solve in some way the question of what will be produced, how it will be produced, and for whom it will be produced. In a "market system," these problems are solved by the operations of markets. What will be produced is determined by the users of products, since by their "money votes" in the markets they encourage the production of those goods and services that are profitable to produce and also discourage the production of unprofitable products. How things will be produced also depends upon market conditions, although in this case it is prices in resource markets that determine the "mix" of productive resources employed in a production process. For whom things are produced depends also on productive resource markets because the incomes of resource owners (hence their purchasing power) depend on the prices they receive and the quantities they sell of such factors of production. Although we shall not be dealing with productive resource markets until the next chapter, this theory of the functions performed by markets explains, perhaps, what product markets do. We shall see later on that some questions have been raised about the generalizations that buyers are sovereign and dictate production.

In examining markets, economists have come to the conclusion that some kinds of markets perform the economic functions described above better than others. That is, they have observed the existence of different types of markets and have contended that market behavior (including performance of the economic functions of markets) depends on the kind of market that exists. The classification system they traditionally employ is different from the one we have been using because they regard different characteristics as being important. The major characteristic of significance is felt to be the number of sellers, leading to the following classification:

Number of Sellers in the Market	*Market Type*
One	Monopoly
Two	Duopoly
A few	Oligopoly
Many	Competitive

Since a purpose of such a classification is to indicate the market power of those selling in the market, a similar classification is sometimes made of the number of buyers to indicate their bargaining power:

Number of Buyers in the Market	*Market Type*
One	Monopsony
Two	Duopsony
A few	Oligopsony
Many	Competitive

In addition to the terms mentioned above, special terms are applied to other market situations—for example, a market in which there is only one buyer and one seller is called "bilateral monopoly." In any case, there is a term to fit every kind of market situation in terms of the number of sellers and buyers present, and according to economists adopting this theory, each market behaves in a certain way. The value of this approach, it is contended, is that by counting the number of buyers and sellers in a particular market we can forecast the results of their interaction.

COMPETITIVE MARKETS. According to traditional economic theory, competitive markets will perform the basic economic functions best (except in those rare cases—such as public utilities—where monopoly is "natural"). In competitive markets, there are a large number of sellers and a large number of buyers. All of the sellers—according to this theory—are attempting to maximize profits, but they find that they can do so only by producing an output that minimizes their average costs, and also that the price they receive under competitive conditions covers only those costs (which include a "normal" rate of profit). Hence, competition among sellers leads to the lowest prices consistent with covering minimum costs as well as forces producers to produce most efficiently. This desirable situation is contrasted with that alleged to prevail under monopoly.

MONOPOLY MARKETS. At the other extreme from a competitive market is the situation in which monopoly prevails—that is, in which only one seller is present. In the absence of other sellers (and in the absence of governmental or other restrictions), he can set his price as high as he wishes. In setting his price, he attempts to maximize profits and hence the price he sets is not as high as he might set it and still make some profit—that is, he takes into account the fact that as he raises the price, some buyers will be "priced out of the market" and, therefore, he will not be able to sell as many units at a higher price as he would at a lower price. Still, the amount sold by the monopolist will be significantly less than the amount sold in a competitive market, and the price will be appreciably greater. Also, the seller will not be producing at his most efficient output. Although profits will be received in excess of "competitive profits," they will not perform their economic function of attracting additional sellers because one seller possesses a monopoly.

Comparison of the theoretical results of monopoly with those of competition leaves no doubt in the theorist's mind as to the relative desirability of competition. Although other market situations exist between these two extremes, they are all regarded as being monopolistic to some degree and as not yielding as desirable results as competitive markets.

A General Theory of Markets

The traditional theory has not had as its sole goal the explanation of market behavior. It has also been concerned with the question of how various kinds of markets allocate productive resources among alternative uses and how income is distributed to those supplying the resources. To accomplish these other purposes, certain simplifying assumptions have been made, including the assumption that only the actions of buyers and sellers are relevant (and that the influences that others might conceivably have on the market act directly upon buyers and/or sellers and *through them* upon market conditions). Although this assumption is useful for certain purposes of economists, it tends to mask the role that individuals and groups other than buyers or sellers play in determining market price and output. For example, the federal government limits the amount of daily price change permitted in some agricultural commodity markets. It does this through regulation, acting neither as buyer nor seller. Although its actions affect buyers and sellers, to really appreciate all of the influences upon markets it seems proper to recognize formally the existence of such third parties. Earlier, we developed a theory of the firm that explained the behavior of a firm in terms of the external and internal influences brought to bear upon it. We can, and in the interests of consistency and realism should, state an analogous theory of market behavior: "The behavior of a market—as evidenced by market price and quantity bought and sold—depends upon the behavior of the buyers and sellers in the market and upon that of others having some influence upon the market." This statement is consistent with traditional theory, but gives explicit recognition to influences of those not buyers or sellers.

HISTORY OF MARKETS

An investigation of the development of product markets shows something of their nature that is not revealed by examination of such markets in the aggregate nor by theories of markets. In the history of markets, product markets (at least in the sense of markets as specific places) came into existence long before commodity exchanges, labor markets, and other places in which productive resources might be acquired. Perhaps this reflects the fact that not until production was conducted on a large scale was there a need for places in which large quantities of productive resources could be readily secured. On the other hand, there has long been considerable production for the market conducted on a small scale, and the development of marketplaces for finished goods served the interests of such producers as well as those of buyers.

Although the nomadic tribes typical of early stages of economic development engaged in some exchange, established marketplaces waited upon the settlement of villages and towns. In these settlements, exchange began to take place at certain times and places. Markets and fairs were established, frequently combining trade with festive activities. The logical development of occasional market periods was the continuous conduct of trade at established places of business by merchants and craftsmen. Traveling merchants traveled to various places to acquire and sell goods, but chiefly conducted their activities in various marketplaces. They apparently did not confine their activities to any specific area, but ventured off to markets far and near in search of profitable trade. Perhaps the existence of markets as areas awaited the rise of the peddler, who purchased his goods in the town and distributed them throughout the surrounding countryside. As producing units grew in size, they began to conceive of their market as being something more than the local marketplace and sent their representatives throughout the region, the nation, and eventually the world in search of customers.

In America, markets did not develop as they did in England and other European countries and elsewhere. Although not all of the native American tribes were nomadic, market institutions were not well developed in the villages and other settlements existing in that part of America that is now the United States. Markets came with the white man, and even then did not follow the traditional pattern. The first permanent colony on our Eastern seaboard was established at Jamestown by the English in 1607. It was not intended to be a self-sufficient economic unit; rather, the object of the settlement was to produce certain products valued in England for shipment to English markets as well as to provide a market for English merchants. Eventually, tobacco became its most important export, and the most important trade took place between the colony and England. The local markets that existed were mainly markets for English products rather than for those of local manufacture. To a very large degree, this characterized all of our colonial experience: overseas markets for American products were more important than local markets, although production for local markets did increase throughout the colonial period.

The American Revolution changed the market situation substantially. Although a large proportion of Americans remained loyal to the English Crown and continued to ship goods to England for sale in markets there (the English, after all, did have control of the major American seaports as well as of the seas), the war created a national market for military goods. American producers were not very well set up to produce for this market, not only because they lacked production facilities but also because communication and transportation were so poor (not to mention the quality of the currency and credit of the revolutionaries). Nevertheless, production for domestic markets increased and sales overseas declined until the peace treaty was signed in 1783.

After the war, the relative importance of domestic markets for American producers declined. Floods of imports from England and elsewhere made it difficult for certain manufacturers to compete in domestic markets, and the opening of the seas to American merchants made overseas markets of great importance again. Interstate trade was inhibited by some actions of state governments until the adoption of the Constitution and the enactment of federal legislation promoting such trade. Matters were such that local markets and foreign markets were of greater importance than regional and national markets, a development which seems somewhat other than what might have been expected from an examination of the rise of markets in Europe.

Conflicts between the English and French, and our consequent involvement during the War of 1812, spurred the development of regional markets for American products. Since each warring nation sought to cut off the international trade of the other, it became increasingly difficult for American merchants to gain access to foreign markets, thereby causing a decline in international trade (especially after the federal government passed legislation restricting trade with the belligerents).

The war between the English and French made it possible for President Jefferson to acquire the vast Louisiana Territory at a bargain price as well as enabled the United States to acquire lands (or at least to settle competing claims) in the Great Lakes region. Between 1816 and 1860, internal development of the lands acquired between 1800 and the beginning of the Civil War (lands out of which some thirty states were eventually created) led to a transformation of American markets. Commercial agriculture was established in the trans-Allegheny west, and with it came markets for agricultural products as well as markets for products desired by farmers. The large metropolitan centers of Pittsburgh, Cincinnati, St. Louis, and Chicago sprang up, providing central locations for the gathering of agricultural products of the region and for the distribution of goods to the newly created villages and towns. Improvements in transportation and communication—that is, canals, steamboats, railroads, and telegraph—created regional and national markets for products that had been sold only locally theretofore.

The existence of mass domestic markets, along with changes in production techniques, made feasible the rise of mass production; the changes in this period set the pattern of American markets that still persists. Mass production made productive resource markets of greater importance. We shall now turn to an investigation of them.

READING: Markets for Petroleum Products *

Petroleum products found a waiting market. For many years a search had been on for a bright-burning, safe and inexpensive illuminating oil. For centuries,

* The material for this original reading is taken principally from Ralph W. Hidy and Muriel E. Hidy, *Pioneering in Big Business* (New York: Harper & Row, 1955).

whale oil had been a major illuminant, giving rise to a major American industry. Its defects, including the growing difficulty of securing adequate supplies, had stimulated search for a superior substitute. None was found until a Scotsman in Glasgow developed a method for extracting a crude liquid hydrocarbon from coal and shale. This "crude" was distilled, with three major products of distillation being secured: the lightest was what we popularly refer to as gasoline (then called "naphtha"); an intermediate product called "coal oil" (kerosene); and a residue, which provided lubricants and paraffin wax. The Scotch process was patented in 1850, and during the following decade many coal-oil manufacturers sprang up in the cities and towns of the United States. Thus, local markets for kerosene were developed before petroleum was employed extensively to produce "coal oil."

During the 1850's "coal oil" was also sold by refiners (distillers) of the crude petroleum which issued from the surface of the earth or which was found in salt-water wells. However, when in 1859 the first oil well was drilled, an "oil boom" was touched off in northwestern Pennsylvania. Annual output of crude oil increased in this region from 2,000 barrels in 1859 to almost 5,000,000 ten years later. Processors of petroleum sprang up in the Oil Regions of Pennsylvania and in the large metropolitan centers where the major domestic markets were. The major product was kerosene, and by 1872 it was being sold in all of the main markets of the world, including Japan, which had only recently been opened to Western commerce. By-products—naphtha, lubricants and paraffin wax—were also sold throughout the world, although on a relatively small scale.

Initially, the petroleum industry was characterized by a high degree of specialization. Crude oil producers sold their products to refiners, or to pipeline operators who ran pipelines to the wells and stored the crude in tanks. In turn, refiners sold their products in various markets. Mainly interested in kerosene, they sold the "top cut" (naphtha) to firms which specialized in redistilling naphtha distillate, and they sold the residue—tar or lubricant stock—to firms manufacturing lubricants and wax. Kerosene was sold through middlemen such as commission merchants, who sold either through wholesalers or at wholesale to retailers. John D. Rockefeller had been a partner in such a mercantile commission house in Cleveland when he perceived the potential of this new industry and entered into the refining aspect of it. During the 1870's, as Standard Oil of Ohio entered into alliances with a number of other firms in the oil industry—principally refiners—it secured the participation of some marketing firms, but the influence of the combination in the product markets was relatively slight. Only limited coverage of the domestic market was attained by the group and almost all sales for export were to foreign merchants.

In the early years of the petroleum industry, the market for kerosene was quite competitive. Many buyers and sellers were present, and price wars broke out in many areas. Although the many refining and marketing firms in the Standard Oil Alliance produced and sold a major share of this product, they did not in any organized fashion attempt to dominate the market. This waited upon formation of the Trust in 1882.

By 1882, Standard Oil firms had expanded their product line substantially. In the early years, they had concentrated upon the production and sale of kerosene, selling the "by-products" to others. Now, companies in the combination produced a complete range of petroleum products: gasoline, naphtha, benzine, illuminating oil, gas oil, industrial fuel oil, paraffin wax, lubricating oils, and greases. Even for a few years after the formation of the Trust, those Standard Oil firms marketing such products made no coordinated attack upon the problem of organizing the market. Until 1886, Standard Oil firms sold mainly to wholesalers not owned by the combination.

The domestic market for petroleum products was rapidly expanding in the early 1880's, although some problems confronted marketers of those wares. Rapid growth in population and industrialization increased the demand for lighting (though electricity and artificial gas were beginning to compete for this market). The construction of railroads and steamships, the mechanization of manufacturing, and the expansion in the number of vehicles meant increased demand for fuel and lubricants. Here, too, there were important competing products: coal was used much more than fuel oil for heat and power generation, and many still preferred animal and vegetable products as lubricants. Even though the trend in consumption of petroleum products was upward, there were substantial seasonal and cyclical fluctuations in sales volume and price.

Difficulties with independent wholesalers led the combination to adopt the policy of expanding the number of wholesaling firms within the combination. Several new marketing companies were added by inducing former competitors and customers to join the Trust. Thus retailers rather than wholesalers of petroleum products became the customers of Standard Oil. In effect, one intermediate market—with its attendant problems—was eliminated.

Competition in product markets continued to be keen in the early 1880's. John D. Rockefeller was an advocate of price competition, expecting that a large volume of sales at a narrow margin of profit would put the combination in a good position. During the depressed market conditions of the period, he advocated reducing prices to the extent necessary to maintain previously attained volume. Not all competition in the markets was open price competition: rebates were given to customers to secure orders; advertising was employed; and heaters, stoves, lamps, lanterns, irons, and other utensils were sold in order to increase consumption of Standard Oil kerosene and gasoline. Through successful competition, but also through acquisition of competing refineries and marketers, the Trust had by the middle of the decade secured from 80 to 85 per cent of the domestic market for petroleum products. This was not in reality one large national market, but an aggregation of a number of local and regional markets with widely varying characteristics, including the degree of competition.

In foreign product markets, Standard Oil met considerably less success. Foreign markets were of special importance, since the bulk of kerosene output of some of the combination's eastern refineries was sold abroad, with Jersey Standard's Bayonne refinery selling for export almost three fourths of its product. Each foreign country was in many ways a separate market, since national governments (and even regional and local governments) established different specification for certain products and prescribed different regulations for the conduct of business. Entrance into some markets—such as those of Russia, France, Spain, and Austria-Hungary—was made difficult by high tariff barriers.

The nature of foreign product markets affected production, packaging, and pricing policies of Standard Oil in the early period, although the combination did not have overseas representatives. Almost all of its exports were disposed of through American commission merchants or agents of foreign importers. New York was the port through which almost three fourths of petroleum exports flowed and, as was true of all Atlantic ports, sales contracts were subject to the rules of the New York Produce Exchange. Thus, as in the case of domestic markets, Standard Oil did not in its early years sell its products to foreign retailers, but confined itself to operations in markets where those performing the wholesale function were the buyers.

Competition for foreign markets grew and eventually forced a change in Standard's policies. Scotch shale oil had been sold in Europe for a number of years before kerosene was exported by Standard. These firmly-established competitors were joined by others manufacturing products from the crude oil fields being developed in Canada, Russia, Austria-Hungary, Java, and Japan. The most rapid development of crude oil production abroad took place in the 1880's, and the resulting growth in foreign refineries led to an increased measure of competition which threatened to drive Standard Oil products from markets abroad. Experienced businessmen such as the Nobels and Rothschilds were attracted to the development of Russian oil, and one alarmist charged the Russian interests with a "quixotic ambition to drive the American oil from the markets of the world."

The initial response of Standard to the new competition was to modify and intensify existing practices. When the results were not particularly encouraging, price competition was decided upon. This began in the Levant, and spread to Bombay, Madras, and Calcutta. Reduced prices overseas meant reduced prices to exporters on the New York Produce Exchange, thus affecting all sales for foreign consumption. Price competition did not seem to adversely affect the refiners of Russian oil at all, and their production and sales mounted. By the late 1880's, it was obvious that stronger measures were necessary if the Standard Oil Trust was to retain its position in the markets of the world.

In 1888, Standard Oil established the first of its foreign affiliates—the Anglo-American Oil Company. Its organization was timely. American kerosene, which had in 1883 enjoyed almost the whole of the market, had seen the Russian product cut its market share to 70 per cent (and during 1882, the volume of American exports actually declined in absolute as well as relative terms). Anglo-American and other foreign affiliates of the Trust were to import and market the refinery products of Standard Oil. Rather than relying on the markets in Atlantic ports, the combination now carried its products in tankers to foreign countries, marketing its goods through its own companies and carrying the fight to its competitors. No quick victory was won. Exports of American kerosene increased between 1888 and 1891, but so did those of the Russian product; the disturbing part of it all was that the total value of the American exports in 1891 was less than it had been in 1888, since prices had declined substantially.

Standard Oil marketing assumed a different form after 1892. The Trust was being dissolved as a consequence of the State of Ohio's action forbidding Ohio Standard from continuing as a member of the Trust. Therefore, the Export Trade and Domestic Trade committees passed from the picture. The constituent companies did not, and carried on their activities in a loose association until 1899, when Jersey Standard became the holding company controlling the policies of the various associated Standard Oil firms.

During the nineties, foreign markets posed a number of problems for Standard Oil. Legislation passed in many countries further regulated markets and restricted entry into them. The Nobel-Rothschild group continued to be fierce competitors, and an attempt by Standard to reach an agreement with them on dividing foreign markets failed. French refiners made it plain that Standard Oil was not welcome as a competitor, but signed an agreement to purchase crude, kerosene, naphtha, and distillate from Standard, with the American firm agreeing to abstain from selling to anyone else in France. Similar agreements were signed with refiners in Spain and Fiume. Sales in other European countries were expanded through the creation of new foreign affiliates. Affiliates were also acquired in Canda, the Imperial Oil Company being the most important acquisition. This reflected Standard's policy of buying out important competitors rather than engaging in extended conflict with them. Although Latin American and African markets were not developed to any extent by Standard, it turned its attention to the Far East. This large potential market was already being tapped by the Russian refiners, and the discovery of crude oil in the area brought Royal Dutch and Shell into the market as tough competitors.

Competition was becoming stronger in domestic markets, too. Although the Standard Oil interests were the dominant firms, new companies were appearing and older ones became stronger. Kerosene continued to be the major product, but the sales of some other products were expanding at a faster rate. The volume of fuel oil sold by Standard Oil refineries between 1890 and 1897 increased almost 750 per cent while that of kerosene grew only by slightly more than 50 per cent. This change was more important than volume figures show, since the price for kerosene was dropping while that of fuel oil increased during the period. The result was that between 1890 and 1897, income from sales of kerosene increased only 5 per cent, while revenues received from selling fuel oil grew almost 1,000 per cent.

To get closer to the market, Standard expanded the number of bulk stations selling to retailers and in a few cases sold products door-to-door to consumers from tank wagons. However, the main buyers of kerosene and stove gasoline continued to be retailers. Price wars occurred in a number of major cities. Standard was rarely the instigator, preferring to cut prices only when necessary to maintain its share of the market. Among other competitive devices, advertising was employed extensively during this period, especially to dispose of surplus gasoline. Since internal combustion engines did not as yet provide much of a market for this product, Standard Oil companies promoted the use of gasoline stove extensively. Despite all such promotional efforts, gasoline continued to take increased space in storage tanks, and Standard was confronted with a "surplus" problem.

During the early years of this century, the markets for petroleum products rapidly changed. Artificial gas and electricity became increasingly more important competitors to producers of natural gas and kerosene for illumination. Coal continued to dominate the market for heat energy. Domestic competitors grew in numbers and importance, reducing Standard's share of the market. In addition—as a consequence of tariff reductions—foreign competition in domestic markets was of substantial significance for the first time in the history of the industry. Public hostility toward Standard Oil was manifested in the passage of a number of laws restricting its freedom to adopt competitive practices employed by it in the past. Offsetting all of these problems was the existence of a seller's market in petroleum products from 1899 to 1911. Sales of fuel oil continued to mount, and the development and sale of automobiles was the outstanding industrial phenomenon of the age. Most automobiles used gasoline as fuel (all of them required lubricants) and by 1911 Standard Oil's sales of gasoline and naphtha exceeded sales of kerosene.

During the first decade of this country, conditions in foreign markets were also dynamic. Demand was shifting from kerosene to the newer products. Competition had been growing much stronger, with a consequent depressing effect upon prices. Although Standard's physical volume of sales remained fairly constant, income from the sale of kerosene declined as did the American combination's market share. Price wars had become the order of the day, and the outlook was for continued disturbed conditions in the market. Although Standard had about 60 per cent of the overseas market (outside of Russia and Austria), it was in no position to control that market.

The dissolution of Standard Oil as a result of a Supreme Court decision in 1911 left Standard Oil Company (New Jersey) a greatly weakened firm. Although good relations with its former affiliates made it easier to market its products, Jersey Standard eventually built up its own marketing organization. Since 1911, the firm has faced increased competition. In large measure, this competition in both domestic and foreign markets has come from its former affiliates. Jersey Standard now finds itself in new markets as a producer of petrochemicals. However, now as in 1911, gasolines account for the largest part of the sales revenue of the company, with heavy fuels running a close second. Kerosene sales have greatly declined in relative importance, and even when diesel oil sales and home-heating oil sales are added to those of kerosene, such products combined are still in third place. Markets have stabilized somewhat, in terms of product sold, but competition still leads to substantial fluctuations in prices and physical volume sold.

SUGGESTED READINGS

Barksdale, H. C., ed., *Marketing: Change and Exchange* (New York: Holt, Rinehart & Winston, 1964). A collection of readings from *Fortune* on new products, changing markets, and developments in margeting institutions and processes.

McCarthy, Jerome, *Basic Marketing: A Managerial Approach* (Homewood, Ill., Irwin Books, 1964). Contains a discussion of consumers in the American and international markets, along with an analysis of why they buy. Also included is a treatment of "intermediate customers" and their buying behavior.

Mee, John F., "Marketing-Dominated Economy," *Business Horizons* (Fall, 1964). Discusses the various stages in the evolution of our economy, using the history of a flour-milling enterprise to show how a firm moves from a "manufacturing" stage to one in which it is "marketing-dominated."

Otteson, Schuyler F., William G. Panschar, and James M. Patterson, *Marketing: The Firm's Viewpoint* (New York: Macmillan, 1964).

CHAPTER 8

PRODUCTIVE RESOURCES AND THEIR MARKETS

Business firms acquire productive resources, use them in the production process, and sell the products. Various classes of inputs are used by business. They are sold to firms by resource owners, but it is useful to regard businessmen as buying the resources in markets, because businessmen frequently look at their purchases in this way, and also it is easier to generalize about the acquisition of resources if we take this view. Resource owners as well as resource markets are important, because the dealings of businessmen in the markets are with the owners of inputs or their agents. Before we examine the markets and the sellers in them, some further explanation of what is meant by productive resources is in order.

PRODUCTIVE RESOURCES

Resources can be generally regarded as "all available things useful in gaining an objective." Business firms have certain objectives that are gained by engaging in production and distribution. The production of goods and services and the distribution of these products then become more immediate objectives that resources are used to gain. Money, men, materials, machinery, and other productive resources are required in business operations. Money is, perhaps, the first essential. The hiring of men and the purchases of materials and machinery must wait upon the securing of currency or credit. Also required is a location for the conduct of business—a place that must either be purchased or rented. Services of parties outside the firm are sometimes hired. These various resources will be classified as money, labor, raw materials, and capital goods, and can be regarded as being acquired in markets.

Money and Money Markets

Both currency and credit make up "money." Currently, credit is a far more important kind of money than is currency. Over 90 per cent of all business transactions are now conducted through credit rather than through currency, and it is little wonder that when businessmen think of the "money market" or the "money markets" they usually have in mind markets in which loans can be secured. However, rather than thinking of credit as opposed to currency (since most credit can be converted into currency), men in business think of "equity money" (ownership money) as opposed to borrowed funds (debt). "Money markets" are usually organized around the provision of ownership funds or loans.

The sale of capital stock by corporations accounts for the bulk of the purchases in the market for equity money (corporations exchange stock for money). Contrary to what is popularly believed, the sales (and purchases) of stocks on the securities exchanges rarely represent sales of stock by corporations. For the most part, stock exchange transactions are sales by investors or speculators to other investors or speculators. When corporations sell an issue of capital stock, they may sell it, either directly to the investors or indirectly through "underwriters" who buy it from the corporation and then sell it through the medium of the stock exchanges or by direct sale. Conditions on the stock exchanges, however, are important to the issuing corporation. When the prices of previously issued shares of comparable stocks are high, the corporation might expect to secure a high price for its new issue; the contrary is true when the stock market is depressed. Also the volume of sales on stock markets gives an indication of whether or not investors are actively interested in the purchase of securities (although the volume of stocks exchanged on the stock exchanges reflects the activities of speculators more than they do those of investors).

SECURITIES EXCHANGES. There are about twenty securities exchanges in the United States, although the New York Stock Exchange is the best known. Individuals and organizations wishing to buy or sell securities on such exchanges do not do so directly; rather, brokers buy or sell for them on a commission basis. However, brokers also play another role (understanding this other role is necessary to a better understanding of the operations of stock exchanges). They also act as "dealers," buying and selling on their account. The dual role played by stock exchange members has on occasion been the source of criticism because their interests as dealers are sometimes in conflict with the interests of their customers, and such conflicts have occasionally been resolved by member firms in their own favor. Since brokers have sometimes acted in dishonest ways in order to secure profits as dealers, the Securities Exchange Commission has proposed that these two functions be separated and that brokers be prohibited from dealing on their own account. Although this proposal has not yet been enacted into law or adopted by stock exchanges as a rule governing their operations, there is some prospect that further limitations will be placed on dealings by stock exchange members who also act as brokers.

In the preceding discussion, it has been indicated that stock exchanges have "members." The exchanges are regarded, quite properly, as non-profit organizations serving their members. Only members are permitted to buy or sell in the exchanges. The oldest and largest, as well as the best-known, organization is the New York Stock Exchange, which now has some 1300 members—individuals, partnerships, and corporations primarily engaged in the securities business as dealers or brokers. About one half of these are partners or officers in firms known as "commission houses" doing business with the buying and selling public. The others gain their profits through dealing or through commissions received from other members for performing special functions.

The New York Stock Exchange apparently originated out of a desire by early American stockbrokers to prevent "rate-cutting" in the purchase and sale of securities on commission. A written agreement was subscribed to by a number of New York stockbrokers in May 1792 under the terms of which they agreed not to buy or sell any kind of stock "at a less rate

than one-quarter per cent Commission on the Specie value." Those signing the agreement also promised to give one another preference in their
negotiations. There were very few stocks to be dealt in at this very early
point in our national history, most of the "stocks" being in fact the securities of the U.S. Government issued to finance or refinance the costs of
the Revolution. The only important corporation stocks that were exchanged were the securities of the Bank of North America and the Bank
of the United States. No building was erected to house the members while
they were conducting their transactions, hence they conducted business
on the street in good weather, and in the Merchants' Exchange during
inclement weather. The War of 1812 brought new issues of government
securities, and the concurrent expansion of banks and insurance corporations gave rise to greater trading. In 1817 a new agreement was drafted,
providing for daily meetings indoors among other things, although the
members of the New York Stock and Exchange Board did not have their
own building until the time of the Civil War. As corporations expanded
and the list of securities traded grew, the activities of the Exchange became of greater importance to business.

At one time, big speculators on the New York Stock Exchange engaged
in considerable manipulation of securities. In some instances, this manipulation affected firms quite directly in that ownership of firms might
have changed hands quite unexpectedly. For the most part, however,
fluctuations of stock prices and of the volume of shares traded had little
impact on the corporations issuing the securities. Nowadays firms are
more concerned with having their securities listed on the New York
Stock Exchange and with changes in the prices of those stocks. Although
new security issues are not sold directly on the Exchange, listing apparently enhances the price of previously issued securities and enables the
issuing corporation to get a better price for new issues. This is because
listing indicates to potential investors that a ready market exists for the
shares they purchase in the event they choose to liquidate their investments. In other words, a market for existing securities may provide opportunity for easier marketing of new securities issues (there is another
side to this coin—depressed conditions on the securities exchanges may
also result in the inability to market satisfactorily a new issue of securities regardless of the soundness of the corporation and the new issue).
Although corporations do not "buy money" through directly selling securities in this "money market," its existence has had both good and
bad effects on corporations whose stocks are listed; stock speculation and
other activities that cause wide fluctuations in prices are a major cause
for concern (especially when they cause stock prices to fall).

OVER-THE-COUNTER MARKET. Not all corporation securities are sold
on stock exchanges. There is another market called the "over-the-counter

market." This actually does not exist as a place, but some financial institutions interested in trading securities not listed on the regular exchanges communicate "bid" and "asked" prices among themselves. Such trading actually accounts for a larger dollar volume than that of transactions on the established exchanges and can be regarded as the market in which new issues as well as previously issued securities can be sold.

MARKETS FOR LOANABLE FUNDS. When businessmen borrow funds, they are actually "buying" in a number of different "markets." Some borrowing is on a "short-term" basis, and other loans are secured for an "intermediate term" or a "long term." Many business firms are in all of these markets because they have need of borrowed funds for different lengths of time. However, since the "sellers" in these markets are somewhat different, there is usually a different price (interest rate) in the various markets.

Short-term borrowing concerns the securing of funds that are to be repaid in a relatively short time—within a year of the time the loan is secured. Most of these transactions are with commercial banks, which do a large part of their business in making this type of loan. There is, at any one time, a bank rate on short-term business loans that tends to be the same for all "prime" customers of commercial banks in an area. Others— such as the federal government—may make short-term loans to business, but usually at rates different from rates that commercial banks charge. Too, some large corporations sell commercial paper (unsecured promissory notes) on the "open market" to "commercial paper houses" because it is possible to secure more funds at a lower rate of interest than can be secured from a commercial bank. Hence, we really see a number of markets in which the business firm can buy the use of money for a short period of time—each market containing a somewhat different group of sellers and a somewhat different interest rate.

Intermediate-term loans (or just plain "term loans") are what business firms are sometimes "in the market" for. These loans are made for periods ranging from one to ten years, with the bulk of them running between five and ten years. These loans are usually secured from banks and insurance companies, and there tends to be a prevailing rate of interest for this type of borrowing, although there is no central market place in which such borrowing and lending goes on.

Long-term borrowing is necessary when a firm requires funds for a period in excess of ten years and finds it impossible or undesirable to secure equity money. Unincorporated firms can secure such funds though long-term loans secured by mortgages on the property of the company. Corporations can do this too, but can also issue bonds (long-term promissory notes) as security for such loans. Many bonds are mortgage bonds, and are little different (on their face) from the promissory notes secured by mortgages issued by unincorporated enterprises. The big difference is that they can be sold in bond markets, which are regularly organized exchanges, thereby enhancing their salability. In addition, some bonds are not backed up by mortgages on the property of the firm. They may be secured by pledges of other corporate securities, or they may have no specific security behind them, being issued on the general credit of the corporation. As in the case of corporate stocks, bonds are not sold by the issuer on the bond exchanges, but are sold directly to investors through investment bankers, who will in turn sell them to investors or speculators (although there is less speculation in bonds than in stocks). Also, as in the case of stock markets, conditions existing on the exchanges influence the price at which the issuing firm can sell the bonds and the ease with which they can be sold.

Bonds are also bought and sold on stock exchanges. We noted that at the time of its origin, the New York Stock Exchange listed government bonds. It still does, but since 1792 corporation bonds have been added to the list, and there are now more than 1,000 different issues of bonds listed on the Exchange. As in the case of corporate stock issues, securities exchanges provide a secondary market for bonds; the generalizations concerning the significance of this market for corporations issuing stocks apply to bond issues as well.

Labor and Labor Markets

Business firms do not buy people—the day of the slave market in America is long past. What is bought by business in the labor markets is the *services* of people. There are two major groupings of markets in which business buys labor services: one group contains markets in which business hires persons as full-time employees of firms; the other, growing in importance, is composed of the "business services" markets, in which personal services are sold to business on a temporary or part-time basis and the individuals providing the services do not become full-time employees. However, the term "labor markets" normally applies only to markets for the services of employees.

There are about 70 million persons in the American labor force— persons who are employed or who are looking for employment. All of these are selling or attempting to sell their services in the labor markets. No one firm, of course, requires the services of such a large number: firms usually are "in the market" for, or actually buying the services of, a limited number of persons and classes of labor. Even for a certain type of labor, there tends to be a number of local markets rather than regional or national labor markets. The number of persons employed or looking for employment, and the wages paid, vary from market to

market even for a particular class of employees. It is not useful, therefore, to attempt to describe the nature of "the labor market" because it
does not exist.

This is not to say that there are not some labor markets comparable to
stock exchanges. In large cities there are a number of "labor exchanges"
in which "buyers" and "sellers" of unskilled labor make employment
bargains; similar offices exist for farm labor; "hiring halls" are quite common in some industries, although unions normally operate them; also,
both private and public employment agencies provide "market places" in
which those buying and those selling labor can meet. However, there
has been a tendency for large business organizations to establish their
own employment offices and not depend on the operation of the labor
exchanges to give them the kinds and quantities of labor they wish to
hire at the wages they are willing to pay. Although such employers
do not buy labor in a marketplace, they are still regarded as employers
who acquire employees in a "labor market" considered to be an area
rather than a place.

CLASSES OF LABOR.   Labor can be classified in a large number of ways.
One of the more useful classifications sorts out employees according to
the industry division in which they are employed. The numbers employed by the firms in an industry reflect both the demand for and the
supply of a certain type of labor. As we might expect, recent years have
seen a decline in the numbers employed in the extractive industries—
especially agriculture and mining. This decline has been more than offset
by the increase in the numbers employed in other industries. Although
manufacturing firms have taken up some of the slack, there has been a
far greater percentage increase in the service industries. Employment in
trade, contract construction, financial institutions, real estate, and insurance has also increased at a greater rate than in manufacturing (*see*
Figure 8–1). Even within industries, there have been a number of
changes in the nature of the labor force.

A reasonable way of grouping employees within an industry is by the
kind of work they do. The most common occupational groupings are
"white-collar," manual, and service workers. There has been a substantial
increase in the number of white-collar workers—managerial, professional,
technical, and clerical employees—during this century (the number now
is about five times that in 1900). Manual ("blue-collar") workers have
also increased in number, but at only about half the rate of increase of
white-collar workers. Service workers outside private households have
increased at almost the same rate of increase of white-collar employees,
again reflecting the fact that service industries and firms are becoming
more important in our business system.

Market conditions involve something more than the numbers of workers offering their services. Wages paid and hours worked also tell us something about the nature of labor markets. There has been, during the past seventy years, a remarkable increase in wages paid. Payments to various classes of labor have changed at variable rates, of course, but the differences in the pay increases are not very marked, with all classes of

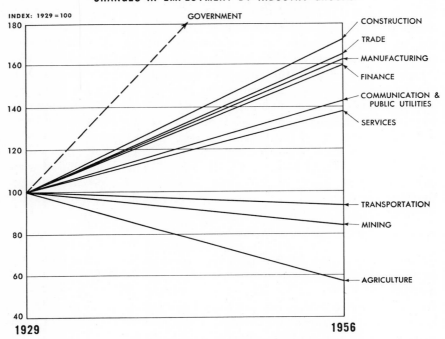

CHANGES IN EMPLOYMENT BY INDUSTRY GROUPS

FIGURE 8–1.

labor being raised in pay by somewhat the same percentage. This is understandable in a nation in which there is a high degree of mobility among various occupations. Manufacturing provides a good example of the increase in wages: in 1890, the average hourly earnings of manufacturing employees was 20¢ per hour; at present, these earnings stand at over $2.00—an increase of more than 1,000 per cent. During this century, there has been a substantial decline in the value of the dollar, but at the same time there has been a great increase in real wages received by all classes of employees. Weekly earnings have not gone up by the same percentage as hourly wage rates, because there has been a decline in hours worked per week from about sixty to forty. Reasons for this decline are twofold: the number of days in the work week has been reduced from six to five and the number of hours worked per day has dropped from ten to eight.

One reason for the increase in wages and reduction in hours has been the rise of another factor in the labor markets—the labor union. Before the turn of the century, only a relatively few occupations were organized to the degree that employees sold their services through unions as bargaining representatives. In 1900 there were less than one million union members; today there are almost twenty million, and the unions have become a powerful force in labor markets, even exerting an influence on wages and hours in unorganized industries.

Much of the labor input purchases by business firms consists of services bought from other business firms. For example, a firm has the alternative of hiring its own bookkeepers and accountants, or securing bookkeeping and accounting services from a firm that specializes in such services. In either case, the firm is purchasing labor services. It should be noted that there has been a recent tendency to purchase an increasing amount of specialized services from persons outside the firm, and that firms providing business services have become a significant factor in the labor markets.

Raw Materials and Their Markets

Almost every firm buys goods that are properly regarded as raw materials—goods that will be consumed in turning out the finished product. One firm's finished product may be the raw materials of another firm. For example, flour is sold by millers to the baking industry; for the baker, flour is a raw material even though the miller regards it as a finished good. As a result, there are a large number of raw materials markets, existing chiefly as areas rather than as places. Published information on raw materials markets as places deals mainly with the products of extractive industries that are purchased by manufacturers on organized commodity exchanges.

COMMODITY EXCHANGES. Many products of the extractive industries are sold on commodity exchanges, which are fixed locations similar to the New York Stock Exchange. These marketplaces are located throughout the United States and tend to be regional markets, although some of them are national in scope and are strongly influenced by conditions on the world market. Commodity exchanges are classified broadly as those involving foods, grains and feeds, fats and oils, textiles and fibers, and metals. Within these broad classifications we find specific markets such as the Minneapolis Grain Exchange, the New York Cotton Exchange, and so on. An important characteristic of these commodity exchanges is that many of them permit trading in contracts for future delivery of a commodity. Such trading permits a business firm to buy or sell a specified quantity of the commodity at a determined price in advance of its raw material needs and thereby to add to the stability of its operations.

The Chicago Board of Trade refers to itself as the "world's largest commodity exchange." This is somewhat misleading: not all commodities are traded on the Chicago Board of Trade; nonferrous metals are traded on the Commodity Exchange of New York; and even in Chicago, the Chicago Mercantile Exchange advertises itself as the "Nation's Market Place" for eggs, butter, potatoes, turkeys, and frozen eggs. In the Chicago Board of Trade, most of the trading takes place in "futures markets" for wheat, corn, oats, rye, soybeans, soybean oil and meal, cotton, cottonseed oil, grain sorghums, and lard. In addition, there is a "cash grain market" in which transactions are made for immediate rather than future delivery. About 90 per cent of the world's trade in futures is conducted on this exchange, but it is the world's largest cash market only for corn and soybeans.

Commodities are traded on exchanges in a number of cities throughout the United States, although there is considerable similarity in the way in which such exchanges operate. As in the case of the Chicago Board of Trade, almost all of them have "cash" and "futures" markets. In the cash or "spot" markets, transactions are usually entered into between someone actually possessing the commodity and someone desiring to acquire the commodity (although most of the transactions are handled by brokers representing such persons). In the futures markets, persons are buying and selling contracts to deliver a certain quantity of a certain commodity at some future date. In some cases, those buying futures actually wish delivery at some future date, and some who sell futures intend to make actual delivery. However, a number of others buy and sell futures with the hope of gaining speculative profits from changes in the price of futures. For example, if a speculator expects futures prices to drop, he will sell a contract to deliver at a future date a certain quantity of a certain commodity at the present price of such contracts; if his judgment is correct, he will be able at some future time to buy a contract to deliver that quantity of that commodity at a lower price. The contract to buy is now offset by the contract to sell, the only difference being the difference between the buying and selling prices, which is pocketed by the speculator. Speculative profits can also be secured in futures trading by buying a futures contract at a relatively low price and selling one at a higher price at some future time.

There are two schools of thought on the effect on markets of such speculation in futures. Those who favor such trading—frequently speculators or those brokers making commissions on trading in futures—suggest that futures trading keeps prices relatively stable and also informs interested parties what the cash price will likely be at some future date. Others have contended that the presence of speculators in the commodity exchanges has caused wide fluctuations in the prices of some commodities and that both those who produce and those who use the commodity are at the mercy of the speculators. Certainly there have been cases in the past where speculators have "cornered the market" in some commodity and have caused great price increases. Although it would seem that those buying in commodity markets would be most resentful of such activity the greatest political pressure to prevent wide fluctuations in commodity prices has come from commodity producers, especially the farmers. For example, futures trading in agricultural commodities on the Chicago Board of Trade is conducted under a license received from the U.S. Department of Agriculture and under rules and regulations established by the Commodity Exchange Authority of that department.

Perhaps one reason that purchasers of commodities have not been greatly concerned by the activities of speculators in futures markets is that the existence of such markets permits them to "hedge" their purchases of commodities so as to avoid any risks that might develop out of fluctuating prices. For example, a wheat miller is in business to make money out of milling, not out of profitable price changes (that is, speculation). If there were no futures markets, a miller might find himself acquiring his raw material at a certain price, and if wheat prices then declined on the cash market, he would suffer a substantial loss in the value of his raw material inventory. Of course, if prices increased after the miller acquired his raw materials, he would make a substantial inventory profit; however, the sums of money involved are so great that this is a risk that millers dare not take. By selling the same quantity of wheat futures at the same time the identical quantity of wheat is purchased in the cash wheat market, the miller effectively "hedges" himself against loss from price fluctuations. When the milled wheat is sold, an identical amount of futures is bought. Since both cash and futures prices normally change in the same direction and by about the same amount, whatever is lost on one transaction is gained on the other, and the miller is assured of whatever profit there is to be gained from milling.

Capital Goods and Their Markets

Every firm employs some capital goods in its operation. These are durable goods that are used over and over again in the production of whatever goods and/or services the firm is engaged in producing. There are two main classes of these fixed assets—structures and equipment. In Chapter 7, we examined the sale of structures and producers durables by some business firms to other business firms. There is, then, little need to say much about who the buyers and sellers are in these markets or how much is bought or sold. One observation that should be made, however, is that this is a market in which total sales vary greatly from period to period, a circumstance that has some importance for both sellers and buyers. Sellers sometimes find themselves with little market for their products. Buyers are occasionally confronted with situations in which capital goods are relatively scarce and can be secured only by paying a substantial premium, if at all.

There are no permanent organized markets for capital goods existing as places. Periodically the makers of a certain kind of equipment will jointly engage in an exhibition of their products and, perhaps, take orders; for the most part, however, their representatives call on prospective purchasers at their place of business. For example, the manufacturers of logging equipment hold an annual "fair" in Eugene, Oregon, at which they demonstrate their products. The fair lasts only a week, and during the balance of the year sales are made to those logging timber by trained salesmen traveling throughout the United States.

The importance of capital goods to American business is hard to overstate. A major reason for our industrial leadership in the world is the great amount of equipment employed in manufacturing. Every year, there is a greater amount of capital goods standing behind the average worker. One indication of this increase in capital is the steady advance in the horsepower available in manufacturing establishments for each production worker employed (*see* Figure 8–2). Horsepower has been substituted for manpower to such a substantial degree that some foresee the day of the automatic factory in which no production employees will be required. Although automation may be a mixed blessing for both business and labor, changes in technology are almost impossible to stop and, consequently, businessmen must keep abreast of changes in capital goods markets or fall behind in the competitive race.

CONCLUSIONS

We have seen that most firms acquire productive resources in markets and, consequently, conditions in those markets are very important to them. Unfortunately for purposes of analysis and description, many of these markets exist as areas rather than as specific places. Although there are means for analyzing market conditions in an area, such markets are quite specific to a particular firm, and it is difficult to generalize about

them. Where resource markets exist as places, we have taken note of
their nature.

The relative importance to business firms of markets for money, men,
materials, machines, and other productive resources would be revealed
by information concerning purchases of these inputs by business during
a given year. Such data, however, are not readily available. Factual in-

HORSEPOWER PER PRODUCTION WORKER
IN MANUFACTURING

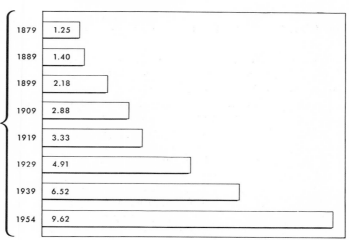

1879	1.25
1889	1.40
1899	2.18
1909	2.88
1919	3.33
1929	4.91
1939	6.52
1954	9.62

COURTESY OF THE COMMITTEE FOR ECONOMIC DEVELOPMENT

FIGURE 8–2.

formation concerning some expenditures by business in resource markets
during 1964 points up the relative importance of labor. Wages and salaries (and various supplementary payments) to employees by business
during that year totaled about $301 billion (almost 60 per cent of na-
tional income). Business purchases of new equipment amounted to only a
little more than $39 billion. The total amount of business borrowing and
sales of stock is almost impossible to determine because there are so many
"money markets." Issues of new corporate securities amounted to almost
$14 billion, but money was secured by both corporate and noncorporate
business in a variety of other markets. Although the total sales in commodity markets are known, no figure is published on the gross amount
of raw materials used by business. Nor are there published data on the
purchases of business services. However, there is a figure on total income originating in business; in 1963, it was $478.5 billion, giving us
some idea of the total payments by business for productive resources

during that year, even though we have difficulty in determining precisely what dollar amounts of specific inputs were purchased.

Many productive resources, especially raw materials, are secured by American business firms from foreign sources. Foreign markets, also, are of considerable importance in the sale of American products. Since the amount purchased is closely related to the amount sold, American purchases and sales in foreign countries will be considered in the next chapter.

READING: Standard Oil and the Crude Oil Market *

The most important productive resource for a refiner is crude oil. Throughout its history, Standard Oil has had to develop means of securing adequate supplies of raw material for its refineries. Although the company eventually decided to engage in large-scale searches for and production of crude oil, initially it relied on purchases of this input in the market. Even today, substantial quantities of crude are purchased from others. Thus, market conditions have always been of importance in determining the policies of Standard and an examination of the development of crude oil and supplies and markets illustrates the general nature of raw materials markets.

After the first successful oil well was drilled in Western Pennsylvania, drillers covered the area with derricks and flooded the market with crude oil. The law governing ownership of crude oil (vesting title in whoever brought it to the surface) encouraged the drilling of as many wells as possible when a new oil strike was made. New oil pools came and went quickly as such drilling practices rapidly exhausted the reservoirs of crude petroleum. Consequently, there was a great fluctuation in both the quantity of crude being produced at any time and the price of it. During 1862, for example, monthly average prices of crude oil ranged from 10¢ a barrel to $2.25. Although some of the producers erected their own tanks for field storage of crude, they did not store large quantities of it. Rather, they turned it over quickly to pipeline operators who (beginning in 1865) ran pipelines to the oil fields and set up their own storage facilities. The pipeline men did not directly purchase the oil from the producers of crude, but gave them certificates for oil received. Oil exchanges were quickly organized for dealing in crude oil certificates, and refiners obtained their raw material supplies by purchasing certificates from the producers and presenting them to those holding the crude in storage.

When John D. Rockefeller and his associates first set up The Standard Oil Company (Ohio), it was essentially a refining firm, purchasing crude oil as needed. Fluctuating crude oil supplies and prices influenced Rockefeller into forming an alliance with other refiners in an attempt to bring about some stabil-

---

* The material for this original reading is taken principally from Ralph W. Hidy and Muriel E. Hidy, *Pioneering in Big Business* and from the second volume in the history of Standard Oil Company (N.J.), *The Resurgent Years* by George S. Gibb and Evelyn H. Knowlton (New York: Harper & Row, 1956).

ity; in the autumn of 1872, a Petroleum Refiners' Association (headed by Rockefeller) was formed to deal with the Petroleum Producers' Association. The two groups attempted to negotiate contracts governing the purchase of crude oil and its allocation among various refiners. (Falling prices had earlier led to the formation of the producers' organization, which originally hoped to be able to curtail production and maintain prices.) This attempt to bring about some measure of stability in the crude oil markets failed and chaotic conditions continued.

To assure themselves of profits and a steady supply of crude, Rockefeller and his associates then established a system of pipelines to gather crude from the producing fields. To strengthen their poition in crude-oil markets, almost all of the refiners in Cleveland, Pittsburgh, Philadelphia, New York, and the "Oil Regions" formed The Central Association under the presidency of John D. Rockefeller in 1875. This organization bought and allocated crude oil supplies for its members. Success attained by this move was only temporary; economic and legal action taken by the producers led Standard Oil to change its policy by 1880 to one of purchasing oil at the market price prevailing on the oil exchanges.

Oil exchanges have since disappeared from the business scene, but at one time were rather lively commodity exchanges. As was true of most such exchanges, the prices were set by buying and selling activities of speculators. Crude oil certificates (representing a certain number of barrels in storage) were bought and sold in large numbers. Although Standard Oil was the largest buyer of crude oil for refining, speculators accounted for the overwhelming proportion of transactions on the oil exchanges and there was no evidence that Standard either attempted to or was able to control the price.

In the 1880's Standard Oil managers reconsidered their policy of not being involved to any great degree in the production of crude oil. The discovery of new oil fields, adverse action by producers dissatisfied with existing crude oil prices and the need for stability of operations led the executives to decide to go into the production of petroleum on a large scale. New oil leases were acquired, and existing operations were purchased. By 1890, the refiners in the Standard Oil Trust were engaged in producing crude oil on a large scale, although the consumption of crude by Standard Oil refineries far exceeded such production. Oil certificates were still purchased on the oil exchanges in order to secure Pennsylvania crude; however, in the oil fields of Indiana and Ohio, attempts to sell and buy crude through trading on exchanges met with failure and the combination bought oil by posting prices at which it would purchase. Since the Standard Oil combination was the largest purchaser of crude, prices on the exchanges tended to follow the posted prices of Standard. In 1895, Standard extended its policy of paying posted prices to the Pennsylvania oil fields. This, along with other developments —such as the decline in the production of crude in those fields—led to a falling off in trading in oil certificates and, between 1896 and 1900, all of the oil exchanges closed.

Since 1900, Standard Oil Co. (N.J.) has satisfied its needs for crude oil through the acquisition of companies with substantial supplies of crude, through acquiring rights to drill for oil and through purchase of crude from producers. In 1900, it purchased the Pacific Oil Company of California which had many wells in the

the fields there. Although additional wells were drilled, crude production was substantially less than the needs of the refineries and Standard was far more important as a buyer of crude petroleum than as a producer of it. Buying practices differed from those adopted elsewhere. Rather than posting a market price each day for different grades of crude, the buyers for the Pacific Coast Oil Co. negotiated contracts to buy from specific producers. Greatly expanded production in the California oil fields early in this century had led to falling prices. As in the oil fields of the eastern United States, producers banded together to secure higher prices for crude and had some success in forcing prices up.

Although Standard had been involved to a slight extent in producing and purchasing crude in the Southwest prior to 1900, the Gulf Coast oil boom following the drilling of the Spindletop well in Texas led to much greater involvement. Participation in the production of crude continued to be limited, but starting in 1901 Standard Oil became one of the largest buyers on the Gulf Coast. The vast outpouring of crude oil from wells in Kansas and Indian Territory (now Oklahoma) led Standard to create the Prairie Oil and Gas Company to produce some crude and buy considerably more for the Standard combine. In its purchasing activities, it adopted the policy of posting prices. However, producers of crude oil flooded the market and Prairie, having limited storage facilities, was obliged to limit its purchases, being unable to buy all offered at the posted price. Producers associations were formed, but were unable to bring about a restriction on output. To discourage production, Prairie cut the posted price to that prevailing on the Gulf Coast. This had no pronounced effect, and it was not until means were developed for transporting and storing the vast outpouring of crude that some stability returned to this market.

In the Midwest, too, there were changes in crude oil markets. The fields in Indiana and Ohio were producing declining quantities of crude, but 1904 saw the beginning of an oil boom in Illinois and by 1907 that state ranked third among the oil-producing states of the nation, preceded only by Oklahoma and California. The Ohio Oil Company of the Standard Oil combine entered these fields on behalf of the refiners and by 1911 became by far the largest producer in the organization.

Despite its growing involvement in production, Standard Oil became more dependent upon others for crude during the early years of this century. Just before 1900, Standard Oil interests produced slightly over one third of the total crude oil production in the U.S. By 1911, affiliates of Standard Oil produced only about one sixth. Since these companies refined 75 per cent or more of the petroleum production in the United States during this period, the bulk of the raw materials used by Standard Oil were secured by purchases of crude oil in the market. Standard Oil managers had looked abroad for crude oil supplies—the oil fields of Russia, Romania, Japan, the East Indies, and Latin America being especially attractive—but did not acquire any substantial quantities from such sources before 1911.

The dissolution decree of 1911 left Jersey Standard, as one of the 34 resulting companies, almost totally dependent upon the market for supplies of crude oil. Standard Oil (New Jersey) had never been a producing company, relying on its affiliates to find and supply it with crude. After its former subsidiaries were divorced from it, one observer commented, "The dissolution left Standard with so little crude production that a good man could have drunk it all!" Initially, no great problem was posed, since the former affiliates were willing to supply crude to Jersey in the manner established prior to 1911. Between 1912 and 1918, almost 90 per cent of Jersey Standard's supplies of crude for its domestic refineries came from its former affiliates. Beginning in 1911, however, foreign crude also became important in domestic operations—principally that obtained from independent producers in Mexico.

The market situation after 1911 was not satisfactory to Jersey Standard's management. Crude oil prices were on the rise and supplies were scarce. The decision was therefore made to engage in the production of crude. Although Jersey itself became involved in such production, the bulk of the expansion of crude production took place through affiliates.

The Carter Oil Company, one of the affiliates remaining attached to Jersey Standard after dissolution, acquired extensive property rights in the Mid-Continent fields (especially Oklahoma). By 1918, it was by far the most important producing affiliate of Standard. Even so, it produced less than 10 per cent of the crude oil requirements of the parent firm's refineries; total production of all affiliated companies was but 17 per cent of the quantity put through the manufacturing plants, and the balance was secured by purchases in uncertain markets.

Market conditions in 1919 and 1920 were especially adverse. Crude oil prices were shooting upward; and though prices of the finished products also rose, Jersey officials were considerably concerned with the problem of finding crude oil supplies to meet a booming market for petroleum products. Early in 1919, one half of the stock of the Humble Oil & Refining Company—the fifth largest producer in Texas—was acquired. Despite the increased supply of crude resulting from this purchase, from the expanded crude production of Louisiana Standard (another Jersey affiliate), and from the producing operations of other affiliates, the demands of the refineries for raw materials actually caused the stocks of crude oil to decline.

In 1921, the market situation changed abruptly. Crude production had caught up with and had passed crude consumption before the end of 1920, and in 1921 the market broke. Prices of crude oil fell to less than one third of their high price of 1920, and rather than being in short supply, crude petroleum glutted the market. Deciding that the situation was temporary, Jersey Standard filled its storage tanks at the low prices prevailing and then adopted measures to bring about greater stability in the future.

Although the company initially decided against a policy of attempting to produce all of its crude needs, it lessened its dependence on the market by expanding its production operations. Humble expanded its operations in Texas, Carter participated in the great oil strikes in Oklahoma, and Louisiana Standard substantially increased its output of crude. By 1927, the total production by the Jersey Standard and its affiliates was 44 per cent of its total refinery throughout as compared to 1912, when total company production was only 11 per cent of its requirements of crude oil.

That trend has continued. Although some of the crude oil requirements of its refineries are presently met through purchases of crude, about 90 per cent of the crude input of Jersey Standard's refineries are the product of its own wells, thereby lessening the company's dependence on uncertain crude oil markets and increasing its bargaining power as well.

SUGGESTED READINGS

Dewhurst, J. Frederick, and Associates, *America's Needs and Resources: A New Survey* (New York: Twentieth Century Fund, 1955). In addition to examining our productive resources and capacities, the authors investigate consumption and capital requirements along with government purchases and foreign transactions.

Jones, Clarence F., and Gordon G. Darkenwald, *Economic Geography,* 3rd ed. (New York: Macmillan, 1965). Discusses the distribution of productive resources throughout the world, among other things.

Lebergott, Stanley, *Manpower in Economic Growth* (New York: McGraw-Hill, 1964). Analyzes the role of manpower in American economic growth since 1800.

Robinson, Roland I., *Money and Capital Markets* (New York: Macmillan, 1964). An assertion that the money and capital markets are the focus of most contemporary financial and economic operations. The interest rates in these markets are considered most important, since they represent costs to many firms as well as being income to others.

CHAPTER **9**

FOREIGN
AND
WORLD
MARKETS

Productive resources are not uniformly distributed throughout the world, nor are techniques of production equally advanced everywhere. Consequently, production of certain goods and services takes place in some countries and not in others. Frequently, potential customers for American business exist in other countries, and American firms desire goods and services available only outside the United States. Where facilitating institutions permit, American firms sell in foreign and world markets and buy in them. These foreign transactions do not amount to a very large part of the U.S. gross national product, but have significance beyond what this quantitative measure indicates.

157

THE DEVELOPMENT OF OVERSEAS MARKETS FOR AMERICAN PRODUCTS

At one time, foreign product markets were of major importance to American firms. The early colonies in Virginia and Massachusetts were established by English merchants who expected colonists to engage in certain extractive and manufacturing industries to produce goods scarce in England and send these products to the mother country. The colonies were also expected to be profitable markets for goods exported to them by the English merchants. Despite the failure of some of the colonies as business enterprises (and the consequent disappointment of the English merchants financing them), they did succeed in producing goods desired abroad and the most important trade throughout the colonial period was export-import trade, with domestic trade and intercolonial trade being far overshadowed by overseas commerce. Even after the American Revolution, such trade was of great importance and continued to be so until 1807, when President Jefferson and Congress decided to restrict such commerce in the hope of avoiding involvement in the conflict between Napoleon's France and England. When it became apparent that it was impossible to avoid becoming involved, the United States went to war with the British for almost three years, beginning in 1812. Since the British navy was much stronger than the American navy, it was able to bring American foreign trade almost to a standstill. Merchants and shippers in New England were reduced to such desperate circumstances that they attempted to secure the secession of some of their states from the American Union in order to renew commercial relations with the British. The treaty ending the war brought a halt to such activity, although a halt had also been brought to the dominant position of foreign trade in American commerce.

The relative decline in the importance of international trade after the War of 1812 was not the result of a decrease in production for and sale in overseas markets. Rather it was the opening up of the interior of the United States and the development of domestic markets that brought about a lessening in the comparative significance of exports and imports. Improved transportation by canals, rivers, lakes, and railroads made production for domestic markets possible and profitable. Although the development of manufacturing after 1800 lessened reliance on others for imports, exports continued to grow. As in the early colonial days, the South was importantly involved in the export of products of the extractive industries. Whereas tobacco had earlier been the most important export, now it was cotton that secured a position of such importance that a southern politician declared that no one dared make war on "King Cotton." However, war did come to the South in the 1860's disrupting overseas commerce for that section of the United States, except as blockade runners were successful in avoiding the navy of the North. Confederate raiders harassed northern shipping, although this had the effect of turning over the carrying trade to the British rather than of halting commerce.

Production for domestic consumption continued to grow in importance after the Civil War, with foreign markets for American manufactured products being of relatively small significance. As manufacturing surpassed agriculture by the end of the nineteenth century, exports continued to decline in their relative importance. This long-term trend was not reversed until after World War II, when the United States found itself occupying a new position in world economic and political affairs and requiring greater concern over the establishment of foreign markets for American products.

THE HISTORICAL IMPORTANCE OF FOREIGN PRODUCTIVE RESOURCES

Foreign productive resource markets played a different role in the development of the American economy. The territory that is now the United States always had a wealth of natural resources; however, it also had for many years a lack of the labor and capital necessary to develop this natural wealth. During the colonial period, the English and Dutch sent some emigrants to develop the natural resources, supplying them with capital. Since many of these colonial enterprises were business failures, and since England did not wish to encourage industries that would compete with those of English manufacturers and merchants, a relative lack of labor and capital continued until after the Revolution. Although economic opportunity attracted immigrants from foreign lands, the flood of immigration during the nineteenth and early twentieth centuries did not satisfy the demand for productive labor. Railroad companies went abroad in search of persons to populate newly opened lands in order to produce traffic-creating agricultural commodities. Some even contracted to import labor for track-laying and other purposes—for example, the Great Northern Railway secured Japanese labor from the Oriental Trading Company through such contracts.

Capital as well as labor continued to be scarce after the American Revolution. England was the premier manufacturing nation of the world at that time, but was unwilling to sell capital goods to American producers, being fearful of the competition this might create. However, since America began to industrialize anyhow—sometimes through pirating the designs of British machinery—and since "free-traders" came to power in England, capital from abroad became more plentiful. As the corporate form of enterprise became widespread in America, securities were sold in Great Britain and on the Continent, with the proceeds being used to acquire capital goods and other essentials from foreign producers. This reliance on foreign resource markets for large parts of U.S. capital requirements was dramatically reversed by World War I, which changed the United States from a "debtor nation" to a "creditor nation" because foreigners liquidated many of their holdings of American securities in order to purchase goods during the war from producers in the United States.

At the present time, American business does not rely greatly on foreign sellers of capital and labor. There are some cases—as in agriculture— where foreign labor is imported because it is cheaper, but this is not an alternative open to many industries. Savings of Americans and American financial institutions are presently able to satisfy the demand of domestic firms for credit and ownership funds; in addition, American capital goods industries are capable of producing the physical capital required by American business (although overseas producers are sometimes able to do so at a lower cost). Now whatever shortages of productive resources confront American business are more likely to be shortages of natural resources. Consequently, firms in the United States attempt to satisfy more of their raw materials requirements either through foreign purchase for manufacture here or through setting up facilities abroad to process natural resources in the nation of their location. This is especially true of firms processing mineral products, such as in the oil-refining industry.

PRESENT IMPORTANCE OF FOREIGN AND
WORLD MARKETS

Exports account for only about 5 or 6 per cent of the U.S. gross national product, and United States imports are, in dollar value, approximately equal to its exports. This relatively small figure obscures the fact that some American firms and industries are dependent on imports, while others depend on the existence of export markets for their profits. Some materials imported are essential to the profitable operation of certain enterprises in manufacturing industries dependent on a cheap and adequate supply of crude foodstuffs and industrial raw materials. What may not be immediately obvious is that if the United States did not import from other countries, it could not export to them, because they would have no dollars with which to purchase American products. They might be able to send gold, but the world's supply is limited; the other alternative, extensively employed after World War II, would be for Americans to give loans and grants to foreign nations so that they might import from the United States. With the prospects of profit from selling in foreign and world markets so inviting to many American businessmen, they are concerned with increasing imports, but others who would be injured by increased foreign competition are concerned with keeping imports down or out.

There have been, in this century, significant changes in the kinds and locations of foreign markets in which U.S. business firms buy and sell. From the beginnings of business in this country, the great bulk of U.S. exports went to European markets and the majority of U.S. imports were purchased there. The goods exported were, before the twentieth century, mainly raw materials and foodstuffs; U.S. imports were chiefly finished manufactures. Now manufactured goods account for about three fourths of U.S. merchandise exports and there has been an increase in the relative importance of raw materials imports. This is a result of a major change in the location of the markets in which the United States buys and sells. About one half of U.S. exports now go to markets in this hemisphere, that is, to Canada and Latin America. Slightly more than one half of U.S. merchandise imports come from the Western Hemisphere, with Latin America alone being more important than Europe as a source of imported goods.

Services are also bought and sold in foreign and world markets. Transportation services, tourist services, and the services of money are the more important ones if we disregard transactions involving the military (since military services are not provided by firms, but by governments). Of these, the most important is the sale of the services of U.S. money. Prior to World War I, Americans bought the use of foreign "capital" in European and British markets; now the United States is a creditor nation rather than a debtor nation, which means that individuals, firms, and governments in the United States buy more securities from or lend more money to individuals, firms, and governments abroad than is the reverse. Of course, this results in the acquisition of dollars by those in foreign countries, which tends to promote the sale of American goods to foreigners.

The shift in the location of the international markets in which American business buys and sells reflects major political changes taking place. In the past, great imperial nations have struggled for overseas markets for their products and for supplies of productive resources that were not native to the mother country. Although the struggle between the Communist world and the Western world is of a somewhat different nature, there are economic aspects to the contest. The intention of the Soviet Union to best the United States in the field of economic endeavor has created problems and challenges for American businessmen as well as for their government. The Soviets are tough competitors in foreign and world markets, because they are willing to do things that do not make economic sense in order to secure political gain. American businessmen, on the other hand, are concerned with the profitable operations of their enterprises and, consequently, are sometimes unable to pay as high a price as the Soviet Union is willing to pay or are unable to charge as low a price as the Soviets might be willing to take. Although some support has been accorded to American business firms by the Congress and Administration in this contest, it still is a difficult situation.

Even those nations allied with the United States in the political contest are providing stiff competition for Americans in international markets. Mention has been made of the formation of a common market in the European Economic Community, in which Western Europeans may sell without tariff and exchange barriers. American businessmen must hurdle such barriers before they can sell in that market, thereby operating under a handicap. Also, since these nations have acquired a technology as advanced as that of the United States, their somewhat lower wage rates enable them to produce competitive goods at lower costs than can American firms.

There are some theoretical reasons for expecting that the importance of international trade to American businessmen will continue to grow. Since each nation has a different endowment of natural resources, and since the kinds and quantities of capital and labor differ among countries, each nation has a comparative advantage in the production of certain goods and services. It may be—as in the case of the United States—that a country has such ample quantities of the various kinds of productive resources that it can produce almost everything it basically requires, without engaging in international trade. Still, so the theoretical argument goes, it would do better to specialize in the production of those things it could best produce and exchange the output in excess of domestic needs for the surplus products of other countries. More generally, if each country specialized in the production of those things it was best suited to produce, gross world product would be at a maximum and (assuming that this product was distributed among the nations of the world in some "equitable" fashion) the gross national product of each country would be at a maximum.

Not all nations subscribe to free trade, which is necessary to maximize specialization in national production and to create the greatest gross world product. This is because, in the past, the nations that were not industrialized saw that the "terms of trade" under which the specialized outputs of various nations were exchanged favored the industrial nations and not those whose products were basically those of the extractive industries. Once a nation is industrialized, however, such terms of trade are in its favor and it pays to specialize. Thus we can expect to see businessmen in the United States (which has reached the highest level of industrial development in the world) tending to adopt the "free trade" point of view and to specialize in the output of those things in which they have a comparative advantage and selling growing proportions of such production in foreign and world markets.

FOREIGN MARKETS

Applying our definition of market as an area or place where buyers and sellers can conveniently exchange, we see that foreign markets exist as places in foreign countries, areas in those countries, a foreign nation as a whole, or even a group of foreign countries. In discussing markets in America, we have examined what is meant by local, regional, and national markets, so the nature of the first three of the above-named foreign markets is familiar to us. Groups of nations as a market is a different concept, but it is useful to conceive of them as comprising a common market in which it is possible for buyers and sellers to engage in trade throughout the area without restrictions being imposed as a consequence of a number of nations being involved. Since World War II, developments in Europe have led to the establishment of a Common Market for a growing number of nations in that part of the Continent not under the control of the Soviet Union. Great Britain may soon join. Nowhere else in the world does there exist such an important group of nations that might properly be regarded as one market. There are other common markets, but for the most part our foreign trade takes place in markets within national boundaries.

One reason that all nations do not form a common market for the products of American firms or a common market in which American firms may buy is that there exist certain barriers to trade. Some of these barriers are economic in nature: foreigners may not have enough dollars or means of securing dollars to buy American products; in turn, American businessmen may not have enough of the currency of foreign countries to enable them to purchase in foreign markets. Many years ago, astute businessmen saw an opportunity to make profits out of this situation and established markets in "foreign exchange"—that is, markets in which an American businessman, for example, can purchase the currency of a foreign country by paying dollars. If governments did not interfere in foreign exchange markets, there would be some price of foreign currency in dollars that would solve the problem of lack of dollars or lack of foreign currency. This, however, points out the major source of restrictions on international trade—government interference.

Governments, to promote their interests or the interests of some of their politically influential citizens, have taken a number of actions that have the effect of restraining foreign trade. Some of these acts deal with exchange rates. Rather than permit a drop in the price of their currency in terms of some foreign nation's currency—for example, in terms of dollars—some nations will hold the price of their currency artificially high, thereby limiting the amount of American purchases in their markets, which has the further effect of reducing the amount of American products sold in their markets. Other nations, in order to secure dollars, will reduce the price of their currency in terms of dollars, which results in greater American purchasing in those nations' markets and in greater sales of American products as the nations acquired dollars. Some nations, also, have adopted controls over the use of foreign exchange, through which they regulate the amount that may be used for certain purposes and specify who may acquire foreign exchange.

There are restraints other than those involving foreign exchange placed upon international trade by governments. Among these are the tariff—taxes on the importation of products from another country, or on exports to other countries. Although in some cases these import duties have been levied as a means of securing governmental revenue, for the most part they have been levied to provide some protection to domestic producers from foreign competition. (An achievement in recent years of the major producing nations of the world has been the reduction of tariff barriers—this has reached the ultimate in the European Common Market, in which tariffs will soon no longer exist on trade among the nations involved.) Some nations have adopted import and export quotas, which further restrict free trade. Since World War I, we have seen a few nations engage in "state trading"—essentially barter transactions—in which one national government exchanges a certain quantity of a given product for an equivalent amount of goods from another nation; this kind of trading further interferes with free international trade.

WORLD MARKETS

Prior to World War I, there were markets in which all buyers and sellers thoughout the world were free to trade and in which one price prevailed. This was largely a result of the "free-trade" policy of Britain, which had led to the establishment of world prices in certain British markets. This situation still prevails to some degree, and some commodities are still bought and sold on a free world market. American producers are influenced more by these circumstances than are American purchasers; there are no taxes on American exports, while importers must pay duties on a number of products bought outside of our national boundaries.

Although we still have world prices for certain products, these world prices are in large measure the result of international commodity agreements rather than the result of the operation of free world markets. Leading producing countries of certain commodities, sometimes in cooperation with the major consuming countries, have drafted a number of agreements governing market conditions for those goods. Production, prices, trade, and trade practices are governed by arrangements among nations concerned with certain basic commodities such as wheat, cotton, coffee, rubber, and tin. Occasionally producers make such agreements directly, with or without government participation, usually through some association of producers. Currently the United States is a party to an international wheat agreement, a sugar agreement, and a coffee agreement.

There are some practical reasons as well as theoretical ones for anticipating that international trade will be of greater importance to American business. Barriers to international trade are coming down, which will encourage specialization and exchange among nations. As a major creditor nation, the U.S. provides dollar credits to individuals and groups abroad; these credits in turn are used to purchase American products. In order to pay for the credit extended, those in foreign countries will have to export things to America. The role of America as a creditor nation is likely to expand rather than to contract, and we can anticipate increased foreign trade as a result. In short, it is possible to look ahead to a day when relatively free world trade will prevail and foreign and world markets will be of much greater importance to American firms than they are at present.

THE IMPORTANCE OF CERTAIN FOREIGN MARKETS

Although free world markets do not at present prevail, some foreign markets are of considerable importance to American business. Earlier, we mentioned the importance of Europe, Canada, and Latin America. Although Africa is not of great quantitative importance as yet to American businessmen, the emerging nations on that continent promise to be of greater significance. New nations are also emerging in Asia, but the highly unsettled conditions there make it difficult to forecast what will eventually develop on the continent, although the re-establishment of Japan as a major trading nation is of great importance.

European Markets

Europe has long been an important market for American products; more is exported by the United States to European countries than to any other major trading area. There has been in Europe an economic revival of astonishing proportions since World War II involving, among other things, a great expansion in European exports and imports. The United States has been exporting more to European countries than it has been importing. In part, this is a result of American efforts to help rebuild the economies of those countries after World War II. Government grants and loans, together with private investment by Americans, gave considerable dollar credits to the Europeans, who used them to purchase American products.

The postwar reconstruction period in Europe is pretty much at an end. Some American government aid still continues, but its objectives tend to be military rather than economic. A pattern for the future is emerging, and it poses opportunities and challenges for American business. Further growth is expected and it is anticipated that by 1970 Europe will have an American-style economy. That is, the big increase in spending foreseen is in consumer expenditures, with spending on appliances and automobiles expected to be more than double the 1955 expenditures on these items. This increase in spending may not be as encouraging to American producers as it may seem because manufacturers in Europe are growing rapidly to fill these demands, and because they still have some protection from American competition. There will, of course, be some increase in U.S. merchandise exports, but the American firms that will gain the greatest share of this growing market will be those that have branches overseas to compete on an equal basis with European producers. American agricultural producers will probably discover that exports of basic farm commodities to Europe will decline sharply as the Europeans increase their farm production and turn to other sources for imports. In the productive resource markets of the world, Europe will again be important, especially in the sale of capital goods, and European exports of such products will pose problems for American producers because European prices tend to be lower.

The Europe of the future may be one large market. Beginning in 1958, Belgium, France, West Germany, Italy, Luxembourg, and the Netherlands joined in a European Economic Community. On January 1, 1959, these six nations took the first step under a program designed to abolish tariffs and other trade restrictions among themselves by 1970. Other European nations (Great Britain, Sweden, Norway, Denmark, Switzerland, Austria, and Portugal) have formed the European Free Trade Association to pursue similar goals and have engaged in essentially the same activities. However, members of the "Outer Seven" are anxious to join the "Inner Six." Although General De Gaulle has been able to veto the British application for membership in the Common Market (as the European Economic Community is also referred to), there is some likelihood that in the future all of the European countries outside the Iron Curtain will be one large foreign market.

The significance of the establishment of a European common market is made clear when we examine past conditions. When Europe consisted of a large number of national markets, each with substantial barriers to imports from others, it was difficult for European businessmen to produce on a large scale and realize the economies of large-scale production because domestic markets were not large enough to absorb the output of mass-production industry. Although substantial trade barriers confronted American businessmen wishing to sell in Europe, still they were able to make some sales since their production costs were low. With the creation of a large domestic market for European producers through "common market" agreements, such businessmen will be able to realize more fully the economies of large-scale production and become more formidable competitors of Americans in Europe and abroad. Some hindrances to participation in the Common Market will confront outsiders, so that the establishment of one large European market will affect American firms in two ways. First, those firms that establish branches within the market will be able to participate in it on a competitive basis with European firms; second, those firms that have no branches in the market will find themselves still confronted by barriers to trading in that market and will find European producers to be tough competitors.

The Canadian Market

After European markets, North American markets are of greatest importance to businessmen in the United States. Although some of these are located in Mexico and Central America, Canada is of considerably greater importance than are the nations south of our border. Not only are exports to Canada more than double exports to the rest of North America, but they have almost doubled since 1950, whereas the exports to others are not appreciably greater. Although Canada at one time was a colonial possession of England, it presently engages in much greater trade with the United States than with the United Kingdom. This is true despite the remaining political and economic ties Canada has with the rest of the

British Empire. In 1867, Canadian trade with the U.S. became greater than with the U.K. By 1891, Canada imported more from its neighbor to the south than from its mother country, although exports were still greater to the United Kingdom than they were to the United States. World War I brought changes that led to both imports from and exports to the U.S. being greater than trade with the United Kingdom. American exports to Canada continue to be greater than imports from that country, showing the relatively greater importance of product markets. Although Canada is well on the way to industrialization, it tends to sell food, feeds, fibers, minerals, and other raw materials to Americans rather than manufactured consumer goods. Some nationalistic Canadians are concerned about the growing economic ties between the two nations; but there is no denying their existence, furthermore, the United States and Canada may eventually become one large market area with integrated economies.

Latin American Markets

South of the Mexican border are a host of countries which not only have provided profitable markets for American products but also supplied various productive resources to U.S. business. Trade with Latin American countries is almost as great as trade with Canada. In the past, each country was essentially a separate foreign market; but now Latin American nations are adopting the common market notion from Europe, and two such market areas are developing.

The nature of trade with Latin America is considerably different from trade with Europe. Many European nations industrialized before the U.S. did. The Latin American countries, on the other hand, are not highly industrialized, although some of them are attempting to speed up industrialization of their economies. The state of economic affairs that has prevailed south of the border has provided a number of product markets for American firms without much competition from enterprises in the countries (although some competition has been provided by producers in other industrial nations); in other words, American manufacturers have found ready markets for their goods. Financial and other services have also been provided by U.S. firms to nations eager for economic development. These goods and services have been paid for by exports of raw materials, in large part. The availability of abundant natural resources and cheap labor in Latin America has encouraged the establishment of productive facilities in those countries by U.S. firms; this has been especially true of firms in the extractive industries, although some manufacturers have also found it profitable to establish branches in Mexico, Central America, and South America.

The common market has come to Latin America. Eight of the largest countries—Argentina, Brazil, Chile, Mexico, Bolivia, Paraguay, Peru, and

Uruguay—formed the Latin American Free Trade Association in 1960. There is also a Central American Common Market, consisting of El Salvador, Guatemala, Honduras, and Nicaragua. The enlarging of Latin American markets encourage the establishment and growth of business in the countries involved, with some consequences for American firms. If these nations are successful in building up their economies and in engaging in greater trade one with another, it may be more difficult for U.S. firms to sell in those markets (unless, of course, they adopt the strategy of establishing branches in those nations). Initially, as these nations industrialize, American producers of heavy industrial equipment stand to make a number of sales even though other manufacturers may be adversely affected. That success will soon attend these plans for common markets is doubtful, since Latin America has a history of political and, therefore, economic instability. In the near future, then, this trading area can be counted on as supplying food and raw materials in exchange for the goods and services provided by industrialized nations such as the United States, although competition from other economically developed countries is increasing in the product markets.

Asian Markets

U.S. exports to Asia are somewhat higher than those to Latin America, although imports are considerably less. The greater amount of exports reflects the existence of a number of programs of the federal government which provides dollars to Asian nations in addition to those they can earn by exporting to the United States. With the exception of Japan, no Asian nation has attained a high degree of industrialization. This would seem to indicate that markets in non-Communist Asia are open to all comers and that Americans are confronted with a number of competitors from other industrial nations in these markets. With the growth of the Japanese industrial economy, it may well be that much of Asia will be tied economically to Japan (although some observers regard China and India as the nations that will eventually hold economic dominion over Asia after they become thoroughly industrialized).

Other Foreign Markets

As nations develop and as economies change to market economies, there is some promise that new product markets will be opened to American businessmen in other foreign countries. Africa is a "sleeping giant" that promises to play a more important role in international trade as it casts off its ties with colonial powers in Europe, although American exports to Africa are now only about one fourth of what they are to Asia. Exports to this trading area have not quite doubled since 1941, while those to other areas have increased about fourfold since then. Australia and Oceania are also becoming more important as product markets and as sources of productive resources for American business firms.

CONCLUSIONS

The outlook, then, throughout the world is for expanded trade and emerging and industrializing national economies that will provide markets for American products and resources for American producers to a degree never before realized, and hardly ever dreamed of. American firms will become international traders, operators, and financiers in order to take advantage of the opportunities created, although it is likely that they will be subject to considerably more international competition than ever before and will continue to be confronted with political and other social problems in addition to economic problems.

The existence of problems for American business in international trade does not mean that there are no means of overcoming the problems. American exports and imports have been steadily mounting. In part, this reflects the development of trade in markets where the competition is not quite so strong or political difficulties not so great, as in Latin America and Canada; it is also the consequence of actions taken in markets where the competition is keen. Many firms having headquarters in the United States have established branches overseas so that they might compete on a more equal basis with foreign-based firms. Also, American businessmen have acted through the government of the United States to solve problems of lack of dollars and other foreign exchange and to remove other barriers to trade. There will always be some opportunities for American business in foreign and world markets so long as productive resources are unequally distributed or so long as they are employed to produce different products. The advantages to nations and to business firms in specializing in certain kinds of products will lead to continuing American participation in markets abroad, although the nature of these markets will constantly change.

READING: America Becomes a Trader * by Gilbert Burck and Sanford S. Parker

Just in the last few years, so quickly that it has gone almost unnoticed, the role of the U.S. in the world economy has undergone its most portentous change in forty years. World War I transformed the U.S. from a debtor nation into

---

* Reproduced by permission of *Fortune Magazine,* in which this article appeared in extended form in October, 1957.

the world's largest creditor and its most reluctant importer—the easy mark of the 1920's who made bad loans to other nations but refused to buy their goods, the Uncle Shylock of the 1930's who hung on to his dollars and piled up most of the world's gold in Fort Knox, the technological prodigy of the early 1940's whose feats in producing substitutes for raw materials threatened to shrink his imports almost to the vanishing point. To be sure, a change seemed probable after World War II thrust vast new world responsibilities on the U.S., even before the Paley Commission predicted that American raw-material resources would have to be supplemented by rising imports. But in fact American imports and foreign investment lagged far behind exports until recently. Only the Marshall plan and military aid to U.S. allies enlarged the flow of dollars abroad.

Suddenly, however, a change is in full swing. Thanks as much to basic economic and technological forces as to any conscious national "policy," and thanks, too, to uncounted thousands of imaginative decisions by individual businesses here and abroad, the U.S. is becoming the great international trader and investor it ought to be. It is entering a complex, competitive international economy of shifting, expanding challenges and opportunities. Although U.S. government aid to foreign countries has risen, U.S. imports and U.S. private investment abroad have recently risen vastly more. Foreign manufactured goods are beginning to fight their way into a country that has been the supreme manufacturer, and over tariff walls to boot. Competition from other nations is cropping up in export markets that had become virtual U.S. monopolies.

They Must Sell to Buy. In one important respect, of course, the foreign market is just like any other market—you can't expect to sell it more than it can pay for. The number of dollars flowing into the pockets of overseas customers depends entirely on the number of dollars they acquired in trading with or getting investment money or aid from the U.S. The number of dollars they spend in any one year does not necessarily equal the number they acquire that year. Between 1948 and 1956 the free world outside the U.S. added $13.4 billion to its gold and dollar holdings, and earlier this year, owing to the closing of Suez and the consequent demand for U.S. oil, it reduced its gold and dollar reserves. But over the years every dollar spent by a foreign country on American goods and services must first be dispensed by Americans as payment for foreign goods and services or gold, or as investment abroad, or as government aid.

The last product in the world one would expect the U.S. to import in volume is the passenger automobile, in whose mass production the U.S. has led the world so long and by so wide a margin. Yet Americans are now snapping up European autos at the rate of 200,000 a year—and despite a 9 per cent tariff. In the U.S., which uses cars hard and pays relatively little for gasoline, the auto industry has logically made big, rugged cars. In Europe, owing to expensive fuel, arbitrary taxation systems, and lower income levels, the auto industry has developed cars with small engines and bodies. Now the American consumer is discovering the peculiar merits of European small cars, and is taking to them in a way that would have seemed impossible a few years ago. The market would seem wide open for European cars for a long time. For only enormous volume, sometimes estimated as high as one million units a year, could enable U.S. manufacturers to turn out a small car very much more cheaply than a large car of the same quality. By then European cars should be well entrenched in the U.S. market.

Besides machinery, vehicles, and newsprint, manufactured imports encompass a fabulous variety of things including glass, leather goods, watches, cameras, embroidery, mouth organs, hair brushes, baskets, pottery, toys, paper products, cotton, wool and silk goods, and thousands of other products. Imports in this sweeping "miscellaneous" category have risen from $1.2 billion in 1954 to about $2.2 billion in 1957, or more than 80 per cent.

How much, then, can total imports of maufactured goods be expected to rise by 1966? Owing in part to the boom in imports of machinery and autos, total imports of manufactured goods have been rising at some $400 million a year. If this were to keep up, imports would double, from $3.7 billion in 1957 to more than $7 billion in 1966. The projecting of manufactured imports is a tricky business because there are no reliable historical relationships to go by. The total wholesale volume of U.S. manufacturing will probably rise from some $200 billion to $300 billion in the next ten years, moreover, and in such a market European and other specialties should find plenty of room. But the effect of tariffs is hard to assay. European manufacturers, always eyeing the escape clause in the U.S. Tariff Act, are often leery of a big commitment in the U.S. market, claiming that the uncertainties of U.S. tariff policy are worse than the rates. Taking all these factors into account, FORTUNE projects the admittedly conservative figure of $5.5 billion for imports of manufactured goods in 1966.

From Oil to Scotch.   Now consider the outlook for imports of oil, agricultural products, semi-manufactures, and raw materials, which constitute the remainder of U.S. purchases of goods abroad. These are headed, in the main, for healthy increases. Imports of crude and residual oil are rising, from $700 million in 1952 to $1.4 billion in 1957. Despite the recent restrictions on imports of crude, there seems no alternative to importing more oil as the years roll on. U.S. oil consumption will double in some fifteen years, and it is highly doubtful that U.S. production and reserves can keep pace. If only because at least twenty-five domestic companies are now getting into foreign oil, protectionism is likely to wane. "Nearly every oil company in the U.S.," says Kenneth Hill of the Chase Manhattan Bank's petroleum department, "will be going abroad if it can afford to." According to the Chase Manhattan official estimates of future needs, the U.S. can be expected to import about $3 billion worth of oil in 1966.

Imported raw materials and semi-manufactures will also be in high demand. Imports of bauxite, aluminum, iron ore, manganese, tungsten, cobalt, and chrome will rise considerably, but imports of other metals like copper, nickel, tin, lead, and zinc will rise more slowly. Imports of wood pulp, lumber, diamonds, and chemicals will also rise substantially. Total dollar volume of all these raw materials and semi-manufactures, which has risen from $3.5 billion in 1952 to an estimated $4 billion in 1957, can be expected to rise to $5.5 billion in 1966.

Agricultural imports, by contrast, have a much less resplendent future. The largest is coffee, which came to $1.4 billion in 1956. Then there is $1.3 billion in crude materials like rubber ($400 million), wool ($240 million), and cocoa ($150 million), and $1.2 billion in processed foodstuffs like cane sugar ($400 million), Scotch and other distilled spirits ($157 million), and canned meat ($145 million). In 1957 agricultural imports will total about $3.9 billion, down from more than $5 billion in 1951, largely because of declines in wool and rubber prices.

Imports of wool and rubber, however, have begun to rise from their low ebbs —but owing to the increase in synthetic substitutes will probably not rise very fast. Although imports of coffee will rise at least a fast as U.S. population rises, production of coffee will expand greatly; and unless European consumption soars, prices may decline, and the value of coffee imports therefore may not rise as fast as physical volume. Imports of manufactured foodstuffs can be expected to rise steadily (imports of canned ham alone have risen from $47 million to $85 million in four years). Thus FORTUNE estimates that imports of all agricultural products will rise to about $5 billion by 1966.

So taking imports of all goods together—manufactured, agricultural, and raw-material—there is good reason to believe they should rise from $13 billion in 1957 to $19 billion in 1966. Assuming that America's total output of goods and services will continue to rise at 4 per cent a year and will therefore come to $615 billion (at today's prices) in 1966, projected goods imports would work out to 3.1 per cent of G.N.P.—about the same percentage achieved by them in 1956 and 1957.

Imported Mountains. As becomes the nation with the world's highest living standard, the U.S. is a large consumer of imported services, and is spending some $5 billion a year for them. The biggest single item in this outlay is transportation—the $1.5 billion the U.S. pays other countries for passenger fares, shipping charges, fleet service, and so on. Since 1950 transportation outlays have been rising faster than imports; they will continue to do so, and should expand by 50 per cent and hit $2.25 billion by 1966. One reason is that they include charter payments for vessels operating under foreign flags but financed by U.S. money. Today there are 380 vessels with a total deadweight tonnage of 6,300,000, and in 1956 the U.S. probably paid out some $150 million to Panama alone for their use.

Almost as large as commercial-transportation "imports" are American travel "imports"—that is, American payments to foreign countries for traveling expenses. The biggest Swiss export, as the saying goes, is mountains, and Americans import a lot of them. American travel outlays have doubled since 1950, and this year will probably come to $1.4 billion—spent abroad by some 1,400,000 U.S. residents. Because their growth rate is slowing down, these outlays will probably increase by only another $1 billion over the next ten years. One reason: foreign-born U.S. residents, who still account for a lot of American travel to Europe, are a steadily diminishing element in the U.S. population.

Invisible Imports. Then there is the $700-million income that foreigners derive from their investments in the U.S.—which is a U.S. "service import" because the U.S. lays out dollars for the use of this capital. Foreign investment in the U.S. totals more than $30 billion, much of it held by central banks as part of currency reserves. More than half of it, therefore, is in the form of bank deposits or short-term U.S. government securities. Only about $5 billion of the $30 billion is in high-income direct investment, and the rest is in stocks and bonds.

The return on this foreign investment, owing in part to rising interest rates, has increased from some $245 million ten years ago to nearly $700 million in 1957. But interest rates probably will not rise much from now on, and foreign accumulations of dollars may slow down. So the return probably will not rise as much in the next ten years as it has in the past ten, and will amount to little more than $1 billion in 1966.

Total imports of services, to sum up, should rise from $5 billion in 1957 to $7.6 billion in 1966, or by about 50 per cent. Therefore total imports of services *and* goods, during the next ten years, should rise from $18 billion to $26.5 billion, or nearly 50 per cent. And imports of services and goods, which rose more slowly than exports during the past few years, should rise much faster, proportionately, in the next ten years. And indeed they *must* rise faster than exports to compensate for the reduced number of dollars that other countries will acquire through U.S. government aid.

No. 1 International Investor. Now look at the colossal, unprecedented rise of U.S. private investment abroad—which, as already noted, increased from an average of $1 billion a year in 1951–55 to $3 billion in 1956 and probably $3.5 billion in 1957. (Some $1 billion of the $3 billion in 1956 went to Canada, $800 million to South America, $700 million to Europe, and $500 million to the rest of the world.)

What the $3 Billion Went For. Of last year's $3-billion *net* investment, $1.8 billion was direct investment, i.e., made by U.S. companies through branches and subsidiaries. Some $1.1 billion of this was made by oil companies. Chase Manhattan reckonings indicate that oil investments will double, rising to $2.2 billion. Corporations outside the oil business invested a total of $700 million (net) abroad in 1956, and this figure will certainly rise over the next ten years. A special survey by FORTUNE of some 500 big corporations suggests that manufacturing companies, whose investment outflow totaled about $270 million in 1956, will increase their outflow at least 50 per cent by 1966, or to some $400 million. Since many companies are thinking of building plants in Europe to take advantage of the common-market trading area, the $400-million figure may turn out to be low. By 1966 U.S. companies will probably be sending more from their foreign subsidiaries and branches to the world markets than from their plants at home.

Mining companies, according to FORTUNE's survey, plan to raise their foreign investment from $90 million to perhaps $150 million—and may go much higher in the event of unusually good "strikes." Trading, finance, and other enterprises, which include companies like W. R. Grace, Anderson, Clayton, Sears, Roebuck, Woolworth, and Household Finance (entering Canada), have been expanding their foreign investment rapidly—and public utilities like American & Foreign Power may expand fast from now on, too. Their total is up from $123 million in 1953 to $330 million, and can be expected to increase by 50 per cent, or to

$500 million in 1966. So the $700 million invested abroad by non-oil companies in 1957 can be expected to increase to more than $1 billion by 1966.

Now consider the prospects for exports of goods. Can the U.S. increase them from nearly $20 billion in 1957 to about $25 billion in 1966? A big chunk of 1957 goods exports—$4.8 billion—is accounted for by agricultural produce, much of it cotton and wheat surplus sold in the world market below U.S. prices and hence subsidized by the U.S. Government. Per capita food production outside the U.S. has not risen much the past five years, and some experts believe that other countries will be in the market for U.S. farm products for a long time. But American efforts to balance domestic agricultural supply and demand will doubtless achieve some success, and the U.S. will probably not be producing such large surpluses by 1966. In fact, more than $1 billion of today's exports are coming out of accumulated surpluses, which are declining. The conclusion seems to be that U.S. agricultural exports will at best hold their own, and will probably decline over the next decade.

Nor do exports of goods other than machinery and vehicles present many possibilities for big increases in U.S. exports.

Thus if there is to be a $5-billion net increase in exports of U.S. goods between now and 1966 most of it will have to be accounted for by vehicle and machinery exports.

On the basis of current trends, it is hard to make a case for the proposition that a world with $35 billion to spend in 1966 will rush out and automatically spend it all on U.S. goods and services. The world demand for U.S. goods and services, in other words, does not appear to be increasing faster than its supply of dollars, and the so-called dollar shortage, which indeed has been easing in the past few years, should continue to ease.

The new international competition, however, should present hardly more than an exhilarating challenge to American business. For one thing, U.S. producers, as they always have, will doubtless find new export opportunities. For another, the world has been accumulating gold and dollar reserves; and when its reserves rise it tends to lift restrictions on imports of U.S. goods. So while the dollar shortage may ease, its very easing will broaden the export market for American business.

Exports depend on Imports. The all-important fact remains: other countries cannot buy U.S. goods and services without dollars, and to an increasing extent they can get dollars only by selling goods and services to the U.S. Thus a big job ahead of the U.S., from a political as well as economic standpoint, is to increase its imports enough so that U.S. business will still enjoy a large and growing export market when U.S. government aid virtually disappears and when annual new U.S. foreign investment is exceeded by annual earnings on previous investment.

As it always does when the U.S. economy develops a few soft spots, U.S. protectionism is erupting again. Several U.S. industries—lead, zinc, whiskey, clothespins—are now urging higher tariffs and the application of escape clauses. The Reciprocal Trade Act, which comes up for extension in 1958, will apparently have a rough time in Congress. FORTUNE's estimate that goods imports in 1966, as they did in 1956, will come to 3.1 per cent of G.N.P. assumes, however, that the protectionist campaign now gathering way will achieve few large or significant gains. The fact is, of course, that the U.S. cannot fully discharge its responsibilities as world leader and creditor unless U.S. trade policy is liberalized further than it has been.

The rest of the world is inexorably moving toward freer trade. The European common-market scheme, whatever its initial discriminations against non-members, will create a huge mass market whose volume of trade with the rest of the world is bound to increase greatly. Given an enlarged and consistent U.S. trade policy and ample international investment, the prospect ahead of the free world begins to resemble the dreams of classical economists: international capitalism enlarging worldwide mass markets through free international trade. In the process of becoming a trader, the U.S. has already contributed enormously to such a prospect.

SUGGESTED READINGS

Dell, Sidney, *Trade Blocs and Common Markets* (New York: Knopf, 1963). An analysis of the origins and significance of trade groupings.

Ellsworth, Paul T., *The Internationl Economy* (New York: Macmillan, 1964). Discusses the bases of specialization and international trade and the development of an international trading system.

Woytinsky, W. S., and E. S. Woytinsky, *World Commerce and Governments* (New York: Twentieth Century Fund, 1955). Examines the volume, composition and patterns of trade throughout the globe.

CHAPTER 10

THE DYNAMIC
NATURE OF
MARKETS

The markets in which businessmen buy and sell are constantly changing. Firms must not only adjust to existing market conditions, but must inquire into what is going to happen in the markets in the foreseeable future. New things will appear on the market; others will pass away. Markets themselves will change in size and location. Changes will occur in the market price and the quantities sold of various goods and services. The relative importance of various buyers and sellers will fluctuate. These changes will take place over varying periods of time, and the estimation of how such variations will occur becomes important. Not only are adjustments made for prospective changes, but the astute businessman also attempts to control the nature and pace of the change whenever possible.

CHANGES IN TOTAL SALES BY BUSINESS

The gross national product of the American economy might be regarded as the total sales of final products of American business, as we have noted previously. If prices do not change in product markets, all fluctuations in the total sales of final products (GNP) will be caused by changes in the quantities purchased by domestic consumers, American business, American governments, and foreign buyers. Over the years, as consumer spending has fluctuated, as business expenditures on capital goods and inventories have changed, as the spending of American local, state, and federal agencies has gone up and down, and as the amount of purchases by foreigners has changed, the gross national product has gone up and down—although there is a general tendency for it to increase from year to year. Such changes are important for business firms because there is some relationship between the total amount of spending for final products and the spending for goods or services in a specific product market.

If we think of all of those producing products for sale in America as being one firm, that "American business firm" will not only make all of the sales of final products but will also make all of the purchases in the resource markets. That is, it will pay out all of the wages and salaries, interest payments, rents, and profits necessary to acquire the resources to produce the gross national product. If we look at who receives these payments (that is, at who supplies productive resources), we discover that individuals, business firms, and governments in the United States and abroad receive them. In short, domestic consumers, American business, American governments, and foreigners receive income from this "firm" as well as purchase products from it. At first glance, this looks like a fine arrangement in which the money received from "The American Business Firm" by those who supply resources to it will be respent by them on its products, and that money will continue to flow in a circle and that sales of final products and purchases of productive resources would not fluctuate (assuming still that prices of final products and resources do not change). *See* Figure 10–1.

But we do see changes in gross national product. During the depressed business conditions of the 1930's, GNP fell to less than one half of what it had been in 1929. Part of this was due to price changes, but a large part of it was due to the fact that consumers, business firms, and governments did not continue to purchase the same quantities of final products they had bought during 1929. That is, consumption spending, business investment, and government expenditures declined. Consumers might have satisfied many of their wants for goods and services and decided to save some of their income. Business firms might have decided that their inventories were too large and that not much additional spending for plant and equipment was justified. Governments might have decided to

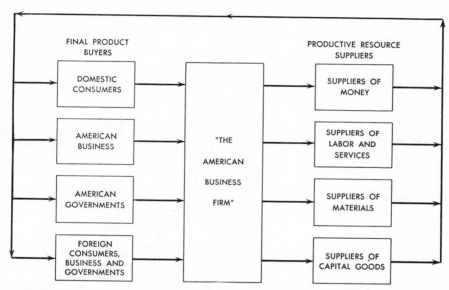

FIGURE 10–1. Circular Flow of Money, or "How Money Would Flow If It Did Flow in a Circle."

use some of their income to retire outstanding debts rather than to maintain expenditures at previous levels. Whatever the reasons for reducing expenditures, during the early 1930's the spending by consumers, business, and governments on the final products of the American economy declined.

Look what happens when the total purchases of the final products of "The American Business Firm" decreases (Figure 10–2). Its income is reduced and it does not require as many productive resources to produce goods and services for a market in which total demand for final products is declining. Consequently, it buys fewer productive resources which, in turn, means less income for those selling them. With reduced incomes from supplying resources, individual consumers, business firms, and governments cut their spending on final products which, of course, means another drop in gross national product. After 1929 GNP did drop in this fashion until 1933, when the aggregate spending by consumers, business, and governments on final products began to increase again.

Since 1933 there has been a long-term upward trend in gross national product. Some aspects of this rise have given businessmen and others cause for concern. For one thing, the increase has taken place partly

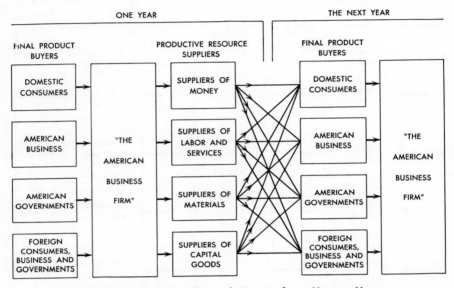

FIGURE 10–2.   The Flow of Money from Year-to-Year.

because of price increases, although there has been substantial growth in the quantity of goods and services sold. Because of price inflation, some firms are unable to compete in foreign markets and others—such as banks —find themselves being paid in cheaper dollars than in which they had loaned or sold. Another development has been that, even though it has increased, the rate of growth of gross national product has been behind that of other industrial nations—including the Soviet Union—and some American businessmen feel that to be an adverse reflection on the U.S. private business system.

Changes in gross national product affect conditions in resource markets as well as in product markets, and, therefore, fluctuations in GNP are of great importance to individual business firms. However, market conditions do not depend solely on changes in GNP. Other influences are at work, too, and we sometimes see the market for a particular product or resource declining while GNP is increasing, and vice versa; therefore, an examination of changes in specific markets and their causes is in order.

THE NATURE OF MARKET CHANGES

Among the most important changes is the change taking place in the kinds of things available in the markets. In large measure, new goods and services come on the market in response to changes in the desires of buyers. More important, perhaps, is that changed technology—new things and techniques available to the producer—will enable businessmen to market products that could not be produced profitably before. In many cases, the appearance of these new products—such as automobiles—will cause old products—such as buggies—to all but disappear from the market. Although some products disappear, all do not do so, and the net result has been a great increase in the number of goods and services sold in markets.

Markets for a certain product may change their size and location. As the population grows and personal income increases, individuals buy more. The market for consumers goods is thereby expanded. Business firms and governments also grow and increase their purchases accordingly. Too, products that were at one time sold on a local market may be sold on regional, national, and even international markets. The location of a marketplace might be changed to suit the needs of the more important buyers and sellers, as happened when the main money market of the world shifted from London to New York.

Even when products traded in a market do not change and little change is noted in the size and location of a market, prices and quantities sold are subject to wide variations. The sales and purchases of a business enterprise are usually recorded by the dollar amount, which somewhat obscures the fact that this value is determined by two variables: the price and the quantity sold. For some final products and resources, we see wide swings in the price and little change in the quantity sold; for others, we note the reverse; and for still others, we note substantial changes in both price and quantity over a period of time. There are no markets in which both the price and the quantity sold stays fairly constant for a long time, and therefore changes in these two market conditions are of paramount importance to businessmen.

We see, on occasion, changes in the parties in the market or influencing the market. Some buyers and sellers are "in the market" for certain products only sporadically, which further unsettles market conditions. Labor unions may appear where there were none before and establish some new influences on labor markets. Governments change, and governmental influence on market conditions therefore changes.

The Length of Market Changes

The time span over which market changes occur can be conveniently classified according to the length of the period in which the fluctuations take place. Those occurring every year are referred to as seasonal. We refer to somewhat longer fluctuations that have a recurrent pattern as "cyclical," and to long-term changes as "secular" trends. In addition, some changes have no regularity and are, understandably, called "erratic."

SEASONAL VARIATIONS. For almost all business firms, sales vary from month to month during a year (the same is usually true for purchases, but we shall use sales as an example). These are called seasonal variations because, at one time, agricultural purchasing was of major importance to merchants: farmers tended to buy goods before the planting season and during the harvest season. Agriculturalists are of less importance now in the markets than they have been in the past, but there are other events—for example, Christmas, the beginning of school, the beginning of a production period—that cause fairly predictable variations in the sales of a firm from month to month. The months of high sales and of relatively low sales are not the same for all firms, but there tends to be a regular pattern for a particular firm or industry.

CYCLICAL CHANGES. Although the same pattern tends to recur during the course of a year, sales are not the same from year to year. A period of years may be experienced in which annual sales climb from year to year, reach a peak, and then fall to a low point before beginning to climb again. This kind of change is called "cyclical." The business cycle has four phases—recovery (rising sales), prosperity (peak sales), recession (falling sales), and depression (lowest sales). The length of the cycle tends to be different for various industries, although we sometimes look at the total sales of final products (GNP) to give us some idea of the phase of the cycle that business generally is in.

SECULAR TRENDS. Through the course of a number of cyclical fluctuations, a definite long-term tendency in the direction of sales may be noted. For most firms, the trend is toward higher sales. Some firms in declining industries, however, see a tendency toward lower sales over a long period of time. It is worth noting that sales of final products by American business as a whole has been on a continually rising trend, although some firms may find their sales—and therefore their purchases—trending downward at the time that business generally is moving upward.

ERRATIC MARKET CHANGES. Dealing with seasonals, cycles, and trends is made easier by virtue of their regularity; unfortunately, some changes are erratic in nature. Strikes are disrupting forces in the markets in which businessmen buy and sell. The labor supply of a firm may be cut off as a consequence of a strike by the employees of the company. Suppliers of other resources may be affected by strikes and be unable to provide things necessary for continued production and sales. Strikes also influence the purchasing power of buyers of final products and can, therefore, influence the markets in which business firms sell in an unpredictable fashion. The other major influence that operates in an irregular fashion is war. There are a number of unpredictable political influences on markets, but none have so strong an effect as those established during times of military conflict. Business firms are confronted by shortages in the markets in which they buy—labor, raw materials, and capital goods are usually in short supply and sometimes unobtainable during wartime. On the other hand, the demand for final products usually increases greatly in such periods, but business firms are unable to satisfy such demands due to the scarcity of productive resources. Although many business opportunities present themselves during wars, rationing, price, and profit controls prevent firms from taking full advantage of the situation.

Tendencies in Certain Markets

There have been, in recent years, certain tendencies discernible in the markets in which American businessmen buy and sell. Changes have been taking place in the relative importance of various classes of final products sold by business as well as in the relative amounts purchased by the major groups of purchasers. There has been an upward trend of considerable significance in the total final sales of business. Also, changes in resource markets have caused businessmen to make adjustments— chiefly by substituting one resource for another. Awareness of the nature of these changes enables businessmen to make appropriate adjustments.

PRODUCT MARKET CHANGES. Since World War II, the production and sale of manufactured goods have been increasing steadily. Purchases of durables and nondurables have increased at about the same rate, although there is a wider cyclical variation in the buying of durables—a condition that might be expected, because purchase of durables is more easily postponed than purchase of nondurables such as food. Sales of services have increased at a somewhat higher rate than those of goods since 1945, and there is even a greater stability in the sale of services than in the sale of nondurables, with very little evidence of cyclical or erratic influences on this market, especially in sales to consumers. (Figure 10–3 shows some important economic changes in the postwar period.)

GROSS NATIONAL PRODUCT AND NATIONAL INCOME

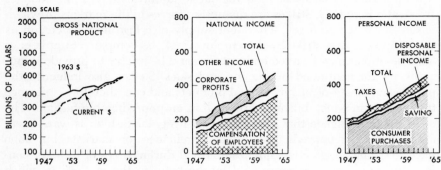

POSTWAR GROWTH IN MAJOR COMPONENTS OF GNP

BY MARKET

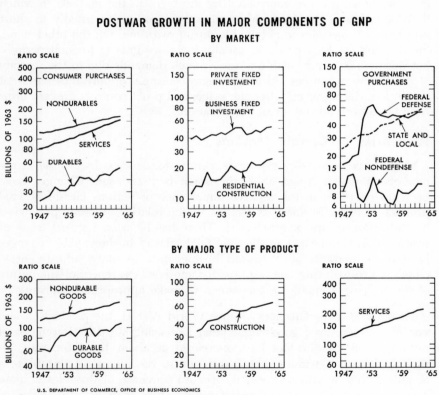

BY MAJOR TYPE OF PRODUCT

U.S. DEPARTMENT OF COMMERCE, OFFICE OF BUSINESS ECONOMICS

FIGURE 10–3.

The relative stability of consumer purchases marks the buying of this group in all final products markets. Buying of final products by business —especially purchases of capital goods—tends to be the most highly fluctuating, while government purchases of goods and services are more stable, although not as constant as consumer purchases. Too, since World War II, governments have tended to purchase a somewhat larger proportion of the gross national product than ever before, although the federal government became an increasingly important purchaser during the 1930's.

LABOR MARKET CHANGES. In American labor markets, there have been some significant developments since 1945. One obvious change has been the great increase in the number of persons in this market. In part, this is a consequence of the large relative increase in the number of women— especially married women—in the labor force. There has also been a relative decline in the number of employed unskilled workers because of the increased education of Americans and the demands by business and other employers for more highly trained personnel. Changes in the needs of employers have resulted in a high level of unemployment of those without needed skills, and there has been what appears to be a "surplus" in the labor markets, although, in fact, certain skilled workers are in short supply. The increases in employment have been in nonagricultural employment and within this classification, employment in nonmanufacturing industries has increased faster than in manufacturing. Employment in agriculture has actually declined.

Labor union membership has increased in number, but not as a percentage of total nonagricultural employment. Actually since 1945 there has been some slight decrease in the percentage of employees who are union members, and union membership seems to have stabilized at about one third of the total nonagricultural employees. It may well be that the trend toward the greater unionization of the labor markets is halted. Changes in the structure of the labor force has increased the relative number of workers traditionally difficult to organize. Legislation since 1945 also has deprived union leaders of some of the influence they and their members could exert on such markets. This is not to suggest that unions do not have much influence on labor markets; an examination of developments in those markets underscores the extent to which labor union activity has changed market conditions.

Wages in almost all labor markets have increased greatly since the beginning of this century. In some fifty years, average hourly earnings of production workers in manufacturing have increased more than ten times. There has been considerable price inflation during this period but, even so, the wages paid for labor services have increased more than proportionately, thereby making the United States the highest-wage nation in the world. Much of this increase has been effected by union activity, with the greatest increase coming after unions organized employees and pressed for higher pay. Wages of nonunion workers in this century have increased by approximately the same percentage as that of unionized employees, but started from a lower level. Too, these labor service prices probably increased as a result of a rise in wages in unionized labor markets.

Hours of work have declined as wages have increased. In 1890, the average workweek in manufacturing stood at about 60 hours. Now it averages about 40 hours. This development too is in large measure the result of union activity; it was in unionized firms that hours were first reduced. The reduction in weekly hours worked has tended to offset, in some measure, the increase in the labor force—that is, as a result of the reduced number of hours worked per week, the number of labor-hours for sale in the labor markets has not increased as rapidly as has the labor force.

MONEY MARKET CHANGES.   In the money markets, certain trends have developed that are likely to continue. Since the passage of the Federal Reserve Act in 1913, and especially since developments during the New Deal period, the federal government has played a stronger role in influencing money markets, and has even become an important buyer and seller in those markets. It has influenced the quantity of money available by controls over lenders and securities markets; too, it has become an important lender, tending to supply funds when other lenders are unwilling or unable to do so. As a large borrower, it has also influenced bond and other money markets by its management of its debt.

The federal government has also exerted, in recent years, great influence on the price of money. Although states had set *maximum* rates of interest for various classes of loans before the central government became more active in money markets, the national government has had great influence on the *prevailing* rate. It has done this by the interest rates it has fixed on home loans, by the interest rate it pays on its debts, and by its buying and selling activities in certain markets in which it attempts to influence the market rate of interest. Although the U.S. does not deal in all money markets, those that it does influence have an effect on almost all of them. The net effect of the federal government's influence on the markets has been to increase the stability of interest rates—the price of money—and to make a more stable quantity of money available.

CHANGES IN CAPITAL GOODS MARKETS.   Capital goods markets have noteworthy cyclical variations and trends. Prices of capital goods are quite stable, and especially are unlikely to decline during periods of recession and depression, although they may move up in periods of recovery. On the other hand, there is a great cyclical variation in the quantity of capital goods sold. During times of recession and depression, very little of these resources is purchased; during recovery and prosperity great quantities are bought by business firms. The most notable trend in this industry is its continuing long-term growth because equipment tends to be substituted for labor wherever profitable, and profitable opportunities increase as wages rise and technology improves.

RAW MATERIAL MARKET CHANGES. In the raw materials markets we note cyclical variations quite different from those prevailing in markets for capital goods. Prices of raw materials tend to fluctuate quite widely, while the quantities brought to the market tend to be relatively stable, although some raw materials are unpurchased by business firms during periods of recession and depression. Some greater stability has been brought to these markets—especially commodity markets—by the action of the federal government in regulating prices, marketing practises, and quantities produced, and by its purchases of "surplus" products in some markets.

CAUSES OF MARKET CHANGES

In specific markets, a number of influences affect sales. In Chapter 7, we enunciated a general theory of market behavior: "The behavior of a market—as evidenced by market price and quantity bought and sold— depends upon the behavior of the buyers and sellers in the market and upon that of others having some influence upon the market." This statement implies that changes in market conditions—such as changes in market prices and quantities sold—depend upon changes in the kind, quantity, and behavior of individuals and groups (mainly buyers and sellers, but not excluding others) having some influence upon the market. In some markets, only changes in the behavior of buyers and sellers are important; in others, new parties may come upon the scene and exert some influence upon market conditions even though they do not act as buyer or seller. For example, it would be difficult to explain the price changes occurring in the steel industry in early 1962 solely in terms of interactions among buyers and sellers in the market for steel. President Kennedy and his administration had considerable impact on the decision finally arrived at. At one time, it was only the behavior of buyers and sellers of steel that was important; now there is asserted to be a "national interest" in what steel prices are and the federal government frequently has an important influence upon steel price changes. Apparently, in order to adequately explain market changes, it is necessary to take into account all those individuals and groups who are able materially to affect market conditions. The degree to which various individuals and groups are able to exert such influence would seem to depend on their objectives and resources and on how they employ their resources. Thus in order to understand why certain changes take place in specific markets, we need to discover which individuals and groups are capable of influencing the market, to determine their objectives, and to examine their resources and the lines of action they adopt to gain their objects.

Changing Technology

Technological change, it has frequently been said, alters market conditions. Technology, however, does not exist unrelated to individuals and groups. For example, technological advancement affects market conditions when someone puts a new product on the market—when Edison could produce electric light bulbs in commercial quantities, he adversely affected the market for kerosene as an illuminant. Thus when competitors alter their products or their production processes as a result of technological advances, it is the activities of competitors and not technology that change market conditions. Conditions in resource markets may also change when someone applies new techniques—a case in point being the application of drilling techniques (which had formerly been used to secure water) to extracting crude oil from the ground. The early techniques of drilling were as crude as the oil sought, but they have become as refined as the final products of the petroleum industry. Advances in the techniques of recovery of oil from beneath the earth's surface brought the price of crude oil down to a low level, causing great quantities of crude to come to the market when oilmen applied such techniques, not when the technology developed.

Changing Income and Tastes

Economists have also noted the importance of changing income and changing tastes in causing market changes. It is, of course, the changes taking place in the incomes and tastes of individuals and groups that cause changes in the product markets. As the American economy has grown, those supplying productive resources and products have increased their incomes and their purchases. Per capita income in the United States is the highest in the world. This has led to something more than just an increased spending on things that were previously purchased. With the elementary needs for food, shelter, and clothing being met with a decreasing fraction of income, more purchasing power has become available to satisfy other wants, no matter how luxurious or frivolous. Businessmen, aware of this, have created a host of new products to meet such wants (and have even attempted to create desires for luxury goods and things unnecessary to existence).

Changes in the Number and Nature of Those Influencing Markets

Increases in individual income and changes in individual tastes are not the whole story of why there has been a great increase in the purchases of those buying in consumer product markets. There has been a great growth in the number of individuals in America since World War II, and as postwar babies reach adulthood their buying power is added to the adult population and greatly increases demand for most products (although we should note that the "teen-age market" has also become a potent force in American business). Population growth also increases business and government buying.

In addition to the changes that buyers and sellers in the markets effect, other parties not involved in buying or selling have become increasingly important. The past century has seen manifold growth in labor unions. They might be regarded only as "sellers" in the labor markets, but much union activity could scarcely be called market activity, although it does influence market conditions. The same period has also witnessed a tremendous increase in the regulatory activities of local, state, and federal government. Such regulations frequently affect markets, and sometimes market prices are determined by government action rather than by interaction among buyers and sellers. Financiers have also attempted to influence firms to conduct themselves in markets in ways different from which they might if this pressure were not present. Trade associations attempt to secure uniformity of action on the part of their members, and this too may change market conditions from what they would be without the presence of such organizations. The number and variety of individuals and groups other than buyers and sellers capable of exerting influence on markets is increasing, and no adequate understanding of any specific market condition or change is possible without taking these individuals and groups into account. A detailed examination of some of the more influential classes of these individuals and groups will be undertaken in Parts II and III.

COMING TO TERMS WITH A CHANGING ECONOMIC ENVIRONMENT

It is beyond the intended scope of this work to deal with the various ways that business firms have developed for coming to terms with market changes. It is sufficient to say that such means exist. In some cases, sophisticated devices have been developed to determine the existing nature of a market and to estimate future changes in it. Too, many firms engage in activities that will create new markets or expand existing ones. The only further point that should be made is that those firms that have not acquainted themselves with techniques of determining market changes and have not concerned themselves with means of coping with changing markets frequently find themselves in economic difficulties. There is, perhaps, no more important reason for business failure than the lack of understanding of the nature of markets in which firms buy and sell and the inability to come to terms with this economic environment.

APPENDIX: Historical Charts

Historical charts graphically demonstrate the fluctuations taking place in the markets in which business firms sell and buy. Figures 10–4 to 10–10 show certain changes taking place in product markets. Some money market developments are illustrated in Figures 10–11 through 10–13. Two charts, Figures 10–14 and 10–15, are concerned with developments in labor markets. Changing prices of raw materials are shown in Figure 10–16, which shows changes in all wholesale prices, and Figure 10–17, which shows price changes of selected raw materials.

All of the charts, except one, have been taken from the 1964 edition of *Historical Chart Book*, issued by the Board of Governors of the Federal Reserve System. The lone exception, Figure 10–9, came from the 1964 *Supplement to Economic Indicators*, prepared for the Subcommittee on Economic Statistics of the Joint Economic Committee of Congress by the committee staff and the Office of Statistical Standards, Bureau of the Budget.

SUGGESTED READINGS

Chambers, Edward J., *Economic Fluctuations and Forecasting* (Englewood Cliffs, N.J.: Prentice-Hall, 1961). Contains a description and analysis of types of economic fluctuations and a historical summary of American business cycles in the four decades since the end of World War I.

Committee for Economic Development, *Economic Growth in the United States* (New York: The Committee, 1958). A brief description of the growth of the American economy up to the present, with a discussion of what may reasonably be expected in the future. Largely a factual and statistical description of economic growth and the conditions that have brought it about.

Gordon, Robert A., *Business Fluctuations* (New York: Harper & Row, 1961). A comprehensive analysis of business cycles, combining theoretical, historical, and statistical approaches and stressing growth and inflation.

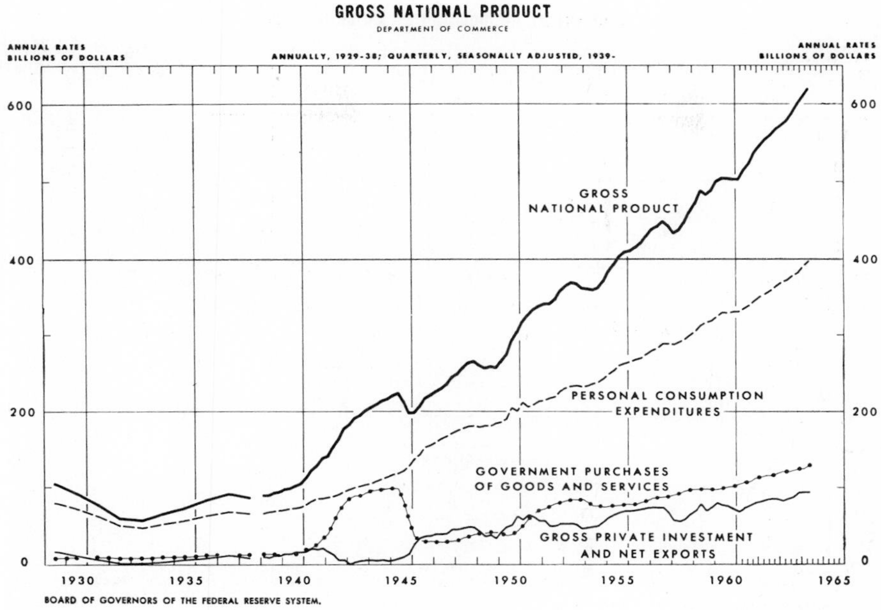
GROSS NATIONAL PRODUCT
DEPARTMENT OF COMMERCE
ANNUAL RATES
BILLIONS OF DOLLARS
ANNUALLY, 1929-38; QUARTERLY, SEASONALLY ADJUSTED, 1939-
ANNUAL RATES
BILLIONS OF DOLLARS
600
400
200
0
GROSS
NATIONAL PRODUCT
PERSONAL CONSUMPTION
EXPENDITURES
GOVERNMENT PURCHASES
OF GOODS AND SERVICES
GROSS PRIVATE INVESTMENT
AND NET EXPORTS
1930
1935
1940
1945
1950
1955
1960
1965
BOARD OF GOVERNORS OF THE FEDERAL RESERVE SYSTEM.

FIGURE 10–4.

INDUSTRIAL PRODUCTION BY MAJOR DIVISIONS

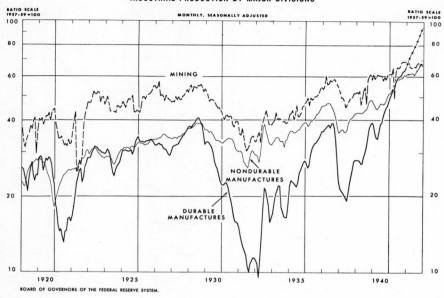

BOARD OF GOVERNORS OF THE FEDERAL RESERVE SYSTEM.

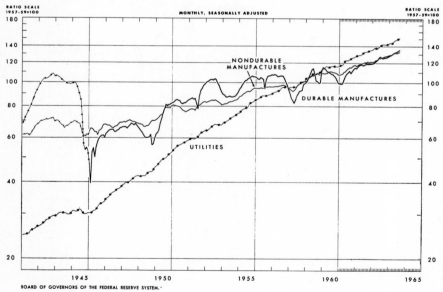

BOARD OF GOVERNORS OF THE FEDERAL RESERVE SYSTEM.

FIGURE 10–5.

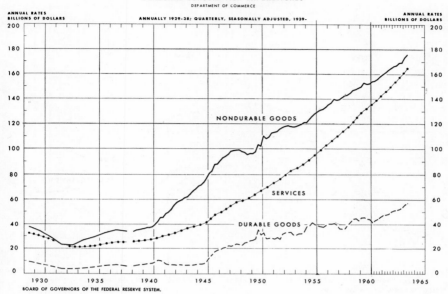

FIGURE 10–6.

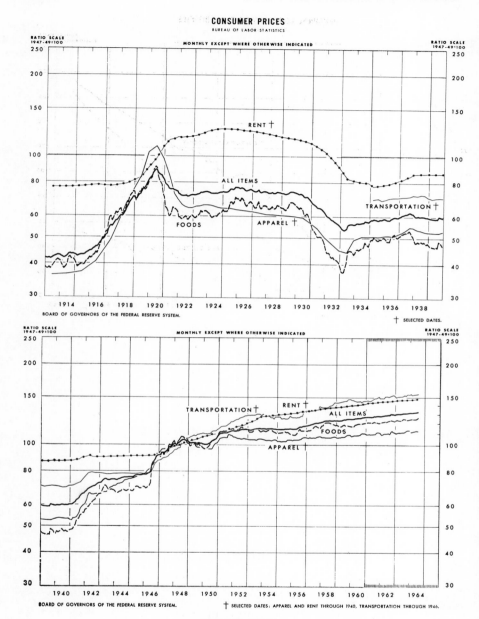

FIGURE 10–7.

BUSINESS EXPENDITURES ON NEW PLANT AND EQUIPMENT

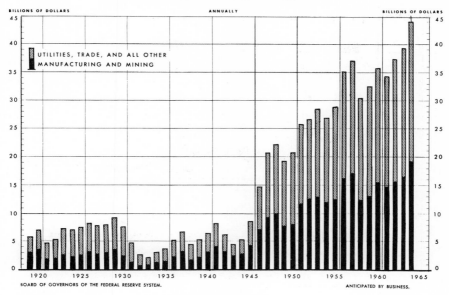

FIGURE 10–8.

FIGURE 10–9.

FEDERAL EXPENDITURES, NATIONAL INCOME ACCOUNTS BASIS, 1947–64.

(Quarterly data. Seasonally adjusted annual rates.)

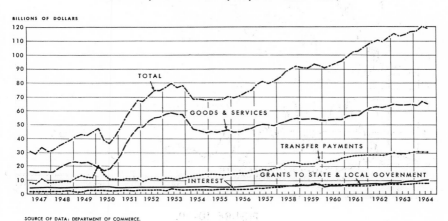

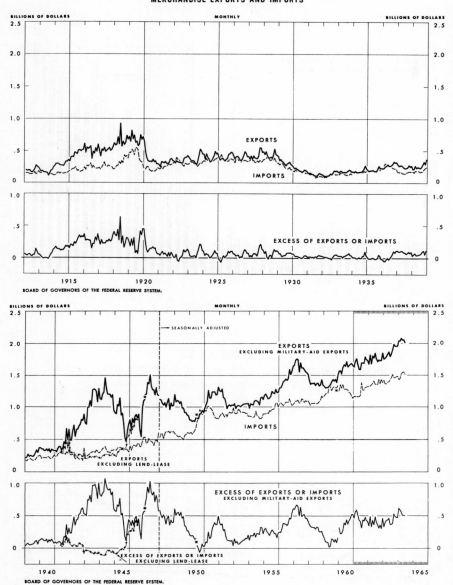

FIGURE 10–10.

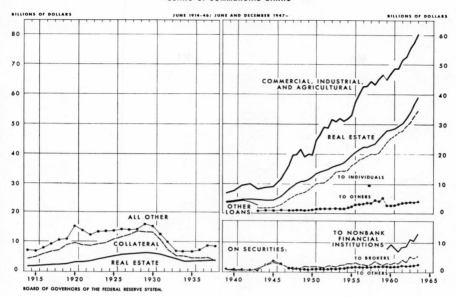

FIGURE 10–11.

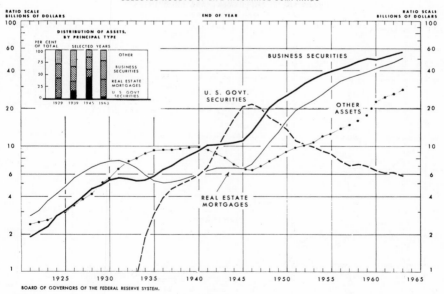

FIGURE 10–12.

LONG- AND SHORT-TERM INTEREST RATES

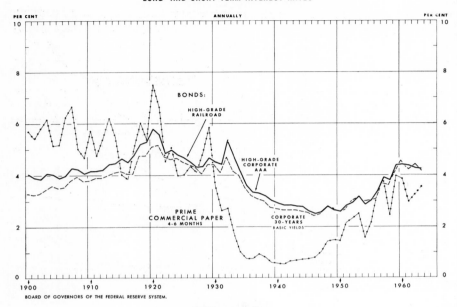

BOARD OF GOVERNORS OF THE FEDERAL RESERVE SYSTEM.

FIGURE 10–13.

LABOR FORCE, EMPLOYMENT, AND UNEMPLOYMENT

BUREAU OF LABOR STATISTICS

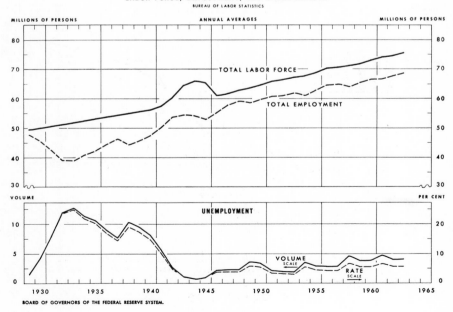

BOARD OF GOVERNORS OF THE FEDERAL RESERVE SYSTEM.

FIGURE 10–14.

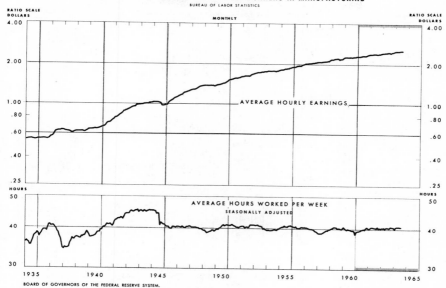

FIGURE 10–15.

FIGURE 10–16.

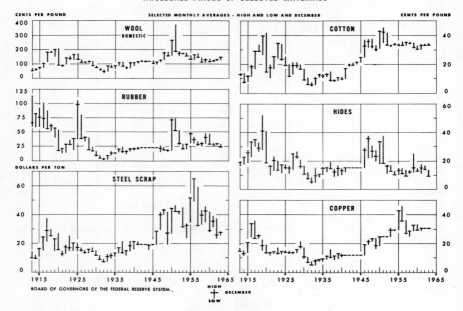

FIGURE 10–17.

CHAPTER 11

THE ECONOMIC RESPONSIBILITIES OF BUSINESS

In recent years heavy emphasis has been placed on the great economic responsibilities of American businessmen and business firms. On every hand, voices are raised beseeching business to assume greater responsibility, not only in the economic arena but also in the social and political spheres. Not only is it urged that more responsible behavior be undertaken in the specific markets in which businessmen deal, but also that businessmen concern themselves with the preservation of free market institutions, price stability, economic growth, and a high level of output and employment generally. In addition, they are asked to defeat the Communist economic challenge. If, it is declared, American men of business do not discharge these responsibilities, dire consequences will follow and the American business system, as we know it, may even expire. An opposing point of view is sometimes heard—that the businessman should not charge himself with responsibility for much beyond the competent profitable operation of his individual enterprise.

PROFIT-MAKING THE BASIC RESPONSIBILITY

Some economic theorists contend that if businessmen attempt to maximize profits they best fulfill their economic function and, therefore, will not have to concern themselves with what their economic responsibilities are. The catch in this is that the economists making this contention are talking about what the results would be if all markets were perfectly competitive. In product markets, no excessive profits could be made by firms while production would be at the maximum consistent with minimum prices, economic resources would be allocated to their best possible uses, productive efficiency in the use of such resources would be at its greatest, and consumers would be sovereign, dictating through their money votes what should be produced. No economist believes that such a world exists, but some would like to see it brought about and, consequently, prescribe profit-maximization without concerning themselves about other economic responsibilities the firm should assume.

A prominent law school dean has added his voice to those of such economists. Eugene V. Rostow, Dean of the Yale Law School, wrote: "The law books have always said that the board of directors owes a single-minded duty of unswerving loyalty to the stockholders, and only to the stockholders. The economist has demonstrated . . . that the quest for maximum revenue in a competitive market leads to a system of prices, and an allocation of resources and rewards superior to any alternative in its contributions to the economic welfare of the community as a whole." Economists and lawyers, in such discussions, generally do not stop without mentioning and approving the duties the law imposes on businessmen for fair dealing with customers, suppliers, and competitors in the marketplace.

RESPONSIBILITIES TOWARD OTHERS IN THE MARKETS

Most economic relationships of the businessman are with buyers and sellers in the markets. In the markets in which business sells—the product markets—there are buyers and other sellers. On the other hand, in the markets in which business firms buy—resource markets—there are sellers and other buyers. In addition, there are sometimes other parties, such as governmental agencies, trade associations, and labor unions, who are attempting to influence market conditions. The relationships with the latter groups fall more aptly under the heading of social and political relationships and will consequently be dealt with under Parts II and III.

Businessmen have normally been aware of their responsibilities to their customers, although they have not always discharged them very well. The philosophy of "Let the buyer beware!" has never dominated the thinking of the majority of American businessmen. Such an attitude is characteristic of the fly-by-night peddler rather than the businessman who intends doing business in one location for a substantial period of time. Consequently, since most firms recognize that their profits depend on customer satisfaction, established businesses have concerned themselves with providing the kinds of goods and services that customers want in quantities and at prices that will insure continued patronage as well as profits.

This is not to say that there are not some complaints that might be made of the ways in which businessmen have dealt with their customers. There are instances in which firms have restricted consumer choice by not making products consumers wanted (the success of the Volkswagen has been laid, in part, to the unwillingness or inability of American automobile manufacturers to make an inexpensive, functional automobile). Some have accused manufacturers of "anti-functionalism," that is, of producing products with nonfunctional features that raise the price without improving the performance of the basic function of the product—tail fins on automobiles being a common illustration. Too, the employment of "hidden persuaders" to "psychologically twist the buyer's arm" has been deplored. The lack of price competition and the sale of the same product to different buyers at different prices even though the circumstances are similar have also been regarded as a failure to meet responsibilities toward customers. Consumer credit has multiplied rapidly since World War II, mainly because business has "sold" it to consumers to the point where some are overburdened with debts. The argument made by businessmen in answering many of these charges is that they are producing only what the market wants, and that the fact that these practices are accepted by consumers is evidence that they meet an economic want. This in turn has raised the counterargument that perhaps businessmen should concern themselves with the economic needs of their customers and the U.S. rather than with some of the frivolous wants of those consumers who happen to have the ability to pay. These issues—as is true of all issues involving the responsibilities of any individual or group—will never be resolved to the satisfaction of all parties concerned, and are introduced merely to show the kinds of questions that are raised concerning the economic behavior of business, without presuming to state what the answers should be in each case.

In the markets in which they buy, businessmen are on the other side of the bargain and it has been suggested that in many cases they have conducted themselves too shrewdly and not responsibly enough. The money markets provide some illustrations of shrewd dealing. Where the managers are also the owners, they have not been obliged to go into the markets for ownership money, although they might borrow from various lenders. However, more and more business is being conducted by corporations, in which the managers are not the owners, and it has been suggested that in the sale of new stock in the corporation the managers do not always disclose all that should be told. Sometimes partnerships and individual proprietorships have not told all to their creditors. Since the thirties, federal legislation has forced greater disclosure of the facts concerning new securities issues and the current operations of corporations. Certainly, it is declared, a business firm owes its owners and creditors full and honest disclosure of its financial condition, of the results of its operations, and what it intends to do with the funds it secures.

In their operations in labor markets, businessmen have yet other responsibilities. Only in recent years has there been much concern on the part of labor with the disclosure of financial facts of the enterprise; this concern has been chiefly the result of the rise of unions. Historically, differences have existed between buyers and sellers over wages, hours, and working conditions. Both buyers and sellers in labor markets agree that there should be "a fair day's pay for a fair day's work," but there has been considerable disagreement on what those two things mean, and unions have usually said that the pay is too low and the work too much. Unions have also declared that businessmen have been unwilling to bargain collectively on certain other conditions of employment and, therefore, labor organizations have sought to enlarge the scope of collective bargaining agreements. Beyond the question of wages, union leaders have sought to secure guarantees of minimum amounts of employment (or at least wages) during a year and also to secure some pension rights for retired employees. The question is: What is business responsibility in the labor markets? It is easy enough to state that business should conduct itself responsibly; it is quite another thing to translate this into specific recommendations.

Market relationships with suppliers of capital goods and raw materials have raised some questions concerning responsible behavior on the part of the purchasing firm, but these are not as vexatious as those concerning dealings with owners, creditors, and labor. Where controversy has arisen, sellers of raw materials—especially farmers—have sometimes stated that purchasing firms have not dealt fairly with them. As is true in the markets in which businessmen sell, certain market practices have been established as "fair practices" and adherence to these rules by both buyers and sellers have been enforced by governing bodies. Provisions in laws, also, are quite clear about what the responsibilities of both parties are.

In the markets in which they buy and sell, firms usually have one or more competitors. What responsibilities, if any, a firm has toward other firms in the same industry and in the same market has been the subject of considerable discussion. One point of view suggests that there is no duty owed to competitors at all, and that each firm should compete fiercely with others buying or selling the same thing. A middle ground in the debate is that there should be a code of fair competitive practices drawn up that will limit the area of competition by banning unfair trade practices. Yet another view is that the competitors should not compete vigorously at all but, rather, should cooperatively establish market conditions that will benefit all in the industry buying or selling in this particular market. If there is a consensus concerning this particular issue, it is probably on that position taken by those in the middle.

RESPONSIBILITIES FOR PRESERVING
FREE MARKET INSTITUTIONS

Many observers have pointed out that there is nothing permanent about the institutions of the American economic system. These institutions have changed in the past and will be changed in the future, it is stated, unless businessmen discharge certain responsibilities. Some have declared that certain business firms have restricted economic opportunity and competition either by direct action to keep others out of markets or by the mere fact of their size. In some industries, such as the steel industry, the largest firms have been quite concerned that they do not become so large that they will be accused of restricting entry into the field or monopolizing the market. Although there is little suggestion that private property will be done away with, there is some indication that greater governmental interference in the markets will take place unless business acts with restraint.

RESPONSIBILITY FOR PRESERVING
ECONOMIC STABILITY

One characteristic of free markets is that the market price is free to fluctuate according to whatever influences are brought to bear in the market by buyers and sellers. What has happened in our recent past is that price changes in most markets have tended upward rather than fluctuated around a relatively stable equilibrium price. This has been a matter of concern to those on fixed incomes, to creditors, and to those who wish to see the United States in a better position to compete in foreign and world markets. Since so many prices are set by managers of firms, they are frequently urged by those in governmental and other influential positions not to raise prices even though their costs may be rising. Although many firms would like to disclaim responsibility for price movements, the fact that others hold them responsible gives them cause to pause and reflect on what their responsibilities really are.

Another aspect of economic stability is stability of output and employment. Unions especially criticize managements for adopting policies that lead to wide swings in production and hours of work. The automobile industry provides a good example: the institutionalization of the "annual model change" has resulted in periods of high employment for production workers during part of the year, but mass layoffs when production lines are being changed over for the new models. Although the United Auto Workers has sought to counter the effects of such business policies through demands for a "guaranteed annual wage," others have urged institutional changes that would make smoother the seasonal fluctuations in output and employment. Some firms have adopted measures that have had this effect, but there is apparently some difficulty in doing so throughout American business.

RESPONSIBILITY FOR PRESERVING HIGH OUTPUT AND EMPLOYMENT

Perhaps the most important responsibility of business, according to those who would assign certain responsibilities to it, is to produce goods and services in sufficient quantity to provide employment opportunities to all who would like to work. At one time it was thought that this question would not arise because there would always be jobs available at some wage rate. The Great Depression of the thirties shattered this belief —many were unemployed for long periods of time, with no jobs to be had at any wage. One result of this situation was governmental action in providing temporary jobs for those unable to find them in private business. Such development was viewed with alarm by some businessmen, and others felt that such governmental action would eventually result in a permanent change in the economic system if permitted to continue. The alternative, of course, is for business to provide enough jobs to make such governmental action unnecessary.

Such responsibility probably should not be assigned to business. Neither individual nor collective action by businessmen is likely to preserve purchasing power at a high level in the face of declining demand for products by consumers and government. At one time, it was thought that if prices were sufficiently flexible, price reductions would help keep output and employment at a high level. However, the experience of businessmen has been the contrary and during the depression of the 1930's, industrial prices were maintained even though sales, output and employment declined greatly. The Employment Act of 1946 recognizes that private action by business is not enough to achieve a stable level of output and employment at a high level and directs the federal government to employ its authority to attempt to solve this problem.

RESPONSIBILITY FOR PRESERVING
A GROWING ECONOMY

High private employment cannot be continued unless business expands rapidly enough to provide jobs for new entrants into the labor force. In the past the output of goods and services has been going up fast enough on the average—although there have been cyclical fluctuations—to require an expanding work force. Some view this development as almost too successful; they feel that the American economy has matured to the point where it can no longer continue to grow at the previously established rate. Under these alleged circumstances, a consequent proposal is that the federal government undertake new projects in order to absorb surplus manpower. This solution is unacceptable to many businessmen who would like to see business rather than government provide employment opportunities. If business is to do this, it means that businessmen must ask themselves what needs to be done to maintain past rates of economic growth and then take the necessary action. The problem is complicated considerably by the fact that productive efficiency needs to be increased in order to provide price stability and that in the past output per manhour (that is, productive efficiency) has been increased very effectively by the substitution of machines for men.

The problem of economic growth is further complicated by developments abroad. The Soviet Union and other industrial nations are expanding their economies at a faster rate than the American economy is growing (when measured by percentage increases in the gross national products of the various countries). As they become more industrialized, they become more formidable competitors of American business in world markets and they tend to have less need for the products of U.S. firms than during earlier stages of their industrial development. Although the United States may be a relatively mature industrial nation, it might profit by following some suggestions about what business might do to increase economic growth. It is urged that a labor policy suited to the maintenance of our international competitive position be adopted—that is, that wage increases by business be tied to increases in national productivity so that prices may be brought down in industries whose productivity is increasing rapidly. A problem, of course, in adopting such a policy is that labor might not stand for it in highly unionized industries. It has also been suggested that by improving management, costs can be brought down despite some increase in the cost of raw materials and labor. It is rather doubtful that businessmen are greatly concerned with lagging national economic growth or can be held responsible for it. Certainly they are concerned with increasing productivity in their particular firms, and to the extent that they are successful they will have done their part. Here again, a large part of the burden needs to be shouldered by government —a fact recognized by the federal government in recent years.

RESPONSIBILITY FOR BEATING THE COMMUNISTS ON THE ECONOMIC FRONT

In many ways, the struggle between the Communist world and the Western world is an economic contest. Since most Western nations, and particularly the United States, rely on private enterprise to perform most of the economic functions, it is up to American businessmen to outperform the Communists. Much hinges, it is declared, on their ability to do so. If economically uncommitted nations see that our way of economic life is superior to that of the opponents, we shall win them over to our side politically as well as economically, thereby enhancing our prospects of winning the larger struggle. If we cannot beat the opposition during a period of competitive coexistence, both the political and economic consequences, it is said, will be unacceptable to us. This contest involves more than growing more rapidly than the Soviet Union.

Part of the contest with the Communists concerns the acquisition of natural resources in foreign countries. In the nineteenth century, many European nations established colonies in foreign lands to gain control over the natural resources needed as raw materials for the industrial development of the imperial country. The United States did not engage in the building of empires to the extent that some European nations including Great Britain did. However, many American firms established branches abroad and engaged in other activity to acquire and develop the natural resources of certain nations, especially in Latin America. The Communists have charged that this is imperialistic exploitation and have encouraged revolutionary changes that may force American firms to discontinue doing business in certain parts of the world. The challenge to American businessmen in this case is to demonstrate that they serve the interests of the nation in which the natural resources are located better than can the Communists. Certainly American businessmen can prove that they have enabled some development to take place that would not have otherwise occurred or that would have taken place at a much slower rate. Whether this will meet the challenge is doubtful, as an analysis of developments in Latin America reveals.

Meeting the Communist challenge is not solely a job for business. With their great resources, the Soviet Union and its satellites are able to carry on economic, political, and propaganda campaigns with which no American business firm could be expected to compete. Although there are a number of ways in which American firms can demonstrate their adequacy —if not supremacy—in performing certain economic functions and their willingness and ability not to abuse their power in their overseas operations, support from the national government seems essential if business is to meet and beat the Communists on the economic front. Such assistance has been forthcoming; it will remain for the future historian to determine whether it has been adequate and timely.

RESPONSIBILITY FOR SOLVING
THE BALANCE-OF-PAYMENTS PROBLEM

Since World War II, the United States has seen an "adverse balance of payments" occurring in a number of years. That is, sales of American products abroad have not generated sufficient income to pay for American purchases overseas. This excess of purchases over sales has been paid for by gold out of U.S. money stock to a point where the amount of gold supporting American currency has dwindled to a level that has caused considerable concern to monetary authorities. Businessmen have been urged to help solve this problem by buying less overseas and by selling more in foreign markets. To such urging, they have responded to a degree. A cursory analysis of the balance-of-payment accounts, however, reveals that it is not business that has caused the problem (in which case its responsibility to solve it is not very well established). Rather it has been the military and foreign aid programs of the federal government that tip the balance from "favorable" to "adverse." Actually the export of goods and services by the private sector of our economy exceeds its imports. It is the fact that the federal government has been "buying" the friendship and alliances of foreign countries as well as purchasing facilities, supplies, and other products for military personnel overseas that has led to a situation in which our total overseas purchases exceed our foreign sales. To ask businessmen to cut back on foreign buying and to purchase more expensive inputs in the United States in order to solve this problem is to ask quite a bit, especially when, in many cases, American firms already are at a competitive disadvantage with foreign producers. Here again is a situation in which government and business action need to be combined to deal with an economic problem.

WHAT *ARE* THE ECONOMIC RESPONSIBILITIES OF BUSINESS?

Businessmen (as we have noted) are continually confronted by persons who declare that business has certain responsibilities and who usually add that businessmen have not properly discharged them. How *should* businessmen regard their economic responsibilities? A few benchmarks might help. A sound management principle states that authority must be equal to responsibility. In other words, if there is no authority—the rightful power to make decisions and take action—there is no responsibility. Very few business firms have, individually, the power to make all of the changes necessary to meet all of their responsibilities as others see them. Collective business action to do so would be contrary to some of our established economic, social, and political institutions. This does not mean that businessmen should not assume some of these responsibilities, but it should be recognized that businessmen do not always have the power to do so. They should ask themselves if they do have the authority, or if they *should* assume the authority to take the proposed action, before feeling responsible for attaining certain objectives. In situations in which their resources are inadequate or in which they do not have the right to act, they have little or no responsibility.

In addition to "outsiders" telling them what their duties are, businessmen themselves have been urging business generally to assume many of the responsibilities listed earlier. This may seem somewhat inconsistent in the light of the inability of most firms, individually, to have much influence. What is being urged is the voluntary action of businessmen to move in the same direction. This type of exhortation stems partly from the fear that if businessmen do not act, governments will—with a consequent change in our economic system.

In the previous discussion, we have concerned ourselves mostly with what the economic responsibilities of business *are not*, so we should briefly attempt to answer the question of what they really *are*. A guiding principle covering such conduct is, I think, the following: "Responsible behavior requires taking into account the interests of all affected parties in proportion to some measure of their interests." What this means, for business behavior specifically, is (1) determining the parties who are materially affected by a particular business action; (2) determining what the interests of those parties are; (3) determining the relative importance of their interests; and (4) taking action in accordance with the results of such analysis. Such action is never going to satisfy all parties. Never will all individuals and groups be convinced that a particular action is responsible. An observer of the administrative process has stated: "It is a thankless and discouraging task at best to undertake to serve so many interests, often conflicting and usually never satisfied." However, it is a task that must be undertaken by business administrators, and long-term business success hinges on its responsible performance.

What the above implies is that businessmen must concern themselves mainly with quite specific economic responsibilities and ignore those which they are without power or without authority to fulfill. In succeeding chapters, we shall examine some of the specific parties (individuals and groups inside and outside the markets) with whom businessmen have relations, the nature of the relationships, and the ways in which businessmen have attempted to come to terms—responsible and otherwise—with those parties. There are some individuals with whom business does not have direct economic relationships but who have an interest in what goes on in markets and the economy generally. These will also be studied because some of them—such as government officials—can exert strong influence on the development of the firm.

READING: The American Economy: Is it Growing Fast Enough? * by the Center of Information on America

We Americans, with considerable justification, are proud of the achievements of our economy. In spite of its ups and downs (including the disastrous Great Depression of the 1930's and the mild recessions of 1949, 1954, and 1958), production of the goods and services we desire has approximately doubled every 20 or 25 years over the course of the past century. Today our population of 178 million enjoys an average standard of living vastly higher than that of the previous generation of Americans and substantially in excess of that achieved anywhere else in the world.

With such a record behind us, it would be easy to be complacent—to be confident that our economy will continue to grow at a satisfactory pace and that its supremacy will remain unchallenged. Many Americans, however, are far from content with our recent economic record. They point with concern to the fact that our national output is increasing less rapidly than in certain previous periods

* Reproduced with special permission from *Vital Issues*, Vol. IX, No. 9 (May, 1960), published by the Center for Information on America, Washington, Connecticut.

and that the economy of the Soviet Union, our major competitor, is developing at a markedly faster rate than ours.

In recent months questions concerning our rate of economic growth have become matters of increasing public concern and controversy. The Joint Economic Committee of the Congress has sponsored extensive studies and conducted lengthy hearings in an attempt to assess the nature of the complex process in which our economy grows. Responsible leaders from many walks of life, including labor union officials, businessmen, economists, and educators, have had much to say concerning the adequacy of the recent rate of growth of the economy and the steps that may be required to improve it. And there are already indications that issues relating to economic growth will play a role in the forthcoming political campaigns.

In order to understand these issues, we must ask several questions: What is economic growth, and how is it measured? What has been the growth record of the American economy in recent years? What factors contribute to growth? Why is the rate of growth of our economy so important? What can be done to improve it?

What Is Growth?   Economic growth, in its broadest sense, refers to progress in satisfying our material needs and wants. As such, it has long been an important ingredient of "the American dream." Our national history has been characterized by economic expansion in many respects—in population, employment, income, stock of capital equipment, and in the range and size of the production of goods and services achieved.

Economists attempt to measure the growth of the economy with several measuring rods. One is the "gross national product," which is the sum total, for a given year, of the dollar value of all goods and services produced by both the private and public sectors of the economy. It is a tally which includes, accordingly, the total market value of all the food, clothing, and other consumer goods produced in a given year, the new houses, machinery, and factories constructed, and the services rendered by government in such diverse fields as providing for our national defense, developing our resources, education, handling the mails, and so forth.

The gross national product, which is usually referred to as the "GNP," is normally expressed (as it is on the first line of Table I, below) in terms of the prices of the particular year or years under consideration. When comparing the GNP's of different years, therefore, it is important to recognize that a part of any difference noted may be the consequence not of changes in the amounts of goods and services produced, but rather of changes in the purchasing power of the dollar. The GNP of $100 billion in 1940, for example, is stated in terms of the value of the dollar of that year, when it could purchase, on the average, somewhat more than twice what a dollar will buy today. To get at real changes in the output of our economy, the effect of price variations must be eliminated in the figures employed. This may be accomplished through a restatement of the GNP's for various years in terms of the prices, or value of the dollar, in a single base year (In line two of Table I and in Table II, we have chosen present-day, 1960 prices). This second, more useful indicator of economic growth we may call the "real gross national product," or "real GNP."

In comparing the output of the economy at different periods of time, we must remember that many important factors in addition to prices may also have undergone change. Of particular bearing on the degree of economic progress achieved will be any changes in population which may have taken place over the period in question. In order to take such changes into account in evaluating the growth record, it will often be helpful to turn to figures expressing real gross national product in per capita terms. Statistics on real GNP per capita readily indicate the degree to which growth in output has kept pace with, or exceeded, the rate of population increase.

Table I. The Growth of GNP, 1929–60 *

	1929	1933	1940	1950	1960 *
GNP ($ billions)	104	56	100	284	490
Real GNP ($ billions at 1960 prices)	203	141	230	356	490
Real GNP per capita ($)	1,680	1,130	1,740	2,360	2,810

* Figures derived from *Economic Report of the President*, January 1960; 1960 figures estimated.

Table II. Fluctuations in GNP Since World War II *

(Real GNP in $ billions, at 1960 prices)

1945	$360	1953	$417
1946	316	1954	409
1947	316	1955	442
1948	328	1956	451
1949	328	1957	459
1950	356	1958	449
1951	385	1959	479
1952	399	1960	490 *

* Figures derived from *Economic Report of the President*, January 1960; 1960 figure estimated.

Many other measurements of economic progress and well-being are employed in assessing the record of economic growth. Figures on average personal or family income, or disposable income (after taxes), and statistics concerning wage rates, profits, and new investment in factories and equipment are often cited. None of these measures satisfied every need, and none takes into account all of the components of economic progress. All of those mentioned, for example, fail to reflect the reduction of the average work week in recent decades (from an estimated 63 hours in 1880, to 46 hours in 1920, and approximately 40 hours today), and the corresponding increase in leisure time which the American worker is free to enjoy. Nor do these statistics pay heed to the degree of individual freedom present in the economy to which they refer. Nonetheless, if one is prepared to recognize their shortcomings, these measuring rods can provide helpful guides in assessing how well our economy is doing.

Our Recent Growth Record.   Examination of these two tables, and review of the studies recently prepared for the Joint Economic Committee, permit us to make three important observations concerning our growth record:

First, the general trend of the economy has been markedly upward. Over the past several decades real GNP has increased at an average (compounded) rate of approximately 3% per year. Taking population increases into account, real GNP per capita has risen, on the average, approximately 1.6% per year. Also worthy of note is an average annual increase in productivity, or output per man-hour worked, of approximately $2\frac{1}{2}\%$, although this has been very unevenly distributed over the various sectors of the economy (being much higher, for example, in agriculture and many parts of manufacturing industry than in construction and services).

Second, the rate of growth of output has been uneven over time—with very little growth, and even declines in output, in periods of recession. Postwar recessions have been very mild, to be sure, in contrast with the Depression of the 1930's, but they have resulted in 12–15 month interruptions in the upward trend of economic activity on three separate occasions since the end of World War II.

Third, the postwar rate of expansion of output has been somewhat less rapid than it was in certain previous periods, and is significantly lower than that of the Soviet Union (whose real GNP is reliably estimated to be mounting at an annual rate of 7–9%, in contrast with our own 3% rate). Much of the explanation of these differences is to be found in the fact that we are now a wealthy and highly developed nation, and that a large part of the expansion which occurs in response to consumers' preferences in our economy is in those sectors (especially services) in which substantial increases in productivity are very unlikely or, at best, difficult to achieve. The lagging postwar growth rate is also attributed in part, by some observers, to the setbacks of the recessions of 1949, 1954, and 1958.

There is widespread disagreement as to how the recent record should be interpreted. It is probably fair to say, however, that the record is neither as bad as it is made out to be by some critics of current governmental policies nor as good as might be hoped for.

Factors Affecting Growth.   Economic growth is a reflection of the effective performance and expansion of many diverse parts of the economy. The amount of growth realized, as one might expect, is dependent on many different, but interrelated, factors.

The level of output depends, first of all, on the size of the population (or, more precisely, the employed portion of the labor force). Growth in output, therefore, may simply reflect an increase in the *quantity* of labor employed. As we all are aware, however, the value of output produced per hour worked is far from uniform among different types of labor, with varying degrees of skill. Accordingly, increases in output may also be the result of improvements in the *quality* of labor utilized—in the health of the labor force, and the degree of education and special skills brought to the job.

The amount which each of us is able to produce also depends in large measure on the nature of the machines and tools with which we work. Much of the growth of output achieved over the course of recent decades in the United States can be traced to a marked increase and improvement in the mechanization and "automation" of the economy. The degree of mechanization realized, of course, is dependent in turn on the development of technology and on the existence of a climate in which those who contemplate investing their money in new factories, machines, and equipment can expect a reasonable rate of profit, or return, on their investment.

In any attempt to explain the growth and successes of the American economy, one must also cite the importance of our political system, and its emphasis on individual freedom and decentralized economic initiative. The growth of our economy is a consequence of the activities of vast numbers of individuals and business firms, each pursuing, within the framework of the law and a degree of public regulation, the profits to be found in an enlarged scale of output.

One must also remember that economic growth is dependent on the workings of the public as well as the private sector of the economy. Government activities in such fields as education, research, development of resources, highways, and public health—to name only a few—have a direct bearing on the capacity of the whole economy to expand.

In even a skeletal listing, such as this, of the factors contributing to growth, one further point must be noted. At certain times the answer to the question, "How much growth?" will be determined not by the *supply* of labor, machinery, inventiveness, and skills, but rather by the extent of the market or *demand* for the goods and services that might be produced. Concern over the absence of markets, which mounts in periods of recession, can result in contractions of output and new investment, and in corresponding reductions or temporary halts in the rate of growth. In recent years the maintenance of appropriate levels of demand or spending in the economy as a whole has increasingly been recognized to be a major responsibility of the monetary and fiscal authorities of the Federal Government. The task assigned to these authorities is by no means simple, nor is it unimportant, for excessive demand or spending (by consumers, investors, and government together) may result in inflation, while inadequate spending will produce or protract recessions and result in lagging economic growth.

The Importance of Growth.   We all have a tremendous stake in the rate at which our economy grows. Unless our output of goods and services increases very substantially in future years, our rapidly rising population will be accompanied by a declining level of consumption per capita. The continuing improvement of our standard of living, which we have all come to expect, is dependent on our achieving a rate of expansion of output greater than that required to offset our mounting population. What not many years ago would have been thought of as an unattainable miracle—an average family income level of $7,000 a year, after taxes—is not only possible but likely to be achieved within ten or twelve years, *if* we can maintain the rate of growth which we have experienced so far this century.

Continued economic growth, moreover, would permit us, in the near future, to eliminate, or at least substantially improve conditions in, many of the troubling "pockets of poverty" or "gaps in our prosperity" which are rightly matters of deep concern for a society of our degree of affluence. The futures of the one-fifth of American families whose incomes are currently less than $2,500 a year will be very much affected by the degree of success realized in expanding our economy.

Also at stake as our future rate of growth is determined is the image of the United States among the uncommitted nations. Part of the communist economic challenge, and of the appeal of communist economic methods in underdeveloped countries, lies in the outstanding growth record of the Soviet economy. Unless our economy, too, continues to display a creditable record of economic growth, our political and economic system, with its emphasis on the role of individual initiative and private enterprise, may be discredited in large portions of the world.

The amount of growth achieved by our economy over the course of the next decade will also have an important bearing on the likelihood of our meeting the challenges we face as a nation in the areas of defense and foreign assistance. An expanding economy will permit the resources which may be required for high-priority defense and foreign assistance projects to be channeled into such uses without the necessity of a cutback in the levels of private consumption. Should we fail to grow rapidly, however, we might well be faced with the difficult and unhappy situation of being able to meet our national security and foreign assistance commitments only through a curtailment of our living standard.

What Can Be Done to Promote Growth? Prescriptions for accelerating the rate of economic growth in the United States fall under as many different headings as there are factors at work in the process by which the economy grows. Although the relative importance of the different proposals is open to debate and the urgency with which they are advocated will vary according to the degree of dissatisfaction with the recent record of the economy, steps to promote growth must be considered in each of the following areas:

Developing Human Resources. The functioning of a complex economy like ours is increasingly dependent on the education and skills of the work force. Individuals whose talents are not fully developed because of poor or insufficient schooling will fail to realize their potentials as productive members of our society. While great advances have already been achieved in both the extent and quality of educational opportunities open to the average American, much remains to be done in this field. During the next decade, according to many independent studies of our educational needs, an extraordinary expansion of our educational system at all levels—grade schools and high schools, and colleges, universities, and professional and technical schools—will be required. Many difficult issues will have to be faced in finding ways of filling our needs for teachers of high quality and financing educational expansion.

A healthier population is also a more productive one, and anything that can be done to step up the rate of advances in medicine will promote the growth of our economy. Improvements in housing, particularly in areas of "metropolitan blight," also merit a place on our agenda for developing our human resources for growth.

Developing Our Material Resources. As our economy expands, our needs for raw materials, for power, water, and other resources can be expected to mount at a rapid rate. Heavy demands will also be placed on our transportation and communication systems. Both private industry and government face massive tasks in these areas if the requirements of a growing economy are to be met.

Research and Technology. Advances achieved in the laboratories of both industry and government are crucially important in improving productivity and contributing to the growth of output. Increased efforts in training scientists, efficiently organizing research activity, and making effective use of laboratory findings will be richly repaid in expanded output.

Preserving a Sound and Competitive Enterprise System. We have previously noted the importance of competitive enterprise and individual initiative in explaining the past achievements of our economy. We must remain on guard in the future to be sure that a climate conducive to vigorous competition is maintained. In particular, our system of taxes, which have assumed increasing magnitudes in recent years, must be critically examined, and if necessary reformed, to ensure that it works to promote rather than stifle incentives and competitive forces.

Stabilizing the Economy. High on the list of major objectives of economic policy are three related goals: maintaining high levels of employment, preventing inflation, and achieving a rapid rate of growth. As is amply demonstrated by the price increases and recessions which have occurred since World War II, the continued and simultaneous achievement of these objectives isn't easy to realize. Of great importance in determining our growth record in the future will be the degree of success accorded our efforts to prevent, or at least to reduce, the length and magnitude of recessions. Difficult problems must be anticipated, in that some of the measures which might be adopted in combatting recession involve at least the risk of contributing to rising prices.

Other Measures. Many additional policies for promoting growth might also be cited. Steps to increase the mobility of labor out of geographical areas or industries of low productivity into other employment where productivity is higher will accelerate the rate of growth. And both the increased markets and the increased competition for domestic producers associated with an expansion of international trade would serve as a stimulus to growth.

The responsibility for a growing economy, as this brief list of measures readily indicates, is widely shared. Each of us has a role to play in determining what our future economic growth rate shall be.

SUGGESTED READINGS

Fenn, Dan H., Jr., ed., *Management in a Rapidly Changing Economy* (New York: McGraw-Hill, 1958). A collection of papers given at a national business conference on changes in the economy and their implication for business.

Malik, C. H., "Job for the Businessman," *Fortune* (November 1958). The author, a Lebanese diplomat and one-time president of the United Nations General Assembly, calls on the U.S. to be more versatile if it is to compete with the economic challenge presented by communism.

Ferry, W. H., *The Corporation and the Economy* (Santa Barbara: Center for the Study of Democratic Institutions, 1959). A discussion of how the corporation can best fulfill its economic mission.

The Social
Environment
of Business

AMERICAN SOCIETY FROM THE BUSINESSMAN'S PERSPECTIVE

In discussing the markets in which American businessmen buy and sell, we noted the presence in those markets of various categories of individuals and groups. These social classes are important to business mainly because of the economic roles they play; however, they sometimes take other kinds of social action—such as political action—which are of significance to the American businessman. In addition, there are some classes of individuals and groups in American society with which businessmen have no important economic relations, but which also attempt to influence business activity through social action. Government agencies and officials are perhaps the most influential, although their activity tends to reflect the actions of other classes of individuals and groups in our society interested in influencing business. The great importance of government requires an extensive treatment, which will be undertaken in Part III of this volume; in this part we shall deal at some length with the nature of American society and its significance for business.

THE NATURE OF AMERICAN SOCIETY

Few words are given the variety of meanings that "society" has been given. Some philosophers, economists, and sociologists have used the term in many different ways, and others suggest that "society" is a useless generalization. To make clear what we mean when we use the term, we shall examine some of the ways in which it has been employed and indicate which of the meanings are and are not relevant to our purpose.

Views of Some Philosophers

Philosophers, especially, have advocated the idea that society is something more than a mere sum of its individual members and should be thought of as possessing independent reality. This conception goes back to Hobbes, Locke, Rousseau, Montesquieu, and other political philosophers concerned with the nature of the "state." The "body politic," according to such thinkers, has its own distinguishing characteristics, including interests that may be different from those of the individuals and groups making up the society. The intellectual heirs of these philosophers, including certain American politicians and others given to speaking in vague generalities, have held that there is a "common good," "general welfare," or "public interest" that has priority over the good, welfare, or interests of some of the individuals and groups making up American society. Such a view of the nature of society is of little value to the businessman because it provides no objective way of determining what "Society" is or what its interests are. He might take the word of some philosopher or politician as authoritative, but there are some good reasons for not doing so.

Not all philosophers hold such a view of society. John Dewey, for example, denied the usefulness of "society" as a generalizing idea because he believed it was devoid of meaning. To pose problems of relationships between the individual and society (such as the proper relation between the individual businessman and society) is as meaningless, he believed, as to make a problem out of the relationship of a letter of an alphabet to the alphabet. He saw society as being made up of a number of individuals and as being nothing more than this. This view, shared by some others, regards society as a plurality of individuals entering into relations of contract for the promotion of their own personal interests. Although businessmen and social scientists might regard this view as being more realistic, it is still not very helpful because for some it carries the implication that to understand American society it is necessary to understand the characteristics of the individuals who make it up. No one could reasonably expect to understand the unique characteristics of each individual in America, although there are ways of dealing with some commonly held characteristics of Americans.

National Character

Some students of society have boldly asserted that there is such a thing as "national character" and that by discovering what it is, the commonly held characteristics of individuals in that nation, and hence the character of that society, will be known. The classic example is Alexis de Tocqueville's study of democracy in America originally published in the 1830's. Greatly impressed by differences between American society and European society, the young French visitor attributed these differences mainly to the "general equality of condition" (democracy) that prevailed in America. It was this essential democracy that seemed to him to be the striking characteristic of the American social condition and one that explained a number of other characteristics of American society. Even today there are some scholars who believe that the idea of "national character" is a useful one, although (as the reading—Historians and National Character—at the end of this chapter will show) there is some considerable disagreement as to what traits are characteristically American.

The Class Nature of Society

Nowadays not all students of society are fully convinced that it is possible to determine traits characteristic of all or even a majority of individuals in the nation or that if it were possible to do so, these would be of as great importance as are the differences among classes of individuals and groups. In other words, it is more usual (and more useful for a number of purposes), some believe, to classify the individuals making up American society and to try to determine the characteristics of those classes.

THE MARXIST VIEW OF SOCIAL CLASS.   The outstanding example of the use of the concept of social class by an economist is that of Karl Marx's. In broad outline, Marx's theory asserted that in the course of making a living in industrialized societies, the members of society become segregated into classes that carry on different functions in industry and therefore occupy different positions in that society. Between such classes, according to Marx, there inevitably arises an antagonism of interests and a consequent class struggle. Although some present students of society agree that society has a class nature, they hasten to point out that they are not Marxists and that Marx had a quite restricted and erroneous view of the class nature of society. For example, it is noted that Marx believed that society consisted solely of economic classes that were concerned only with their economic class interests, that violent class conflict was inevitable, and that one class—the proletariat—could emerge victorious and establish a classless society. Modern believers in the "pluralistic" nature of society point out that there are many classes in society based on other than economic foundations, that conflict among classes is not inevitable (that is, they believe in the possibility and probability of conciliation and compromise), and that society will continue to be composed of social classes.

Sociologists' Views of Social Class.   When sociologists discuss the class structure of America, they are usually concerning themselves with socioeconomic classes. In their studies of individuals in various parts of the United States, they have perceived stratifications in American society. They point out that the individuals studied also regarded themselves as falling into roughly three classes: lower, middle, and upper. By studying the different characteristics of such classes, sociologists feel they have something more meaningful to say than those who talk about national character (which implies that all individuals in a nation share common characteristics).

In addition to a "horizontal" classification of individuals into socioeconomic classes, sociologists also make "vertical" classifications. Such groupings separate individuals in a society according to their race, religion, national origin, or a number of other characteristics other than socioeconomic status. Such groupings, when combined with socioeconomic classifications, make for a much greater number of social categories, and some distinctions can be discovered—for example, between the characteristics of upper-class Catholics and of lower-class Protestants.

Despite the greater utility in determining the characteristics of society achieved by horizontal and vertical analysis of the social structure, such studies still do not adequately serve the businessman in understanding society as it confronts him. Such analysis *is* of help in determining something of the nature of the market for which he is producing—for example, knowledge of the characteristics of the upper class is helpful if he is producing expensive items aimed at those with higher incomes. Too, recent studies of the "Negro market" point up the relevance of knowledge of ethnic groups to business. It might be added that ethnic groups are important to the businessman outside the marketplace, as the picketing, boycotts, and "sit-ins" by individuals and groups of "the Negro movement" amply demonstrate. Still, more frequent usage by the businessman of a somewhat rough-and-ready classification of the individuals with whom he comes into contact reveals that the data of his experience do not fit into the categories we have been discussing. Businessmen regard people as, for example, customers, suppliers, union members, government officials, competitors, or as falling in a host of other classifications that do not result from the sociologists' horizontal and vertical analysis of society.

The Group Nature of Society

Some sociologists have suggested other ways in which society might be viewed that correspond more closely to the view of the businessman. Herbert Blumer has said:

> A society has an organization. It is not a mere aggregation of disparate individuals. A human society is composed of diverse kinds of functional groups. In our American society illustrative instances of functional groups are a corporation, a trade association, a labor union, an ethnic group, a farmers' organization. To a major extent, our total collective life is made up of the actions and acts of such groups. These groups are oriented in different directions because of special interests.[1]

Others agree that American society is an associational society or a "mosaic of sub-cultures." Since the values that individuals hold are largely determined by their group membership and culture, there is in America a variety of groups, each of which has members holding values different from, and sometimes in conflict with, those of another group. A political scientist who has developed an essentially sociological theory of politics has stated:

> The chief social values cherished by individuals in modern society are realized through groups. The number is countless and the variety of these social groupings is abundant and complex. No aspect of the life of the individual is untouched by them. Modern man is literally conducted from the cradle to the grave by groups, for he is born in a family, goes to school in organized classes, goes to church (perhaps), plays with boyhood gangs, joins fraternities, works for a corporation, belongs to various associations—cultural, civic, professional and social—and is carried off to his immortal reward by a business enterpriser with the solemnity appropriate to such ceremonies.[2]

[1] Herbert Blumer, "Public Opinion and Public Opinion Polling," *American Sociological Review*, Vol. 13 (1948), p. 544.
[2] Earl Latham, *The Group Basis of Politics* (Ithaca, N.Y.: Cornell U.P., 1952), p. 1.

As Latham notes, such groups are countless and in order to deal with them in a general way we must classify them (although it should be noted that the business firm deals with a limited number of groups and is able to determine the relevant characteristics of the specific groups with which it is in contact). Our concern, then, will be with classes of individuals and groups in American society with which business firms have quite direct dealings.

The classification scheme we shall employ is not a comprehensive one—not all of American society will fit into the classes we shall establish. This is not a major problem, however, because we are interested only in those classes that influence business activity in some fashion. By placing individuals and groups with common interests and objectives in one category, we can generalize about them so as to give a realistic view of society as the businessman sees it.

INDIVIDUALS AND GROUPS IN THE BUSINESS ENVIRONMENT

Some categories of individuals and groups have fairly continuous economic relationship with business. Among these are customers and customer groups, owners, creditors, employees and unions, other suppliers, and competitors and trade associations. Also, there are some business groups such as chambers of commerce interested in business activity on local, state, regional, national, and international levels. These business associations have only limited economic relationships with business firms, but exert influence of other kinds.

Other individuals and groups perform functions that are essentially noneconomic, but the pursuit of their goals by the parties involved has, nonetheless, an impact on business. Among these are writers, operating through various communications media, who have some influence on beliefs about business. Cartoonists also have had some impact on the "public image" of business. Intellectuals of various kinds have had differing influences on business. In this classification we find philosophers, preachers, professors, and others who feel that they are in a position to state the ideal nature of the social condition and to pronounce moral judgments about existing conditions, including the way in which business operates. There are community groups that have certain goals and make demands on business to help them attain those goals. Government agencies and officials directly and indirectly influence firms. Last, but certainly not least, are politicians and political parties. (See Figure 1–1 which shows the important categories of individuals and groups confronting the firm.)

THE FIRM'S RELATIONS WITH SOCIETY

These individuals and groups are important to business for two reasons: their goals are sometimes in conflict with the attainment of the goals of business, and they have resources with which to attempt to secure their goals. The extreme view held by Karl Marx and his followers is that industrial society inevitably becomes segregated into classes having antagonistic interests and that a continuous struggle of classes will take place until a classless society is achieved. There are other possible kinds of relationships between business and other social groups, however, and class warfare is not necessarily a consequence of incompatible aims. That is, accommodation, cooperation, and even assimilation are possible.

The Undesirability of Conflict

The reason that conflict relationships are undesirable is fairly obvious. A business firm is attempting to reach a certain goal or goals. When it is confronted by a group striving to reach an opposing goal, business can reach its objective(s) only with greater difficulty than if it were unopposed—if it can reach them at all. Recall that the general social principle previously referred to as "Walton's Law" states: "The results of any social interaction depends on the objectives and resources of the parties, and the way in which the resources are managed." The significance of this self-evident proposition for conflict situations is clear: when parties with objectives in conflict with those of a business firm have sufficient resources and manage them well, they can strongly influence the degree to which that firm can reach its objectives and the ease with which it does so. Not all conflict relationships can be avoided, in which case a firm may try to do something about the relative resources of the other party in order that it may emerge victorious from the conflict. However, it is sometimes possible to structure some other kind of relationship.

Ways of Avoiding Conflict

The major ways in which conflict relationships can be changed to more desirable relations are through accommodation, cooperation, and assimilation. Accommodation refers to the structuring of arrangements under which parties whose goals are in conflict do not change their objectives but agree to an arrangement by which they can function without open warfare. Some union-management agreements are of this sort; they are more in the nature of a "truce" rather than the giving up of fundamental aims that are in conflict. In some cases in which it is possible to substitute compatible objectives for those in conflict, cooperation can replace conflict. There are some union-management relationships that are cooperative because both parties are in pursuit of the same object or see that a certain line of action will help them to reach their different, but harmonious, objectives. In some circumstances, individuals and groups who are involved in some kind of relationship can come to share the same sentiments, values, and goals—the process of assimilation—and conflict disappears. In business relationships, assimilation would require a firm either to change its objectives or to get other parties to change theirs, or both.

COMING TO TERMS WITH THE SOCIAL ENVIRONMENT

The record of American business amply illustrates the necessity of taking into account influential groups in the social environment of business. Customer dissatisfaction brought about a movement for government regulation of the railroads in the latter part of the nineteenth century—a movement leading to ever-increasing governmental controls. Owners have on occasion staged "stockholders' revolutions" and have thrown out managements with which they were dissatisfied. Creditors have sometimes taken similar action or have sought a greater voice in management when their objectives have not been attained. The growth of the ability of labor unions to influence the operation of business needs no elaboration. The activities of competitors have brought many firms to the edge of bankruptcy and have frequently pushed them over the brink. Less immediate has been the impact of writers, cartoonists, philosophers, ministers, and college professors, whose main influence has been to shape public opinion toward business. When they have created an "unfavorable image," such adverse public sentiment has, on occasion, supported economic, social, and political action hostile to business. At times, groups in the community in which a firm does business have turned hostile when they feel that their interests are being adversely affected by the behavior of that firm.

To come to terms with important social classes—through conflict, accommodation, cooperation, or assimilation—certain steps are necessarily taken. First of all, it is necessary to identify them. This is usually a simple matter because individuals and groups important to the management of a firm normally bring themselves to the attention of the manager(s). Second, it is necessary to identify their objectives, together with some estimate of their relative importance. Identification of objectives is not an easy matter, since quite frequently the stated objectives of individuals and groups are not their real objectives, or the objectives of the leaders of a group may not be those of the membership (as is sometimes said to be true in labor unions). Third, it is useful to have some idea of the resources of the individuals and groups in question and of how much of these they are willing to commit to the attainment of their various objectives. This too is difficult to determine; in fact, some firms, in the past, even resorted to hiring spies to ferret out such information, especially with respect to labor unions and competitors. Finally, it is necessary to know something about the lines of action open to individuals and groups in contact with the firm and what action they are likely to take. In practice, a firm needs such information about every important individual and group with which it has dealings, and the information it acquires will be quite specific to them. We shall, in succeeding chapters, examine certain important individuals and groups and look at certain useful generalizations concerning their identity, objectives, resources, and lines of action.

After information has been secured on the various groups in contact with business, important decisions need to be made. If conflict seems inevitable, the firm may want to increase its resources relative to the opposition. This would be done in the expectation of winning out. Where there seems little to be secured in open conflict, a firm may wish to establish some sort of accommodation. Sometimes there may be some promise in attempting to get others to change their objectives, leading to cooperation or even assimilation. It may well be that the managers of a firm may wish to change some of their own more immediate objectives, although still retaining certain long-run goals. The action any firm may wish to take depends on the specific situation, of course, but it might properly be pointed out that in the past, little of lasting value has been gained for business through conflict. Many important social issues have been decided against business, and although it has sometimes won "battles" it has frequently lost the "wars." Consequently, business firms now are turning more toward accommodation, cooperation, and assimilation with the hope that their basic objectives may be more adequately secured by such action.

If business firms are going to attempt to change the objectives of opposing parties, some knowledge of the way in which opinions are formed is necessary. Some studies of the opinion of the general public with respect to business have been made. These will be examined in some detail in Chapter 20, but it is in order to point out here that general public opinion with respect to business generally is of little significance to any specific business firm. As we have indicated in the discussion above, a firm is confronted with a number of social categories or "publics." It is the opinion of a specific influential "public" toward it that a firm must concern itself with, and not with views of the general public toward business.

In part, attitudes toward business have a psychological basis in the personalities of individuals; more important, however, are the cultural and social bases of the attitudes of members of a particular group. The various bases of public opinion will also be examined in some detail in Chapter 20, but it should be noted here that one result of such an examination will be the conclusion that objectives of other groups (which are based on attitudes, in part) are difficult to change. If cooperation or assimilation is to take place, it may be necessary to change at least some of the more immediate objectives of the firm.

KINDS OF SOCIAL ACTION

The variety of activities of individuals and groups is great; fortunately, actions taken by those having some relationship with the business firm fall into a relatively small number of categories. Such activity is normally economic, political, legal, or "educational." There are other important actions, of course, although many of them are illegal or unethical. For example, individuals and groups having an interest in what a firm does may engage in "espionage" to discover certain business secrets; "labor piracy" may deprive a firm of some of its trusted employees; or, customers may use articles purchased (such as party dresses) and then demand a refund. However, the more important and usual activities are those previously named.

Economic Action

Those taking important economic action are buyers, sellers, competitors, and government. Individuals buy or refuse to buy, thus affecting the fortunes of the firm. Frequently groups purchase or refuse to buy, bringing to bear concentrated economic power. When, for example, a large number of consumers refuse to buy until a firm meets its terms, this boycott can have a pronounced effect on the firm's policies and upon the results of its operations. One big buyer can have a similar influence, as in 1962 when the federal government threatened to discontinue its purchases of steel from firms that had announced price increases regarded by the Kennedy administration as being unwarranted. Sellers, likewise, when they are important individual suppliers or when they organize, can bring their economic influence to bear upon the firm, thereby forcing it to adopt policies or affecting the results of its operations in ways other than would exist if this power was not wielded.

The economic roles played by governments go beyond buying and selling. Taxes on firms are important determinants of business policy and of the outcome of business operations. However, governments also provide direct and indirect subsidies to some firms. Too, governments are concerned with maintaining a favorably "economic climate" for firms falling within their jurisdictions. For example, the federal government, through its controls over money and credit and through its taxing and spending policies, attempts to bring about economic growth and prosperity.

Sometimes private groups ask contributions of businessmen. Since they usually assert that such contributions of money, goods, or services should be made by corporations as "good corporate citizens," such contributions are similar to tax payments, although no legal power exists by which such contributions can be exacted involuntarily. Such claims are growing in importance, but as yet are a relatively unimportant kind of economic activity.

Competitors sometimes compete and sometimes cooperate. The nature of the competitive action adopted by competitors strongly influences the behavior of a firm. When competitors cooperate (in such matters as advertising, selling, or buying), their economic power is added to that of the firm, enabling it to reach its objectives with greater ease. The specific kinds of action taken by competitors (as well as that of buyers and sellers) and their impact on the firm will be discussed in Chapters 13–17.

Political and Legal Action

By political action, we mean attempts to influence public policy and its administration. Many groups, when their economic power is limited but their political resources are substantial, will attempt to secure their objectives through favorable legislation or through favorable administration of existing laws. Securing desired statutes and friendly administration of the laws may lead groups into activity aimed at influencing elections. Also, because the administration of the laws is partly in the hands of the courts, some actions are aimed directly or indirectly at influencing judicial decisions.

The existence of certain laws and the court system makes it possible for individuals or groups to initiate (or to threaten to initiate) law suits, to defend against suits, and to delay final court decisions. Such actions are quite usual in conflict relationships because violence is frowned upon and the parties in conflict are normally obliged to conduct their contest in the political arena or in the courts. The nature of law in the U.S. and the American court system will be examined in considerable detail in Part III, as will be the other aspects of the governmental and political processes.

"Educational" Action

Education generally concerns itself with attempts to influence knowledge, attitudes, and/or skills of individuals. Except for groups engaged in formal education, few of those confronting business firms are concerned with developing skills of those whom they are attempting to "educate." Instead they are usually concerned with presenting information favorable to their cause or with structuring desired attitudes through "information" or "propaganda" campaigns. This action is rarely aimed directly at the firm; more frequently it is directed toward other individuals and groups in a position to influence the firm.

CONCLUSIONS

Business firms cannot, except at their peril, ignore society. In order to achieve their objectives, they must come to some sort of terms with various influential individuals and groups in their environment. Some of these are organized and others are not, but in any case those in any one category have certain common objectives and also have resources with which to attempt to reach those objectives. Frequently the objectives of these classes are in conflict with those of the business firm. In order to avoid the consequences of conflict, it is necessary to do something about the objectives of the parties (including those of the business firm) to the social interaction. If conflict is inevitable, something needs to be done about the "balance of power." In any case, an investigation must be made of the objectives, resources, and lines of action of the classes with whom social relations are had. To such an investigation we shall next proceed.

Finally, since businessmen are inevitably involved in relationships with a number of individuals and groups, it is necessary for them to arrive at a social philosophy not unreasonably at odds with the interests of others. At the end of this Part, we shall deal in considerable detail with the question of what social responsibilities have been urged upon the businessman and what philosophy he ought to adopt.

READINGS: Various Views of the Nature of Society

[*The following readings illustrate different ideas held as to the nature of society. In the first, a Yale historian takes a look at how historians have employed the concept of "national character" and what they have regarded it as being. Next are some excerpts from De Tocqueville's book, indicating his view of the Ameri-*

can national character. Karl Marx was one of the earliest proponents of the idea of social class and made certain assertions concerning the class structure of industrial society and the outcome of what he regarded as the inevitable conflict between two classes of such societies. Although many students of society regard his views as being erroneous, they are presented here because they are important and provocative. His most influential follower, Nikolai Lenin, summarizes the views of Marx in a discussion of the class struggle. Finally a group of sociologists sets forth what it regards as being the true nature of social class in America, challenging the Marxian view in the process.]

Reading: Historians and National Character * by David M. Potter

The concept of national character, then, ranks as a major historical assumption and one which has colored the writing of a vast body of historical literature. It might be supposed that, in the case of such a basic concept, far-reaching attention would have been given to the rationale of the subject and that the idea would have been defined and elaborated with rigor and precision. Yet the fact is that historians have done very little either to clarify or to validate this concept which they employ so freely. The looseness with which the term "national character" is used and the inconsistent meanings which attach to it are striking evidence of the lack of adequate analysis. Because of these deficiencies, and especially because of the way in which the idea of national character got mixed up with doctrines of race, the entire concept has been called into very serious question, and it will be necessary, at a later point in this discussion, to examine this philosophical rejection of the concept. First, however, the inadequacies, the abuses, and the confusion in the use of the concept by historians need to be scrutinized.

The most basic ambiguity of all is that historians vary widely in their notion as to what constitutes national character. To some writers it implies an absolute quality, persisting without change from one generation to another and manifesting itself universally in all the individuals who compose the national group. To others it is little more than a statistical tendency for the individuals in one country at a particular time to evince a given trait in higher proportion than the individuals of some other country. This approach is essentially relativistic, and it contrasts with the absolute approach both in regarding national traits as changing responses to changing conditions and in regarding national character as something which may be found in a large enough proportion of the people (and which exists as national character, pragmatically, only because it is found in them) rather than as something which inheres in all the people (and is found in them, mystically, because it is the national character).

Despite the insight which Hippocrates and Herodotus had originally shown in recognizing that, if conditions determine character, character will change with conditions, it was unfortunately true that many later historical writers seemed to accept the absolute view, which ultimately found its most extreme expression in the early nineteenth century. Today it can no longer be taken seriously in its literal form, and we can only smile at such manifestations as Herder's assertion

* Reprinted with the publisher's permission from David M. Potter, *People of Plenty* (University of Chicago Press, 1954), pp. 8–11.

that the Teutonic vocal apparatus was naturally formed for the enunciation of German speech and that it would be a perversion for the Teutonic larynx to dally with any other language. But, in a more subtle form, the concept of a character which is shared in common by all people still commands impressive support. For instance, Otto Bauer has argued that national character is far more than a mere similarity of traits in diverse individuals and that it is, rather, a "community of character." Community of character, he contended, does not imply that individuals of the same nation will be similar to one another but that "the same force has acted on the character of each individual. . . . While . . . similarity of character can only be observed in the majority of the members of the nation, the community of character, the fact that they all are the products of one and the same effective force, is common to all of them without exception."

Many other writers whose view is far less carefully refined than Bauer's have held to the absolute point of view by setting up what Weber would have called "ideal typical" images to personify the character of given nations and then evaluating individual citizens according to the extent to which they correspond to these types. Thus John Bull remains the "typical Englishman," and the old-fashioned Yankee remains the "typical American" for many writers, despite the fact that the vast majority in the English and the American population do not now conform to these types, if, indeed, they ever did. In this case, there is no longer a mystical assertion that all Englishmen or all Americans are alike, but there is still an arbitrary assumption that specific qualities are peculiarly British or American and that the extent to which an individual is truly British or American depends upon the extent to which he possesses these qualities.

Against these fixed notions of national character, the few critics who concern themselves with the subject have made such headway as they can. Writers like Hans Kohn and Carlton J. H. Hayes have shown clearly that traits which are deemed more intrinsic to the "character" of a nation will change markedly and rapidly as historical circumstances change. Thus at the beginning of the eighteenth century the English were considered volatile and unstable in political affairs, while the French seemed steady and even phlegmatic by comparison. But a century later these conceptions had been reversed, and it was the French who were regarded as political weathercocks. Other writers have accepted the idea that traits of national character are essentially tendencies which ebb and flow with the waxing and waning of historical forces. For instance, Frederick Jackson Turner conceived of American traits as developing under the impact of frontier forces, and he spoke with foreboding of what would happen to these traits when the frontier no longer existed to perpetuate them.

But, though many historians have adopted these more tenable concepts of what constitutes national character, most of them have done so implicitly, without much discussion of their premises, and the fact remains that there is no agreement, no uniform understanding, within the profession, as to what is meant by "national character" or as to what elements go to make it up.

Not only have historians failed to agree on what they mean by "national character," they have also failed to agree on what kind of qualities should be taken into account as composing it.

Reading: The Democratic Character of America ° *by Alexis de Tocqueville*

Amongst the novel objects that attracted my attention during my stay in the United States, nothing struck me more forcibly than the general equality of condition among the people. I readily discovered the prodigious influence which this primary fact exercises on the whole course of society; it gives a peculiar direction to public opinion, and a peculiar tenor to the laws; it imparts new maxims to the governing authorities, and peculiar habits to the governed.

I soon perceived that the influence of this fact extends far beyond the political character and the laws of the country, and that it has no less empire over civil society than over the government; it creates opinions, gives birth to new sentiments, founds novel customs, and modifies whatever it does not produce. The more I advanced in the study of American society, the more I perceived that this equality of condition is the fundamental fact from which all others seem to be derived, and the central point at which all my observations constantly terminated. . . .

Gradually the distinctions of rank are done away; the barriers which once served mankind are falling down; property is divided, power is shared by many, the light of intelligence spreads, and the capacities of all classes are equally cultivated. The State becomes democratic, and the empire of democracy is slowly and peaceably introduced into the institutions and the manners of the nation. . . .

The time will therefore come, when one hundred and fifty millions of men will be living in North America, equal in condition, all belonging to one family, owing their origin to the same cause, and preserving the same civilization, imbued with the same opinions, propagated under the same forms. The rest is uncertain, but this is certain; and it is a fact new to the world, a fact which the imagination strives in vain to grasp.

Reading: Class Struggle † *by Nikolai Lenin*

That in any given society the strivings of some of the members conflict with the strivings of others; that social life is full of contradictions; that history discloses to us a struggle among peoples and societies, and also within each nation and each society, manifesting in addition an alternation between periods of revolution and reaction, peace and war, stagnation and rapid progress or decline—these facts are generally known. Marxism provides a clue which enables us to discover the reign of law in this seeming labyrinth and chaos: the theory of the class struggle. Nothing but the study of the totality of the strivings of all the members of a given society, or group of societies, can lead to the scientific definition of the result of these strivings. Now, the conflict of strivings arises from differences in the situation and modes of life of the classes into which society is divided.

The history of all human society, past and present (wrote Marx in 1848, in the *Communist Manifesto;* except the history of the primitive community,

° Excerpted from Alexis de Tocqueville, *Democracy in America,* Vol. I (Cambridge, Mass.: Sever and Francis, 1863), pp. 1, 9 and 558.

† Reprinted from Nikolai Lenin, *The Teachings of Karl Marx* (New York: International Publishers Co., Inc., 1937), pp. 18–19.

Engels added), has been the history of class struggles. Freeman and slave, patrician and plebeian, baron and serf, guild-burgess and journeyman—in a word, oppressor and oppressed—stood in sharp opposition each to the other. They carried on perpetual warfare, sometimes masked, sometimes open and acknowledged; a warfare that invariably ended either in a revolutionary change in the whole structure of society or else in the common ruin of the contending classes. . . . Modern bourgeois society, rising out of the ruins of feudal society, did not make an end of class antagonisms. It merely set up new classes in place of the old; new conditions of oppression; new embodiments of struggle. Our own age, the bourgeois age, is distinguished by this —that it has simplified class antagonisms. More and more, society is splitting up into two great hostile camps, into two great and directly contraposed classes: bourgeoisie and proletariat.

Since the time of the great French Revolution, the class struggle as the actual motive force of events has been most clearly manifest in all European history. During the Restoration period in France, there were already a number of historians (Thierry, Guizot, Mignet, Thiers) who, generalizing events, could not but recognise in the class struggle the key to the understanding of all the history of France. In the modern age—the epoch of the complete victory of the bourgeoisie, of representative institutions, of extended (if not universal) suffrage, of cheap daily newspapers widely circulated among the masses, etc., of powerful and ever-expanding organizations of workers and employers, etc.—the class struggle (though sometimes in a highly one-sided "peaceful," constitutional form), has shown itself still more obviously to be the mainspring of events. The following passage from Marx's *Communist Manifesto* will show us what Marx demanded of social sciences as regards an objective analysis of the situation of every class in modern society as well as an analysis of the conditions of development of every class.

Among all the classes that confront the bourgeoisie to-day, the proletariat alone is really revolutionary. Other classes decay and perish with the rise of large-scale industry, but the proletariat is the most characteristic product of that industry. The lower middle-class—small manufacturers, small traders, handicraftsmen, peasant proprietors—one and all fight the bourgeoisie in the hope of safeguarding their existence as sections of the middle class. They are, therefore, not revolutionary, but conservative. Nay, more, they are reactionary, for they are trying to make the wheels of history turn backwards. If they ever become revolutionary it is only because they are afraid of slipping down into the ranks of the proletariat; they are not defending their present interests, but their future interests; they are forsaking their own standpoint, in order to adopt that of the proletariat.

In a number of historical works Marx gave brilliant and profound examples of materialist historiography, an analysis of the position of each separate class, and sometimes of that of various groups or strata within a class, showing plainly why and how "every class struggle is a political struggle." The above quoted passage is an illustration of what a complex network of social relations and transitional stages between one class and another, between the past and the future,

Marx analyzed in order to arrive at the resultant of the whole historical development.

Reading: Social Class in America ° by W. Lloyd Warner, Marcia Meeker, and Kenneth Eells

Our great state papers, the orations of great men, and the principles and pronouncements of politicians and statesmen tell us of the equality of all men. Each school boy learns and relearns it; but most of us are dependent upon experience and indirect statement to learn about "the wrong side of the tracks," "the Gold Coast and the slums," and "the top and bottom of the social heap." We are proud of those facts of American life that fit the pattern we are taught, but somehow we are often ashamed of those equally important social facts which demonstrate the presence of social class. Consequently, we tend to deny them or, worse, denounce them and by so doing deny their existence and magically make them disappear from consciousness. We use such expressions as "the Century of the Common Man" to insist on our democratic faith; but we know that, ordinarily, for Common Men to exist as a class, un-Common superior and inferior men must also exist. We know that every town or city in the country has its "Country Club set" and that this group usually lives on its Gold Coast, its Main Line, North Shore, or Nob Hill, and is the top of the community's social heap. Most of us know from novels such ,as those of Sinclair Lewis of the Main Streets that run through all our towns and cities, populated by Babbitts or, more explicitly stated, by "the substantial upper-middle class;" and by now, thanks to another group of novelists such as Erskine Caldwell, we know there is a low road, a Tobacco Road, that runs not only by the ramshackle houses of the poor whites of the South, but by the tarpaper shanties of the slums and river bottoms or Goat Hills of every town and city in the United States.

The "superior people" of Marquand's New England, "the North Shore crowd," divided into a top level of "old families" with a set of values and a way of life rated above those of the "new families," are matched by Philadelphia's "Main Line" families in Christopher Morley's *Kitty Foyle* and by similar groups in many other novels which report on the dominance of "the upper clases" in all regions of the United States. Reading them, together with similar novels reporting on Suburbia and Main Street for the middle classes and those on the Tobacco Roads and the city slums for the lower levels, gives one the understanding that throughout the towns and cities of America the inhabitants are divided into status levels which are ways of life with definite characteristics and values. Talking to and observing the people of these communities demonstrate that they, too, know how real these status levels are, and they prove it by agreeing among themselves about the levels and who belongs to them in their particular city.

Although well aware of social class, social scientists have been more concerned with their theories and with quarreling among themselves about what social class is than with studying its realities in the daily lives of the people. Until recently, they have lagged behind the novelists in investigating what our classes are, how they operate in our social life, and what effect they have on our individual lives.

° Reprinted by permission of the author and the publisher, From *Social Class in America*, W. Lloyd Warner, Marcia Meeker, and Kenneth Eells (New York: Harper, 1949), pp. 5–10.

But recent scientific studies of social class in the several regions of the United States demonstrate that it is a major determinant of individual decisions and social actions; that every major area of American life is directly and indirectly influenced by our class order; and that the major decisions of most individuals are partly controlled by it. To act intelligently and know consciously how this basic factor in American life affects us and our society, it is essential and necessary that we have an explicit understanding of what our class order is, how it works, and what it does to the lives and personalities who live in it. Our most democratic institutions, including our schools, churches, business organizations, government, and even our family life, are molded by its all-pervading and exceedingly subtle but powerful influence.

The researches on social class in the several regions of the United States make it possible to fill in much of the missing knowledge necessary to give Americans such explicit understanding of social class and to answer some of the important questions we raise about it when adjusting to the realities of our existence. Reduced to their simplicities these questions are: What is social class? How are social classes organized? And how do they function in the individual and the community? How do we use such knowledge to adjust ourselves more satisfactorily to the world around us? What is the effect of class on buying and selling and other problems of business enterprise, on the problems of personnel, on school and education, on the church and religion, on the acceptance and rejection of the communications of mass media such as the radio, magazine, newspaper, and motion picture? And, above all, are there effective and simple techniques of studying and applying the social-class concept so that those who are not specialized class analysts can apply such knowledge to the practical problems of their business or profession or to the research problems of the scientist?

The answer to this last important question is "yes;" the answer to the others will be found in this volume. The authors believe that they present a sufficient description here of how to do these things to enable interested people to deal with problems arising from social class. They recognize that further refinement is necessary and that modifications and improvements will have to be made, but the fundamental elements are now known sufficiently well to provide this set of instructions adequate to the identification and measurement of social class in America. Most of the book—all chapters between this and the last—will deal specifically with these instructions.

The Structural Imperative—Why We Have a Class System.   The recognition of social class and other status hierarchies in this country comes as no surprise to students of society. Research on the social life of the tribes and civilizations of the world clearly demonstrates that some form of rank is always present and a necessity for our kind of society.

Just as students of comparative biology have demonstrated that the physical structure of the higher animals must have certain organs to survive, so students of social anthropology have shown that the social structures of the "higher," the more complex, societies must have rank orders to perform certain functions necessary for group survival.

When societies are complex and service large populations, they always possess some kind of status system which, by its own values, places people in higher or lower positions. Only the very simple hunting and gathering tribes, with very small populations and very simple social problems, are without systems of rank; but when a society is complex, when there are large numbers of individuals in it pursuing diverse and complex activities and functioning in a multiplicity of ways, individual positions and behaviors are evaluated and ranked. This happens primarily because, to maintain itself, the society must co-ordinate the efforts of all its members into common enterprises necessary for the preservation of the group, and it must solidify and integrate all these enterprises into a working whole. In other words, as the division of labor increases and the social units become more numerous and diverse, the need for co-ordination and integration also increases and, when satisfied, enables the larger group to survive and develop.

Those who occupy co-ordinating positions acquire power and prestige. They do so because their actions partly control the behavior of the individuals who look to them for direction. Within this simple control there is simple power. Those who exercise such power either acquire prestige directly from it or have gained prestige from other sources sufficiently to be raised to a co-ordinating position. For example, among many primitive peoples a simple fishing expedition may be organized so that the men who fish and handle each boat are under the direction of one leader. The efforts of each boat are directed by the leader and, in turn, each boat is integrated into the total enterprise by its leader's taking orders from his superior. The same situation prevails in a modern factory. Small plants with a small working force and simple problems possess a limited hierarchy, perhaps no more than an owner who bosses all the workers. But a large industrial enterprise, with complex activities and problems, like General Motors, needs an elaborate hierarchy of supervision. The position in a great industrial empire which integrates and co-ordinates all the positions beneath it throughout all the supervising levels down to the workers has great power and prestige. The same holds true for political, religious, educational, and other social institutions; the more complex the group and the more diverse the functions and activities, the more elaborate its status system is likely to be. We will amplify this point later.

The studies of other societies have demonstrated one other basic point: the more complex the technological and economic structure, the more complex the social structure; so that some argue (the Marxians and many classical economists) that technological advancement is the cause of social complexity and all class and status systems. It cannot be denied that economic and technological factors are important in the determination of class and status orders. We must not lose sight of the fact, however, that the social system, with its beliefs, values, and rules, which governs human behavior may well determine what kind of technology and what kind of economic institutions will survive or thrive in any given tribe or nation. In any case, social complexity is necessary for economic advancement. Furthermore, social complexity is a basic factor determining the presence or absence of class.

The Marxians have argued that the economic changes our society is undergoing always result in a class war in which "the proletariat" will be triumphant and out of which a "classless society" will result. The authors do not agree with them for several reasons. The principal reasons are: (1) the presence of a class order does not necessarily mean class conflict—the relations of the classes can be and often are amiable and peaceful; (2) classless societies (without differential status systems) are impossible where there is complexity for the reasons previously given. Russia's communistic system, supposedly designed to produce a pure equalitarian society, necessarily has citizens who are ranked above and below each other. Generals, there, outrank privates; commissars, the rank and file; the members of the Politburo, the ordinary comrade. Occupants of these higher ranks in Russia tend to associate together; those of the lower ranks form their own groups. Their children are trained according to the rank of their parents. This means that the younger generation learns these status differences, thereby strengthening status differences between levels and fostering the further development of social class in Communistic Russia.

All this has occurred despite the fact the Russians have removed the means of production from private hands and placed them under the control of the State ("the people"). The economic factor which by Marxian doctrine produced social classes is largely absent; yet social hierarchies and social classes are present for the reason that Russia is a complex society and needs them to survive.

These status trends in Russia will undoubtedly continue, for her population is vast, her peoples diverse, her problems immensely complex; and elaborate systems of co-ordination and control are necessary for such a nation to maintain itself. The Communist ideals of economic and political equality cannot produce perfect equality within the complexities of Russian life.

But let us return to the United States. We, too, have a complex, highly diverse society. We, too, possess an elaborate division of labor and a ramified technology. And we, too, possess a variety of rank orders built on the need of maintaining unity and cohesion in making our common enterprises successful. Men occupying high and low positions possess families. Their families and their activities are identified with their social position. Families of the same position tend to associate together. They do this informally or through cliques, associations, or other institutions. This social matrix provides the structure of our class system. Children are always born to their families' position. Through life they may increase or decrease their status. The family thereby strengthens and helps maintain our class order. Social status in America is somewhat like man's alimentary canal; he may not like the way it works and he may want to forget that certain parts of it are part of him, but he knows it is necessary for his very existence. So a status system, often an object of our disapproval, is present and necessary in our complex social world.

SUGGESTED READINGS

Cutlip, Scott M., and Allen H. Center, *Effective Public Relations*, 3rd ed. (Englewood Ciffs, N.J.: Prentice-Hall, 1964). A widely used public relations text which identifies the various "publics" with which business has relations and outlines the "ecology" of p.r.

Houser, Theodore V., *Big Business and Human Values* (New York: McGraw-Hill, 1957). A study of the experience of Sears, Roebuck in dealing with customers, suppliers, the community and other "publics." Written by the chairman of the board of directors of that company.

McGuire, Joseph W., *Business and Society* (New York: McGraw-Hill, 1963). A discussion of certain aspects of business and its social environment, and of some issues arising out of those interrelationships.

CHAPTER 13

CUSTOMERS

Under most circumstances, customers make their influence felt in the market. Their buying behavior affects the kinds of products sold as well as the market price and quantity sold. However, the history of American business reveals a number of instances in which individual and organized customers have not been satisfied with playing such a limited role in determining what business firms do. In the realm of economics, they have organized boycotts of products or firms. Sometimes they have coupled their refusal to buy with the establishment of purchasing or competing organizations. Customers have taken political as well as economic action, with the result that certain industries have been confronted with new government agencies and officials administering legislation passed as a consequence of the political influence that irate customers have been able to wield. These laws have also made individual legal action more effective. Various classes of customers have different objectives, resources, and available lines of action. The most useful classification is that which regards customers as being composed of domestic consumers, business purchasers, and governments.

DOMESTIC CONSUMERS

Purchases for household consumption account for about two thirds of the sales of final products in the American economy. At one time, the motivation of these customers was regarded as being fairly simple: domestic consumers wished to purchase any given product at the lowest possible price. With the advent of notions such as "conspicuous consumption," views of consumer desires were changed—perhaps too drastically —to those in which the consumer was now looked upon as a rather irrational purchaser, subject to emotional appeals and willing to pay a high price for certain articles known to have a big price tag. The truth seems to be that consumer motivation is quite complex, varying from person to person and from article to article, and that consumer behavior is a mixture of the rational, irrational, and nonrational.

Rational behavior has been traditionally regarded as the act of purchasing any given article at the lowest possible price. The argument has gone like this: Individuals wish to maximize their satisfactions; increased real income (goods and services that can be used to produce satisfactions) will increase satisfactions; therefore, with a given money income, to maximize satisfactions a person (if he is rational) will purchase a certain kind of product at the lowest possible price, since this will maximize real income. Unfortunately, considerable evidence has accumulated that persons buy some consumer goods and services to impress others and that others are impressed when they know that the product has a high price tag. This has sometimes been regarded as irrational, since the effect of such behavior is to reduce the amount of real income one can secure from a given money income (although it may well be that greater satisfactions accrue to the purchaser acting in this fashion—that is, he may be rational after all). Too, some purchasing may be "nonrational" in the sense that it is habitual or customary.

The question of consumer motivation has been a fascinating but puzzling one for firms. Not only are there a great variety of motives, but they have different effects on the buying behavior of different consumers, and even their influence on a particular buyer varies from moment to

moment, hour to hour, day to day. Some observers think they see trends
—for example, it has been suggested that consumers now buy more to
express themselves rather than to impress others. Some firms have tried
to determine what consumers want and why through various research
programs, including motivation research. Such research has not always
yielded results of unerring accuracy (as Ford found out when it brought
out the Edsel after lengthy and painstaking research). Nevertheless,
some continuing study of consumer wants and motives is essential because
consumers can adversely affect the fortunes of a firm if that firm incor-
rectly estimates the nature of its customers.

The most important action taken by consumers is market action. When
they are dissatisfied (that is, when firms inaccurately assess their wants
or do not concern themselves with what their customers really want),
they refuse to buy. This has led some to declare that the consumer is
sovereign. Regardless of their motivations, consumers, it is said, dictate
what will be produced and in what quantities. The business system,
according to this view, is geared to satisfy consumer wants as expressed
in the way in which consumers use their purchasing power. Although
some businessmen and business organizations publicly subscribe to this
ideology, there is considerable evidence that at least some consumers do
not. An opposing opinion is sometimes urged on the part of the consumer according to which firms decide what they want to produce and
then try to force it upon the unsuspecting consumer through advertising
trickery, fancy packaging, and outright fraudulent misrepresentation.
Although most consumers do not hold such an extreme view, some
consumers not believing in their sovereignty have taken influential individual action outside the market.

Other than refusing to buy, influential individual action is quite limited. A customer, of course, can complain (the complaint department is
the subject of a number of cartoons about business). Complaints are
sometimes carried to court, and there have been instances (as in the
case of the California company that distributed polio vaccine that caused
rather than prevented the disease) in which companies have had to pay
very substantial sums in damages. However, much influential consumer
action has been taken by groups rather than by individuals.

Consumer Organizations

Organizations of consumers have been created for both practical and
ideological reasons. In most cases, they have been seen as a solution to
problems which could not be solved by domestic consumers acting in an
individual capacity. An individual purchaser of consumer goods can do
little about the price and the quality of the goods he or she purchases.
Quite evidently, organization is necessary to secure the necessary influ-

ence. More than this, however, is involved in the "consumers' movement"; some consumer groups have believed in the "cooperative commonwealth" as an article of faith; they have set up consumers' cooperatives and taken other actions because they believe that those who consume should also own the means of production and distribution—a belief falling somewhere between socialism and capitalism.

There is a rather wide variety of consumer organizations in the U.S. Among the most important are the consumer cooperatives that compete with, and that have replaced, some retail firms. A number of consumer organizations engage in product testing and information programs. These are the major kinds, although a number of others have appeared on the business scene—including Impulse Buyers Anonymous, formed by some women in Arlington, Virginia, to help one another stiffen their sales resistance, and the Anti-Digit-Dialing League, a band of irate San Francisco Bay area telephone customers who complained to the California Public Utilities Commission about the "scheme" of Pacific Telephone and Telegraph Company to substitute numbers for letter prefixes.

Consumer Cooperatives. Consumer cooperatives have been operating in the United States since before the Civil War. In 1845 a consumer's retail cooperative movement was launched in New England. The New England Protective Union contained slightly over 400 participating groups by 1855, but passed out of existence during the financial panic of the late fifties. After the Civil War, American farmers established consumer cooperatives on a large and enduring scale. Farm groups went beyond performing the retail function, and established wholesale and producing cooperatives. Such organizations have been joined by cooperative credit unions (a type of financial institution), cooperative housing associations, cooperative health associations, and cooperative burial associations. In addition to these cooperative groups, engaged in purchasing and producing in order to reduce the cost to the consumer, other consumer groups are performing other functions.

Consumer Information and Education Groups. Some consumer groups engage in product testing and information. The largest of such groups at the present time is the Consumers Union. This organization developed out of Consumers' Research, Inc., which was set up in 1929 to test products and advise members about their price and quality. Both organizations are still in existence, along with another relatively small group, the Inter-mountain Consumers' Service. The membership of these groups is now something over one million. The number of persons reached by them might be somewhat greater because all three publish periodicals, and it is likely that the readership is greater than the membership. How influential these groups are with consumers is difficult to determine because there is little way of knowing to what extent their recommendations concerning products are followed by those receiving this information. Letters to the editors of the publications indicate that some businessmen whose products are tested are influenced by what they read, as they state they have made changes in their products to make them more acceptable to the testing organization. (An assessment of the influence of the Consumers' Union is contained in a reading at the end of this chapter.)

Other organizations engage in consumer education. A group that has done much to promote this is the American Home Economics Association, which is especially interested in the formal education of consumers in high schools and colleges. Such education is aimed at helping home-makers purchase more economically and may influence the sales of busi-nessmen selling higher-priced goods. This association was joined in the movement to educate consumers by the Consumer Education Association and the short-lived Institute for Consumer Education at Stephens Col-lege. In addition, many general education groups—such as the National Education Association—have supported the movement to provide more consumer information through the school curriculum.

ORGANIZED CONSUMER BOYCOTTS. One line of action adopted by cer-tain consumer groups has been the boycott. A concerted refusal to buy, if continued for any length of time, is a powerful influence on business firms. The depression of the thirties brought forth a number of spectac-ular examples. One was the Detroit meat strike in the summer of 1935 in which housewives attempted to get butchers to close their shops until the meat packers lowered wholesale prices. This movement led to the formation of the Women's League Against the High Cost of Living, a more permanent organization. Meat prices did not decline as a result of this action, but the group took credit for halting the rapid rise in meat prices. More influential was the League of Women Shoppers, which apparently had a close tie to labor unions. It picketed and boycotted stores that were regarded as being unfair to labor and claimed to have influenced firms into signing union contracts or making other conces-sions to striking employees. There are at the present time certain prod-ucts—such as books regarded as being immoral by church groups—that some groups refuse to purchase. However, as in the case of boycotts by organized Negroes, much of this activity is aimed at promoting the in-terests of labor, particular races, and the members of certain religious groups rather than the interests of consumers generally.

CONSUMER POLITICAL ACTION. One of the most important types of action taken by consumer groups has been political action. Just after the beginning of this century, the American Pure Food League was organized by such groups as the General Federation of Women's Clubs and the National Consumers League and supported the drive for the passage of the Pure Food and Drug Act in 1906. Some thirty years later, the more highly organized consumer groups existing at that time pressed for the passage of the Food, Drug and Cosmetic Act of 1938. One objective of consumer organizations has been the creation of a Department of the Consumer in the federal government, but legislation providing for this has not been forthcoming. However, there are a number of government agencies that do look out for the consumer's interest; the establishment of these units has been partly in response to the political pressure of organized consumer groups.

As has been indicated, a considerable part of the political influence of consumer groups has stemmed from their alliance with other influential groups. The American Association of University Women has paid considerable attention to consumer problems and has given support to consumer groups in their various activities. The National League of Women Voters and the National Federation of Business and Professional Women's Clubs have also supported consumer interests, as has the National Congress of Parents and Teachers, in which the influence of housewives is strong. Welfare organizations, including the National Federation of Settlements, have been very much concerned with consumer problems and have supported the "consumer movement." Religious groups, especially the Federal Council of Churches of Christ in America and its successor—the National Council—have supported consumer activity and have been keenly interested in the cooperative movement. Producer groups such as labor unions and farm organizations have supported organizations of consumers on many occasions and have engaged in activities to protect their interest as consumers as well as producers.

The "consumer's interest" has also been promoted by liberal politicians (or at least by those who feel that there is some political advantage to be gained by posing as the champion of the consumer). Before his untimely death, Senator Kefauver of Tennessee took a number of actions in the consumer's interest. As chairman of the Senate Subcommittee on Antitrust and Monopoly, he had the committee investigate pricing in the steel, the automobile, the bread, and the drug industries. Some legislation followed these investigations. In 1959, he introduced a bill that would have created (had it passed) a Department of Consumers to be headed by a Secretary having cabinet status. There was not sufficient political support for the establishment of such a department, but President Kennedy took up where Senator Kefauver left off. In March 1962, he sent to Congress an omnibus "Consumers' Protection and Interest" measure requesting a batch of new laws as well as the strengthening of existing

programs. Although Kennedy did not propose a new cabinet department, he did appoint a 12-member Consumers' Advisory Council, which
is attached to the Council of Economic Advisers, part of the White House
staff. After the assassination of President Kennedy, Lyndon B. Johnson
continued to give consumers representation in the White House.

Some states have passed laws and created agencies to protect consumers. Early in 1959, the California legislature passed a bill creating the
Office of Consumer Counsel. The person occupying the position has the
functions of recommending consumer legislation, testifying in behalf of
the consumer at hearings conducted by government agencies, and making reports to the people on matters of interest to consumers. Some other
states have taken similar action (although in the case of New York,
Governor Rockefeller eliminated the position of consumer counsel, turning over that function to the Bureau of Consumer Frauds in the attorney
general's office). In Michigan, the Michigan Consumer Association—a
nongovernmental body—has pressed for legislation in behalf of the consumer, including the creation of a position for a consumer representative
in the state administration, but its initial efforts in this direction were
not successful.

The reaction of business firms to the consumer movement has been
varied. Advertising firms and organizations and some business firms advertising and distributing on a national scale have fought some aspects of
the movement because their interests are quite directly threatened. Other
firms, such as chain stores, have welcomed consumer support and even
developed their own consumer organizations in fighting repressive legislation. Still others have engaged in publicity activities to sell business,
national brands, and advertising to the American public. Some retailers
have met the consumer halfway through the National Consumer-Retailer
Council, set up in 1937 for the discussion of the mutual problems of the
retail seller and the household buyer. Better Business Bureaus (organizations of business firms) have promoted business by taking action to
protect the domestic consumer. In general, retailers seem more inclined
to cooperate, while manufacturers and advertising firms tend to regard
their interests in conflict with much of what the consumer movement
stands for.

BUSINESS CUSTOMERS

Although the largest portion of the final products of business is bought
by domestic consumers, many intermediate products are sold by one
business firm to another. Even finished goods sometimes go through the
hands of wholesalers and retailers before finally arriving in the hands
of the ultimate consumer. Before a finished product reaches the con-

sumer, it (or parts of it) might have been sold to five different business buyers (ignoring some middlemen) as Figures 13–1 indicates. This is not always the case in manufacturing, because many firms have "integrated"

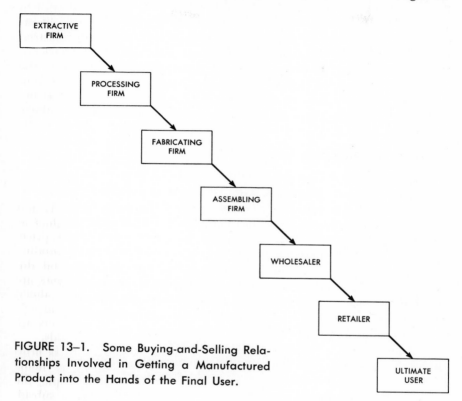

FIGURE 13–1. Some Buying-and-Selling Relationships Involved in Getting a Manufactured Product into the Hands of the Final User.

the functions of extracting raw materials, processing them, fabricating basic materials into various parts and assembling them, and even selling the finished products at wholesale and retail. Each firm in the chain usually sells to a number of business buyers, but each purchaser may buy a significant percentage of the product, thereby making business buyers of somewhat greater importance than domestic consumers, who rarely buy a significant part of the products of a firm as individuals. The sales by some firms to other business firms are so large in dollar volume, and represent the sole outlet for so many firms, that such purchasers warrant special attention.

Motives of Business Buyers

It is usually contended that the motivations of this class of customer are much different from those of the domestic consumer. A popular marketing text declares: "The purchase of industrial goods, in contrast to most consumer-goods purchasing, is motivated by rational considerations." This statement is later modified by the amendment that industrial buying "is not without its nonrational motives, such as personal friendships, political influence, favoring a family connection, or bowing to the dictates of a powerful director.... In general, however, rational considerations prevail." [1] Accumulating evidence indicates that there is not such a great distinction between the two types of customer as the above remarks indicate, and that in any case the business firm needs to be aware of what this class of purchaser wants and of what lines of action are sometimes taken when they do not get what they want.

Behavior of Business Buyers

Insofar as their behavior is "rational," business buyers of goods and services are mainly concerned with getting a good quality product at the lowest cost. Lowest cost does not necessarily mean lowest price, since a higher-priced machine, for example, may result in lower production cost per unit of output because of its greater efficiency and durability. This "cost-consciousness" does not mean that such buyers are not price conscious, however, and a number of their actions are aimed at securing a lower price from the seller. Although the behavior of groups of these purchasers are of interest and importance, individual buyers are of much more importance here than in the case of consumer goods.

Quite frequently a firm that sells its products to other business firms is in a position in which it is dealing with a few "big customers." Some are such big buyers that they set the purchase price. For example, the Humble Oil & Refining Company (the chief domestic operating subsidiary of Standard Oil of New Jersey) posts prices it will pay crude oil producers in the Texas and Louisiana oil fields. Also, it has been suggested that some mail-order houses that buy a large portion of the total output of some small manufacturers are in a position to tell them what price they will pay, and sometimes can force price concessions. Sometimes big customers are also suppliers of a firm, and demand reciprocity, in effect, saying, "If you don't buy from us, we won't buy from you." The Antitrust Division of the Department of Justice recently secured an indictment against General Motors, one of the charges being that GM used its position as the largest shipper of freight over the rails to induce railroads to buy locomotives from its Electro-Motive Division. The antitrusters charged that GM offered to route its freight over the roads that bought its locomotives and took freight business away from carriers that

---

[1] Edward A. Duddy and David A. Revzan, *Marketing*, 2d ed. (New York: McGraw-Hill, 1953), p. 290.

bought locomotives from competitors. General Motors replied that it was not guilty of such monopolistic practices. There is no doubt, however, that "reciprocity" is widespread.

Big customers demand and receive other kinds of special consideration. This may only involve preferential treatment in filling an order. Sometimes it may involve rebates (or kickbacks as they are sometimes called). Big buyers may even solicit contributions from their suppliers. In 1958, to help pay for events celebrating its 100th anniversary, Macy's obtained $540,000 from 750 of its suppliers. The suppliers received no special promotion of their products in exchange for their contribution. The Federal Trade Commission ruled that the practice was illegal, even though there was no evidence that Macy's threatened suppliers or applied overt pressure on them, stating: "Vendors, as a practical matter, could not refuse Macy's request.... We hold that the practice of a large buyer using the leverage of its size and importance to exact ... substantial gifts ... solely for the buyer's advantage is an unfair practice."

Because they are such big buyers and have quite a bit at stake in their dealings with their suppliers, business customers are much more likely to take political and legal action than are consumers. Very few firms have sufficient political resources to get certain candidates elected or laws passed, but in organized groups they have been more successful. The National Automobile Dealers Association has been instrumental in getting Congress to pass legislation promoting the interests of auto dealers since World War II. Traffic associations (organizations of buyers of transportation services) usually appear before regulatory commissions to oppose the requests of railroads for increases in rates or the discontinuance of certain service. After 19 electrical equipment companies pleaded guilty to fixing prices in 1961 and 10 more did not contest the charges, the entire group was confronted with some 1,500 damage claims brought by their customers—utility companies, the federal government, cities, and other purchasers. These suits asked damages mounting into many millions of dollars, and though many were settled out of court for less than the sum claimed, this still was dramatic evidence of the power of customers to take adverse legal action.

There are a number of groups of business purchasers. One of these is the National Association of Purchasing Agents, which is especially interested in the promotion of "rational" purchasing. Its influence is perhaps not considerable as compared to those organizations of buyers confronting certain firms and industries. Mention has already been made of purchasing cooperatives set up by farmers. In a number of instances they have replaced retailers and wholesalers and have been in a strong position to secure special concessions from manufacturers with whom they now deal directly. Farm groups have also been politically active; one consequence of such action has been the legislative or administrative reduction in the prices of goods and services sold to farmers—railroad rates provide a good example. Some manufacturers have been confronted by organized groups of retailers. Retail buying groups have been organized to pool the purchases of a number of retailers and have been able to force manufacturers to make price concessions.

GOVERNMENTS AS BUYERS

Governments are big buyers. Not only is the amount of goods and services they buy from business large in dollar amount but they also are relatively few in number, and the amount each buys is sufficiently important to make the market and other actions of individual governments quite significant. State and local governments conduct themselves in a much more "rational" manner in their purchasing activities than does the federal government; we shall therefore say no more about them but shall examine the important objectives and activities of the national government as a buyer.

Agencies and officials of the federal government buy as Congress permits them to buy. Congress holds the purse strings and it not only determines the amount to be spent in performing various governmental functions but also directs the manner in which the amount will be spent. This does not mean that the executive branch is not important. It proposes, through the President's Budget, how much should be spent on what. Congress, however, reviews these requests and never gives the executive branch exactly what it asks for; not only does it sometimes give less than is asked, it sometimes gives more. Although some agencies and officials have refused to spend money appropriated by Congress for certain matters, such refusal is rare. In addition to determining how much will be spent on certain functions Congress, through other legislation, determines what functions the federal government will perform.

The objectives established by Congress for federal purchasing are not always "rational"—that is, the federal government does not always look for the lowest price for a product meeting its specifications (as state and local governments normally do). It may try to support certain prices by paying something more than the "market price," as in the case of some products of agriculture and other extractive industries. It may concentrate its purchases in "depressed" regions or in states whose Congressional representatives have considerable influence. Those in control of the legislative and administrative branches may wish to buy in such a way as to counteract fluctuations in the "business cycle" (cutting back expenditures during inflationary periods and increasing them during recessions). Congress may pass laws denying contracts to those firms that discriminate on bases of color and creed in their employment policies. Some of its laws apparently oblige those receiving government contracts to pay the union scale prevailing in the area in which the work is being performed.

Because the federal government is such a big buyer, it holds the power of business life or death over some companies, especially those in the defense industries. The Defense Department does not employ this power lightly (and cannot, for it is Congress that passes the defense budget), but in making decisions on big contracts (such as the TFX fighter contract, which finally was allocated to General Dynamics) it gives a great boost to the business of the company receiving the contract and adversely affects the companies that bid for the business and lose. In its position as the biggest buyer, the Defense Department is sometimes dissatisfied with the deal it has made and "renegotiates" the agreement to force the company to return some of its "excess profits" from sales under the contract.

Purchasing agencies of governments are more likely to take legal action when they feel they have justified grievances against vendors than are other classes of buyers. This may be owing to the fact that they are likely to be subjected to public criticism if they seem to make poor purchases (many election campaigns and numerous legislative investigations resound with charges and countercharges concerning "ill-advised" government purchases). Too, because the costs of such suits are borne by the public, there are only negligible disadvantages in taking legal action, while the potential gain is great. Whatever the reason, the federal district court's decision in the recent price-fixing case in the electrical equipment industry [1] gave rise to a large number of damage suits by federal, state, and local agencies that contended they had been overcharged as a result of the conspiracy.

Perhaps it should be pointed out that while governments have substantial power to wield in their relationships with business (including the buying relation), businessmen also possess considerable influence over the buying activities of government and do not stand powerless before federal, state, and local agencies. The role of business in the political process will be examined more fully later. Generally speaking, in every buying and selling relationship both buyers and sellers are able to bring some influence to bear. The firm, as a buyer, is confronted by a number

---

[1] In 1960, the federal government brought an antitrust suit against General Electric, Westinghouse, three other corporate defendants and a number of individuals charging them with conspiring, among other things, to fix prices of certain electrical equipment. The final judgment in 1962 was in favor of the government. A detailed treatment of the case is contained in a book by Clarence C. Walton and Frederick W. Cleveland, Jr., *Corporations on Trial: The Electric Cases* (Belmont, Cal.: Wadsworth, 1964).

of kinds of sellers taking many different kinds of influential actions. Because labor is so important an input for most firms, we shall next examine the influences brought to bear by those supplying labor and services.

READING: U.S. Business' Most Skeptical Customer *
by Philip Siekman

Consumers Union, the biggest, probably the most influential, and certainly the most vocal adviser to the American consumer, sometimes makes it seem that the emptor who does not damn well caveat every minute will be scandalously swindled, if he is not electrocuted or mutilated by one or another of the machines or appliances he may be tempted to buy. This summer, for example, C.U.'s publication, Consumer Reports, announced the results of C.U.'s latest appraisal of powered rotary lawn mowers. C.U.'s technicians and consultants had tested forty-four models by twenty-four manufacturers whose products probably account for 85 per cent of power-mower sales in the country. The verdict: "None was clearly acceptable"; thirty-one were "excessively hazardous", thirteen were given a grudging "conditional acceptance."

C.U. notwithstanding, something like three million power rotary mowers will be sold this year, bringing the total in use to about 20 million, which suggests that Americans are willing to live—and cut grass—a little more dangerously than C.U.'s technicians think they should. But this should not be taken as an indication that nobody listens to C.U. A great many people do.

The fact is that this little outfit, with an annual budget of less than $4 million, can and does make itself felt. In at least one industry, thumbs down from C.U. can kill a product. In some markets its approval can double sales. And more than once in its twenty-five years, C.U.'s unpopular (at the time) preferences have turned out to be harbingers of a turn in popular taste and buying patterns. Take automobiles, for example: C.U. has been denouncing "giantism," tail fins, overpowering and over-chroming in American cars for twenty years. It hailed the short-lived Hudson Jet in 1953 and last year righteously reminded its readers that the Jet was pretty much the same size as Detroit's newest compacts. C.U. was an early and enthusiastic champion of both the Volkswagen and the Rambler.

Now it appears that C.U.'s opposition to annual model changes in appliances is at last finding some backing in industry. Last June [1959], President George Romney of American Motors said that his firm's Kelvinator division was eliminating annual model changes in its appliances because "attempts to forcibly outdate products that are meant to have a long and useful life . . . are being questioned by the consumer with increasing intensity." These words could have appeared without change in Consumer Reports, which uses the same portentous tone of voice to warn against the dangers of radiation fallout as it does to denounce a clam chowder without clams.

Who reads Consumer Reports? The magazine has 700,000 subscribers and an

* Reprinted by permission of Fortune Magazine (September 1960), Vol. LXIII, No. 3, pp. 157–159, 224–229.

additional 150,000 readers who buy it at the newsstand. Counting in library and "pass along" readers, something over two million families consult it more or less regularly.

As customers, these people can be hard to sell. In fact, a true-blue Consumers Union consumer in full cry is an awesome sight. A used-car salesman encountered one of these a few years ago in the person of a medical student armed with a C.U. article entitled "How to Buy a Used Car." The student brought his wife along with him. He had her and the salesman stand on the bumpers, jumping up and down, while he sat at the wheel. He then went methodically through the twenty-nine items on the C.U. check list to the growing astonishment of the salesman—a man more accustomed to buyers who choose by the time-honored tire-kicking and door-slamming techniques. The student spent two and a half hours going over the car—and he was not yet sold. He asked the salesman, "Do you mind driving this around the block while I get into the trunk?" The salesman obligingly locked his potential customer in the trunk and gingerly chauffeured him around the block. Back at the lot the salesman said, "I don't know what that was supposed to prove, but I hope it came out all right." "I was listening to the differential," the student explained, and closed the deal.

Surveys of *Consumer Reports'* readers suggest that they are well-to-do (the median income is around $9,000 a year) and that as many as three-fourths of them have gone to college. A less impersonal description of the *Reports* audience was provided by a reader who wrote in not long ago and remarked that the magazine appeared to be written by and for a man:

1. Who reads and talks highbrow intellectual stuff.
2. Who lives in Manhattan—but has relatives newly moved to the suburbs.
3. Who has only recently outgrown the habit of condemning corporations, advertising, and old-fashioned ideas.
4. Whose wife uses words about everyday things like "integrated," 'group," "motivation."
5. Whose knowledge and interest in such varied outdoor activities as gardening, golf, boating, fishing, hunting, walking is genuine but new, limited. The limitation: he doesn't realize that some readers have been doing some of these things for many years in different places than Long Island.

The letter went on to say that "This set of clichés applies largely to myself," prompting the editors of the *Reports* to reply in unaccustomed levity: "Never send to know for whom the *Reports* toils; it toils for thee."

"C.U. Put Us in Business." Three questions are most often raised about C.U.:

1. Is C.U. big enough or influential enough to affect sales?
2. Is its testing competent?
3. Is it biased, generally anti-big-business?

C.U.'s influence on sales is hard to measure across the board. However, there have been isolated instances in which its impact was traceable, and tremendous.

The most recent instance, and one of the most spectacular, developed out of a December, 1959, rating of dishwashers. Two R.C.A. Whirlpool models were said to be "superior by a clear margin." What happened after that, according to Charles Reinbolt, manager of the Whirlpool Specialty Products Division, was "so fantastic that every morning when I wake up I shake myself wondering how long it can keep up." At the beginning of that December, Whirlpool had what it assumed was a twenty-seven-week supply of the highly rated dishwashers. Within a month, 80 per cent of this stock was gone. Production was doubled. Even so, two months later the two models that C.U. liked were on sixty to ninety days' back order. Reinbolt figures that Whirlpool will sell twice as many dishwashers this year as it did in 1959, and he is convinced that C.U.'s rating is largely responsible for this big jump.

Another instance of an increase in sales being traceable to a good rating from C.U. also occurred last year. After two Porter-Cable hand sanders were given a top rating in May, sales abruptly rose 15 to 20 per cent.

In 1954 a top rating was given to two washing machines manufactured by the Norge Division of Borg-Warner. Judson S. Sayre, chairman of the division, says simply, "C.U. put us in the washing-machine business."

In one market—admittedly a rather small one catering to a special kind of buyer—C.U.'s word is gospel. This market is for high-fidelity audio equipment. One New York retailer of audio components says that after a piece of equipment gets a high rating, "sales go up fantastically." He adds pityingly, "And Lord help the ones they say are no good." Edgar Villchur, president of Acoustic Research Inc., gives major credit to good ratings in Consumer Reports for the rise in his sales from $1,350,000 in 1958 to $2,900,000 in 1959. A high rating given in December, 1958, to a small speaker made by a Japanese firm resulted in such a demand for the speaker that four companies in Japan are now busy producing it.

Some hi-fi manufacturers have concluded that the only thing to do about a poor rating from C.U. is to remove the product from the market. At least one manufacturer, however, has refused to haul down his flag: he is suing C.U., claiming that an unjustifiable poor rating on his loudspeaker practically put him out of business.

On the other hand, no appliance or automobile manufacturer interviewed by *Fortune* would say that his sales have ever been hurt by an unfavorable C.U. rating. Most manufacturers concede that C.U. has "some" effect on their sales, but they doubt that it is an appreciable effect. American Motors, for example, will say no more than that C.U. "probably helped" Rambler, although Volkswagen sales personnel say forthrightly that *Consumer Reports* was a major factor in the success of their car in this country.

The fact seems to be that in very large markets and for very large companies it is hard to determine how many sales have been generated by favorable C.U. ratings. As an executive of a big television manufacturer said, C.U. had no influence on his sales, but "they can make or break a small firm."

One reason for the difficulty in tracing C.U.'s influence, except on rare occasions, is that it seldom singles out one brand or model for either unqualified praise or unmitigated condemnation. In fact, readers sometimes complain that the ratings are so heavily qualified and expressed in such technical language that only an engineer can determine which model C.U. favors. Often, in some product tests, it gives an acceptable rating of one degree or another to almost every brand examined. Frequently two or three brands share an equally good rating. Now and then one product may be given the accolade of "best buy," indicating that it offers the most for the money, but this is infrequent. (Otherwise, price is not considered in ratings, though the list price is always noted.)

A Gadget for Ball-Point Pens. Is C.U.'s testing adequate? It is with some qualifications that will be pointed out.

For the bulk of its testing C.U. relies on its staff of thirty-five technicians and engineers, plus a varying number of consultants. Most of the staff technicians hold degrees in science or engineering; three are Ph.D.'s. Most were employed in industry at one time: Ashton Lyon, head of the chemical division, was manager of organic-chemical research for Air Reduction; Mitchell Cotter, head of the audio division, was an engineer with a scientific-instruments company; Thomas Jacoby, who now runs C.U.'s textile testing, was in charge of chemical research development at Alexander Smith and chief chemist for another large carpetmaker.

The technical staff works in 18,000 square feet of laboratory space in a converted optical factory at Mount Vernon, New York. C.U. also maintains an automobile laboratory in Connecticut and occasionally farms out research projects to consultants to carry out in their own labs. Testing equipment, for the most part, is standard stuff used in industry, although C.U. has developed some gadgets of its own to test, among other things, current leakage, ball-point pens, refrigerator performance.

Test samples are purchased from retail outlets in various parts of the country by shoppers who do not reveal that they work for C.U. When possible, they insist on factory-packed merchandise. Any model that performs either exceptionally well or exceptionally badly is rechecked with other samples. (The 1959 Whirlpool dishwashers were tested with six samples.)

At the outset, each sample is carefully examined to make sure it matches the manufacturer's published specifications; automobiles are run for 2,000 miles before the testing starts. Any aberration that shows up is then corrected by authorized servicemen.

C.U. testing begins with the tests used by industry for its own products. In some cases C.U. has devised additional techniques, such as "naturally soiled" rugs for vacuum cleaners, and where it seems to make sense, products are also tested in the homes of employees and volunteers. Gas and electric ranges are put through fifty-five checks, refrigerators get forty, portable electric heaters thirty.

Industry engineers who have been skeptical about C.U.'s technical adequacy usually change their minds when they take the trouble to inspect the setup at Mount Vernon. "I think that generally the people who have gone through its facilities," says an engineering executive of a large electrical-products firm, "have a favorable opinion. Any manufacturers who are just sitting there complaining about their ratings—my advice to them is to look to their products."

There is some informed criticism of Consumers Union's testing methods. One objection is that the organization can afford to test only a limited number of samples of some products. The automobile industry particularly is unhappy about this because C.U. usually buys only one car of each model. A second objection is that C.U. is weak on testing durability of many products: travel irons can be run until they burn out, but it takes too long to test the longevity of, say, a car or a refrigerator.

A third criticism is that C.U. makes "subjective" evaluations. Frequently its technicians find excessive shock hazard in electric appliances that have received the blessings of the Underwriters Laboratories. The objection most frequently voiced by manufacturers is that C.U. is "subjective" in weighing various factors in performance. For example: a washing machine was once downgraded by C.U. because it "tangled the wash." The manufacturer concedes that this was true but he objects to the weight given this factor in the over-all rating of a machine that was good at getting dirt out of clothes, which was what it was designed to do.

Are the Ratings Biased?   Another question raised about C.U. by business-men concerns its attitude toward business. There is a belief that C.U. is innately hostile to big business—if indeed it is not hostile to capitalism and free enterprise—and that it consistently rates small-company and mail-order-house products over those manufactured by the giants of American capitalism. The facts do not bear out this allegation. A statistical study made some years ago by Eugene R. Beem and John S. Ewing, published in the *Harvard Business Review,* concluded that no such bias was shown in C.U. ratings. Products marketed by Sears, Roebuck and Montgomery Ward under their own labels (often, of course, manufactured by "big business") receive their share of poor ratings, just as items under the trademarks of such companies as General Electric, General Motors, and R.C.A. frequently get top marks. "Sears products were rated below the average of their competition 45.8 per cent of the time . . . Montgomery Ward products . . . 42.1 per cent of the time . . ." and "the biggest national advertisers were rated above the average of all their competitors 65.2 per cent of the time . . ."

It is true that *Consumer Reports* often seems to speak in an irritated tone of voice when dealing with a heavily advertised product, and that a severely en-forced policy of "no commercialization" is not calculated to endear this non-profit organization to men whose function is necessarily commercial. A number of manufacturing executives grumbled to *Fortune* that C.U.'s "holier-than-thou" attitude was personally offensive to them. An executive with a company that manufactures TV sets commented sourly: "I think Mr. Warne and Mr. Masters (C.U.'s president and director), when they run themselves a tub of water in the morning and step into it, they are a little disappointed that they can't stand on the surface."

C.U.'s "no-commercialization" policy prohibits any use of its reports in promo-tion and sales. A retailer who exhibits the magazine on his sales floor is inviting trouble with C.U., and any advertiser who mentions C.U., *Consumer Reports,* or even a "leading independent consumer testing agency," might just as well call his lawyers the same day he places his advertisement.

On at least one occasion, however, an astute manufacturer has outwitted C.U. on "commercialization." In January, 1958, in the course of a report on tars and nicotine in cigarettes, C.U. noted that the Parliament filter did a passable job. The Philip Morris Co., which makes Parliaments, placed an advertisement in eighty-six newspapers that said only: "For the latest report on filter cigarettes, see page 24 of the January Issue of *Consumer Reports*. Parliament Cigarettes." C.U. immediately squawked, whereupon Philip Morris promptly apologized, and asked how it could make amends. C.U. wanted a public apology, so the cigarette manufacturer, with C.U.'s approval, ran another ad that said in effect: "We're sorry that we told you to check page 24 of the January issue of *Consumer Reports* for the latest information on filter cigarettes."

Director Dexter Masters admits that C.U. didn't come out of this skirmish very well, and says that it would handle the problem differently next time. But he insists that C.U. has to do whatever it can to maintain its reputation "for integrity" with its subscribers, and that "no commercialization" is one means to that end.

Guinea Pigs and Un-American Activities. Consumers Union has long been plagued by the confusion and acrimony that attended its birth. This story goes back to 1929, when F. J. Schlink, an engineer with the American Standards Association, an industry-supported coordinating group, established the first consumer-products testing organization. It was called Consumers' Research, Inc. Four years later Schlink and another A.S.A. engineer, Arthur Kallet, published an exposé of "dangers in everyday food, drugs and cosmetics" in a book called *100,000,000 Guinea Pigs*. The book, and Consumers' Research, were widely discussed.

In 1935, C.R. employees went on strike. Schlink refused to bargain. Kallet, then secretary of C.R., sided with the strikers. The strike was brief, bitter, violent, and a failure. With ten other C.R. employees Kallet left to set up Consumers Union of U.S. In May, 1936, they sent the first copy of their magazine to 3,000 readers.

Two years later trouble began for Kallet and his crew. It arrived in the person of J. B. Matthews, a former Consumers' Research vice president and self-proclaimed ex-fellow traveler. Matthews told the House Un-American Activities Committee, then headed by Martin Dies of Texas, that Consumers Union was a Communist front. Subsequently, a number of governmental and private anti-Communist groups took up the charges, though C.U. was never on the Attorney General's list of subversive organizations.

After the war the chorus of denunciation became persistent. In 1948 and again in 1951, the Un-American Activities Committee noted five separate citations of C.U. as a Communist front. The Cincinnati Public-school system banned *Consumer Reports*. Somewhat belatedly, C.U. began in earnest to refute its critics. Finally, in February, 1954, the Annual Report of the House Un-American Activities Committee stated: "After hearings and thorough study, the committee finds there is no present justification for continuing this organization as one that is cited, and future reports and publications will reflect that this organization has been deleted from the list of subversive organizations and publications."

That settled it for almost everybody but Schlink. He remains convinced that C.U. is a Communist plot. Schlink is still in the consumer-guidance business, but he is far behind C.U. He says the circulation of Consumers' Research's *Bulletin* is now 100,000, the same total he claimed in 1948, and about one-ninth of the present circulation for C.U.'s *Reports.*

At the outset, C.U. expected that a great deal of its support would come from labor unions and their members, but it hasn't worked out that way. Originally two editions of Reports were published: one aimed at the middle-income families and a cheaper one aimed at union members, somewhat narrower in the range of products tested. The cheaper edition didn't take—labor appeared totally un-interested—and it was dropped after a few years. The middle class apparently welcomed guidance, and circulation of *Reports* soared from 100,000 in 1945 to its present 850,000. After teetering on the edge of bankruptcy during World War II, when there were few consumer products to rate, C.U. concentrated on the college-educated middle class. Thus, from testing low-priced items—canned food, aspirin, shoe polish, children's underwear—as it did in its early years during the depression, C.U. turned to big-ticket items like TV sets, dishwashers, washing and drying machines, and other mechanical paraphernalia now deemed indispensable to the good life of middle-income groups.

"I Was Fired."   In the early fifties, as more money became available, Warne increased such "educational" activities as conducting consumers' conferences and giving speeches to academic and other groups on the subject of consumer goods. Kallet, who oversaw the office and testing work as director, became more and more concerned about Warne's programs, which, in his words, "made heavy demands on the time and attention of the staff . . . at what I considered to be an intolerable cost to the quality of C.U.'s technical work."

Warne now says that the issue was not the reason for his open break with Kallet. But nobody at C.U., including the principals, can agree on any other reason. In any case, Warne brought the matter to the C.U. board in 1957, charg-ing that Kallet had "narrowed C.U.'s concept" and "abrogated the board's right to set basic policy." Warne won with a vote of nine to eight. Kallet refused to resign. He announced publicly, "I was fired," and retained his membership on the board, which is elected by mail vote of subscribers to the *Reports.* Still a board member, Kallet now publishes The Medical Letter, a newsletter in which drugs are evaluated for physicians.

Kallet was replaced as director by Dexter Masters, a journalist and novelist who had worked off and on for C.U. since 1936, and Warne continues to push C.U.'s nontechnical work. Under his prodding, C.U. has been giving financial support to research projects in the field of consumer behavior. It has backed the well-known Survey Research Center at the University of Michigan; initiated the Committee on Consumer Attitudes and Behavior, now known as the National Bureau of Economic Research; aimed at determining methods for predicting consumer buying and trying to "clear up such mysteries as why Americans buy 5,500,000 cars one year and seven million the next."

Not for Amateurs. Despite increased activity in these so-to-speak extra-curricular areas, testing and reporting on consumer products remain C.U.'s principal purpose. And this will continue so long as its officials believe, as they do with some reason, that buying anything from a wheelbarrow to a car is too serious a matter to be left to the uninitiated.

SUGGESTED READINGS

Adelman, Morris A., *A & P: A Study in Price-Cost Behavior and Public Policy* (Cambridge, Mass.: Harvard U.P., 1959). In part, a study of the buying methods of the Atlantic and Pacific Tea Co., including its relations with large and small suppliers and the influence the company was able to bring to bear upon those firms supplying it.

Campbell, Persia, *The Consumer Interest* (New York: Harper & Row, 1949). An interesting study by a one-time adviser to President Kennedy. Contains a chapter on the "Consumer Movement."

Hopkinson, Tom M., "New Battleground—Consumer Interest," *Harvard Business Review* (September–October, 1964). The author proposes that managements open their corporate blinders and let in some consumer-relations thinking and change policies in order to deal with growing problem of dealing with proposed restrictive legislation in interests of the consumer.

Voorhis, Jerry, *American Cooperatives: Where They Came From, What They Do, Where They Are Going* (New York: Harper & Row, 1961). A former Congressman and leader in the "cooperative movement" discusses the role of consumers in that movement.

CHAPTER 14

SUPPLIERS
OF LABOR
AND
SERVICES

In acquiring resources with which to conduct its operations, the firm necessarily has relationships with a number of suppliers. For the most part, these contacts take place in the "market." However, there are a number of interrelations that do not conform to commonly held notions of buying and selling activity. Suppliers of certain resources—particularly labor—have on occasion been unwilling to accept the results of the operation of the market and have taken action toward the purchasing firm in order to secure a more satisfactory situation for the seller. For many firms, labor is the most costly input and the suppliers of labor have been a very important class in the social environment of business. We shall, therefore, first turn our attention to individuals and groups in this category.

There are three major subclassifications of suppliers of labor and services—independent contractors, agents, and employees. Most firms purchase certain labor services from individuals and groups on an occasional basis. Accounting and bookkeeping services, engineering services, management consulting services, and employment services are examples. The persons from whom these services are secured are not employees of the purchasing firm, but perform the service under some type of contract, and are regarded as being independent contractors. Some persons providing services to a firm on a full-time basis are not regarded—at least in the eyes of the law—as employees. A law firm retained by a business acts as its agent in legal matters (the word "attorney" means "agent"). There are other kinds of agents—such as selling agents—and the legal duties and responsibilities of agents toward the firm and their relationships with the firm differ from those of employees and independent contractors. The most numerous of the suppliers of labor are employees, however, and are of greatest significance because independent contractors and agents gain their objectives through market action, for the most part, while employed workers have posed great problems because of their frequent unwillingness to accept "the judgment of the market."

There is, perhaps, good reason for employees not to accept the market's judgment of the value of their labor. In the theory of perfectly competitive labor markets, it is assumed among other things that there are a large number of buyers and sellers of labor in such a market (which would give buyer and seller equal bargaining power), and that the buyers have perfect knowledge of the productivity of the labor they purchase which, in turn, determines the wage rate they are willing to pay for any given amount of labor. Such conditions are rarely, if ever, met with in practice. It is part of the folklore of labor that employers possess greater bargaining power (which is true in most cases when an individual employee bargains with an employer) and that they use their great power to exploit labor by paying workers something less than their value (which is less true). Even though employers might possess greater bargaining power, they lack precise knowledge of the productivity of any given employee. In some cases this might make employers cautious so that they will not employ a person unless there is no doubt that his productivity is considerably greater than the wage paid; in other instances, however, employers pay wages considerably in excess of the productivity of the worker. In any case, lack of exact knowledge of how much an employee is worth creates a range of wage rates that the employer is willing to pay for certain work, and the precise rate paid an employee depends on the bargaining power of both employer and employee and how they use it. It is perhaps natural for persons to believe that they are being paid something less than their true value, and when individual bargaining by them does not succeed in raising their wages they turn to collective bargaining.

A satisfactory rate of wages is not all that employees want, although a "rational" view of suppliers of labor leads to the conclusion that what they want is the highest price or money income possible from the rendering of their services. Such a notion might be fairly accurate with respect to individual contractors and agents, although they want other things— such as fair treatment—as well. The great difficulties confronting firms in their dealings with employees is a consequence of the fact that employees want many other things besides satisfactory wages, and that when they regard wages as being satisfactory other things become *more* important than wages. Businessmen who have paid more than the going rate of wages in a particular labor market have found that they have had labor problems because they have either ignored or inaccurately estimated what workers want in addition to a fair wage, or because they were unable to help workers satisfy their wants.

WHAT WORKERS WANT

The identification of objectives of workers is a difficult task. First of all, workers are not all alike. In a large manufacturing corporation, the employees include members of top management, middle management, and supervisory forces, as well as office and production workers. Those responsible for the direction of the affairs of the company know quite well what managers want, but have a less clear notion as to what supervisors and those on the bottom of the organizational structure want.

One way in which the problem of determining what workers want might be resolved is to examine certain fundamental human needs. One list includes:

1. Physiological needs—food, rest, shelter, etc.
2. Safety needs—protection against danger, threat and deprivation.
3. Social needs—association with and acceptance by others, giving and receiving friendship and love.
4. Ego needs—self-esteem and good reputation.
5. Self-fulfillment needs—realization of one's potential.[1]

Although this seems to be a reasonable listing of what humans ultimately want, what workers want from management is the granting of some more

[1] This list is based on a discussion of basic needs in Abraham H. Maslow, *Motivation and Personality* (New York: Harper, 1954), Chapter 5.

immediate demands or claims that will help them attain those ultimate goals. For example, the General Electric Company conducted a study of what its plant employees wanted, and came up with the following list:

1. Good pay and other material benefits.
2. Good working conditions.
3. Good bosses.
4. A fair chance to get ahead.
5. Steady work.
6. Respectful treatment.
7. Full information.
8. Important and significant work.
9. Rewarding associations on the job.[2]

Many other studies have been made of what workers want and although there are many similarities, there are some differences too. What employees want and the relative importance to them of what they want is greatly influenced by the specific employment situation.

Although needs and wants are not necessarily the same, managements have learned to concern themselves with both. The lack of recognition of employee needs and wants by business, or the unwillingness or inability by firms to help satisfy them, has led to worker frustration and to worker activity which has been detrimental to the attainment of the firm's objectives. Some individual workers have looked for a better employment situation elsewhere, but more commonly a solution to their problems has been sought through individual and collective action while staying in the employ of the firm. At one extreme, individuals have not worked at anything approaching their full potential, but have done just enough to get by. At the other extreme, they have actively engaged in various acts of sabotage that have seriously hampered the achievement of the goals of the firm. For most employees, individual action has rarely secured results that were altogether satisfactory. However, they have discovered that organized action can secure objectives that individual action cannot. Consequently, employee organizations have grown and have introduced a new element into the environment of business firms.

EMPLOYEE ORGANIZATIONS

There are essentially two kinds of organizations of employees that have been important to businessmen—those which are just an organized group of the firm's workers which have no connection with external organizations and those which are affiliated with some group outside the firm.

[2] General Electric Company, *Employee Relations News Letter,* December 31, 1954.

Businessmen have sometimes encouraged the development of employees' organizations within the firm, especially when there was some prospect that workers might join an outside union. Little difficulty has been experienced in relationships with such "inside unions" because they have rarely had the resources with which to reach their objectives if they were in opposition to the goals of the management. One consequence of this, however, has been the replacement of inside unions with outside unions that possess greater power. The objectives of organizations wholly within the company have been mainly recreational, fraternal, and benevolent, and those of outside unions have come to be chiefly economic in nature. It might be argued that, by definition, only "outside unions" are in the environment of the firm and therefore relevant to our study; in any case, their objectives are more likely to be in conflict with those of the firm and their resources also relatively great, thus giving cause for their extended examination.

Outside Unions

Although the "union movement" is sometimes spoken of, what we see when we examine outside unions is a number of different union types with distinctive structures, varying objectives, different resources, and employing various courses of action. Craft unions are quite distinct from industrial unions, and their differences have occasioned conflict between them. Local unions do different things than do the national unions to which they belong. There are a number of different kinds of federations of unions. Differences in objectives permit us to differentiate between "reform unionism," "political unionism," and "business unionism." We shall, therefore, examine a number of kinds of unions rather than deal with "the labor movement," which implies common objectives, united leadership, and joint action.

UNIONS CLASSIFIED BY OBJECTIVES. There is a great variety of union objectives, and various employee organizations pursue somewhat different goals. It is possible to classify unions according to the major goals they see, although it should be kept in mind that each organization pursues a number of objectives and that there are sometimes distinct differences between the goals of the leaders and those of the members.

Business Unionism. Most of the unions we are aware of are exponents of "business unionism." The phrase refers to both the objectives and the means employed to gain those objects. It suggests that unions want the same thing that business is regarded as wanting—the highest possible price consistent with other objectives. In order to get the highest possible wage rate (the price of labor), it is declared that such unions employ monopoly methods similar to those it is alleged that businessmen use.

Restrictions on entrance of individual sellers of labor into a particular labor market are created by making union membership a condition of employment; and by restricting entrance into the union, the number of sellers in the market can be controlled. By these limits on the amount of labor available, the union is then in a position to ask and get higher wages. There is some evidence that unions pursuing the goal of higher wages are interested not only in hourly wage rates, but in weekly, monthly, and annual earnings of their members, and it may be that in some cases the highest hourly rate will not result in maximum earnings over a longer period of time. However, it is fairly accurate to describe most American unions as being essentially interested in the highest wages for their members, that is, as subscribing to business unionism.

Reform Unionism. Unions have now, and have had in the past, objectives other than maximum wages. Social reform was, and is, such a goal. Some large organizations of the past, such as the Knights of Labor, were greatly interested in improving physical conditions of work and changing the social structure so as to promote industrial harmony. Although "reform unionism" as the central principle about which labor organizations are formed is dead, some unions interested mainly in the wages, hours, and working conditions of their members are also concerned with the promotion of the welfare of other groups, especially when this promotes the interests of the union. In these activities, unions are sometimes engaged in political action, which leads us to "political unionism."

Political Unionism. Some workers' organizations have been interested in gaining their goals through political means. There have been some political parties established by labor groups in the United States—the American Labor Party, the Socialist Party, the Communist Party, and so on—which have attempted to gain political control through the elective process. They have had little success, although some municipalities have elected labor candidates to local office and there have been some members of state and national legislatures who ran on labor party tickets. This lack of success in establishing an effective labor party has encouraged labor unions to act as political pressure groups, attempting to elect friendly candidates of some other party and pressuring legislators and administrators to do their bidding. Samuel Gompers, for many years president of the AFL, thought he perceived a lesson in the failures of labor parties in the late nineteenth century and urged union members to abstain from the formation of such organizations, instead telling them to "reward our friends and punish our enemies" at the polls. Here they have had some substantial success, with the consequence that local, state, and federal legislation, and the administration of those laws, have become more sensitive to labor groups and to their influence.

Before we leave the subject of goals of unions, we should deal with the matter of the difference between the goals of the membership and those of the leadership. Recent studies of trade union wage policy have shown that in order to understand the demands made by union leaders that led to lengthy strikes and great economic hardship for those members out on strike, we must understand that the goals of union leaders are in large part "political." That is, they want to continue as leaders of the union for whatever satisfactions they derive from occupying such positions and when their security is threatened—as by the leader of a dissident faction—they may respond by making demands on companies that will very likely result in strikes that adversely affect the members. Also there have been instances of corrupt union leaders who have entered into contracts that were disadvantageous to their membership in exchange for under-the-table payments from the firm. The moral is that managers must concern themselves with the objectives of both union leaders and union members if they are to come to terms with unions in some satisfactory fashion.

RESOURCES AND ACTIONS OF UNIONS. To the extent that union objectives have been gained, they have been secured because the resources of unions—and those of their friends—have been superior to those of groups which have opposed them or because their strategy has been more effective. Some of the power of unions is economic in nature—by controlling the supply of labor, they have been able to secure a number of economic objects. Unions also have considerable political power, although not as much as the number of union members might indicate. (There have been a number of instances where candidates opposed by union leaders have been voted for by union members.) Most of the lines of action taken by unions are economic or political in nature, although they sometimes engage in educational and other activities as well.

The major economic activities of unions are well known. Through their control over the supply of labor, they attempt to secure certain concessions from firms. The threat of a strike is frequently sufficient to gain a part of what is demanded, if not all. Although union leaders do not like to call their members out on strike, they will do so if they are not conceded enough. The strike funds of the union provide strikers with some income during the strike and give the union considerable bargaining power. Especially among industrial unions, the leaders will frequently call strikes on only one firm at a time in the expectation that the firm cannot long afford to have its plant idle while its competitors have the entire market to themselves. Also, this minimizes the drain on the strike fund. Firms in some industries have dealt with this by declaring: "A strike on one is a strike on all," or by setting up strike insurance funds out of which the struck firm is paid. Although such employer strategy has proved effective in some industries, there are labor leaders who are willing to strike an entire industry in order to gain their objectives. The use of their economic power in such a heavy-handed fashion has turned public opinion against a number of unions and it is possible that in the future such activity will be prohibited by law, or at least limited to some degree. To forestall this, unions engage in political activity.

To gain their objectives and to confound their enemies, unions are involved in a number of kinds of political action. The history of labor legislation from the turn of the century up to the end of World War II shows that unions scored a host of victories in the political arena. Beginning in 1947, with the passage of the Taft-Hartley Law, the tide has run the other way. Still, on balance, labor unions have many more laws favoring them than they did in the 1890's. They continue to press for favorable legislation and the AFL–CIO, through its Committee on Political Education, has attempted to reward its friends and punish its enemies at the polls. Although labor still has friends in public office, it has not made political gains similar to those of the New Deal period. In addition to elections and legislation, unions also concern themselves with influencing the policies and decisions of administrative agencies such as the National Labor Relations Board.

Among other union actions important to business are educational activities and disputes among unions. Much of the educational activity of unions is propaganda designed to put business in a bad light—"high prices" and "excessive profits" are common objects of attack—while attempting to establish that unions are responsible for attaining a number of socially desirable objects, but do not cause inflation. Some union educational activity is aimed at preparing their members to do a better job in both the industry and union, and to help them adjust to technological changes; however, this is a relatively minor aspect of union operations. When unions war with one another, the effects can be desirable or undesirable insofar as managers of firms are concerned. To the extent that a firm's operations are not affected, such warfare depletes the resources of the unions and makes them less formidable opponents of management. However, disputes over job jurisdiction sometimes puts management in impossible situations—no matter which union is given jurisdiction, the other will go out on strike or take other adverse action.

We should not conclude the discussion of union activity leaving the impression that the parties are unalterably opposed. Although it is perhaps inevitable that unions and managements will be adversaries in a number of arenas, still there are times when unions cooperate. Perhaps the most extreme examples of union cooperation are seen in the garment industry, in which unions perform a number of services for firms, including making loans to keep them in business (and union members employed). Also, students of labor history point out that the long-term trend

is away from open conflict and toward greater labor-management cooperation.

THE STRUCTURE OF AMERICAN UNIONS.   Various unions in the United
States have structured relationships among themselves and with organizations in other countries. An understanding of this structure is essential to
an adequate comprehension of American labor. In part, the structure reflects the organization of workers into craft or industrial unions, somewhat different types of "business unions." Also, the fact that unions
initially conducting their activities in one locality (as well as in one
craft or industry) saw advantages in forming associations with other
unions has resulted in a fairly complex set of interrelationships.

Craft and Industrial Unions.   One basis for distinguishing among
unions is by the nature of the work the union members perform. Prior to
the spread of the factory system of production throughout the United
States, organizations of journeymen in various crafts—such as shoemakers,
carpenters, and printers—had already been established. These skilled
workers, performing all of the tasks in a particular production process,
banded together to protect and promote their economic interests in the
sale of their labor to masters, who kept shops. Even after many industries
had adopted factory methods, unions continued to be organized on a
craft basis, with a number of classes of skilled employees being represented by various unions within one firm. Although there were a number
of attempts to organize all of the production workers within a firm into
one union during the 1800's, little success attended such efforts until this
century. Since that time, the numbers and power of industrial unions (as
unions of all employees of a firm, regardless of kind or level of skill are
called) have grown enormously. Craft unions are still of great importance, too, but the growth of industrial unions is the outstanding development in union organization during this century to date.

Local and National Unions.   Members of an organized craft or industrial union are involved in an organization having certain geographical
characteristics. Initially, unions had only a local basis. Although there
might have been organizations of workers possessing the same craft in
various localities, these unions had no interrelationship. Later, as it was
apparent that certain objectives could be promoted thereby, regional and
then national organizations of the local unions developed. Those firms
presently dealing with industrial unions find themselves confronted by a
situation in which the national headquarters of the union makes the more
important decisions concerning demands for better wages, hours, and
working conditions, while the local union concerns itself mainly with the
grievances individual members may have against the employer. There
is another union organization between the local and the national union;
this is the "joint board," which is a centralized body of all the locals of

a particular national union in a city or other region. In many cases, the officers of the joint board have more power than the officers of the local unions.

In illustrating the relationships among locals, joint boards, and national

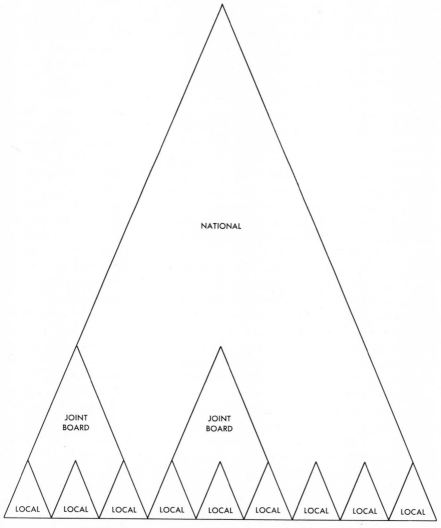

FIGURE 14–1. The Structure of a National Union.

unions, we might use a pyramid (pyramids are frequently used as representations of organizations based on a large membership and having one person—such as a union president—at the top, as in Figure 14–1). Although accurately indicating relationships among locals, joint boards, and the national union of members of craft or industrial unions, the pyramid may give the wrong impression as to where the greatest power or influence resides. That is, the national leaders do not always make the most important decisions, especially in craft unions in which the joint boards make the decisions as to what wages and other concessions will be demanded of management (although in industrial unions such as the United Auto Workers, such decisions *are* made by the national officers). In any national union, there are certain well-defined functions performed at the various levels of organization, although the national leadership is generally most powerful.

Federations of Unions. Local and national unions have formed organizations embodying a number of craft and/or industrial unions. These federations of unions also have a geographical structure. Before the appearance of national organizations of local craft unions, groups of organized workers in different crafts in a particular locality formed a council through which they tried to promote the common interests of those craft unions. These are usually called central labor unions (or "city centrals") or labor councils (for example, King County Labor Council). Even after national unions developed, there still were reasons for the establishment and maintenance of such councils in cities and counties. Also, mainly to promote the political objectives of unions within a state, federations of local unions have been established to deal with state legislatures and executive departments (these are called, logically, "state federations"). On a larger scale, national unions have formed federations for various purposes. The AFL–CIO (American Federation of Labor and Congress of Industrial Organizations) is such a federation of a number of national unions. A logical, and the ultimate, development has taken place in the formation of international federations of trade unions, which hold conventions of union representatives from a number of nations.

By using pyramids again, we can show graphically the nature of the most important federation of national unions in the United States, the AFL–CIO, as in Figure 14–2.

Leaders of the AFL–CIO might deny it looks like Figure 14–2, since the two federations—the American Federation of Labor and the Congress of Industrial Organizations—merged into one federation in 1955. However, although there is no longer a CIO in existence as a federation separate from the AFL, the industrial unions that were the members of the CIO are members of the Industrial Union Department whose head—Walter Reuther—was the president of the CIO. The I.U.D. holds separate conventions and blames many of its difficulties on the old AFL craft unions. There remains much jurisdictional conflict between craft and industrial unions in the AFL–CIO and some observers feel that the merger can't last, in which case the two large federations of national unions would again have separate existence.

It should be pointed out that there are other federations of some con-

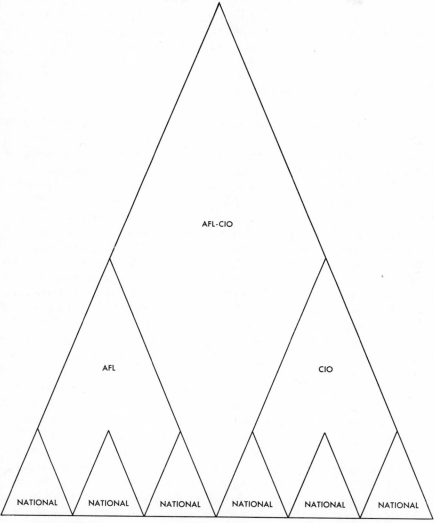

FIGURE 14–2. The Structure of the AFL–CIO Federation.

sequence. For example, there is a Railway Labor Executives Association that performs many functions similar to those of the AFL–CIO. There are also some important national unions that never have been members of a federation (such as the brotherhoods of locomotive engineers and firemen); some that have withdrawn (the most important being the United Mine Workers); and some that were "kicked out" (as was the Teamsters' brotherhood). Therefore, we ought not to confuse the AFL–CIO with "the American labor movement" because there are some important unions that are independent of it and have quite different objectives, and because the AFL–CIO by no means represents a united movement with common objectives, common interests, and common leadership.

THE HISTORY OF UNIONS IN AMERICA

A better understanding of the nature of American unions is gained from examining their development. One kind of union we are familiar with goes back almost to the Revolutionary War. Before the Declaration of Independence, some skilled artisans had joined together in benevolent societies, but the first local unions of journeymen, carpenters, printers, shoemakers, and the like were not formed until the 1780's, and 1790's. In addition to the welfare activities of providing members and their families with financial assistance in the event of serious illness, debt, or death of the wage earner, these unions frequently sought higher wages, minimum wage rates, shorter hours, and the "closed shop." Strikes were called by local printers' and shoemakers' unions against master craftsmen in order to secure their demands. Although a number of local craft unions developed in the early years of the nation, their growth was hindered by the application of legal doctrines holding that combinations of workmen to raise wages were a conspiracy against the public or—even if unions were regarded as lawful—that strikes, boycotts, and other measures adopted to secure union objects were illegal.

Perhaps as a consequence of the unfavorable legal environment, unions began to engage in political activity to change laws, and "political unionism" appeared on the labor scene. In Philadelphia a number of craft unions formed the Mechanics' Union of Trade Associations in 1827. This group soon began to nominate and elect candidates to "represent the interests of the working classes" in the Philadelphia city council and the Pennsylvania state legislature. Local labor parties also sprang up in other states. With the rise of these political organizations, much of the strictly economic activity of trade unions declined, as did the number of craft unions. Although these new groups were successful in getting their candidates elected for a short time, they failed to attain their aims and passed rather quickly out of existence.

Business unionism replaced political unionism by the middle of the 1830's, and "city centrals" began to spring up in cities other than Philadelphia. Organization of union groups beyond a single local area was first tried in 1834 when city central bodies from seven cities met in New York to form the National Trades' Union. This first national federation was the victim of the financial panic of 1837 and the depression which followed it, as were the endeavors of cordwainers (shoemakers), carpenters, typographers, and others to establish national organizations of local unions of their particular crafts.

New attempts to establish national unions met with success in the 1850's. The printers' union held a national convention in 1850, and by 1859, the stonecutters, hat finishers, molders, machinists, and locomotive engineers had established national organizations. This decade was marked by the occurrence of a number of strikes of unions in almost every known craft. However, employer resistance to unions was declining and collective bargaining was becoming established practice in several leading trades.

As each war thence forward was to do, the Civil War gave a tremendous boost to labor organization. Some indication of this growth is revealed by the fact that the number of local unions in the northern states increased from about 80 to almost 300 during 1863 and 1864. The number of city centrals also grew and in 1864 again attempted to establish a nationwide labor federation. This International Industrial Assembly of North America was short-lived, but the number of national unions steadily grew (with 13 new ones appearing between 1861 and 1865). The national unions formed became relatively permanent, with some of them (plasterers, cigar makers, bricklayers, and masons) continuing to the present.

After the Civil War, American labor unions went through a period of ferment and change lasting until World War I. Great fluctuations occurred in union membership, although the trend was steadily upward. National labor federations appeared and disappeared, although one was to emerge as the first permanent federation. Whether the "labor movement" would adopt "business unionism," "reform unionism," or "political unionism" as a guiding principle was not settled until late in the period.

The National Labor Union, formed in 1866, was the first postwar attempt at establishing a national federation. Basically a loose federation of city centrals, it also included local and national unions and various social reform organizations. It veered away from its early trade union goals and aimed at political and social reform. One social change called for was the development of producers' cooperatives, stemming from a belief in such cooperation as a means of freeing workers from the "control" of capitalism. To gain the financial resources to develop such enterprises, the National Labor Union joined the politically inclined farm groups in the "Greenback" movement for large issues of paper money and easy credit. The year 1872 saw the end of the National Labor Union, along with the National Reform and Labor Party, which it supported in the election of that year. A few of the cooperatives survived for a time, but the National Labor Union left no enduring organizations.

Shortly after the appearance of the N.L.U. came the Noble Order of the Knights of Labor. Initially a small local union of Philadelphia garment workers established in 1869, it expanded slowly as other craft unions joined. Its greatest growth came between 1879 and 1886, when its membership swelled from 10,000 to more than 700,000. At the peak of its power, the Knights had a national organization exercising centralized control over a number of district assemblies, each of which was composed of five or more local assemblies (these were of two kinds: trade assemblies including members of only one craft, and mixed assemblies that admitted members from a wide range of occupations including some businessmen). The Order had the broad aim of replacing the existing competitive society by a cooperative one. Reliance was placed on educational and political methods to achieve this objective, rather than on collective bargaining, and strikes were to be employed only as a last resort.

During the eighties, however, trade unionists gained influence in the organization and the Knights engaged in a series of strikes for better wages. Some of these were quite successful, but internal conflict between those favoring collective bargaining and traditional trade-union practices and those committed to political means and basic social change led to the decline of the Knights of Labor, with most of its craft union membership joining the new federation of national craft unions.

This new organization, called the American Federation of Labor, was created in 1886 when the Knights at their annual convention refused to respect the jurisdiction of some of the large craft unions. Several of the latter left and founded the A.F. of L., absorbing through amalgamation the Federation of Organized Trades and Labor Unions, formed in 1881 by six prominent craft unions and some other labor groups. In 1886, the A.F. of L. had some 138,000 members; however, it doubled its membership during the next twelve years, while the Knights saw their membership drop from 700,000 to 100,000 between 1886 and 1890. Thereafter, the Order continued to lose members, although continuing in existence until 1917.

In the three decades following 1890, the A.F. of L. firmly established its position as the principal national federation of American unions. From a membership of one-half million in 1900, it increased this number to 2 million by the outbreak of World War I. It was challenged for the leadership of the "labor movement" by some politically radical organizations—the Socialist Labor Party (which attempted in 1895 to form a rival body—the Socialist Trades and Labor Alliance), the Socialist Party, and the Industrial Workers of the World. The IWW was formed in 1905 by radical political and union groups and aimed at the "abolition of the wage system" and the organization of unskilled factory workers and of migratory labor. Although it had some success—notably in the wheat fields, mines, and lumber camps of the West—its militant tactics caused it to come into public disfavor and to be outlawed in several states. After 1913, it declined rapidly and no longer contended with the AFL for supremacy. The A.F. of L. was given considerable recognition during World War I by the friendly Wilson administration, and the economic conditions of the period also aided its growth in numbers and influence.

Employer opposition, the unfavorable political climate, and unsettled economic conditions combined to reduce the size and power of the A.F. of L. between 1920 and 1933. From a 1920 membership of about 5 million, the number of members declined to about 3½ million in 1923, staying at about this level for the next decade. Important strikes were lost in the steel, coal, and railroad industries. Employers were able to establish the "open shop" in many industries and also to substitute company unions for those affiliated with the national federation.

The New Deal brought changes in the economic and political climate and reduced the power of employers to resist the organization of their firms. Section 7(a) of the National Industrial Recovery Act of 1933, and its successor legislation, the National Labor Relations Act of 1935, firmly established the right of workers to organize for collective bargaining purposes (the latter law also prohibited employer-dominated company unions). The numbers and influence of organized labor reached a new peak, with the only dark cloud a conflict between industrial and craft unions.

Many new industrial unions had been chartered by the A.F. of L. after the New Deal legislation promoted the organization of industries which had previously been unorganized by unions. By 1935, differences between craft and industrial unions in the A.F. of L. led to the establishment by some of the industrial unions of a "Committee for Industrial Organization." The executive council of the A.F. of L. (dominated by craft unions) told the committee to disband: the CIO refused to do so, whereupon the A.F. of L. suspended the ten international unions making up the committee. Nine of the ten and some 32 other "organizing committees" established to recruit workers in unorganized industries then reorganized the committee into the Congress of Industrial Organizations. The CIO had considerable success in organizing the automobile, textile, and steel industries, and by the beginning of World War II, total union membership in the U.S. had climbed to between 10 and 11 million, more than double that existing when the CIO began its organizing campaigns.

World War II provided organized labor with another opportunity to extend union organization and influence. Union membership steadily increased at the rate of about one million workers per year, with the greatest gains for labor being recorded in the shipbuilding, aircraft, automotive, and other industries engaged in production of war goods. For example, the United Auto Workers reported a total dues-paying membership of 1,052,000 in 1945, the largest membership of any national union up to that time.

For a brief period after the war, unions gained a number of objectives important to them, including substantial wage increases (which were offset in large part by increased prices), but they also met with adversity. The economic environment was changing rapidly. Automation and other improvements in manufacturing technology changed the nature of labor markets to ones in which the old skills and unskilled labor were not in such great demand. Labor unions have not had much luck organizing the new professional and technical employees, and the number of union members has remained at about 17 million, only 2 million more than at the end of World War II. Changes in the political environment also reduced the influence of unions. The Taft-Hartley Law of 1947 and the Landrum-Griffin Act of 1959 both placed greater restraints upon unions and attempted, in part, to redress the "balance of power" in favor of employers.

As it exists today, organized labor in the United States is made up of more than 200 national unions, most of which are affiliated with the AFL–CIO. The number of local unions chartered by national unions is estimated to be more than 70,000. In addition to these locals, some locals are directly affiliated with the AFL–CIO where no appropriate national union exists. Also, the AFL–CIO maintains city and state organizations which their affiliated unions are expected to join. Each state in the Union has a state federation and there are approximately 1,000 city centrals and county councils.

The question of what the future outlook is for union development and union activity is discussed in the Reading at the end of this chapter.

READING: The Future of American Unionism *
by Daniel Bell

Where U.S. labour goes from here is a difficult question, for the trade union movement is now at an impasse. The source of its difficulty lies deep in the facts of present-day American life.

* From: Daniel Bell, "Capitalism of the Proletariat?" Encounter (February 1958), pp. 21–24. Reprinted in The End of Ideology, Daniel Bell (New York: Glencoe Free Press, 1960).

1. Union membership has reached its upper limit. In the last five years U.S. unions have ceased to grow. In fact, the proportion of the unionised in the work force has actually declined.

Today there are roughly 16 million workers (plus another 850,000 members of Canadian affiliates) belonging to American trade unions as against two million a quarter of a century ago. Measured against a labour force of 65 million persons, this is slightly under 25 per cent; seen more realistically as a proportion of the wage and salaried persons (i.e., excluding farmers, self-employed professionals, and small businessmen) the unions have organised about 30 per cent of the employee group of the society. But in organising this 30 per cent, they have reached a saturation mark; they have organised as much of their potential as they can.

If one distinguishes between blue-collar and white-collar workers, then it is likely that about 75 per cent of the blue-collar force—factory workers, miners, railway men, building craftsmen, and labourers—belong to unions. In coal and metal-mining, in railroad and construction, in public utilities, unions have organised between 80 and 90 per cent of the blue-collar force. In basic manu-facturing—auto, aircraft, steel, rubber, ship, glass, paper, electrical equipment, transportation equipment—about 80 per cent of plant and production workers are organised. The remaining obstacle in the unorganised units is their small size. A U.A.W. survey, for example, showed that 97 per cent of the unorganized plants within the union's "jurisdiction" have less than fifty workers. These plants are extremely difficult to organise. The social relations within a small firm are very different from those in a large one—the identification with an employer is greater; employer counter-pressure is easier; the cost of the union of reaching and servicing these places is very high and often "uneconomic," since unions, as business organisations, have their cost and efficiency problems as well. The only unorganised industries are oil, chemicals, and textiles. In oil and chemicals, wages are extraordinarily high because labour costs are only a slight element in total costs, and workers are organised in independent unions. In textiles, the old paternalistic and southern mill-village pattern has been strong enough to resist unionisation.

What then of the other fields? In the trade and service fields, employing about fifteen million workers, unions have only a slight foothold—in restaurants, hotels, laundries—but usually only in the metropolitan centres where other unions have been able to help organisation. Most of these units are small, and thus difficult to organise.

In the white-collar and office field (banks, real estate, insurance, as well as the office forces of the large industrial companies), unions have failed signally. In plants where the blue-collar force is organized, the firm usually follows the practice of granting tandem wage increases to the office workers, so that the latter have no need or incentive to join a union. In the insurance companies and in white-collar employment generally, there is a high turnover. Jobs are held by young girls, recruited directly from school, who leave for marriage after five or six years, and who are reluctant to join a union. In general, white-collar workers in the U.S. shrink, for status reasons, from identifying themselves with the dirtyhanded blue-collar workers. In European and Asian countries, teachers and civil service employees may consider themselves the leaders of the working class. In the U.S. these groups seek to emphasise the differences between them.

2. Unions have reached the limits of collective bargaining. This may be a startling statement, but yet it is one of the most important facts tending to re-shape the American labour movement. By the "limits of collective bargaining" I mean simply the growing awareness by unions that they can obtain wage and welfare increases equal only to the increases in the productivity of the country. Such a story may be an old one to unions in Europe, who are sensitive to the trade positions of their countries, but it is new in the U.S.

Even the idea of productivity is a relatively recent one. (It is, perhaps, one of the reasons why Marx's analysis of capitalism has been proven wrong. For Marx, wealth was gained through "exploitation." Now we can see that wealth, private corporate wealth and national wealth, increases only through increases in productivity.) The turning point in American labour history, I think, came with the idea of the annual productivity wage increase. This is the conception that the workers are entitled each year to a wage increase, above and beyond the change in the cost-of-living. One may argue as to how much productivity has advanced—whether it is 2 per cent or 3 per cent or 4 per cent; these are statistical questions. What is settled is the fact that each year the living standard of the worker will advance—in the case of the auto workers, about 3 per cent. (If one compounds the 3 per cent increase, then the living standard will have doubled in a little over twenty-five years.) Curiously, the idea of the productivity wage increase was not a union but a corporation innovation, by General Motors. The company offered such a wage increase in return for a five-year contract, guaranteeing labour peace.

Today the idea of the productivity wage increase has spread throughout most of the basic American manufacturing. In this way a strong demand factor is built into the economy, thus holding off a downturn of the business cycle. But wage rises are geared to the most productive sector of the economy, while inefficient firms, or industries which by their nature cannot increase productivity (barbers, waiters, etc.), have to match these increases. This leads to a strong inflationary impact on the economy.

Such questions aside, the importance of the productivity wage increase is that, despite the lingering rhetoric of militancy, unions have accepted the idea of limits to what can be obtained through economic bargaining. I do not mean to suggest that there will be no more bargaining. But we have here the bureaucratisation of bargaining in the establishment of limits.

3. The rise of the salariat. A third crucial change in the nature of the American labour movement arises from the shifting composition of the work force. Briefly put, the proletariat is being replaced by a salariat, with a consequent change in the psychology of the workers. The trend arises in part from the fact, as Colin Clark long ago noted, that with increasing productivity, greater output is being achieved with a smaller industrial work force, while the demand for new services, entertainment, education, recreation, and research means the spread of more and new middle-class occupations. But we have appreciated less the changes in the work force within the giant manufacturing firms themselves. For with the increases in production have come increases in research, merchan-

dising, sales and office force, etc. In the chemical industry, for example, from 1947 to 1952, production increased 50 per cent; the blue-collar force increased 3 per cent; the white-collar force by 50 per cent. In the fifteen largest corporations in the country, the salaried work force is already one-third to one-half of the hourly-paid production force. For example:

	Hourly Workers	Salaried Workers
DuPont	52,000	31,000
Standard Oil	30,000	27,500
Westinghouse	70,000	40,000
Ford	135,000	40,000
G.M.	360,000	130,000

These salaried groups do not speak the old language of labour. Nor can they be appealed to in the old class-conscious terms. Their rise poses a difficult problem for the leadership of the American labour movement.

4. *The loss of élan and the disfavour of the public.* The labour movement, in its present form, is less than twenty-five years old, and the men on top are the men who built it. But they are no longer young—the average age of the A.F.L.-C.I.O. executive council is in the middle sixties—and they have lost their élan. The organising staffs, too, are old, and there is no longer the reservoir of young radicals to rely on for passing out leaflets at the plant gates.

But more than this, there is a crisis in union morality and public confidence. It is not simply a problem of racketeering. Racketeering is shaped by the market. It has always had a hold in the small-unit construction trades, the long-shoremen, and the teamsters, where the chief cost to an employer is "waiting time," and where one can therefore easily exact a toll from employers. And one finds no racketeering in the mass-production industries. Even in the fields where "shake-downs" are common, racketeering is on a considerably smaller scale today than twenty-five years ago when the industrial gangster flourished in the U.S. The real sickness lies in the decline of unionism as a moral vocation, the fact that so many union leaders have become money-hungry, taking on the grossest features of business society, despoiling the union treasuries for private gain. And where there has not been outright spoliation—typical of the teamster, bakery, textile, and laundry unions—one finds among union leaders an appalling arrogance and high-handedness in their relation to the rank-and-file, which derives from the corruption of power. Such gross manifestations of power have alienated a middle-class public which, for twenty years, was tolerant of, if not sympathetic to, unionism.

It is quite possible that the labour movement may sink, slowly, slothfully into the market role of being a junior partner to industry, as is now the case with the building trades. But it is more likely, in my opinion, that in the years ahead we will find U.S. labour seeking to re-define itself as a social movement.

One reason is that, with politics becoming so intertwined with bargaining, the need to extend labour's political power means that the unions will have to play a more direct role in the Democratic Party and will have to build a liberal coalition in order to strengthen their own position in that party. A subtle change in the political process itself, moulded by the spread of mass media and mass communication, reinforces this tendency. This is the emergence of what may be called "symbol" groups (or those bearing ideological tags) as against the "interest" groups (with their single focus on protecting the specific tangible interest of a specific, tangible group). For in a mass society, where public opinion is king, various groups are more than ever forced to assume some coherent identity and clothe their aims in national or general-interest terms. This is particularly true where the poll concept of democracy takes hold, for polls can only formulate problems in symbolic terms, such as: what should The Farmer do (without worrying about the complication that "The Farmer" is a whole spectrum of persons), or what should Labour do, without enquiring further as to the meaning of such a generic term as "Labour."

But not only the nature of polls, the new process of informal group representation in government as well becomes a shaping element in this fusion of coherent identities. Thus "Business" is asked to name its representatives to a government advisory board; and "Labour" is asked likewise. Political issues become national in scope, and "Labour" as a symbolic group is asked to define "its" attitude toward such issues; and it has to learn to compose its internal differences in doing so. One of the pressures for unity between the A.F. of L. and C.I.O., for example, was the need to have a single set of spokesmen to speak for "Labour" on various national issues.

More directly, the tendency towards the transformation of the union into a social movement gains ground in the undisputed emergence of Walter Reuther, aged fifty, as the top spokesman for U.S. labour, a move which awaits only the retirement of George Meany. Reuther is not popular with his peers. He makes them uncomfortable. He is no back-slapper. He will not relax. His vices are few and his energies are enormous. Like the Jansenist confronting the "whiskey priests," his example calls them to account for their own moral failures. Yet there is no one else who can lead them. And Reuther, temperamentally and biographically, is an ideologue; and his concept of the labour movement is ideological.

What will be the political and ideological content of this new unionism as a social movement? This is difficult to say. The "left" ideology has in recent years become utterly exhausted; and the idea of nationalisation holds no appeal. Most likely we shall see the re-emergence of a rather more emphatic version of "Labourism," insisting more vigorously than ever before on such matters as better housing, more schools, adequate medical care, the creation of a more "humanistic" work atmosphere in the factory, and the like. These are generally prosaic in nature, and it takes great skill on the part of an individual to dramatise them. Whether Reuther can do it or not, remains to be seen.

SUGGESTED READINGS

Beal, Edwin F., and Edward D. Wickersham, *The Practice of Collective Bargaining* (Homewood, Ill.: Irwin, 1963). Describes the parties involved, their relations with one another and with government and the general public. Union and management organizations for collective bargaining are explained as natural reactions to the historical, economic, and political environment within which collective bargaining occurs.

Pelling, Henry, *American Labor* (Chicago: U. of Chicago, 1960). A brief historical study of the "labor movement" with an interpretation of its main features against the background of social and economic development.

Peterson, Florence, *American Labor Unions: What They Are and How They Work* (New York: Harper & Row, 1963). A factual presentation of the history, structure, and operation of American labor organizations.

CHAPTER 15

SUPPLIERS
OF MONEY

Financial resources are secured by firms from owners and creditors. In most businesses, the owners are also the managers and, therefore, there is no social class of owners in their environment. As closely held corporations have grown larger, however, they have been obliged to secure ownership funds from individuals and groups outside of the management of the firm and have, consequently, been involved in relations with a social class (that of "shareholders") which is, in practice if not in theory, outside of the firm and which wishes to influence the management of the business. Most business firms have creditors, and though some of their borrowing might be from members of the firm, for the most part it is not, and so lenders become an important external influence on the operations of business. As in the case of customers and the suppliers of labor, outside owners and creditors are sometimes not wholly satisfied with the results of market activity alone and pursue other lines of action to secure their objectives. Since those who supply money are sometimes represented by others, firms have been thrown into contact with, and have been influenced by, a number of "third parties."

In the history of American business, some students have perceived a stage of "financial capitalism." This era was said to extend from 1873 to 1929. The earlier year was selected as the beginning of the period, since this was the year in which the financial house of Jay Cooke (the great financier of the Civil War) failed. The failure came about because the financier was unable to control the management of the Northern Pacific Railroad, which continued to make large expenditures despite the inability of Cooke to raise the necessary funds. Consequently, according to the historians adopting this view, other financiers employed the lesson learned from Cooke's failure and adopted a number of measures that would ensure control over the financial policies of companies in which they had some interest. Although investment and private bankers were leaders in this movement, commercial banks and insurance companies—important lenders to business—were also involved. The year of the great Wall Street "crash," 1929, is sometimes regarded as the end of the period, with financial capitalism being supplanted by "national capitalism" and "managerial capitalism" under which the nation and corporate managements, respectively, assumed control over the policies of business. However, there is some evidence that (although underground) financial capitalism is far from dead, for various kinds of financial institutions still exert considerable influence over business, as we shall see.

CREDITORS

As with other social classes in the environment of American business, creditors of importance to a firm can be individuals or groups. On occasion, a firm may borrow funds from an individual who is in a position to make substantial loans. Also, businessmen may borrow from a number of individuals—a corporation, for example, sells bonds (which really means borrowing money on a long-term promissory note) to a number of buyers who have no organization. Too, a firm usually buys many of its inputs on credit from various suppliers, and these trade creditors normally do not band together. The most important lenders of money to firms are financial institutions of various kinds, and these have had great influence on business firms, either through individual or group action. Although their name might lead us to think of commercial banks as being the most important institutional lenders to business, we ought to revise our views. During the period of 1948–1960, life insurance companies alone provided more than half (some 53 per cent) of the new money borrowed by American business. This statistic will help explain why such financial institutions play such an active role in their relations with the firms borrowing the funds.

What Creditors Want

Lenders basically want their money back—with interest—when the loan matures. Theoretically, the market rate of interest compensates the lender for undergoing the risk that may get neither principal nor interest. However, in practice, lenders are not always willing to view the matter in this way and, accordingly, take action to insure the safety of the principal as well as to get the interest due them. To achieve these objectives of security and income, they pursue a number of more immediate objectives. They want, for instance, to know something of what the borrowing firm intends to do with the funds and what prospects it has of paying back the loan. (It has been suggested that some lenders set such rigorous standards that about the only persons who can get a loan are those who can prove that they don't need one!) Even when they are prepared to grant loans, creditors may want to take certain protective measures to increase the probability of payment of interest and principal. These measures include the placing of certain restrictions on the use of the borrowed funds; in some cases, conditions are included in the loan agreement providing for other restrictions on what the management might do with the firm's resources—for example, a corporation might be required not to pay dividends until the loan is repaid. Furthermore, to insure that the debtor firm does what it has promised to do, lenders sometimes demand representation in the policy-making body or management of the firm; in corporations, this may mean having a representative on the board of directors.

Resources and Lines of Action of Creditors

The basic resource of creditors is credit. They are in a position to withhold loans or refuse to renew loans if the borrowing firm does not meet their demands. Where they have representation on the policy-making body of a firm, they may be sufficiently influential to determine the direction the business takes and the policies it follows in attempting to reach such a goal. Although the era of financial capitalism is said to be in the past, there still are instances in which creditors exert many important influences on the operations of a firm beyond the influence they have in the money markets.

Among things done by creditors to protect their interests have been restricting dividend payments, forcing changes in managements, and even encouraging mergers among firms when managements might prefer to preserve their separate corporations (which would also preserve their positions and all that goes with them). For example, Sharon Steel entered into a revolving-credit term loan agreement with several banks under which it could borrow up to $10 million from time to time until June 30, 1963, repayable by 1968. In order to secure this loan, the steel company agreed to limit its dividends. Sometimes removal of the head of a corporation from a position of power is a condition of extending a loan. The farm equipment industry provides illustrations: late in 1961, a credit line of $140 million was extended to J. I. Case in exchange for new management and new policies; the president of Motec resigned early in 1962 apparently as a consequence of pressure from banks and other lending institutions that felt that the company was attempting to expand too rapidly, especially when the agreement between the banks and Motec was said to stipulate that none of the lines of credit extended should be used for acquisitions. Perhaps the outstanding recent case of the removal of a manager as a condition of making a loan was the agreement by Howard Hughes to turn over control of Trans World Airlines to a group of trustees representing banks and insurance companies. Although Hughes (through his ownership of the Hughes Tool Co., which owns 78 per cent of TWA stock) still owns the airline, the voting trust prevents him from exercising any control over it. In 1962, a study by the House Antitrust Subcommittee noted that a handful of big lenders (Metropolitan Life Insurance Company, Equitable Life Assurance Society, Prudential Insurance Company, Chase Manhattan Bank, Chemical Bank of N.Y. Trust Company and First National City Bank of N.Y.) held most of the $1.1 billion in outstanding loans to the "big four" airlines—American, Eastern, United, and TWA. The committee was especially concerned because—in true financial capitalistic fashion—the lenders were playing a major role in arranging mergers among the airlines to which they had made loans.

If a business fails to repay either the interest or principal on loans when such payment is due, the creditor has certain legal lines of action he may pursue. He may go to court and secure a judgment against the debtor. Under extreme circumstances, if the debtor does not pay, the creditor or creditors may force the borrowing firm into bankruptcy, hoping that enough can be realized from the forced sale of the assets of the firm to repay the creditors, regardless of whether or not the owners salvage anything. At times a less extreme measure is resorted to. Rather than forcing the firm to go through the rigors of bankruptcy, creditors demand a reorganization of the capital structure of the borrowing firm; a not uncommon result of reorganization is the replacement of the original owners by the creditors. This has been the rule in railroad reorganizations, where some bondholders have wound up holding the capital stock of the corporation. Although the actions of creditors with respect to borrowing firms are not frequently made public information, the role they play in their nonmarket relations with business firms is very important. More frequently, though, we hear of the behavior of owners.

OWNERS

Every firm has an owner or owners. For most firms, the owners are also the managers and consequently do not appear as an external force. In individual proprietorships and partnerships, the owners are the managers—with some exceptions in the case of partnerships. The kind of business firm in which the owners are frequently not the managers is the corporation, especially the large corporation, and when we think of owners as being outside the firm we are usually thinking of stockholders in large corporations.

Theoretically, the corporation is a body of stockholders doing business as one person. In practice, stockholders have in many cases become so divorced from the actual operations of the firm that they are properly regarded as being outside the firm. This has been recognized as a fact by those firms that have set up departments of stockholder relations, which are counterparts of departments of industrial relations (which deal with unions) and of customer relations. Again in theory, the stockholders elect a board of directors to carry out the wishes of the owners, and the board, in turn, elects certain persons to the management of the corporation and controls the activities of the firm in the interest of the owners. This view is a proper one of relatively small, or even large, family-controlled corporations. In many big corporations, however, the management has been able to get itself—or its candidates—elected to the board of directors and the myriad of small stockholders have little control over the directors or the operations of the company even though they might, collectively, own a majority of the common stock. This "splitting of the corporate atom" (that is, the separation of ownership from control) has been widely observed, and when we talk about "the firm" in the case of certain large corporations, the managers rather than the stockholders become the objects of our attention. Although managers may have gained control over the corporation, they must still concern themselves with what the stockholders want, since frustrated owners may take a number of courses of action embarrassing to them.

We should not think of stockholders only as individuals; there are a number of stockholder groups of importance. Even individual stockholders differ in their nature and behavior: there are persons who hold the majority or a significant minority of the shares of a corporation; there are small, but vocal, stockholders who attempt to influence corporate managements even though their holdings are so insignificant in amount that they can elect no directors nor get any resolutions adopted; and there are the small, but docile, stockholders, who make no attempt to influence the management. Stockholders groups are becoming increasingly important. This is in part owing to the fact that institutional buyers purchase by far the largest portion of new stock issues. In 1960, slightly over one half of the total net additions to stocks were purchased by noninsured pension funds, which included both union-administered and corporate pension funds. About 30 per cent of the additional shares was purchased by investment companies. Individuals, including personal trust funds, purchased only about 3 per cent of the total net addition, with the remainder being bought by other institutions and foreigners. Organized groups of small stockholders have been formed in recent years to promote their interests, thereby adding to the growth in importance of stockholder groups. Holding companies have long been important. Before examining such groups, however, we shall discuss individual shareholders.

What Owners Want

The motivations of owners are somewhat more complex than those of creditors. It is fairly obvious that many owners—such as *most small* stockholders in large corporations—do not want to be bothered with the management of the firm's operations. This attitude is what makes it possible for managers to secure control of some corporations. Perhaps the only safe generalization to make concerning the objectives of all stockholders is that they want a good income from their investment, with some security for the amount invested.

Income from investment in shares of the capital stock of a corporation can come from dividends paid on the stock or from selling the stock at a higher price than the purchase price. The peculiarities of the federal income tax make it preferable for many stockholders to receive their income through selling the stock at an appreciated price rather than through the receipt of dividends; consequently, they want the management to take action that will cause the price of stock to rise, which may mean retaining earnings rather than paying them out in dividends. Other investors may count on fairly continuous payment of cash dividends of a certain amount, and their wants may be in direct opposition to those who want a rising price. Even security of investment may be relatively unimportant to "speculative investors," who hope to get rich quick by investing in corporate stocks that promise a very high return in the immediate future—large dividends for a few years may return a sum larger than the initial investment and even if the entire amount originally put into the corporation is lost, it still will have been profitable. What all this may mean is that what owners want is quite specific to the kind of owner we are talking about.

Resources and Actions of Stockholders

All stockholders—regardless of whether they hold many or few shares or whether they are individuals or shareholding groups—have certain resources in common. That is, they have certain legal rights. Some of these are common-law rights which have been established as a consequence of judicial decisions on legal issues involving the relation between the corporation and the shareholder. Under the common law, shareholders have rights to the profits of the corporation, the right to elect the directors, the right to establish policies by passing resolutions, the right to receive annual reports from the corporation, the right to hold directors responsible for their actions, the right to inspect the corporation's records, the right to vote on mergers, the right to vote on corporate charter changes and certain pre-emptive rights to purchase portions of new stock issues. Added to this impressive list of common-law rights are some that have stemmed from laws passed by state and federal legislatures—for example, the Securities Act of 1933 gives the shareholder certain rights to information. Although all shareholders possess these legal rights, only a few—the large and/or aggressive— exercise them. For the most part, the small owners are scattered, unorganized, and indifferent. Other resources of shareholders vary widely, as do the lines of action taken. The kinds of action taken are related to the type of owner, so let us proceed to an examination of the various classes of stockholders in the environment of corporations.

BIG INDIVIDUAL STOCKHOLDERS. The stockholders having a majority of the shares of voting stock are, of course, in a position to control the corporation through their influence on the composition of the board of directors. Surprisingly enough, stockholders owning a minority of the voting shares of corporation stock are frequently more important than those holding a majority. This situation arises when an individual or group owns the largest single block of voting stock, even when this is considerably less than one half of the total shares outstanding. This minority interest—if the majority is unorganized—can control the corporation. The DuPonts, having only about 23 per cent of the common stock of General Motors, were held to have controlling interest of that corporation. A holder of only about 5 per cent of the stock of Safeway Stores was able to bring about a change in the top management of that concern. Consequently, what important minority stockholders want in circumstances when the majority is not organized is of prime importance to the management. Although control can frequently be secured by the holder of the largest minority of shares, sometimes a challenger may appear and a "proxy fight" (a scramble to secure the votes of a majority of the voting shares) ensues. In many giant corporations, the shares of voting stock are so many, so expensive, or so unobtainable that those seeking control will attempt to gain authority from other holders to vote their shares (that is, they seek to gain their "proxy") rather than try to secure ownership of a majority of shares. Such proxy fights make the headlines of the financial dailies because they determine who will control many of the large corporations in the U.S. Since World War II, individuals holding substantial minority interests have challenged other minority stockholders having control of Montgomery Ward, the New York Central railroad, Chrysler, the Allegheny Corporation, and other giant firms. They have not always been successful in taking over control, but they have gained some concessions and have influenced policies adopted by boards of directors.

THE SMALL, BUT VOCAL, STOCKHOLDER. The small stockholder not having an important block of stock or unable to organize an influential group rarely is in a position to determine any fundamental objectives or policies of a corporation. Most of them are aware of this and choose to dispose of their stock if they become dissatisfied with the performance of the management rather than to rebel. On occasion, however, managements are confronted with small, but vocal, shareholders who demand that important changes be made in the way in which the affairs of the corporation are conducted. The prime example of this kind of owner is Lewis Gilbert, the self-styled "corporation gadfly." Such shareholders are rarely able to command a majority of votes, but by using publicity as a major weapon they are sometimes able to gain concessions from corporation managements.

Small, but vocal, stockholders regard themselves as workers in the cause of "corporate democracy." They regard managements, where they control corporations, as being dictatorial; one small stockholder went so far as to compare the position of small stockholders in such corporations to that of the Russian people:

> We should try to understand that Russia is much more like a giant corporation than it is a political state; since the state owns all resources and means of production. The Russian people are the stockholders in the corporation, and Khrushchev is the chairman of the board of directors. Like the small stockholder in America, the Russian stockholder can exert no control over the management of the corporation, but must take whatever dividends the board allows after it has deducted the generous salaries of management.

Lewis Gilbert admits to being the author of the phrase "corporate democracy," but others have enlisted in the movement as well. The most prominent is Wilma Soss, founder of the American Federation of Women Shareholders in Business, to which she has said:

> We shareholders own the corporation. All these Prussian-faced directors are just our employees—laboring people, you might say. Naturally, we the owners have the right to give the hired help a few constructive suggestions from time to time and I am always astonished that they are not more appreciative.

Among the suggestions made by Mrs. Soss is that every corporation have a woman on its board of directors because women own a large portion of the outstanding shares of corporations.

"Corporate democrats" are very much in evidence at annual meetings. They ask pertinent and impertinent questions of officers and directors (Gilbert once asked Douglas MacArthur, then Chairman of Remington-Rand, why he had not purchased shares in the company, and let the general know that he was not pleased by the response of the former army officer that he bought Defense Bonds instead). This gives a clue to one of the objectives of "corporate democrats": management ownership of stock so that managers will have the shareholder's point of view. The resolutions they introduce (which are almost invariably voted down) also reflect their objectives, which one writer listed as being unlimited freedom of speech at stockholders meetings; accessible meeting places; cumulative voting for directors; elimination of the stagger system of electing directors; appointment of professional or public directors; the naming of independent auditors by shareholders; freedom of shareholders to nominate candidates for directors on the proxies sent out by management; freedom to originate resolutions on such proxies; post-meeting reports of the annual meeting; and, the aforementioned management ownership of stock.

The influence of "corporate democrats" is hard to assess. As we noted, they rarely have any of their resolutions adopted, although managements may modify their proposals to prevent any substantial number of shareholders from voting for those of Gilbert, Soss, and so on. "Corporate democrats" have had little luck in getting their nominees elected to boards of directors, although they do claim some success in getting election procedures modified. However, their embarrassing questions may have some impact. Gilbert contends that many an executive's yacht has been discontinued as a result of shareholders' complaints about luxurious executive living. Executive salaries and pensions have also been attacked, but with less apparent success. By bringing management practices out into the open, there is perhaps less chance of managers acting contrary to the interests of the shareholders.

THE SMALL, BUT DOCILE, STOCKHOLDER. The average small stockholder is not vocal. He is an absentee owner who does not want to be bothered about managing the firm. Normally he feels no class interest and does not care to organize to protect his interests. He is disfranchised, since he has only one slate of directors to vote for—that which the management lists on the ballot requesting his proxy. Although he has many legal rights, he usually confines himself to exercising his right to sell his share(s) if dissatisfied with the management. Finally, he is usually ineffective in whatever attempts he may make to influence the management because he lacks the resources with which to gain such an end, or if he possesses them, realizes the folly of employing them in such fashion.

REPRESENTATIVES OF STOCKHOLDERS. Large corporations with many stockholders are occasionally confronted with individuals or groups who claim to represent the interests of the scattered owners. For such firms, relations with individual holders of shares of company stocks are usually limited to one-way communications in which the management of the corporation—through annual reports, stockholders' meetings, requests for proxies, dividend checks—gives some account of itself and what it has done. Some individual stockholders may write the management, and even visit the company, and are usually received cordially. Also, some individual shareholders speak up in meetings. However, the channels of communication and influence are fairly limited for individual stockholders and managements have been more inclined to give heed to those who represent a large group of owners.

One owner's representative to whom most managements of large corporations are very sensitive is the investment banker. Large corporations do not normally sell shares of their stock directly to the ultimate owners, but sell them through one or more investment bankers (such a group is known as a syndicate). These bankers are in the relatively permanent business of selling corporate stocks to ultimate owners, and are concerned about their reputations as merchants of good securities. Where managements take actions that seem contrary to the interests of the security owners—and therefore to the reputation of the investment bankers—the financiers, as representatives of the owners, sometimes take a hand. This type of influence reached its peak during the period of "Financial Capitalism" in the United States. Large investment bankers, such as J. P. Morgan and his associates, insisted on some measure of control over the corporations whose securities they sold in order to protect the interests of the owners and, therefore, their own. There is not as much financial control over corporations now as there once was, but investment bankers are still important.

It might be expected that other financial institutions would also exert considerable influence on the managements of corporations whose securities they held. However, institutional shareholders—such as investment trusts, insurance companies, trust companies, pension funds—rarely exercise their considerable power to throw poor managements out or to influence the policies of a corporation. Their representatives do not make speeches at annual meetings, nor do they introduce resolutions or nominate directors. They do not want to be saddled with managerial responsibilities or be responsible if their candidates do a poor job. This does not mean, however, that they are without influence. They do vote the shares in their trust, and they may vote against the management. Also, if they decide to disinvest in a particular corporation, the market price of the company's securities might fall (since this seems to reflect on the management of the corporation, executives are quite anxious for the good opinion of the institutional investors and give heed to suggestions made by them).

Some investors' organizations do control the management of corporations. These are the holding companies, which hold the securities of other corporations, and when they hold a controlling interest, possess undisputed control. However, such organizations do not represent the interests of the small investor in the operating company; rather, they act in behalf of the owners or managers of the holding company.

There are other representatives of shareholders of some importance; of these, some are temporary organizations and others are permanent. At a critical point in a company's history, some attempt may be made to organize the widely scattered stockholders of a large corporation into a group to take effective action on some particular matter. Such organizations rarely last after the crisis is past. Some permanent organizations of relatively small shareholders have been set up, but as yet their influence is nominal. One of these is the American Federation of Women Shareholders in Business, headed by Mrs. Wilma Soss, which we have already mentioned. There are two others: the Investors League and United Shareholders of America, Inc. The late B. C. Forbes, who published *Forbes* business magazine, founded the first of these, which originally took the name Investors Fairplay League, merged with the American Federation of Investors and in 1945 adopted the name of Investors League. The League does not believe in "rabble-rousing at stockholders meetings," concerning itself instead with legislation in the interests of investors. Specifically, the League has concerned itself with lobbying and propagandizing for elimination of "double taxation" of dividends, elimination of the capital gains tax on the appreciation in price of securities, and for other laws that would increase the profits of corporations and the income of investors. United Shareholders of America, Inc., is a "split-off" from the Investors League. Feeling that the ties of the League with corporations were too close, Benjamin A. Javits (brother of Senator Jacob K. Javits of New York) organized the United Shareholders in 1950. It has legislative aims similar to those of the League, but also concerns itself with the kind of stockholder relations corporations have (giving awards to those which, in its judgment, have good relations). Although there is some doubt that United Shareholders is sufficiently critical of corporate practices, it has come out against such things as the stagger system of electing directors. However, there is not much evidence that any of these organizations appreciably influence either legislation or corporate managements.

If there is any tendency in the ability and interest of corporate stockholders to influence management, it is probably increasing. However, in the foreseeable future, there appears to be little prospect of shareholders seriously challenging managers for the control of corporations in those firms where the management has secured this power. Although stockholder influence may be increasing, managements may be freeing themselves somewhat from their dependence on creditors. Since World War II, many firms have been able to generate substantial inflows of money through sales and, therefore, have not had to approach either owners or creditors for additional sums.

READING: Shareholders at Their Annual Meeting,* Standard Oil Company (New Jersey)

The shareholders' meeting of a large firm such as Jersey Standard is revealing. It shows how little influence individual shareholders and stockholder groups representing only a small percentage of the outstanding stock exert in large cor-

* Excerpts are from the reports of the 77th and 79th meetings of the shareholders in Standard Oil Company (New Jersey) held in 1959 and 1961. Reprinted by permission.

porations where the management has the proxies of the bulk of the stockholders. Jersey had some 680,000 shareholders in 1961, of which some 3,800 attended the meeting in person (just over one-half of one per cent). However, well over 75 per cent were represented by proxy and more than 85 per cent of the outstanding shares were voted. Since the management had the bulk of the proxies under their control, there could be no doubt as to the outcome of the voting for directors and on resolutions. However, resolutions proposed by some shareholders, their behavior at the meeting and the response of management indicates the objectives of some of the owners, the way in which they proposed to secure those objects and also something about the goals of the managers.

In 1959, Lewis Gilbert, a leader in the movement for "Corporate Democracy," introduced a proposal that the number of directors of the corporation be increased from fifteen to sixteen, explaining it in the following manner:

> I have a few comments. One of the management's replies to our proposal is in regard to the importance of the full-time director. We agree completely. This has nothing to do with the fact that an extra outside director can be on the board. The possible areas of conflict which can occur when we do not have an outside director—and naturally we would prefer to see him elected through the right of cumulative voting—are shown when options and such emoluments are under review, as the interests of management and the shareholders are not always one and the same.

The Chairman of the Board of Directors, Eugene Holman, disagreed that there was any possibility of conflict between the interests of stockholders and management in his response to Gilbert:

> The board is not opposed to increasing the number of directors, if and when it finds that a larger number can more effectively serve the stockholders. It already has the authority to change the number and does so from time to time. Full-time directors devoting their entire efforts to the company's interests can, in our opinion, deal more effectively with this company's problems. Firsthand knowledge of its business interests, its organization and personnel, which comes from daily association . . . , is essential for the directors in this company, with its complex and worldwide interests. As has been demonstrated over the years, the board has been able to recommend directors with a variety of experience and a high degree of ability and effectiveness from among the full-time personnel of the company and its affiliates. The proper discharge by each director of his responsibilities to the stockholders as a whole precludes, in our opinion, any possible areas of conflict between the interests of stockholders and management.

Having previously nominated members of the management for election to the board of directors, the management used their control of the proxies to elect management men to the board and, subsequent to the shareholders' meeting, in their role as the board of directors appointed themselves as officers of the company. The Gilbert resolution aimed at getting an "outside" man on the board gained only 2.57% of the vote.

In 1961, Gilbert and his associates tried again, with the assistance of Mrs. Wilma Soss, the head of the Federation of Women Shareholders in American Business, Inc. This time their resolution proposed the election of directors by cumulative voting—which procedure would entitle each stockholder to as many votes as equal the number of shares he owns multiplied by the number of directors to be elected and would enable him to cast all such votes for a single candidate. This procedural change would permit a minority of the shareholders to gain minority representation on the board of directors. Discussion of the proposal led to the following exchange between Gilbert and President M. J. Rathbone:

MR. LEWIS D. GILBERT—I am again grateful for the fine support we are going to have from so many independent shareholders on this particular point. I would like to point out, of course, that the vote against these proposals includes the unmarked proxies and includes the fiduciary proxies, the bulk of which always vote with the management.

I would also like to point out that this is a New Jersey corporation and as such, of course, can have cumulative voting.

THE PRESIDENT—This question has been presented to us twice before, once in 1952 and again in 1956. In both years it was rejected by something over 97 percent of the shares voted.

Your management believes that the proposed change in voting rights is neither appropriate nor necessarily in the interests of the shareholders. Directors elected through cumulative voting tend to be representatives of separate groups of shareholders, each one looking after some special interest and not working together as the most effective team for the maximum benefit of all. We believe it is important to the shareholders that the board continue to be a cohesive group working together effectively, and that every director represent all shareholders rather than some special group.

Our entire board reviews the recommendations of every individual put up for a director. We never recommend a director for election unless he is acceptable to the whole board. Such a procedure cannot fail to give Jersey an efficient, smooth-working, teamlike board.

We recognize, of course, that Mr. Gilbert and the others who recommend this proposal are sincere in feeling that the change would be an improvement. It is a difference of opinion. We have not been persuaded, and remain unpersuaded that there is anything to be gained for the shareholders of Jersey by instituting cumulative voting for directors.

MR. GILBERT—In closing the discussion on this particular point, I would like to make a few observations. I was delighted to see that, just as with the place of the meetings and some of the other fine things the board has adopted over the years after they were aired at stockholder meetings, we are trending toward an outside director sooner or later.

After hearing the views of our board, I would say that one thing they object to most is that they couldn't have the exclusive right of deciding who would be on it, and that they would be unhappy if they had to have somebody they didn't apparently know. I agree that directors should be happy (Laughter) but their happiness is a very secondary consideration. It is the welfare of the entire body of the shareholders which is of the greatest importance.

This time, the resolution gained the support of 2.86% of the shares.

Mrs. Soss had been involved in another proposal to protect what she regarded as the shareholder's interest. In 1959, she and her associates had proposed a change in Jersey Standard's stock option plan—a plan which many shareholders regard as desirable, since it gives managers a proprietary interest (and presumably the shareholder's point of view). The proposed change would have required those managers acquiring stock under the plan to hold their shares for at least three years and to pay 100% of the market price of the shares, among other things. She supported her resolution with the following statement:

> These are the reasons for this proposal: When questioned at the last annual meeting, officers were vague about disposal of optioned stock granted to increase proprietary interests. The mandatory holding period makes abuse of option privileges more difficult. The Senate Sub-committee on Antitrust and Monopoly noted in its majority report of March 13, 1958, that ownership of stock creates a direct interest in affairs of the corporation, but ownership of options creates a direct interest in stock market valuations. Other companies have added holding clauses such as we have suggested. One had added the non-cumulative installment provision, preventing exorbitant profit taking at the end of an option period possibly accruing from conditions which may be unrelated to actual company business.
>
> As you have seen, some of our officers from time for one reason or another have sold optioned stock which they have had for a proprietary interest.

The management of the company regarded stock option plans mainly as a means for providing incentives for managers rather than giving them the shareholder's point of view. Consequently, it opposed the Soss resolution and made its own proposal for a change in the stock option plan. The Chairman put it this way:

> There is on the agenda a management proposal for a second incentive stock option plan for executives. This plan is an integral and important part of the company's executive development program. Your directors consider that one of their most important functions is to attract, develop, and keep managerial leadership of the highest caliber. The specific provisions of this plan, including the 100 per cent purchase price, have been very carefully formulated. Various limitations which we believe safeguard appropriately the interests of all concerned have been written into the plan.
>
> The further restrictions included in this stockholder proposal would preclude the individual from exercising his right to manage his financial affairs to suit his personal financial situation. This would tend seriously to dimin-

ish the value of the plan. While different plans might well be suitable for other companies, it is the considered judgment of the board of directors that the second incentive stock option plan best fits this company's executive development program and its competitive situation in industry. For these reasons, the management opposes this stockholder proposal.

Another shareholder—apparently Mr. Gilbert—spoke for the Soss proposal:

On behalf of the owners of over 30,000 shares of stock, we are 100 per cent behind this restricting resolution. Everything in it speaks for shareholder protection, and the shareholders of the United States have the right to be protected just as much as American management or American labor.

Remember, options dilute your equity, and if the stock is sold it helps keep your stock and my stock and everybody's stock down. It also keeps dividends down, because the more stock there is outstanding, the more the company has to earn to pay any given dividend. And may I remind you as taxpayers that every time we have special benefits for a special class, all the rest of us pay increased taxes.

When the ballots were counted, the restrictions proposed by some shareholders were found to have the support of only 3.19% of the shares; the management's proposal was approved, gaining slightly over 96% of the votes.

Another resolution to protect the shareholders' interests, as one shareholder viewed them, proposed to limit corporate gifts to charitable, educational and similar organizations. No funds were to be given except for purposes in direct furtherance of the business interests of the corporation. The representative of the proponent spoke as follows in behalf of the resolution:

Mr. Watson Washburn—I represent Mrs. Alice Vandergrift Gordon. Her grandfather was one of the associates of John D. Rockefeller in the early days of Standard Oil, and she has always taken great interest in the welfare and progress of the company. She is very regretful that she can't be here today because of illness, and has asked me to represent her.

The reasons for this resolution, given in the proxy statement, are as follows: Your directors are giving millions of dollars of your corporation's money to charity. This seems wrong. Your company is supposedly run solely for the stockholders' benefit. It is not an eleemosynary institution. Many stockholders undoubtedly feel that charity begins at home. Others who can afford donations are certainly entitled to choose their own beneficiaries. The current practice is especially reprehensible when as here nearly $10,000,000 have been given since 1955 to educational institutions, many of which now teach socialism and ridicule businessmen, savers, and investors, as recently explained in the well-documented best-seller, Keynes at Harvard.

Actually your company has made unrestricted grants to 429 different educational institutions in this country in the last five years. By merely inspecting the list one could say that some of them were not the kind of college where they encourage companies like ours and stockholders like ours. For example among the men's colleges Harvard, Yale, and Princeton have been the beneficiaries of the company's donations; and among the women's colleges, Smith, Vassar, and Sarah Lawrence. Those are just examples of places where, on the whole, left-wing-doctrines are taught in the economics departments.

In his response, the president of the company indicated his belief that corporate giving was in the interest of the stockholders:

> We in the Jersey Company believe in being good corporate citizens. We think the principle of corporate giving is well established. It is encouraged by our tax laws; it has been upheld in our courts; and the public has come to expect it of corporations. Perhaps this was not so, say, some twenty-five years ago, but it is today. In our judgment these contributions are extremely important if Jersey is to merit the good will of the public, which is essential to the prosperity of your company.
>
> When you're a good corporate citizen, it is often necesary to give support to private institutions from which you expect no direct dollar-and-cents benefit—hospitals, community service organizations, the Red Cross, colleges, universities, and so on. If good citizens, corporate and individual alike, did not support these institutions, they would have to turn to the government for support—and that, certainly, is not the way to advance the cause of free enterprise.
>
> As to the merits of giving to one institution, or one type of institution, over another, the possibilities for discussion are infinite. As we normally do in such a situation, we call upon a competent staff to gather information, to study the various facets of the problem, to appraise and analyse the facts, to evaluate the direct and indirect benefit to the company and its shareholders, and to make recommendations to the board. Your directors are then in a position to make a sound decision, and I assure you that in every instance the shareholders' interests are paramount.

In this case, the management had some support from a stockholders' group and from Mr. Gilbert.

> A SHAREHOLDER—I represent a group of independent investors, the United Shareholders of America. Our president, Mr. Benjamin A. Javits, had intended being here today but has asked me to come in his stead. Before I read his statement on this resolution, may I make my own personal observation?
>
> Is it preferable to have government interfere in this matter of endowments to universities and colleges? We feel that, as an organization, we certainly don't want any more government interference because we are dedicated to the free enterprise system which has served us so well in this country.
>
> (The shareholder then read a statement from Mr. Javits, opposing the resolution and supporting management's position, in which he stressed the need for industrial leadership, and not just political leadership, in the achievement of social and educational objectives under democratic capitalism.)

GILBERT—I am supporting the management position. I certainly think that management has an obligation in regard to social duty; and in giving wise contributions over the years, we are benefited and so is the entire system. But I do think that the holders should be told in the Annual Report if we give exceptionally large contributions to any one charity or cause in one year.

PRESIDENT—Thank you, Mr. Gilbert, We'll take that suggestion into consideration.

This shareholder's resolution secured slightly more support than had the others, receiving 3.05 per cent of the shares voted in favor.

Although the management soundly defeated all proposals which it did not make, it did not want the shareholders making the proposals and other suggestions to feel as though the management was indifferent. That the company's officers were not unalterably opposed to making a change in the board's composition is revealed in a brief discussion between an identified shareholder (again probably Gilbert) and the company's chairman:

On behalf of the holders of 30,000 shares, I want to record our objection to the continued all-inside working board. We have felt this way for quite a while, and we are going to continue to urge over the years that this policy be ended.

THE CHAIRMAN—This is a policy to which we give periodic consideration. We don't have a closed mind on it. We may change our policy one of these days. We feel that a working board gives us a considerable advantage in that all members pretty much understand all of the phases of the business.

The president of the firm responded in similar vein to a suggestion concerning scholarships for employees:

May I just say this, that I hope you shareholders will agree with me when I say that we are receptive to your suggestions. We may appear a little obdurate once in a while, but if the suggestions are sound and keep coming up, sometimes we find that they impress us eventually.

All of the above seems to indicate that individual shareholders and stockholders' organizations representing only a small minority of the shares have little or no influence on the management of Jersey Standard. It is difficult to say whether or not the management's stock option proposal was put forward to counter the proposition of some shareholders, but it may have been and, if so, indicates that such resolutions have some influence, even if not passed. Although it might be easy to conclude that here is an example of the management of a large corporation—firmly in control of the votes—being indifferent to its shareholders, it is probably more accurate to state that Jersey Standard had learned the hard way that although the interests of its shareholders are important, other interests have to be taken into account as well.

SUGGESTED READINGS

Gilbert, Lewis D., and John J. Gilbert, *Annual Report of Stockholder Activities at Corporation Meetings* (Published annually since 1939 "for and in the interests of American Stockholders by Lewis D. Gilbert and John J. Gilbert, 1165 Park Avenue, New York 28, N.Y.") Lively reports of the activities of "Corporate Democrats" in their attempts to influence managements.

Jacoby, Neil H., and Raymond J. Saulnier, *Business Finance and Banking* (New York: National Bureau of Economic Research, 1947). An examination of the changing relationships between commercial banks and business enterprises since 1900.

Livingston, J. A., *The American Stockholder* (Philadelphia: Lippincott, 1958). A fairly objective study of various kinds of stockholders and their activities by a syndicated financial columnist.

CHAPTER 16

SUPPLIERS
OF MATERIALS

In conducting their operations, business firms use materials, machines, and structures as well as men and money. Relations with suppliers of plant and equipment are relatively infrequent and are, for the most part, market relationships. However, the contacts a firm has with those who supply it materials are fairly continuous, and such suppliers frequently exert influences on the managers of an enterprise beyond normal market pressures. Figure 16–1 shows the flow of materials through the hands of the manufacturer into the hands of the ultimate user. It does *not* show the entire flow of materials, since those supplying materials to manufacturers have their suppliers, and these in turn have theirs, and so on. However, manufacturing firms are involved with the major classes of suppliers of materials, and hence the figure presents a fairly complete view of the kinds of materials suppliers.

In the following treatment, suppliers of capital goods, suppliers of parts for assembly, and suppliers of supplies will not be discussed in any great detail because they, for the most part, restrict themselves to market action. On occasion some of them have "conspired" against their customers (as in the case of the electrical equipment industry) and charged prices that were probably higher than they would have been had the

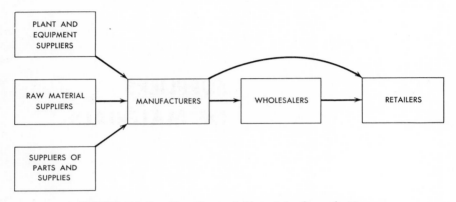

FIGURE 16–1. The Flow of Materials through Firms.

price-fixing conspiracy not taken place. However, this is still market action. Suppliers of parts and supplies have rarely enjoyed the opportunity to enrich themselves greatly at the expense of the firms that are their customers—partly because there is considerable competition among such suppliers and partly because their customers have a "make-or-buy" option available to them which they do not have when purchasing equipment.

Suppliers of raw materials and suppliers of goods for resale (especially manufacturers) have engaged in political and other nonmarket action in addition to collective action in the markets. These have had considerable influence, not only on the prices paid by business firms buying such supplies but on other aspects of the activities of the buyers as well. In discussing the major classes of materials suppliers, we shall be concerned with their collective activities inside and outside the market through which they hope to attain their objectives.

RAW MATERIALS SUPPLIERS

Raw materials are those goods that a firm alters physically and incorporates into its final products. For example, a flour-milling concern purchases wheat and converts it into flour. The mill may sell the flour as a final product or it may use the flour in the production of other products. In any case, wheat is a raw material for the miller. A baking firm would regard flour, along with other ingredients, as raw materials for the production of bread. Every manufacturing firm has certain inputs that are the raw materials out of which it makes its products. Producers in the extractive industries are among the more important suppliers of such goods, although many manufacturers buy their raw materials from other manufacturing firms.

Suppliers of Agricultural Products

In the history of American business, there has been no other group of suppliers of raw materials as influential on the purchasers of their products as have been American farmers. Agricultural producers have frequently been dissatisfied with market conditions—as sellers as well as in their role of buyers. This dissatisfaction has led them to take a number of actions beyond selling as individuals in the market in order to get higher prices, and they have been quite successful in such endeavors. They have marshaled their economic bargaining power through group action; they have employed their great political resources to secure results they could not get through collective economic action; finally, they have enjoyed a favorable public opinion and have allied themselves with sympathetic individuals and groups in order to gain their goals.

Mention has been made in Chapter 13 of the attempts by farmers to promote their interests as consumers through collective economic action; in addition, they have cooperated to promote their interests as sellers. In 1889, a group of Iowa farmers established the first cooperative grain elevator. Prior to this time, the agriculturalists were obliged to sell, as individuals, to the owner of the local grain elevator, who, in turn, sold the commodity on the organized grain exchanges at the major railroad terminals in the nation. From this first step, taken to increase the price received in the local market, farmers' cooperative grain associations have grown so that they are sometimes in a position to influence prices on the major grain exchanges. Perhaps the grandest attempt to do so took place during the 1920's, when two large wheat growers' cooperatives tried to acquire virtually all of the wheat produced in the United States and to withhold it from the market until the prices rose to a satisfactory level. This attempt failed. Since that time, wheat farmers have turned to political measures to secure what they could not gain through economic means. Much grain is still sold by farmers' cooperatives, and they claim that they have been able to secure a higher price for their members, or, as the buying firm sees it, to charge higher prices to buyers.

There have been, of course, organizations of sellers of agricultural commodities other than wheat. For the most part, the main objective of all of these organized groups has been to raise the price received by the agricultural producer. Early in this century, the producers of tobacco went on "strike" against the American Tobacco Company, the biggest buyer prior to its dissolution in 1911 under the Sherman Antitrust Act. This withholding action, which kept the bulk of the tobacco crop from reaching the market, resulted temporarily in a higher price for tobacco leaf. In recent years, producers of the major nonperishable agricultural commodities have relied on legislation rather than on economic action to keep the price of their products high. However, sellers of perishable or specialty farm products still are engaged in cooperative activity that raises the price to the business firm that processes or resells the product.

Periodically, we see news reports concerning action taken by a group of milk producers, livestock producers, fruit growers, or other producers of perishable agricultural products that has the effect of increasing the price. Milk producers, operating under federal legislation, have carved the nation up into a number of "milksheds" (marketing areas from which milk producers outside the area are barred). In these markets, the representatives of the producers (usually some kind of cooperative) set the prices that creameries must pay (subject to the approval of the U.S. Department of Agriculture). Livestock producers also engage in cooperative marketing of their products. In Illinois recently, six livestock marketing associations voted to consolidate into a new organization called the Illinois Producers Livestock Association. This new group has a membership of some 35,000 livestock producers who expect that the consolidation will result "in greater returns to farmers through increased volume and efficiency and increased bargaining power." To the extent that its increased bargaining power secures higher prices for livestock, this raises raw material prices to meat packers. In California, where there are many associations of growers of perishable agricultural products, reliance is also placed on the increased bargaining power stemming from cooperative marketing. For example, there is a California Canning Peach Association, which bargains with the cling-peach canners to gain as high a price as possible for its farmer members.

All such cooperative marketing activity aimed at raising farm prices is legal, although manufacturers engaged in interstate commerce are frequently prosecuted under the antitrust laws for doing essentially the same thing. This state of affairs reflects the great political resources of agricultural producers, and has an interesting history. Congressional representatives from the farm states were major supporters of antimonopoly legislation when the Sherman Antitrust Act was passed in 1890. Farmers hoped that this would reduce the prices of things that they bought (through breaking up the "Barbed-Wire Trust," the "Harvester Ring," and so on) and did not expect that the legislation would be used against farmers' organizations. At the time of the passage of that act, some spokesmen for agriculture urged "counter-combination" as the solution for the farmer's poor bargaining position and some large cooperative marketing organizations were established shortly after the passage of the Sherman Act.

To the dismay of the farmers, associations of manufacturers were not (in the early judicial interpretations of the Sherman Act) held to come under the law and the U.S. Supreme Court refused to order their dissolution. Furthermore, during the "farm strike" of tobacco producers against the American Tobacco Company, some actions of the farmers were held to be contrary to the antitrust law and those agriculturalists involved were fined. This led to an attempt by agrarians to exempt the activities of agricultural and horticultural associations from the Sherman Act. The Clayton Act of 1914 did contain a provision that seemed to do this, but later Supreme Court decisions held that certain activities still came under the prohibitions specified in the law. However, agricultural cooperative marketing legislation passed in the 1920's permitted groups of agricultural producers to cooperate in activities aimed at raising the prices of farm products. Although this legislation did not exempt farmers from the antitrust laws, it took the enforcement of such laws against farmers from the U.S. Attorney General and turned it over to the Secretary of Agriculture (normally a friend of the farmer, who does not make it his business to prosecute farmers for trying to raise their prices through collective action).

An interesting aspect of the farm legislation permitting cooperative marketing as a means of raising farm prices is that such marketing has not been effective for all crops. The grand schemes of the wheat growers during the 1920's failed, and these producers (along with the producers of other basic nonperishable agricultural products) have turned to price-support activity by the federal government to keep prices high. The maintenance of high domestic prices and the piling up of surpluses of some of these crops under price-support programs have had adverse influences on a number of processors of agricultural products. For example, American cotton textile mills have been obliged to pay a high, government-supported price for cotton. In order to help cotton planters dispose of some of their surplus production, the federal government has been giving them an export subsidy to enable them to meet lower cotton prices in other countries. Foreign cotton textile producers have been buying this cheap cotton, manufacturing it into textiles and re-exporting the manufactured product to the United States, where it can be sold cheaper than textiles produced by American manufacturers. Not only are cotton mills in the U.S. injured by this increased competition in domestic markets but they find it almost impossible to compete in foreign markets because the domestic price of the raw material is higher than its price overseas. Although the federal government has tried to do something for American textile producers (since they come from politically important states), it is difficult to accomplish much because agrarian political pressure is maintained for retention of price-supports on cotton and prevents permitting the domestic price of cotton to fall to the level of prices in other parts of the world.

Other Extractive Products Suppliers

Producers in other extractive industries have also taken action to promote their interests. Late in the nineteenth century, the Standard Oil Company of New Jersey had a virtual monopoly on refining capacity in the United States. Crude oil producers contended that the company was using its position to keep the price of the basic commodity low and took action to get a higher price for crude. Miners of metallic ores, especially silver, have employed various means (including political action) to secure increased prices for their products. Fishermen, too, have formed cooperative marketing organizations to improve their bargaining position with respect to those firms that buy from them. In short, there is almost no field in the extractive industries in which organizations have not sprung up to raise the price of these raw materials. The exceptions exist chiefly where the processing firm also owns the sources of the basic commodities.

Suppliers of Other Raw Materials

Not all firms use the products of extractive industries as their raw materials. Automobile manufacturers buy sheet steel from the steel mills, for example, and do not produce their own from iron ore, coal, limestone, and so on. However, the motivation of suppliers of steel and other goods to be transformed in the production process is similar to that of the farmer and other firms in the extractive industries. Basically, they want to get the best price for their products. To secure the best price, they have engaged in cooperative action to raise or maintain the price. It should be stated that in such price-setting activities, some regard has to be given to the necessity of maintaining a desired volume of sales and to the possibility of antitrust suits; for agricultural producers, this is frequently unimportant because the federal government will purchase and stockpile those surplus commodities that processing firms do not buy and will not sue farmers for engaging in cooperative marketing. Consequently, for suppliers of certain raw materials, the highest price is not necessarily the best price.

Some firms have kept down the price of raw materials by owning the sources of supply. In the lumber industry, many large firms own substantial tracts of timber and even engage in "tree farming" to assure themselves of a perpetual supply of the raw material. Other lumber companies rely on the sale of timber from government-owned lands, but frequently complain that agencies such as the U.S. Forest Service appraise the stumpage at too high a price. Steel companies get a major share of their raw materials from "captive" iron and coal mines; that is, from mines they own. This gives them considerable leverage over other suppliers and enables them to hold down prices on "noncaptive" tonnage. An interesting question is raised thereby: Why haven't processors of agricultural products acquired "captive wheat fields," "captive tobacco fields," and so on?

SUPPLIERS OF PARTS FOR ASSEMBLY

Most manufacturing firms purchase parts to be assembled into final products, along with those parts which it makes. Automobile companies, for example, make certain of the components of a car or truck, but purchase many other finished parts from other suppliers. In addition to wanting a fair price, such suppliers want the continued patronage of the purchaser. This limits their demands for high prices, because they understand that the automobile firm has a "make-or-buy" alternative open to it with respect to many purchased parts. Producers of automobiles do not exercise this option lightly because they know that the supplier is in a position to favor his loyal customers in times of scarcity. The Ford Motor Company, which points out that it has thousands of suppliers, has said, in effect: "We depend on suppliers in good times, in bad times and at all times. If we treated them unfairly in bad times, they'd treat us poorly in good times. We'd lose out in the long run." However, Ford has exercised its "make-or-buy" option on occasion; recently it purchased the Autolite Company and made a number of its own electrical components, thereby cutting out the Champion Sparkplug Company, which had previously supplied many of its requirements. Competition among such suppliers is relatively great, and there is not much evidence of their organizing to raise prices to buyers.

SUPPLIERS OF GOODS FOR RESALE

Wholesalers and retailers purchase goods to be sold again without any physical alteration or incorporation into another product. Wholesalers buy

from firms in the extractive and manufacturing industries; retailers sometimes buy from firms in those industries, but they also buy from wholesalers. Such suppliers are essentially interested in low distribution costs
(which means greater income to them) and in the sale of the goods at
the right price and desired volume in wholesale and retail markets. When
they have not secured these objects through individual bargaining in
the market, they have taken other action to improve their situation; frequently this has been at the expense of those purchasing the goods for
resale. The activities of agricultural marketing cooperatives have already
been mentioned in relation to their supplying raw materials to processing
firms. In addition, such cooperatives have taken over important wholesaling functions when they have felt that existing middlemen were not
performing effectively. Their entrance into the retail field has not been
as extensive, but the actions of these producers indicates one of the most
potent actions available to suppliers of goods to wholesalers and retailers—replacement of the middleman by a producer-controlled organization.

Manufacturers as Suppliers

Wholesalers and retailers purchase from manufacturers, and even
where retailers have no direct relations with manufacturers the producers
are able to influence the ultimate seller. The last century has seen an
astonishing growth in the number of goods sold at retail. This has been,
in part, a result of the development of manufacturing techniques enabling
firms to mass-produce goods on a scale undreamed of prior to the Civil
War. To permit firms employing such devices to produce near their capacities, it is essential that mass distribution also take place. Prior to the
great growth in manufacturing, wholesalers had built up their businesses
by performing many functions that manufacturers were not equipped to
undertake. The cost of doing these things was reflected in a relatively
high spread between the price received from the retailer and that paid to
the manufacturer. Also, a wholesaler would handle the identical or similar
products of a number of manufacturers; he gave no special promotional
effort to selling any one of these to retailers unless there was some special
inducement from a manufacturer to do so (in which case the products of
the other manufacturers were slighted). As manufacturers grew larger,
developed distinctive brands, and engaged in a number of costly activities to promote those branded products, they became dissatisfied with
wholesalers on two main counts: the wholesaler's margin was regarded as
too high and his promotional activity was regarded as too limited.

Wholesalers have generally been reluctant to reduce their margins or
to increase their promotion of any particular brand at the expense of

the brands of their other suppliers. Many manufacturers have therefore felt obligated to take other steps. The biggest of these has been the bypassing of the wholesaler entirely. Manufacturers have frequently developed their own sales forces to deal directly with retailers—a move made easier by the growth in the size of retailing firms and *their* desire to bypass the wholesaler. Consequently, wholesalers have been squeezed out of some industries, have had to develop new sources of supply, have adopted "private brands," or have integrated their operations with both manufacturers and retailers. There are even a number of instances of manufacturers taking over the retail function, and some retailers have found their own suppliers competing with them. Manufacturers of books, aluminum siding, and appliances, among others, have been engaging in this practice, which has increased to such an extent that a congressional Small Business subcommittee conducted an investigation to determine the impact on independent small businessmen of competition from suppliers.

As retailers have come into closer relations with manufacturers and as nationally advertised brand names have been developed by manufacturers, the producer has been making greater claims on the seller. One demand has been for volume sales, as we might expect, but others—such as good service to the customer—have also become important. A refiner of gasoline presses the retail gas dealer to provide good service as well as volume sales, and when the dealer fails to do so for any extended period of time, he might find his lease canceled—as many of these retailers operate stations leased to them by the manufacturer. A similar circumstance occurs when dealers sell certain goods under a franchise from the manufacturer; this contract may be canceled or not renewed if the retailer has not performed according to the manufacturer's desires. This is characteristic of automobile manufacturers, for example. On occasion they have forced franchised dealers to buy more cars than they wanted, employing the threat to cancel the franchise if the dealer refused. Also, they limit the area in which dealers might sell; General Motors even established a Dealer Relations Board to adjudicate disputes among dealers when a charge is made by one that another has trespassed on his territory. When GM discovered that its franchised dealers were selling new cars to discount dealers in the Los Angeles area, it brought pressure on them to discontinue the practice. Although auto dealers have had some success in securing legislation and court decisions limiting the influence of the manufacturers upon them, a considerable amount of manufacturers' influence still exists.

One of the most significant developments in manufacturers' influence on retailers has been in the field of pricing. At one time, mass-production manufacturers wanted low retail prices in order to expand the demand for their products. An outstanding instance of this was the price policy of the Ford Motor Company that revolutionized distribution of automobiles. Since Ford wanted—and received—a satisfactory manufacturer's price for its Model T, this meant that the cost of wholesaling and retailing had to be cut substantially. Means of doing this were found, and a new era in production and distribution was ushered in. More recently, some manufacturers of consumers goods have felt that a low price for their products—which had resulted as a consequence of low-cost manufacturing and low-cost distribution—was a reflection on the quality of the goods. Also, when products are used as "loss leaders," some other retailers will not be willing to stock them. As a consequence, some manufacturers have adopted a policy of "resale price maintenance" and have attempted to control the retail price by various means. Some retailers— usually those operating on a high margin—have hailed these developments while others—normally those wishing to advertise certain products at unusually low prices in order to attract patrons—have condemned them. In any case, it has meant that retailers have found their suppliers attempting to influence the retail price to a very large degree. This is in sharp contrast to the previous practice of selling to wholesalers or retailers at a certain manufacturer's price and permitting them to price the merchandise as they saw fit.

To aid them in "resale price maintenance," manufacturers have had certain legal resources. Congress and some states have passed legislation permitting manufacturers to make contracts with retailers to maintain prices; such contracts have been binding not only on the retailer signing the agreement but also on other retailers in the state even though they have not signed such a contract. Court decisions and changes in statutes have recently modified this situation, but it still exists. Furthermore, the manufacturer can legally employ the more drastic measure of refusing to sell to a price-cutter. They are reluctant to do so, of course, since the retailer can turn to another source of supply. Consequently, the manufacturer is more inclined to seek legal means of bringing the retailer "in line" rather than to discontinue supplying him.

The "resale price maintenance movement" has taken a rather interesting turn. Originally, it was the manufacturers who advocated the establishment of legal rules permitting manufacturers to enter into agreements with retailers to fix the retail price of their products. Manufacturers had such authority until 1908, when court decisions limited this power. (The producers of manufactured products had unsuccessfully contended that they had a proprietary interest in goods carrying their trade name or brand and that, therefore, they should have the authority to determine what the retail price should be.) However, since about 1920, the greater pressure for "fair trade" has come from distributors. The rise of consumer cooperatives, chain stores, and supermarkets caused merchants doing business in the traditional fashion to lose business to each new type of distributor; consequently, they turned to the manufacturers and demanded price protection from them rather than change their merchandising methods. A relatively small proportion of manufacturers producing trademarked or branded products were and still are interested in trying to maintain retail prices. One of the companies heavily committed to "fair trade"—which it has written off as a lost cause after trying unsuccessfully to police retailers of its products—was General Electric. When it distributed its products through a number of distributors, it had difficulty checking up on price-cutting; and when it did discover violations, the company found that investigation and legal expenses made it unprofitable to bring the price-cutters to "justice." However, it has adopted the somewhat different strategy of selling certain trademarked products only to franchised dealers under agreements in which the dealers agree to abide by the stated price. The dealers with whom such agreements are made are willing to submit to such a condition in exchange for a local monopoly of the products and a protected margin.

Wholesalers as Suppliers

With the changes taking place in distribution, wholesalers have lost much of their influence over retailers and what they want is important only to a declining proportion of retailers. Since many retailers are now buying direct from manufacturers and even engaging in their own manufacturing as well as their own wholesaling activities, the main objectives of wholesalers have been to maintain what business they have and to develop new accounts for those they have lost. They can do this only where they can perform wholesaling services more efficiently than can the manufacturer or retailer. In some circumstances they have been able to do this, but they have also found salvation in many cases by integrating with retailers and/or manufacturers. For a long period in the history of American wholesaling, the number of wholesalers declined as a consequence of manufacturers and retailers taking over the wholesaling functions. In recent years, there has been a resurgence in the number of wholesalers. However, owing to their vulnerable economic position, they are not able to exert the kind of influence on retailers that manufacturers can exert.

In the markets in which they buy and sell, business firms are subject to influences exerted by competitors in addition to those brought to bear on them by suppliers and customers. Competitors also take political and other kinds of action that may adversely affect a firm. However, as in the case of almost every other class of individuals and groups in the environment of the firm, some of their influence is beneficial, as we shall see in the next chapter.

READING: The Platform of the Populists

[*Political action taken by farmers to gain their objectives is usually organized action. Since the Civil War, a number of farmers' organizations, and political parties promoted and supported by agrarian groups, have been established. Many of these has disappeared, but others have endured and still wield considerable political power. The first major organization was the Order of Patrons of Husbandry (now known more simply as "the Grange"). The "Granger Movement" resulted in a large number of state laws regulating business. Many of these were passed in the 1870's, and Granger influence still persists. However, farmers began to form new alliances during the 1880's, and the Northern Alliance and the Southern Alliance joined hands to support a Peoples' Party—a political organization seeking victory in the nation's capital as well as on the state level.*

A Civil War general from the farm state of Iowa was the Peoples' Party choice for President in 1892, but secured only a minor fraction of the votes. In 1896, William Jennings Bryan was the coalition candidate of the Populists and Democrats for the Presidency, and came close to being elected. The 1896 election was the high point in political activity for the Alliances, and those farm groups have since disappeared from the scene. However, the twentieth century has witnessed the rise of a number of new farmers' organizations, many of which espouse Populist principles. Much of what the Peoples' Party stood for, as reflected in its campaign platforms, has been enacted into law—chiefly during the New Deal period. Some present-day political commentators have gone so far as to label President Lyndon B. Johnson a Populist, but this seems a dubious proposition. Texas was at one time an important center of agrarian political activity, but oil has changed the nature of that state's politics considerably.

The following* is taken from the platform adopted by the Peoples' Party at Omaha in July of 1892. Although they were not successful in capturing the Presidency in either 1892 or 1896, it is interesting to note how many of their planks have become law—partly because other parties adopted them.]

Assembled upon the 116th anniversary of the Declaration of Independence, the People's Party of America, in their first national convention, invoking upon their action the blessing of Almighty God, puts forth, in the name and on behalf of the people of this country, the following preamble and declaration of principles:—

The conditions which surround us best justify our cooperation: we meet in the midst of a nation brought to the verge of moral, political, and material ruin. Corruption dominates the ballot-box, the legislatures, the Congress, and touches

**Excerpted from:* Edward Stanwood, *A History of the Presidency* (Boston: Houghton-Mifflin, 1898) second edition, pp. 509–513.

even the ermine of the bench. The people are demoralized; most of the States have been compelled to isolate the voters at the polling-places to prevent universal intimidation or bribery. The newspapers are largely subsidized or muzzled; public opinion silenced; business prostrated; our homes covered with mortgages; labor impoverished; and the land concentrating in the hands of the capitalists. The urban workmen are denied the right of organization for self-protection; imported pauperized labor beats down their wages; a hireling standing army, unrecognized by our laws, is established to shoot them down, and they are rapidly degenerating into European conditions. The fruits of the toil of millions are boldly stolen to build up colossal fortunes for a few, unprecedented in the history of mankind; and the possessors of these, in turn, despise the republic and endanger liberty. From the same prolific womb of governmental injustice we breed the two great classes—tramps and millionaires.

The national power to create money is appropriated to enrich bondholders; a vast public debt, payable in legal tender currency, has been funded into gold-bearing bonds, thereby adding millions to the burdens of the people. Silver, which has been accepted as coin since the dawn of history, has been demonetized to add to the purchasing power of gold by decreasing the value of all forms of property as well as human labor; and the supply of currency is purposely abridged to fatten usurers, bankrupt enterprise, and enslave industry. A vast conspiracy against mankind has been organized on two continents, and it is rapidly taking possession of the world. If not met and overthrown at once, it forebodes terrible social convulsions, the destruction of civilization, or the establishment of an absolute despotism.

We have witnessed for more than a quarter of a century the struggles of the two great political parties for power and plunder, while grievous wrongs have been inflicted upon the suffering people. We charge that the controlling influences dominating both these parties have permitted the existing dreadful conditions to develop without serious effort to prevent or restrain them. Neither do they now promise us any substantial reform. They have agreed together to ignore in the coming campaign every issue but one. They propose to drown the outcries of a plundered people with the uproar of a sham battle over the tariff, so that capitalists, corporations, national banks, rings, trusts, watered stock, the demonetization of silver, and the oppressions of the usurers may all be lost sight of. They propose to sacrifice our homes, lives and children on the altar of mammon; to destroy the multitude in order to secure corruption funds from the millionaires.

Assembled on the anniversary of the birthday of the nation, and filled with the spirit of the grand general and the chieftain who established our independence, we seek to restore the government of the Republic to the hands of "the plain people," with whose class it originated. We assert our purposes to be identical with the purposes of the National Constitution, "to form a more perfect union and establish justice, insure domestic tranquillity, provide for the common defence, promote the general welfare, and secure the blessings of liberty for ourselves and our posterity." We declare that this republic can only endure as a free government while built upon the love of the whole people for each other and for the nation; that it cannot be pinned together by bayonets; that the civil war is over, and that every passion and resentment which grew out of it must die with it; and that we must be in fact, as we are in name, one united brotherhood of freemen.

Our country finds itself confronted by conditions for which there is no precedent in the history of the world; our annual agricultural productions amount to billions of dollars in value, which must, within a few weeks or months, be exchanged for billions of dollars of commodities consumed in their production; the existing currency supply is wholly inadequate to make this exchange; the results are falling prices, the formation of combines and rings, the impoverishment of the producing class. We pledge ourselves, if given power, we will labor to correct these evils by wise and reasonable legislation, in accordance with the terms of our platform. We believe that the powers of government—in other words, of the people—should be expanded (as in the case of the postal service) as rapidly and as far as the good sense of an intelligent people and the teachings of experience shall justify, to the end that oppression, injustice, and poverty shall eventually cease in the land.

While our sympathies as a party of reform are naturally upon the side of every proposition which will tend to make men intelligent, virtuous, and temperate, we nevertheless regard these questions—important as they are—as secondary to the great issues now pressing for solution, and upon which not only our individual prosperity but the very existence of free institutions depends; and we ask all men to first help us to determine whether we are to have a republic to administer before we differ as to the conditions upon which it is to be administered; believing that the forces of reform this day organized will never cease to move forward until every wrong is remedied, and equal rights and equal privileges securely established for all the men and women of this country.

We declare, therefore,—

First. That the union of the labor forces of the United States this day consummated shall be permanent and perpetual; may its spirit enter all hearts for the salvation of the republic and the uplifting of mankind!

Second. Wealth belongs to him who creates it, and every dollar taken from industry without an equivalent is robbery. "If any will not work, neither shall he eat." The interests of rural and civic labor are the same; their enemies are identical.

Third. We believe that the time has come when the railroad corporations will either own the people or the people must own the railroads; and, should the government enter upon the work of owning and managing all railroads, we should favor an amendment to the Constitution by which all persons engaged in the government service shall be placed under a civil service regulation of the most rigid character, so as to prevent the increase of the power of the national administration by the use of such additional government employees.

*   *   *

First, Money. We demand a national currency, safe, sound, and flexible, issued by the general government only, a full legal tender for all debts, public and private, and that, without the use of banking corporations, a just, equitable, and efficient means of distribution direct to the people, at a tax not to exceed two per cent per annum, to be provided as set forth in the sub-treasury plan of the

Farmers' Alliance, or a better system; also, by payments in discharge of its obligations for public improvements.

(a) We demand free and unlimited coinage of silver and gold at the present legal ratio of sixteen to one.

(b) We demand that the amount of circulating medium be speedily increased to not less than fifty dollars per capita.

(c) We demand a graduated income tax.

(d) We believe that the money of the country should be kept as much as possible in the hands of the people, and hence we demand that all state and national revenues shall be limited to the necessary expenses of the government economically and honestly administered.

(e) We demand that postal savings banks be established by the government for the safe deposit of the earnings of the people and to facilitate exchange.

Second, Transportation. Transportation being a means of exchange and a public necessity, the government should own and operate the railroads in the interest of the people.

(a) The telegraph and telephone, like the post-office system, being a necessity for the transmission of news, should be owned and operated by the government in the interest of the people.

Third, Land. Land, including all the natural sources of wealth, is the heritage of the people, and would not be monopolized for speculative purposes, and alien ownership of land should be prohibited. All land now held by railroads and other corporations in excess of their actual needs, and all lands now owned by aliens, should be reclaimed by the government and held for actual settlers only.

Resolutions

WHEREAS, Other questions have been presented for our consideration, we hereby submit the following, not as a part of the platform of the People's party, but as resolutions expressive of the sentiment of this convention.

1. *Resolved,* That we demand a free ballot and a fair count in all elections, and pledge ourselves to secure it to every legal voter without federal intervention, through the adoption by the States of the unperverted Australian or secret ballot system.

2. *Resolved,* That the revenue derived from a graduated income tax should be applied to the reduction of the burden of taxation now resting upon the domestic industries of this country.

3. *Resolved,* That we pledge our support to fair and liberal pensions to ex-Union soldiers and sailors.

4. *Resolved,* That we condemn the fallacy of protecting American labor under the present system, which opens our ports to the pauper and criminal classes of the world, and crowds out our wage-earners; and we denounce the present ineffective laws against contract labor, and demand the further restriction of undesirable immigration.

5. *Resolved,* That we cordially sympathize with the efforts of organized workingmen to shorten the hours of labor, and demand a rigid enforcement of the existing eight-hour law on government work, and ask that a penalty clause be added to the said law.

6. *Resolved,* That we regard the maintenance of a large standing army of mercenaries, known as the Pinkerton system, as a menace to our liberties, and we demand its abolition; and we condemn the recent invasion of the Territory of Wyoming by the hired assassins of plutocracy, assisted by federal officials.

7. *Resolved,* That we commend to the favorable consideration of the people and the reform press the legislative system known as the initiative and referendum.

8. *Resolved,* That we favor a constitutional provision limiting the office of President and Vice-President to one term, and providing for the election of senators of the United States by a direct vote of the people.

9. *Resolved,* That we oppose any subsidy or national aid to any private corporation for any purpose.

10. *Resolved,* That this convention sympathizes with the Knights of Labor and their righteous contest with the tyrannical combine of clothing manufacturers of Rochester, and declares it to be the duty of all who hate tyranny and oppression to refuse to purchase the goods made by said manufacturers, or to patronize any merchants who sell such goods.

SUGGESTED READINGS

Buck, Solon J., *The Granger Movement* (London: Oxford University Press, 1913). A study of the first major "farmers' movement" after the Civil War, indicating the varied objectives and activities of Grangers.

Hicks, John D., *The Populist Revolt: A History of the Farmers' Alliance and the Peoples' Party* (Reissued as a Bison Book by the University of Nebraska Press, Lincoln, Nebraska). The classic history of the Populist movement.

Saloutos, Theodore, and John D. Hicks, *Agricultural Discontent in the Middle West, 1900–1939* (Reissued as a Bison Book by the University of Nebraska Press, Lincoln, Nebraska). A study of farm organizations and their activities since the beginning of this century.

Shannon, Fred A., *American Farmers' Movements* (Princeton, N.J.: Van Nostrand, 1957). Describes both the violent uprisings and the peaceful organizations by which American farmers have tried to improve their economic condition.

Stern, Louis W., "Approaches to Achieving Retail Price Stability," *Business Horizons* (Fall 1964). A discussion of means adopted by manufacturers to secure the desired retail price: fair trade, restricting distributors, "shortening the channel," franchising dealers, and others.

CHAPTER 17

COMPETITORS
AND COOPERATORS

In the markets in which it buys and sells, a firm is confronted with a number of competitors. There are two extreme views of competitors: they can be regarded simply as the other firms in the same industry and/or market, or they can be regarded more broadly as all of the individuals and groups who have something to sell to a certain class of customer or who wish to buy from a certain set of suppliers. That is, it is possible to consider General Motors (in its selling activities) to be in competition with all other producers of consumer goods and services and even with governments, which want part of the consumer income for public purposes, or to be in competition with only three other American automobile manufacturers. We shall view competitors in the narrow sense—that is, as the other producers in the same industry who are supplying the same or similar goods or services in a firm's product markets, or those who are seeking to secure some of the same productive resources used by the firm.

To deal with competitors effectively, it seems desirable to classify them into different kinds of competitors because the kind of competitive activity depends to some degree on the kind of competitor confronting the firm. Normally, we think of competitors as being other private business enterprises. However there are others: cooperative enterprises which, although private, are either consumer- or producer-owned rather than investor-owned; government enterprises, which do not pursue profit objectives and can stay in operation indefinitely without fully covering costs; foreign competitors, including co-ops and governments in addition to business firms; and "do-it-yourselfers." Although there is not much information on competition by those engaging in "do-it-yourself" activity, some have estimated that such action actually increases gross national product to some 20 to 25 per cent more than the figure reported by the Department of Commerce. Certainly there are a number of industries whose expansion and existence has been threatened by this kind of competition.

Competitive activity is not only market action. Do-it-yourselfers satisfy their own wants through direct action rather than through purchasing goods and services in the market; although their actions affect market conditions, they do not enter the market. Also, when governments acquire financial resources through taxation or acquire land through powers of condemnation and eminent domain, such acts can hardly be referred to as market action in which governments bid against others for the resources. Too, when we examine in some detail the competitive activities of other business firms, we shall note that much of it is not market action.

PRIVATE FIRMS AS COMPETITORS

Even in the major classification of private business firms, we see various subclasses of competitors. Some are fierce competitors, others are conservative competitors, and yet others are cooperative competitors (although some observers feel that when firms selling in the same market cooperate, they can scarcely be termed competitors). Such a subclassification is useful because it gives us some idea of the behavior that may be expected from firms falling into a particular category. Another kind of subclassification would separate big competitors from small ones, on the grounds that this distinction also reflects differences in behavior that might be expected. For example, big competitors usually provide price leadership that smaller firms follow (U.S. Steel and General Motors are such leaders, although their leads are not always followed). Since big firms have substantial resources, they can act in ways in which a small firm may not be able to act.

It may have been noted that we did not define business competitors as other firms that are in the same industry buying or selling in the same markets. This is not because this view does not have some merit nor because it is impossible (although difficult) to define an industry and determine who is in it, but because firms from other industries have a way of entering product and resource markets, thereby enlarging the number of competitors. Examples abound: trucking firms compete with railroads for traffic; oil companies make containers to compete with tin cans; real estate brokers and accountants compete with lawyers; television competes with mass-circulation magazines for advertisements. Such firms are not normally regarded as being in the same industry, but their competition is real.

It is difficult to generalize about the objectives of other business firms selling in the same product markets. Fierce competitors are out to win the competition and to drive the other firms from the industry or market. However, there are instances in which firms have seen the futility of competition as a means of gaining satisfactory market shares and profits. In these cases, the producers may aim at a relatively stable situation that will be profitable to all firms in the industry, although they may also wish to keep new competitors from entering the product markets. There is perhaps an intermediate position between fierce competition and "stabilization of the situation" through cooperative action. Some industries are competitive, but the firms operate under accepted "codes of fair competition" that may prohibit price competition and other "unfair methods of competition."

If a firm is a "fierce competitor," it may find the other firms in the industry taking action against it. The range of action taken is wide: in extreme cases, the other producers may buy out the overly competitive firm or they may seek to drive it out. When the United States Steel Corporation was being formed at the beginning of the century, the organizers of the combination did not feel safe until they were able to get Andrew Carnegie to sell his steel-producing interests to it. Carnegie was a tough and profitable competitor, who was threatening to expand his production of steel when the other firms in the industry were losing money and concerned with excess capacity. If such a firm is in a relatively weak financial position, the other firms may cut prices until the fierce competitor is driven into bankruptcy, although such price wars may be concluded as soon as the original price-cutter sees the advantages of not competing on a price basis. In one instance, a seller of dairy products who was unwilling to raise the price of a quart of milk from 22 cents to 23 cents when the other stores in the area did found himself facing a situation in which the others sold milk at about 9 cents a quart to make the holdout see the error of his ways. Also, the irate competitors may—in cooperation with other groups—have sufficient political influence to secure legislative and/or administrative action against the firm whose competition is regarded as being unfair. The history of the Standard Oil Company of New Jersey provides illustrations of other refiners working to get the largest unit in the industry declared monopolistic and illegal.

In American business, the era of fierce price competition has almost come to a close. Experiences of business firms—especially manufacturers —during the latter part of the nineteenth century led them to conclude that no one really won such contests when they extended for long periods of time. Firms with large investments in their operations could, and did, continue in production for years even though all of their costs were not covered. Wisdom soon became the better part of valor, and producers began to cooperate more and compete less. Competition is not disappearing, but it is taking different forms. Businessmen continue to be competitive in nature, but tend to compete on bases other than on that of price as their expenditures on advertising and personal promotion of products indicate. There are differences among industries, too, insofar as price competition is concerned. Those manufacturing and retailing firms selling to the domestic consumer appear to be more inclined to engage in competitive pricing practices than are those in the extractive and processing industries or those firms that sell equipment to business and government buyers.

COOPERATIVES AS COMPETITORS

Mention has been made of cooperative economic activity undertaken by farmers, labor unions, and consumers. There are very few industries in which some group has not at one time or another attempted to operate a cooperative, nonprofit firm. These have not posed very great threats to profit-oriented enterprises except where the cooperatives have had special advantages. When the Grangers in Iowa began to produce farm equipment in competition with existing firms, they soon went bankrupt. Such failures helped bring about the decline of the Grange after the middle 1870's. What investor-owned firms object to in the operations of such organizations at the present time are the tax and other legal advantages cooperatives have. Such competition is regarded as being unfair, and sometimes the differences in costs resulting from those advantages make it impossible for the profit-oriented firm to continue in business.

Some cooperatives are consumer-owned and aim at providing their members with goods and services at lower prices or with products they might otherwise have difficulty in getting. Mutual savings banks, savings and loan associations, and credit unions are essentially cooperative enterprises whose objectives are to make funds available to their members when they are unable to secure them elsewhere or when the cost of securing funds from other sources is high.

The main goal of a credit union has been stated as "ridding the world of unscrupulous money lenders and loan sharks." Such action is not aimed at commercial banks, many of which make personal loans at lower rates than those charged by credit unions, although some "small loan" companies have been affected. Rural electric cooperatives came into existence to "serve the unserved," and with the helping hand of the federal government they have become quite formidable competitors, especially as they have expanded their operations to include suburban and even urban areas. College co-op bookstores not only have become the biggest sellers of textbooks but many of them retail anything from pencils to expensive clothing.

Other cooperatives are producer-owned, and aim at expanding producers' incomes, partly through getting a larger share of the consumer's dollar and partly through raising the price of the product. Most such co-ops in the U.S. are organizations of agricultural producers. The Allied Grape Growers (an organization of some 1,500 California agriculturalists) process their grapes into wine, transport and bottle that product, and wholesale it to retailers throughout the United States. The loans, grants, and other kinds of federal support given such co-ops have made them formidable competitors, indeed, and they have in many cases replaced private business enterprises in the processing and marketing of agricultural products.

GOVERNMENTS AS COMPETITORS

Since the beginning of our national history, certain economic functions have been performed by governmental units. What concerns some firms is that the business activity of government is expanding and that government enterprises do not compete "fairly." In 1933, a special committee of the House of Representatives made an exhaustive study of government enterprises that competed with private business and found 232 such activities still lingering on from World War I. The committee reported:

> The evidence in general indicates that the operations of the Federal Government in the field of private enterprise has reached a magnitude and diversity which threatens to reduce the private initiative, curtail the opportunities and infringe upon the earning powers of tax-paying undertakings while steadily increasing the levies upon them.

Since 1932, there has been an expansion rather than a contraction of government-operated enterprises. During the New Deal period, there was a great growth of business activity on the part of the federal government, especially in the electric utility industry. World War II brought a further growth in the ownership and operation of business enterprises by government. In 1954, the Director of the Bureau of the Budget, Mr. Rowland R. Hughes, pointed out that

> The Federal Government today operates over a hundred business-type activities. . . .
>
> For a country which is the citadel and the world's principal exponent of private enterprise and individual initiative, this is rather an amazing list.[1]

Government operation of business enterprises is of concern to private business not only because it competes but because the competition is felt to be unfair. The commission studying the organization of the executive branch of the federal government declared that

> The Government business-type enterprises, except in a few instances, pay no taxes, and pay little or no interest on the capital invested; they seldom charge depreciation and frequently their directing personnel is not included on their payroll. Likewise the "fringe benefits" of Government personnel in most instances are not included in their costs. Moreover, in addition to the fact that most of them pay no taxes, they deprive the Government of taxes which would otherwise be paid by private enterprise if it conducted these operations. Therefore, their claims of financial success are often wholly invalid; and, worse, with the advantages they receive from the Government, they are unfair competition.[2]

Competition with private business comes from state and local government as well as from the federal government; we shall indicate, more specifically, the nature of such competition when we examine the political environment of business in Chapters 26 and 27.

---

[1] Commission on Organization of the Executive Branch of the Government, *Business Enterprises, A Report to the Congress,* May 1955, p. xviii.

[2] *Op. cit.,* p. xii.

FOREIGN COMPETITION

Private enterprises located in other countries and business activities of foreign governments also provide competition for American businessmen in resource and product markets. The keenness of such competition is well illustrated by recent developments in the automobile and oil industries. Foreign cars are being sold in increasing numbers in American markets, invading what was at one time the almost exclusive preserve of domestic producers. American producers of petroleum products have found their position in certain foreign markets threatened by the Soviet Union's sale of gasoline and other refinery products at a price below that charged by others. Such competition is difficult to deal with, unless some support comes from the United States government.

Foreign competition is increasing for two main reasons: barriers to international trade are being removed, and producers abroad are expanding production. Most of the removal of barriers to trade has come about through governmental action, although improvements in transportation and communication have helped. Government has also been important in the expansion of industrial production abroad. The U.S. has carried on foreign-aid programs that helped the industrialized nations of Western Europe rebuild their industry after World War II and that have also helped "emerging nations" industrialize. The Soviet Union and its satellites have embarked on programs of "forced" industrialization, and these Communist countries have become important competitors in foreign markets (although their products have been kept out of many U.S. markets by a combination of public and private action). As foreign producers have expanded their production and put it on a low-cost basis, they have invaded American markets. Some of this competition is regarded as being unfair—U.S. steel producers have accused foreigners of dumping their surplus production on American markets at prices below the cost of production; also, some manufacturers complain that foreigners have copied American products and processes that were patented and have flooded our markets with imitations. Although it is likely that American firms will be able to adjust to these changing economic conditions, the period of adjustment will be painful in many industries.

Foreign competition is not limited to competition in product markets. Businessmen and governments in other countries also compete with American firms for resources. American fishermen have been very much concerned by the "invasion" of their traditional fishing grounds by foreign fishing vessels, and the domestic industry is declining rapidly as a result. When such competition for resources is conducted by governments (as is true of the greatly expanded fishing activities of the Soviet Union), it is difficult to meet and beat. Too, much of the political activity of the Soviet Union is aimed at bringing countries possessing desired natural resources into her sphere of influence, which may deny access to certain resources to some American firms.

Foreign competitors are not always fierce competitors. On a number of occasions they have joined with American businessmen and cooperated in the establishment of market quotas, fair prices, and fair practices. This cooperation has taken place in transportation, but the more effective agreements have been in the extractive and processing industries. Under government sanction, agreements have been reached with respect to many agricultural commodities that move in international trade. There have also been many cartels—agreements among firms in different nations to divide markets and maintain prices. These have usually been established by firms engaged in processing products of mines, such as lead, zinc, and nickel. The federal government has not encouraged American producers to engage in such arrangements—in fact, it has discouraged them; consequently, some secrecy surrounds the activities of these groups and their impact on businessmen in the United States is not clear.

THE NATURE OF COMPETITION

Traditionally, economists have concerned themselves almost exclusively with price competition. Given their particular objectives, this has been logical. However, the range of important action taken by competitors is great. In addition to varieties of price competition, competitors engage in product, advertising, service, and "unfair" competition and are also involved in political, legal, and other influential actions. Although this may be quite apparent to the perceptive observer of the business scene, some illustrations may strengthen this point.

Some competition *has* been price competition. Price wars among gasoline retailers, rate wars among the airlines and rate wars among savings institutions (which compete for investment funds) have made headlines in recent years. The competition for engineers and other technical personnel has been, in large measure, price competition. In many cases, price competition has not been so open. Discounts have been given from list prices and new classes of service (as in the airlines) have been created with little change in the quality and quantity of service, but with some reduction in price. Product improvement with no change in price is also disguised price competition. The sale of unbranded products at considerably lower prices than identical branded goods is also a kind of price competition, as is the increase in the amount or quality of service with no change in price.

Service competition takes other forms, Automobile manufacturers and dealers have extended the warranty period on new cars, as have others in the consumer durables industries. Independent appliance dealers have combatted the price competition of discount houses by contending that their service is superior. Some sellers of manufactured products compete in the financing of "big ticket" items, where a low monthly payment or low down payment may be more important to the buyer than the total price paid.

Firms compete through advertising and for distribution channels. When the Ford Motor Company brought out the ill-fated Edsel, it spent vast sums on promotion and in building a dealer organization (which meant luring dealers away from other manufacturers in many cases).

As the automobile industry amply illustrates, competition also takes place in research and styling. So important are new products and new styles that firms engage in "espionage" and in "pirating" away employees of their competitors when they have valuable information. Attempts have been made to retain the advantages of research through patenting certain products and processes, but this involves a firm in investigating and prosecuting those infringing on its patents. Sometimes style change may not take place in the basic product, but only in its package, yet this is an increasingly important competitive device.

Beyond espionage and piracy, there are other kinds of unfair competition. Much advertising downgrades the product of a competitor in addition to boosting the advertiser's goods. Some advertising is unfair and deceptive. Unauthorized producers have sometimes entered protected markets (as when dental laboratories and dental technicians illegally sold false teeth when this field is reserved, by law, to dentists).

To protect themselves from unfair competition, to gain a competitive advantage and to harass competitors, firms have engaged in political and legal action. A firm will frequently find that its competitors are trying to influence lawmakers to establish rules that work to its disadvantage and that when such laws are secured, its competitors seek to have the rules administered to reduce the firm's ability to compete. Currently lawyers and real estate brokers are engaged in legislative battles in various states over which group shall be permitted to draw up real estate contracts (a field which lawyers would like to reserve to themselves). In merger hearings before administrative agencies, competitors of those attempting to merge (as in the railroad and airline industries) seek to block the mergers or else ask some concessions as the price of their acquiescence. Legal action can also be effective. One embittered small businessman (after his costly experience in a court fight with a large competitor) told his fellows:

> ... you must appreciate that any large corporation under our present judicial system can attack any small competitor on the flimsiest pretext. There is no machinery in our legal setup to prevent the Federal Courts from being used as a useful tool of destruction by a large business, ethics notwithstanding.
>
> Given the full-time legal department in a big company . . . , due process becomes an ideal tool for minimizing competition.

Legal suits can be time consuming and costly, and for a firm with limited resources they can mean the difference between business success and failure.

Confronted with a great variety of competitors employing a wide variety of competitive devices, it is not so surprising that business firms have frequently turned to cooperation to mitigate the "evils of competition."

COOPERATION AMONG COMPETITORS

Cooperation among business firms has taken a number of forms. At one extreme, there is the "gentlemen's agreement" to refrain from or to engage in certain practices; at the other is formal combination of competing firms into one organization with one policy-making group. In every industry, however, there are some businessmen who are not "gentlemen," and who take advantage of the fact that others in the industry are abiding by an agreement to alleviate the problems confronting all producers in a field. Where there are relatively few firms in an industry or market, and when entrance into the field is difficult, combinations or agreements are usually effective. Such conditions do not always prevail, however, and where there are many firms and entrance into the market is easy, cooperation usually takes the form of associations to promote the interests of their member firms. Such associations and their activities are somewhat more effective than are general understandings among firms in an industry, and their widespread development testifies to the importance attached to them by businessmen.

Trade Associations

Almost as long as there have been well-defined industries, the members thereof have found advantages in associating to promote their interests. In England and on the Continent, these took the form of merchant and craft guilds. The guild system of Europe was never strongly established in America and the establishment of a permanent association of businessmen in a specific industry did not come into existence until after the Revolutionary War. Stock brokers in New York in the 1790's formed the group that has since become the New York Stock Exchange. As manufacturing grew, manufacturers organized groups to help deal with problems confronting all of the firms engaged in a certain line of production. These have been joined by associations of distributors and those in the service trades. At first these associations were local and regional, but many of them have also formed national organizations. A recent count of national business associations revealed that approximately 2,000 were in existence, of which about 1,800 were trade associations. Local, county, state, and regional groups bring the total number of such trade groups in the United States to over 10,000.

Trade associations pursue a number of objects. To increase the sale of the products of the industry, they engage in advertising activities. The good name of the industry is promoted through publicity and public relations. When member firms are threatened by adverse legislation or when favorable laws are sought, the association goes to work to secure a better "legal environment" for its members. Associations also represent the industries before administrative bodies. In some industries, the association engages in collective bargaining with unions. In addition to educating outsiders as to the industry's problems and needs, the associations also carry on information activities for the member firms through the gathering of statistical and other information on conditions in and confronting the industry. One of the main objects, however, has always been "industrial self-regulation" through which prices, production, and services have been controlled in the interests of all of the members of the industry.

The devices employed by trade associations to influence prices and production are many. The promotion of uniform methods of cost accounting (or "cost education") and the publication of average costs in the industry (including profit) strongly suggest what the price of a product should be, and other means are employed to persuade members to charge that price. Statistical activities may affect prices by influencing the production policies of member firms—that is, statistics on the amount of production, inventories, unfilled orders, idle capacity, and sales, and the interpretation of these data suggest certain production policies. Some trade association statistics report prices being charged by others in the industry, thereby influencing pricing policies quite directly. Even standardization of products, standard terms of contracts, and so on, seem to lead to standardization of prices. Although a number of means exist to secure agreements on prices, this does not mean that success has been attained.

The results of attempts at self-regulation through trade associations have been mixed. A major problem has been the difficulty of enforcing decisions. In the ordinary course of events, there are few sanctions the association can employ. Throwing nonconforming firms out of the group is of little value, since no influence can thereafter be had on them (although the desire of firms to be members in good standing might cause the threat of expulsion to have some effect). For the most part, the association must rely on persuasion, attempting to convince an errant firm that all in the industry would suffer if all were to behave the way that firm is acting, and that unless all conform to the decisions made, eventually none will. Briefly, during the New Deal period, trade associations were given the right to bring legal sanctions to bear against members who did not conduct themselves according to the "codes of fair competition" drafted under the National Industrial Recovery Act of 1933. After that law was declared unconstitutional in 1935, such measures were no longer open to associations. As a matter of fact, their activities in attempting to bring about some stability and profitability to their industries have frequently been held to be in conflict with the antitrust laws. Consequently, little publicity is given to this aspect of trade association activity, although it is in all probability the most important objective sought.

The demise of the National Industrial Recovery Act and, therefore, the "codes of fair competition" established under that legislation does not mean that governments do not encourage the drafting of such codes and that they will not enforce them. One extreme example is found in the code of ethics of the bar association in a state—the professional association of lawyers. It contains certain rules governing members of the bar that will be enforced by the judiciary, and flagrant violation may lead to disbarment (in which circumstance, the attorney disbarred is not permitted to practice law before the courts). Other professional groups have been able to secure some control over the licensing of practitioners in their industry, and, consequently, over the behavior of those in the profession. One "antitrust" law—the Federal Trade Commission Act—permits the Commission to approve certain trade practices established by the members of an industry as being "fair" and to prosecute violators of this code for engaging in "unfair trade practices" (much the same sort of situation as prevailed under the National Industrial Recovery Act). Attempts by industry associations to secure control over practices and practitioners through legislation have been fairly successful, and are likely to grow in importance.

Employers' Associations

As we have noted, trade associations frequently conduct labor relations activities for the members of an industry; however, this function
is sometimes performed by employers' associations. That is, trade associations have been mainly concerned with the product market, while employers' associations have been concerned with the labor market. A
standard definition of an employers' association is: A group which is
composed of, fostered by, or controlled by employers, and which seeks
to promote the employers' interest in labor matters. Normally, these are
associations of employers in a particular industry and/or area. In the
past, their main activities were aimed at keeping unions from organizing
an industry or gaining a foothold in a particular area; now their major
function is to engage in collective bargaining with unions so that the
members of an industry can deal on a united basis and, therefore, with
greater influence. Such associations are local, regional, and national in
scope. Beyond collective bargaining, they have attempted to shape
legislation and influence administration of labor laws at various governmental levels. The legislative activity of the associations has usually been
aimed at reducing the power of unions, and at limiting union and
governmental determination of wages, hours, and working conditions;
however, there have been instances in which the interests of unions and
employers have coincided and the two groups have worked together for
the passage of legislation such as workmen's compensation laws.

As in the case of trade associations, organizations of employers had
some predecessors in the few guilds that had developed in colonial
America. Although some craft-guilds were established in the colonies,
they were not as powerful as their English and other European counterparts. However, they did have some influence in establishing wages,
hours, and working conditions. With the coming of the factory system,
other employer associations sprang up—first in a locality, then in a
region, and by the Civil War some nationals had been created. One of
the early national organizations—the American National Stove Manufacturers and Iron Founders' Association, permanently organized in
1866—prepared a notice to be posted in its members' shops stating its
purposes among which was "resisting any and all action of the Molders'
Union which shall in any manner interfere with our right to control our
own workshops and to manage our own business."

Although employers' associations were not successful in keeping unions
out, they have been more successful in presenting a common front to
labor. From the standpoint of a firm this means it must sacrifice some

of its freedom to determine labor matters as best it can. This is a freedom that most employers give up willingly because their bargaining power is greater when one agency bargains on behalf of a large number of firms.

By some observers, the National Association of Manufacturers is regarded as an outgrowth of the employer association movement. However, since a number of industries are represented in the NAM and since it takes in the entire United States, we shall examine it as a general business organization rather than as an association of employers.

READING: Trade Association Activity * by Clair Wilcox

[*Although trade associations are undoubtedly quite important in their influence upon the policies adopted by their members, there is scant information on their activities. This may be a consequence of the fact that some such actions are illegal or that the association feels they may be regarded unfavorably by the public. In any event, it is necessary to go back to the period before World War II to find a scholarly study of their activities which shows, among other things, the impact of association actions on price decisions of members of the association. The Temporary National Economic Committee was a Congressional committee established in 1937 to investigate various aspects of the American economy. In the following reading, an economist for the T.N.E.C. presents his findings.*]

The trade association movement is a product of the past 30 years. The few associations that were formed during the latter half of the nineteenth century were, in the main, impotent, clandestine, or ephemeral. Trade organization, in the twentieth century, took its initial impetus from the enunciation of the rule of reason by the Supreme Court in 1911 and from the publication of a popular book on "The New Competition" by Arthur J. Eddy in 1912, both statements holding out the hope that competitors might cooperate in common activities and remain within the law. The formation of associations was further stimulated in 1917 and 1918 by the function assigned to them by the War Industries Board in the procurement of supplies, and again in 1933 and 1934 by the opportunity afforded them to adopt and administer codes of fair competition under the National Industrial Recovery Act. In 1940 there were more than 8,000 trade associations—local, regional, and national—in the United States, some 2,000 of them national in scope.

The functions performed by trade associations for the benefit of their members are numerous and diverse. Many of them do not appear to be inconsistent with the preservation of competition; many others may involve the imposition of restraints. Typical association activities include cooperative industrial research,

---

* *Excerpt from:* Clair Wilcox, *Competition and Monopoly in American Industry,* T.N.E.C. Mono. 21 (1940), pp. 225 ff.

market surveys, the development of new uses for products, the provision of traffic information, the operation of employment bureaus, collective bargaining with organized labor, mutual insurance, commercial arbitration, the publication of trade journals, joint advertising and publicity, and joint representation before legislative and administrative agencies, all of them undertakings that may serve a trade without disservice to its customers. But they also include the establishment of common cost accounting procedures, the collection and dissemination of statistics, the operation of price reporting plans, the standardization of products, terms of contracts, and price lists and differentials, the provision of credit information, the interchange of patent rights, the administration of basing point systems, the joint purchasing of supplies, and the promulgation of codes of business ethics, each of them practices which may operate to restrain competition in quality, service, price, or terms of sale. As Adam Smith remarked in 1776, "People of the same trade seldom meet together, even for merriment and diversion, but the conversation ends in a conspiracy against the public or in some contrivance to raise prices."

Cost Accounting. Conspicuous among association activities is the promotion of cost accounting, or, in association parlance, cost education. As described, by Burns, this educational work is carried on through six grades. In the first, the association provides its members with standard forms for use in cost determination. This is expected to eliminate any price cutting that might arise from ignorance of costs. It may also carry the suggestion that no seller's price should fall below his costs as set forth on the standard forms. In the second grade, the association prescribes detailed procedures for computing costs, showing its members the proper way to figure charges for materials, the proper way to compute depreciation, and the proper way to distribute overhead. This is designed to reduce the price disparities that might result from the employment of diverse methods of calculation. In the third grade, the association suggests a uniform mark-up. Each of its members is encouraged to add the same percent of profit to his costs to get his price. But one member may undersell another if he has lower costs. In the fourth grade, however, the association publishes some sort of an average of the costs of all the firms in the trade. Where this figure is adopted by members in place of their individual actual costs, it affords a basis for the establishment of a common price. But prices may still vary if members do not add a uniform mark-up to the uniform cost. In the fifth grade, therefore, says Burns, "Some associations have taken the final step and included an allowance for profit in the so-called average costs. Average costs then become merely a suggested selling price, uniform for all, and provide a means by which to define and detect price cutting and a stimulus to attempts to eliminate it." In the sixth and final grade, the association undertakes to enforce adherence to the average "costs". Through editorials published in trade journals, through resolutions passed at association meetings, and through conferences and correspondence between association officials and members of the trade, it endeavors to persuade all sellers that they should adopt the common estimate of "cost" and therefore charge a common price.

Not every association has carried cost education through all six grades. But every student of the activity has recognized that it is subject to abuse. Whitney, for instance, lists three methods of controlling price: direct, through price fixing; indirect, through persuasion; and technical, through cost accounting. The Federal Trade Commission quotes a statement made by the secretary of the National Association of Cost Accountants at a meeting of the American Trade Association executives: "I cannot see a great deal in uniform costing unless it does lead to an exchange of information and a comparison of costs with a view to securing a certain amount of cost standardization which is something entirely different from uniformity of method. . . . It is perfectly true that the exchange of information is likely to have an influence on price levels in the industry, but why shouldn't it?" Accordingly to the Commission, "These words sum up very well the philosophy of cost accounting and cost comparison as a trade association activity." The study of average cost data by the members of an industry "will promote uniformity of practice in computing costs and generally influence them in the direction of uniformity of prices." It is, moreover, "the natural tendency of trade associations to include everything possible in costs and thus to swell the amount". The Commission therefore concludes: "Among the many legitimate kinds of trade association activities which may easily and imperceptibly pass over from the stage of useful service to that of abuse and even illegality, there are probably few more prone to this sort of transition than cost-accounting work."

Statistical Activities.   The statistical activities of trade associations may affect prices by influencing the production policies of member firms. Association statistics cover such matters as the volume of production, inventories, unfilled orders, idle capacity, shipments, and sales. Reports on the volume of production may show output as a ratio of capacity and compare it with some ratio designated as "normal". They may compare output with orders or with shipments. They may compare it with the quantity produced during some "normal" period in the past. Such comparisons are likely to carry the suggestion that production is getting out of hand. The consequent curtailment amounts, says Burns, "to adapting production to demand and avoiding the accumulation of unsold stocks. It is implied that when demand declines there is only one proper response, viz., an equal reduction of output." In some cases, association reports have compared changes in the volume of one member's output with changes in the total output of the trade. "These calculations are aimed at deterring the firm whose sales have been falling from attempting to increase its sales by increased sales effort or price cutting at a time when the sales of all firms are falling. Thus a 'demoralized market' is avoided. Such an interpretation of the statistics must tend to fix the distribution of business between firms. Insofar as price cutting is deterred when business falls off, there is also a tendency to maintain unchanged prices." Reports on the volume of inventories likewise "are likely to be used as a guide to production policy, production being diminished when stocks are accumulating and increased when stocks are falling. . . . The existing price of the product tends to be maintained and production adjusted to changes in demand at the unchanging price." So, too, with reports on unfilled orders. If they reveal an increase in the volume of such orders, output may rise; but if they reveal a decline, it is probable that output will be curtailed and the established price maintained. Reports on the volume of idle capacity may have a similar effect. They serve to warn the members of the trade that a price cut may provoke a price war. They may also deter existing firms from adding to their equipment and new firms from entering the field, even though it might be possible to put the added capacity to work at a lower price. Whitney's three methods of price control are paralleled by three methods of controlling production: direct, through quota systems; indirect, through persuasion; and technical, through the collection and dissemination of statistics.

Price Reporting Systems. Trade association statistics cover prices as well as production. Through their price reporting systems, association members make available to one another, and sometimes to outsiders, information concerning the prices at which products have been, are being, or are to be sold. It is argued that such systems, by increasing the amount of knowledge available to traders, must lessen the imperfection of markets and make for more effective competition. Whether they do so, in fact, depends upon the characteristics of the industries which use them and upon the characteristics of the plans themselves.

For a price reporting system to increase the effectiveness of competition in a trade, many conditions must be fulfilled. As for the characteristics of the trade: Sellers must be numerous, each of them relatively small, and no one of them dominant. Entrance to the field must not be obstructed by legal barriers or by large capital requirements. Otherwise a reporting system may implement a price agreement, or promote price leadership, and facilitate the application of pressure against price cutters. Moreover, the market for the trade must not be a declining one. Supply, demand, and price must not be subject to violent fluctuation. The product must consist of small units turned out in large volume and sales must be frequent. Otherwise sellers will have a stronger incentive than usual to restrict competition and, even though numerous, they may agree upon a common course of action. Under such circumstances, a price reporting plan may serve as a convenient instrument for the administration of a scheme of price control. And finally, the demand for the product of the trade must be elastic, falling as prices rise and rising as prices fall. Otherwise it is not to be expected that the provision of fuller information would force a seller to reduce his price.

So, too, with the characteristics of the reporting plan itself: The price reports must not be falsified. If members do not return their lowest prices, if the association excludes such prices from the figures it reports, competitive reductions to meet the lowest figure actually charged will not occur. The reports must be available to all sellers on equal terms. If they are not, the sellers who fail to see them will not be informed of lower prices that they otherwise might meet. The reports must also be available to buyers. If information is withheld from them, they cannot seek out the seller who has filed the lowest price or compel another seller to meet this price to make a sale. The reports must not identify individual traders. The reporting agency must be neutral, keeping each seller's returns in confidence and transmitting the collective information to all concerned. If price cutters are openly or secretly identified, those who desire to sell at higher prices may employ persuasion or even sterner methods to bring them into line. The prices reported must be limited to past transactions. If current or future prices are exchanged, sellers will hesitate to cut their charges to make a sale, since they will know that lower figures will instantly be met. Each seller must be free to change his price at any time. If a seller cannot cut a price until sometime after he has filed the lower figure, thus affording his rivals an opportunity to meet it instantly, the chances that he will do so are accordingly reduced. The plan must carry no recommendation as to price policy. If the publication of average "costs" suggests the figures to be filed, if uniform charges are voted at trade meetings, then the reporting system becomes a method of policing the observance of a common price. The system, finally, must make no provision for the supervision of prices charged or for the imposition of penalties on those who sell below the figures they have filed. If association officials supervise the filing and persuade sellers whose quotations are low to raise them, if penalties are imposed on those who quote figures below those recommended or sell at figures below those quoted, then the reporting plan becomes but an incident in the whole price fixing scheme. When every one of these conditions is fulfilled, a price reporting system may promote effective competition. But where any one of them is unsatisfied, price reporting is likely to implement the non-competitive arrangements within the trade. It follows that competition must more often be diminished than increased through the operation of price reporting plans.

Standardization.   The standardization of products, terms of contracts, and price lists and differentials, though frequently advantageous to buyers and sellers alike, is also subject to abuse. Standardization of products contributes to convenience and lessens waste. But it may limit competition in quality, restrict the consumer's range of choice, and by eliminating the sale of cheaper grades, compel him to buy a better and a more expensive product than the one that he desires. Standardization of the terms of contracts saves time, prevents misunderstanding, and affords a common basis for the comparison of prices. If limited to such matters as allowable variations in the quality of goods delivered, the time when title passes, and the method to be employed in the settlement of disputes, it does not restrain competition. But a trade may go on to establish common credit terms, create uniform customer classifications, eliminate or standardize discounts, forbid free deals, limit guarantees, restrict the return of merchandise, minimize allowances on trade-ins, fix handling charges, forbid freight absorption, discourage long-term contracts, and agree upon a common policy with respect to guarantees against price declines. In the judgment of the Federal Trade Commission, "the standardization of terms of sale, and of elements in the sales contract, appears to be entirely desirable, and at least as beneficial to the buyer as to the seller, and yet it is hard to arrive cooperatively at such standardization without an agreement on some element in the price paid." At best, such an agreement restricts the scope of competition and deprives buyers of options which they are entitled to enjoy. At worst, it serves to supplement other elements in a comprehensive scheme of price control, preventing indirect departures from the established price and facilitating its enforcement through the operation of a price reporting plan. So, also, the standardization of price lists and differentials involving the selection of a single variety or size of product for use as a base in quoting prices and the adoption of a system of uniform extras and discounts for use in computing the prices of other varieties and sizes, contributes to the convenience with which negotiations may be carried on. But here again, as the Trade Commission has observed, "the simplification of the process of quotation doubtless facilitates agreement on prices between sellers; and the devising of a base price list, or of standard differentials, by an association may be accompanied by elements of agreement that are contrary to the anti-trust laws."

Credit Bureaus.   The provision, through a central bureau, of information on credit risks increases the safety with which credit may be granted. If confined to the exchange of ledger data on individual buyers in response to specific requests and accompanied by no recommendation as to policy, it helps the members of a trade without injustice to their customers. But an association may go on to limit the freedom of members to extend credit where they please, to circulate black-lists, to boycott delinquent debtors without affording them a hearing, to set up uniform terms to govern the extension of credit, and to employ the denial of credit as a means of controlling the channels of distribution or enforcing the maintenance of a resale price. . . .

Cooperation or Conspiracy?   . . . It is impossible to measure the extent to which members of trade associations are actually engaged in cooperating to serve the public and in conspiring against it. The line between cooperation and conspiracy is not an easy one to draw. The courts, to be sure, must attempt to draw it. Price reporting, for instance, is held to be legal if reports are confined to past transactions, is of uncertain legality if they cover current or future transactions, and if members are required to adhere to the prices they have filed, and is illegal if essential information is withheld from buyers, if sellers are identified, if members agree upon the prices they will file, and if adherence to these prices is enforced by detailed supervision and by the imposition of penalties. But no one say with confidence how many of the price reporting systems now in operation fail to overstep this line. . . . Nor can there ever be assurance that the merriment, diversion, and conversation, of which Adam Smith once spoke, do not lend to the conspiracies or contrivances to raise prices which he feared, unless an agent of the Federal Government is placed in every trade association office to read all correspondence, memoranda, and reports, attend all meetings, listen to all conversations, participate in all the merriment and diversion, and issue periodic reports on what transpires. No such systematic oversight is now authorized by law.

SUGGESTED READINGS

Bonnett, Clarence F., *History of Employers' Associations of the United States* (New York: Vantage Press, 1956). The book covers the period from the first recorded association to the year 1900 (another book by the author, *Employers'*

Associations in the United States deals with some association activities in the present century). It traces the development of ancient associations in the Old World to furnish a background.

Judkins, Jay, *National Associations of the United States* (Washington, D.C.: Department of Commerce, 1949). A directory and review of the services and accomplishments of trade associations, professional societies, labor unions, farm cooperatives, chambers of commerce, better business bureaus, and other organizations which play a prominent part in American economic life.

CHAPTER 18

GENERAL
BUSINESS
ORGANIZATIONS

The social environment of business contains a number of individuals and groups influencing business firms outside the markets in which business buys and sells. Some of their objectives may be economic in nature, but the activities engaged in to attain those objectives are rarely undertaken in markets. Others have goals that are not economic, and also have lines of action outside market activity available to them; when their interests are in conflict with those of business firms they may take action against business. Not all relationships of business to these individuals and groups are in the nature of a conflict and frequent cooperation takes place. Regardless of the nature of the relationship, however, certain demands are made of firms and accordingly an awareness of the nature of such classes in the surroundings of business is essential to an adequate understanding of the environment of the firm.

Some groups in the environment of business may be classified as "general business organizations." They are organizations of businessmen, professional men, firms, trade associations, and so on, from a number of industries. Some are less general than others. Chambers of commerce, for example, have the broadest representation from various industries. On the other hand, manufacturers' associations draw their members from a smaller segment of American business, although a great variety of manufacturing industries are represented in organizations such as the National Association of Manufacturers. Chambers of commerce and manufacturers' associations have the greatest membership of the various general business organizations, but there are others of influence and interest. One of these is the Committee for Economic Development, which is a relatively small organization of men from big business plus some educators. Better Business Bureaus and their national association are also organizations of businessmen from a large number of industries, but do not appear to be as influential as those previously mentioned. Then there is a scattering of various small groups of some interest but not of great influence.

CHAMBERS OF COMMERCE

Chambers of commerce have their origin in the merchant guilds of the Middle Ages. The first organization to have the name "chamber of commerce" was formed by the town council of Marseilles, France, in 1599. This points up a distinction between such organizations as they developed in England and other European countries and those established in the United States. American chambers have no governmental status, while those abroad are frequently associated with their governments. Possessing governmental power, these early commercial organizations regulated trade in the interests of the government as well as in those of the merchants.

The first chamber of commerce in America was formed in New York in 1768 (eight years before the Declaration of Independence). Colonial merchants in that city had found collective action effective in securing repeal of the 1765 Stamp Act, which had burdened trade, and decided to form a permanent group because "mercantile societies have been found very useful in trading centers for promoting and encouraging commerce, supporting industry, adjusting disputes relative to trade and navigation, and procuring such laws and regulations as may be found necessary for the benefit of trade in general." They were able to secure a royal charter for their activities in 1770, and after the Revolutionary War continued as the Chamber of Commerce of the State of New York. Charleston, South Carolina, formed a chamber in 1773, and by 1801 additional chambers had been formed in the other seaport cities of New Haven and Philadelphia. By 1870, there were chambers of commerce in 40 major American cities; and by 1900, over 3,000.

Although the New York City chamber took the name of Chamber of Commerce of the State of New York, the first state chamber of commerce made up of a number of local chambers was not formed until just before the beginning of this century. Ohio businessmen took the lead in this movement, and some thirty states have followed Ohio's example.

A logical development after the establishment of state chambers would seem to be the creation of a U.S. Chamber of Commerce. Although the present National Chamber dates from 1912, it had a predecessor, which appeared before the establishment of any state federation of local chambers of commerce. In 1859, the Boston chamber urged the establishment of a Board of Trade as a part of the executive branch of the national government, an agency to be similar to the Board of Trade in England, which had official status. This proposal was not adopted, but a National Board of Trade (without governmental status) was established in 1868, having as its purpose: "to create unity and harmony of action in reference to commercial usages, customs and laws, and especially in order to secure proper consideration of questions pertaining to the financial, commercial and industrial interests of this country at large. . . ." Initially, this group had 32 organization members and contacted the President, department heads, and Congress to promote its objectives. It did not, however, grow with the increase in the number of local and state chambers and lost its representative character.

To give a unified voice to business in the nation's capital, several federated business organizations met in 1911 with the Secretary of Commerce and Labor and suggested to him that a conference be called in Washington to establish a new national business federation. President Taft included in a message to Congress during December of that year the suggestion that some better system be established to enable business to communicate its views to government. Accordingly, a National Commercial Conference was scheduled for April 1912, and it created the Chamber of Commerce of the United States. Since the various types of chambers perform somewhat different functions, we shall examine them separately.

Local Chambers of Commerce

At the present time, chambers of commerce in cities and counties play fairly well-defined roles. They are composed of the business and professional men and women of a locality interested mainly in increasing total spending in the local markets. A second basic objective (which promotes attainment of the other primary goal) is community improvement. To promote the interests of the firms making up the majority of the membership, a number of lines of action are taken to bring more money into the local markets in which the business firms sell. These typically fall under the general headings of industrial development, trade development, civic development, agricultural and natural resources development, transportation development, and publicity.

Local businessmen will secure increased sales if existing firms will expand their payrolls through increased operations and also if new firms can be encouraged to begin operations in the area. To expand present manufacturing operations and to encourage new "industries," industrial development is undertaken. This involves assisting present firms in meeting their needs and solving their problems and aggressively encouraging and promoting the establishment of suitable new firms, both from within and without the locality.

Trade development deals with expanding and improving retail and wholesale trade and with attempts to increase tourist business and conventions. By making the locality a more attractive center for retail shopping, more persons will come into the local market and, presumably, spend more money. Adding more wholesalers will have the effect of adding more payrolls to be spent in the community. Tourists and conventioneers also bring additional money into the community.

Agricultural and natural resources development directly or indirectly results in increased purchasing power in the markets in which local businessmen sell. New firms and better firms in the extractive industries realize a greater income from the sale of their products and consequently have more to spend in the local market. The development of natural resources for recreational uses attracts tourists who will make purchases in the locality.

Civic development and transportation development have indirect effects on purchasing power in the local market, but are influential to a significant degree. Through civic improvement and the development of the area's educational and cultural assets, more firms and individuals are attracted to the community as a place in which to locate. Improvement of roads and other transportation facilities also attracts new settlers as well as enlarges the area of the local market. By having some influence on legislation and regulations affecting transportation—with an eye to securing efficient service and low rates—not only are new firms attracted, but local firms are in a better position to compete with firms in other areas.

Publicity and public relations activities play important roles in the carrying out of the programs of local chambers of commerce. Outside the market area, communication must be made with tourists and firms looking for business locations. Those individuals and groups in the area who are not members of the chamber are urged to support programs sponsored and/or favored by the business group. Legislators and other political figures not in the immediate locale must be contacted for the same purpose. These activities and the other programs cost money, hence the biggest demands made on business firms by local chambers are for funds. In addition to money, the time of members of firms is requested in order to plan and carry out programs through committee action.

Some local chambers are concerned with the poor teaching of economics and business in the public schools. To influence the administrators and teachers, they have established Business-Education Day programs. Educators are invited to visit business firms and talk to businessmen so that they will have some notion of what business is really like. To reach the students, the Junior Achievement program has been supported as a means of teaching teen-agers the economic facts of life. Under this program, high school students form companies to manufacture and sell products, with advice and financial aid from businessmen. Feeling that there is "much ignorance, half-baked information and superstition" on the part of high school pupils, the J.A. program is regarded by at least one local chamber as an important means of counteracting "the attacks that are being made against the free-enterprise system and of bolstering the poor teaching in economics offered by public schools."

Most firms do not feel there is any conflict between their activities and those of local chambers; on the contrary, they are willing to cooperate to improve "the business climate" in the community. However, some see no direct benefit from chamber of commerce action—or feel that the action will take place even if they do not cooperate—and are unwilling to give time or money to such organizations. Sometimes the chamber will urge businessmen to go along on specific programs—such as keeping retail establishments open on certain nights—which may appear contrary to the interests of a particular firm. Firms outside the community are frequently in conflict with a local chamber: railroads, for example, are pressured for better service and lower rates even though this increases costs and reduces revenues of the carrier. Also, retailers on the fringes of the trading area of a particular community see the chamber group as threatening to take customers away from them.

Since local chambers represent the businessmen of one locality, on occasion they are in conflict with other local chambers because each attempts to promote business in its particular community. A recent example of this was the proposal of the Philadelphia Chamber of Commerce to relieve the congestion of New York's air space by having all flights between Western Europe and the eastern part of the U.S. transferred from New York's airports to Philadelphia. The New York Chamber took a dim view of this proposal, of course.

There is some evidence that the influence of local chambers of commerce is declining in some communities. Special business organizations established to promote conventions and tourism or to preserve the downtown shopping area have taken over some functions that local chambers used to perform, as have certain local and state governmental agencies. The strong political stands taken by some chambers have been regarded as keeping some business out of the locality (for example, the support of "right-to-work" laws by a local chamber makes it difficult for a city to attract labor union conventions). Still, they remain the most influential general business organizations in localities, and there is little likelihood that they will soon disappear from the scene.

State Chambers of Commerce

Some problems confronting businessmen generally within a particular community may not be possible of solution at the local level. This is most frequently true of political problems. A local chamber may have some influence with local authorities, but the most important legislation concerning business stems from state legislative halls and the Congress. In order to provide a spokesman generally for business at the state capital, state chambers of commerce have been formed. Not every state has one. In some states the chamber of commerce from the major city may represent the position of business, or another general business association operating under another name may do so. The object of a state group is to improve conditions for business generally throughout the state and not for any particular locality. Consequently, it works for favorable legislation and to some extent promotes the state as a place to do business in, to live in, or to visit.

National Chamber of Commerce

The Chamber of Commerce of the United States of America achieved rapid growth after 1912 and has become the major general business organization in the U.S. A recent statement declared that it speaks for more than 3,600 Organization Members—local, state, and regional chambers of commerce, and trade and professional associations—and for more than 25,000 Business Members—firms and individuals. The affiliated organizations have a combined membership of more than 2,750,000, so the National Chamber speaks for almost 3,000,000 individuals (assuming the unlikely circumstance that they were unanimous in their views). Not only has there been a great growth in membership, but there has also been some change in the programs of the national organization.

Initially the purposes and programs of the National Chamber were limited. A major objective was to focus business sentiment on legislation concerning business. The organization saw itself as expressing the business opinion of the entire nation and made itself available for conferences with the executive and legislative branches of the federal government. Also, it aimed at making more available and more useful the work of various governmental bureaus. Too, it encouraged the organization of businessmen in all parts of the country, in order to secure concerted action; once organized, the National Chamber aimed at making them more effective. Finally, the federation provided trade information to its members. The justification for such activity was set forth in an early publication:

> The need for unity of action by the business forces of America is pressing. With the increasing tendency toward federal regulation of domestic commerce and with the fast growing importance of our foreign trade, business becomes more and more dependent upon national rather than state or local regulation and legislation. The progress of leading European nations in commercial development, the organization and increase of their foreign and domestic trade, are largely to be attributed to the ability of their commercial interests to act in concert through national commercial bodies.

Currently the objectives of the organization are expressed in less clear fashion, although the activities of the U.S. Chamber indicate its aims. First, the National Chamber finds facts on matters of importance to the nation's business, analyzes those facts, interprets the findings, and disseminates its conclusions. Second, the National Chamber develops a policy position on such national issues, normally by taking a poll of its members. Once a position is taken, the chamber attempts to influence public opinion to be favorable toward this view. Also, it works in Washington to get congressional and administration support for the position as well as works through local businessmen, inspiring them to communicate with their Congressmen. Finally, the National Chamber continues to service its member organizations, attempting to make them more effective.

International Chamber of Commerce

As might be expected, the final development in the chamber of commerce movement has been the creation of an international group. The International Chamber of Commerce is a world federation of national bodies representing trade, industry, banking, transportation and, in general, all branches of economic activity (including in its membership chambers of commerce, trade associations and federations, syndical chambers, etc.). It is also a central organization for enterprises whose activities extend to the international level and that are interested, therefore, in the improvement of international business relations.

The International Chamber was formed in 1919 and now has members from 66 countries. Its members are interested in the expansion of world trade and develop policy positions that it feels will promote that objective. Some of its contacts are with international organizations (both governmental and nongovernmental), but it relies on its National Committees to secure the cooperation of national governments and other organizations within a nation. Although it might seem logical for the U.S. Chamber of Commerce to perform this function, a separate National Committee exists in the United States. This committee is made up of representatives of the leading trade associations in various industries as well as individual commercial and industrial firms. Policies of the International Chamber are developed by commissions studying issues confronting businesses involved in world trade. Four major problem areas and groups of commissions exist: economic and financial policy; production, distribution, and advertising; transport and communications; and law and commercial practice. To the extent that the International Chamber is able to get its policy recommendations adopted, it creates a more favorable legal and economic environment for those firms engaged in international business.

MANUFACTURERS' ASSOCIATIONS

Somewhat less general in their membership than chambers of commerce are organizations of manufacturers without regard to type of manufacture. While they are not truly general business associations—they normally admit only manufacturers to their memberships—they speak for a substantial portion of the business community. Manufacturers' associations had their origins in the craft guilds that governed wages, hours, and conditions of employment in a number of handicraft industries prior to the rise of the factory system in the United States. With the development of modern manufacturing, associations of manufacturers in a particular industry were organized to deal with labor problems. In some instances, the organizations encompassed a number of manufacturing industries in a locality. A further development was the creation of state bodies, and eventually, a national organization. The groups functioning on the state and national level are mainly concerned with securing legislation favorable to them. Not all state groups bear the title of manufacturers' association, some being referred to as "associated industries" or even "employers' associations."

On the national level, the National Association of Manufacturers speaks for the bulk of American manufacturers. It has some 19,500 members, 83 per cent of whom employ 500 workers or less. Formed in 1895, the declared objectives toward which the association works are (1) the promotion of the industrial interests of the United States; (2) the fostering of the domestic and foreign commerce of the United States; (3) the betterment of the relations between employers and their employees; (4) the protection of the individual liberty and rights of employer and employee; (5) the dissemination of information among the public with respect to the principles of individual liberty and ownership of property; (6) the support of legislation in furtherance of those principles and opposition to legislation in derogation thereof. The permanent committees of the N.A.M. give some clue to the matters with which it is concerned. They are agricultural cooperation; economic policy; economic security; educational cooperation; employment relations; governmental finance; healthful working conditions; industrial economics; industrial financing; industrial practices; national defense and industrial mobilization; patents and trade-marks; public relations; relations of government to industry; scientific research study of depressions; tariff and transportation. Essentially, the group acts to influence public opinion and legislation.

OTHER ASSOCIATIONS OF BUSINESSMEN

The Committee for Economic Development is another national organization in which businessmen from a number of industries are influential. Its membership is small—approximately 200 leading businessmen and educators—but the business members occupy very important positions in American economic life. The stated objectives of this group are to make recommendations for business and public policy that will preserve and strengthen our free society, and that will maintain high employment, increasing productivity and higher living standards, greater economic stability, and greater economic opportunity for all. These objectives are promoted through research and discussion and through dissemination of the findings to bring about increased public understanding of the importance of the objectives and the ways in which they can be achieved. The National Planning Association pursues similar objectives through similar means, but includes representatives from labor and agriculture as well as those from business.

A question might be raised as to why the CED is necessary, since the National Chamber and the NAM claim to be the national spokesmen for business. A clue to the answer may be in the fact that the bulk of the membership of both of these large national business organizations consists of small and medium-sized firms, while the membership of the CED is pretty much a roster of executives from the largest corporations in America. Although the big firms also belong to the U.S. Chamber and the NAM, they may well feel that those organizations tend to have their policies influenced too much by smaller firms. Also, the possibility exists that business members of the CED feel that the NAM and National Chamber are not constructive enough in their recommendations, as they have implied: "CED believes that by enabling businessmen to demonstrate constructively their concern for the general welfare, it is helping business to earn and maintain the national and community respect essential to the successful functioning of the free enterprise capitalist system."

Better Business Bureaus are another class of general business organizations. They are nonprofit corporations established by business and professional firms in a community and claim to be the only business groups that carry on continuing public relations programs based on action to maintain the "integrity" of the business community, to maintain the confidence of the people in the area in the reliability of the local market as a place in which they can buy with faith and satisfaction, and to maintain an environment which is conducive to better customer relations, higher productivity of promotional expenditures, and better profits.

The Better Business Bureau movement originated in 1912, and has grown enormously. There are some 125 local Bureaus with more than 150,000 business firm members, which give time and money to promote the Bureaus and their objectives. The local organizations have formed a national Association of Better Business Bureaus. Also, there is a National Better Business Bureau which has as its members 2,175 national advertisers, advertising agencies, media, trade associations, direct selling companies, and chambers of commerce. Its concern is to promote honesty in the field of national advertising.

Members of local Better Business Bureaus apparently feel that their interests are promoted mainly by action against "unethical" firms. One of its activities is taking action against firms engaging in misrepresentation and deception in advertisements. Each local BBB has close liaison with advertising media, advertising agencies, government agencies, and advertisers, and attempts to eliminate "badvertising." Misrepresentation of a product, service, price, or value by an advertiser in order to attract customers unfairly diverts trade from responsible business firms; such misrepresentation is sought out and attacked. In the activities of BBBs, there is some evidence of concern with keeping outsiders from entering the domestic market, whether they are "ethical" or not. In Seattle, for example, the general manager of the BBB urged the City Council to retain a license rule requiring heavy fees for "special auctions" of merchandise brought in from outside the city limits because the law was designed to protect the Seattle field for Seattle merchants. On occasion,

local Better Business Bureaus will issue public warnings of itinerant peddlers of faulty roofing jobs, furnaces, aluminum siding, and so on.
Although there are some "gypsies" who do engage in such fraudulent
selling, the main purpose of such warnings seems to be to protect the local
market for local businessmen.

The influence of Better Business Bureaus is difficult to assess. In instances in which advertising and selling practices are fraudulent or otherwise illegal, calling the attention of authorities to such practices does
have impact. On the other hand, where such activities are not illegal, the
influence of a BBB is considerably less. The Better Business Bureau of
Metropolitan New York has contended that the evidence did not support
the Sperry & Hutchinson Company's contention (contained in its advertising) that its green trading stamps were "worth more" than other
stamps issued in the New York area. Despite this, S & H ignored the BBB
pleas to modify its ads, and although the bureau contacted those providing the advertising media, none of the media used by the company balked
at the wording of the ads.

There are, as we mentioned in the beginning, a number of other general business organizations, in the sense that more than one industry is
represented in the group. There are various small–business organizations
that try to promote, mainly through political action, the interests of that
class of businessmen. Christian Business Men's organizations attempt to
promote Christianity in business life. Industrial development is sometimes
carried on by corporations set up by businessmen in a community who
see such organizations as a means of attracting new establishments
(which means new payrolls and increased sales for some local business
and professional men). Occasionally, businessmen will form special corporations to conduct fairs and expositions which, it is hoped, will attract
visitors who will spend in the locality.

As we look at the community, we also see other individuals and groups
attempting to influence the behavior of firms, and having some impact on
the results of their operations; although we have examined some—local
labor unions, local trade associations, and so on—others merit examination.

READINGS: Objectives and Activities of General Business Organizations

[*Most large organizations develop some formal statement of their objectives
and activities. General business organizations are no exception, and, given their
belief in the value of publicity, these formal statements have been made public.*

*The following excerpts from publications of some of the business groups dis-
cussed in the chapter shed additional light on the nature of those organizations.*]

Reading: The National Chamber: What It Is, What It Does, and Why °
by U.S. Chamber of Commerce
[*In the following reading, the objectives of the U.S. Chamber of Commerce
are stated by that organization. Since the relative importance of objectives are
indicated by the activities undertaken by an organization, the major areas of
activity engaged in by the National Chamber are also included.*]

The Chamber of Commerce of the United States—the National Chamber—
is a national federation of businessmen, firms and organizations.

The National Chamber was brought into being on the recommendation of
President William Howard Taft who saw the need for "a central organization"
to give Congress the benefit of the thinking of the business community on national problems and legislative issues affecting the economy and the future of
the country.

In April, 1912, President Taft called a meeting in Washington of representatives of commercial and trade associations—and, at this meeting, the first
steps were taken to form the National Chamber.

In its first year, the Chamber's membership totaled 82 local and state chambers
of commerce, and trade associations. The federation has grown steadily in size
ever since—and in the scope and effectiveness of its work.

The National Chamber represents all business and industry, large and small,
and every section of the country. It is composed of

—More than 3,600 Organization Members—local, state and regional chambers
of commerce, and trade and professional associations; and
—More than 25,000 Business Members—firms, corporations and individuals.

In dealing with national questions, the National Chamber works not only in
Washington but also on the community level, on a nation-wide basis. It works
through its affiliated organizations—in partnership with its underlying membership of more the 2,750,000 local business and civic leaders—and with its Business Members.

While the National Chamber and its members work to uphold and strengthen
four basic principles—limited government, individual freedom, free competitive
markets, steady economic progress—the specific purposes back of all the work of
the Chamber federation are these:

1. To strengthen and improve the competitive enterprise system.
2. To keep the economy dynamic and expanding—to create new job opportunities—and to raise the level of living of the American people.
3. To preserve our representative form of government, with proper checks
and balances, and with limitations on its powers.

° Reprinted with permission of the U.S. Chamber of Commerce from its *Progress
Report* for 1960 and the *Progress Report, 1963–64.*

4. To encourage the solution of local and national problems through voluntary organized action, and thus to remove excuses for intervention by the federal government.

5. To reduce non-essential government spending.

6. To halt inflation by getting rid of causes of inflation.

7. To equip and encourage businessmen and others to be better informed, more active and more responsible citizens.

8. To emphasize the worth and dignity of the individual.

9. To advance the political and economic interests of the United States in world affairs.

10. To keep the country productive and strong against the threat of war.

The Chamber's activities divide themselves broadly into five areas:

Facts

The National Chamber is a research organization, a fact-finding organization.

It searches out the facts, analyzes the facts, interprets the facts—and disseminates the information to businessmen, public officials, educators, editors, students, writers.

For its own use, the National Chamber wants to find out accurately everything there is to know about today's big national issues and problems—and it wants the thinking people of the country to have this dependable information.

Policy

The National Chamber is a policy-making organization, a policy-establishing organization.

Through a democratic procedure, which has been developed and perfected over a period of more than 48 years, the Chamber determines where business in general stands on national issues—and specifically what the business community recommends should be done to resolve national problems.

The Chamber keeps these established policies current—adjusted to meet changing conditions.

The Chamber uses these policies as its strict guide in planning and carrying out its whole program of work.

Responsibility

The National Chamber is an opinion-development organization.

It works to encourage and equip its own members and others to be more active in national affairs—to assume greater citizenship and governmental responsibility.

Through its major training and action programs—which are conducted by local firms, and by local organizations of businessmen—the National Chamber shows individuals how to train and prepare themselves: to be more articulate spokesmen for private business; to express their views more effectively to their elected representatives in Washington; and to be more influential in politics.

At the same time, the National Chamber works to build a better public under-

standing of national issues and problems—and to create increased public sentiment in favor of the philosophy of competitive enterprise, individual initiative
and self-reliance.

Action

The National Chamber is an action-getting organization.

It works vigorously, positively—and effectively—to implement the policies
of business on national issues.

Through its Washington office, the Chamber takes advantage of every opportunity to let Congress and the Administration know where business stands on
legislative proposals, and to show why the recommendations of business are in
the public interest.

Through its nation-wide network of local Congressional Action Committees,
the National Chamber inspires local businessmen to communicate with their
Congressmen and to give them their informed views on national issues affecting
business.

Service

The National Chamber is a service organization.

The Chamber helps America's voluntary organizations of businessmen grow
in usefulness, each in its own field, and on the national scene. It keeps them
pulling together in the same direction to achieve their common goals, to keep
the economy dynamic, and to preserve individual freedom.

Reading: The NAM: Its Nature, Its Creed, and Its Work,° *by President
Rudolph F. Bannow and the NAM Board.*

The National Association of Manufacturers is a non-profit, voluntary membership organization representing the bulk of this nation's manufacturing capacity.
Of our some 19,500 members 83% employ 500 or less, 46% employ 100 or less
and 25% employ 50 or less. Since its inception in 1895, NAM has been the national spokesman for American Industry. It speaks out frankly and firmly for
competitive free enterprise, the system of economics which has made America
a great nation. It uses all effective means to convince fellow citizens that the
preservation of this system will benefit all America—not just industry.

THE NATIONAL ASSOCIATION OF MANUFACTURERS CREDO,
Adopted by the Board, December 4, 1956.

The National Association of Manufacturers is a voluntary organization of many
thousands of member companies, located in every state, representative of industry of all sizes from the smallest to the largest, and dedicated to the economic
and social well-being of the nation and the freedom and progress of the American
people.

The purposes of the National Association of Manufacturers are defined as
follows:

° Reprinted by permission of the National Association of Manufacturers from *NAM
Viewpoints (Industry Believes),* 1961, and "A Message to Educators," by President
Rudolph F. Bannow.

* To formulate policies and objectives based on the enduring economic, social and governmental principles embodied in the Constitution of the United States, and without regard to partisan political considerations or the fortunes of any political party or candidate.

* To provide leadership in bringing about a steady improvement: (a) in the economic strength of the nation; (b) in the contribution of industry to the public welfare; (c) in the operation of the American system of free capital and free labor so as to afford opportunity and incentive for the individual to progress and provide for the well-being and security of himself and his family.

* To assist manufacturers in appraising the significance of social, legislative, and economic trends as they affect industry, people, the community and the nation.

* To contribute to a continuing improvement in the relations and cooperation between employer and employee, between government and industry, and between the public and industry.

* To join with others in bringing to the public and to government the viewpoint of manufacturers as to how national and international issues affect industry and the future of every citizen.

* To help create understanding of how the American free competitive enterprise system works for the benefit of every individual.

* To formulate its policies and conduct its operations so as to merit the respect and support of the American people.

The work of the National Association of Manufacturers begins with the formulation of industry viewpoints on the major public issues and affairs of our times. These are issues of significance not only to manufacturers, but to all citizens, for they go to the heart of the well-being of our people.

These beliefs are derived from the distilled research, discussion and conclusions of 13 large policy committees, representing more than 3,000 member companies of all types and sizes, and from all industries. When stated by such committees and adopted by a majority vote, they become subject to a vote of a two-thirds majority of the NAM Board of Directors before final adoption and publication in "Industry Believes." The final determination of policy is a function of the Board, and no individual or executive group of either staff or members may stand between a committee recommendation and the Board of Directors.

Reading: The Committee for Economic Development *

The Committee for Economic Development is composed of 200 leading businessmen and educators.

CED is devoted to these basic objectives:

* Reprinted by permission of *The Committee for Economic Development*.

1. To develop, through objective research and discussion, findings and recommendations for business and public policy which will contribute to the preservation and strengthening of our free society, and to the maintenance of high employment, increasing productivity and living standards, greater economic stability and greater opportunity for all our people.

2. To bring about increasing public understanding of the importance of these objectives and the ways in which they can be achieved.

CED's work is supported by voluntary contributions from business and industry. It is nonprofit, nonpartisan and nonpolitical.

The trustees, who generally are Presidents or Board Chairmen of corporations and Presidents of universities, are chosen for their individual capacities rather than as representatives of any particular interests. They unite scholarship with business judgment and experience in analyzing the issues and developing recommendations to resolve the economic problems that constantly arise in a dynamic and democratic society.

Through this business-academic partnership, CED endeavors to develop policy statements and other research products that commend themselves as guides to public and business policy; for use as texts in college economic and political science courses and in management training courses; for consideration and discussion by newspaper and magazine editors, columnists and commentators, and for distribution abroad to promote better understanding of the American economic system.

CED believes that by enabling businessmen to demonstrate constructively their concern for the general welfare, it is helping business to earn and maintain the national and community respect essential to the successful functioning of the free enterprise capitalist system.

SUGGESTED READINGS

Brady, Robert A., *Business As a System of Power* (New York: Columbia U.P., 1943). Contains a chapter on the NAM, although the treatment is not a balanced one.

Schriftgiesser, Karl, *Business Comes of Age: The Impact of the Committee for Economic Development, 1942–1960* (New York: Harper & Row, 1960). A lively account of the individuals and issues involved in the development of the CED, along with some estimate of its impact on economic policies.

Shreve, Earl O., *The Chamber of Commerce of the United States of America* (New York: The Newcomen Society in North America, 1949). A brief historical sketch of the National Chamber by a former president of the organization.

Steigerwalt, Albert K., *The National Association of Manufacturers, 1895–1914.* (Ann Arbor, Mich.: Bureau of Business Research, Graduate School of Business Administration, University of Michigan, 1964). A history of the NAM in its early years.

CHAPTER 19

BUSINESS
AND THE
COMMUNITY

Business firms conduct their operations in communities. Although we sometimes hear the region or nation spoken of as a "community" and some even speak of the "world community," our concern in this chapter will be mainly with the local community—the town or city in which a firm does business.

Towns and cities in America exist because of business. Early towns developed as places for conducting trade, in which local artisans and merchants as well as traveling merchants were engaged. In America, many communities were originally established upon some basic industry —commercial agriculture, mining, fishing, manufacturing, and so on—

which led to names such as farming community, mine town, fishing village, and mill town. Although forts and churches also provided nuclei about which communities grew, nowadays the basis for the existence of an urban community is business. As business grew in these villages and towns, they developed into cities. In urban communities, businessmen are men of power. They command resources of people, money, and goods. They are community leaders, occupying positions of influence in many community organizations. However, their leadership is sometimes challenged and sometimes firms find the "business climate" in a community distinctly unfavorable. Therefore, although communities depend upon business, sometimes community action adversely influences the operations of firms; hence, the community is an appropriate object of study for those who wish to understand the significant relationships between business and its environment.

THE NATURE OF THE COMMUNITY

The American community is American society in microcosm. Analyzing it presents the same problems as does analyzing American society as a whole and yields much the same answers. As in the case of society, some look at the community as having independent existence, with certain needs and wants. Employing such a view, one sociologist declares that the following is what communities want of business:

    1. A fair share of the taxes.
    2. A non-nuisance operations—no problems of parking, traffic congestion, air-water pollution, noise.
    3. A good operation—wages, hours, working conditions and other operating aspects that are good.[1]

There is some evidence that not all communities want these things, and even though it may be reasonable to assume that a community might want them, pressure for attaining them is not exerted by the community as a whole. It is only when individuals and groups within the community make some conscious effort to achieve them that they are secured if business firms do not voluntarily supply them. Accordingly, as in the study of society, we shall focus on individuals and groups making up the community rather than on the community as a whole.

Those sociologists who conceive of society as being composed of socio-economic classes have made numerous studies of particular communities. The results of their research have appeared in books titled *Hometown, Middletown, Yankee City,* and so on. However useful this view might be

[1] William Cole, *Urban Society* (New York: Houghton, 1958), pp. 267–268.

to sociologists, it is of no greater value to businessmen in studying the community than it is in studying American society; the examination of groups in specific communities leads us to employ a different classification.

In examining communities, some have been impressed by the large number and variety of groups existing. In the small college town of Amherst, Massachusetts, there are—not counting student organizations and government groups—

> well more than one hundred Clubs, Lodges, Leagues, Guilds, Tribes, Granges, Circles, Unions, Chapters, Councils, Societies, Associations, Auxiliaries, Brotherhoods, and Fellowships. Their specialties or special interests, to name a few, include cards, cameras, stamps, gardens, churches, teachers, speakers, voters, horses, business, service, golf, nature, eating, fishing, gunning, parents, grandparents, ancestors, needlework, temperance, travel, and kindergarten.[2]

It would be impossible to deal effectively with each group found in a small town or even with only each group that has some impact on the decisions and operations of business firms. Again, it is essential to classify these groups into some meaningful categories if we are to achieve an understanding of the nature of the community.

Some sociologists have been concerned with classifying the organized groups to be found in any community. These groups are regarded as economic, occupational, political and governmental, civic and welfare, social, religious, educational, ethnic, racial, cultural, health and recreation groups. We have already dealt with economic and occupational groups, which include business firms, trade associations, unions, chambers of commerce, and so on. The discussion of political and governmental groups in the environment of business will be deferred to Part III. Some of these classes of groups impinge upon the firm only rarely, and so we shall not specifically examine social, ethnic, racial, and cultural organizations. This leaves us the civic and welfare groups, health groups, religious organizations, educational organizations, and recreational groups to deal with. Although we shall confine our discussion to certain classes of community groups, we should point out that in some communities there are powerful individuals who exert considerable influence not related to their membership in any organization. However, since they are difficult to classify and generalize about, we shall only mention them in passing, if at all.

Although we shall not discuss government at any length at this point, it should be indicated that under its "police powers," local government

[2] William L. Doran, *Univ. of Mass. Alumni Bulletin*, Vol. 31, December 1948, p. 4. Quoted in Earl Latham, *The Group Basis of Politics* (Ithaca, N.Y.: Cornell U.P., 1952), pp. 2–3.

takes action to promote the health, safety, welfare, and morals of the community. It is not alone in this field, however, since some community organizations also take such action. These groups are—for the most part—self-appointed guardians of the public good, although some claim divine authority for their actions. Regardless of whether or not their activities are authorized or of what the source of their authority may be, they do possess power to influence the firm and are, therefore, important objects of investigation.

It should be added—as the following discussion will confirm—that most businessmen are well aware of their position of leadership in the community, and consequently are concerned with meeting legitimate demands and even some requests that business may not properly be asked to grant. One problem confronting the firm is that these demands are so great in number and variety that even the resources of business are inadequate to meet them.

CIVIC, HEALTH AND WELFARE ORGANIZATIONS

Organizations devoted to civic improvement are organized for attaining such objectives as better housing and neighborhoods, better boys and girls, reform of adults, aid to the handicapped and underprivileged, better community health and for a variety of philanthropic purposes that, it is said, will improve the community. Sometimes businessmen have established service clubs to carry on such activity. In other instances, they serve on the governing boards of such organizations and actively participate in their campaigns—especially in fund-raising.

Service Clubs

Every urban community of any size has one or more service clubs. Some of the more prominent are the Active, Kiwanis, Lions, Optimist, and Rotary clubs. These are organizations of business and professional men who perform community service among other things. In some respects, they are similar to chambers of commerce—they have occasionally acted in lieu of such chambers in cities or towns in which the commercial associations did not exist—and seek community improvement to achieve better business opportunities for their members. There are other motivations, of course, and the members of service clubs discharge some of their community responsibilities through the programs of these organizations. As might be expected, these groups are not in conflict with business generally, although they might bring pressure to bear on certain firms to live up to what is felt to be their proper obligations. What service clubs want of their members is very similar to what chambers of commerce want— they want business firms to be represented by membership in the organizations, they want their money to promote the programs of the group, they want members to volunteer their time to carry out projects, and they want cooperation of other kinds.

The nature of service clubs is better understood from an examination of their activities. A somewhat cynical view of their nature and behavior was expressed during the 1920's by Sinclair Lewis in *Elmer Gantry:*

> The Rotary Club was an assemblage of accountants, tailors, osteopaths, university presidents, carpet manufacturers, advertising men, millinery dealers, ice dealers, piano salesmen, laundrymen and like leaders of public thought who met weekly for the purposes of lunching together, listening to addresses by visiting actors and by lobbyists against the recognition of Russia, beholding vaudeville teams in eccentric dances, and indulging in passionate rhapsodies about Service and Business Ethics. They asserted that their one desire in their several callings was not to make money but only to serve and benefit a thing called the Public.

There is some realism as well as cynicism in this characterization. Service clubs serve the interests of their members as well as those of the community, although these are not necessarily in conflict, as an illustration from real life may show. Eugene, Oregon, is a university town which had been host to the state basketball tournament for a number of years prior to 1962. That year, Portland, with a brand-new coliseum, was trying hard to wrest the tourney away from Eugene. The Eugene Active Club— which sponsored the tournament—was much concerned about the prospect of the games being played in Portland because it would mean a loss of some $750,000 to the "community" in money that would be spent for lodging, food, admissions, and incidentals in Eugene. It would also mean a loss of some $5,000 of income to the club, which relied mainly on this source to support its various child welfare projects. It was finally decided to continue holding the tournament in Eugene, thereby promoting both the business interests of members of the Active Club as well as community welfare.

Community Chests

Many civic, health, and welfare groups have united in the appeal they make for funds. Businessmen have usually occupied the most important positions in these United Appeal, United Fund or Community Chest drives. In addition to their time, they have been asked to contribute money and to cooperate in the solicitation of their employees by those conducting the campaign. Businessmen have responded to the demands made upon them for a number of reasons. Some do so out of a sense of social responsibility mixed with feelings of humanitarianism and civic pride. In addition to these motives, businessmen share a general concern that if they do not meet community needs, governments will be looked to by these groups to meet the needs they feel require fulfillment. Such intervention might lead to increased business taxes, increased government control, and decreased prestige for businessmen in their role as community leaders. Another reason for supporting drives that "put all the begs in one ask-it" is that this probably reduces the total demand on the time, money, and cooperation of businessmen for such projects.

Adverse Action

Sometimes civic, health, and welfare groups take action that is directly adverse to the interests of some business firms. The boycotts and political activity of units of the National Association for the Advancement of Colored People is well-known. Local chapters of the American Cancer Society and units of the National Tuberculosis Association engage in campaigns to educate school children in what those groups consider to be the dangers of smoking. Although the American Medical Association and American Dental Association are really professional groups having some of the characteristics of trade associations, they are concerned with community health and their attacks on certain treatments and products and their endorsement of others have quite directly affected certain firms and industries. Firms in the outdoor advertising industry have been the object of attack by "roadside councils" and "highway protection committees," which seek to cut down the interference of billboards with the scenery.

EDUCATIONAL ORGANIZATIONS

In any community—especially cities—there are a large number of groups engaged in both formal and informal education. Elementary and secondary public schools have little direct contact with business firms—at least as compared with publicly-supported colleges and universities. It is mainly the private educational organization—especially the private college or university—that looks to business for time, money, and cooperation. Some educational organizations do not run schools, operating mainly through the mails, distributing literature to those to be educated. Although they may not be situated in the same locality as a firm, various educational organizations still may look to it for support.

Public Elementary and Secondary Schools

In the early nineteenth century, there was little public schooling at any level. Some employers were obliged to educate their own employees in order to secure an educated workforce. The "public school movement" removed some of the burden of employee training from business, although it substituted tax burdens instead. Especially where public education had a vocational orientation, the value to business of such education was clear. Although the tax burden on business has been quite heavy, the chief complaint of business has been that public elementary and secondary schools are doing an inadequate job of educating students in an appreciation of business. That is, that schools are consciously or unconsciously influencing students to adopt unfavorable attitudes toward business. Business organizations have undertaken a number of programs to change what they regard as an unfortunate state of affairs; it is likely, however, that such adverse influence is nominal and that, on balance, the effect of this type of formal education is greatly beneficial for business.

Colleges and Universities

The activities of institutions of higher education are of somewhat greater importance to business than are those of the elementary and secondary schools. Most graduates go to work for business firms, and college education—especially in highly technical fields—is of great value to business. However, the demands on business for support of colleges and universities are correspondingly greater. Too, there is considerable suspicion in the minds of many businessmen that in some institutions of higher learning teachers and teachings are hostile to business. Even where such hostility does not exist, it is sometimes felt that ignorance, on the part of professors, of the true nature of business leads to the implanting of false notions in the minds of the students.

To implement their programs, colleges and universities need money. Although they receive some tuition income and funds from governments (even so-called private colleges and universities have received in recent years substantial research grants and other governmental funds), they have looked to business for additional money. In the case of public institutions, these requests are normally limited to pleas for scholarship funds, although funds for other programs may be requested as well. It is particularly the private college or university that makes requests for substantial sums from businessmen. Buildings, and even entire colleges or universities, have been named for those businessmen making such contributions. For many years, businessmen have been given honorary degrees and positions of honor and influence on the governing bodies of those institutions. There are other devices of more recent vintage aimed at separating businessmen from their money, and though these have met with considerable success there still recur statements that business fails to give its "fair share."

Some businessmen are greatly concerned over certain "undesirable" aspects of higher education. It is no secret that socialists hold positions on college faculties. Although only a small minority of them are members of the Communist party, they all share the belief that private business is inadequate in solving the problems of modern industrial society and that government enterprise should be substituted in many, if not all, areas of economic enterprise. Even though not socialists, most professors are quite "liberal" in their views. To the extent that such faculty members are influential—and their influence is considerably exaggerated, as is probably true of the influence of any college professor—student attitudes toward business become unfavorable. This outcome cannot be regarded as a conscious product of higher education and it is quite unrealistic to regard it as a major influence of colleges and universities (although some individuals and groups do so regard it and urge businessmen to withhold financial support from those schools "teaching wrong doctrines.") Certainly, the great expansion of education in business administration in institutions of higher learning reflects the commitment of such schools to the private enterprise system.

Some collegiate education concerning business that may have the effect of creating unfavorable attitudes in the minds of students is the product of ignoring business and ignorance of business. This charge can quite properly be made against colleges and universities as a whole. The increased study of business in colleges and the improved education of professors are remedying this situation. Business firms are sometimes asked—by organizations such as the Foundation for Economic Education—to be hosts to ignorant professors to give them a comprehensive picture of the operations of their firms through interviews and observation, to pay their transportation costs and to provide living expenses while they are visiting the firm. Although most professors participating in such programs are from departments of economics and schools of business, enough professors from English, political science, sociology, history, and other departments participate to lead to the conclusion that there will be less unfavorable influence on student attitudes stemming from ignorance of business or ignoring it.

Other Educational Groups

There are relatively few organizations whose only concern is education, other than elementary and secondary schools, colleges, and universities. Correspondence schools may indirectly serve business by providing their students with useful knowledge, skills, and attitudes, but their direct relationship with business is small. There are also some private vocational schools that supply business firms with educated employees, but their direct influence upon business through making demands on businessmen is negligible. The Foundation for Economic Education illustrates the type of educational organization that aims at improving the education of educators, but this type is very few in number.

However, there are a host of organized groups that carry on "educational" activities as part of their program. In many cases, these are organizations propagating a particular point of view. Where they feel that businessmen share their point of view, they ask for business support. The general business organizations almost uniformly engage in such action, and chambers of commerce promote "Business-Industry-Education" days, during which educators visit business firms to gain some better understanding of business, and businessmen visit schools to secure a clearer picture of what schools are doing. All such activities require the time, money, and cooperation of businessmen, and they are increasing.

Some of the educational activities of organized groups adversely affect some firms. A case in point is the attempt to discourage students from smoking before they get to college. The joint health-education committee of the American Medical Association and the National Education Association has called for the home and school to "initiate education" to curb smoking at ages prior to the usual beginning of the practice. The American Cancer Society distributes anticigarette filmstrips to secondary schools. To the extent that such educational activity is effective, the cigarette industry is unfavorably influenced.

RELIGIOUS AND MORAL ORGANIZATIONS

Although there has been a relative decline in the influence of organized religion, it is still of great importance. Not only do churches and other religious groups have considerable influence on attitudes toward business, they sometimes take social action adverse to the interests of some firms and businessmen. They are occasionally joined in such action by moral organizations—whose morality may or may not have a religious founda-

tion—that are insistent on forcing their morals on others, with consequences sometimes adverse to certain business firms.

Churches and Business

Generally, it might be concluded that churches are now more favorably
disposed toward business than in the past. At one time the love of money
was regarded as being the root of all evil; in the recent past, however, it
has quite commonly been stated that it is one's Christian duty to become
rich. Voltaire once said: "All generalizations are false, including this one."
Certainly no generalization about the attitude of religion toward business
can be accurately applied to all churches and other religious organizations because they vary so much among themselves. Here, as before, it
is necessary to classify the phenomena under examination in order to
deal with them effectively.

The most common classification of organized religion is Protestant,
Catholic, and Jewish. It has been popular to regard Catholic economic doctrines as being somewhat inimical to the development of business and to tie the "Protestant Ethic" to the rise of capitalism. Business
virtues and moral virtues became intertwined—those who succeeded in
their earthly endeavors were obviously the recipients of heavenly blessings, according to this idea. Catholic and Jewish scholars have protested
that the economic doctrines of their religions were not antibusiness and
that the development of capitalism did not depend upon the Protestant
Reformation. A moderate view is that although the "capitalist spirit" has
existed for thousands of years, the Protestant Ethic reinforced it and gave
it additional moral sanction.

There is some scientific support for doubting the influence of churches
on the economic attitudes of their parishioners. In a study titled "Religious Affiliation and Politico-Economic Attitude," Wesley and Beverly
Allinsmith examined the politico-economic attitudes of members of eight
major religious groups in the U.S., including Protestants, Catholics, and
Jews.[3] They discovered that although the various denominational groups
possessed different socioeconomic status (with corresponding variations
in politico-economic opinions and behavior), the economic opinions of
individuals within any denomination were related more to their individual socioeconomic status than to their membership in any particular religious group. There was one marked exception to this general conclusion:
Jews of whatever individual socioeconomic status tended to exhibit similar politico-economic attitudes. Whether this is a product of their religion
or some sort of "pressure" for Jewish people to identify with other Jewish
people is not clear. In any case, the authors concluded that "Protestants

[3] *Public Opinion Quarterly* (1948), Vol. 12, pp. 377–389.

are a very diverse lot and that ordinarily, at least on politico-economic issues, the trichotomy 'Protestants, Catholics, and Jews' represent a meaningless oversimplification."

Regardless of their influence of organized religion on the economic attitudes of their members, churches have exerted considerable pressure on business in other ways. Where they hold political power, they can have restrictive legislation passed and enforced. The Massachusetts Bay Colony in New England (Boston) was a community in which the Puritans held political power and passed laws governing prices and restricting profits. There are still some communities and states in the U.S. in which one religious group predominates and is able to secure legislation in accordance with its moral laws. Even where this is not true, various churches may jointly support legislative proposals in accordance with their teachings and their influence may be the determining force in their passage. Laws prohibiting selling liquor, conducting business on Sunday, showing "immoral" movies, and selling "indecent" literature—all reflect such influence.

Some chuches are able to exert economic as well as political influence. Where a church's membership is large, boycotting a particular businessman unless he conforms to the desires of that church can be quite effective. Picketing of nonconforming establishments can also inflict financial loss. In their economic and political action, churches sometimes form larger groups for the attainment of certain objectives. Within a particular community, associations of ministers have arisen and have frequently been able to get business firms—especially retail firms—to suspend operations on the Sabbath, so that more parishioners will go to church. These local groups have their counterparts in state councils of churches and in the National Council of Churches, which have educational and political programs through which they attempt to persuade individuals and influence legislation, with some apparent effect.

Moral Groups

There are a number of other organizations that seek to impose their moral standards on the community, sometimes with detrimental influences on certain kinds of business. Some have some church connection —the Legion of Decency and National Office for Decent Literature are associated with the Roman Catholic Church. Some have no specific church affiliation. The Watch and Ward Society—which had threatened magazine dealers with prosecution if they handled what the Society regarded as an obscene issue of the *American Mercury*—was characterized as a "secular organization of blue-nosed puritans." In another passage in *Elmer Gantry*, Sinclair Lewis succinctly deals with the nature of moral organizations and their activities earlier in this century:

> He [Elmer Gantry] would combine in one association all the moral
> organizations in America. . . . The Anti-Saloon League, the W.C.T.U. and
> the other organizations fighting alcohol. . . . Vice Societies doing such mag-
> nificent work in censoring immoral novels and paintings and motion pictures
> and plays. The Anti-Cigarette League. . . . The associations making so brave
> a fight against Sunday baseball, Sunday movies, Sunday golfing, Sunday
> motoring and other abominations whereby the Sabbath was desecrated and
> the preachers' congregations and collections were lessened.

The influence of such groups—along with that of some churches—has
been quite strong in the past. In part, the "noble experiment" of prohibiting the sale of intoxicating beverages during the period 1920–1933 was
a product of the activities of these groups. The impact of Prohibition on
manufacturers, wholesalers, and retailers was fatal to many of those enterprises. The present influence of such groups is probably less than it has
been, but there are some occasions when they can adversely affect business firms.

RECREATIONAL GROUPS

At first glance, it would not appear that organizations interested in
promoting recreation would be of much consequence to business. However, in a number of circumstances they have felt their interests threatened by business firms and have taken action against certain businesses.
For example, sports fishermen have been concerned by the pollution of
streams by manufacturing firms and have worked for antipollution legislation. The same class of sportsmen has been concerned by the construction of dams by electric utility firms, and have vigorously protested their
construction in hearings before utility commissions. These protests have
sometimes delayed construction or have required costly changes in plans.
Groups interested in preserving certain areas for hunting, camping, hik-
ing, and for just enjoying the sight of them have been able to prevent the
commercial exploitation of forest lands. The pressure of such groups has
been so great, in some cases, that firms have attempted to settle for
multiple use—including business use—of certain natural resources.

A number of community organizations aim at influencing attitudes
toward business; an examination of the "public image of business" and
who creates it and how will add to our understanding of the importance
of such groups.

READING: The Minister Guides the Manager Toward More Effective Community Action,* by David G. Colwell '40, Pastor, Park Hill Congregational Church, Denver, Colorado

[*In the following reading, a minister critically examines the role played by businessmen in community groups.*]

As a parish parson, I have a special stake in the businessman's "sense of social responsibility": I am on the receiving end of a great deal of it.

This perspective, acquired both from my own profession and from my association with a wide variety of community groups, has given rise to two observations:

1. Businessmen are appreciably more effective when they use real care and responsibility in selecting the groups which they will join.

2. Businessmen have much more to offer to community organizations than they generally make available to them.

I start from the premise, of course, that the community needs top business talent to help in the solution of its far-reaching problems. I am also assuming that executives today feel an obligation both to their firms and to themselves as citizens to join in the task of managing and shaping the environment in which they live and operate. Furthermore, I am assuming that a man's obligations as a citizen and as a member of a corporation are not in conflict. Rather, it seems to me, one of the assets a company can provide for the community as a whole is the devoted skills and informed minds of its best people. At this point the obligations of the company coincide with the businessman's obligations as a person.

The question I am asking, then, is: How can the business manager fulfill this responsibility with the maximum degree of productivity?

First of all, I would like to see businessmen utilize their non-office time and talents in as competent a fashion as they do their professional assignments. Often, I find, managers do not allocate their extra-curricular hours and their particular skills carefully and thoughtfully in order to get the maximum production from them. Let us turn to the hypothetical case of Mr. A, for example:

Mr. A is a senior officer in one of our country's business firms. His background is excellent: good family environment in his formative years, good education which he finished formally by two years in the nation's leading graduate school of business administration. His work leading to the MBA degree showed that he not only has a good mind, but that he also is capable of that self-discipline which is so important if the good mind is to be put to constructive use.

* Reprinted by permission from the *Harvard Business School Bulletin*, February 1959.

The Redoubtable Mr. A. Some years later, we find him in a dominant position in the world of business. He has achieved this eminence through the positive application of his abilities. He has worked long and hard for his firm, and its welfare has become one of the consuming interests of his life. The business community recognizes him as a progressive and competent leader.

Mr. A is a member of one of the larger churches of the community which he attends with some regularity. He is a devoted father and husband though he sometimes feels guilty about being out of touch with his adolescent children. In the annual membership and fund drive for the YMCA, he is happy to participate; that is, he makes a substantial contribution, attends a couple of luncheons and allows his name to be used in one of the teams. He also makes a few telephone calls to friends and acquaintances seeking their participation. For the past years, Mr. A has served on the Board of the Community Chest.

The Mayor of the City asked him to serve as a member of one of the citizen advisory committees concerned with planning the city's future growth patterns, but he felt that he could not accept because of the press of time and the demands of business; he also admitted privately to a kind of instinctive suspicion of government which was not allayed by the fact that the Mayor was a member of a political party which he views with some apprehension.

Mr. A is a member of one of the community's prestige golf clubs and of the old long-established downtown club; at both of these places he meets his friends and finds congenial and relaxing surroundings. He is a member of the Chamber of Commerce and one or two other trade associations. While he rarely attends, leaving this chore to some of his junior executives, he keeps an eye on what is going on and exercises considerable influence through the occasional well-directed telephone call as well as through the younger men in his firm. His duty to participate in the political life of the community is fulfilled by voting, after considerable study, in both the primary and general elections; in making a contribution to his party's campaign chest; and in engaging in heated discussion of political matters at the club or at lunch. These discussions rarely take the form of debate, because the basic presuppositions of his friends and associates seem to support his own rather consistently.

In short, Mr. A is a good person with many of what we are pleased to call the old-fashioned virtues. He is highly respected by those who know him; he is absolutely honest; he is intelligent; he works hard. His personal life and habits are excellent. Here is a person who leads the kind of life and holds a position in the community for which many of us strive.

How to Cheat Your Community. I suspect that all of us know large numbers of men like Mr. A, and have a very high regard for them. But let me say something about him from my particular point of view. I must admit that I am concerned about the Mr. A's of our communities because they are shortchanging the rest of us, denying us the benefits of their substantial talents in the very places we need them most.

Don't misunderstand me—I am not making the familiar plea simply for

MORE community activity on the part of businessmen. What I am asking for is more EFFECTIVE participation in the ways and positions that really count, that are important in shaping the community.

Community activities can be divided roughly into three categories:

1. Those which are primarily concerned with the economic health of the area, or the upgrading of specific business, industries, or management functions. I would place the Chamber of Commerce, the service clubs, trade associations, some civic improvement organizations, national associations of business specialists, and so on in this category.

2. Those well-directed, well-established and fully accepted organizations where the top business leaders can lend their names and considerable prestige to support fund raising and other public relations programs. Such essential and excellent groups as the Community Chest, the YMCA, the YWCA, the Red Cross, and Scouting I would list in this group.

3. Community undertakings which require a stand for a point of view not generally held, or potentially controversial, and often demanding some positive, hard, creative work in a pioneering venture. Here I include organizations like the Urban League, Foreign Policy Association, Welfare Councils, Committees for Better Schools, citizens groups that carry advisory or quasi-governmental functions, political activity, and working boards of churches.

It is my observation that business executives are very sparsely represented in the third group, somewhat more often found in the second and, of course, dominant in the first. In contrast to this breakdown, the lawyers, teachers, doctors, public career men—yes, and pastors—abound in the second and third kinds of community endeavors. Conceivably, they might occasionally have a contribution to make to the first sector, but—except for service clubs—they are seldom on hand.

I must admit, of course, that there are many distinguished exceptions to this generalization, but these men, for whom we are all grateful, do not negate the validity of the statement. I should like to be convinced that I have misstated the situation either in my own city or in other urban centers, but I know of no compelling evidence that will prove me wrong.

As a matter of fact, the Editors of the *Bulletin* made available to me some of the many analyses compiled by reunion classes of the B-School over the past several years, and these documents tend to support my thesis. Similar questions appeared in all various questionnaires, and the answers were all too uniform. Many times, for example, alumni were asked: "What are your non-business activities (hobbies, memberships, civic affairs participation, etc.)?" Without attempting to make an exact statistical study of the answers, I should judge that something under 50% of the men reporting listed civic organizations in my third category, outside of mere membership in a church, as objects of their interest. As the *Bulletin* pointed out in October, somewhere under 15% of those graduates reporting were involved in government, citizens' quasi-governmental bodies, or in politics at any level.

Active—But How and Where?   By way of contrast, the great majority of the men queried and responding listed participation in club activities of one kind or another, and a large percentage reported association with one of the service clubs, or the groups in my Category II. It is also apparent that HBS is well represented on Chambers of Commerce and similar groups with specific business interests.

I have to go on to say that the answers to the questions give little real indication of the level of participation. I can testify from all-too-frequent experience that it is possible to list a church membership correctly with figures but that such a compilation gives no clue to the vitality of faith and commitment of the men and women on the rolls.

One cannot help but wonder why it is that the same segment of our society that has shown real creative skill in pioneering new techniques and procedures in the world of commerce generally absents itself from any real and substantial participation in the wider corporate affairs of men. The question becomes especially pointed when it is clear that the initiative and drive shown so abundantly in business are so sorely needed by the total society.

I do not mean to indicate that I think the organizations I list in Categories I and II—the established welfare and youth groups, and the business organizations —are superfluous. Of course they are not. But in terms of the shaping of our society and our communities, in their immediate impact on the kind of city or nation in which we will live, they are not as significant. Zoning and city planning, race relations, our public school system and what it teaches, our political system and who runs it—these are the areas where the battles are being fought and where the decisions are being made.

Are Executives Shrinking Violets?   As a clergyman, I cannot help but worry over an attitude which apparently prohibits the participation of top economic leaders in those significant parts of our common life which are actually or potentially controversial—those which may expose a man to the neccessity for making a moral commitment and expressing an ethical conviction.

Why is our friend Mr. A so reluctant to get into the thick of the action? Why does he avoid the places where, as a businessman, he can exert the most leverage? Why does he not thoughtfully assign a part of his non-business time to the community projects which are really biting into the problems of the day?

Partly, I suspect, because he is a human being like the rest of us and he likes to associate with his own kind. In most of his contacts with others he finds himself in organizations where there is a similarity of points of view, and it is basically the business point of view. Oh, there are some professors and social workers scattered around on these various boards—and even an occasional labor leader for window-dressing—but the real core are men who have pretty much the same orientation and subscribe to about the same set of mores.

We can't blame Mr. A for this; I am much more comfortable in a roomful of parsons than nuclear physicists. But if Mr. A insists on talking only to himself and those who mirror his views, he is not going to have much influence on what goes on around him. It isn't until he gets out into the scrimmage that his word and his idea is going to reach to the next man—where he is going to make clearer the business point of view and show up the weaknesses of the opponents—even if he does get roughed up a bit in the process.

I might also suggest, here, that this is the only way Mr. A is going to learn and grow. Presumably his slant on every issue is not 100% right; conceivably he has not kept completely abreast of the times in everything; maybe he has inadvertently slipped into rigid and unrealistic grooves and mind-sets in some areas.

One of the real problems of our society centers around the parochial nature of the minds of men. There are certain things that we all know; there are things that we like; there are things that come to us easily. Because this is true, we tend to avoid those fields which are unfamiliar or difficult, or in which we feel inferior. But in succumbing to this temptation we cut ourselves off from the broadening influence of new vistas and new knowledge; we tend to fall into ruts of thought and attitude, ruts which soon deepen into great canyons and continually close in our vision.

Furthermore, in the business world, it is easy to make a virtue out of this weakness. Mr. A can justify his limited perspective by referring to the heavy demands of his job. For this, he gains much respect among his peers and superiors. The fact that his devotion to his work brings such substantial and tangible benefits within the business community both to himself and to his firm bolsters him in his strict attention to the grindstone.

More Pies Than Fingers. Certainly the press of business these days is a defensible reason for limiting one's non-business obligations. I do not want to get involved here in the argument of the relative amount of time a manager should spend in the shop vis-à-vis his "outside" activities. I suspect this varies with the individual, his interests, his position in the company, the weight of business pressures at any given moment, and so on. All I am saying is that the businessman should beware of simply slipping easily into the kind of community group which comes most naturally to him; instead, he should look at the whole spectrum objectively to see where he can be most effective in dealing with the major issues of the day.

I should say at this point that Mr. A has avoided one pitfall which has trapped many of us at one time or another: he has not signed himself up in so many projects outside his company that he cannot do justice to any of them. How many times do we fail to say a firm "No" when we should, and thus end up on one more letterhead, with one more group expecting us to produce? We have all fallen for the eager nominating committee chairman or project promoter who says, "Oh, but really, it won't take much of your *time*. We just want your advice now and then!" Before we know it, we have been stretched out so thin and taut that we haven't the time or the energy to carry all our outside obligations. At that point life becomes a round of missed meetings, juggled commitments, and guilt feelings.

As a pastor, I can say fervently that I would much rather have a prospective church committee member give me an honest and straightforward "No" than a half-hearted "Yes," only to let me down when I need him to do some real work.

Mr. A Nails the Board.   Now, what happens to Mr. A when he gets on a board or a committee of some kind? How effective is he when he does participate? Suppose he accepts the nomination as an officer in the church to which he belongs and which he attends. In due course he is elected. In attending the meetings of the board, which has the responsibility for the whole life of the church, he finds himself in a world that is both strange and familiar. He knows some of the other board members by sight, some by reputation, and one or two rather well.

The nature of the church comes up for discussion, and because he is a responsible kind of person, Mr. A wants to help in the discussion. Every man needs to get new and strange things into a currency that he can handle, so he tries to see it in terms of that which he knows and understands best: his work. He makes a tentative remark, and encouraged by the respect given it he goes further.

He may say, for example, that the church should be run on a sound, business-like basis. If he means that thorough records should be kept, the funds should be wisely spent, the relationship of programs to objectives should be worked out carefully, no one would disagree. As a matter of fact, helping the church establish itself efficiently and think in these terms may be just what the powers-that-be had hoped Mr. A would undertake as an officer. Consequently, his first comment is likely to be greeted with enthusiasm by his colleagues.

Warmed by this initial responsiveness, he pushes on—and suddenly he finds the room turning chilly. His associates begin to wonder if he isn't talking about objectives, and critically, too. They hear him say that the budget must always be planned to leave a surplus at the end of the year, projects should be on a pay-as-you-go basis, the minister should realize that he is the board's executive, so the morning service and the content of the church school should reflect the board's wishes and opinions.

All this makes perfectly good sense in the context of a business organization, but in a non-profit service organization like a church it is out of place. The fact is that different organizations have different aims and methods of achieving them. We know this in principle, but in practice we all have an overpowering need to feel competent. As a result, too many of us are unwilling to accept the discipline that a new kind of situation forces upon us. We keep wanting to reduce everything to the familiar terms where our feeling of competence can assert itself. I suppose that for our time the classic statement of this point of view was former Secretary of Defense Wilson's famous remark identifying the good of General Motors with the good of the country. In short, business leaders often cut down their effectiveness in community groups by failing to take into account the particular frame of reference within which these organizations move.

A Manager Gets the Deep Freeze.   But what happens to Mr. A in the board meeting when the temperature goes down? At this point, he can go in several directions: If he is a person who is not accustomed to being directly challenged by anyone except people in the high echelons of business—or maybe his wife— he will either fight back or he will retire from battle. If he fights back, he will repent his harshness and, being a good person, will be penitent, embarrassed, and uncomfortable. If he feels that everyone is against him, and he is fighting a lone battle for the good and the true, he will retire within himself and make no further contribution to the meeting—or maybe even to the committee.

Mr. A often runs into difficulty with the whole way the meeting is run, too. With his business background, he chafes under the more informal, casually unstructured gatherings of volunteers. Nothing ever seems to happen, everything has to stop until Mrs. C gets through her long, irrelevant harangue, the chairman isn't very clear about what is going on, there may or may not be minutes and agenda. Furthermore, and this is as frustrating as all the others put together, no one seems to have the vaguest notion of what should be brought before a board of directors and what should be decided by the staff. One minute poor Mr. A is listening to an endless discussion of whether the Easter Sunday programs should be done in puce or chartreuse; the next moment someone is rather lightly raising the issue of the long-range building needs of the church. But far more time goes into the color of the orders of service than into the plans for possible expansion.

Grit or Pearl in the Oyster?   Unfortunately, Mr. A is likely to throw up his hands in the face of this seeming confusion and refuse to attend any more meetings, or to participate in the ones he does attend. Things do get done, of course, but with such apparent waste of time and wheel-spinning that he wonders why he is tossing away his valuable hours in *this* operation instead of "getting something done."

Even more irritating is the result when, several years later, he tries to do something about the mess as chairman. People get mad and buck him, the staff simply doesn't produce what he wants them to, no one seems to understand what he is trying to do, old Mrs. C resigns in a flap, and poor Mr. A comes to dread every session.

From the standpoint of the organization, either Mr. A's retirement from the scene of battle or his forceful attempt to impose business procedures on a non-business organization are regrettable. The fact is that most volunteer organizations are needlessly unbusinesslike in their procedures, planning, control, differentiation of board and staff functions, financial structure, and so on. Many of them do tend to ride off in all directions on worthy projects without pinning down objectives and fitting the program into them in an orderly fashion.

If Mr. A can be sympathetic and tolerant, he can do an educational job on these people that will mean a tremendous step-up in power for the organization. But it will take patience, devotion, understanding and time to get everyone talking the same language and even respecting each other's particular competencies.

It may also take some changes in his point of view on issues like the open-ended discussion in committee meetings. I am sure that the process of arriving at group decisions is a waste of time at many points, and there are times when the group ought to accept the idea of the best informed. But there are also times when, with patience, the group itself will come to a far more profound understanding than any of its members had when they gathered together. Those of us who are used to structure must learn that there are times when the truth is found through group searching, and the man who has drive and ability also needs to learn patience.

The matter of goals presents a different kind of problem. I have known a number of businessmen who walked into their first committee meeting only to be struck by an awful sense of incompetence or inferiority. Everyone else seems to be an expert on international affairs or adult education or city planning or race relations and he feels himself lost. He may even feel such a sense of incompetence in this group where the goals are in the difficult fields of the intangible that he finds it necessary to absent himself from further participation upon some plausible excuse—which is usually the lack of time.

This is a real problem for the talented man. In his major work he has competence; his excellence is widely recognized and used, and that is why he was appointed to this committee in the first place. It is hard for him to be in situations where he feels incompetent because he is not used to it and it threatens to destroy something within him. His very real difficulty is compounded by the fact that others knowing of his competence elsewhere have a tendency to expect it here also. The one who is used to the exercise of leadership finds it hard to follow, but it may be that in the process of setting goals in a voluntary organization his role is that of an indispensable participant rather than a leader. On the other hand, as I have said, when it comes to policies and procedures he may well be leading the parade.

More Than a Blank Check.   One final point: too often businessmen like Mr. A are placed on community committees because, in the eyes of the group, "He can get us some money; and even if he won't raise any himself, his name will help." I think businessmen resent being considered no more than walking moneybags—I know I would. Many organizations have never really considered the help and professional know-how the business executive can offer them, and this is to their discredit and disadvantage.

In defense of these people, though, it is true that too many businessmen have made their major contribution an exclusively financial one. A famous biographer has said that he can never really write an accurate biography of an individual unless he can get access to his old check stubs. There is a lot of truth in his remark, but nevertheless it is not always possible to measure our affections and our real commitments in terms of our financial involvement. Helped a good deal by the income tax provisions, business leaders have been generous with their financial support of various community enterprises, including those which hold no hope of immediate return like the church. I suspect, however, that too many of us have used the financial gift as a substitute for ourselves.

Is it not true that the successful businessman quite accurately reveals his basic identity in terms of how much of himself he gives to the various groups, including his family, which compete for him? People outside the business community will look on the manager as a professional with something unique to offer instead of just a source of dollars and prestige only to the degree that businessmen participate effectively in significant community organizations.

Our friend Mr. A might well be lost to further participation in the real working committees of the church—or other similar groups—through any one of the above or a host of other frustrations without really being aware of why his interest has dimmed. We have a way of being blind to our own real motives. Some years ago I was part of a group in which I held a point of view that was different from the majority. I told myself that the matters under discussion did not benefit me directly, nor could I see how the discussion could be relevant to my situation. My attendance became less frequent and my participation fell off until I finally dropped out altogether.

Getting the Maximum Mileage.   Many times, we ought to extricate ourselves from involvement with some group or other, but in this case, I have since come to the conclusion that there were two things about me that caused my disinterest:

1. I was not as well versed in the subject as were the others. Though I did not enjoy the feeling of incompetence, I was unwilling to do the study necessary to close up the gap.
2. I really didn't want to listen to someone else's point of view.

And there you have it; I should hazard a guess that I am not greatly different from other people at this point and that we all fall prey to this weakness.

Let me summarize what I have said. I hope no one will interpret this article as a generalized, overworked pitch for social responsibility. My concern is with getting the maximum mileage out of the hours now being spent on projects outside the company's walls. This means more businessmen in the top echelons of those organizations which are devoting themselves to the central problems of our life today—action groups, controversial endeavors, political and quasi-political committees, associations for public education. Even more important, it means a closer look at the kind of contribution managers are making. Is their participation expressed in a few telephone calls, a check, attendance at occasional meetings—or is it a positive and active commitment? The latter is time-consuming, challengng, and difficult, but, like anything else, it is all the more rewarding to all concerned.

As a parson, I can't help but point out here that the extent of our activity in any cause or organization is directly related to its relevance to us. I don't invest myself in anything that does not have relevance to my understanding of life, my ultimate values.

Implementing Good Intentions.   Among the questions that were asked of the reunion classes at the Business School was one apparently designed to get at these fundamentals. The answers revealed a definite correlation between a man's activities and group associations and the kind of view he held of life. If he expressed a belief that his purpose was beyond himself and his family, he was apt to be involved in the community in at least one crucial point. If his philosophy of life focussed basically on himself and his circle of friends, then his group identities were of this kind. Unfortunately, the latter was the far greater number.

Increasingly, businessmen are paying attention to the relevance of the community's well-being to them and their companies. But their efforts to do something to implement this understanding can end in frustration and irritation unless they are tackled with the objectivity and vigor which characterizes the manager's approach to any other business problem.

SUGGESTED READINGS

Economic Education in the Schools: Report of the National Task Force on Economic Education (New York: Committee for Economic Development, 1961). Findings of a committee appointed by the CED and the American Economic Association to investigate the state of economic education in the high schools, and recommendations made to improve that condition.

Form, William H., and Delbert C. Miller, *Industry, Labor and Community* (New York: Harper & Row, 1960). Describes the impact of industry upon a community; analyzes the interrelationships between business and labor with political organization, mass communication, education, welfare, religion, and the family.

Pope, Liston, *Millhands and Preachers* (New Haven, Conn.: Yale, 1942). A study of the actual role played by the church in the industrial community of Gastonia, North Carolina. Criticizes the relationship between the textile mills and the churches.

CHAPTER 20

THE IMAGE
OF BUSINESS

The ways in which individuals and groups behave toward business firms are conditioned by their "image" of business. In the following discussion, we shall use the terms *opinion* and *image* interchangeably, since they both connote the view that a person holds concerning a specific subject. Generally, public opinion is quite favorable toward American business, although this fact may be somewhat misleading because what influential individuals and groups in American society think about a particular firm is of greater significance than the opinion of the general public toward business generally. Since some individuals and groups act on the basis of their opinion of business, if businessmen are to counteract hostile action they must learn something of the way in which opinions are formed and then take appropriate action. An examination of the "business image" and the bases on which it rests provides some clues as to what effective action might be taken by business to create favorable opinions.

THE PUBLIC'S OPINION OF BUSINESS

Although the "image" that the public has of business might be discovered in a number of ways, in recent years great reliance has been placed on public opinion polls to reveal the business image. It may be somewhat surprising—at least to those businessmen who feel they are surrounded by a hostile and unappreciative public—to discover such polls to show that a substantial majority of Americans apparently hold the view that business generally has done a good job and that the profit system is desirable.

A poll conducted for *Fortune* magazine in 1949 concerned itself with the way in which the public viewed profits and the profit system. Only 1 per cent of those polled said that profits were not necessary to make our economic system work and that the government should take all of them away in taxes. The other 99 per cent felt that profits were necessary, but varied in their views as to how much profit (if any) should be taxed away, with slightly over half agreeing with the statement, "There shouldn't be any top limit on profits, but the government should tax big profits at a higher percentage rate than small profits." Responses to other questions echoed this sentiment concerning big and small profits (which appeared to be tied to attitudes concerning big and small business). Some opinions were unfavorable. Slightly more than half of the respondents felt that the following statement was more true than false: "In the long run, most of the profits of big business get into the pockets of the big bankers and financiers in Wall Street." Also, opinion was almost equally divided on the question of whether or not big corporations tried to give the public a true picture about the profits they make. Despite the evidence of general approval of the profit system, the *Fortune* writer saw in this poll some cause for alarm, stating that a conflict was going on in this country between capitalism and socialism, "some of it surely based on the idea of the misuse of large profits and the Wall Street myth" and that business needed to learn to make itself, in deeds, a less inflexible obstacle to the people's desire for participation in the profit economy.

The Opinion Research Corporation did a survey on big business, which *Look* reported in 1955. This poll discovered that an overwhelming majority of those American adults questioned answered that big business was a good thing for the country, in general. Of all those polled, 80 per cent stated big business had been good for the nation and only 8 per cent indicated that it had not been good (a 10 to 1 ratio). Even when the general public was broken down into various income classes, men and women, Republicans and Democrats, union members and workers not members of unions, about 80 per cent of each group—regardless of income, sex, political affiliation, or union membership—stated that big business was good, generally. When asked what was good about big business, the respondents stated that big business provided many jobs, that it promoted research, that it was the backbone of defense production, that it lowered prices through mass production, that it promoted national growth and prosperity and that it improved our standard of living. The principal fear of big business was that it might harm small business or tend to become monopolistic. Although some (16 per cent) were concerned about the amount of power held by big business, an equal number felt that big government posed the greatest problem of bigness, but three times as many felt that power of big labor unions posed the biggest problem of bigness. As in the *Fortune* poll, the *Look* poll revealed that the general public was poorly informed concerning some facts about business, but this apparently did not adversely affect the opinions of large segments of the public.

THE PROBLEMS OF POLLS

Other polls have dealt with the public's opinion toward business and have yielded other answers, but perhaps we should raise the question, Do any of these answers mean anything? A number of students of public opinion polls say "no" or "maybe or maybe not."

Polls are conducted using the survey technique. That is, not all members of the American public are polled. A "sample" is taken that the pollsters hope will be representative of the entire public involved. These samples are not ever perfectly representative of the population from which they are drawn (except in very rare circumstances), and some big mistakes have been made in drawing samples (perhaps the classic illustration was that sample employed in the 1936 *Literary Digest* poll that yielded the conclusion that Alfred Landon would defeat Franklin D. Roosevelt by a handsome margin in the presidential election of that year —Landon carried only 2 of the 48 states, and the *Literary Digest* suspended publication).

Even when samples are representative, the responses given by those polled may lead to inaccurate conclusions. The way in which questions are phrased, who does the questioning, and how the interview is conducted—all influence responses. Even when no disabling defect comes from this source, respondents may not tell the truth. Mark Twain, in his autobiography, discusses an incident in which he refused another author permission to publish his view on free love:

> I said that if I, or any other wise, intelligent, and experienced person should suddenly throw down the walls that protect and conceal his *real* opinions on almost any subject under the sun, it would at once be perceived that he . . . ought to be sent to the asylum. I said I had been revealing to her my private sentiments, *not* my public ones; that I, like all other human beings, expose to the world only my trimmed and perfumed and carefully barbered public opinions and conceal carefully, cautiously, and wisely my private ones.

If all surveys were perfectly conducted and all the respondents answered truthfully, there is still one fundamental reason that their results may not be too meaningful: They probably have not given the proper weight to the opinions of those who count. Survey results can quite accurately predict the outcomes of elections (when polls are well-conducted and truthfully answered) because each voter has one vote. Most issues confronting business are not resolved by ballots, but by the pressure brought to bear by interested parties. Some may have more influence than others—for example, the opinion of a union leader might be of much greater importance to the management of a firm than that of the union members, since the head of the organization may have the power to call a strike or take other hostile action even though a majority of the union membership might not favor such action (this has led to the passage of federal legislation requiring a poll of the membership of a union on the employer's last offer before certain action can be taken by a union leader). In short, public opinion polls do not tell how much influence is possessed by those with different opinions. Nor do they always indicate which individuals and groups hold what opinions, nor which of them are concerned enough to act on their opinions, nor whether the opinions are subject to change. Consequently, what the businessman must do to discover important public opinion is essentially what we have been doing: he must view society as being composed of individuals and groups with different opinions and varying power to act upon their opinions. Discovering the opinions of those who count in his world is the way to determine relevant public opinion. This is not to say that surveys have no value in determining public opinion, but rather that they must be used with care and that the information gained from them must be supplemented by data secured by other means.

BASES OF OPINION

When the opinions that count have been determined, it is possible that they are erroneous or hostile. Under such circumstances, businessmen and business organizations may wish to attempt to change these opinions. In order to do so, it is necessary to determine what individual opinion is determined by (since there are influential individuals confronting business and since important groups are made of individuals—public opinion being the opinions of the individuals in a public). Individual opinion on a specific issue is determined partly by the individual's attitudes and partly by an analysis—however limited—of the information available to the individual on that issue. Attitudes and analyses in turn have certain determinants, as Figure 20–1 indicates.

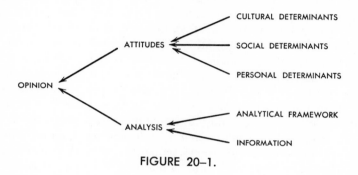

FIGURE 20–1.

Each of these influences on opinion will be examined, for by doing so we can examine the likelihood of changing opinions through changing or using in some way a specific determinant.

Information and Analytical Frameworks

The "facts" available to a person are the raw material of analysis, but they do not alone determine the results of an investigation. Every investigator examines data through some analytical framework that tells him which facts are meaningful and which are not. Such frameworks also suggest relationships among data which are regarded as being meaningful and which, consequently, influence the conclusions arrived at by the analyst. (Figure 20–1 is such an analytical structure.) Some individuals do not have a very highly developed analytical scheme, and facts may not influence their analysis in any determinable way. On the other hand, other individuals have developed such rigid theoretical frameworks that they are quite limited by them in the conclusions they reach in their analysis. An example that shows how restrictive theory can be (since many analytical frameworks are based on theory) is the Marxist-Leninist theory of the development of industrial societies. Any Socialist or Communist believing in this theory and using it as a basis for his analysis will come to quite predictable (and wrong) conclusions regardless of the data given him. This happens because all data that do not fit are discarded and because the theory provides for only one interpretation of that information employed. The reason for stressing this point is to indicate that providing persons with information will not necessarily lead them to come to the conclusion the information-provider wishes them to reach.

Information campaigns conducted by business and other organizations have been notoriously unsuccessful in inducing the desired behavior in specific publics. Increasing the flow of information is not the solution because part of the problem seems to lie in the fact that many individuals do not want to expose themselves to or absorb the information. This is partly accounted for by the fact that in any public there seems to be a "hard core of chronic know-nothings," people who do not want to be informed and cannot be influenced regardless of the amount, nature, or level of information. Knowing something about the psychological characteristics of the other members of a "public" might be of value in the conduct of an information campaign. For example, it is known that interested people acquire the most information. Discovering the interests of a public may lead to a more effective information program. More importantly, people seek information compatible with their existing attitudes. Investigation of those attitudes may suggest more effective ways in which information may be presented. A problem presented by this, perhaps, is the fact it may not have the desired result of changing unfavorable opinion to favorable views. That is, there is ample evidence that individuals exposed to the same information change their views differently, not because they employ different analytical frameworks, but because of their attitudes.

Attitudes and Their Determinants

Since attitudes are obviously very important in opinion formation, those who would mold or understand public opinion must understand the nature of attitudes and their determinants. We shall regard an attitude as being a general state of feeling about something. All individuals have general feelings about a number of things, including attitudes toward business. Their specific opinions concerning certain aspects of business are strongly influenced by the general way in which they feel about business. No one is perfectly rational (in the sense that his opinion rests solely on the facts and some reasonable analysis of them) and the conclusions drawn as the result of an analysis that has been made are conditioned in some degree by the attitudes a person possesses. The readiness to become motivated toward a particular objective (whether in harmony or conflict with business objectives) is dependent on our attitudes

—that is, our values are part of our attitudes. Because attitudes play such an important role in the determination of opinion and movement toward certain goals, examination of the determinants of attitudes is essential. These determinants can be regarded as cultural, social, and personal.

CULTURAL DETERMINANTS.   All individuals in a common culture have certain similar attitudes or beliefs that are part of their "culture pattern." It would be erroneous to regard all Americans as having identical culture patterns, even though they share a common American culture. Membership in various social classes—economic or otherwise—in American society seems to have a greater impact on the economic attitudes of individuals than does the national culture they share. The influences of culture are sometimes separated into conventions and folkways, respectively. Conventions are ideal types of thought and behavior that have developed over a long period of time and that present standards for thought and behavior. American ideals indicate the attitudes Americans ought to hold. Folkways are the actual types of thought and behavior.

The influence of culture is regarded as being very important (especially by specialists in the study of culture). A cultural anthropologist has declared: "Man is a creature of his culture in the sense that his behavior—his acts, thoughts and sentiments—are largely molded by it." [1] This strong statement is weakened somewhat by the addition of others pointing out that man is also a creator of his culture—in that since actual behavior can never match idealized standards, man sometimes initiates variations that might become folkways. Also, man might be a manipulator within the framework of his culture. That is, man sometimes uses the mores and morals of his culture to his own advantage, marshaling them to strengthen his position or to coerce associates into aiding him, or he may even inspire others to make sacrifices that will aid him. If men find themselves in difficult situations, they frequently flaunt folkways, ignore mores, and take refuge in "higher principles" (morals), sometimes claim supernatural endorsement (furnished or suggested by religious morals), or adopt arguments of expediency (which may be derived from the mores of a dominant group).

Some scholars have attempted to explain unfavorable attitudes toward business as a consequence of the alleged failure of businessmen to live up to American ideals. There are a number of ideals associated with the notion of democracy that Americans are said to cherish. One of these is social democracy—the idea that each man is as good as the next. This implies that social classes based on economic status ought not to exist,

[1] Leo W. Simmons, *Sun Chief* (New Haven: Yale Univ. Press, 1942), quoted by Alfred McClung Lee in "Social Determinants of Public Opinions," in Daniel Katz, Dorwin Cartwright, Samuel Eldersveld and Alfred McClung Lee, eds., *Public Opinion and Propaganda* (New York: Holt, 1954), p. 102.

and the existence of socioeconomic classes with businessmen in the upper classes seems to give evidence that businessmen do not believe in this kind of democracy. A prevalent view of political democracy is that each individual ought to have equal political influence—a notion manifestly not shared by many men of business. To the extent that economic democracy involves a belief in equal economic opportunity, it can be shown that such equality of opportunity does not always exist and that businessmen have sometimes restricted it. Although the frequent failure of business to live up to these ideals is sometimes used to explain hostile attitudes, it is much more likely that something more fundamental is involved. Group membership or some unfavorable personal experience is more frequently found to determine hostile individual attitudes.

Although we see considerable evidence of cultural influence in American life—or at least evidence of manipulative behavior within the cultural framework—it is likely that culture has less influence on Americans than does group membership. After all, America is a sort of "melting pot" in which the distinctive cultural characteristics of immigrants become lost after the passage of a few generations and it is doubtful that a distinct American character has emerged—at least one that dominates our acts, opinions, and attitudes. Rather, we seem to be a multigroup society in which individuals are members of a number of groups. These groups have their ideals and mythology that they pass on to new members and perhaps are more important "creators of the image" than are the agents of the transmission of American or "Western" culture.

SOCIAL DETERMINANTS. By "social determinants," I mean the influences that cause individuals to adopt the attitudes and opinions of the groups of which they are members (or at least that cause them to appear to adopt such attitudes and opinions). Americans are members of a large number of groups and knowing something about their group membership tells us much more about their attitudes than does the fact that they are Americans. For example, obituaries reflect the fact that such memberships indicate who a person is and what he stands for—they indicate the family he is a member of, his church affiliation, his business or professional affiliation, the clubs he belonged to, the important organizational positions he filled, and so on. To know that a man is a member of an "old family," a Presbyterian, a leading merchant, former president of the local chamber of commerce, a Rotarian, a Princeton alumnus is to know quite a bit about what his attitudes are.

Why do individuals adopt (or seem to adopt) the attitudes and opinions of groups of which they are members? There is, for one thing, "the urge to identify." Individuals wish to be recognized as being members in good standing of certain groups, and by expressing the opinions associated with those groups such recognition is secured from those inside and outside the group. Too, group pressures are brought to bear on individuals to adopt (or at least express) certain attitudes and opinions— that is, certain "social rewards and punishments" are available to the leaders of the group to keep members "in line." It should also be pointed out that leaders of the group may be able to influence the views of the members (by some definitions, a characteristic of leadership is the ability to influence the thought and behavior of followers). Yet another reason that persons apparently adopt group attitudes and opinions is that they wish anonymity, which they secure by echoing the views of the group.

A foreign observer of the American scene found social influences on opinion quite important. James Bryce stated:

> In examining the process by which opinion is formed, we cannot fail to note how small a part of the view which the average man entertains is really of his own making. His original impression was faint and perhaps shapeless; its present definiteness and strength are mainly due to what he has heard and read. He has been told what to think, and why to think it. Arguments have been supplied to him from without, and controversy has embedded them in his mind. Although he supposes his view to be his own, he holds it rather because his acquaintances do the like. Each man believes and repeats certain phrases because he thinks that everybody else on his side believes them, and of what each believes only a small part is his own original impression, the far larger part being the result of the commingling and mutual action and reaction of the impressions of a multitude of individuals, in which the element of pure personal conviction, based on individual thinking, is but small. . . .
>
> When some important event happens, which calls for the formation of a view, pre-existing habits, dogmas, affinities help to determine the impression which each man experiences and so far are factors in the view he forms. But they operate chiefly in determining the first impression, and they operate over many minds at once. They do not produce variety and independence: they are soon overlaid by the influences which each man derives from his fellows, from his leaders, from the press.[2]

Since Bryce's time, other students of opinion formation have laid more stress on personal influences on attitudes than did Bryce.

PERSONAL DETERMINANTS. Psychologists see attitudes as deriving from the experiences of the individual. This view, of course, is not necessarily in conflict with the views of those who point out the importance of the culture and the group in conditioning attitudes. That is, individuals have experiences as members of groups and cultures. However, psychologists

[2] James Bryce, *The American Commonwealth* (New York: Macmillan, 1914), Vol. II, p. 253.

point out that some individual experiences are unique and not associated with membership in a group or culture and that some attitudes stem from the ability or inability of individuals to satisfy certain personal needs. Psychologists, generally speaking, study individuals and attempt to explain individual, group, and cultural attitudes as resulting from individual experience and needs, whereas sociologists and cultural anthropologists study social and cultural institutions and attempt to explain individual and group attitudes as deriving from those institutions.

All individuals have certain psychological needs. In order to satisfy them, they tend to adopt certain attitudes. In order to defend the favorable image that an individual has of himself, he sometimes represses impulses within himself that would require him to take a different view of himself. For example, persons who are not financially successful may adopt the attitude that their failure is the fault of the economic system or of some other economic class rather than admit to themselves that they are at fault. Certain attitudes, then, are adopted as "ego defenses." In psychology, there are a number of "schools of thought," and each group differs somewhat in respect to how attitudes are shaped. Other groups do not stress "ego defense," but may see attitudes shaped by responses to the rewards and punishments offered by society, or by some other influences.

There are several ways in which attitudes are enmeshed with personality factors. Attitudes may reflect or express the person's central values. They may gratify certain basic needs and be consistent with his characteristic behavior. Also, they may be part of his attempt to construct a stable and meaningful world within which he can order his life. Finally they serve to express his identification with and to promote his acceptance by his favored social groups.

Whatever does determine the attitude of an important individual and group is a matter of concern to business. In order to create a more favorable "image" generally and to influence the attitudes of specific individuals and groups, a number of programs have been adopted by firms and other business organizations.

CHANGING UNFAVORABLE PUBLIC OPINION

Some businessmen and business groups have believed that too much unfavorable opinion of business exists and have tried to do something about it. One major measure employed has been the information campaign, which is based on the assumption that hostile opinion is the result of the absence of adequate information or the presence of misinformation. The results of such campaigns—although much money has been spent on them—have not been encouraging. Objective appraisals of the effects of mass persuasion campaigns indicate that significant changes in attitudes, opinions, and behavior are the exception rather than the rule.

Business has also attempted to change certain attitudes to more friendly ones because attitudes play an important role in opinion formation. Institutional advertising—the promotion of private business as a desirable social institution rather than advertisement of the products of business— has been a major means employed. Business firms and groups have "elaborated the latent consequences" of business activity by pointing out that they pay substantial taxes, provide employment, purchase large amounts of goods, promote technological progress, and so on. It is shown how these activities benefit certain individuals and groups in the society, the society as a whole, and that sacred social institutions and values are promoted by business action. Institutional advertisers also attempt to humanize themselves in the eyes of the public by exhibiting characteristics of personal warmth, patriotism, willingness to work, and wisdom. They deny that they have certain undesirable characteristics such as being cold and impersonal, that firms are run by small groups of rich and powerful men, that they are monopolistic and uncompetitive, and that they are greedy for profits. Certain characteristics of business, however, cannot be denied, and where institutional advertisers feel that those traits may be looked upon as undesirable, they attempt to convince their audience that these aspects of business are beneficial to society. This has been referred to as the technique of "conversion"—in which "profane" values are converted into "sacred" values. To the extent that persons may think that profits are undesirable, emphasis is laid on the use of profits in such a way as to contribute to social values. The virtues of bigness are pointed out for those who might disapprove of "big business." Attempts are also made to secure some "ego-involvement" between the audience and the company, industry, or private business system so that an attack on business will be regarded as an attack on the public. Even though business may not contribute to certain respected values, it associates itself, through institutional advertising, with the family, religion, science, the American way of life, and so on.

Institutional advertising normally addresses itself to cultural values, but also points out how business promotes the objectives of certain groups as well. In addition to addressing themselves to the general public, businessmen and business organizations have sometimes addressed themselves to specific groups. In doing so, they have concerned themselves with the nature of the "group mind" and how best to address themselves to the group. There is an optimistic view of the group mind that holds that groups are interested in gaining knowledge about the issue confronting it and that given sufficient information a group is capable of forming sound, intelligent opinions (whereas if it is ignorant of the true conditions, it acts irrationally, and is swayed by instinct and emotion). Unfortunately, as we have noted, there are enough cases in which information programs have failed to cause some to take a dim view of the "group mind" and regard it as being "unreasoning." That is, groups are conceived of as being more emotional (hence, less rational) than individuals, although more responsive to appeals to their nobler emotions than those that are ignoble. Such groups, it is felt, require an idol to personalize its ideals and a villain against whom hostility can be directed. The basic assumption that the group mind is unreasoning, dominated by instinct and emotion, easily influenced, fickle, unstable, and of low intelligence should be challenged, perhaps, even though we see some evidence of its existence. Rather than to proceed on *any* assumption concerning the "group mind," those who would influence the attitudes of members of a group would do well to examine the characteristics of that specific group and tailor a program accordingly.

To aid in understanding changes in the attitudes of individuals, it is helpful to turn to the psychologists and their findings on how attitudes may be changed. One problem in applying such findings is that there are a number of "schools" of psychological thought.

The Gestalt school sees individuals as striving toward a more stable organization of their psychological field—that is, they say that individuals try to reconcile conflicting impressions, seek to know what the world is like and make sense of it. According to this view, attitudes and opinions can be changed through attacking the perceptions of an object (that is, by attempting to show its true nature) and by attacking the frame of reference within which it is perceived. This approach assumes that individuals are essentially rational and will change their attitudes and opinions if they are presented with facts and reasons that accord with their own beliefs and assumptions.

Another psychological school sees attitudes shaped by the rewards and punishments received for exhibiting certain attitudes. To change attitudes, then, one must apply rewards and punishments in the proper manner. Unfortunately, perhaps, business does not have much in the way of rewards and punishments that it can employ to create desired attitudes—although an exception certainly should be made for the case of employer-employee relationships.

Yet another school holds that the attitudes a person possesses reflect his need to preserve a favorable self-image. In order to defend this favorable self-image, a person represses impulses within himself which would require him to take a less favorable view of himself and his attitudes may therefore be regarded as "ego-defenses" in which the attitude reflects the impulses in himself that he does not wish to recognize. In order to change such attitudes, the recommended treatment is catharsis —the free ventilation of thought and feeling in an accepting interpersonal atmosphere and by direct interpretation of the thoughts and feelings ventilated. By revealing to the individual concerned the internal conflicts and by forcing him to recognize the impulses he did not wish to recognize, his self-image changes and he no longer feels obliged to defend his ego by adopting certain attitudes. However valuable such a view might be to psychiatrists, it is of limited utility to businessmen. Lack of time, money, and training makes it difficult to put it into practice (even if a hostile union leader could be persuaded to come into a corporation president's office and freely ventilate his innermost thoughts and feelings).

Although business has availed itself of much of the knowledge concerning cultural, social, and personal determinants of attitudes and opinions, it is not certain that its activities in attempting to create a more favorable image have met with much success. Businessmen do not have a monopoly on the channels of communication and the good effects of their various programs—such as information campaigns—may be canceled out by the activities of opposing individuals and groups. That is, there are other creators of the business image in addition to businessmen and business organizations. To an examination of the activities of the former, we shall turn in the next chapter.

READING: How High School Students Feel About Business * by U.S. Chamber of Commerce

More than half the students who graduate from our high schools do not go on to college. They enter the work force (with time out for armed service obligations) . . . they go into offices, stores, shops, plants, factories . . . they become the employees that help make the wheels of business and industry turn.

Their attitudes toward American business (and businessmen) . . . their opinions about our economic system . . . their views on competition and productivity, on technology and freedom—are extremely important. Important because business management needs their cooperation in increasing efficiency and productivity— factors responsible for raising living standards; important because in a few years their votes and their influence will help determine the local, state and national laws that shape the future of our business system.

Businessmen, certainly, should be concerned about the attitudes of our high school students toward business and the free market economy.

What are those attitudes? . . . those opinions?

* Reprinted from the February 1959 issue of *Explaining Your Business News Bulletin,* Vol. 6, No. 2, by special permission of the Chamber of Commerce of the United States.

Survey of 1,443 High School Students.   A recent survey of 1,443 high school students in thirteen high schools in a typical industrial county is revealing. The survey was made among tenth, eleventh and twelfth grade students for General Electric by the Opinion Research Corporation of Princeton, N.J. The primary purpose was to measure the students' economic beliefs and information. The questions were related to these six major areas of business principles and practices:

°How the system shares the fruits of production
°Profits—their size and function
°Competition—in theory and in practice
°Productivity and living standards
°The role of capital
°Freedom and government control

The survey did not require knowledge of high-level economic theory. Achieving a good score, however, did require some knowledge of the basic facts of our industrial history, an ability to distinguish between fact and myth about the business world and respect for economic and individual freedoms fundamental in our form of society.

Average Score 47.1.   The average score was 47.1 out of a possible 100. If the students had been blindfolded, if they had just guessed at the answers, they could have (by the laws of chance) made a score of 45.7.

However, the low score, the survey report emphasizes, is "not a reflection of antagonism to the business system." Only about one student in twenty places major stress on the faults of the system.

Yet, their conception of the principles and practices of our business system is far from accurate. Sixty-five per cent of the students, for example, think that the average profit on sales is more than 10%. The exact breakdown follows . . .

Profit on Sales	*Students*
Less than 3%	3%
3% to 6% (correct answer)	11%
7% to 10%	20%
11% to 15%	20%
16% to 25%	26%
More than 25%	19%
No choice	1%

The students not only felt profits were high; they assumed almost every company operates at a profit. Seventy-seven per cent said that few companies operate at a loss. Actually, about one third of all corporations show no net income every year.

Importance of Profit Incentive Not Recognized. The importance of the profit incentive is not recognized by the majority of students . . . as evidenced by the answers to this question . . .

"The American business system cannot function without . . ."

	Students
Keeping the profit incentive alive	37%
More government planning and control	26%
A public works program in bad times	24%
Reduction of taxes on business	13%

The survey revealed that the students do not understand how our economic system shares its wealth . . .

"On the average in a manufacturing company each dollar divided between workers and owners goes roughly . . ."

	Students
80¢ to workers, 20¢ to owners (correct)	14%
60¢ to workers, 40¢ to owners	28%
40¢ to workers, 60¢ to owners	40%
20¢ to workers, 80¢ to owners	18%

U.S. Department of Commerce data for manufacturing companies (1939 to 1952) show the divisions of profits and employees' compensation to be 14% for profits, 86% to employees.

Misunderstandings About How Our System Shares the Wealth. These additional questions on the sharing of the wealth also indicate lack of information . . .

	Students
Dividends have increased as fast or faster than wages in the past 30 years	73%
Workers' pay has not kept pace with output	64%
Wages suffered as much or more than dividends in the depression of the 1930's	60%
Owners get too much compared with employees	56%
Wealth is becoming too concentrated	46%

Commenting on these replies, the survey report says, "Possibly these questions cover more of our economics history than high school students can be expected to know. But if students are to appraise our system they need to understand its accomplishments as well as its shortcomings."

Competition Accepted in Principle but Questioned in Practice.   The students accepted competition in principle, but questioned whether it worked out in practice. For example . . .

> 81% deny that competition is wasteful.
> 70% say companies grow big through service, not through unfair use of economic power.
> 68% agree that companies seek profit by lowering prices, not by keeping them high.
> 63% deny that companies set prices where they please.

Yet only 44% choose competition over price controls in normal times. And the majority of students didn't realize there is no real job security unless a company can meet its competition, as evidenced by the following answers . . .

"In a manufacturing company the best protection for job security is . . ."

	Students
Ability to meet competition	31%
A strong and able union	49%
Company-wide seniority rules	11%
Having the government guarantee jobs	9%

The students indicated they did not feel competition is operating in the American economy in answering questions like these . . .

	Students
In many industries one or two companies are so large as to be practically monopolies	77%
Some industries have little or no competition	47%
Meeting the competition is a real problem only for small companies, not big companies	43%
Similar prices in one industry is evidence that competition is not operating	41%

Thumbs Down on Productivity.   The importance of productivity—a key factor in raising living standards—seemed to escape the students because 71% answered "No" to the question, "Should a worker produce all he can?" When asked the "most practical way for workers to increase their living standards," 66% said, "Get more of the company's money" and only 34% said, "Produce more."

The fundamental principle of individual incentives and rewards inherent in our economic system seems little understood by the students—54% agree with this basic tenet of Marxist doctrine: "The fairest kind of economic system is one that takes from each according to his ability and gives to each according to his needs."

When asked, "Which has done the most to improve living standards in this country?" they said:

	Students
Organized labor	56%
Business management	16%
The government	14%
No opinion	14%

The myth that machines destroy jobs rather than create them was echoed by the students when 66% said that there are fewer and fewer jobs as factories put in more and more machinery. The way technological progress benefits everybody was apparently lost upon 76% who said that owners, not workers, get most of the gains of increased output due to new machinery.

So went the results of this survey of 1,443 high school students. Further evidence that businessmen are neglecting the important job of explaining the facts about business. Further evidence that chambers of commerce in communities all over America have a man-sized task cut out for them . . . for chambers are supposed to be *spokesmen for business*.

SUGGESTED READINGS

Eells, Richard, and Clarence Walton, *Conceptual Foundations of Business* (Homewood, Ill.: Irwin, 1961). Discusses the basic values upon which our business society is said to rest, and which presumably conditions behavior of members of that society.

Glover, John D., *The Attack on Big Business* (Boston: Division of Research, Graduate School of Business Administration, Harvard University, 1954).

Riley, Jr., John W. (ed.), *The Corporation and Its Public* (New York: Wiley, 1963). Placing the corporate image in its broader social and cultural context, this text clarifies the concept of the "corporate image."

CHAPTER 21

CREATORS
OF THE
BUSINESS
IMAGE

The opinions that individuals hold of any particular business firm are, as we have seen, conditioned by a number of influences. Actions of the management of a firm are interpreted as having certain meanings, either by individuals or by spokesmen for the groups of which they are members. Such interpretations, as we have also seen, are influenced by cultural forces. Each culture has certain ideals, and in a particular culture, actual behavior is measured against ideal behavior and when differences are found between the two (as there inevitably are), that behavior is condemned for falling short of the ideal. The ideals of any particular subculture in American society of which a person is a member are probably more influential in shaping an individual's view of a particular business firm than are American ideals, but the latter are also of some significance. Their importance is heightened because those who transmit "American ideals" and those of the "Western world" have frequently criticized business for its failure to measure up to the ideal. In addition to those transmitting cultural values are various individuals and groups having, wittingly and unwittingly, some influence on our view of business. In the following pages, we shall briefly examine the influence of schools and scholars, churches, intellectuals, writers, cartoonists, government agencies, and officials, and—last, but certainly not least—business itself.

Cultural and social values are generally transmitted by speaking, writing, or some other form of visual presentation. However, it is not useful to adopt such a classification for analysis because individuals and groups in one class of those who influence our image of business may adopt a variety of techniques. It has been pointed out by a student of the public relations of business that our cultural cargo is heavy with ancient ideals which color our view of business: "There is . . . considerable evidence that disdain for trade and hostility to gain depend heavily upon cultural inheritances from the pre-industrial stages of western civilization." [1] Evidence of this is seen in fictional portrayals of businessmen in novels, in television plays, and in hostile political oratory. This inheritance is traced to the Greek philosophers, whose views have been invested in the humanities—philosophy, poetry, and literature. However, something more than cultural influences seems to motivate those who create the image of business, and to this we shall also address ourselves.

INTELLECTUALS

Students of business and society have dealt with intellectuals as though they were a separate social class. Intellectuals have been defined as those who consider only large issues and intellectual concepts and do not waste time on "less important" problems. Another writer regards them as "those who report, interpret, analyze and comment upon public affairs and who exercise a considerable long-range influence on popular judgment. In default of a more apt name, this group of scholars, journalists and speech-makers is referred to as 'the intellectuals.' " [2] Unfortunately, as this latter statement indicates, there are a number of subclasses within the general classification of intellectuals, and scholars constitute such a subclass. It should be noted that only *some* scholars are regarded as intellectuals (a

---

[1] See the reading at the end of this Chapter for the source of this statement and a fuller discussion of this topic.

[2] Max Ways, "Labor Unions Are Worth the Price," *Fortune*, May 1963, p. 112.

judgment which students and faculty members will readily assent to). For our purposes, we shall want to deal with scholars, journalists, and speechmakers whether or not they are intellectual, since their influence does not depend upon the possession of that particular trait. However, since much has been written about the intellectual and his relation to business, we shall examine him briefly.

Intellectuals are important to business because they see part of their function as that of "social critic." They observe the contemporary scene, find fault with it, and propose changes. What their objectives are in so doing are not very clear (it has been suggested that they are pursuing the ideal republic in which the philosophers will reign supreme), but their statements reveal their values. Such statements are sometimes anti-business (Thoreau said, "There is no glory so bright but the veil of business can hide it effectively.") or they at least reveal a deep-seated suspicion of business motives.

A recent study of the intellectual's challenge to the corporate executive pointed out a number of interesting characteristics of the intellectual.[3] One intellectual surveyed saw the relationship between the intellectual and the executive as one of fundamental antipathy: "The intellectual looks down on the businessman as an inferior breed of human. And the businessman looks at the intellectual as a queer kind of person who is soft in the head and best avoided." Although intellectuals conceded that business had done a good job in raising material levels of living, they wondered why business leaders did not apply their talents to the attainment of social goals and apparently felt that executives were power-hungry manipulators intent on feathering their own nests, while only incidentally raising the standard of living. They also saw the need for a stronger role for the national government, higher personal standards and greater stress on ethics by businessmen, less materialism and more emphasis on humanistic values, more labor-management cooperation, more attention to the quality of products, and less advertising ballyhoo.

A question might be raised as to the influence of intellectuals. The study mentioned felt it to be quite strong: "The average businessman may not realize the importance of the intellectual in shaping the business climate—in antitrust, tax incentive, public spending, government controls and other areas." Also, there is an often-repeated statement made by an English intellectual (John Maynard Keynes, the economist, in his book *The General Theory of Money, Interest and Employment*[4]):

> The ideas of economists and political philosophers, both when they are right and when they are wrong, are more powerful than is commonly under-

[3] This study was reported in "Business-Eye View of the Egghead," *Business Week*, January 27, 1962, p. 134.
[4] (New York: Harcourt, Brace, 1936), p. 383.

stood. Indeed, the world is ruled by little else. Practical men, who believe themselves to be quite exempt from any intellectual influences, are usually the slave of some defunct economist. Madmen in authority, who hear voices in the air, are distilling their frenzy from some academic scribbler of a few years back.

Thus there are some observers who feel that the writings and speeches of intellectuals are quite influential. Before we accept this judgment, however, we should examine the process by which ideas influence action, since the ideas of intellectuals are influential only when they are in positions of power or when they have some impact on the actions of powerful individuals and/or groups.

In order to estimate realistically the impact of intellectuals, it must be recognized that at times men seize upon the ideas of high-minded writers to rationalize their behavior when they are, in fact, driven by quite different motives. For example, the ideas of the classical economists are frequently given credit for the passage of the Sherman Antitrust Act of 1890. However, in examining the circumstances surrounding the passage of that law, we note that the leadership of the Republican party was with good reason concerned about losing the support of farmers in the Middle West, who, suffering from declining prices and casting about for a scapegoat, blamed business for the distressed condition of agriculture. Although both farmers and politicians invoked the classical economists in their condemnation of "monopoly," it seems that they were scarcely philosophical antimonopolists, but that they employed these ideas to rationalize action based on quite different grounds. Also, we might suggest that the invocation of the words of an intellectual does not indicate that ideas and actions have been shaped by the person uttering those words, since intellectuals may only express in better words opinions already held by those employing the language of the intellectual. Finally, the selection of an intellectual's words might also involve an "appeal to authority" when it is felt that one's own words do not carry great weight.

It should not be concluded that intellectuals have no influence, but rather that they are most influential when occupying positions of power. They are beginning to permeate business, "getting into every nook and cranny of business life, particularly in staff positions." They have long been influential in government, not so much as elected officials as in appointive positions. President Franklin D. Roosevelt had his "Brain Trust," and President Kennedy surrounded himself with a number of academic intellectuals, principally from Harvard University. It may well be that intellectuals in positions of business and government power are more susceptible to the influence of other intellectuals than "practical men" might be, and to the extent that "big thinkers" are also in a position to take "big action," intellectuals do have considerable influence.

SCHOOLS AND SCHOLARS

Education is informal as well as formal. Parents and other associates outside the classroom or lecture hall play an important role in shaping our values and in molding our opinions. Our formal education seeks to foster certain attitudes as well as to transmit knowledge—this applies to both secular and religious education. It is difficult to generalize about the informal education a person receives, but the impact of formal education on the "business image" can be evaluated.

Elementary and Secondary Public Education

There is little or no education in business and economic affairs in the elementary and secondary public schools. This has been a cause for concern on the part of some business groups that feel that those coming out of the public schools have little real knowledge of business and, worse, that they have unfavorable attitudes toward business. These deficiencies, from the business viewpoint, are somewhat unintended products of public education. The very fact that education about business is not incorporated into curricula tends to give the impression that business is not very important. So-called business courses tend to be narrowly vocational and do not really deal with business. Educators, of course, think that education is important—especially education in the traditional academic disciplines. This tendency to set education and educators above business and businessmen and to frown upon vocational education (by all except those engaged in vocational education), leads to reinforcement of unfavorable attitudes toward business. Furthermore, in courses in which some views toward business might consciously be dealt with—in social studies, history, and English courses—the resulting "image" of business is not very favorable.

College Education

College education offers no great improvement over secondary schools in creating favorable opinion. This, however, is not the result of a lack of attention to education about business. In departments of economics, sociology, political science, history and other social sciences, the American economy and American business are investigated. Such studies are not only analytical, but critical as well—college professors in these fields usually regard themselves as critics of the social order. Businessmen would not mind so much, perhaps, if these self-appointed critics were as critical of government and labor as they were of business. Outside of the social sciences, there are others who examine the American businessman and find him wanting. In literature courses, for example, considerable emphasis is given to writers and writings critical of business. Even in departments and schools of business, some faculty members are critical of the morals of American businessmen. They tend to be somewhat more sympathetic, since they are more aware of the problems; however, their status in the academic community depends somewhat on their exhibiting the same attitudes as their colleagues throughout the institution. Partly in self-defense, therefore, many business-faculty members are moralistic in their treatment of business; they criticize past businessmen for their "immoral" conduct and urge students to conduct themselves more morally when they enter the business world. Finally, it might be said that academic careers attract persons whose social-political-economic views tend to be considerably "left" of those of businessmen and this, too, influences the way in which college teachers deal with business.

THE HISTORIAN AND BUSINESS. Among academic scholars, perhaps the most influential group has been the historians. This is true not so much because of their lectures to college classes, but because they write prolifically for a wide, general audience and because their writings are not as obscure as those of other scholars. However, many historians have substituted "the folklore of the robber barons" for the much less lurid truth about business. A prominent American historian, Allan Nevins, who has written a number of works on the history of business took his fellow historians to task for doing an injustice to business history. He saw a number of reasons for this: social prejudice, which relegated the businessman to an inferior position unworthy of historical treatment; the regarding of business as being dull; a view of business as being conducted on a low ethical plane; the fact that many historians were socialists; and the psychology of the historian. This situation is being remedied, with many competent academic historians writing the stories of companies and businessmen from records freely opened to them. However, it will be some time before a balanced picture emerges.

THE ECONOMIST AND BUSINESS. Academic economists are also of some importance in creating the image, and generally they paint a black picture. At one time English businessmen were the chief economic theorists, but businessmen have generally given way to academics in this field. College economists have taken upon themselves not only the description, analysis, and explanation of economic phenomena (including business activity) but the prescription of the ideal economic order as well. For example, traditional economists have urged competition among a large number of firms in an industry as the ideal method for achieving basic economic objectives. When they investigate the structure of American industry and observe business behavior, they note situations in which one or a few firms are dominant in an industry and they also point out the many restrictions on competition established by business. To the extent that economists can influence individuals to love competition and hate monopoly, and then demonstrate that American business is not perfectly competitive, they create an unfavorable image. Perhaps the major factor keeping their work from having greater impact is the obscurity of their discourse, although some—such as John Kenneth Galbraith and Kenneth E. Boulding (who are not-so-traditional economists)—have written for general audiences with consequent substantial influence.

It should be pointed out that very frequently academic economists appear as expert witnesses before governmental investigating bodies and, thereby, influence some individuals and groups possessing considerable power to influence business. The publicity given such testimony is also an important factor, since news publications normally print the more sensational aspects of the hearings including that dealing with unethical or illegal business practices.

A final point that should be made about academic economists is that not all of them are hostile to big business (which is frequently regarded as the enemy of competition). John Maurice Clark, for many years a professor of economics at Columbia University, concluded that industries made up of thousands of small companies that appeared, on the surface, to be intensely competitive were less competitive than they appeared to be and, further, that they served the public interest badly. He named homebuilding and small retailing as typical of industries populated by a multitude of small, inefficient companies that frequently took refuge in "guild-like" behavior in which accepted trade customs took the place of active competition. Although no believer in monopoly, he favors a situation in which companies are strong and rich enough to invest in research and to develop new and better products, resources, and more effective operations. Also, many economists teach in schools of business administration and, as they become more aware of the problems confronting businessmen, tend to become somewhat more sympathetic.

BUSINESS PROFESSORS AND BUSINESS. The fact that greater sympathy toward business exists in college of business administration faculties does not mean that they are not critics. Recently the oldest collegiate school of business administration in the United States—the Wharton School of the University of Pennsylvania—issued a report on the mutual fund industry, which the chairman of a trust fund sharply attacked, declaring the professors' theories " . . . so devoid of practicability as to be shocking and bizarre. . . . " A member of the Harvard Graduate School of Business Administration was chairman of the Business Ethics Advisory Council set up by the Kennedy administration after the price-fixing scandal in the electrical equipment industry. Other Harvard Business School professors have lectured businessmen on their social responsibilities and ethics at annual conferences held by that school and in various publications. Evidence that some businessmen do not feel that collegiate business schools are on the side of business is contained in a 1962 address by the president of the NAM in which he urged such schools "as the academic custodians of business knowledge, to become seriously concerned about the rash of insistent attacks on our free business system," implying that such concern was lacking.

There are other educational organizations disseminating views that businessmen regard as unfriendly. The Center for the Study of Democratic Institutions of the Fund for the Republic has published a number of critical commentaries. In one, it has declared: "The complexity and interdependence of the scientific-industrial state calls for national planning. The individualism of the eighteenth and nineteenth centuries is a casualty of technology, as are old theories of private property. Government must intervene more and more in the nation's industrial life." Whatever influence such views possess is largely due to the use of such publications in college courses.

Religious Education

Religious education deals even more consciously with social values. Sacred scriptures and preachers in the pulpit lay down moral laws concerning conduct, including some governing business behavior. Catholic economic doctrines have been quite restrictive of certain kinds of business activity, especially prior to the Protestant Reformation. A fairly large group of scholars holds that Protestantism—especially Calvinism—led to the development of "the spirit of Capitalism," which in turn played a crucial role in the development of modern business. Prominent Catholic scholars have attacked this view, pointing out that early Protestant preachments concerning business were not much different from those of the Catholics. Other scholars have argued that the social attitudes and economic practices associated with Judaism had been the primary source of the spirit of capitalism. Although almost all of the major religions in the United States have modified their moral laws to permit greater latitude to business conduct, they still uphold standards of morality to which they expect business to conform and are occasionally critical of business for failing to do so.

The effect of teachers and preachers on the attitudes and opinions of their audiences is difficult to assess. What evidence there is seems to indicate that their impact is not very significant and that they do not achieve any great transformation. Studies of students' attitudes prior to entering college and after leaving it show little changes in their economic attitudes, indicating that other forces are of greater importance. It has been suggested that these attitudes have become fairly well fixed prior to college entrance, and consequently are little changed by whatever the collegiate experience is. Too, it has been shown that socioeconomic status is more important in determining politico-economic attitudes than is religious affiliation for most persons, with the possible exception of the Jews.

The study dealing with religious affiliation and politico-economic attitude, mentioned in Chapter 19, investigated eight major religious groups in the U.S. Catholics, Jews, and members of six Protestant denominations were studied to determine whether or not there seemed to be any relationship between membership in a particular religious body and politico-economic attitudes (which could be, at the extremes, either "liberal or conservative"). Also, since sociologists were conducting the study, an investigation was made to determine whether or not there was any relationship between socioeconomic status and politico-economic attitude. The study concluded that any differences existing in the attitudes of members of various religions appeared to be primarily due to differences in socioeconomic makeup of the various religious bodies (that is, some of the Protestant churches were "upper-class," others were "middle-class," and yet others appealed mainly to individuals having low socioeconomic status). Also pointed out was the fact that there were wide variations in politico-economic attitudes *within* a particular denominational group, and that such differences were associated with socioeconomic stratification within the group—that is, those members of a particular denomination who were in the upper socioeconomic classes tended to have more conservative politico-economic views, and vice-versa. The only marked exception to the observed relationships between status and attitudes was noted among the Jews, who held liberal attitudes regardless of their status. This, however, was regarded not so much as a product of religious teaching as of a "cross-pressure" on individual members of this religion to identify with other Jewish people.

WRITERS

A large part of the adult audience is not reached by formal secular or religious education. Their schooldays are over, and they may never have

gone to church or are not in current attendance. Teachings and preach-
ings may have some residual influence, but their attention is given to
new "teachers" who communicate with them through different media.
One medium is the written word. There are many kinds of writers having
some impact on an individual's attitude toward and opinion of business,
but they can be broadly classified into those writing fiction and nonfiction.

Writers of Fiction

Poets, playwrights, novelists, and short–story writers—all have dealt
with morality and have sometimes dealt with the failure of business to
meet the moral standards set. From the day of Charles Dickens to the
present, the most common theme in novels concerning business has been
profits versus principles. Recent novels of business have been somewhat
more sympathetic, but still do not seem to illuminate the business scene;
rather, they seem consciously structured to create moral conflicts to test
businessmen. It is not surprising that fictitious managers and others in
influential business positions are frequently found wanting. Still, in novels
concerning American business, there seems to be emerging a less unfavorable picture of the businessman. There are seldom found the virulent
attacks characteristic of the Socialist novelists of the turn of the century;
writers of the caliber of Upton Sinclair are no longer to be found attacking the morals and mores of businessmen. There has been a recent fad
in the writing of the "business novel," but none of them has been regarded
as great literature, although Cameron Hawley's *Executive Suite* has sold
well over a half-million copies. The impact of business novels on public
opinion is difficult to assess, although it has been said that Upton Sinclair's *The Jungle* played a major role in reforming the meat packing
industry early in this century.

The impact of short–story writers is essentially the same as that of
novelists, although their audience is somewhat larger because their works
are widely published in periodicals. Poets write for a much more select
audience, and it may be properly concluded that they have little influence,
and that those whom they influence are of no great consequence insofar
as being able to affect the activities of business.

In recent years, playwrights have turned with renewed vigor to an
examination of business morals. The Broadway stage has produced *Death
of a Salesman, Born Yesterday, Solid Gold Cadillac,* and *How to Succeed
in Business Without Really Trying.* Financially successful enterprises
themselves, they have made fun of business or have raised serious moral
questions about business operations. In any case, the image has been an
unfavorable one. Writers for the movies have produced scripts critical
of the American economic system and of the role of business in that

system. An investigation by the House Un-American Activities Committee centered on the "Hollywood Ten" who were alleged to have Communist leanings. Some of these were writers. A similar investigation of the television industry led to the dismissal of some writers who were suspect in the eyes of the congressional investigators. It might be said that writers for radio and television are considerably more cautious in their writings than are those who write for movies and stage, since business sponsors are reluctant to be linked with scripts that attack business. When Edward R. Murrow produced a program dealing with the ways in which some firms and businessmen used sex to promote business, the sponsor's reaction was swift. Some firms, industries, and general business organizations have attempted to counter whatever adverse influence there might be in certain television scripts by sponsoring their own programs which are laudatory of the American business system, their industry, or their firm.

Writers of Nonfiction

Those who purport to write the literal truth fall into two major classifications. There are the journalists, columnists, editorialists, and others who write for periodicals of a nonscholarly nature. Then there are the scholarly writers of articles, research monographs, histories, biographies, and textbooks. The first group does not tend to be especially critical of business. Most nonscholarly periodicals (with the major exception of the labor press) are run on a business basis and are basically pro-business. Although certain business practices, businessmen, and business firms may be attacked, these are exceptional cases and such writers generally "project a favorable image of business." Scholars, especially those in academic halls, tend to be much more critical of business, as we have seen. Their writings as well as what they say in the classroom, reflect this critical attitude. Social, economic, and business histories deal critically with business. There is good reason to suspect that historians have not dealt adequately or fairly with business—with some blame for this resting upon businessmen as well as on historians. Economists, political scientists, and sociologists have also been critical of business in their writings. To the extent that textbook writers build on the findings of such scholars, textbooks also reflect these critical views.

CARTOONISTS

A strong case can be, and has been, made for the contention that cartoons have had a greater impact than novels, plays, and works of nonfiction. Cartoons, after all, are probably seen by people who do not, for various reasons, read novels or serious works, or who do not go to plays. Caricaturists work in blacks and whites in the realm of morals as well as on paper. The oversimplified message of the cartoon may, consequently, have a great impact on the public image of business. Cartoons might be classified into those with serious intent—editorial cartoons—and those that intend to amuse us. Editorial cartoons have tended to become less critical of business as time has passed (again with the major exception of those in the labor press) for the same reasons that journalists are not strongly critical of business in their writings. Cartoons on the editorial pages of the daily paper are much more likely to attack labor or government than business.

Cartoons that have the primary objective of entertainment may still have a great influence on individual attitudes toward business. Certainly the "General Bullmoose" that Al Capp has created is not designed to picture the big businessman as a very sympathetic character. Some cartoons—such as the more subtle and sympathetic ones appearing in the *New Yorker*—have pictured the businessman as having a number of human, and sometimes undesirable, traits.

UNIONS AND GOVERNMENT

Foremost among other individuals helping to shape the image of business are union leaders. Especially when negotiation of new union contracts is under way, the leaders of unions are given to making public statements declaring the profits of the firm or industry to be excessive, saying that either prices should be reduced to the consumer or that more should be paid labor. Walter Reuther, the president of the United Auto Workers union, has especially been given to making such statements, and has taken companies to task for increasing executive bonuses while calling for workers to hold the line on wages. The head of the International Union of Electrical Workers, James B. Carey, harassed the management of General Electric, after conviction of that company, along with some others, of conspiracy to fix the prices of heavy electrical equipment, by publicly calling upon the company to fire the employees involved, to sue them for damages, to require them to repay their income from bonuses and stock options, and to form an "impartial panel" to determine whether the chairman of the board should have been aware of the price-fixing (which knowledge he had denied). Union publications, which perhaps are not as widely noted, also carry a number of attacks on business.

Government agencies and officials engage in a number of investigations of business, and their reports can have substantial influence. When the Public Health Service issued a report on the relation between cigarette smoking and various diseases, there was a marked (although short-lived) influence on the consumption of cigarettes and the prices of tobacco company stocks. Secretary of Commerce Luther Hodges published a book entitled *The Business Conscience* in which he made it quite clear (through illustrations of bad business practices) that business had some soul-searching to do. Those who occupy, or are candidates for, elective positions are frequently prone to attack business in the belief that such attacks will get them the support of politically important groups.

BUSINESS AS A CREATOR OF THE IMAGE

Individual businessmen, firms as a whole, trade and professional associations, and general business organizations all have substantial influence on the image of business by what they do and say. They are, of course, committed to creating a favorable image. Their efforts do not very often meet with success, as noted in the preceding chapter.

The ways in which businessmen and business groups conduct themselves in their relations with the individuals and groups in their environment have the greatest influence. Unfortunately, this conduct does not always result in a "favorable image." Consequently, business has engaged in a number of activities aimed at improving the image. Such activities cover a wide range: speeches are made; articles and books are written extolling a businessman, firm, industry, or the business system; institutional advertising is done; educational programs are undertaken; contributions are given, both of time and money; and so on. These attempts to influence opinions, attitudes, and analyses seem to have had little impact. Perhaps it is because, as Emerson said: "What you are shouts so loud that I can't hear what you say." At any rate, one investigation (reported in a book by William H. Whyte entitled *Is Anybody Listening?*) revealed that almost no one paid the slightest attention to the "Freedom Forums" and expensive institutional advertisements extolling "the American way of life." Others have poked fun at the attempts by business to influence opinion. This does not seem to have put a halt to business attempts to improve the image, but the question still remains as to what effect such efforts have.

With moral judgments being made about business by a number of individuals and groups, the question that has confronted—and perplexed —some businessmen has been what their real responsibility to society is. In the next chapter, we shall discuss the responsibilities of business.

READING: A Profit Should Not Be Without Honor *
by William C. Halley

Of all the foes the public relations man must face, one of the most durable is that ancient Western prejudice: The notion that commercial activity and making a profit are not quite pure and not quite admirable.

This idea seems amazingly impervious to the impact of events. For, during the life span of a man now passing his fiftieth birthday, the United States has actually doubled the quantity of goods and services produced for each man, woman, and child within its borders. This is a remarkable record of improved material welfare and one in which the nation's industrial and business community takes understandable pride. Producing goods is its function in life and it has marvelously succeeded.

Just an Ordinary Man. The businessman's prideful reverie, however, is frequently fractured by his feeling that a pervasive air of disapprobation and hostility dogs his achievements. Like Professor Henry Higgins of *My Fair Lady*, he knows he is just an ordinary man. Yet he is sometimes astonished at the stereotypes of himself which are nourished in literature,† in television plays of the *Patterns* stamp, and in the barbs of hostile political oratory. Not only is he variously depicted as socially irresponsible, profit-mad, unduly selfish or ruthless; he is also blamed for an unbelievable number of national woes.

Worse—and this, alas, may be the unkindest cut of all—although the businessman builds plants, creates social wealth, and provides society with useful services, he is still, sad to report, "in trade." His spirit is reputedly vulgarized by single-minded pursuit of personal gain and it is maintained that anyone, given a hard heart and an itching palm, could duplicate the businessman's achievements. In the novel *Ulysses*, for example, James Joyce skewers the merchant with six words: He is one "who buys cheap and sells dear." And that, presumably, is that.

Such condescension the modern business manager naturally finds offensive. He does not wish to be considered a saint, but neither does he think of himself as depraved. Why, he wonders, when three out of four Americans are engaged in business activity, is production of goods "merely material." Do the businessman's tangible and demonstrably useful efforts really represent less than a noble calling? Or do the stereotypes concerning him really express beliefs and ideals that may have been appropriate to the past, but are anachronisms now?

There is, in fact, considerable evidence that disdain for trade and hostility to gain depend heavily upon cultural inheritances from the pre-industrial stages of Western civilization. Like men at any time, we look at the world not with the unclouded eye of the young child, but with the compound vision provided by the past. As Anatole France put it, "We are already old when we are born."

* Reprinted by permission from *Public Relations Journal*, January 1958 issue.
† See "The Fictional Business Leader: Unflattering Is The Portraiture," by Dr. Robert A. Kavesh, *Public Relations Journal*, June 1956.

Ancient and Ultra-Modern Ideals.   Thus, our mental cargo can include both ancient and ultra-modern ideals, existing side by side. The problem, obviously, is that an old way of thinking—however valid and useful in its own time and setting—may be inapplicable to new social circumstances. As the historian of science, W. P. D. Wightman, writes, "Ideas, like persons, are born, have adventures and die. But unlike most persons, they do not disappear from this mortal stage; their ghosts walk, often to the confusion of new ideas."

In this regard, it is interesting to note that many of the labels applied to businessmen are as old as the Athenian hills, deeply ingrained in our culture and crushingly embodied in received opinion. The dualism of "worthy" and "unworthy" pursuits that irritates the businessman is similarly evident in industry's parent, science, where we see sharp distinctions drawn between so-called "pure" and "applied" branches. Such prejudices, it would seem, are remarkable in a people whose lives are eased at every moment by the applications of discovery and the products of industry. Clearly, these airs have the tang of ancient snobberies and can clearly be seen as far back as the ancient Greeks.

To the Greek philosophers, according to Benjamin Jowett, the eminent classical scholar, "probably no feeling was more deeply implanted than that which taught the essentially vulgar character of retail trade. . . . The wealthy aristocrat might employ his slaves in a workshop, or let them out for hire as artisans and mechanics; he could not, without social degradation, to use Plato's humorous language, 'open a shop or keep a tavern.' "

This bias is evident as early as 600 B.C., as reported in the apocryphal story of Thales, one of the Seven Wise Men of ancient Greece. Twitted by friends for his poverty, Thales took time off from philosophic contemplation long enough to corner the olive market, wax rich, and prove there was nothing to it. Then he went back to contemplation.

Plato and Aristotle.   Plato and Aristotle, laying the foundations of Western culture, were quite explicit on the inferiority of the people who do the world's work. Plato graded humanity from the bottom up, assigning artisans, workers, and tradesmen to the task of providing vulgar necessities. Higher came the warriors, whose noble task was war; and sitting upon the shoulders of all were the philosopher-kings, whose job was to think the nation's thoughts. For Plato, contemplation and Pure Knowing constituted the worthy life; the task for man was to abhor the vulgar and embrace the finer things.

Aristotle disagreed with his master on many things, but not upon such points as these. Though we may cluck over his acceptance of slavery as the natural lot of inferior mortals, we are inclined to smile appreciatively over his contempt for trade.

"Citizens," he says in his Politics, "must not lead the life of crafts-workers or tradesmen, for such a life is ignoble and inimical to virtue. . . . To be always seeking after the useful does not become free and exalted souls." In his educational advice, he stresses that useful arts should be taught to slaves, but not to children who should not learn any skill that deforms the body or enables them to earn money.

"At Thebes," he notes approvingly, "there was a law that no man could hold office who had not retired from business for ten years."

The disdain for practical, worldly pursuits, first voiced by the Greeks, became part and parcel of our Western inheritance. The suspect nature of business and its deleterious effects upon motives and character were sanctioned not merely by theology, but by the aristocratic traditions and rigid class alignments which characterized society from Roman patrician to Eighteenth Century gentlemen. In philosophy, poetry, and literature—the whole body of what is generally labeled the humanities—these notions are implicit, inherited anew by every school child. Only in natural science has subject matter been fully updated—and that after a battle with Aristotelian theories which would have horrified that great, primal thinker.

Uncritical Acceptance.   Yet, in a nation like the United States, we must work constantly to amend and alter our views of life as circumstances change and new social patterns emerge. Uncritical acceptance and nourishment of cultural relics like the "unworthiness of worldly pursuits" is forcing new wine into old bottles, and can exact a heavy social cost. It has before and it can again.

For not until Adam Smith in the Eighteenth Century did any philosopher worth his salt consider economic effort as deserving of detailed and systematic description. The same bias against the worldly and the merely useful repressed the progress of natural science and its offspring, modern industry, for nearly two thousand years.

In addition, an incalculable social loss was sustained when this bias diverted from society's needs vast stores of brainpower. The reluctance of gentle persons to associate themselves with menial tasks meant that the bulk of early industrial activity was undertaken by horny-handed men beyond the pale of "decent" society—barbers, blacksmiths, machinists, and other humble folk. It must be said, in fact, that the bounties of mass production were thrust upon the race by social lepers while the cultivated minds concerned themselves with ends not so demonstrably useful.

As in the past, so in the future there is no reason to think that timeworn modes of looking at business will provide the insight and vigor needed by an industrial civilization. What we have developed in America is something entirely new in the history of the race: An industrial democracy of unexampled fruitfulness. Its novelty was noted as early as 1840 by de Tocqueville who wrote that, in America, ". . . the greatest undertakings and speculations are executed without difficulty because the whole population is engaged in productive industry. . . . The Americans arrived but as yesterday on the territory which they inhabit, and they have already changed the whole order of nature for their advantage."

De Tocqueville, of course, had not seen anything yet, but there is serious doubt that the bulk of our nation today sees as much as the Frenchman did a century ago.

Major Educational Challenge.   Thus, a major educational challenge is presented to the business public relations man: To build a realistic, down-to-earth understanding of the role business and industry have played in creating this society. He must bridge the enormous gaps which exist between the business world as it is and the pictures which linger in our American heads.

To do this most effectively will undoubtedly require a considerable deepening of the business public relations man's function in the future. It seems likely that more and more he must undertake to provide what amounts to basic education in social and economic history—background on an industrial past about which the nation is incredibly uninformed. His publications, his speeches, all his utterances must touch upon a central historical theme: The integral role of industry and business in building American civilization.

This kind of program will begin at the beginning. It will recreate the feeble, agricultural society of colonial times—a society of hard labor, dependent upon Europe, prey to invasion. Most important, the program will chronicle in detail the transformation of that society: The rise of domestic manufactures, the improvement of technology, the fantastic saga of American invention.

Ideally, the man using the power lathe will develop a lively awareness of what he owes to steam and electrical pioneers. The TV watcher will know that the frontier was conquered not by Wyatt Earp, but by the mass-produced plow, the steamboat, the locomotive. The short work week and the widespread ownership of property—the high wages and the greater leisure—these will be revealed not as gifts from God, but as the logical results of high productivity and the substitution of mechanical energy for human sweat.

Ambitious Communications Program.   Such a communications program is ambitious, unquestionably, but the pressing need for it can clearly be seen in the misconceptions and contradictions which characterize opinions about business. For example, one of the requisites for large-scale production is the large production organization—a pool of skills, talents, and tools geared to enrich not just itself but society as a whole. Yet, as the 1956 Presidential campaign indicated, the spectacle of citizens applauding blanket condemnations of "big business" is far from uncommon.

In a nation whose population is currently growing at the rate of about 3.5 million a year, we hear presumably serious cries that business is too big, that it should be splintered, that its growth should be stopped by hook or by taxes. Supplying tomorrow's needs will actually call for larger units than we have today. Yet, if current debate is any guide, this is a fact which runs head-on into much of our folklore.

There are other signs of basic confusion. The ancient stereotypes of philistinism and the most primitive economic notions are married to myths of the exploited worker; of large business smashing small; of anti-social concentrations of power; of ruthless, irresponsible business managers. Side by side with revolutionary rises in family income, leisure, and possessions are excoriations of the technology which has produced the abundance we enjoy.

Fundamental Misconceptions.   All these are symptoms of fundamental misconceptions and misinformation about the nature, the history, the activities, and the contributions of business and the businessman. Removing them will require deep-down content in the public relations program. It is a big job, for as that doughty battler for science, Francis Bacon, reported more than two centuries ago, the multitude is, in reality, "ready to give passage to that which is popular and superficial than to that which is substantial and profound." Time, he said, seems to be a river "which carrieth down to us that which is light and blown up, and sinketh and drowneth that which is weighty and solid."

But the public relations man's educational job must be attempted. For it seems obvious that the greatest danger to the well-being of business and industry is a nation which does not know how it got this way.

SUGGESTED READINGS

"The Business Novel Fad," *Fortune* (August 1959). A discussion of the rash of business novels published after World War II and what kind of "image" emerged from them.

Cheit, Earl F., ed., *The Business Establishment* (New York: Wiley, 1954). Concerns itself with some "creators of the business image" and also is an example of a work that may have some influence on opinions held of business. Topics discussed are reflections on a changing business ideology; businessmen in American fiction; the evolution of the American creed; why managers cultivate social responsibility.

Packard, Vance, *The Waste Makers* (New York: McKay, 1960). An example of current nonfiction that creates an "unfavorable image." Packard examines modern marketing practices and concludes that many businessmen seek to make their fellow Americans more greedy and prodigal and that "durability is a dirty word" among the producers of goods.

CHAPTER 22

THE SOCIAL
RESPONSIBILITIES
OF BUSINESS

Ever since World War II—or at least since the postwar demand for goods and services was satisfied—a great debate has raged over what the responsibilities of business are. The 1961 price-fixing case in the electrical equipment industry gave new impetus to the discussion. The issue is not yet settled and it is likely that the debate will not be concluded in the foreseeable future. Part of the problem in the discussion has been that there is no clear understanding—or at least no agreement—on what business and society and their interrelationships are. In the preceding chapters we have attempted to provide some clarification. Even if all parties to the debate on responsibilities were to agree to the views presented, the argument would still continue, since there would be disagreement on what the responsibilities of business are even within this framework. The difficulty is not that there are no answers to what business responsibility is, but that there are too many answers. Different debaters hold different views on what the social responsibilities of business are. Not so surprisingly, the views that various parties hold tend to reflect their interests.

BUSINESS ETHICS

A predominant theme in the discussion is that business should conduct itself ethically. No one has disagreed—or would disagree—with this proposition. The question is: Whose ethics? There are a number of ethical standards espoused by a number of parties. Usually, ethical principles do not stand alone but are a part of an ethical code that may contain principles that would, in some cases, prescribe conflicting courses of action. Therefore, even if a certain set of ethical principles were agreed on, the question of which should be given priority under a certain set of circumstances would still have to be answered. We shall sidestep this issue, since it appears to be impossible to secure agreement on what principles ought to govern business conduct. Some, however, are worthy of examination.

Christian Ethics

It is sometimes suggested that there would be no problem of irresponsible business behavior if businessmen would conduct themselves "in a Christian manner." To the extent that businessmen are not Christians, such ethics have no relevance, or at least no influence. Assuming that they all were Christians, the problem still would not be solved because there are differences among various Christian churches and ministers as to what doctrines—including ethical ones—are the proper ones. We have already mentioned that the "Protestant ethic" presumably differed from the economic doctrines of the Catholics and has been regarded by some as supporting the rise of capitalism. However, there have been a number of Protestant ministers who believed Christianity and capitalism to be incompatible and who therefore supported socialism as a solution to the ethical dilemmas posed.

A professor of sociology at a leading divinity school has suggested that churches as well as individuals might be classified according to socioeconomic status. That is, there are upper-class, middle-class and lower-class churches in the sense that the members they serve are drawn pretty much from these various socioeconomic classes. The significance of such a classification, for our purposes, is that there seem to be quite separate and distinct economic doctrines associated with upper-class churches as opposed to middle-class and lower-class churches. More favorable views of business and capitalism are part of the doctrines of the upper-class churches than they are of the others. There have been cases of business-men changing churches from those in which they felt ill at ease—owing to an alleged discrepancy between their behavior and Christian ethics—to ones in which no such incompatibility was seen or in which capitalism was regarded as a manifestation of God's will. Each church sees its doctrines as the true ones, but the lack of close agreement leaves even Christian businessmen without a uniform benchmark for their behavior.

The "Individualistic Ethic"

Within churches and without, some voices are heard urging the busi-nessman to act so as to maximize individual freedom and opportunity. In recent years, partly as a consequence of the publication of such books as *The Organization Man*,[1] in which the author deplores the stifling, conformist influences on individuals by organizations (including business firms), this issue has been a matter for public discussion. Many business-men subscribe, at least publicly, to this point of view, since they feel the heavy restraints of government activity on their individual freedom. Un-fortunately, within a business firm it is frequently necessary to have the individual members working for the goals of the business, which may be in conflict with their own goals or which restricts their freedom to develop their own personalities without restraint by the organization.

In their dealings with customers, suppliers, and unions, the require-ments of successful business operation occasionally influence business managers to restrict individual freedom. For example, much has been written in recent years about the ethics of "motivational research" aimed at finding the psychological motivations of buying behavior. One objec-tion to the use of such studies is that by "psychologically twisting the buyer's arm" the seller is limiting the free rational choice of the consumer. A firm that buys large quantities of goods from other companies that, in turn, buy large quantities of the product turned out by the industry of which the firm is a part, frequently demands and gets "reciprocity," which is a limitation on the freedom of its suppliers to buy from whom-ever they choose. In order to preserve their "right to manage," many firms have restricted the freedom of their employees to join unions. It

[1] William H. Whyte, Jr. (New York: Simon & Schuster, 1956).

should be pointed out that such activities may be necessary, from the business point of view, but that they are also in conflict with the individualistic ethic. This conflict between individualistic beliefs and organizational needs has sent some businessmen "scrambling for a faith which will bridge the gap."

The "Social Ethic"

Some of those who have found that the individualistic ethic does not fit the realities of the business situation have sought to substitute other principles, including the social ethic. One definition (by a believer in "individualism") of the social ethic is that "body of thought which makes morally legitimate the pressures of society against the individual." Such an ethical proposition is a hard pill to swallow for many businessmen who believe in individualism or who find the individualistic ethic a good rationalization for positions and actions they wish to take. However, some businessmen profess a belief in a social ethic, although they phrase it differently. Frank Abrams, at one time the board chairman of Standard Oil of New Jersey, has said: "The job of professional management is to conduct the affairs of the enterprise in its charge in such a way as to maintain an equitable and workable balance among the claims of the various directly interested groups—stockholders, employees, customers, and the public at large." The ethical principle embodied in this statement proposes that businessmen discover who the various directly interested groups are, determine their claims, and then make decisions and take action that will maintain an equitable *and* workable balance among the claims. Special note should be taken of the phrase "and workable," since it implies that there are some equitable solutions that may not be workable or that there may be some solutions to the problem of social responsibility that may be workable but may not be equitable. More will be said later about the problem of putting responsible business behavior into practice.

I have stated an ethical principle I call, again somewhat immodestly, "Walton's Moral Law" that is a social ethic of sorts and that squares with Mr. Abrams' statement. To quote myself: "Responsible behavior involves taking into account the interests of all parties concerned in proportion to some measure of their interests." Few, I think, would quarrel with this proposition, although many may question its practical significance. The major problem in putting it into practice, quite obviously, is to secure some measure of the interests of the parties and, frankly, I know of no universally acceptable objective way of measuring interests. This is not a fatal defect, however, since looking at the problem in this light leads one to ask the right questions:

1. Who are the parties at interest?
2. What are their interests and how important are they?
3. Are the interests of some parties being given disproportionate weight?

Such an approach will, it seems to me, tend to make problems of responsible business behavior quite concrete.

It should be pointed out that a belief in a "social ethic" is not necessarily incompatible with a belief in the "individualistic ethic." Individuals have some rights and so does "society." It has been urged: "Let each one be all that he is capable of being within the legitimate requirements of society." This emphasizes the fact that not all social requirements or pressures are legitimate, and that a maximum amount of individual freedom should be permitted within the legitimate needs of other individuals and groups. There still remains the ethical problem of determining which demands of others are legitimate, but at least it should be recognized that both an individual and others have some rights and that on occasion one must give way to the other.

Self-serving Ethics

It is not so surprising that those who urge businessmen to behave "responsibly" promote ethics that serve their particular interests. When labor groups, consumer groups, stockholder groups, and other interested organizations suggest principles of proper business behavior, they are usually urging codes of business conduct that will result in more for labor, consumers, owners, or whatever group is making the suggestion. Since turn-about is regarded as fair play, many businessmen have adopted ethical codes that serve the special interests of business. However, many businessmen have also thought about ethical principles that would harmonize the interests of all concerned.

Ethical Codes Adopted by Business

Firms that have consciously adopted codes of business ethics have drawn them from three major sources—from within the firm, from an industry code, or from codes drafted by some general business organization. General Electric's management engaged in extensive study of what the proper objectives of the firm were and concluded, in part, that they should be:

> To design, make, and market all Company products and services with good quality and with inherent customer value, at fair, competitive prices.

To attract and retain investor capital through attractive returns as a continuing incentive for wide investor participation and support.

To cooperate with suppliers, distributors, retailers, contractors, and others who facilitate the production, distribution, installation, and servicing of Company products and systems.

To meet the Company's social, civic, and economic responsibilities with imagination and with voluntary action which will merit the understanding and support of all concerned among the public.

Unfortunately, although G.E. engaged in such a thoughtful and direct expression of its ethical standards, some of them seem to have come into conflict with the ethics of the industry and industry ethics won out (at least this is one possible interpretation of General Electric's participation in the price fixing conspiracy in the electrical equipment industry).

As was pointed out in the discussion on trade associations, one of the more important functions of such groups is to draft codes of conduct for the member firms in a particular industry. General business organizations, such as the National Association of Manufacturers, require their members to support certain codes of business practices. Members of the NAM subscribe to the following:

1. We will strive at all times to conduct the affairs of this company to merit public confidence in American business and industry and faith in our free private competitive enterprise system.

2. We will see that our employees are given every opportunity to progress with the company and are appropriately compensated for their work.

3. We will deal fairly with customers and suppliers and extend to them the same treatment we wish to receive ourselves.

4. We will compete vigorously to serve our customers and expand our business, but we will avoid unfair or unethical practices.

5. We will seek through sound management practices to produce the profit necessary to the continued progress of the business and so fulfill our responsibilities to our stockholders, employees, customers, community and nation.

It is not clear what sanctions the NAM has at its command to enforce this code, and it is probable that its influence is less than that of an industry code.

Codes Established by Government

Governments are involved in establishing codes beyond those already mentioned. Laws provide a legal code of behavior that those individuals and groups coming under the law are supposed to conform to, and penalties are usually provided for those who are convicted of violating the code. There is a prevalent view that such legal codes are not adequate and that moral or ethical codes are required to reinforce them. On occasion, government officials have urged businessmen to go beyond what is required by law and behave in accordance with certain ethical principles suggested by the public officer. Businessmen, knowing that such statements cost the official nothing and may bring him some political profit, may under such circumstances sympathize with the view expressed by Mark Twain: "To be good is noble; but to show others how to be good is nobler and no trouble."

There was a recent attempt to draft an entire code of business morals by the federal government. After the price-fixing scandal in the electrical equipment industry in 1961, Secretary of Commerce Hodges invited clergymen, educators, businessmen and labor leaders to Washington for a conference on business morals with the object of drafting rules for business behavior. The administration took the position that the price-fixing incident was morally as well as legally wrong, and that general business organizations, trade associations, and other business groups should join in a crusade to establish higher business morality.

President Kennedy's Business Ethics Advisory Council issued a report that did not contain a specific ethical code. Instead, it enunciated what must be regarded as a "social ethic":

> Business enterprises, large and small, have relationships in many directions with stockholders and other owners, employees, customers, suppliers, government, and the public in general. The traditional emphasis on freedom, competition, and progress in our economic system often brings the varying interests of these groups into conflict, so that many difficult and complex ethical problems can arise in any enterprise. While all relationships of an enterprise to these groups are regulated in some degree by law, compliance with law can only provide a minimum standard of conduct. Beyond legal obligations, the policies and action of businessmen must be based upon a regard for the proper claims of all affected groups.[2]

Instead of urging a specific code upon business, the Business Ethics Advisory Council urged the American business community "to hasten its attainment of those high ethical standards that derive from our heritage and traditions." The heritage and traditions referred to were "our religious heritage and our traditions of social, political, and economic freedom," which impose on all men high obligations in their dealings with their fellow men, and which make them all stewards of the common good. However, the Council was somewhat ambivalent, since it also pointed out that new ethical problems were being created constantly by the ever-

[2] *A Report to the President from the Business Advisory Council*, January 16, 1962, p. 1.

increasing complexity of society and that businessmen, therefore, must continually seek to identify new and appropriate standards.

In order that businessmen might develop their own ethical codes, the Council asked some questions to aid in the examination by American businessmen of their ethical standards and performance. It was stressed that these were not all the questions that would have to be considered by each business enterprise if it were to achieve the high ethical standards deriving from our heritage and traditions. Some questions dealt with the existence of codes of ethics in business firms and the awareness by officers and employees of the ethical standards established to guide the members of the firm. Others concerned compliance with laws and regulations, conflicts of interest, expenditures for gifts and entertainment, and relations with customers and suppliers.

Perhaps the Council did all it could do under the circumstances. The great variety of religions in America; varying views of the nature of our social, political, and economic heritage; and differences in relationships and responsibilities confronting various firms—all combine to make it impossible, from a practical standpoint, to establish an ethical code that would be pertinent to all firms in all industries. The net result of the Council's deliberations, however, seemed little more than a general injunction to "do good" plus some suggestions as to what businessmen might think about in order to reach that vague objective.

THE DIFFICULTY OF "RESPONSIBLE" BUSINESS BEHAVIOR

There are difficulties confronting the business firm that wishes to act responsively and responsibly beyond those created by different and often irreconcilable views of what business "ought to do." The lack of authority or power may hamper the firm in the discharge of duties that others feel it should take on. The fact that other parties interested in business behavior have influence over what a firm does further limits its ability to act ethically. Finally, it has its own needs to consider.

Lack of Power or Authority

Frequently, business firms find themselves powerless to discharge responsibilities which they may otherwise be willing to assume. Owing to economic conditions, they may find themselves in distressed financial circumstances and unable to pay interest to creditors, dividends to shareholders, wages to employees, bills of suppliers, and so on. Competitive pressures may prevent a firm from paying as high wages as it would like.

Pressures of high costs may keep it from charging as low a price or as giving as high quality a product as it would like to do. Even if a management had the economic power to pay higher wages or charge lower prices, a question would remain as to whether or not it would be legitimate for it to do so. There is a school of legal thought that declares that the sole responsibility of the managers of a corporation is to the stockholders and that management is not authorized to take actions contrary to the interests of the owners—for example, since one of the rights of shareholders is to the profits of the enterprise, managers cannot properly take action that will reduce profits. We find a useful touchstone in that managerial maxim that declares that authority and responsibility must go hand in hand. Although others might like managers to assume certain responsibilities, if they are without authority to do so they cannot properly be charged with those duties.

Presence of Other Powerful Parties

Since the interests, and ethics, of the parties capable of influencing business are frequently different from those of the firm, and since they have certain powers with which to pursue their objectives, this establishes additional limits on what a firm can do. The phrase "politics is the art of the possible" applies to business policy as well as to government. If certain business behavior will give rise to "countervailing power," at least a second thought must be given to the matter by the manager. Perhaps the most prudent approach, as has been suggested before, is one in which the likely reaction of various influential groups is assessed before action is taken.

To put it another way, what is ethical is not always practical. "Walton's Social Law" points out that social phenomena are determined by actions taken by interested parties to attain certain objectives with whatever resources they are willing to commit to the attainment of those ends; Walton's Moral Law" suggests that responsible behavior means taking into account the interests of the parties in proportion to some measure of those interests. What we see in the real world are a number of situations in which some parties have resources or powers to determine an issue that are *not* in proportion to their interest in that issue. One such case, it has been suggested, is the determination of the price of a product. What has been said is that the consumer—who has a very strong interest in this matter—has almost no influence on the price, but that business firms through their monopoly power and unions through their control over the supply of labor and, hence, labor costs have influence disproportionate to their proper interest in what prices should be. The question, therefore, confronting a firm sometimes is: How much of the resources of the firm should be employed in attempting to counteract the influence of those parties whose influences are regarded as being in excess of their legitimate interest in what a firm does? It may well be that the establishment of the necessary amount of countervailing influence would create such a drain on the resources of the firm that it would have difficulty in attaining its other goals. Consequently, we should not be surprised—and perhaps we should be somewhat sympathetic—when we see business firms acting in what may be regarded as an irresponsible fashion. It may be that they are not really irresponsible, but that they lack the power to counteract those forces pushing them into a certain line of behavior.

In fulfilling its social responsibilities, then, the firm must keep a number of things in mind. In behaving responsibly toward society, it is limited by what it *can* do—by its lack of authority or power, by the probable adverse consequences of certain acts, and by its own needs. Within these limits, firms may develop certain business ethics that take into account the culture or cultures in which they operate. Since these ethics will be culturally determined, there is no need—nor is it desirable, since few ethical principles will cover all cases—to discuss here further what they ought to be.

THE PUBLIC RELATIONS MOVEMENT

As business came under attack from a number of individuals and groups in American society alleging that businessmen were acting in unethical, immoral, irresponsible, and illegal ways, it initiated a movement to counter these attacks. For lack of a better term, this might be called the "public relations movement." Public relations has a number of definitions. One quite appropriate to our discussion is: "The activities of an organization in building and maintaining sound relations with special publics—such as customers, employees and stockholders—and with the public at large, so as to adapt itself to its environment and interpret itself to society." Other definitions place more emphasis on the publicity aspect of public relations—for example, "public relations is the building of a favorable image of an organization through good works and good communication." Initially public relations placed more emphasis on publicity than on structuring harmonious relations with various publics, but nowadays the latter is given stronger emphasis.

History of Public Relations

Businessmen have always had some relations with various segments of society or the public. When business was small, these relationships were face to face and quite personal. As business grew larger, managers of business firms had fewer and fewer direct relations with the various publics with which the firm had dealings. In some cases, this led to a lessened awareness of the interests of the public and to a more self-centered concern with the interests of the managers of the firms. There were a few extreme cases in which the attitude of managers were properly characterized as: "The public be damned!" Such a sentiment was actually uttered by William H. Vanderbilt, son of the man who put together the New York Central railroad. Taken out of context, this statement has been regarded as being characteristic of the attitudes of big business generally in the period between the Civil War and the beginning of this century. Certainly there were occasions on which Cornelius Vanderbilt, his son, and men like them took actions contrary to the interests of their customers and others, and contrary to the law as well. Some of these actions were justified, but some were not. In any event, big business firms in the latter part of the nineteenth century found themselves confronted with an increasing number of hostile organized groups—such as labor unions and farmers' organizations—which were able to take direct action affecting the firms or were able to secure legislation adverse to the interests of big business.

Initially the response of big business was to fight these groups. A number of battles were won, but the war seems to have been lost. Farm groups, labor organizations, and other hostile bodies grew in strength and became more successful in both economic action and political action. As a consequence, a new attitude developed in business: "If we can't lick 'em, get them to join us." Thus "public relations" was born.

In its infancy, public relations was concerned almost solely with publicity. Journalists and other skilled publicists were employed by business to demonstrate that there was no conflict between the interests of business and the public and to enhance the reputations of firms and businessmen. Publicity would win the war, according to its advocates. A pioneer public relations man, Ivy Lee, wrote a book entitled *Publicity* in which he declared: "I believe in telling your story to the people. If you go direct to the people and get the people to agree with you, you can be sure that ultimately legislatures, commissions and everybody else must give way in your favor."

Publicity did seem to meet with some success. In the 1920's, public attitudes toward business were more favorable. Whether or not this was a consequence of publicity is not certain, but what is certain is that this condition did not endure. During the depression years, business came under severe attack, often unfair. A favorite political slogan of the Democrats in 1932 was: "Hoover blew the whistle, Mellon rang the bell, Wall Street got the signal, And the country went to hell." Certainly businessmen did not conspire to create a business depression and they were help-less individually and collectively to prevent it. Regardless of the truth of the matter, the "public image" of business suffered during the Great Depression and it was quite obvious that publicity was inadequate to repair the damage.

Some firms have moved out of what has been called "the public be pleased, but fooled" stage which characterized the bulk of the early public relations activities of businessmen, firms, trade associations, and general business organizations. This new stage of "the public be fully served and fully informed" has not yet fully replaced the former stage, but there are a number of examples of genuine business concern with the nature of the responsibilities of business toward the various publics with which a firm has relations.

Some viewers of business behavior are slightly skeptical about why managers cultivate social responsibility. It has been said that they are preaching the "Gospel of Social Responsibility" to justify their position of power in modern society and to fortify their image in addition to pro-moting new understanding of their place in society. Since, it is suggested, older business ideologies—which had the objective of relating certain attributes of business to some more commonly esteemed values so as to bestow honor upon business—were not in accord with the facts of mod-ern business, it became incumbent upon business to develop a new ideol-ogy to fill the ideological gap. What is in the minds of managers—as we have noted earlier—when they say and do certain things is difficult to determine, but there is probably something more to the "social respon-sibility movement" than an attempt to discover some new phrases that will somehow, through publicity, result in a favorable image.

Big business, especially, has learned the penalties accruing to behavior that important individuals and groups regard as irresponsible. The con-cern of the managers of many large organizations with the problem of social responsibilities seems genuine.

READING: Have Corporations a Higher Duty Than Profits? * by Fortune Magazine

Is a manager primarily responsible to society or to stockholders? New theories of corporate law and ethics abound, but should be warily examined. More often than not they conflict with the principles of a free-market economy.

Like any healthy institution, corporations change; but in the last few decades American corporations have changed so drastically as to raise the question of whether the old kind of corporation did not die to be replaced by a different

* Reprinted by permission from the August 1960 issue of *Fortune*.

institution under the same name. For in essence the old corporation was organized around an intention to make a profit for its shareholders. The modern corporation, although continuing to make profits, often *seems* to have other (some would say "higher") motives. To explain actual corporate behavior new definitions of management responsibility are being invented. For instance, Frank Abrams, the highly respected retired board chairman of Standard Oil of New Jersey, says: "The job of professional management is to conduct the affairs of the enterprise in its charge in such a way as to maintain an equitable and workable balance among the claims of the various directly interested groups—stockholders, employees, customers, and the public at large."

When a corporate manager shifts his focus of interest from profits to doing equity among groups of claimants, does he really improve his ethical position? Profits, at least, can be measured and they also form a way of measuring efficiency. Equity gives no clue to efficiency. A manager can *say* he is putting "fairness" or "the good of society" ahead of profits, but the suspicion arises that he is merely escaping from accountability into a realm where there are no checks upon his power. The old way of describing the manager's responsibility had at least the advantage of clarity: the manager's power came from a property right delegated to him for a specific purpose—profits; his scope was limited by this delegation and his performance could be tested in the market. In the new theory the manager is part of a self-perpetuating class, which appears in many lights to be superior to the group it replaced; but neither the legitimacy of its power, nor the limits, nor the tests of performance are clear.

Who cares, so long as it works? Quite a lot of thoughtful people have been concerned for thirty years about whether the corporation will continue to work well unless its managers and the rest of society have a clear and agreed-upon theory of the nature of their responsibility. Recently the discussion has taken on new impetus without, however, arriving at any solid consensus.

Three new books, *Power Without Property* by Adolf A. Berle Jr., *The Meaning of Modern Business* by Richard Eells, and *The Corporation in Modern Society*, a collection of essays edited by Edward S. Mason, professor of economics at Harvard, address themselves to such questions as: What justifies the corporation's power? What are its limits? To whom is it responsible? Within these books can be found the main lines of present discussion on how the corporation fits into legal and social theory. The principles in debate affect the day-to-day decisions of every business executive—whether he knows it or not—on problems ranging from investment to labor relations to plant locations. Moreover, the pervasive question of the relation of private enterprise to government may turn in the end on which theory of the corporation the U.S. accepts.

Splitting the Atom of Property.   The present debate over corporate responsibilities goes back to the publication in 1932 of *The Modern Corporation and Private Property* by Adolf A. Berle Jr. and Gardiner C. Means. At that time the authors noted a two-fold development, which was increasingly concentrating capital assets in the hands of salaried managers and depriving the stockholders of any effective control over their property. Thus, while a centrifugal force was dispersing ownership and thinning out the power of the individual stockholder, a centripetal force was bringing together great aggregations of wealth and bestowing economic power upon a new class of managers. Long before, the classical economists had shown that the capitalist, in seeking his private advantage in competitive markets, contributed indirectly to the public good. But the manager had no property interest in the capital he controlled, hence no claim on profits. At the same time, the concentration of economic means in his hands gave him power over prices and the ability to extort a disproportionate share of the consumer's income.

More recent statistical research has not borne out the thesis that industrial concentration is increasing. Berle himself is willing to admit that there has been no significant change in the ratio of concentration over the last fifty years. But his thesis concerning the separation of ownership from control is widely accepted today in one form or another. This has led Berle, in *Power Without Property*, to shift his ground and lay emphasis on absolute size and the fact of concentration itself, rather than the growth of concentration. Indeed, concentration and the absolute size of the business firm are formidable to contemplate. According to the *Fortune* directory of leading U.S. industrial corporations, the 500 biggest firms accounted last year for more than half the sales of all manufacturing and mining companies, and for over 70 per cent of the profits. The fifty biggest accounted for 28 per cent of all manufactured or mining output and 40 per cent of profits. This represents an enormous concentration of economic power in the hands of a small class of professional managers. They are presumed to be working for their more numerous but less influential stockholders. They are said to be freed from the constraints of the competitive market, and responsible to no one. "What Mr. Berle and most of the rest of us are afraid of," writes Mason, "is that this powerful corporate machine, which so successfully grinds out the goods we want, seems to be running without any discernible controls. The young lad mastering the technique of his bicycle may legitimately shout with pride, 'Look, Ma, no hands,' but is this the appropriate motto for a corporate society?"

The Financial Mix.   At least, one might argue, the corporate managers must assure a flow of profits to the stockholders high enough to facilitate additional financing and the flotation of new stock issues. But Berle points to the large proportion of new capital which is internally generated—that is, retained from earnings or drawn from depreciation allowance. Thus it would seem that corporations have become largely independent not only of the individual suppliers of risk capital but of the money markets controlled by large banks and other lending institutions.

Berle estimates that from 1947 to 1957 capital accumulated by corporations amounted to $292 billion, 60 per cent of which was internally financed, 20 per cent drawn from bank credit, and another 20 per cent from capital markets. But more than half of this last percentage was money handled by the investment staffs of insurance companies and pension trusts. Berle is of the opinion that only 5 per cent of the vast total capital accumulation was supplied from the voluntary savings of individuals.

Private Civil Servants.   The important new development, from the point of view of Berle's thesis, is the growth of pension trusts with large sums invested in common shares carrying voting rights. It is here that the "fission of property" becomes complete; for the beneficiary of the funds held in trust has no voice at all in the affairs of the corporation in which the trust owns stock. The fund trustees, who could exercise the voting rights to sway management, tend to go along with the incumbency or sell out. Nevertheless, the situation is appreciably changed. While the power of the individual stockholder continues to wane, there has been a reconcentration of common-stock holdings, and in the hands of institutional investors. Where power exists, Berle thinks, men will sooner or later use it:

"In point of present fact, trust fund custody is held by a dozen large banks and insurance companies. It would be easy to say that this handful of banks and insurance companies will wield the power nucleus looming over the economic horizon; certainly this is the best forward guess one can make. . . . A relatively small oligarchy of men operating in the same atmosphere, absorbing the same information, moving in the same circles and in a relatively small world, knowing each other, dealing with each other, and having more in common than in difference, will hold the reins. These men by hypothesis will have no ownership relation of any sort. They will be, essentially, non-statist civil servants—unless they abuse their power to make themselves something else."

Berle makes no recommendation to pass on the voting rights to the beneficiaries of the pension funds or to break up the actual or potential power in the hands of trustees. He tends to believe in some kind of mechanism of countervailance whereby power engenders its own limitation. The discretionary power for good or ill, now vested in corporate managers and shortly, if Berle is right, to be shared with fiduciary agents, will be limited by the moral restraints of what he calls the "public consensus," that body of settled moral principles of which public opinion is the fluctuating expression. Moreover, he believes that the boards of publicly held companies have already developed a "corporate conscience" and are primarily concerned with their good reputation in the business community and in the eyes of the public at large.

But Berle's argument does not stop at an appeal to moral principle. The public consensus is the breeding ground of "inchoate law"—the seeds of legal growth that may reach the stage of statutory enactment or administrative law. His final solution to the problem of concentrated economic power would be a national planning agency to coordinate the existing regulatory bodies. Berle does not think that the number of present government agencies needs to be greatly augmented, but their power should be extended in some cases and action should be taken in conjunction with institutions of business society. Thus the civil servants of the state would act in concert with the civil servants of the corporate bureaucracies.

The Other-Directed Corporation.   In *The Meaning of Modern Business* Richard Eells rounds up much material on corporate responsibility and kindred subjects and tries to build it around what he calls three models of the large-scale business enterprise: the "traditional corporation," the "metrocorporation," and the "well-tempered corporation." The first is an instrument for making money for its stockholders. Any moral obligations or social responsibilities it may assume flow from this primary imperative to make money. If its directors and managers assume a wide range of responsibilities, they do so because, under the circumstances, it is the most prudent policy for the corporation. On the other hand, the metrocorporation is a quasi-public body that mediates between the interests of a large number of "contributor-claimant" groups: security holders and customers, employees and suppliers, competitors, local communities, the general public, and governments. The well-tempered model is a mean between these two extremes, but it is hard to see how it differs from the metrocorporation, which Eells condemns. The only clear difference that *seems* to emerge is that, whereas the directors of the metrocorporation regard profits as secondary, for the well-tempered model they are still primary but relative to "coordinate" functions, such as "controlling the economic process," "participating in the governmental process," and "contributing to the cultural process." But this distinction turns out to be elusive, if not illusory. For it is impossible to attach a definite meaning to the expression "profits are secondary" or even to "profits are primary but coordinate with other functions." If profits are secondary, then they can *always* be sacrificed for the sake of fulfilling obligations that are primary; but since profits are an indispensable condition of the corporation's existence, this is tantamount to saying that the corporation can sacrifice its existence and at the same time fulfill its obligations to the community. Again, to say that profits are a primary function, coordinate with other functions, amounts to saying that these other functions are also primary and hence of equal importance. So what does the corporation do in the event of a conflict?

Eells's well-tempered corporation is nothing by David Riesman's "other-directed" personality writ large. "What is required," says Eells, "is a sensing operation in which the antennae are delicately attuned to many wave lengths and pointed in many directions. Investors, customers, suppliers, competitors are obvious groups from which incoming messages have to be assessed. But the *potential* suppliers of equity capital, goods, and services, the *potential* customers, the *potential* competitors, as well as the 'public at large' and especially its representatives in local, state, national, and international governments, are all extremely important sources of intelligence about the reputation of the company and its impact upon social institutions."

How the corporation is to introduce order into this babel of voices, Eells does not exactly say. With a multitude of voices demanding now this, now that, is it not more honest, and for that matter simpler, to do one's duty and steer by rational self-interest?

Abstaining from Profits.   Eugene V. Rostow, dean of the Yale Law School, obviously thinks that the old theory is preferable to the new. He writes in his contribution to *The Corporation in Modern Society*: "The law books have always said that the board of directors owes a single-minded duty of unswerving loyalty to the stockholders, and only to the stockholders. The economist has demonstrated with all the apparent precision of plane geometry and the calculus that the quest for maximum revenue in a competitive market leads to a system of prices, and an allocation of resources and rewards, superior to any alternative, in its contributions to the economic welfare of the community as a whole. To the orthodox mind, it is therefore unsettling, to say the least, to have the respected head of the Standard Oil Co. of New Jersey (he means Frank Abrams) equating the management's duty to stockholders with its obligations to employees, customers, suppliers, and the public at large."

Rostow's argument turns, of course, on the key term, "competitive market." Writers like Berle and Eells think this term is largely inapplicable to the present capitalist economy in America. They contend that capitalism has entered a new phase, and under conditions incompatible with the classical assumptions of Adam Smith and Ricardo. It is true that in markets where there are many traders, or at least to which many traders have easy access, the forces of competition will bring prices down to a point where they just cover costs and thus eliminate monopoly profits. And to be sure, in oligopolistic markets, where one big company exercises price leadership, it is possible that profits may represent an extortionate levy on the consumer's purchasing power. The question of whether or not corporations should assume social responsibilities and become arbiters of social justice largely resolves itself into a question about the effective functioning of the market mechanism. If the market is functioning and regulating the flow of income to different functional classes within society, then attempts to find an equitable distribution, based on a notion of just prices, wages, and profits, can only wreck the mechanism. And this is Rostow's view of the present situation. "If, as is widely thought, the essence of corporate statesmanship is to seek less than maximum profits, postwar experience is eloquent evidence that such statesmanship leads to serious malfunctioning of the economy as a whole."

Rostow is arguing there that the market will regulate the flow of income to different groups, and that modern corporate "statesmanship" is attempting to reroute funds against the current. No doubt if capital does move in response to changes in the structure of relative prices, then a policy of holding prices down, motivated by public benevolence or whatever, can lead to misallocation of resources and widespread diseconomy. The question then is: to what extent is the rate of investment actually sensitive to changes in prices and resultant profits?

The Invisible Hand of Oligopoly. There is some evidence that oligopolistic markets are allocating resources with tolerable efficiency. Numerous buyers and sellers, acting independently, are but one criterion of competitive performance. Free entry into markets and the fact that capital, labor, and other resources actually do move into areas where profits are highest indicate that the economy is still performing in a relatively healthy manner. And this would seem to be the case in many industrial sectors dominated by oligopoly. John Lintner sums up the latest findings in his contribution to *The Corporation in Modern Society:* "An impressive recent study (*The Investment Decision* by John R. Meyer and Edwin Kuh) investigated the factors determining the plant and equipment expenditures of approximately 700 firms in the early postwar period. The study included virtually all the companies, large and small, listed with the Securities and Exchange Commission, in seventeen different manufacturing industries accounting for the bulk of plant and equipment expenditures in all manufacturing. The authors found that the rate of profitability, the level of sales, and the degree of pressure of sales upon current capacity were uniformly the most important factors determining the current rate of investment outlays among these firms—we may add, just as would be expected, if market mechanisms were functioning efficiently. . . . Other things being the same, the amount of new investment was not only correlated with profitability and increasing sales, but the reliance on the financial markets for outside capital was also closely associated with the rate of growth of the firm."

This evidence that the market still does its work should not incline us, however, to assume that there is no danger from oligopoly. Antitrust prosecutions, or the threat thereof, are needed to spur competitive performance. But even if our markets worked less well than they do, we should beware of any shift in fundamental theory that would assign either to corporation managers or to government the functions now assigned to the market. Once we subordinate the market, either a businessman must become a public official or a public official must become a businessman. Either way, the principle of a division of labor between government and market will be violated. From this point of view, managerialism is the worst solution of all; for it is highly repugnant that a corporate manager, not publicly elected and hence not subject to popular recall, should have a special responsibility for what the managerialists call the process of government. At least a socialist government can be defeated at the polls.

Longevity Is the Key.   But to reject modern theories of managerialism does not give us what we need: A theory that covers the actual contemporary behavior of corporate management and is at the same time compatible with our economic and political principles. The old theory that a corporation is organized around profits for stockholders will serve, provided it is properly understood. A clue may be contained in one of the earliest and most famous statements about the corporation. In 1612, Lord Coke observed that it "is not subject to imbecilities or death of the natural body or various other cases." The corporation is not immortal, but it frequently outlives those who at any given time are its masters. The implications of this peculiarity were obscured in the days when the corporation existed in a business world dominated by flesh-and-blood traders. In such a world the corporation was thought of as another "person," an agent who happened to have a special legal form. In the twentieth century, when the corporation has become the dominant and almost the only business unit, its true characteristics have become more apparent. Men see that their corporate creature has a great potential for expansion—or rather projection—along the line of time. No longer is corporate effort concentrated on expansion in "space," meaning *this year's* profits, *this year's* volume of sales, *this year's* share of the market. The modern businessman is interested not only in current yields but also in the more remote prospects of profitability. His strategy is to make inroads into the uncertainty of the future by combining alternatives, spreading risks, fostering the good repute of his organization. Peter Drucker, a leading exponent of managerialism, feels that economists have not taken into account this shift of business horizons, and that, influenced by Ricardo, they have conceived the capitalist too narrowly on the analogy of the stockjobber: "Ricardo was a London stockjobber, and he built his system in that image. No other vocation could have furnished so pure a model of 'economic man in the market.' The stockjobber works without employees and without organization. The time element does not enter into his activity. He turns over his entire capital immediately; for the first rule of the stockjobber's profession is to clear the books and liquidate all positions every day. Every morning, therefore, the stockjobber starts business anew, as it were from scratch. Every evening he liquidates his business completely. His is an almost timeless world—very much like the universe of the Newtonian physicists."

Starving the Stockholders.   Compared with such primitive forms of economic endeavor, the corporate capitalist enterprise has always been characterized by continuity of operations and long-range calculations. The modern businessman, as opposed to the capitalist adventurer of the mercantile period, seeks to make profits by methods of continuous application and constant increment. He does not necessarily seek "the big quick profit," insofar as such behavior implies a ruthless treatment of persons and resources. But he does, if he is rational, try to augment the total mass of profits over an extended period, and he may be willing to "sacrifice" current yields to this end.

One of the grievances of stockholders is that management is always plowing profits back into the business and not giving them their "fair" share. To defend himself against this charge, the businessman need not invoke some as yet unformulated rule of justice when the rule of long-term profit maximization will do perfectly well. If he adheres to this formula, he will have some basis for deciding what part of profits to reinvest and what to distribute to the stockholders. In fact, modern managers every day make some sacrifice of present gain for the sake of future advantages and the stockholders are not hurt because this emphasis on the future enhances the value of their investment and its liquidity.

A manager who pays labor more than he "must" may be able to justify that course by his concern for the company's future far more rationally than if he says he is giving labor a "fair" share.

Frank Abrams is one of those who use *both* theories to explain modern corporate practices. Sometimes he speaks as if the main role of management is to do justice between the competing claims of stockholders and other groups. Sometimes he seems to take the view that a long-range concern for profits is enough to guide the managers. We suggest that the second view is the right one and that it makes the first unnecessary.

The difference between the two views has an important bearing on the great discussion of twentieth-century political economy, an argument turning on the questions: Shall private business function in a free market within a broad framework of law? Or shall business be deemed an instrument through which the state attempts to replace the market and allocate goods in accordance with the state's idea of what various groups of citizens ought to have?

SUGGESTED READINGS

Selekman, Benjamin M., *A Moral Philosophy for Management* (New York: McGraw-Hill, 1959). A professor at the Harvard Business School shows how the businessman faces a constant dilemma—to keep his business efficient and profitable on the one hand, and on the other hand to see that it squares with the concepts of traditional morality and American democracy.

Bursk, Edward C., ed., *Business and Religion: A New Depth Dimension in Management* (New York: Harper & Row, 1959). Twelve distinguished business executives, teachers, and theologians provide "insights on ways to realize ethical ideals in the business world."

Bowen, Howard R., *Social Responsibilities of the Businessman* (New York: Harper, 1953). A college president (and former economics professor) urges certain responsibilities upon businessmen and suggests that certain tangible benefits will result from the acceptance of those responsibilities by top business leaders.

Fenn, Jr., Dan H., ed., *Business Responsibility in Action* (New York: McGraw-Hill, 1960). A collection of discussions of quite specific responsibilities of business stemming from a national conference of businessmen at the Harvard Business School.

PART III

The Political Environment of Business

CHAPTER 23

THE POLITICAL
ENVIRONMENT
OF BUSINESS

With the passing of every year, American business seems to have a greater number of increasingly complex relationships with government. At local, state, national, and even international levels, new agencies and officials come into existence and exercise some influence on the conduct of business firms in the United States. Not all such influences, of course, are adverse. Governments are promoting business as well as regulating it, taxing it, buying from it, selling to it, and competing with it. Administrative agencies and officials operate under the laws establishing them, and those statutes which have later become their responsibility. The laws, in turn, are established under the constitution or other organic act creating the governmental unit in question. Most laws and all constitutions are drafted by representative bodies, although in some parts of the United States, "direct democracy" results in the passage of laws through referendums submitted to the citizens within a particular area.

Where representative political institutions prevail, the tendency has been for various groups interested in the passage of certain legislation to play an active part in the elective and legislative processes. After laws are passed, the interested groups attempt to influence those engaged in the administrative process to interpret the legislation in a favorable fashion. Where little success has been had by an interested party in influencing elections, legislation, or the administration of a law, the courts are sometimes looked to in the hope that the judicial process will provide some relief, or at least delay the enforcement of a law. Business interest groups frequently find themselves in the political arena with some of the economic and social groups we have previously discussed, and the result of the striving of official and nonofficial groups for various goals determines the nature of the governmental influences on business at any particular moment.

GOVERNMENT RELATIONS WITH BUSINESS

When the relations that business firms have with government are discussed, government regulation, taxation, and competition receive the greater part of attention. Although these are certainly important influences, the role of government as promoter of business should not be ignored. Without certain governmental services, American business as we know it today could not exist. Government agencies and officials, operating under various laws, also make substantial purchases from business, grant subsidies to it, and make special concessions—such as tax concessions—to it. Such promotion of business is as old as the Constitution, and it has been only within the last century that government regulation and competition have become important. Finally, governmental agencies sometimes sell goods or services necessary to the operation of certain firms.

Government Promotion of Business

All firms receive certain services from the governmental units in the area in which they are located. The institution of private property on which our business system rests would have little meaning if it were not protected by the courts and law enforcement officials. State and local governments spend large portions of their budgets on streets and high-ways, which are of benefit to merchants, manufacturers, and other busi-nessmen. Expenditures for education provide firms with literate and trained work forces. The spending of the federal government on defense is so great that not only firms but entire industries are dependent for their life on that spending. Without subsidies received from governments, some firms and industries could not have come into existence and they could not continue to exist without loss except for continuing aid. It is true, of course, that business firms pay taxes, but many of them pay considerably less than the cost of services and subsidies received, while some pay more. The growth of business taxes, especially those levied by the federal government, has been so great in this century as to be a matter of con-siderable influence upon firms.

Government Taxation of Business

As state and then federal government grew in importance relative to local government, so did their taxes on business. The reliance of local governments on taxation of real estate and personal property has long been important to businessmen whose investments in land, plant, equip-ment, and inventories are quite substantial. State taxes on business took on added significance with the development of the corporate form of enterprise. In this century, the corporation income tax of the federal government has overshadowed all other types of business taxation, with larger corporations at one time paying over one half of their net profits to the U.S. Treasury. The federal government has levied other important business taxes, including duties on imports and excises on certain manu-factured products. For some firms, the tax laws and the way in which they are administered can mean the difference between success and failure. It is small wonder, then, that businessmen are much concerned with this aspect of their relations with government.

Government Regulation of Business

Governments prohibit certain kinds of business firms and business acts and regulate others. Perhaps the most striking illustration of prohibition was that forbidding the manufacture and distribution of alcoholic bev-erages during the twenties and early thirties. That is in the past, but it is still illegal to engage in certain kinds of business—the distribution of narcotics by those not in the "ethical drug" industry provides a current example. Even where governments permit certain types of industry to exist, certain practices—such as "unfair labor practices" and "unfair trade practices"—are outlawed. Although there is a host of prohibitions in laws affecting business, they are greatly overshadowed by the restrictions placed on business in doing what it may legally do.

There is no industry in the United States that is not regulated in some way by some governmental agency. This governmental regulation is so great in some instances that the industry feels it is being "strangled to death" by it—an attitude that prevails in the railroad industry, for example. Common carriers, communication firms, combinations, business practices, prices and pricing practices, production, banking, and reorganization are among the industries and business activities that come under regulation by local, state, and federal government. To catalog the range of regulatory activities is beyond the scope of this book. Our purpose is to examine what lies behind the regulatory and other governmental activities as they apply to business.

Commercial and Competitive Relations

Earlier we made note of the importance of American governments as purchasers of the final products of the national economy. Many firms, and even entire industries, depend for their sales, profits, and very existence upon such purchasing. All government expenditures are not for final products, however, and certain resources—especially money and labor—are purchased by governments for use in their productive activities. Governments are important sellers as well as buyers. Although some final products are sold, the bulk of government sales (if we do not regard services "paid for" through taxes as part of such sales) have been of natural resources, commodities that have been stockpiled, and the products of "public utility" enterprises—mainly water and electricity.

Government buying and selling inevitably put it into competition with some private business firms, but other activities also create competitive relationships. The federal government is a big buyer of certain agricultural commodities under its price-support programs. This, of course, raises the price to some firms. Other commodities are also bought in large quantity, affecting their availability as well as their price. Governments as employers compete with business for certain kinds of labor. In the money markets, government agencies compete for loanable funds. Government purchases of plant and equipment are also made in competition with firms. The federal and state governments have been in the "land business" for years, and though not many sales are currently made of government lands, these properties are sometimes leased and timber and mineral rights sold. Some of the buying and selling activities conducted by government are intended to provide competition with business, as in the case of those hydroelectric installations that are intended to serve as "yardsticks" to measure the performance of private electric companies and to keep private rates "competitive." These commercial and competitive relations of governments to business have been growing in importance; we shall give them further examination when dealing with various levels of American government.

Government Relations Are Social Relations

The businessman does not deal with that metaphysical creature, "The State." He has relationships with individuals and groups occupying official positions who act in the name of the state and possess governmental power. The objectives of his firm and industry are promoted by officials in certain governmental departments—those who provide useful information, those who make loans or give subsidies to business, and those who render other services helpful to the businessman. Tax assessors, tax collectors, and other tax administrators are flesh-and-blood persons. Members of regulatory bodies are also human. The significance of the fact that business has dealings with humans in governmental positions rather than with an impersonal "State" lies in the recognition that all individuals have certain attitudes, values, objectives, and resources. Coming to terms with government means coming to terms with people who are capable of being influenced as well as capable of influencing business.

GOVERNMENT OFFICIALS

Government officials are persons either elected or appointed to offices in the local, state, or federal government. Traditionally, a distinction has been made among them according to the functions they perform. The main branches of government are the legislative (law-making), executive (law-administering) and judicial (law-enforcing). In practice, there is considerable overlap of these functions in many governmental offices, especially in those nominally administrative. The President of the United States, known also as the Chief Executive (administrator) of laws passed by Congress, has also been referred to as the "Chief Legislator," since he represents all the people of the nation, makes proposals as to what laws should be passed, and has the power to veto legislation he does not approve. Many administrative agencies have been referred to as "quasi-judicial" because they conduct investigations much as judges do, make decisions as to the legality of certain acts, and issue orders to enforce their rulings. Those officials of greatest importance to business and the ways in which they operate will be dealt with in some detail in following chapters. Since they have the power of the government behind their actions with respect to businessmen, their objectives—both those contained in the law and their personal goals—are of considerable importance.

Because those who make laws, administer them, and enforce them are either elected or appointed by elected officials, it is necessary to understand the nature of the elective process. A realistic examination of this process shows that those elected are supported by certain groups who feel they will gain most by the election of a particular candidate. Since those who are elected to office are, for the most part, realistic politicians, they appoint or concur in the appointment of appointive officials who are satisfactory to the groups on whose support the elected officials rest. These groups are not limited to political groups, but extend to a host of economic and social groups, some of which we have already examined.

Administrative Officials

When government influences business, its point of contact with the businessman usually is the administrative official. It is little wonder that those businessmen who are affected adversely by government speak disparagingly of the "bureaucrats" who tie them up in the "red tape" of administrative procedures. However, it is true that government administrators cannot proceed arbitrarily against business firms. They must do so in accordance with the law and the rules and regulations established for the conduct of an agency. The decisions they make are not the result of a slot-machine process in which information is fed into the agency and a decision is automatically issued; they are in the nature of interpretations of laws, rules, and regulations. The interpretation made in any particular case reflects not only the facts and the rules, but also the attitudes of the administrator plus whatever pressures are brought to bear on the official by various interested parties. Consequently, the range of action open to the businessman who wishes to influence administration stretches beyond changing the law. Businessmen who do not like certain administrative decisions can press for a change in the administration, for a change in the rules and regulations adopted by an agency, or for a change in a decision. If the official is elected, his defeat in forthcoming elections may be sought; if he is appointed, pressure may be brought to bear on the appointing official to secure the resignation of the unsatisfactory (from the businessman's standpoint) officer. Getting rules and regulations changed is a difficult process, but sufficient political pressure can bring about a change (which is easier to accomplish than changing the law). Perhaps the easiest change to bring about is a change in a particular decision, and if presentation of facts do not bring about the desired decision, political pressure may. Proceeding against an administrator, rules and regulations, and particular decisions is not always the most satisfactory or permanent way of securing favorable decisions and, consequently, seeking changes in the law under which agencies operate is important.

Legislative Officials

As we have noted, laws under which administrators operate are normally made by elected representatives. Whether serving in town board, city council, county commission, state assembly or Congress, the elected legislator holds office because his views are satisfactory to a sufficiently large number of groups in his constituency. If he does not understand who his supporters are or what they want, or if he acts too independently of their desires, he will probably lose his post. According to the major exponent of this view, in the legislative process:

> The legislature referees the group struggle, ratifies the victories of the successful coalitions, and records the terms of the surrenders, compromises and conquests in the form of statutes. Every statute tends to represent compromise because the process of accommodating conflicts of group interest is one of deliberation and consent. The legislative vote on any issue tends to represent the composition of strength, i.e., the balance of power, among the contending groups at the moment of voting. What may be called public policy is the equilibrium reached in this struggle at any given moment, and it represents a balance which the contending factions of groups constantly strive to weight in their favor.[1]

If this view of the legislative process is realistic, then there are a number of implications in it for businessmen confronted with laws they regard as undesirable. When legislation is pending, business interest groups might form coalitions among themselves and whatever other groups would like to see the law develop in a certain fashion and attempt to secure the balance of power. When laws are already on the statute books, such a coalition might bring about a change in the law by having friendly legislators introduce measures to effect a change and then attempt to influence a majority of lawmakers to vote for them. If a legislator is unwilling to vote the "right" way, his removal from the legislative body at the next election may be sought by business groups.

When laws are the product of "direct democracy," as through the initiative and referendum process, then business groups—if they wish to influence law—must attempt to influence the electorate directly.

[1] Earl Latham, *The Group Basis of Politics* (Ithaca, N.Y.: Cornell U.P., 1952), pp. 35–36.

Judicial Officials

In some respects judges perform functions similar to administrative functions, but in other ways they make laws. As do officials in the executive departments, judges have certain evidence presented to them; they weigh the evidence and make some decision according to a rule of law either established by a legislative body or by precedent. Since judges have some leeway in interpreting laws, and have even been known to overthrow statutes as unconstitutional or to make decisions contrary to established precedents, they play a role in making the law as well as administering it.

Judges are also subject to some group pressures, although perhaps to a lesser degree than administrative officials or legislators. Where judges are appointed for life terms, they require no group support for continuance in office, except in the rare circumstances when their impeachment is sought. However, since they are appointed and confirmed by elected officials, group pressures do influence to some degree who will secure a lifetime appointment. If judges are elected, then their decisions must be pleasing to the groups supporting them if they wish to continue in office. When business groups are dissatisfied with judicial decisions, they sometimes find the same alternatives open to them as when they are dissatisfied with an administrative decision or with the decision of a legislative body. However, they have still another very important recourse. They can seek to change a decision of a lower court, or to delay a final judicial decision or the implementation of such a decision by availing themselves of the appeals procedure provided in American courts.

NONOFFICIAL INDIVIDUALS AND GROUPS

In the political arena, there are individuals and groups who have no official status but who, nonetheless, are intent on and capable of influencing public policy and its administration. Many of these we have already examined, pointing out that some of their influence on business firms stems from political action. Business itself plays a prominent part. Some firms have their own spokesmen, while others rely on trade associations and general business organizations. Labor unions, farm groups, and even some organizations of consumers employ whatever political resources they have to influence the outcome of legislative, administrative, and judicial decisions. There remains one important class of nonofficial individuals and groups to be discussed: politicians and political parties.

There is no mention of political parties in the U.S. Constitution; rather it appears to establish a structure of government in which partisan politics has no place. However, it has long been recognized by practical men that organization is an important resource by which various objectives can be secured; and shortly after the adoption of the Constitution in 1789, political parties appeared on the scene.

The existence of partisan politics in the U.S. poses a perplexing problem for business firms. Favors can be expected if the party a businessman or firm supports holds public office; however, if it is out of office and the businessman or firm is strongly identified with it, governmental favor might be withheld. Some practical businessmen—such as John Jacob Astor—solved the problem by being friendly with both major parties. In any event, a firm must decide upon some policy because politicians continually confront businessmen with requests for support, explicitly or implicitly suggesting that contributions of time, money, and so on, will gain the firm some of its desired objectives.

THEORIES OF POLITICS

Political theorists have attempted to explain why governments do what they do. A number of theories are alleged to explain the American political process, and the businessman must select one (or perhaps develop his own) that seems best to explain that process. In the preceding discussion in this chapter (and throughout this book) we have adopted what has been termed "realist political theory."

"Realist Political Theory"

The "realists" do not believe that such things as "the public will" or "the public interest" exist. Instead, they believe in the existence of a number of public wills and public interests (although, since these are the interests of special publics rather than that of the public as a whole, they may be—and are—referred to as "special interests"). The function of government, according to those supporting this political theory, is to provide some means by which these "publics" can gain access to agencies and officials and to provide for harmonious adjustment of conflicts among their interests. In other words, the function of government is to provide "public harmony," that is, "the continuous readjustment of conflicting interests, with a minimum of disturbance of existing equilibria." Legislators are regarded as spokesmen for dominant constituency and pressure-group interests, performing mediatory functions and also acting as a kind of interest group. The judiciary and political parties are seen as performing essentially the same function as legislators, while administrators, including the Chief Executive, act as catalysts through which conflict among special interests is transformed into the public interest.

Some of the leading proponents of "realist" theory stress the importance of groups almost to the point of excluding individuals as being of any consequence in the political process. Earl Latham, in his book *The Group Basis of Politics,* sees policy as emerging out of the struggle of groups. However, the difference between such a view and one that sees public policy as being determined by the interaction of individuals and groups is more apparent than real. The difference is chiefly in the definition of *group;* we have been using the term to refer to an organization, whereas Latham and others espousing a group theory of politics include both individuals and organizations within their definition of *group* (while we have used the term *class* instead). In any event, realistic theorists recognize the importance of individuals such as the President of the U.S., governors of states, and so on.

"Realists" conceive of public policy as being a "resultant" of the influences exerted by special-interests groups. In Chapter 3, we suggested the utility of such an idea for explaining business policy as well (noting that it had been adopted from students of public policy). One writer has conceived of the political process as being analagous to the play of mechanical forces: "Were it possible to plot pressure groups objectively as parallelograms of forces and compute the resultant, significant predictions might be made not only as to what party platforms are likely to be, which parties will win, but also as to significant trends in public policy." [2] The practical significance for business behavior of adopting this view is the implication that businessmen, if they wish to attain a certain result, must exert a certain amount of influence in the "right" direction, must gain the support of other influential individuals and groups so that they also will exert their influence in the same direction, and must try to minimize the influence of those exerting pressure in the "wrong" direction.

The products of interaction among individuals and groups in the political arena are manifold. The very structure of American government has been determined in this way, with a number of works having been written about the U.S. Constitution as the product of individuals and groups representing certain economic interests. State constitutions, statutes, administratively determined rules and regulations, decisions of administrators and judges—in short, all the rules governing relationships among individuals and groups are determined by this process. Political parties, party platforms, and who holds office in political parties and the

---

[2] H. L. Childs, "Pressure Groups and Propaganda," in *The American Political Scene,* edited by E. B. Logan (New York: Harper, 1936), p. 225.

government are likewise products of such interactions. If this view of the political process in American life is indeed realistic, its adoption should be urged; however, we should note the existence of some competing views.

"Rationalist Political Theory"

Some commentators on the political scene in America subscribe to a "rationalist" theory of the political process. They conceive of the existence of a "Public" and a "Public Will." Believing the ultimate source of public-policy goals to repose in the people (the Public), they regard it as being in the public interest to "rationalize" governmental decision-making processes so that they will result in the carrying out of the Public Will. Such a "rational" political process would include the following elements: the organization of political parties that would concern themselves with defining the Public Will (those most successful in so doing would see their candidates elected to public office); legislatures, whose membership would in the main be composed of members of that political party best understanding the Public Will, would then translate the Public Will into law; the Chief Executive, also a member of that party, would oversee the faithful execution of the law; and, the Courts, dominated by members of the majority party either through election or appointment, would enforce the law.

This view is "unrealistic" in more ways than one. Certainly, it does not seem to explain the facts of American political life. It suggests no course of action to the business firm that wishes to influence its political environment other than to attempt to influence public opinion—one of the less effective measures that might be taken, according to studies dealing with political action by business. Even so, the "rationalists" are more realistic than the "idealists."

"Idealist Political Theory"

The "idealists" view the public as an inadequate, incompetent source of public policy. Rather than the "Public Will," it is "Natural Law" that should govern decision-making by legislators, chief executives, administrators, and judges. Political parties have no place in their scheme of things, since they, as well as special-interest groups, bring pressure to bear on the decision-makers, who should be guided only by the natural law in serving the public interest. How the "Natural Law" is to be discovered indicates that some doubt exists as to its nature—that is, it is proposed that officials, since they have some personal discretion in decision-making, should consult this higher law which is, apparently, found only in the conscience of the official. Ideally, the "idealists" say, we should expand the scope of official discretion and the proportion of elected officials. What this assumes is that the public—although an inadequate, incompetent source of policy—will, in its wisdom, elect officials who, dedicated to the "public good" and guided by the "Natural Law," will be able, as George Washington was alleged to have been able to do, to rise above political party and the pressures of special-interest groups and represent all of the people. Thus we will have a highly moral official world, populated by "the Independent Congressman, the Strong President, the Good Administrator and the Wise Judge." Such "Philosopher Kings" will serve the "public interest."

It is not seriously suggested by the idealists that this is the kind of political system we have—rather, it is an ideal we should aspire to. On occasion, political figures and those commenting on public affairs will employ the language of the idealists, but when they do we can quite realistically suspect that they are doing so to promote their special interests. In any case, some implications this theory has for the political behavior of businessmen are that they are not to join special-interest groups or support political parties—advice business would be wise not to heed, given the nature of the real political environment.

In the following chapters, we shall deal in greater detail with the interrelations between business and various aspects of its political environment. First, we shall deal with the U.S. Constitution and the role it plays in such relationships; then, we shall discuss the kinds of laws of importance to business that the Constitution permits. Since the roles of federal, state, and local governments are somewhat different under our governmental structure—as set forth in the Constitution and state constitutions—we shall examine those agencies and officials of major significance to businessmen at each level of American government. Increasingly, businessmen in the United States are affected by foreign and international governments; therefore, a chapter will also be devoted to agreements, agencies, and officials on the world economic scene. Legislators, administrators, and judges tend to proceed in much the same way, regardless of the level of government, and since understanding these political processes gives the businessman not only some knowledge of how government acts with respect to business but also of the role that business plays in these processes, we shall examine the legislative process, administrative process, and judicial process. In conclusion, the question will be raised as to what the political responsibilities of business are in the light of the political environment that confronts businessmen, firms, industries, and the business system as a whole.

READING: The Political Process * by Earl Latham

The struggle of groups to survive in their environments and to carry forward the aims and interests of the members, if entirely uninhibited, would produce violence and war. Social disapproval of most of the forms of direct action reduces this struggle to an effort to write the rules by which groups live with each other and according to which they will compete for existence and advantage. . . . As groups come to put away gross forms of coercion in their dealings with each other, by equal degree the area widens within which the behaviors of each are subject to codification by rules. The struggle for advantage, for benefits for the group, for the self-expression and security of their members tends then to concentrate upon the writing of these rules to the advantage of the parties-in-interest. These rules take the form of statutes, administrative orders and decrees, rules and interpretations, and court judgments.

We come then to the apparatus of the state which, through its manifold offices—legislatures, councils, agencies, departments, courts and other forums—maintains a system of instrumentalities for the writing and enforcement of the formal rules by which society is governed. But all of these instrumentalities are themselves groups and they possess a sense of group belonging and identification which is very strong. . . . It is a part of the political consensus—the understood and agreed conditions of life in a civil society—that certain groups will be permitted to act in unilateral relations with others. Such groups are distinguished from others only in their possession of the characteristic of officiality. The designation "official" is the sign manifest that the bearer is authorized by social understanding to exercise against all groups and individuals certain powers which they may not exercise against him.

The principal function of official groups is to provide various levels of compromise in the writing of the rules within the body of agreed principles that forms the consensus upon which the political community rests. This is the role they play in the restless flux of effort on the part of groups to dominate, neutralize or conciliate the environment in which they seek to survive.

The legislature referees the group struggle, ratifies the victories of the successful coalitions, and records the terms of the surrenders, compromises, and conquests in the form of statutes. Every statute tends to represent compromise because the process of accommodating conflicts of group interest is one of deliberation and consent. The legislative vote on any issue tends to represent the composition of strength; i.e., the balance of power, among the contending groups at the moment of voting. What may be called public policy is the equilibrium reached in this struggle at any given moment, and it represents a balance which the contending factions of groups constantly strive to weight in their favor.

* *Excerpted from:* Chapters I and VI of *The Group Basis of Politics* by Earl Latham. Copyright 1952, by Cornell University. Used by permission of Cornell University Press.

In this process, it is clear that blocs of groups can be defeated. In fact they can be routed. Such groups do not possess a veto on the proposals and acts that affect them. What they do possess when they are defeated is the right to make new combinations of strength if they are able to do so, combinations which will support a new effort to rewrite the rules in their favor.

In these adjustments of group interest, the legislature does not play the inert part of cash register, ringing up the additions and withdrawals of strength, a mindless balance pointing and marking the weight and distribution of power among the contending groups. For legislatures are groups also and show a sense of identity and consciousness of kind that unofficial groups must regard if they are to represent their members effectively. In fact, the two houses of Congress have a conscious identity of special "house" interest and a joint interest against the executive establishment. . . . the dignity of a Congressman is an expression of his official group interest, and it cannot be invaded lightly. Legislators have to be approached with a certain amount of deference and tact; they may be pressured, but some forms of pressure will be regarded as too gross. . . . A Congressman, like men everywhere, comes to his position carrying in his mind a mixture of ideas, principles, prejudices, programs, precepts, beliefs, slogans, and preachments. If he mistakes the pattern of his support or acts too independently of its desire, he may lose his seat, as some Congressmen have, after only one term.

The function of the bureaucrat in the group struggle is somewhat different from that of the legislator. Administrative agencies of the regulatory kind are established to carry out the terms of the treaties that the legislators have negotiated and ratified. The administrative agency of the regulatory kind is like an army of occupation left in the field to police the rule won by the victorious coalition. . . . The defeated coalition of groups, however, does not cease to strive to wring interpretations favorable to it from the treaties that verbalize its defeats. Expensive legal talent is employed to squeeze every advantage which wit and verbal magic can twist out of the cold prose of official papers. The regulatory agencies are constantly besought and importuned to interpret their authorities in favor of those for the regulation of whom they were originally granted. Nor do the losing coalitions of groups confine their fight against unfavorable rules to the bureaucrats appointed to administer them. They constantly seek to rewrite the rules in their favor through compliant legislators. Where the balance of power is precarious, the law will remain unsettled until the balance is made stable.

The function of the judge is not unlike that of the bureaucrat, for the judiciary, like the civilian bureaucracy, is one of the instrumentalities for the administration of agreed-on rules. But the responsibility rests with the judge more than with either the legislator or the bureaucrat to develop a more or less objective system out of statutes, administrative decrees and the causes of private clients (according to Cardozo, the function of the judge is creative and original in those many interstices of the law left vacant by the statutes and administrative decrees). The judiciary is superior to the bureaucracy in performing this important and fateful task, and it is in this superiority that its distinguishing characteristic lies. All other distinctions (procedural mainly) between the judges and the bureaucrats are secondary.

In the small universe of official groups the same phenomena of struggle for self-expression and security take place that may be witnessed in the various nonstate communities of society. In fact, some interesting variants are thrust into the entire political process by the state of rivalry which often characterizes the relationships among the official groups. . . .

Congress is traditionally suspicious of the President and historically has sought to dominate the executive establishment. . . .

It has been pointed out that overlapping but different combinations of economic groups are marshaled behind the President and Congress. . . . The rivalry between Congress and the executive establishment would be natural and expected because of the group interest of each of these sets of functionaries, but the struggle is exacerbated by the support that each of the contestants is given by alliances and coalitions of groups whose interests are at stake in the outcome. The leverage in this contest is with Congress.

The rivalry between the judiciary and the executive has sometimes emerged in spectacular form as in the duel between Jefferson and Marshall or F.D.R. and the Supreme Court before 1938 . . . but the most enduring struggle has really taken place below the surface of public events and out of the public gaze in the silent war waged by the judiciary against the regulatory agencies. The chief characteristic of the regulatory agency of the quasi-judicial kind is that it combines in one instrumentality the legislative, the executive and the judicial powers.

It might be mentioned that even with the structure of official agencies in one branch of the federal government, competition of group interest takes place. . . . (Army, Navy and Air Force rivalry is an outstanding example.) State departments of health are often in conflict with state departments of industry over matters which fall within the jurisdiction of both. In states with unintegrated state administrations—where the chief administrative officers are elected by voters—the attorney general may frequently be at odds with the governor whose office he covets. Legislative committees may contest for jurisdiction of certain bills. The vital position held by committees in the legislative processes of Congress intensifies the efforts of partisans in the group struggle to get their favored view before the committee with the power of life and death over legislation. Even within departments and bureaus, subgroups form and contest with one another.

The group struggle, therefore, is apparent in the universe of unofficial groups and it is apparent in the universe of official groups. But these are not separate universes. They are one. Official groups are inhabitants of one pluralistic world. That world is an aggregation, a collection, an assemblage, a throng, a moving multitude of human clusters, a consociation of groups, a plurality of collectivities, an intersecting series of social organisms, adhering, interpenetrating, overlapping —a single universe of groups which combine, break, federate, and form coalitions and constellations of power in a flux of restless alterations.

Official groups, because of their officiality, have a leverage in many group situations which makes them valuable allies and stern foes. Before 1937, for example, business groups could combine with courts (i.e., judicial groups) to defeat combinations of other official groups such as presidents, Congressmen, and administrators. . . . the new judges now reflect more closely the aspirations of the new groups that came to power in 1933—the farmer, the small businessman, the industrial worker, the consumer, the aged, the buyers and holders of securities, and so on. . . .

Since 1937, a new alliance has been formed between Congressmen and economic minorities, an alliance which sometimes circumvents the judges. It was such a combination which temporarily set aside the Supreme Court decision which brought insurance companies under the antitrust laws by reversing sixty years of precedent. . . . Much less has been heard of the finality of Supreme Court announcements since 1937, although the traditional respect for the independence of the judges is strong, and the advocates of legislation to reverse the judges proceed with some caution toward their goals. In any event, the judges, including the members of the Supreme Court, would seem more clearly since the New Deal to perform the function which they performed before the New Deal, namely, that of serving as one more level of official compromise in the never-ending march and counter-march, thrust and parry, among economic groups, enforcement agencies, legislators, and executive functionaries. If the Supreme Court is not now looked upon by business groups with the same friendly eye as heretofore, it is because the judges for the first time in the history of the Court are less conservative than Congressmen.

A summary view of the struggle over S. 1008 shows policy emerging as a by-product of group actions and interactions. The congressional phase was set in motion by the Cement Case of 1948. In this case, the F.T.C. had successfully appealed to the Supreme Court to sustain the Commission order requiring the Cement Institute to dissolve. The character of the Cement Institute as a structure of power in its internal organization and its external relations was well documented by the Commission in its findings. Industrial groups, like the steel and oil companies and the cement interests, believing themselves to be adversely affected by the Cement Case, then turned to Congress to persuade it to rewrite the rules, so as to protect pricing practices said to have been endangered and cast in doubt by the pronouncements of the Supreme Court.

Friendly subgroups of Congress carried forward this campaign in the last session of the Eightieth Congress and in the opening months of the Eighty-first. Thereafter, the leadership passed into the hands of O'Mahoney, usually the spokesman for the opposition to any relaxation of the antitrust laws. This anomaly was not fully appreciated at the outset, but when it was the leadership of the deserted opposition in the House passed to another of its established champions, Patman of Texas. In the Senate, Douglas took on O'Mahoney's traditional role. Before the full import of the anomaly was appreciated, however, O'Mahoney had succeeded in obtaining an official consensus in support of his measure, a combination which included the Federal Trade Commission and the Department of Justice, official groups sometimes opposed to each other. The resistance of Douglas and his supporters in the Senate helped to weaken this official consensus, and the Federal Trade Commission then withdrew its support, having previously been put in the embarrassing position of supporting action to repudiate policies it had sought to develop. But the O'Mahoney alliance of private and official groups outside of Congress, joined with Republicans and Dixiecrats within Congress, was able to push through the measure and send it on its way to the White House.

The Patman-Douglas coalition was not fully effective until S. 1008 was out of the Senate and in the White House. When it became apparent to the White House that O'Mahoney was committing the President to the support of business and other groups to which the Patman-Douglas combination was opposed, the White House had to decide whether to seek new friends at the risk of losing old and established friends. It chose to maintain its reputation and stand with the latter.

It has been said that Congress represents minorities, while the President represents the majority. To the extent that this is true, the White House had to decide what the majority view was, or was likely to be. . . . The fact that Congress had enacted a bill did not necessarily mean that it was an action that the popular majority would approve if informed about it. . . . The President believed that the majority view was that professed by the small business groups.

Those who scorn the vocatian of the politician, those who view the history of S. 1008 as just another example of the perfidy of politicos bent upon perpetuating themselves in office at whatever cost, reckon too low the value of this flexibility of opinion, judgement and action and the democratic process. There is a jest which says that the politician is the man who can rise above principle. Actually he does not, because he serves the principle of toleration and compromise, without which the democratic process would not function at all. Only authoritarian systems push upon the people bodies of fixed principles without counting the desires of the people. Only totalitarian governments profess to know what is best for the people despite the evident assurances of the people to the contrary.

Democratic politicians must reflect the consensus, and most of the time of legislators and chief executives is spent in determining what the consensus is. There are no infallible signs, and the White House guess on the balance of power could have been wrong. Congressmen are vulnerable to particular pressures brought by powerful groups who hope to identify their particular group interests with the national interest, and the pressures of these groups are acutely felt in the small constituencies at home. Besides this, Congressmen continually seek to forecast the reactions of incipient and unorganized groups, which, although not immediately organized and aroused, might become so. The President is generally less vulnerable to the direct presures of organized groups because his constituency is national and not local; and for pressure groups to defeat him requires an expenditure of effort and money sometimes out of keeping with the value of the prize which this effort wins. But he is not less responsive than the Congressman in his anticipation of the reactions of the incipient and unorganized groups.

SUGGESTED READINGS

Johnson, Arthur M., *Government-Business Relations* (Columbus, Ohio: Merrill, 1965). Contains discussions of the public policy process, the partnership of government and major economic groups, governmental restraints on business, government ownership of productive facilities, and summarizes changes in government-business relations from 1900 to 1964.

Schubert, Glendon, *The Public Interest* (New York: Free Press, 1960). A systematic examination of statements made about the public interest, classifying them as examples of "rationalist," "realist," or "idealist" theory.

Truman, David B., *The Governmental Process* (New York: Random, 1951). Examines political behavior from party platforms to judicial opinions, and systematically discusses the role played by interest groups in the American governmental system.

CHAPTER 24

BUSINESS
AND THE
U.S.
CONSTITUTION

The way in which American governments can influence business is conditioned by what written constitutions permit them to do and prohibit them from doing. Some state constitutions were in effect prior to the adoption of the Constitution of the United States in 1789 and determined the powers of state governments and the local governments those states created. Other states have adopted similar instruments since 1789. When the Constitution of the United States was adopted, it forbade states to do certain things at the same time that it gave the federal government certain powers. Therefore, in any state in which a firm carries on business there are two constitutions of importance to it—the state constitution and

453

the Constitution of the United States. It is neither feasible nor desirable to go into the provisions of state constitutions here. However, since the U.S. Constitution is the supreme law of the land, some of its provisions—along with its origin and development—are worth noting.

ORIGIN OF THE CONSTITUTION OF THE UNITED STATES

In the period between the Declaration of Independence in 1776 and the adoption of the Constitution in 1789, a new central government was created under a document providing for a confederation of the states that had declared themselves "free and independent." In fact, at the same time that a resolution favoring a declaration of independence was introduced in the Continental Congress, it was accompanied by another resolution urging a constitution for the "United Colonies." The Articles of Confederation were drafted and submitted to the states in 1777, with all the states except Maryland ratifying this instrument by 1779. In 1781, after Maryland won certain concessions from other states, it also ratified the Articles. The Continental Congress had been in fact exercising the powers that the document eventually granted to it. However, those powers were inadequate to the effective functioning of a federal government. Furthermore, the existence of thirteen sovereign states created a number of problems, especially for businessmen.

Under the Articles, the Continental Congress had little power to promote or protect the interests of business. It was unable to negotiate effective commercial treaties with other nations because it was incapable of guaranteeing compliance with such treaties by the state governments. Consequently, the British closed the West Indies to American trade and discriminated against New England merchants doing business in English ports. Congress was powerless to retaliate in kind because all states would not honor such an arrangement. Also, states carried on commercial warfare among themselves, with New York laying taxes on imports that were to be re-exported to New Jersey and Connecticut, while those two states—in retaliation—taxed interstate commerce with New York. In a number of states, an alliance of those favoring paper money—small farmers, artisans, and other debtors—was able to secure state issues of paper money and other legislation easing the burdens of debtors to the disadvantage of creditors, who were mainly businessmen. In Massachusetts, armed bands of farmers closed courts in the interior of the state and threatened to lay siege to Boston unless the state legislature passed laws to inflate the money supply (and deflate its value).

Some states took action to deal with the commercial rivalry that existed. Maryland and Virginia drafted an agreement in 1785 to resolve disputes over regulation of commerce on the Potomac. In the hope that such agreement could be extended to cover all states in the Confederation, the two states issued an invitation to the others to join in a convention to consider a common interstate commercial policy. This convention met in Annapolis in 1786, but was not successful in gaining the objective of its proponents because only five middle states were present. However, rather than give up, the five adopted a resolution to be sent to each state calling for the holding of a constitutional convention in Philadelphia the next year.

In 1787, the Constitutional Convention met and drafted the Constitution; it was finally adopted by a sufficient number of states in 1789, and is the fundamental instrument governing state and federal governments. Many of its provisions affect business directly and indirectly, as we shall see. There have been a number of interesting interpretations of why some of these specific provisions were inserted. Historian Charles Beard has written *An Economic Interpretation of the Constitution of the United States,* in which he contends that the movement for a new Constitution was supported by substantially all of the merchants, moneylenders, security holders, manufacturers, shippers, capitalists, financiers, and their lawyers, and that the bulk of the opposition came from non-slaveholding farmers and debtors. Although this interpretation has been challenged by other historians, there is no denying that the document reflects an attempt by some economic interest groups to change the "rules of the game" in their favor.

CONSTITUTIONAL PROVISIONS OF IMPORTANCE TO BUSINESS

The U.S. Constitution contains a host of provisions of importance to business, and the majority of them have had the effect of promoting the interests of businessmen. Some of the clauses gave Congress powers it did not previously have; others prohibited Congress from doing certain things; still others prohibited states from passing legislation that might have the effect of injuring business. Since 1789, a number of amendments to the Constitution have been made, and many of these are also of significance to businessmen. Since the significance of some constitutional provisions may not be readily apparent, we shall examine them briefly.

Provisions Granting Certain Powers to Congress

The first power granted Congress under the Constitution was the power to "lay and collect Taxes, Duties, Imposts and Excises," with all duties, imposts and excises to be uniform throughout the United States. Under the Articles, Congress had no power to tax and was obliged to ask states to supply it with revenue to conduct the Revolutionary War and for other purposes. Since 1789, a number of taxes have been imposed on business, and it may be difficult to see how the tax power of Congress is of much benefit to business. However, tax revenues permit the federal government to conduct many programs of benefit to business, and certain taxes—such as tariffs, or duties levied on imports—have been used to keep foreign producers from competing too strongly with domestic producers.

"To BORROW MONEY . . ." Associated with the congressional power to levy taxes is the power to borrow money on the credit of the United States and to pay the nation's debts. During the Revolutionary War, the states and the Continental Congress had done considerable borrowing abroad. Under this provision, the new national government not only paid its debts but assumed the war debts of the states as well. This had the effect of improving U.S. credit in the creditor nations (since there had been some indication that much of this debt would be repudiated), which improved the overseas market for future sales of American securities, both public and private. (It is interesting to contrast the experience of the United States with that of the Soviet Union, which repudiated the debts of the Czarist governments. The economic development of the U.S.S.R. has been hindered by the unwillingness of foreign investors to lend to a nation that repudiated debts incurred by an earlier government.) A number of speculators in America became rich as a consequence of buying the promises to pay of American governments at low prices when there was some doubt if or when they would be paid, and then having them paid off at face value. These are the "security holders" mentioned by Beard, but there were other motives behind this provision besides enriching speculators. Some members of the convention felt that evidences of debt guaranteed by the government could be employed as currency in a country that had little coin to use for that purpose. To the extent that such paper could be used for circulating media, business throughout the United States would be promoted.

"To REGULATE COMMERCE . . ." A provision of great importance is that giving Congress power "to regulate Commerce with foreign Nations, and among the several States, and with the Indian Tribes." Although trade with the Indians is no longer as important as it was at one time, the commerce power has been employed in a variety of ways. It gives the federal government the right to engage in commercial treaties with other nations and requires states to observe those treaties. Although in many cases this power has been used to promote the interests of American businessmen, there have been instances in which it has had adverse effects on those engaging in foreign trade—during Jefferson's administration, for example, embargoes were placed on trade with England and France;

more recently, restrictions on trade with Cuba and other Communist countries have adversely affected some businessmen. However, at the time of its adoption, it led to commercial treaties and economic relations with other nations not possible under the Articles.

In the early years of our national existence, foreign trade was of greater importance than interstate commerce. However, as we noted earlier, the restrictions placed on interstate trade by state governments was a considerable burden to those businessmen buying in, selling to, and shipping to or from other states. The Constitution gave Congress the right to regulate such commerce in the "commerce clause" and in other provisions it prohibited any requirement that "Vessels bound to, or from, one state be obliged to enter, clear, or pay Duties in another." Initially the regulation of interstate commerce by Congress was aimed at promoting such trade. However, one hundred years after the Constitutional Convention, and under the authority of the "commerce clause," Congress passed an "Act to Regulate Commerce" establishing the Interstate Commerce Commission and providing for the regulation of interstate railroads by the federal government. Since 1887, many other congressional acts regulating business have been passed under the authority of the commerce clause so that nowadays its greater importance seems to lie in its authorizing the regulation of business rather than promotion of business interests.

"TO ESTABLISH ... UNIFORM LAWS ON ... BANKRUPTCIES." The significance of the clause giving Congress the power "to establish uniform Laws on the subject of Bankruptcies throughout the United States" has persisted. Under the Articles of Confederation, a number of states had passed laws relieving debtors of their obligations to pay their just debts. Many of these laws made it so easy for debtors to avoid paying that creditors were unjustly burdened. This constitutional provision took the power to make any bankruptcy laws away from the states and vested that authority in Congress, which presumably would be more conservative in the laws it passed. To further protect the interests of creditors, the Constitution contained clauses prohibiting states from making anything but gold and silver coin legal tender in payment of debts and from passing any law impairing the obligation of contracts (including the obligation to pay debts legally contracted). To this day, all bankruptcies are filed under federal bankruptcy statutes that attempt to insure justice to creditors as well as to provide some means of relief to debtors who are unable to pay.

"TO COIN MONEY, REGULATE THE VALUE THEREOF ..." Another clause of considerable significance is that giving Congress authority to coin money and regulate its value. Allied with this is a provision dealing with the punishment of those guilty of "counterfeiting the Securities and current Coin of the United States." In yet another provision, states were forbidden to coin money or issue "Bills of Credit" (paper currency). Thus the power over money was firmly established in the hands of the federal government and taken away from the states, which had in many cases issued paper money in such high volume that the issuers were unable or unwilling to redeem the money in gold or silver, with consequent inflation (again working a hardship on creditors who received bad money in exchange for good). Although "sound money" has not always stemmed from this congressional power, the situation is undoubtedly superior to what it would be if states had continued to have the power to create currency.

Actually the Continental Congress had the power to issue money under the Articles of Confederation. However, it had no power to levy taxes— although it did borrow money—and consequently had little surplus revenue consisting of gold or silver with which to redeem the paper money it did issue. This paper money quickly depreciated in value, giving rise to the phrase "not worth a Continental." Since the adoption of the Constitution, Congress has adopted laws providing for the acquisition of gold and silver and for stating the value of its paper currency in terms of such precious metals (although the federal government no longer redeems paper money by paying out gold, and in recent years there has been a shortage of silver that may result in a situation in which paper money will be redeemed only through another issue of paper money). However, the federal government has a number of powers it employs to combat inflation and deflation and thereby regulate the value of money. Maintaining a relatively stable value of American currency provides businessmen with some certainty that the dollars they take in during some future time will be as valuable as those they have given out in the past and thereby encourages them to engage in long-range business programs they might otherwise not engage in.

In addition to having the power to regulate the value of currency issued by the United States, Congress also has authority to regulate the value of foreign coin. It has not used this power to any great extent, and it has mainly left to dealers in "foreign exchange" the function of fixing, through market action, the exchange rate between American and foreign currency. There is some exception to this, however, in that the United States is now party to an international agreement establishing the International Monetary Fund, which fixes, through the action of member governments, exchange rates among the currencies of the more important commercial countries. This constitutional clause permits the United States to be a member of such an agreement, and authorizes its actions in carrying out decisions of those directing the IMF.

To "FIX THE STANDARD OF WEIGHTS AND MEASURES." In the Department of Commerce at the present time, there is a Bureau of Standards. It operates under legislation passed by Congress under its power to "fix the Standard of Weights and Measures." When tons were a different number of pounds, and pounds a different number of ounces (with the weight of the ounce unsure), trade was difficult because the same trade term meant different things to those engaged in exchange. The same was true when quart, gallon, yard, and so on, all meant different things in different places in the United States. By standardizing weights and measures, commercial intercourse was enhanced; the work of the Bureau of Standards is of continuing importance to American businessmen.

"To ESTABLISH POST OFFICES AND POST ROADS." Congress was also authorized by the Constitution to "establish Post Offices and post Roads." At the present time, it is difficult to envision the problems of communication and transportation confronting businessmen in the late eighteenth century. Not only was there no telephone or telegraph, there was also no good postal service. Letters and parcels went by private carrier—ships or stages—and service was uncertain, infrequent, slow, and costly. The creation of government post offices with regular and certain service made it possible for businessmen to engage in speedier and more frequent communication with others in the United States, thereby aiding the growth of business. As we shall note in Chapter 26, the Post Office Department has engaged in a number of influential activities other than carrying the mail. By giving Congress the power to establish post roads, transportation of goods as well as letters has been promoted. Before the federal government engaged in road construction, roads were very poor (although there were some exceptions in the case of toll roads; however, since it was costly to travel great distances over toll highways, this inhibited commerce). Most of the highways today in the United States, whether state or federal, are financed largely by Congress under its authority to establish post roads. It is significant, perhaps, that the Bureau of Public Roads is in the Department of Commerce, which has as its main objective serving the interests of business.

"To PROMOTE THE PROGRESS OF SCIENCE AND USEFUL ARTS." Also in the Department of Commerce is the United States Patent Office. It operates under legislation passed by Congress under its power "to Promote the Progress of Science and useful Arts, by securing for limited Times to Authors and Inventors the exclusive Right to their respective Writings and Discoveries." In modern terms, this clause permits inventors to patent their inventions and writers to copyright their writings (along with giving certain other artists the sole right to reproduce their creations). Without patent rights, very few firms could afford to spend large sums in research and development of new products only to see the design copied by those who did not make such expenditures. Normally, under the patent laws and this constitutional provision, a patent is granted for a period of seventeen years, giving the inventor the exclusive right to produce his patented product (although he may sell or assign that right to others). There seems to be little doubt that manufacturing has been promoted by this clause.

TO "PROVIDE FOR THE COMMON DEFENCE." The "common Defence" is specifically provided for by a number of Constitutional provisions. Congress has the power to declare war. Although it has done so on a number of occasions, only in the early years of our national existence were such wars carried to our shores and borders. Some of the discussion of the origins of the Constitution leads to the conclusion that the war power was regarded as useful in pointing out to the French, Indians, British, and Spanish that the United States was willing to go to war in order to protect the territory it claimed as well as in attempting to acquire lands claimed by others. Whether we have gone to war with other nations on their territory overseas or defended the homeland, the interests of business have been promoted thereby—not only by the protection afforded, but also by the purchases made to prosecute such wars.

In the early days of the republic, a considerable amount of concern was exhibited over the attacks made upon American merchantmen on the high seas. The Constitution gave Congress power to provide and maintain a navy and to "define and punish Piracies and Felonies committed on the high Seas." Some of the earliest successes of the U.S. Navy were against the Barbary pirates, who were capturing American merchant vessels in the Mediterranean. To permit merchantmen to protect themselves, Congress was empowered to "grant Letters of Marque and Reprisal, and make Rules concerning Captures on Land and Water." That is, it was given authority to permit merchant vessels to retaliate by arming themselves and capturing vessels of other nations whose ships were raiding American commerce. Although merchantmen are still armed during wartime, they seldom go on the attack. However, they are still protected by the Navy, which convoys them through danger zones.

On a few occasions, Congress has employed its power to call "forth the Militia to execute the Laws of the Union, suppress Insurrections and repel Invasions." There have been some labor strikes of national importance leading to the calling out of the troops. During the American Railway Union strike of 1894, for example, the military arm of the federal government was used to protect the U.S. mails and, incidentally, the interests of the firms being struck. There have been occasions on which the federal government has declared it will use the troops to operate certain establishments in the event of a strike, and this usually works to the advantage of the business firms.

Less obvious from an examination of the war powers of Congress is that the operation of some firms and industries can be taken over during periods of national war emergency. During World War I, for example, the railroads of the United States were operated by the U.S. Railroad Administration. During the Korean War, President Truman tried to seize the steel industry when a strike threatened, but the Supreme Court said that he had no power to do so, as Congress had not authorized such action.

Provisions Prohibiting Certain Congressional Actions

Although considerable power was given Congress by the Constitution, it prohibited the exercise of certain other powers that a sovereign state might otherwise employ. Some of these were and are of significance to businessmen. Since some southern states imported large numbers of slaves for work on the plantations, their representatives at the Constitutional Convention secured a provision preventing Congress from putting an immediate halt to the slave trade through the proviso that "the Migration or Importation of Such Persons as any of the States now existing shall think proper to admit, shall not be prohibited by the Congress prior to the Year one thousand eight hundred and eight." Not all of the states in the south supported this provision because some—Virginia and Maryland —had a surplus of slaves and sold their excess to those operating plantations in the Carolinas and Georgia. The conflict between these two groups of states resulted in the compromise contained in the Constitution.

RESTRICTIONS ON THE TAX POWER. Of greater current importance are some provisions dealing with taxation. Taxes on exports are forbidden. A proviso that was to raise an important constitutional issue was the one declaring: "No capitation, or other direct, Tax shall be laid, unless in Proportion to the Census. . . . " At the time of the drafting of the Constitution, income taxes were not a means employed by the federal government to secure revenue. The first federal income tax was levied during the Civil War by the Republicans as a means of securing additional revenue to prosecute the contest with the South. The legislation providing for such taxation remained in effect until 1872. In 1894, a new income tax law was passed, and promptly came under attack as being unconstitutional. This was somewhat surprising, since a Supreme Court decision in 1881 had upheld the constitutionality of the Civil War legislation. Even more surprising was the fact that the Supreme Court now held the federal income tax law to be unconstitutional on the grounds that it was a direct tax on property and that, therefore, it needed to be levied in proportion to the population of the states in order to be constitutional.

Eventually, the problem of the constitutionality of a federal income tax was resolved by the Sixteenth Amendment to the Constitution. It provides that "the Congress shall have power to lay and collect taxes on incomes, from whatever source derived, without apportionment among the several states, and without regard to any census or enumeration." This amendment was ratified by a sufficient number of states in 1913, and since that time both individual and corporation income tax laws passed under this constitutional provision have been of increasing importance to American business.

RESTRICTIONS ON THE COMMERCE POWER.   To further insure equality of treatment of interstate trade engaged in by water routes, a prohibition on certain congressional action was inserted into the Constitution. Although the national legislature was given power to regulate interstate commerce, it was explicitly pointed out that "no preference shall be given by any Regulation of Commerce or Revenue to the Ports of one State over those of another; nor shall Vessels bound to, or from, one State be obliged to enter, clear, or pay Duties in another." It is hard for us nowadays to imagine the existence of a condition in which commercial rivalry among states was so keen that not only were states prohibited from interfering with interstate commerce but some doubt existed as to whether or not some influence on Congress might not result in a situation in which some states would be discriminated against by congressional action.

Prohibitions on State Action

We have already mentioned a number of actions prohibited to the states by the Constitution: the prohibition on coining money and issuing paper currency; the prohibition on making anything but gold and silver legal tender in payment of debts; the prohibition on passing laws impairing the obligations of contracts. Perhaps it should be pointed out that the federal government has made its paper money legal tender in payment of debts, but that such paper money is backed in at least fractional amounts by gold and silver. There were other provisos of significance in addition to those we have already mentioned.

One other provision of great importance dealt with taxes that states might levy on imports and exports. It declared:

> No State shall, without the Consent of the Congress, lay any Imposts or Duties on Imports or Exports, except what may be absolutely necessary for executing its inspection laws; and the net Produce of all Duties and Im-

posts, laid by any State on Imports or Exports, shall be for the Use of the Treasury of the United States; and all such Laws shall be subject to the Revision and Control of the Congress.

Thus, the Constitution disposed of a problem confronting merchants during the period of the Articles of Confederation. Such state taxes had the effect of reducing the income and trade of merchants engaged in interstate commerce and their prohibition meant that this means could no longer be employed to inhibit trade among the states. However, this does not mean that there have been no restrictions established by states on interstate commerce. As this portion of the Constitution indicates, states may establish inspection laws and inspect goods coming into or leaving a state. Sometimes these inspection laws have been used to keep out goods from "foreign states," or at least to restrict such commerce.

Amendments to the Constitution

The Constitution provided certain procedures for its amendment. Since its adoption in 1789 it has been amended by the addition of more than twenty new articles (although one amendment cancels an earlier amendment). We have already mentioned the Sixteenth Amendment dealing with federal income taxation. Others adopted before and after that amendment have also become of great significance.

THE "BILL OF RIGHTS." Just after the ratification of the Constitution by the required number of states in 1789, ten amendments were proposed and adopted. These articles, called the "Bill of Rights," are usually regarded as the price some states extracted from others before agreeing to ratify the original document. In the Bill of Rights is the Fifth Amendment, which we have heard much of in recent years owing to its employment by persons who wish to avoid testifying before certain bodies, since the amendment prevents American governments from compelling persons from being witnesses against themselves in any criminal case. However, it is not this portion of the Fifth Amendment that has been of significance to business. Another part provides that no person shall "be deprived of life, liberty, or property, without due process of law; nor shall private property be taken for public use, without just compensation." The value to business of a provision prohibiting government from taking business property for public use without proper compensation is quite obvious. However, the first portion is also of great importance. The Supreme Court has declared corporations to be persons coming under the protection of the Fifth Amendment; thus a corporation may not be deprived of property without due process of law. Among the property rights of a corporation is the right to its profits, and on occasion government action that has reduced the profits of corporations has been stricken down by the Supreme Court on the ground that it violated this provision. The same terminology was repeated in the Fourteenth Amendment to the Constitution, adopted shortly after the Civil War, but now applying specifically to state action: "No State shall ... deprive any person of life, liberty, or property, without due process of law. ..." This amendment has also been used to preserve corporate property against state action that the Supreme Court has said to be in violation of the "due process" clause.

THE SEVENTEENTH AMENDMENT. At first glance, the Seventeenth Amendment seems to have nothing to do with business. It provides that "the Senate of the United States shall be composed of two senators from each State, elected by the people thereof ...." Prior to the ratification of this amendment in 1913, senators were chosen by the legislatures of their states. Over the years, considerable popular condemnation of this practice was voiced. In part, it was due to the fact that in some cases state legislatures had been bribed to appoint certain senators. More important to us was the charge that the Senate had become a "rich man's club," and that businessmen (owing to their wealth) were said to dominate the Senate and use their position of political power to dominate other economic groups.

Proposals to provide for direct election of senators were advanced as early as 1828. However, it was not until radicals and reformers began to gain political power that serious efforts to so amend the Constitution were made. In the 1890's, charges were made that the Senate was filled with "venal-minded corporation lawyers, retired millionaires, and corrupt state bosses, who represented the will of the 'interests' and not that of the people." Cartoonists depicted the Senate as a group of "overstuffed moneybags, each marked with the label of the 'oil trust,' 'sugar trust,' 'money trust,'" or some other combination. There was some truth to the charges. Senator Camden of New Jersey frequently looked after the interests of Standard Oil and it has been suggested that "Senator H. B. Payne of Ohio was for years the faithful servant of the Standard Oil Company, and Senator Joseph Foraker of Ohio was later revealed as a pensionary of the same concern." Other senators had been corporation lawyers and yet others had been businessmen of some consequence—Marcus A. Hanna of Ohio was a retired steel manufacturer and was regarded as the "power behind the throne" of William McKinley, who was elected President in 1896 and 1900. The House passed amendments to provide for direct election of senators in 1893, 1894, 1900, and 1902, but the Senate either ignored such proposals or voted them down. Upon the publication of the "wholesale bribery" of the Illinois legislature in order to elect William Lorimer to the Senate in 1911, the movement received new strength and both houses of Congress passed an amendment and submitted it to the states. Since its ratification, the nature of the Senate has changed substantially.

THE EIGHTEENTH AMENDMENT. For slightly more than a decade, an amendment to the Constitution prohibited certain kinds of business. The Eighteenth Amendment declared: "After one year from the ratification of this article, the manufacture, sale, or transportation of intoxicating liquors within, the importation thereof into, or the exportation thereof from the United States and all territory subject to the jurisdiction thereof for beverage purposes is hereby prohibited." All those engaged in the manufacture, sale, transportation, exporting, and importing of alcoholic beverages did not go out of business; they either turned to other pursuits or operated illegally. There was, in fact, so much illegal operation of enterprises in this group of industries that it was eventually seen that the "evils of Prohibition" outweighed the "evils of Drink." The Eighteenth Amendment went into effect in 1919 and was repealed by the Twenty-first Amendment in 1933. The repeal was not total, since Article XXI of the Amendments prohibits the "transportation or importation into any State, Territory or possession of the United States for delivery or use therein of intoxicating liquors, in violation of the laws thereof." That is, states are permitted to be "dry" and if they so elect, then it is illegal either to send or to import alcoholic beverages into such a dry state. Some states have adopted prohibition laws, and this has had some continuing effect on the liquor business.

THE IMPLEMENTATION OF THE CONSTITUTION

Although we have called the U.S. Constitution the "supreme law of the land," this is somewhat misleading. This characterization is quite accurate in those cases where certain actions are prohibited; however, a number of provisions are only permissive of certain governmental action, and do not require that certain things be done. That is, Congress, the President, and the Supreme Court are given powers they do not need to carry out. Thus the implementation of the Constitution depends upon the willingness of the national legislature, the Chief Executive, and the highest court to carry out certain provisions as well as on the ways in which they choose to do so. Not until Congress affirmatively acts, and the President approves, do many provisions become part of the law affecting business. Even so, the Supreme Court reviews—when petitioned and when it chooses to do so—such legislation to determine whether it regards such laws as being consistent with the Constitution. In many cases it has not.

As a Chief Justice of the Supreme Court once said: "The Constitution is what the Court says it is." Judicial review of legislation and other aspects of the nature and activities of legislatures and courts will be discussed in Chapters 30 and 31.

THE DEVELOPMENT OF THE CONSTITUTION

The ways in which the Constitution has developed should now be clear. Some amendments have been made when politically powerful groups were able to get Congress to propose amendments to the states. Some changes in the Constitution have also come about as a consequence of changed interpretations of it by the Supreme Court—for example, the upholding of the constitutionality of federal incomes taxes in 1881 and the declaration of their unconstitutionality in 1895. Of these two means of securing changes in the Constitution, the latter is most common. This was given recognition by President Franklin D. Roosevelt, who proposed adding some judges who would vote the "right way" to the Court after some New Deal legislation had been declared to be unconstitutional by a close vote. Businessmen adversely affected by some decisions of the Supreme Court on what is constitutional may work toward the same end of securing the appointment of justices who will interpret the Constitution the "right way." Since Supreme Court justices are appointed by an elected officer—the President of the United States—and approved by an elected body—the United States Senate—it is apparent that any impact business can have on the Constitution will depend mainly on what success they have in getting the "right people" nominated and elected in political campaigns. This is not the only way in which a desired interpretation can be secured, since the Court will hear arguments from attorneys (including lawyers representing business) concerning the proper interpretation of the Constitution. The question may be properly raised of how influential such arguments are with a group that regards itself as the experts in the field, and whose members already have quite fixed attitudes on most constitutional issues.

Congress has passed a host of laws under its constitutional powers. Some of these we shall examine, along with other aspects of law as it confronts the firm, in the next chapter.

READING: Excerpts from the Constitution

[Space does not permit anything approaching a thorough discussion of those portions of the Constitution that are of importance to a complete understanding

of the political environment. A thorough examination of that document reveals that many (if not most) of the provisions that deal with substance rather than procedure directly or indirectly affect business. The following articles, or portions thereof, concern themselves with the powers of state and federal government and are, therefore, the basis for the ways in which American governments influence business decisions and operations.]

Preamble. We the People of the United States, in Order to form a more perfect Union, establish Justice, insure domestic Tranquility, provide for the common defence, promote the general Welfare, and secure the Blessings of Liberty to ourselves and our Posterity, do ordain and establish this Constitution for the United States of America.

Article I. *Section 8.* The Congress shall have Power to lay and collect Taxes, Duties, Imposts and Excises, to pay the Debts and provide for the common Defence and general Welfare of the United States; but all Duties, Imposts and Excises shall be uniform throughout the United States;

To borrow money on the credit of the United States;

To regulate Commerce with foreign Nations, and among the several States, and with the Indian Tribes;

To establish an uniform Rule of Naturalization, and uniform Laws on the subject of Bankruptcies throughout the United States;

To coin Money, regulate the Value thereof, and of foreign Coin, and fix the Standard of Weights and Measures;

To provide for the Punishment of counterfeiting the Securities and current Coin of the United States;

To establish Post Offices and post Roads;

To promote the Progress of Science and useful Arts, by securing for limited Times to Authors and Inventors the exclusive Rights to their respective Writings and Discoveries;

To constitute Tribunals inferior to the supreme Court;

To define and punish Piracies and Felonies committed on the high Seas, and Offenses against the Law of Nations;

To declare War, grant Letters of Marque and Reprisal, and make Rules concerning Captures on Land and Water;

To raise and support Armies, but no Appropriation of Money to that Use shall be for a longer Term than two Years;

To provide and maintain a Navy;

To make Rules for the Government and Regulation of the land and naval Forces;

To provide for calling forth the Militia to execute the Laws of the Union, suppress Insurrections and repel Invasions;

To make all Laws which shall be neccessary and proper for carrying into Execution the foregoing Powers, and all other Powers vested by this Constitution in the Government of the United States, or in any Department or Officer thereof.

Section 9.   The Migration or Importation of Such Persons as any of the States now existing shall think proper to admit, shall not be prohibited by the Congress prior to the Year one thousand eight hundred and eight, but a tax or duty may be imposed on such Importation, not exceeding ten dollars for each Person.

No Bill of Attainder or ex post facto Law shall be passed.

No capitation, or other direct, Tax shall be laid, unless in Proportion to the Census or Enumeration herein before directed to be taken.

No Tax or Duty shall be laid on Articles exported from any State.

No preference shall be given by any Regulation of Commerce or Revenue to the Ports of one State over those of another: nor shall Vessels bound to, or from, one State be obliged to enter, clear, or pay Duties in another.

Section 10.   No State shall enter into any Treaty, Alliance, or Confederation; grant Letters of Marque and Reprisal; coin Money; emit Bills of Credit; make any Thing but gold and silver Coin a Tender in Payment of Debts; pass any Bill of Attainder, ex post facto Law, or Law impairing the Obligation of Contracts, or grant any Title of Nobility.

No State shall, without the Consent of the Congress, lay any Imposts or Duties on Imports or Exports, except what may be absolutely necessary for executing its inspection Laws; and the net Produce of all Duties and Imposts, laid by any State on Imports or Exports, shall be for the Use of the Treasury of the United States; and all such Laws shall be subject to the Revision and Control of the Congress.

Article II.   *Section 1.*   The executive Power shall be vested in a President of the United States of America. . . .

Section 2.   . . . He shall have power by and with the advice and consent of the Senate to make treaties, provided two-thirds of the Senators present concur; and he shall nominate and by and with the advice and consent of the Senate shall appoint ambassadors, other public ministers and consuls, judges of the Supreme Court, and all other officers of the United States whose appointments are not herein otherwise provided for, and which shall be established by law; but the Congress may by law vest the appointment of such inferior officers as they think proper in the President alone, in the courts of law, or in the heads of departments.

Section 3.   He shall from time to time give to the Congress Information of the State of the Union, and recommend to their Consideration such Measures as he shall judge necessary and expedient; he may, on extraordinary Occasions, convene both Houses, or either of them, and in Case of Disagreement between them, with Respect to the Time of Adjournment, he may adjourn them to such Time as he shall think proper; he shall receive Ambassadors and other public Ministers; he shall take Care that the Laws be faithfully executed, and shall Commission all the Officers of the United States.

Article III. *Section 1.* The judicial Power of the United States, shall be vested in one supreme Court, and in such inferior Courts as the Congress may from time to time ordain and establish. The Judges, both of the supreme and inferior Courts, shall hold their Offices during good Behaviour, and shall, at stated Times, receive for their Services a Compensation which shall not be diminished during their Continuance in Office.

Section 2. The judicial Power shall extend to all Cases, in Law and Equity, arising under this Constitution, the Laws of the United States, and Treaties made, or which shall be made, under their Authority;—to all Cases affecting Ambassadors, other public Ministers and Consuls;—to all Cases of admiralty and maritime Jurisdiction;—to Controversies to which the United States shall be a Party;—to Controversies between two or more States;—between a State and Citizen of another State;—between Citizens of different States;—between Citizens of the same State claiming Lands under Grants of different States, and between a State, or the Citizens thereof, and foreign States, Citizens or Subjects.

In all Cases affecting Ambassadors, other public Ministers and Consuls, and those in which a State shall be Party, the supreme Court shall have original Jurisdiction. In all the other Cases before mentioned, the supreme Court shall have appellate Jurisdiction, both as to Law and Fact, with such Exceptions, and under such Regulations as the Congress shall make. . . .

Article IV. *Section 1.* Full faith and credit shall be given in each State to the public acts, records, and judicial proceedings of every other State. . . .

Section 3. . . . The Congress shall have power to dispose of and make all needful rules and regulations respecting the territory or other property belonging to the United States. . . .

Article V. The Congress, whenever two-thirds of both Houses shall deem it necessary, shall propose Amendments to this Constitution, or, on the Application of the Legislatures of two-thirds of the several States, shall call a Convention for proposing Amendments, which, in either Case, shall be valid to all Intents and Purposes, as part of this Constitution, when ratified by the Legislatures of three-fourths of the several States, or by Conventions in three-fourths thereof, as the one or the other Mode of Ratification may be proposed by the Congress. . . .

Article VI. All debts contracted and engagements entered into before the adoption of this Constitution shall be as valid against the United States under this Constitution as under the Confederation.

. . . This Constitution, and the Laws of the United States which shall be made in Pursuance thereof; and all Treaties made, or which shall be made, under the Authority of the United States, shall be the supreme Law of the Land; and the Judges in every State shall be bound thereby, any Thing in the Constitution or Laws of any State to the Contrary not withstanding.

Amendments.   *Amendment V.*   No person shall be held to answer for a capital, or otherwise infamous crime, unless on a presentment or indictment of a Grand Jury, except in cases arising in the land or naval forces, or in the Militia, when in actual service in time of War or public danger; nor shall any person be subject for the same offence to be twice put in jeopardy of life or limb; nor shall be compelled in any criminal case to be a witness against himself, nor be deprived of life, liberty or property, without due process of law; nor shall private property be taken for public use, without just compensation. (December 1791.)

Amendment IX.   The enumeration in the Constitution, of certain rights, shall not be construed to deny or disparage others retained by the people. (December 1791.)

Amendment X.   The powers not delegated to the United States by the Constitution, nor prohibited by it to the States, are reserved to the States respectively, or to the people. (December 1791.)

Amendment XIV.   Section 1.   All persons born or naturalized in the United States, and subject to the jurisdiction thereof, are citizens of the United States and of the State wherein they reside. No State shall make or enforce any law which shall abridge the privileges or immunities of citizens of the United States; nor shall any State deprive any person of life, liberty, or property, without due process of law; nor deny to any person within its jurisdiction the equal protection of the laws. (July 28, 1868)

Amendment XVI.   The Congress shall have power to lay and collect taxes on incomes, from whatever source derived, without apportionment among the several States, and without regard to any census or enumeration. (February 25, 1913)

Amendment XVII.   The Senate of the United States shall be composed of two Senators from each State, elected by the people thereof. . . . (May 31, 1913.)

Amendment XVIII.   After one year from the ratification of this amendment article the manufacture, sale, or transportation of intoxicating liquors within, the importation thereof into, or the exportation thereof from the United States and all territory subject to the jurisdiction thereof for beverage purposes is hereby prohibited.

The Congress and the several States shall have concurrent power to enforce this article by appropriate legislation. (January 16, 1920)

Amendment XXI.   Section 1.   The eighteenth article of amendment to the Constitution of the United States is hereby repealed.

Section 2.   The transportation or importation into any State, Territory, or Possession of the United States for delivery or use therein of intoxicating liquors, in violation of the laws thereof, is hereby prohibited. (December 5, 1933)

SUGGESTED READINGS

Beard, Charles A., *An Economic Interpretation of the Constitution of the United States* (New York: Macmillan, 1961 [Macmillan Paperback Edition]). Originally published in 1913, this classic conceives of the Constitution as being in large measure an economic document, with its form determined by the economic interests represented at the convention.

Cortner, Richard C., *The Wagner Act Cases* (Knoxville, Tenn.: U. of Tenn., 1964). An examination of the constitutional doctrines at issue in the five cases, with greater attention devoted to the maneuvering of the interest groups involved.

Dumbauld, Edward, *The Constitution of the United States* (Norman, Okla.: U. of Okla., 1964). The United States judge for the Western District of Pennsylvania gives the text of each clause of the Constitution, an account of its origin and evolution, and analyzes its meaning according to the decisions of the Supreme Court.

CHAPTER 25

LAW AND
THE AMERICAN
BUSINESS
FIRM

The ways in which governments influence business are determined in part by law. However, the laws confronting businessmen are truly astonishing in their number and variety, and they are not all laws governing the actions of agencies and officials at different levels of American government. Laws, broadly defined, are those rules governing behavior. This definition encompasses more than human behavior. For example, there are scientific laws that "govern" the behavior of physical objects. The "law of gravity" is such a principle. Some scientific laws (such as "Walton's Law") also attempt to explain human behavior. The social sciences generally are concerned with discovering the principles that appear to govern the relationships among individuals and groups.

Our concern in this chapter will not be with scientific laws but with those principles that state how individuals and groups *ought* to conduct themselves. This distinction between rules that generally seem to explain behavior and those that are intended to prescribe action has sometimes been referred to as the difference between scientific laws and moral laws. Moral laws set standards for conduct; laws passed by Congress under its constitutional powers are of this nature. However, there are other kinds of moral laws and an adequate understanding of law as it confronts the American business firm requires some understanding of the general classifications into which rules setting standards for human behavior fall. There are so many such laws that no single book can possibly contain all of them (the sight of the many law books that contain only part of those laws is sufficient to convince anyone that it is impossible to know all such law). However, as in other cases in which we have had to deal with a great number of specific things, we can solve the problem by classifying laws. Therefore, in the following pages, we shall examine some different classes of moral laws and take a brief look at some laws of considerable importance to American business.

CLASSES OF LAWS

Laws can be classified in a number of ways. Some legal scholars (operating in a field called analytical jurisprudence) have attempted with more or less success to establish a systematic classification of all rules of law so that each falls only into one class. However, we shall examine some moral laws that are outside the field of "legal law" and our classification will not be the same. Too, since there are a number of ways in which moral laws may be classified, any given law may fall into more than one of the following classes.

Natural Law

It is part of the tradition of Western civilization that a higher law exists that should govern the actions of men. Such a notion goes back to the Greek philosophers. Plato, for example, argued for the establishment of a republic governed by ideal laws (although he recognized that in practice laws would fall short of the ideal). The idea of a natural moral law that should determine legal law has had a number of proponents, although they have looked to different sources for this higher law. The Greek philosophers, of course, felt that philosophers were the proper persons to declare what that law was. That is, ideal laws were apparent only to the eye of the philosopher. Important religious thinkers saw divine origins of the natural law: the laws of St. Augustine's City of Man were copies of the laws of the City of God. During the medieval period, the Catholic Church regarded natural law as an aspect of divine law. More recently, "idealist" political philosophers have suggested that natural law can be discovered by search of one's conscience.

Although there have been some written legal and moral codes said to be based on the natural law, that law is by its nature unwritten. Too, since the law as it does exist differs (at least in the minds of many observers) from natural law, perhaps natural law is not too important to businessmen. Business must concern itself with existing and potential law rather than with law as it should be (as stated by priests and philosophers). The reason for this is obvious. Natural law is not enforceable unless it is embodied in the "positive law"—that is, in the law as it is. Some writers on the law make a distinction between "positive law" and "normative law"—law as it is and law as it should be. Natural law falls into the latter category, and while businessmen and others may wish to appeal to a higher law to justify their actions, courts apply rules of law as they exist.

Written Law

Most laws governing the relations of businessmen with others are written. This is not true of all such laws: there is more in the "unwritten law" than just natural law. We all observe certain rules of conduct that are not recorded anywhere. For example, on every college campus there are certain unwritten rules governing the behavior of students and faculty. Violation of those rules will lead to the imposition of certain social sanctions. However, the courts will not enforce all such rules. There are some unwritten rules that the courts *will* enforce. These are the traditional legal doctrines that are not embodied in any single authoritative formulation, but that judges feel to be proper rules of law, which they apply to specific cases. However, the bulk of the rules of law governing the rights and responsibilities of the businessman are expressed in formal legislative enactments, in the recorded opinions of judges who have applied certain rules to particular cases, and in the rules and regulations issued by administrative bodies.

Not all written laws are drafted by agencies and officials of government. Almost all of us are members of a number of private, voluntary associations that frequently have written constitutions, bylaws, and other rules to govern the behavior of the membership. Religious organizations have moral codes to guide their members. The Catholics have, in addition to the Ten Commandments, canon laws and other written pronouncements to govern members of the Church. Even if businessmen are not members of any religious organization, they probably are members of chambers of commerce, service clubs, and trade associations, all of which have written rules by which their members are to abide. The business corporation has a constitution (the charter granted by the state within which the firm is incorporated) and certain bylaws adopted by the governing board. Some of these written rules of private associations will be enforced in the courts. For example, if officers of a business corporation exceed the authority granted to them by the corporate charter and its bylaws, they may be subjected to suits by those adversely affected by such action. Courts will uphold the claims of plaintiffs in such suits if they are convinced that officers of the corporation acted beyond the powers granted them, that they did so in bad faith, and that their actions resulted in injury to the interests of some individual or group. Mainly, however, it is the written rules of law promulgated by government that concern businessmen; and hence we shall confine our remaining discussion to such laws.

GOVERNMENTAL LAWS

It is possible to classify rules of law that have been promulgated by various agencies and officials of government in many ways. Since each way throws some light on a very complex subject, we shall look at a variety of different classifications of what is essentially the same thing: the body of written law.

Classifications of Law According to Who Writes the Law

Earlier we noted that some written law stemmed from legislative bodies. Legislatures exist at different levels of government—there is the Congress of the United States, and there are also state legislatures, county boards of commissioners, city councils, town boards, school boards, and so on. All perform a legislative function—they draft written rules of law, which are normally called statutes or ordinances. Occasionally, constitutional conventions are convened to draw up or amend the constitution governing a particular governmental unit. This is nowadays a rare occurrence, with constitutions being amended by means other than calling a constitutional convention, but such assemblies in the past have created the U.S. Constitution as well as those governing territories and states. The constitutions they have created are a fundamental part of the written law. Although other means do exist for the establishment of constitutional provisions and statutes other than by action of a legislative body, for the most part they are the product of legislatures.

ADMINISTRATIVE LAW. Elsewhere we have noted the great growth in rules established by administrative bodies. To businessmen affected by certain governmental units these laws may be of greater importance than statutes, since they more specifically state what public policy is and how it will be implemented than do the acts of legislatures. This rule-making function is essentially a legislative one. The ability of administrative agencies to "legislate" is limited. Their authority to do so is a delegated one—the legislature establishing the agency can, within limits, delegate some of its law-making power to that agency. An administrative body can establish rules only within the limits of the delegated authority to do so. (Perhaps we should point out that some courts have held that legislative bodies may not delegate their law-making authority; however, they have not prohibited agencies from making rules but have regarded such rule-making as "filling in the details" of statutes passed by legislatures rather than as an exercise of delegated legislative power. This has not made any significant difference in the power of administrative agencies and officials to make valid and binding rules and, consequently, the number of "administrative laws" has outgrown the number of statutes and constitutions passed by representative legislative bodies.)

COMMON LAW. Judges also make laws. They do not do so in the same way that legislatures pass statutes or administrative bodies establish rules. Some matters that have come before courts for adjudication have had to be decided even though no constitutional provision, statute, or administrative rule had been established governing that particular subject. Without such a guide, judges have had to develop their own rules to govern such matters. Over the years, many judicial decisions have been handed down and recorded. In such recorded judicial opinions, a rule of law is either explicit or implicit. These written opinions have guided other judges in deciding similar cases, since courts generally apply the principle of *stare decisis*—the rule that prior decisions in cases involving the same question of law provide rules of law that courts deciding subsequent cases should follow. Such rules of law are called "common-law rules" to distinguish them from statute law.

Common-law rules do not appear in written works in the same form as do statutes. Federal legislation, state statutes, city ordinances, and so on, are usually collected in bound volumes in an orderly fashion. The rules of common law are found throughout a host of volumes reporting the decisions of judges in different jurisdictions. For example, the common law followed by American courts originated in England (during the colonial period, colonial courts used English law in deciding cases and the states continued to do so after the American Revolution). Thus we sometimes see references made to ancient decisions of English courts when common-law rules are applied by American judges. What has happened since 1776 is that, although many states have adopted constitutions specifically adopting the common law except when changed by statute law, each state has also developed some common-law rules of its own. Unfortunately, each state, in developing new common-law rules governing new situations, has not always established exactly the same rules as any other state, so we now have a situation in which each state has its own common law that differs somewhat from that of any other state in the Union. Although there has been some attempt to bring about some uniformity in the United States by having all states adopt certain statutes superseding the common law, this movement has not been wholly successful, and consequently the business firm doing business in more than one state must concern itself with the sometimes differing common-law rules governing the conduct of business in each state. Such rules of law are to be found in the written decisions of state courts. There are some principles of common law that are generally accepted by courts throughout the United States, and the American Law Institute has prepared "Restatements of the Law," which are publications purporting to contain common-law rules deduced from numerous court decisions that attempt to put the common law into the same form as statutes.

INTERNATIONAL TREATIES. Treaties with other nations are a rather unusual part of the written law of the land. The President of the United States is given the power to make treaties by Article II of the Constitution. Although the Constitution also provides that the advice and consent of the Senate is necessary before a treaty is binding, the initiative for drafting such an international agreement is clearly in the hands of the President. Normally the Secretary of State acts for the President in making international treaties (which makes it convenient for those opposed to a certain treaty to attack the State Department when they would hesitate to attack the President—for example, in recent years commercial fishermen in the Pacific Northwest have complained that the State Department has been "selling them down the river" by negotiating treaties providing other nations greater fishing privileges in the North Pacific).

Treaties, together with the Constitution and laws passed by Congress under its Constitutional powers, are the supreme law of the land. They have had considerable impact on American business, mainly beneficial. Shortly after the Constitution was adopted in 1789, John Jay negotiated a treaty with the English that was of considerable value to American merchants. Since that time, others of value have been made—such as those involving agreements concerning patents and copyrights—although on occasion the desire of the President to attain certain objectives may have adverse influences on some industries (as in the case of the commercial fishermen noted above).

Rules of Law and Maxims of Equity

Written rules of law are by their very nature universal in their application to all persons falling into the classes covered by the law. Although there is much to be said for the uniform application of legal principles, there may be instances when to do so will give inadequate remedy to some injured party. Aristotle defined equity as being "the correction of the law, where, by reason of its universality, it is deficient." American courts have followed the English precedent of making a distinction between law and equity. At one time, courts of law in England confined their remedies to the assessment of money damages—that is, they were concerned essentially with cases in which one party complained of injury by another and asked for money damages as a remedy. These courts refused to give other kinds of relief to the injured party, such as requiring the one performing a wrongful act to do, or refrain from doing, something. Since they were not always able to secure adequate relief in courts of law, plaintiffs began to petition the king of England for other remedies. Eventually, the king delegated to his chancellor the authority to hear such petitions and, in due course, courts of chancery (taken from the title of the king's officer) or courts of equity were established to decide such matters. "Maxims of equity" as opposed to "rules of law" governed the decisions of such courts and the remedies they provided differed from those granted by courts of law. Since American courts were patterned on the judicial system of England, at one time courts of general jurisdiction in the United States were divided into courts of law and courts of equity. However, as a consequence of a movement to "merge law and equity," this division has all but disappeared in the U.S. court system, although the distinction between rules of law and equity continues to be of importance.

Courts hearing cases in equity decide them by reference to principles known as maxims of equity. Since the object of the equity court is to do justice (it has been suggested that what one gets in a court of law is law and not necessarily justice), statutory rules of law and precedents are less important and the decision is supposed to be based on "moral rights" and "natural justice." However, the judges are not without written guidelines. Maxims of equity have been developed (such as, "equity will not suffer a right to exist without a remedy") and these have been adopted by courts sitting to decide cases in chancery or equity. The existence of equity courts employing certain equitable maxims in deciding special cases has complicated the legal environment of the businessman, although it may be that the net result is favorable. What appears to be true is that the importance of equity proceedings is increasing, and that in the future more reliance will be placed by courts on equitable maxims and less upon the relatively rigid rules of law.

Public Law and Private Law

Some students of the body of law divide it into public law and private law. The distinction concerns the subject matter of the law (since both are made by public agencies such as legislatures and courts). Public law involves matters in which the public has some interest. Laws defining crimes and establishing penalties for violation of the law are public laws because the public has an interest in seeing that certain actions are punished. What this means, in reality, is that it is not necessary to show that any specific individual or group is injured by an action before punitive measures can be applied to the transgressor. An agent of the public— some governmental agency or official—can commence a criminal action against the person violating the law in the name of "the people" in a certain jurisdiction. Criminal law is not the only kind of public law. Constitutional law and administrative law are also types of law that are enforced by some public agency in the name of the general public, although, since there is no general public in reality, such agencies sometimes appear to be acting in the interests of certain special publics.

Private law, on the other hand, concerns itself with the proper relationship of one individual with another, not with the relation of an individual to some abstract "public," and affords remedies for wrongs done to one person by another. Many laws governing the behavior of businessmen are private laws. The law of contracts is one of the most obvious illustrations. Businessmen make a number of contracts with others—mostly with suppliers and customers. Although the contracts (whether written or oral) spell out some of the duties and rights of the contracting parties, there is a vast body of legal rules governing contractual relationships. Thus contract law supplements and limits the provisions of an agreement between two individuals. If a provision of an agreement is contrary to the law of contracts, the courts will not lend their power to a person attempting to secure the carrying out of that provision. Therefore, businessmen must be careful how they draw up contracts, since the courts may refuse to enforce them unless their provisions are in accordance with the law and since such enforcement will be in line with the law of contracts.

In addition to the law of contracts, private law has another major subdivision: the law of torts. A tort is a wrong committed by one person against another (this is very similar to a crime, except that a crime is considered to be a wrong committed by one person against the public or society). The similarity between crimes and torts is well illustrated by some provisions of the antitrust laws. Section 1 of the Sherman Antitrust Act declares:

> Every contract, combination in the form of trust or otherwise, or conspiracy, in restraint of trade or commerce among the several States, or with foreign nations, is declared to be illegal. Every person who shall make any such contract or engage in any such combination or conspiracy shall be deemed guilty of a misdemeanor, and, on conviction thereof, shall be punished by fine not exceeding fifty thousand dollars, or by imprisonment not exceeding one year, or by both said punishments, in the discretion of the courts.

Here, quite clearly, is a criminal law. Any person engaging in the prohibited activity is subject to fine and/or imprisonment. No private person need complain to the courts of a violation of the law—the Department of Justice conducts investigations and brings criminal charges against businessmen and firms that seem to be engaging in such illegal activity. When the "price-fixing conspiracy" in the electrical equipment industry was discovered by the Justice Department, and when charges were brought by it in a federal court, the judge convicted several businessmen and firms of violating the Sherman Act, levied fines, and even sentenced some corporate executives to jail terms. The Clayton Act, which amended the Sherman Act in 1914, has a provision stating:

> Any person who shall be injured in his business or property by reason of anything forbidden in the antitrust laws may sue therefor . . . and shall recover threefold the damages by him sustained. . . .

Thus the federal antitrust statutes incorporated a common-law principle from the law of torts that provided that anyone injured by a "combination in restraint of trade" had a right to recover money damages from those engaging in such a combination. Under this provision of the Clayton Act, many customers of firms in the electrical equipment industry sued to recover three times the money damages they allegedly sustained because they paid excessively high prices for equipment owing to the price-fixing conspiracy.

Commercial law is an important part of private law. At one time, there were separate rules of law governing commercial relationships and separate courts existed to adjudicate commercial disputes. Feudal lords often provided courts to attract merchants to their towns at fair times, and the decisions made by the judges of these courts evolved into a body of law governing commercial relationships. This *lex mercatoria* (law merchant) was eventually incorporated into the English common law and is part of our legal inheritance. Many textbooks on business law state the generally accepted common-law principles governing contracts and business torts in addition to discussing certain statutes of importance to businessmen. In the United States, no separate courts exist similar to the commercial courts of feudal England and medieval Europe, but the legacy of these courts is seen in the private law governing business relationships.

Laws Classified According to Their Influence on Business

Earlier we indicated that government activity influenced business in a variety of ways. That is, government promotes, taxes, regulates, competes with, sells to, and purchases from business. Since these activities are carried on under laws, we have promotive laws, tax laws, regulatory laws, and laws governing government competition with and government sales to and purchases from business. As with the other classifications, it would be possible to put the body of laws influencing business into the classes indicated, but they are so numerous it is neither possible nor desirable to do so here. Rather, our objective is to indicate the general classifications into which such laws fall, since the names of the classes are widely employed in literature that students of business read. Perhaps by examining some laws regulating business, we enhance our understanding of the classes of the body of law in the environment of the business firm.

LAWS REGULATING BUSINESS. As we noted in an earlier discussion of government regulation of business, such regulation takes many forms. However, we might conceive of all laws permitting government regulation as being concerned with the regulation of business practices. Although we cannot possibly deal here with all such laws, examination of the development of some of the rules of law governing business practices illuminates the nature of regulatory law as it confronts business.

Regulation Under the Common Law. The *lex mercatoria* was part of the private law governing relationships between buyers and sellers, and regulated business practices in the sense that it spelled out the rules governing commercial relationships. However, since "the public" as well as individual buyers or sellers might be injured by certain illegal business practices, the common law of England included rules making certain business actions criminal offenses (a part of the public law). In small English communities during the medieval period, it was possible for merchants to affect the supply of food and other necessities in order to raise their prices. Consequently, the common law began to contain rules prohibiting forestalling (preventing the entry of goods into the market), regrating (buying of foodstuffs with the intention of selling them in the same market at a higher price) and engrossing (purchasing large quantities of growing crops with the object of selling the produce at enhanced prices). These early rules of law were aimed at individual action, but there were other common-law rules that made joint action by merchants to control the market a criminal offense. Such action was regarded as a "conspiracy to monopolize" and such conspiracies were illegal.

English common law also contained certain rules governing "restraints of trade." Originally this referred to contracts in which an individual agreed not to engage in a certain business. Such agreements were frequently made when one person sold his place of business to another and, as part of the bargain, agreed not to open a new establishment in competition with the enterprise he had just sold. Initially, common-law courts held such agreements void and unenforceable (for example, the seller might open a new establishment in violation of the agreement and the buyer of the original firm could not secure any remedy from the courts for any injury resulting from the violation because the courts held such agreements contrary to public policy). However, the rules of common law governing such agreements changed and eventually English courts (and their American followers) began to regard such contracts valid, so long as the restraint of trade was "reasonable."

Restraint of trade has taken on another meaning in American law. In the United States, competitors in the same market have occasionally made agreements with one another to fix prices, restrict output, divide the market, or pool earnings. American common-law courts held such agreements to be contrary to public policy (although they were not made criminal offenses) and would not enforce them if one of the parties to such an agreement complained that the contract had been violated by another party to it. If all competitors in a market made such an agreement, the result was a monopoly. Some students of the common law have pointed out that although monopoly has never been an offense as such, where monopoly results in restraint of trade then an agreement by competitors to establish a monopoly is illegal.

Not all of the English common-law rules governing business practices found their way into American common law. For example, American state governments did not engage in criminal prosecutions of businessmen for engrossing, forestalling, or conspiracy to monopolize. The doctrines concerning restraint of trade were adopted, and new meaning was given them by applying them to contracts and combinations entered into for the sole purpose of restricting competition. However, a number of factors combined to lead to dissatisfaction with common-law rules and to pressure for statutes governing business practices.

In part, the public prosecution of violators of the rules of common law was weak. Little provision was made in the various states for aggressive prosecution of those engaging in contracts, combinations, and conspiracies in violation of common-law rules. Also, the common law did not provide much in the way of penalties for engaging in the illegal practices. About the only penalty available was that of refusing to enforce such contracts; such refusal might have had some influence because a party to such an agreement might gain a temporary advantage by increasing output or cutting prices, even though the contract prohibited members to the agreement from doing so. Too, only the United States had jurisdiction over interstate commerce, and since such contracts might cover firms doing business in a number of states, no one government was in a position to proceed against the members of the agreement in all of their places of business. (It should be pointed out that the federal government does not enforce common-law rules, and when no federal statute exists permitting federal agencies to proceed against those engaging in certain business practices, they may not do so, even though there is a violation of common law by those engaged in interstate commerce.) Obviously, the solution (at least for those who regarded certain business practices as a public problem) was the passage of statutes by state legislatures and Congress.

Statutory Regulations. State statutes preceded federal regulatory legislation, and state constitutional provisions came before state legislatures passed laws. Maryland, in a constitutional provision adopted in 1776, declared monopolies: "odious, contrary to the spirit of a free government and the principles of commerce, and ought not to be suffered." Such constitutional declarations did not always lead to the passage of statutes by state legislatures, and without such legislation they had little effect. It was not until after the Civil War that states began to adopt statutes prohibiting monopolistic combinations and regulating certain business practices.

It was in the Middle West and Texas that antimonopoly forces were first able to secure state statutes regulating business practice generally. Farmers in these areas felt that operators of railroads, warehouses, and manufacturing plants were engaged in conspiracies or monopolies that had the effect of reducing prices the farmer received and of increasing the prices he paid. Some of this legislation was aimed at specific business practices—for example, state legislatures set maximum railroad rates and charges for storage of grain by statute. However, much of the legislation (although aimed at specific practices) contained a general condemnation of monopoly and restraints of trade. Since the 1870's, more than forty states have adopted such laws by act of their legislatures. There is considerable variety in the laws passed by various states, but essentially state laws make illegal agreements or combinations to restrict output or raise prices. Although these actions may have been illegal under common-law rules, positive penalties for engaging in such activities are provided for in the statutes, and public officials are charged with the enforcement of the laws.

Federal regulation was pressed for when it became obvious that action under state law was inadequate to meet the wishes of those proposing regulation of business. Since states could not regulate matters that involved interstate commerce, federal law was necessary if such regulation was to take place. The first regulatory federal statute was the Interstate Commerce Act, passed in 1887. It, however, applied only to railroads and some other transportation agencies, and the first federal law regulating business generally was not passed until 1890, when the so-called Sherman Antitrust Act was passed.

Some students of the antitrust laws regard the Sherman Act as adopting the common-law rules. Certainly an examination of provisions of that law supports such a contention. Earlier we quoted a section of that law which declares every contract, combination, or conspiracy in restraint of trade among the states to be illegal. Another section states that "every person who shall monopolize, or attempt to monopolize, or combine or conspire with any other person or persons, to monopolize, any part" of interstate commerce is guilty of a crime. Although the rules are essentially common-law rules, the penalties that might be assessed against those found guilty are considerably greater than those the common law provides.

Since the passage of the Sherman Antitrust Act in 1890, a number of other federal statutes regulating business practices have been passed. In 1914, the Clayton Act (which was also previously mentioned) and the Federal Trade Commission Act were enacted by Congress. The first of these amended the Sherman Act, while the second declared certain "unfair methods of competition" to be unlawful. There were in existence prior to 1914 some common-law rules dealing with unfair competition—that is, the law of "competitive torts" held misrepresentation, misappropriation, diversion of trade, interference with trade relations, and attacks on competitors as being unfair competition, and any businessman injured by such action could sue for damages or other relief. These common-law doctrines were now incorporated in a federal statute, and what had previously been in the realm of private law now became public law. The Clayton Act also prohibited certain kinds of practices, not so much on the grounds that they were unfair as in the belief that they tended to lessen competition or to create monopolies in certain lines of commerce.

Judicial Interpretation of Federal Statutes. Although, in theory, there is no common law governing the actions of the federal government, federal courts have, in practice, evolved certain rules that have the effect of common-law rules. That is, in deciding cases, federal judges have been obliged to interpret the statutes governing the particular cases brought before them. In doing so, they have occasionally introduced some rules of law that do not appear in the statutes and that sometimes appear contrary to the letter of the law. An outstanding example is the "rule of reason," which the Supreme Court developed in applying the provisions of the Sherman Act to specific cases.

The first section of the Sherman Act specifically declares *every* contract, combination, or conspiracy in restraint of trade to be illegal. In an early prosecution by the Justice Department under this law (the Trans-Missouri Freight Association case), the defendants urged the Supreme Court to adopt a "rule of reason," contending that Congress intended to outlaw only those trade restraints that were "unreasonable," and therefore unlawful at common law. At this time (1897) the Supreme Court was unwilling to adopt such a rule, pointing out that the statute condemned every combination restraining trade, whether that restraint was "reasonable" or not. Any change, the Court said, would have to be written into the law by Congress and could not be made by the Supreme Court "by a process of judicial legislation wholly unjustifiable."

In 1911, the Court reversed its position and adopted a "rule of reason." Although it upheld previous findings that the Standard Oil Company and the American Tobacco Company violated the Sherman Act, it also declared that both were combinations in "unreasonable restraint of trade" and implied that "reasonable restraints of trade" were legal. Justice Harlan dissented from the enunciation of a "rule of reason," saying that the Court was thereby usurping a legislative function by reading new words into the statute and thereby modifying what was clearly the letter of the law. Nonetheless, although Congress has never changed this wording of the Sherman Act, the federal courts (under the leadership of the Supreme Court) have applied a rule stemming from common law and legislated by judges.

Regulatory Laws and Classes of Legal Law. Our objective in dealing with some laws regulating business was to show how they fell into the classifications we had earlier established; a summary might serve to strengthen the points made in the preceding discussion. Initially, we set up a classification scheme of constitutional law, statute law, administrative law, and judge-made law. As we noted, some state constitutions contained prohibitions of monopolies. Federal and state legislatures have passed antitrust statutes. Under the Federal Trade Commission Act of 1914, the Commission has adopted certain rules stating what "unfair methods of competition" are illegal under that statute; these administrative rulings have the force of law. Judge-made law was evident in the traditional common-law rules governing restraints of trade and in the "rule of reason" adopted by the U.S. Supreme Court in 1911.

Another distinction we made was between rules of law and maxims of equity. In a court of law, a person injured by the actions of another person or persons violating laws regulating business can only secure money damages. However, by suing in a court of equity, that court (operating under the maxims of equity) may give certain equitable relief—such as issuing an injunction prohibiting the person or persons violating the law from continuing that action (that is, a "cease-and-desist" order might be issued). As we saw, when regulatory laws are violated, both money damages and injunctions can be secured.

Also, we distinguish between public law and private law. Under the common law, some business practices were regarded as a private wrong by one person against another—for example, we mentioned the common law of "competitive torts," which are rules declaring certain actions by one businessman to be wrongs against other businessmen. Some of these common-law principles became incorporated into public law (in the case of the common law of "competitive torts," the rules were implicitly included in the Federal Trade Commission Act) which declared certain actions contrary to public policy and provided for prosecution of violators of the law by public agencies (such as the Federal Trade Commission). Thus it is possible for some actions to be contrary to both private and public law, that is, to work an injury both on some specific person or persons and "the public."

In succeeding chapters, we shall examine more thoroughly the processes by which the various classes of laws are made. However, since the relations of business with government are with agencies and officials rather than with the law, we shall first examine these relations at different levels of government: national, state, local, foreign, and international.

READING: The Standard Oil Case of 1911 *

[*The following reading illustrates a number of points concerning the law confronting business. Mainly concerned with the Sherman Antitrust Act of 1890, it also refers to the common law concerning restraints of trade and monopolies. It shows why it was necessary to pass a federal statute governing such matters. This case has special significance in that the Court enunciated a "rule of reason" (although one Justice dissented, saying that the statute plainly forbids all activities of certain kinds and not just those which "unreasonably" restrain trade). That is to say, through "judicial legislation" the Supreme Court modified the statute passed by Congress, illustrating how judges make laws. The reported arguments and opinion of the Court (221 U.S. 1) cover more than one hundred pages; the record presented to the Court consisted of twenty-three volumes of*

* Cases adjudged in the Supreme Court of the United States at October Term, 1910. *The Standard Oil Company of New Jersey, et al.* v. *The United States.* Appeal from The Circuit Court of the United States for The Eastern District of Missouri. Argued March 14, 15, 16, 1910; restored to docket for reargument April 11, 1910; reargued January 12, 13, 16, 17, 1911—Decided May 15, 1911.

printed matter, aggregating about twelve thousand pages, "containing a vast amount of confusing and conflicting testimony relating to innumerable, complex and varied business transactions, extending over a period of nearly forty years." All that has been reproduced here is a "syllabus" of the opinion of the Supreme Court.]

The Antitrust Act of July 2, 1890, c. 647, 26 Stat. 209, should be construed in the light of reason; and, as so construed, it prohibits all contracts and combinations which amount to an unreasonable or undue restraint of trade in interstate commerce.

The combination in this case is an unreasonable and undue restraint of trade in petroleum and its products moving in interstate commerce, and falls within the prohibitions of the act as so construed. . . .

Allegations as to facts occurring prior to the passage of the Antitrust Act may be considered solely to throw light on acts done after the passage of the act.

The debates in Congress on the Antitrust Act of 1890 show that one of the influences leading to the enactment of the statute was doubt as to whether there is a common law of the United States governing the making of contracts in restraint of trade and the creation and maintenance of monopolies in the absence of legislation.

While debates of the body enacting it may not be used as means for interpreting a statute, they may be resorted to as a means of ascertaining the conditions under which it was enacted.

The terms "restraint of trade" and "attempts to monopolize," as used in the Antitrust Act, took their origin in the common law and were familiar in the law of this country to and at the time of the adoption of the act, and their meaning should be sought from the conceptions of both English and American law prior to the passage of the act.

The original doctrine that all contracts in restraint of trade were illegal was long since so modified in the interest of freedom of individuals to contract that the contract was valid if the resulting restraint was only partial in its operation and was otherwise reasonable.

The early struggle in England against the power to create monopolies resulted in establishing that those institutions were incompatible with the English Constitution.

At common law monopolies were unlawful because of their restriction upon individual freedom of contract and their injury to the public and at common law; and contracts creating the same evils were brought within the prohibition as impeding the due course of, or being in restraint of, trade.

At the time of the passage of the Antitrust Act the English rule was that the individual was free to contract and to abstain from contracting and to exercise every reasonable right in regard thereto, except only as he was restricted from voluntarily and unreasonably or for wrongful purposes restraining his right to carry on his trade. Mogul Steamship Co. v. McGregor, 1892, A.C. 25. . . .

This country has followed the line of development of the law of England, and the public policy has been to prohibit, or treat as illegal, contracts, or acts entered into with intent to wrong the public and which unreasonably restrict competitive conditions, limit the right of individuals, restrain the free flow of commerce, or bring about public evils such as the enhancement of prices.

The Antitrust Act of 1890 was enacted in the light of the then existing practical conception of the law against restraint of trade, and the intent of Congress was not to restrain the right to make and enforce contracts, whether resulting from combinations or otherwise, which do not unduly restrain interstate or foreign commerce, but to protect that commerce from contracts or combinations by methods, whether old or new, which would constitute an interference with, or an undue restraint upon, it.

The Antitrust Act contemplated and required a standard of interpretation, and it was intended that the standard of reason which had been applied at the common law should be applied in determining whether particular acts were within its prohibitions.

The word "person" in §2 of the Antitrust Act, as construed by reference to §8 thereof, implies a corporation as well as an individual.

The commerce referred to by the words "any part" in §2 of the Antitrust Act, as construed in the light of the manifest purpose of that act, includes geographically any part of the United States and also any of the classes of things forming a part of interstate or foreign commerce.

The words "to monopolize" and "monopolize" as used in §2 of the Antitrust Act reach every act bringing about the prohibited result.

Freedom to contract is the essence of freedom from undue restraint on the right to contract.

In prior cases where general language has been used, to the effect that reason could not be resorted to in determining whether a particular case was within the prohibitions of the Antitrust Act, the unreasonableness of the acts under consideration was pointed out and those cases are only authoritative by the certitude that the rule of reason was applied; United States v. Trans-Missouri Freight Association, 166 U.S. 290, and United States v. Joint Traffic Association, 171 U.S. 505, limited and qualified so far as they conflict with the construction now given to the Antitrust Act of 1890.

The application of the Antitrust Act to combinations involving the production of commodities within the States does not so extend the power of Congress to subjects dehors its authority as to render the statute unconstitutional. United States v. E. C. Knight Co., 156 U.S. 1, distinguished.

The Antitrust Act generically enumerates the character of the acts prohibited and the wrongs which it intends to prevent and is susceptible of being enforced without any judicial exertion of legislative power.

The unification of power and control over a commodity such as petroleum, and its products, by combining in one corporation the stocks of many other corporations aggregating a vast capital gives rise, of itself, to the prima facie presumption of an intent and purpose to dominate the industry connected with, and gain perpetual control of the movement of, that commodity and its products in the channels of interstate commerce in violation of the Antitrust Act of 1890, and that presumption is made conclusive by proof of specific acts such as those in the record of this case.

The fact that a combination over the products of a commodity such as petroleum does not include the crude article itself does not take the combination outside of the Antitrust Act when it appears that the monopolization of the manufactured products necessarily controls the crude article.

Penalties which are not authorized by the law cannot be inflicted by judicial authority.

The remedy to be administered in case of a combination violating the Antitrust Act is two-fold: first, to forbid the continuance of the prohibited act, and second, to so dissolve the combination as to neutralize the force of the unlawful power.

The constituents of an unlawful combination under the Antitrust Act should not be deprived of power to make normal and lawful contracts, but should be restrained from continuing or recreating the unlawful combination by any means whatever; and a dissolution of the offending combination should not deprive the constituents of the right to live under the law but should compel them to obey it.

In determining the remedy against an unlawful combination, the court must consider the result and not inflict serious injury on the public by causing a cessation of interstate commerce in a necessary commodity.

SUGGESTED READINGS

Corley, Robert N., and Robert L. Black, *The Legal Environment of Business* (New York: McGraw-Hill, 1963). After considering the origins of law, the authors turn their attention to contemporary jurisprudence, presenting law as established by judicial decision, and by administrative action. Also analyzed are major environmental factors and trends in areas such as taxation, regulation of commerce, competition, and labor-management problems.

Kempin, Jr., Frederick G., *Legal History: Law and Social Change* (Englewood Cliffs, N.J.: Prentice-Hall, 1963). A colorful history of law and legal institutions from Norman times to the present. Presents the historical background of existing legal institutions and concepts in the context of the ideas and social conditions which originally gave rise to them.

Weissman, Jacob, *Law in a Business Society* (Englewood Cliffs, N.J.: Prentice-Hall, 1964). Discusses the nature of law and business and the way in which the law views property and business behavior.

CHAPTER **26**

BUSINESS
AND THE
FEDERAL
GOVERNMENT

Without a doubt, the federal government has become greatly important
to American businessmen since 1789. This is true whether we examine it
in its activities as promoter, regulator, taxer, buyer, seller, or competitor.
These activities are carried on by seemingly countless agencies and officials functioning under the U.S. Constitution and laws passed by Congress. It would be impossible to deal with all of the laws, agencies, and
officials of the federal government of importance to business in the brief
span of a chapter, but some of the important powers of Congress, the
President, and the federal courts will be touched upon, along with the
major administrative agencies that carry out the intent of Congress and
the President.

DEVELOPMENT OF THE FEDERAL GOVERNMENT'S POWER

The federal government has not always had the power it presently exercises. Before federal agencies and officials can act, there must be constitutional and congressional warrant for their behavior. For a brief period prior to the adoption of the present Constitution, the federal government operated under the Articles of Confederation. Under those Articles, our governmental structure was something like that of the United Nations (*see* Figure 26–1). The thirteen colonies in 1776 declared them-

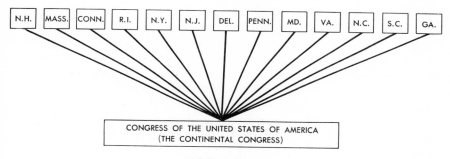

FIGURE 26–1.

selves to be "free and independent states" with the "full power to levy war, conclude peace, contract alliances, establish commerce, and do all other acts and things which independent states may of right do." One thing these states did was to adopt the "Articles of Confederation and Perpetual Union." Only very limited powers were granted the Continental Congress by this document—for example, it had no power to tax or to regulate commerce. In some states, during the period the Articles were in effect, governmental powers were employed to the disadvantage of business. Disillusioned businessmen joined with others to form a new federal government, with greater power to advance the interests of business and with some restrictions on the powers of the states to act contrary to the business interest.

Article I of The Constitution of the United States sets forth a host of important powers of the Congress, as we have seen. Important powers were also given to the President. Under the Articles of Confederation, the Continental Congress held executive power as well as legislative authority. Now the executive power is vested in a President, along with military powers, treaty-making power, and the power to appoint certain administrative officers with the advice and consent of the Senate. The only other power of importance to business specifically granted the President by the Constitution is the veto power.

The judicial power is vested in the Supreme Court, and in inferior federal courts established by Congress. The jurisdiction of federal courts is somewhat limited, since it shares judicial power with state courts.

The power of the federal government has grown from the time of the adoption of the Constitution for a number of reasons. Perhaps most important has been the fact that Congress has passed legislation carrying out its enumerated and implied powers, creating a vast bureaucracy possessing considerable delegated authority to act. Too, the Congress, the President, and the Supreme Court have acquired other powers not specifically granted by the Constitution, although they apparently are not in conflict with it. As the head of a political party, the President has certain powers to compel members of that party—including members of Congress—to do his bidding. The Supreme Court has taken upon itself the power to declare legislation and executive actions unconstitutional under certain circumstances. Also, by interpretation of the Constitution, the Court has expanded the powers of Congress and the President.

In part, the growth of the powers of the federal government stem from its placing the states in a subordinate position in the structure of American government. The states had initially been in a dominant position and the federal government was granted power by the people and the states, which reserved those powers not delegated to the United States government nor prohibited by the Constitution to the states. The framers of the Constitution apparently contemplated that states were to be at least on the same level as the federal government, if not in a superior position. The constitutional question of whether or not states (as sovereign governmental units establishing a federation or existing on an equal level with it) could withdraw from the Union was settled by force of arms during the 1860's. In the century following, the federal government has established its supremacy over the states and has used its other powers—including the power of the purse—to make the states subordinate to it.

DEVELOPMENT OF THE FEDERAL BUREAUCRACY

No specific executive departments were established by the Constitution. Since 1789, they have been created by Congress in the exercise of its powers and have grown in number and influence. Although each agency or major official position was initially created by Congress under some law, the tendency has been, in many cases, for Congress to pass additional legislation increasing the activities and influence of existing agencies and officials. The purposes for which agencies and official positions have been created are indicated in the U.S. Government Organization Manual, a publication listing the thousands of federal agencies and officials existing at present. From examining some of the major cabinet departments and independent agencies we can get some understanding of the many administrative activities of the federal government and of how they influence American business.

The Cabinet Departments

The Cabinet is a creation of custom and tradition, going back to President Washington. It is presently composed of the heads of the ten executive departments of which the President is Chief Executive (as well as the United States Representative to the United Nations). These executive departments have been created at various times in our national history and have grown immensely. They affect business in a surprisingly large variety of ways.

At the time of the organization of the new federal government under the Constitution, only three departments were created—the War Department, the Foreign Affairs Department, and the Department of the Treasury. Since that time, the Department of Foreign Affairs has had its name changed to the Department of State and the War Department has become the Defense Department. Also created in 1789 were the positions of Attorney-General and Postmaster-General, who have since become the heads of the Justice Department and Post Office Department—cabinet departments created in 1870 and 1872, respectively. The only other cabinet department created in the early years of the new government was the Navy Department—established in 1798—now also a part of the Defense Department.

During the nineteenth century, two entirely new cabinet departments were created. The Department of the Interior was formed in 1849 and the Department of Agriculture in 1862, although the latter was not given cabinet status until 1889.

In this century, some departments important to business were created and given cabinet rank. In 1903, the Department of Commerce and Labor was established and separated into two cabinet departments in 1913. Since World War II, the Department of Health, Education and Welfare was formed and the Department of Defense consolidated the activities of the departments of War and Navy.

From the beginning, the activities of the cabinet departments served to promote the interests of business. The War Department and Navy Department protected the commerce and property of American businessmen at home and abroad. The first Secretary of the Treasury was concerned with developing a tax system that would encourage manufacturing and with establishing a sound currency. A system of post offices and post roads improved communications and transportation, especially important to businessmen. As their missions became more complex, the activities of the major executive departments began to have other impacts, and in each department we see a number of influences being exerted upon business.

DEFENSE DEPARTMENT.   Although the Defense Department is still important as a protector of the lives and property of Americans, its buying behavior and competitive activities are also of great consequence. Many billions of dollars are spent each year for national defense purchases from business, and the ability to secure contracts to supply such needs means the difference between success and failure for many firms. Although protection and purchases promote the interests of business, there is considerable competition with private enterprise within the Defense Department, especially during military emergencies. Considerable manufacturing and maintenance work is conducted; military transportation of personnel and goods frequently takes away traffic that private carriers might otherwise secure; the supply of goods at retail for service personnel competes with merchants; the provision of medical, dental, and hospital services competes with some private enterprises; and, the housing of military personnel takes potential tenants away from landlords. Conscious efforts have been made since World War II to reduce such competition, but substantial amounts of it still remain.

TREASURY DEPARTMENT.   Normally, the Treasury Department is thought of in connection with taxes. Its Internal Revenue Service administers the corporate income tax laws, individual income tax laws, and a number of other pieces of tax legislation that are aimed at securing revenue from business. This agency concerns itself with something more than just following the letter of the law, since it issues rules and regulations having the force of law (unless successfully challenged). By changes in rules—such as the rules governing how much depreciation business firms will be permitted to charge on their plant and equipment —the Internal Revenue Service can in effect change the amount of tax the firm will be obliged to pay during a certain period. Nor is the I.R.S. the only important tax agency in this department; the Bureau of Customs administers the tariff laws that provide for taxes on goods imported into the United States. Here again, the way in which the law is administered has some impact on business. Although tax rates are set by Congress, rules and procedures for administering the law are established by the Bureau of Customs and it may adopt some which are more effective in minimizing foreign competition (a major object of present-day tariff legislation) than others might be.

Administering tax laws is not the sole function of the Treasury Department. It exercises considerable regulatory powers over the banking industry. The National Bank Acts passed by Congress about a century ago created the position of Comptroller of the Currency (the currency he controlled consisted of the national bank notes provided for by that legislation). The privilege of note issue has since been taken from national banks, but the banks still form an important industry and are regulated in a variety of ways by the Comptroller. In recent years, his approval of their establishment of branches and of merging with one another has greatly increased the size and importance of some national banks.

STATE DEPARTMENT. Although it has little direct contact with business, the State Department performs a number of functions of importance to American firms. In its conduct of foreign affairs, it is concerned with protecting and promoting the interests of business. Through the threat of use of the nation's military or other powers, it has been able on many occasions to prevent hostile foreign governments from taking adverse action against the property and personnel of American firms in foreign countries. Through the international treaties it drafts in league with other nations, it attempts to promote the interests of certain industries. In recent years, it has been involved in making agreements under the Reciprocal Trade Agreements Act that have resulted in expanded foreign markets for American producers. It should be pointed out that some agreements entered into by the State Department have adverse influences on firms in some industries. In order to gain wider foreign markets for American goods through reciprocal trade agreements, it is usually necessary to admit foreign producers into our domestic markets on more favorable terms than in the past (by reducing tariffs on imports, for one thing). This has the effect of exposing American producers to greater foreign competition, and may well cause certain manufacturing industries to suffer substantial losses. However, the department aims at the general improvement of conditions for American business and it usually has that effect.

JUSTICE DEPARTMENT. Perhaps the most important unit to businessmen in the Justice Department is the Antitrust Division. Charged, along with the Federal Trade Commission and other agencies, with administering the antitrust laws, it attempts to regulate the size and practices of business involved in interstate commerce. Since it is mainly big business that is involved in such trade—and since making an example of the "naughty big boys" is presumed to have a chastening effect on small business firms that misbehave—it has been the larger businesses that have been prosecuted by the Antitrust Division. Some of the giant firms of the past have been "dissolved" as a consequence of such prosecution; the major cases involved those companies controlling the bulk of the output of the petroleum refining and tobacco industries, that is, Standard Oil of New Jersey and the American Tobacco Company. These dissolutions took place more than half a century ago. In recent years not much effort has been expended by the Antitrust Division in trying to break up big business. However, it still achieves considerable success in prosecuting firms for engaging in restrictive practices (as the electrical equipment industry case shows) and it is alert in fighting mergers that it feels might restrain trade or tend to monopolize certain markets. One interesting aspect of its anti-merger activity is that on occasion the Antitrust Division has opposed the merger of firms which have secured the approval of other federal officials—such as the Comptroller of the Currency—who also exert some regulatory authority over business.

In a minor way, the Justice Department is involved in competition with private business. The Federal Prison Industries, Inc.—a government corporation—produces and distributes a number of products that compete with those of private business. Although the main object is to keep "idle hands" busy, goods produced by such poorly paid labor have provided stiff competition for some manufacturers (it is, of course, the demands of certain groups such as farm groups for inexpensive goods that determine the kind of things produced in federal prisons).

POST OFFICE DEPARTMENT. The Post Office Department promotes business generally and some industries specifically. When the Constitution gave Congress the power to establish post offices and post roads, it was concerned with improving communication and transportation for businessmen especially. The need for current market information and the ability to reach markets expeditiously and inexpensively was important to businessmen of the new nation and the establishment of the Office of Postmaster General as soon as the Constitution was adopted testified to the new government's willingness to meet this need. The services offered by United States Post Offices have expanded greatly since the beginning of the republic; one of the more important services is the carrying of parcel post. The existence of an inexpensive and dependable postal service gave rise to the mail-order industry and the nation's largest retailer—Sears, Roebuck & Co.—got its start as a small mail-order firm. Some industries—such as publishing and direct-mail advertising firms— have received a hidden subsidy as a consequence of the delivery of their mail at something less than cost.

Post roads are no longer a concern of the Post Office Department, but it still concerns itself with transportation. By determining whether mail will move by air, water, highway, or rail, it affects transportation industries quite directly. With the advent of airmail and the intercity transportation of mail by trucks, the railroads lost a lucrative amount of business. Expenditures by the Post Office Department on carrying of mail by air has involved, in some cases, a subsidy to air carriers to promote the growth of that industry.

Although business generally and some industries specifically are promoted by the activities of the Post Office, others have been adversely affected. The development of parcel post brought gloom to the express industry and many of the big names in that industry in the nineteenth century—Wells-Fargo and Adams Express—are no more. There still is a railway express agency (as well as air express), but in part the existence of such private carriers depends on Congressional limitations on the size and weight of objects which may go by mail. Not so well known (and not of much current importance) are the banking activities of the Post Office Department. In addition to providing money orders, a service that is in competition with that of certain private financial institutions, there exists a Postal Savings System. Postal savings provided a safe repository in a day when banks experienced considerable financial difficulty and sometimes were obliged to go out of bustiness, with substantial loss to the depositors. The insurance of deposits in financial institutions by agencies of the federal government has made the Postal Savings System less important, but at one time it was an important competitor for savings, especially in rural areas.

INTERIOR DEPARTMENT. At one time, the federal government held title to vast stretches of land in the interior of the United States. Although many of these lands have been disposed of through sale and grant, there still remain considerable public lands under the jurisdiction of the federal government. In the middle of the nineteenth century, the Department of the Interior was created to administer laws governing the disposition and use of federal lands, and to perform "housekeeping" functions for the federal government. Since that time, it has grown to be a department of natural resources. In addition to its custody of some 760 million acres of land, the department has responsibilities relating to petroleum and gas, solid fuels, electric power, fish, metals and minerals. More fully, it engages in the conservation and development of mineral resources and the promotion of mine safety; in the conservation, development, and utilization of fish and wildlife resources; in the coordination of federal and state recreation programs; in the administration of the nation's great scenic and historic areas; in the reclamation of the arid lands of the West through irrigation; and in the management of hydroelectric power systems.

In conducting these activities, the Interior Department promotes, regulates, and competes with private enterprise. Its Bureau of Land Management sells timber to firms in the forest products industry, making it possible for them to exist without acquiring their own lands. The same bureau negotiates leases with mining enterprises and with those wishing to graze livestock on public lands, thereby promoting the interests of firms in these industries. The major regulatory functions performed by the department are those in relation to mineral resources. It administers laws restricting imports of crude petroleum and petroleum products and allocates such imports among various firms. Thus the interests of some firms engaged in petroleum production and refining are advanced, while others have their activities restricted. The Bureau of Mines conducts a number of programs designed to conserve and develop mineral resources and to promote safety and healthful working conditions in the mineral industries. Competition comes mainly from the various power administrations in the department—the Bonneville Power Administration, the Southeastern Power Administration and the Southwestern Power Administration. These agencies compete for dam sites—and normally are given preference over privately owned electric companies in the allocation of such sites—and by giving preference in power sales to public bodies and cooperatives they foster strong, and perhaps unfair, competition by such agencies with investor-owned electric utilities.

AGRICULTURE DEPARTMENT. The Agriculture Department was the first major executive department of the federal government established to promote the interests of an economic class. It has grown to be one of the largest cabinet departments, with a budget second only to that of the Defense Department. In conducting its activities, it is basically concerned with the promotion of the interests of the commercial farmer, but its actions have an impact on other industries as well. For example, promotion of the agricultural interest has led to the regulation of commodity exchanges and the meat-packing industry. Farmers have long been concerned about the wide fluctuations of prices on agricultural commodity exchanges, feeling that activities of traders on those exchanges resulted in an undesirable market situation for certain farm products. As a result of the political influence of farmers, trading practices are now regulated by the Commodity Exchange Authority in the Department of Agriculture. Through meat inspection by an agency of the Department, the processing activities of meat packers are controlled so as to insure a larger market for wholesome meat (and, thereby, a larger market for livestock).

Competition with private enterprise is involved in a number of programs of the Agriculture Department. This is particularly true of the loan programs. From various agencies in the department, loans can be secured on better terms than private financial institutions can or will give. Too, the crop insurance program of the Department of Agriculture provides such insurance at premiums below that at which any private agency could sell crop insurance because most of the administrative expenses are financed by annual appropriations of Congress.

Not all of the Agriculture Department's activities affect other industries adversely. The Forest Service, in its operation of the national forests and in its research programs, promotes the interests of the forest products industries by making timber available and by publishing the products of its research.

DEPARTMENT OF COMMERCE. Early in this century, a Department of Commerce and Labor was established. A decade later, in 1913, the department was reorganized as the Department of Commerce when all of its labor activities were transferred to the newly created Department of Labor. Since that time, it has been the businessman's department with statutory functions of promoting foreign and domestic commerce, fostering manufacturing industries, and aiding the development of the transportation facilities of the United States.

A large part of the activity in this department is aimed at developing and disseminating information useful to business. It conducts the various censuses through the Bureau of the Census. The Office of Business Economics collects, analyzes, and publishes other statistical information of value. Coastal and geodetic surveys are conducted, and nautical and aeronautical charts are published. Commodity weights, measures and standards are established in the Bureau of Standards, thereby facilitating business transactions.

Legal monopolies of certain products are granted by the Patent Office of the department. Without patent protection for their processes and products, some firms could not have grown and prospered. The inexpensive and expeditious movement of products has been facilitated by the activities of the Bureau of Public Roads (although the railroad industry suffered when people and products began to move long distances over public roads). Other services of this department have promoted other industries, and the Department of Commerce continues to grow in importance for American businessmen.

DEPARTMENT OF LABOR. Although its main object is to serve the interests of labor, some functions performed by the Labor Department also promote the interests of business. It concerns itself with forecasting the need for certain kinds of labor and through its education and information programs attempts to insure that a trained work force of proper quality and quantity is available at the time it is needed. Through the activities of the United States Employment Service, it assists employers to find employees at the same time it aids the unemployed secure employment (although these activities, partially conducted through state employment services, have been regarded as unfair competition by private employment agencies). Activities of the department in attempting to prevent labor-management disputes before serious work interruption occur are also in the interests of management as well as labor.

In promoting the interests of labor, the Department of Labor sometimes is involved in regulatory activities. The Fair Labor Standards Act and labor laws covering public contracts are administered by divisions of the department. Employers are obliged, under those laws, to pay certain minimum wages, provide certain overtime compensation, observe certain standards with respect to the employment of child and convict labor, and comply with certain safety and health standards. Employers violating the rules established under such legislation may find themselves prosecuted by the Solicitor of Labor.

HEALTH, EDUCATION AND WELFARE. The most recently established cabinet department is the Department of Health, Education and Welfare. In its health programs, it sometimes adversely affects some industries—the Public Health Service report on the relationship between cigarette smoking and health being a recent case in point. The Food and Drug Administration also performs a regulatory function in promoting purity and requiring truthful and informative labeling of those commodities covered by the Food, Drug and Cosmetic Act and allied legislation.

Almost all educational activity promotes the interest of business, but the Office of Education engages in the performance of functions of special importance to employers. Its Division of Vocational and Technical Education administers a number of laws aimed at increasing vocational and technical training. To the extent that such activity is carried on by public bodies, business firms are not obliged to engage in it.

Among its other agencies, the department's Social Security Administration is perhaps best known. This agency administers the old-age, survivors and disability insurance programs of the federal government and to the extent that these are expanded as a result of efforts by the Social Security Administration to expand social insurance, payroll taxes of business firms are increased. A lesser known activity of the agency is its credit union program, which encourages the expansion of credit unions. This results in increased competition for other financial institutions, both for loans and for savings, and may have an adverse impact on the earnings of some investor-owned enterprises.

Independent Agencies

There are a large number of "independent agencies" existing as administrative units of the federal government. Just who or what they are independent of is not very clear, although it is apparently the objective to make them somewhat independent of politics and the President. Independence is insured by limiting the members of any one political party who may serve on the commissions controlling most of the independent agencies and by providing that the President may not remove any member of such a commission (although he still retains the power to appoint such members, subject to the approval of the Senate). As a result, the independent agencies form what has sometimes been called a "fourth branch" of the federal government, "wholly disconnected from the executive department," with duties which are in large measure "quasi-judicial" and "quasi-legislative."

Insofar as business is concerned, the more important of the independent agencies are those involved in the regulation of certain business practices or industries. A recent study of their nature and activities is included as a reading at the end of this chapter. However, other independent agencies are involved in promoting the interests of business, in taxation, in buying from business, and in competing with private enterprises.

If we ignore, for the moment, the independent agencies involved in regulation, we note that the bulk of the others having some relations with business directly or indirectly promote the interests of various industries. Some of these are engaged in financial activities. The Farm Credit Administration oversees four agricultural bank systems providing short-term, intermediate-term, and long-term credit for individual farmers and for agricultural cooperatives. To supplement, rather than compete with, private financial institutions, an Export-Import Bank aids importers and exporters. The Federal Home Loan Bank Board has jurisdiction over the Home Loan Bank System, federal savings and loan associations, and the Federal Savings and Loan Insurance Corporation, which insures deposits in such institutions, thereby encouraging depositors to leave their savings. A similar insurance program is carried on by the Federal Deposit Insurance Corporation for commercial banks. Finally, the Housing and Home Finance Agency includes in its operations the Federal Housing Administration—which, among other things, provides insurance for mortgage loans on housing—and the Federal National Mortgage Association, which provides a "secondary market" for mortgages and enables institutions holding mortgages to liquidate them without substantial loss.

Some independent agencies engage in research and development activity that benefits business. The National Science Foundation supports basic research that may have a number of practical applications in various industries. Already the research conducted by the Atomic Energy Commission and the National Aeronautics and Space Administration has been put to use by private business. Even the Tennessee Valley Authority—regarded chiefly as a competitor—conducts research in agricultural fertilizers and makes its findings available to private producers rather than engaging in large-scale fertilizer production itself.

Other agencies provide other services. Assistance in resolving labor-management disputes before costly work stoppages occur is provided by the Mediation and Conciliation Service and by the National Mediation Board (which serves only rail and air carriers). Shippers and water transportation companies have benefited greatly from the operations of the Panama Canal Company and the St. Lawrence Seaway Development Corporation (although some transportation industries—especially the railroads—have suffered as a result of improvement of water routes by these two agencies).

Some independent agencies hear appeals from businessmen (and others) from decisions of those government departments under the jurisdiction of the President and Cabinet and sometimes give relief from orders of such departments. The Federal Coal Mine Safety Board of Review hears appeals from orders of the Bureau of Mines. A Tax Court of the United States hears appeals on tax issues and contract renegotiation matters and sometimes renders decisions in favor of businessmen and against other federal agencies. Public investigations on the influence upon certain industries of tariff laws and trade agreements are made by the Tariff Commission, which sometimes recommends relief for industries adversely affected by those laws and agreements.

There is little competition with business by independent agencies. The TVA has provided a considerable amount of competition for investor-owned utilities in the Tennessee Valley, but other than this agency and the Veterans Administration—which might be regarded as providing some competition in medical, hospital, and insurance services—there are no others of any consequence, with one possible exception. The General Services Administration is known mainly as the "housekeeper" of the federal government and is important as a big buyer—procuring supplies and equipment as well as contracting for construction on behalf of most of the civilian agencies. However, it is also engaged in the stockpiling of strategic and critical materials, which sometimes places it in the position of competing with buyers of such materials and of competing with sellers when it declares some of the stockpile to be "surplus."

Although the activities of the federal government are of great and growing importance to business, those of state and local governments are also important. Early in our national history, when the federal government was weak, states and their subdivisions were the businessman's main contact with government. Since their importance to business has continued and grown, no study of the political environment of business would be complete without an examination of activities of states, to which we shall turn in the next chapter.

READING: Independent Regulatory Commissions

[*In 1947, the Eightieth Congress established a Commission on Organization of the Executive Branch of the Government (more familiarly known as the "Hoover Commission" after its chairman, Herbert Hoover). Among the agencies examined were the "independent regulatory agencies" mentioned briefly in the text. Since these agencies regulate business, their further study is warranted. The following reading is an excerpt from a report by the Hoover Commission.*]

The Nature of the Independent Regulatory Commission

In the Federal Government the independent regulatory commission has a history of over 70 years. During that period this type of agency has developed to meet new needs for regulating various industries or types of activity.

The Interstate Commerce Commission, the first of these Federal agencies, was created in 1887 with limited powers to regulate railroad rates and service. After an early period of frustration, the Commission became firmly established, and Congress expanded its powers and assigned to it new areas for regulation, such as pipe lines (1906), motor carriers (1935), and water carriers (1940). Its procedures, organization, and prestige have greatly influenced the later development of the independent commissions.

Under President Wilson, the independent commission was used in several fields. In 1913 the Federal Reserve Board was established to control money and credit and supervise member banks. In the next year the Federal Trade Commission was created with responsibility for restraining unfair methods of competition and enforcing the Clayton Act passed at the same time. Two years later the United States Shipping Board was set up to develop the merchant marine; after various changes, this agency was succeeded by the present Maritime Commission created in 1936.

In the late 1920's two more independent commissions were established to regulate hydroelectric power projects and radio, respectively. The Federal Power Commission, first set up in 1920 as an interdepartment committee, was converted into an independent commission in 1930 on the recommendation of President Hoover. Originally authorized primarily to license private power projects on streams under Federal control, its authority was extended in 1935 to the regulation of interstate transmission of electric energy, and in 1938 to the regulation of interstate gas pipe lines. The Federal Radio Commission, initially created in 1927, became the Federal Communications Commission in 1934 and was made responsible for the regulation of radio, telephone, and telegraph.

Under President Roosevelt three other new commissions were established in addition to the Maritime Commission and the Federal Communications Commission. In 1934 the new Securities and Exchange Commission took over from the Federal Trade Commission the administration of the Securities Act of 1933 (regulating disclosure of information regarding new security issues) and was also assigned the Securities and Exchange Act of 1934 (regulating stock exchanges and dealers); in 1935 the Public Utility Holding Company Act was placed under its supervision. Thereafter, its duties were extended by the Bankruptcy Act (corporate reorganization), Trust Indenture Act (1939), Investment Company Act (1940), and Investment Advisers Act (1940).

In 1935 the National Labor Relations Act created an independent Board to administer the provisions of the act. Finally in 1938, the Civil Aeronautics Act established the independent Civil Aeronautics Authority to regulate air transportation and air commerce.

Even this short summary reveals the important fact that the independent commissions reflect a substantial period of experience and development. Their use has not been limited to any one period. Beginning in 1887, every decade has seen the creation of new commissions or the extension of existing commissions into new fields. So steady an evolution, under such varied political auspices, indicates that these agencies respond to a real need.

Areas of Regulation

At first glance the nine commissions appear to engage in a heterogeneous series of activities, and in fact their duties do cover a wide range. For purposes of discussion, however, they may be divided into general types according to their areas of regulation. On this basis they fall into four groups:

1. Three commissions regulate carriers: Interstate Commerce Commission (rail, motor, and water carriers and pipe lines); United States Maritime Commission (ocean carriers); Civil Aeronautics Board (air carriers).

2. Two regulate other utilities: Federal Power Commission (electrical and gas utilities); Federal Communications Commission (telephone, telegraph, and radio).

3. Two regulate finance and credit: Securities and Exchange Commission (security exchanges and security issues generally, and holding companies); Federal Reserve Board (money and credit, and member banks).

4. Two regulate practices in special fields affecting industry generally: Federal Trade Commission (unfair trade practices), National Labor Relations Board (unfair labor practices and collective bargaining).

General Character of Functions

Defining Standards of Conduct

The point to be emphasized is that the bulk of commission activity is establishing standards and rules to govern conduct for the future. The commissions are engaged far less in prosecuting wrongdoers to punish them for past offenses, than in prescribing and defining the future privileges and duties of the persons subject to regulation. In large measure this involves making and applying policies to carry out the objectives and standards of the statute.

In part, this is done by making formal rules or regulations, often after extensive investigations and hearings; in part, duties and privileges are fixed by decisions in specific cases, after hearing; and in part, by informal conferences, opinions, and rulings. Of course, most of the commissions also do some policing and enforcement to require compliance with their regulations, but that is not a major activity compared with defining the duties and standards. A brief review of the commissions will illuminate this point.

Regulating Utilities

This fact about the work of the commissions clearly appears in the regulation of carriers and other utilities (Interstate Commerce Commission, Civil Aeronautics Board, Maritime Commission, Federal Power Commission, and Federal Communications Commission). With certain exceptions, they engage mainly in regulating—

1. Rates, by fixing maxima or minima, and by forbidding discrimination or preferences;
2. Service, by prescribing the standards to be met by the regulated company;
3. Entry, by granting or refusing certificates, licenses, or permits required by a carrier, utility, or other person in order to furnish or extend service;
4. Finances, by granting or refusing approval for new securities, acquisitions, mergers, and similar actions, and by prescribing accounting standards and methods;
5. Safety, by prescribing regulations regarding equipment, personnel, procedures, and other matters affecting the safety of operations.

Moreover charges, service, competition, finances, and safety are all closely related. The policies and standards as to any one will affect one or more of the other areas. Basically, therefore, each commission is engaged in establishing a coherent framework of policies, standards, and conditions within which the industry carries on its operations.

Regulating Finance and Credit

While their authority and duties are different, the Federal Reserve and Securities and Exchange Commission also illustrate this same fact. In its control of credit and money, the Federal Reserve is clearly establishing the conditions for the future; and on a small scale, the same is largely true of its supervision of member banks, although it may rarely have to enforce its regulations or statutes. The Securities and Exchange Commission has more enforcement duties but is still engaged mainly in defining the standards of disclosure, rules of conduct for the securities markets, and the structure and finances of holding companies; formal proceedings to apply sanctions are only a minor part of its job.

Regulating Unfair Practices

The Federal Trade Commission and National Labor Relations Board appear at first to be exceptions. In part this is due to the fact that their typical proceeding is brought by a complaint against an individual or concern for unfair practices. But the appearance is somewhat misleading. The Federal Trade Com-

mission was created primarily to clarify and develop the standards to govern
business conduct respecting competition. Under the major statutes, the Federal
Trade Commission has power only to order the person to cease and desist from
specific conduct for the future. In other words, the order defines the standards
for future conduct, although cast in a form similar to a prosecution and based on
evidence of past activity.

While the Labor Board does impose sanctions as to past conduct in some
cases, an important part of its work is also to prescribe the duties of the parties
and to establish the guides for collective bargaining.

Significance

In short, each of the commissions is largely engaged in making policies and
defining standards of conduct within the framework of the statute. In great part,
this is carried on through quasi-judicial procedures, but it involves more than
adjudications of a court. In making decisions or regulations defining a standard
of conduct, prescribing a duty, or granting a privilege, the commission must act
in the light of the conditions in the industry and the statutory objectives.

SUGGESTED READINGS

Commission on Organization of the Executive Branch of the Government,
Staff Study on Business Enterprises Outside the Department of Defense (Washington, D.C.: Government Printing Office, 1955). A detailed study of those
business enterprises which are either "not necessary to the efficient conduct of
the government" or are "competitive with private enterprise" and their effect
upon private business.

Dimock, Marshall E., *Business and Government* (New York: Holt-Dryden,
1961). This is the fourth edition of a thorough treatment of the relationships
between American business enterprise and the federal government.

Landis, James M., *Report on Regulatory Agencies to the President-Elect* (New
York: Ad Press, 1960). A detailed analysis of the various functions of the regulatory agencies.

U.S. Government Organization Manual (Washington, D.C.: Government
Printing Office). Issued annually, this manual covers the creation, authority,
organization, and functions of all branches of the federal government. Contains
a section on the Courts, another on Congress and its powers, and comprehensive
statements on the executive departments and agencies.

CHAPTER 27

STATES,
LOCAL
GOVERNMENTS
AND BUSINESS

The great relative growth in the importance of the federal government has somewhat obscured the fact that state and local governments also occupy important positions in the political environment of American business. It is only during the past century that the national government has come to play a role in which it touches the life of every businessman and firm. Before the Civil War, state and local governments had much more influence on all but a few firms. Also, the relative growth of the federal government's impact on business makes us less conscious of the fact that there has been, in absolute terms, a substantial growth in the functions of state and local governments as they impinge on business.

For most firms, what is done in city, county, and state governments is still of greater importance than what goes on in Washington, which directly influences small business chiefly through taxation. Larger firms having greater contacts with federal agencies and officials still retain many important relations with governments within state boundaries.

POWERS OF STATE GOVERNMENTS

The powers that states have over those within their boundaries are continually changing. The Declaration of Independence declared:

> That the United Colonies are, and of right ought to be, Free and Independent States . . . and that as free and independent states, they have full power to levy war, conclude peace, contract alliances, establish commerce and to do all other acts and things which independent States may of right do.

The Articles of Confederation reasserted the existence of the thirteen states as "sovereign nations." That document, drafted in 1777, gave the Continental Congress some authority, but made it clear that: "Each State retains its sovereignty, freedom, and independence, and every power, jurisdiction, and right, which is not by this confederation expressly delegated to the United States, in Congress assembled." In Chapter 24, we dealt with the problems that arose during the brief period when the Articles were in force and with the pressures that were generated for the strengthening of the federal government and resulted in a new basic instrument of government.

The Constitution of the United States went into effect in 1789, and this document, its amendments, and interpretations determine the present power of the states. Under the Constitution, the states gave the federal government greater authority and gave up some powers they previously had. The question of whether the document created a nation or a group of "united nations" was finally settled by force of arms in the 1860's. However, the development of government in the United States makes it useful to think of states having those powers which any sovereign nation has, except as limited by the Constitution and interpretations thereof by the Supreme Court. In short, the federal government is a government of delegated powers; state governments retain those powers not explicitly or implicitly given the federal government or taken by it. Since sovereign power is supreme power, a state government may do whatever it chooses to do, except as the Constitution and the federal government limits it, and the distribution of governmental power between the nation and the states has left the states supreme in many fields.

The powers that a state government exercises within constitutional and federal limits are those it chooses to exercise. Every state of the American Union has a constitution—a written document setting forth the basic law by which the state is governed, the structure of the state government, the basic individual rights of citizens of the state and, frequently, a number of trivial and temporary details. State constitutions are adopted and amended by representative bodies or by the vote of the electorate. The citizens of a state, either directly or through their representatives, determine the form of state government. Not only are constitutions developed in this fashion but also legislation. State laws, so long as they conform to the state and federal constitutions, create agencies of the state that have some impact on business within that state. It is mainly in this relationship between state administrative officials and business that the influence of state government is felt.

The Power to Incorporate Groups

Among the powers of states is the power to incorporate a number of individuals into a body possessing certain powers and privileges granted by the state. There were some business corporations having charters from colonial governments or from Parliament prior to the American Revolution, but incorporation was more usual during that period for religious, educational, and political bodies. Since then, states have employed their power to grant corporations (since obtaining corporate capacity is regarded as a privilege conferred by the state rather than an inherent right) to greatly expand the number and size of business corporations to the point where such business organizations have become the dominant units of American business.

Originally, in the United States, special acts of state legislatures were required before the privilege of incorporation could be secured. Although some turnpike, bridge, canal, dock, water, fire, banking, and insurance companies were incorporated by states prior to 1800, only something more than 300 business corporations were established before that time. Business groups exerted pressure on state legislatures to make the incorporation process easier and to make the corporate form available to all legitimate businesses meeting certain qualifications. North Carolina and Massachusetts passed laws approximating general acts of incorporation prior to 1800, and other states adopted similar laws after that year, but it was not until 1837 that a state (Connecticut) passed a law permitting incorporation for any general business purpose.

Since that time, additional laws have been passed by state legislatures under their power to create corporations, which have promoted the development of this form of business organization. Owners of corporations had their liability in event of bankruptcy limited to the amount of their investment. Corporations were authorized to conduct business outside of the state of incorporation. They were permitted, also, to exchange corporate shares directly for acquired property. Permission was given to issue stock in unlimited amounts. Power was granted to acquire and hold the stock of other corporations. Limitations were removed on the duration of the corporate charter and, in theory if not in practice, corporations were given perpetual life. Although this is not a complete catalog of all the authority granted to corporations by states, it should be obvious that this state power has been of major importance to American business.

The Police and Tax Powers

Also among the powers of states are the so-called police power and the power to levy taxes. The power to promote the health, safety, welfare, and morals of inhabitants of a state is known as the police power. This broad power justifies many actions of states, so long as that action is not in violation of the federal Constitution or that of the state itself. Under the police power, many states have passed laws regulating business activity, statutes promoting certain kinds of private business, and legislation creating state-owned enterprises that compete with privately owned enterprises. Within the limits of the U.S. Constitution, states may levy various taxes, many of which affect business directly. Beyond the general property tax and the corporate income tax, there are special corporation levies, license taxes, unemployment insurance taxes, sales taxes, and severance taxes (taxes on the separation of natural resources from their natural location). Taxes on business have been used as a means of regulating business as well as of raising revenue. An outstanding example has been the taxation of chain stores, the objective of which is to restrict the growth of such stores rather than to provide income for the state.

STATE AGENCIES AND OFFICIALS

The power of the state is brought to bear on businessmen and other citizens through various government agencies and officials. Although officers of the state operate under the statutes and constitution of that government, businessmen have their relationships with men and not with those laws. The notion that American government is a "government of laws and not men" is a pleasant fiction: American government is both of these and it is with men rather than with laws that firms have contacts. Different administrators enforce the same laws in quite different ways;

hence, the businessman who is to deal realistically with government must know something of the nature of government administration.

State governments have a chief executive officer and a number of other administrative officials. Governors of states usually possess restricted executive powers; they commonly share the administration of a state with a number of other officials who have been elected to office by the people. Although some administrators are appointed by the governor (a growing practice), there are still many who are not, and among these are many with whom businessmen must concern themselves. Despite the rather limited executive powers of governors, they have played an increasingly larger role in legislative matters. The combination of the "governor's program" of legislation and the veto power makes the chief executive the "chief legislator" as well. It is perhaps the law-making role rather than the executive position of the governor that is of greater significance to business. Other officials of state, whether elected or appointed, have more direct influence on business. These officials perform functions that can be classified as regulatory, promotive, competitive, and tax administration.

State Regulation of Business

Regulation of business by states aims at the maintenance of competition, the restriction of competition, protection of public health and safety, prevention of fraud, and assurance of adequate service at reasonable rates from businesses "affected with a public interest." It is somewhat paradoxical that states that have passed laws prohibiting monopolies and restraints of trade have then permitted agreements to restrict competition under certain conditions. The maintenance of retail prices under state "fair trade" laws is an outstanding example of such restraint of trade. Too, it has been suggested that the regulation of professions and trades is aimed at creating monopoly situations in which those in a particular occupation might eliminate "unfair competition" and raise prices. This latter type of regulation has led to the establishment of a number of boards of examiners having official status.

The protection of public health and safety is aimed at by many laws and many agencies. State pure food and drug acts prohibiting the sale of diseased or adulterated food products, establishing standards of purity for drugs, and dealing with the labeling of medicines exist in every state. Departments of health normally enforce such laws. Industrial accident commissions or their counterparts require the observance of certain minimum conditions of safety in factories. Safety in mining and transportation is also the concern of states. The health and safety of women and children are protected by labor laws establishing minimum ages for certain types of work and excluding women from specific occupations. Such legislation and its administration has had greater impact since the adoption of workmen's compensation laws, which require employers to contribute to a fund for employees who become ill or injured as a result of their occupation. Many states have also required that firms change practices that contribute significantly to stream and air pollution, and have set up agencies to police such businesses.

To prevent fraud, states have passed a number of laws. Almost all of them have statutes prohibiting fraudulent advertising. The misrepresentation of products by sales persons or the imitation of competitors' products are frequently declared to be illegal. Many states provide for uniform sales contracts, partly to prevent fraud. Most states have "blue-sky laws," aimed at the fraudulent sale of worthless corporate securities. State securities commissions, or similar agencies, approve the sale of stocks and bonds before they may be lawfully sold. To further promote this objective, many state governments regulate security dealers as well as the sale of securities. It should be noted that there is little uniformity as to which agency enforces certain legislation, although there is great uniformity among laws from state to state. In some states, there is no securities commission and enforcement lies in the hands of the railroad commission, the bank commissioner, the insurance commissioner, the secretary of state, or the attorney-general.

A recent development in state government has been the establishment in some states of Consumer Fraud Bureaus. These differ from Better Business Bureaus in that they are state agencies possessing governmental powers of enforcement, but the other agencies are voluntary, business-supported organizations relying heavily on self-regulation (although Better Business Bureaus frequently turn over consumer complaints to public authorities for prosecution). Attorneys for states can secure injunctions against fraudulent practices of companies and even—in some extreme cases—may seek the dissolution of corporations when they engage in persistent consumer fraud. The New York State Consumer Frauds and Protection Bureau, the oldest in the nation, was established in 1957 as a division of the Attorney General's office. Since that time, Alaska, California, Connecticut, Illinois, Kansas, Massachusetts, Michigan, Minnesota, Missouri, New Jersey, Ohio, and Washington have created similar fraud units.

A number of state agencies have been established to regulate specific industries. In order to protect public health and safety, states have regulated the sale of intoxicating liquor by prohibiting its sale in some states, by engaging in the sale of liquor in state stores while denying the right to such sale to private business, or by regulating the sale of liquor under some licensing system. To provide some measure of security for depositors, states also supervise banking. By requiring the holding of minimum amounts of capital and reserves, by placing restrictions on the purposes for which loans might be made, and by demanding special requirements of the stockholders of the bank, the interests of depositors are protected. A banking commissioner normally enforces banking laws, and makes periodic investigations of banks to ensure their conformance with the law. Insurance, too, is an industry subject to strict public regulation by the states. Almost every state has an insurance commissioner, or officer with similar title. In addition to control of companies chartered by the state, he licenses companies from other states and also exercises supervision over insurance agents and brokers. Under certain circumstances, he may revoke a company's license to do business. Insurance rates also come under the jurisdiction of the insurance commissioner, and he may make some changes in the rates that companies propose to adopt. This function is similar to that performed by public utilities commissions.

The regulation of business by states extends most completely over those industries affected with a special public interest. Almost all of the transportation industries—railroads, common carrier truck lines, bus lines, air lines, pipelines, water carriers—are subject to state control. Firms in the communications industries—telephone and telegraph—also are regulated as such because they too are regarded as public utilities. Firms distributing electricity and gas also come under the supervision of public utility agencies. This list is not complete, but it illustrates the nature of industries whose service and rates are subject to public regulation by states.

The supervision of public utility industries lies in the hands of a public utility commission or commissioner, although in some states such a body might be called the railroad commission or public service commission. For most firms in these industries, the most important control exercised by the state agent or agency is the control over the rates the companies may charge. Not only are maximum rates established, but frequently the entire schedule of rates for various services are controlled by public utility commissions. The prescriptions of these agencies as to the service which a company must provide has an important impact on the costs of a public utility. With their influence on income and costs, public utility commissions influence profits strongly, and commonly aim at keeping the profits of firms affected with a public interest from being excessive.

In addition to the extensive regulation of certain industries, specific practices of all firms are subject to state regulation. In some states, hiring practices are subject to regulation to prevent discrimination "because of race, creed, color, or national origin." Such regulation is usually enforced by a Fair Employment Practices Commission. State labor commissions concern themselves with collective bargaining practices of employers. Unemployment insurance contributions are required of most employers in the United States and the administration of the funds are in the hands of state agencies.

There is, in short, almost no private industry or firm that is not touched by some aspect of state regulation. The amount of such regulation is great and growing, and, consequently, a matter for increasing concern on the part of American business.

State Promotion of Business

The promotion of the interests of business by state government has a long history. Some of the disputes among states during the period of the Articles of Confederation stemmed from legislation passed by each state legislature to promote the interests of businessmen of its particular state by making it more difficult and expensive for businessmen from "foreign states" to do business in the "domestic" state. Even though the Constitution reduced the power of states over interstate commerce, states still possess ample powers to enable them to promote the interests of businessmen under their jurisdiction.

Some of the "general activities" of state governments have the effect of promoting the interests of businessmen as well as of other citizens. Traditionally, education and highway construction have been important state activities. To the extent that state governments engage in educating the youth (and sometimes adult citizens) of the state, an educated labor force is made available. Also, education leads to higher income, and hence those businessmen engaged in the production and distribution of consumer goods and services benefit for this reason. Transportation costs are reduced and markets are widened when states engage in the construction of highways. Not all business is promoted by the building of roads, since new highways may change the routes taken by drivers and cause substantial decreases in the business of motels, roadside restaurants, and so on. Beyond such general activity, however, states have engaged in more specific action to promote business.

At one time, in order to encourage certain industries to develop, states were owners and creditors of some firms. This activity took place mainly in the nineteenth century, when state legislatures in the trans-Allegheny West and in the expanding South sold bonds and employed the proceeds either to make loans to railroad, banking, and other corporations or to purchase securities from them. In the unsettled economic conditions of the times, such corporations frequently went bankrupt, and state governments were unable to pay the interest or principal due on the bonds they had issued. The consequent financial embarrassment led many states to alter their constitutions, prohibiting the issuance of state bonds for such purposes. Such prohibition is fairly uniform among the states today, although many states presently provide some financial assistance in order to lure new plants, which indicates a resurgence of this kind of business promotion. At the present time, financial assistance tends to take the form of state lending to development corporations or of insuring mortgage loans to builders of new plants.

As noted above, states have created development agencies to help attract new manufacturing plants. New Hampshire, which began this activity in 1955, provides an illustration of such action. The Industrial Park Authority of New Hampshire has broad powers and can acquire sites that it prepares for occupancy by putting in roads and sewers and building plants (although it can also lend money to others to build plants or it can insure 50 per cent of a mortgage loan to build a plant). When the state agencies build the plants, they normally lease them to manufacturers. Some states secure funds for such operations through tax revenues or through the sale of bonds. Where states are prohibited from directly engaging in such activity, they have established private development corporations that are created by action of the state legislatures rather than under existing corporation-chartering provisions. These "development credit corporations" engage in activities beyond those undertaken by state agencies and make loans for working capital and debt retirement in addition to loans for building.

Many states try to encourage location of new plants through advertising. Most states have an agency bearing the title Department of Business Development or some similar name. Such agencies engage in research on factors important to business location and disseminate the information developed to interested business firms.

States employ some of their powers in rather unusual ways in order to promote business. Their use of the power to tax provides a number of illustrations. Some states have passed laws permitting local units of government to exempt new plants from property taxes for a specified number of years. Louisiana is an outstanding example, having for more than a quarter-century granted either directly, or through local units of government, 10-year exemptions from payment of property taxes to firms investing in new plants. It has been chiefly oil and chemical firms that have benefited, with the list of beneficiaries including Standard Oil of New Jersey, Allied Chemical, American Cyanamid, Dow, U.S. Rubber, Kaiser, Ethyl, and Shell. On occasion, discriminatory taxation has kept firms out —or at least has restricted their operations. The prime example has been taxation of chain stores: the amount of tax per unit increases with the number of stores in the chain. The objective of such activity has been to promote the interests of independent retailers suffering from the competition of chains. Regulatory powers have also been employed to protect some industries from outside competition—as in the case of some state restrictions on importation of fruits and vegetables from other states. Too, the regulation of oil production by the Texas Railroad Commission is deemed to be in the long-run interests of the owners of producing wells.

State Taxation of Business

Taxes levied on business firms by states are great in number and importance, and are growing in complexity. All states impose property, license, gasoline, motor vehicle, alcoholic beverage, and insurance company taxes as well as incorporation and qualification fees for corporations. In addition to these, some states levy franchise, corporate income, personal income, special intangible, bank share, capital stock, severance, chain store, admissions, tobacco, stock transfer, document recording, sales and use taxes. A firm doing business in more than one state finds itself confronted by different taxes and different administration of taxes that are essentially the same. Not all taxes fall upon the business ultimately: if business firms could not "shift" the burden of taxes forward to consumers through higher prices and/or backward to those who supply it with labor, money, and materials, very few could support such a burden. In some ways, then, business firms are tax collectors rather than taxpayers. There are, of course, some taxes that cannot be readily shifted, and these impose burdens on business and even influence their location. Too, as we noted before, some taxes or their administration can be used to promote the interests of firms as well as to extract money from them. In the administration of property taxes, for example, some states in the Pacific Northwest have adopted policies on the taxation of standing timber that have encouraged some firms to establish tree farms and produce timber as a crop.

State Purchases from and Sales to Business

The significance of the amount of goods and services bought by state governments has been dealt with earlier. It is not only quantities that are significant; the kinds of things purchased by states is important as well. State purchasing agents frequently operate under "buy-at-home" policies that require purchases from vendors in the state or at least attempt to restrict purchases to American products. These policies are usually the result of pressure by business firms who have, of course, their interests promoted by such action. Sales to business by states are confined almost entirely to natural resources, such as timber from state-owned lands.

State Competition with Business

A few activities undertaken by states compete directly with private business firms. Public education does compete with private education, although most private education is conducted by nonprofit organizations. Some vocational schools that are operated as business enterprises may suffer from such competition, but it is likely that many of those who attend the public institutions would not be customers of the private organizations.

Although competition with business is not very general among the states, a few states have provided some interesting exceptions. In Oregon, around the beginning of this century, the state created a State Portage Railroad that competed directly with another portage railroad in the state. The Oregon Railroad and Navigation Company had an effective monopoly of transportation on the Columbia River because it had the only portage railroad at some falls on the stream. It discriminated against other steamboat lines (since it also operated boats on the Columbia) by charging very high portage rates on goods carried by those lines but only a nominal portage rate on goods it carried. Shippers and other transportation companies complained to the state legislature, which used its powers of eminent domain to acquire land from the O. R. & N. and then authorized the construction of a competing portage railroad to force shipping rates down and prevent discrimination against other lines.

At the present time, North Dakota probably leads all of the other states in competitive activity by state institutions. Beginning about the time of World War I, the state legislature has authorized the creation of state banks, state grain elevators and flour mills, and even a state brewery. In some of the farm states, the state prisons turn out such things as binder twine at low prices; but, generally, state prison industries are not very important competitors.

We might end our discussion of state government and business by concluding that there are a host of state governmental activities of importance to business; that the number of agencies and officials conducting such important functions is increasing and every industry is involved in some relationships with state agencies and officials; and that state governments tend to be of more importance to small business than are federal agencies and officials.

LOCAL GOVERNMENTS AND BUSINESS

Local governments are created by the state. A city is a municipal corporation, possessing a charter granted by the state giving it certain authority and responsibilities. A municipality is merely a creature of the state, and the state possesses authority over its structure and functions. A county does not even have a corporate existence; it is a local sub-division of the state. Once a city has a charter from the state, it can pass its own laws and govern itself, so long as it does so within the provisions of its charter and the laws of the state. Since state legislatures grant city charters as well as pass legislation governing the conduct of municipal corporations, states have a great measure of control over cities as well as counties. There are other units of local government other than cities and counties: towns, townships, villages, boroughs, and special districts are found throughout the United States. However, most of these other types of local governments are found in rural areas in which few firms are located and consequently have little of the impact on business that city, county and state governments do. For the purposes of our discussion, we shall deal only with counties, cities, and special districts.

Counties

Initially the county was designed to serve as an administrative unit of the state in rural areas. The functions given to counties by state constitutions and laws are usually concerned with protecting life and property, safeguarding health, constructing and maintaining roads, assessing and collecting taxes, conducting elections, administering justice, supervising the school system, and providing administrative services to special districts. In rural areas, only commercial farmers and small-town businessmen would be affected by county government. However, large urban areas with a great variety of business operations come under the jurisdiction of county governments as well. Since the activities of county agencies and officials differ little from those of other local governments, all will be discussed jointly.

Cities

All states create incorporated units of local government. In some states, towns and villages are incorporated in addition to cities, but cities are the major class of municipal corporations. As a corporation, a city possesses a charter granted by the state conferring certain rights and privileges and imposing certain obligations. It does, therefore, resemble a business corporation; but this resemblance is superficial, for business corporations receive protection against arbitrary state action denied to cities. It has been held by the courts that municipalities are merely the creatures of the state, created for the express purpose of doing the state's will, and exercising only such powers as the state may choose to confer.

However, they do have some greater governmental power than do counties, which have been described as "quasi-corporations" having their powers, duties, rights, privileges, and very existence dependent upon the state legislature, except as constitutional provisions limit legislative control.

Upon incorporation, a city is obliged to assume certain governmental functions necessary for the public safety, health, and welfare. These include police and fire protection, and providing for streets and traffic control. In addition, there are some functions which are optional—that is, through action of the city council or by a vote of the citizens a city may have parks, planning, sewers, libraries, an airport, and even may purchase, construct or operate municipally owned utilities. Since some of these functions are the same as those performed by special districts or counties, we shall not discuss further what cities specifically do.

Special Districts

This term is applied to any local government unit that is not a city, town, village, township, or county. They are municipal corporations formed to perform a special function—that is, special districts are created under state law to provide special services for the residents of a certain area. Usually, since the special services provided are normally those which a city provides its citizens, special districts are found outside the corporate limits of a city or other municipal corporation. However, this is not always true. In recent years, special districts have been created that encompass entire cities and portions of the surrounding territory.

As a rule, a special district comes into being by petition and vote of those residing within certain defined boundaries and has a governing board that has the power to raise its own revenue to perform a specific governmental function. The name of a district normally indicates its function. In addition to school districts, there are fire districts, water districts, sewer districts, drainage districts, road districts, soil conservation districts, hospital districts, rural library districts, housing authorities, park districts, transit authorities, port districts, airport districts, and public utility districts. As we have previously noted, almost all of these are functions that counties and cities do or can perform and therefore it is not necessary to deal separately with the influence of each class of local government on business firms.

Regulation of Business by Local Governments

Firms are regulated by local agencies and officials concerned with health and sanitation. Slaughterhouses; the production, handling and distribution of milk; the examination of food handlers and sanitary conditions in hotels and restaurants; air and stream pollution—all come under the control of local government.

Many regulations deal with housing and land use. City planning and zoning regulate the location and operation of business firms. Building and housing codes affect building contractors and landlords.

Where public utilities are privately owned, they also come under the control of local government (especially cities). Frequently, such regulation has been so restrictive as to force out of business some utility and transportation companies and, therefore, we see few cities still having privately owned public mass transportation firms. Electric and gas utility companies have sometimes compensated for the low rates forced upon them by cities by charging higher rates to customers outside the jurisdiction of the city.

Cities sometimes regulate certain kinds of business activity while promoting public morality. Some kinds of enterprise may be prohibited, and others are watched and regulated carefully. Regulating closing hours of bars, and prohibiting the sale of alcoholic beverages to minors, presumably promote the morals as well as the health and safety of the citizenry. In some cities, boards of theater supervisors or censors determine which films and stage shows might be seen. Also, the sale of obscene books is frequently prohibited (although it has been suggested that the effect of banning a book is normally to promote rather than to stop or curtail its sale.)

Promotion of Business by Local Governments

The ways in which local governments promote business are very similar to those that states adopt. Development corporations are established under state law to acquire properties, to build plants and lease them to manufacturers, and to make loans or insure mortgage loans by private lenders. Tax relief is provided for new firms (although apparently low taxes are not so influential in attracting industry as it is sometimes thought because local taxes are usually only a small part of a firm's costs, and higher taxes sometimes mean more local government services, many of which benefit business). Local governments advertise their locality as a good place in which to do business, and the competition among port representatives for foreign cargoes has been keen. In some states whose governments hope to lure industry by passing "right-to-work" laws and to discourage unionization by other legislation, cities have passed ordinances requiring union organizers to pay high fees ($1,000 per day in Star City, Arkansas) in order to conduct their activity. Some towns have gone beyond the traditional inducements of free sites, municipal plant financing, and tax exemption and have paid the moving expenses of companies, have trained work forces without charge, and have even made cash gifts to some firms.

Of course, local governments promote the interests of business firms already within their boundaries by providing general and special services for them. On occasion, housing subsidies have been granted (although this usually has been for public housing) and tax exemption has been granted for the construction and operation of private housing.

Local Government Taxation of Business

In addition to frequently administering state taxes, local governmental units levy some taxes of their own on business. Their property taxes are in addition to state property taxes and are the most important kind of local tax. Some local governments levy sales taxes and income taxes in addition to those levied by the state. Business license fees, admissions taxes, and amusement device fees are also important sources of tax income for municipal corporations. However, the increase in and expansion of federal and state taxes as compared to local taxes make local taxation of relatively minor importance, and in recent years the tax powers of local government have been used more to entice industry than to extract additional revenue from business.

Local Government Competition with Business

Somewhat surprisingly, there is more competition with private business by local governmental units than by state government. This is especially true of the larger cities that have established housing authorities and provided public housing in competition with private landlords. Public recreation facilities attract some who might otherwise patronize facilities under private ownership. Municipally-owned-and-operated on-street and off-street parking places also provide rivalry (in Boston, the Massachusetts Parking Authority operates a 1,450-car parking garage under the Boston Common and planned to provide free bus service to downtown shopping points, a policy fought by the Independent Taxi Drivers Asso ciation).

Perhaps the greatest area of competition by local government is in public utilities. Many municipalities operate public transportation systems which, as was true in San Francisco some years ago, compete directly with privately owned companies. The combination of public competition and public regulation has resulted in a situation in which very few private mass transportation companies exist in the larger cities. Publicly owned electric and water enterprises are quite common, with municipally owned electric utilities being formidable competitors in the western United States. The "public utility district" is a relatively new kind of special district; in the Pacific Northwest such organizations—either individually or collectively—have gained control over a number of important dam sites and, therefore, are important generators and transmitters as well as distributors of electric power.

We might conclude that local government is quite important to business, although there do not seem to be as many agencies, officials, and activities of importance as there are at the state level. This, again, is due to the fact that local governments are creatures and agents of the state and are given fewer powers and governmental functions than the state exercises. However, all firms are within the jurisdiction of some unit of local government and local government is of major importance to those firms doing business solely in one place.

READING: Cases on Constitutional Law

[*Although the powers of state governments are determined by the Constitution, what the Constitution means is what the Supreme Court says it means. There has been a tendency for the Court to interpret that document more liberally as time passes, and the two cases * that follow demonstrate that tendency. In the first, only certain classes of businesses are mentioned as being "clothed with a public interest" so that they are proper subjects of state regulation, although a general principle concerning the power of states to regulate business is stated. The second case reaffirms that general rule and makes it quite clear that there are no classes of business that might not be regarded as being "affected with a public interest."*]

Munn v. Illinois: 94 U.S. 113 (1877)

[*This is one of a group of cases known as the Granger Cases, six cases decided at the same time involving the validity of regulatory legislation inspired by the Grange. The others involved railroad regulations. The principal opinion for the group was written in the Munn case, in which Munn and Scott, Warehousemen, were charged with violating an Illinois statute fixing maximum prices for grain storage and handling.*]

MR. CHIEF JUSTICE WAITE delivered the opinion of the court.

The question to be determined in this case is whether the general assembly of Illinois can, under the limitations upon the legislative power of the States imposed by the Constitution of the United States, fix by law the maximum of charges for the storage of grain in warehouses at Chicago and other places in the State having not less than one hundred thousand inhabitants, "in which grain is stored in bulk, and in which the grain of different owners is mixed

* 94 U.S. 113 *and* 291 U.S. 502.

together, or in which grain is stored in such a manner that the identity of different lot or parcels cannot be accurately preserved."

It is claimed that such a law is repugnant—

1. To that part of sect. 8, art. 1, of the Constitution of the United States which confers upon Congress the power "to regulate commerce with foreign nations and among the several States";

2. To that part of Sect. 9 of the same article which provides that "no preference shall be given by any regulation of commerce or revenue to the ports of one State over those of another"; and

3. To that part of amendment 14 which ordains that no State shall "deprive any person of life, liberty, or property, without due process of law, nor deny to any person within its jurisdiction the equal protection of the laws."

We will consider the last of these objections first.

Every statute is presumed to be constitutional. The courts ought not to declare one to be unconstitutional, unless it is clearly so. If there is doubt, the expressed will of the legislature should be sustained.

The Constitution contains no definition of the word "deprive," as used in the Fourteenth Amendment. To determine its signification, therefore, it is necessary to ascertain the effect which usage has given it, when employed in the same or a like connection.

While this provision of the amendment is new in the Constitution of the United States, as a limitation upon the powers of the States, it is old as a principle of civilized government. It is found in Magna Charta, and, in substance if not in form, in nearly all the constitutions that have been from time to time adopted by the several States of the Union. By the Fifth Amendment, it was introduced into the Constitution of the United States as a limitation upon the powers of the national government, and by the Fourteenth, as a guaranty against any encroachment upon an acknowledged right of citizenship by the legislatures of the States.

When one becomes a member of society, he necessarily parts with some rights or privileges which, as an individual not affected by his relations to others, he might retain. "A body politic," as aptly defined in the preamble of the Constitution of Massachusetts, "is a social compact by which the whole people covenant with each citizen, and each citizen with the whole people, that all shall be governed by certain laws for the common good." This does not confer power upon the whole people to control rights which are purely and exclusively private, Thorpe v. R. & B. Railroad Co., 27 Vt. 143; but it does authorize the establishment of laws requiring each citizen to so conduct himself, and so use his own property, as not unnecessarily to injure another. This is the very essence of government, and has found expression in the maxim "sic utere tuo ut alienum non laedas." From this source come the police powers, which, as was said by Mr. Chief Justice Taney in the License Cases, 5 How. 583, "are nothing more or less than the powers of government inherent in every sovereignty, . . . that is to say, . . . the power regulates the conduct of its citizens one towards another, and the manner in which each shall use his own property, when such regulation becomes necessary for the public good."

From this it is apparent that, down to the time of the adoption of the Fourteenth Amendment, it was not supposed that statutes regulating the use, or even the price of the use, of private property necessarily deprived an owner of his property without due process of law. Under some circumstances, they may, but not under all. The amendment does not change the law in this particular: It simply prevents the States from doing that which will operate as such a deprivation.

This brings us to inquire as to the principles upon which this power of regulation rests, in order that we may determine what is within and what without its operative effect. Looking, then, to the common law, from whence came the right which the Constitution protects, we find that when private property is "affected with a public interest, it ceases to be—juris privati—only." This was said by Lord Chief Justice Hale more than two hundred years ago, in his treatise "De Portibus Maris", 1 Harg, Law Tracts, 78, and has been accepted without objection as an essential element in the law of property ever since. Property does become clothed with a public interest when used in a manner to make it of public consequence, and affect the community at large. When, therefore, one devotes his property to a use in which the public has an interest, he, in effect, grants to the public an interest in that use, and must submit to be controlled by the public for the common good, to the extent of the interest he has thus created. He may withdraw his grant by discontinuing the use; but, so long as he maintains the use, he must submit to the control.

But we need not go further. Enough has already been said to show that: When private property is devoted to a public use, it is subject to public regulation. It remains only to ascertain whether the warehouses of these plaintiffs in error, and the business which is carried on there, come within the operation of this principle.

Under such circumstances it is difficult to see why, if the common carrier, or the miller, or the ferryman, or the innkeeper or the wharfinger, or the baker, or the cartman, or the hackney-coachman, pursues a public employment and exercises "a sort of public office," these plaintiffs in error do not. They stand, to use again the language of their counsel, in the very "gateway of commerce," and take toll from all who pass. Their business most certainly "tends to a common charge, and is become a thing of public interest and use." Every bushel of grain for its passage "pays a toll, which is a common charge," and, therefore, according to Lord Hale, every such warehouseman "ought to be under public regulation, viz., that he . . . take but reasonable toll." Certainly, if any business can be clothed "with a public interest, and cease to be 'juris privati' only," this has been. It may not be made so by the operation of the Constitution of Illinois or this statute, but it is by the facts.

We conclude, therefore, that the statute in question is not repugnant to the Constitution of the United States, and that there is no error in the judgment.

Judgment affirmed.

Nebbia v. New York: 291 U.S. 502 (1934)

MR. JUSTICE ROBERTS delivered the opinion of the Court.

The Legislature of New York established, by Chapter 158 of the Laws of 1933, a Milk Control Board with power, among other things, to "fix minimum and maximum . . . retail prices to be charged by . . . stores to consumers for consumption off the premises where sold." The Board fixed nine cents as the price to be charged by a store for a quart of milk. Nebbia, the proprietor of a grocery store in Rochester, sold two quarts and a five cent loaf of bread for eighteen cents; and was convicted for violating the Board's order. At his trial he asserted the statute and order contravene the equal protection clause and the due process clause of the Fourteenth Amendment, and renewed the contention in successive appeals to the county court and the Court of Appeals. Both overruled his claim and affirmed the conviction.

The question for decision is whether the Federal Constitution prohibits a state from so fixing the selling price of milk.

The more serious question is whether, in the light of the conditions disclosed, the enforcement of Sec. 312 (e) denied the appellant the due process secured to him by the Fourteenth Amendment.

Under our form of government the use of property and the making of contracts are normally matters of private and not of public concern. The general rule is that both shall be free of governmental interference. But neither property rights nor contract rights are absolute; for government cannot exist if the citizen may at will use his property to the detriment of his fellows, or exercise his freedom of contract to work them harm. Equally fundamental with the private right is that of the public to regulate it in the common interest. . . .

The Fifth Amendment, in the field of federal activity, and the Fourteenth, as respects state action, do not prohibit governmental regulation for the public welfare. They merely condition the exertion of the admitted power, by securing that the end shall be accomplished by methods consistent with due process. And the guaranty of due process, as has often been held, demands only that the law shall not be unreasonable, arbitrary or capricious, and that the means selected shall have a real and substantial relation to the object sought to be attained. It results that a regulation valid for one sort of business, or in given circumstances, may be invalid for another sort, or for the same business under other circumstances, because the reasonableness of each regulation depends upon the relevant facts.

The reports of our decisions abound with cases in which the citizen, individual or corporate, has vainly invoked the Fourteenth Amendment in resistance to necessary and appropriate exertion of the police power.

The court has repeatedly sustained curtailment of enjoyment of private property, in the public interest. The owner's rights may be subordinated to the needs of other private owners whose pursuits are vital to the paramount interests of the community. The state may control the use of property in various ways; may prohibit advertising billboards except of a prescribed size and location, or their use for certain kinds of advertising; may in certain circumstances authorize encroachments by party walls in cities; may fix the height of buildings, the character of materials, and methods of construction, the adjoining area which must be left open, and may exclude from residential sections offensive trades, industries and structures likely injuriously to affect the public health or safety; or may establish zones within which certain types of buildings or businesses are permitted and others excluded. And although the Fourteenth Amendment extends protection to aliens as well as citizens, a state may for adequate reasons of policy exclude aliens altogether from the use and occupancy of land.

Laws passed for the suppression of immorality, in the interest of health, to secure fair trade practices, and to safeguard the interests of depositors in banks, have been found consistent with due process. These measures not only affected the use of private property, but also interfered with the right of private contract. Other instances are numerous where valid regulation has restricted the right of contract, while less directly affecting property rights.

The Constitution does not guarantee the unrestricted privilege to engage in a business or to conduct it as one pleases. Certain kinds of business may be prohibited; and the right to conduct a business, or to pursue a calling, may be conditioned. Regulation of a business to prevent waste of the state's resources may be justified. And statutes prescribing the terms upon which those conducting certain businesses may contract, or imposing terms if they do enter into agreements, are within the state's competency.

Legislation concerning sales of goods, and incidentally affecting prices, has repeatedly been held valid. In this class fall laws forbidding unfair competition by the charging of lower prices in one locality than those exacted in another, by giving trade inducements to purchasers, and by other forms of price discrimination. The public policy with respect to free competition has engendered state and federal statutes prohibiting monopolies, which have been upheld. On the other hand, where the policy of the state dictated that a monopoly should be granted, statutes having that effect have been held inoffensive to the constitutional guarantees. Moreover, the state or a municipality may itself enter into business in competition with private proprietors, and thus effectively although indirectly control the prices charged by them.

The milk industry in New York has been the subject of long-standing and drastic regulation in the public interest.

But we are told that because the law essays to control prices it denies due process. Notwithstanding the admitted power to correct existing economic ills by appropriate regulation of business, even though an indirect result may be a restriction of the freedom of contract or a modification of charges for services or the price of commodities, the appellant urges that direct fixation of prices is a type of regulation absolutely forbidden. His position is that the Fourteenth Amendment requires us to hold the challenged statute void for this reason alone. The argument runs that the public control of rates or prices is "per se" unreasonable and unconstitutional, save as applied to businesses affected with a public interest; that a business so affected is one in which property is devoted to an enterprise of a sort which the public itself might appropriately undertake, or one whose owner relies on a public grant or franchise for the right to conduct the business, or in which he is bound to serve all who apply; in short, such as is commonly called a public utility; or a business in its nature a monopoly. The milk industry, it is said, possesses none of these characteristics, and, therefore, not being affected with a public interest, its charges may not be controlled by the state. Upon the soundness of this contention the appellant's case against the statute depends.

We may as well say at once that the dairy industry is not, in the accepted sense of the phrase, a public utility. We think the appellant is also right in asserting that there is in this case no suggestion of any monopoly or monopolistic practice. It goes without saying that those engaged in the business are in no way dependent upon public grants or franchises for the privilege of conducting their activities. But if, as must be conceded, the industry is subject to regulation in the public interest, what constitutional principle bars the state from correcting existing maladjustments by legislation touching prices? We think there is no such principle. The due process clause makes no mention of sales or of prices any more than it speaks of business or contracts or buildings or other incidents of property. The thought seems nevertheless to have persisted that there is something peculiarly sacrosanct about the price one may charge for what he makes or sells, and that, however able to regulate other elements of manufacture or trade, with incidental effect upon price, the state is incapable of directly controlling the price itself. This view was negatived many years ago, Munn v. Illinois, 94 U.S. 113. The appellant's claim is, however, that this court, in there sustaining a statutory prescription of charges for storage by the proprietors of a grain elevator, limited permissible legislation of that type to businesses affected with a public interest, and he says no business is so affected except it have one or more of the characteristics he enumerates. But this is a misconception. Munn and Scott held no franchise from the state. They owned the property upon which their elevator was situated and conducted their business as private citizens. No doubt they felt at liberty to deal with whom they pleased and on such terms as they might deem just to themselves. Their enterprise could not fairly be called a monopoly, although it was referred to in the decision as a "virtual monopoly." This meant only that their elevator was strategically situated and that a large portion of the public found it highly inconvenient to deal with others. This court concluded the circumstances justified the legislation as an exercise of the governmental right to control the business in the public interest; that is, as an exercise of the police power. It is true that the court cited a statement from Lord Hale's "De Portibus Maris", to the effect that when private property is "affected with a public interest, it ceases to be 'juris privati' only"; but the court proceeded at once to define what it understood by the expression, saying: "Property does become clothed with a public interest when used in a manner to make it of public consequence, and affect the community at large" (p. 126). Thus understood, "affected with a public interest" is the equivalent of "subject to the exercise of the police power"; and it is plain that nothing more was intended by the expression. The court had been at pains to define that power (pp. 124, 125) ending its discussion in these words:

"From this it is apparent that, down to the time of the adoption of the Fourteenth Amendment, it was not supposed that statutes regulating the use, or even the price of the use, of private property necessarily deprived an owner of his property without due process of law. Under some circumstances they may, but not under all. The amendment does not change the law in this particular: it simply prevents the States from doing that which will operate as such a deprivation."

In the further discussion of the principle it is said that when one devotes his property to a use, "in which the public has an interest," he in effect "grants to the public an interest in that use" and must submit to be controlled for the common good. The conclusion is that if Munn and Scott wished to avoid having their business regulated they should not have embarked their property in an industry which is subject to regulation in the public interest.

The true interpretation of the court's language is claimed to be that only property voluntarily devoted to a known public use is subject to regulation as to rates. But obviously Munn and Scott had not voluntarily dedicated their business to a public use. They intended only to conduct it as private citizens, and they insisted that they had done nothing which gave the public an interest in their transactions or conferred any right of regulation. The statement that one has dedicated his property to a public use is, therefore, merely another way of saying that if one embarks in a business which public interest demands shall be regulated, he must know regulation will ensue. . . .

The touchstone of public interest in any business, its practices and charges, clearly is not the enjoyment of any franchise from the state, Munn v. Illinois, supra. Nor is it the enjoyment of a monopoly; for in Brass v. North Dakota, 153 U.S. 391, a similar control of prices of grain elevators was upheld in spite of overwhelming and uncontradicted proof that about six hundred grain elevators existed along the line of the Great Northern Railroad, in North Dakota; that at the very station where the defendant's elevator was located two others operated; and that the business was keenly competitive throughout the state. . . .

It is clear that there is no closed class or category of business affected with a public interest, and the function of courts in the application of the Fifth and Fourteenth Amendments is to determine in each case whether circumstances vindicate the challenged regulation as a reasonable exertion of governmental authority or condemn it as arbitrary or discriminatory. Wolff Packing Co. v. Industrial Court, 262 U.S. 522, 535. The phrase "affected with a public interest" can, in the nature of things, mean no more than that an industry, for adequate reason, is subject to control for the public good. In several of the decisions of this court wherein the expressions "affected with a public interest," and "clothed with a public use," have been brought forward as the criteria of the validity of price control, it has been admitted that they are not susceptible of definition and form an unsatisfactory test of the constitutionality of legislation directed at business practices or prices. These decisions must rest, finally, upon the basis that the requirements of due process were not met because the laws were found arbitrary in their operation and effect. But there can be no doubt that upon proper occasion and by appropriate measures the state may regulate a business in any of its aspects, including the prices to be charged for the products or commodities it sells.

So far as the requirement of due process is concerned, and in the absence of other constitutional restriction, a state is free to adopt whatever economic policy may reasonably be deemed to promote public welfare, and to enforce that policy by legislation adapted to its purpose. The courts are without authority either to declare such policy, or, when it is declared by the legislature, to override it. If the laws passed are seen to have a reasonable relation to a proper legislative purpose, and are neither arbitrary nor discriminatory, the requirements of due process are satisfied, and judicial determination to that effect renders a court "functus officio". "Whether the free operation of the normal laws of competition is a wise and wholesome rule for trade and commerce is an economic question which this court need not consider or determine." Northern Securities Co. v. United States, 193 U.S. 197, 337–8. And it is equally clear that if the legislative policy be to curb unrestrained and harmful competition by measures which are not arbitrary or discriminatory it does not lie with the courts to determine that the rule is unwise. With the wisdom of the policy adopted, with the adequacy or practicability of the law enacted to forward it, the courts are both incompetent and unauthorized to deal. The course of decision in this court exhibits a firm adherence to these principles. Times without number we have said that the legislature is primarily the judge of the necessity of such an enactment, that every possible presumption is in favor of its validity, and that though the court may hold views inconsistent with the wisdom of the law, it may not be annulled unless palpably in excess of legislative power.

The law-making bodies have in the past endeavored to promote free competition by laws aimed at trusts and monopolies. The consequent interference with private property and freedom of contract has not availed with courts to set these enactments aside as denying due process. Where the public interest was deemed to require the fixing of minimum prices, that expedient has been sustained. If the law-making body within its sphere of government concludes that the conditions or practices in an industry make unrestricted competition an inadequate safeguard of the consumer's interests, produce waste harmful to the public, threaten ultimately to cut off the supply of a commodity needed by the public, or portend the destruction of the industry itself, appropriate statutes passed in an honest effort to correct the threatened consequence may not be set aside because the regulation adopted fixes prices reasonably deemed by the legislature to be fair to those engaged in the industry and to the consuming public. And this is especially so where, as here, the economic maladjustment is one of price, which threatens harm to the producer at one end of the series and the consumer at the other. The Constitution does not secure to anyone liberty to conduct his business in such fashion as to inflict injury upon the public at large, or upon any substantial group of the people. Price control, like any other form of regulation, is unconstitutional only if arbitrary, discriminatory, or demonstrably irrelevant to the policy the legislature is free to adopt, and hence an unnecessary and unwarranted interference with individual liberty.

Tested by these considerations we find no basis in the due process clause of the Fourteenth Amendment for condemning the provisions of the Agriculture and Markets Law here drawn into question.

The judgment is affirmed.

SUGGESTED READINGS

"Blue books," issued by states. Almost every state has a "blue book" which is the counterpart of the *U.S. Government Organization Manual*. As such, it sets forth in some detail the governmental structure along with valuable information on those agencies and officials of importance to business. In states that do not issue such volumes, the state universities frequently publish such information.

Dahl, Robert A., *Who Governs?* (New Haven, Conn.: Yale, 1961). This investigation into the political structure of an American city—New Haven, Connecticut—offers a major reinterpretation of the location of political power in our democratic society.

MacDonald, Austin F., *American State Government and Administration*, 6th ed. (New York: Crowell, 1960). Discusses the history of American state government, federal-state relations, state constitutions, legislatures, executives, and courts. Also includes material on state control over local governments and the nature of the latter units. Chapters on the state and business and the state and labor are of special importance.

CHAPTER 28

BUSINESS, FOREIGN AND INTERNATIONAL GOVERNMENTS

For an increasing proportion of American firms, the actions of foreign governments and groups of nations are of major importance. Those firms engaging in exporting, importing, and foreign investment—including the establishment of branches in other countries—find their activities coming under the direct influence of other nations; many not engaging in such operations are indirectly affected. Since foreign nations possess all of the powers of sovereign states, they consequently conduct themselves toward business in a manner already familiar to us. They promote, regulate, tax, compete with, sell to, and buy from American business. In addition, some foreign governments have expropriated the property of

U.S. firms. Although there is no world government confronting the firm, there are a number of international agreements and agencies created by groups of nations. Those of especial importance to business aim at promoting and regulating international trade.

FOREIGN GOVERNMENT AND AMERICAN BUSINESS

It is difficult to generalize about foreign governments. Some nations are quite undeveloped economically and others are not far behind the United States. Many foreign countries are politically unstable while others have experienced no radical changes in their government for centuries. In almost all, the government plays a larger role in economic affairs than is true in the United States. Since foreign governments differ, their impact on American business differs.

Foreign Promotion of American Business

Foreign nations are sometimes interested in encouraging American investment. Such investment in foreign countries takes two major forms: the establishment of foreign branches by American firms and the provision of capital and credit for establishing and developing productive enterprises. It is chiefly the economically underdeveloped countries of the world that encourage such investment (although no nation has reached the high level of industrialization that the U.S. has attained and, consequently, even governments of some of the more economically advanced nations promote American investments). India, for example, is attempting to promote industrial development at a rapid rate. Since capital is relatively scarce in that country, the government is encouraging American investment by granting certain tax concessions, by providing a sheltered domestic market for the new producers, and by providing for the free remittance of earnings to American owners. Along with incentives to foreign investors, there are frequently certain restrictions—such as limiting foreign investors to a minority position in the control of enterprises established with foreign capital. In short, though foreign nations frequently wish American investment, they still want to control their own destinies; these motives sometimes work at cross-purposes, limiting the extent to which foreign investment is promoted.

In addition to investment, foreign countries are frequently anxious to promote trade with the United States. They may wish to export certain goods to the United States or to import some products. In order to promote such trade, a government might set a rate of exchange between American currency and the currency of its own country to make such trade especially attractive to business firms in America. Sometimes foreign governments proceed even more directly—by sending trade missions to the United States to develop the desired trade under conditions favorable to American businessmen.

Foreign Regulation of American Business

A nation may regulate only those activities carried on within its boundaries, but this may involve branches of American firms or trade in goods bought or sold by such firms. American branches abroad are subject to the same regulations as are "native" firms, but there are in addition some special regulations affecting them. As earlier noted, in many countries there is considerable resentment of the fact that such a large portion of business activity is conducted by American-owned firms. Therefore, many nations—although wishing to retain American investment in their economy—have passed laws limiting American firms to a minority position in the ownership and control of what are essentially foreign branches of U.S. firms. Too, restrictions are placed by foreign governments on the operations of such branches as well as investment in them.

In its control over its own currency, a foreign nation may have an important impact on American business. It can change the legal exchange rate between its currency and dollars to one disadvantageous to American-owned firms that wish to change some of the foreign currency for U.S. currency. It may even place restrictions on the conversion of such currency into dollars or on the removal of funds from the country. Since one of the major motives for American investment abroad is to obtain good earnings that can be converted into dollars and paid to American investors, such restraints inhibit investment. Trade is also affected by currency controls. Exchange rates may make selling in a foreign country unprofitable; although, when this is true, buying from such a country may be highly profitable for some businessmen. Restrictions on the conversion of foreign currency into dollars also has an adverse effect on trade. Not many firms that sell in a particular foreign country wish to buy things of exactly the same total value as their sales; inability to convert foreign currency into American currency thereby limits the ability and willingness of our firms to sell abroad.

A nation may possess fairly extensive regulations governing exports and imports. These are usually tied up with its tariff laws, and hence will be discussed together with taxes levied by foreign governments on American business.

Foreign Taxation of American Business

Taxes imposed by foreign nations on American business firms and products are not much different from those imposed by American governments. Income taxes, property taxes, excise taxes, sales taxes, severance taxes, corporation taxes—all are to be found in other countries and are levied upon U.S. firms doing business in them. In some cases, tax concessions may be made to encourage American investment, but in others taxes are levied with an especially heavy hand on foreign branches of U.S. firms. Of special note are import taxes. A foreign nation may severely limit the degree to which an American firm may enter its markets by levying high taxes on imports. In some instances, even a relatively high tariff has not prevented the substantial importation of American goods and in order to insure that the quantity imported would not exceed certain amounts, many nations have also established import quotas. Import taxes and quotas can be got around by establishing a producing branch in the foreign country; but, as we have seen, these too are subject to the taxes of the nation that wishes to discriminate against American-owned business firms.

Foreign Government Competition with American Business

In almost every other country in the world, a larger proportion of the nation's business is conducted by government than is true in the United States. To the extent that such governmentally owned and operated enterprises are in competition with American business firms, they are usually competitors almost impossible to beat. Certainly this is true when the competition is on their "home grounds." The foreign government may even prohibit competition with its enterprises, and this ends the matter. Even when the competition is on "neutral ground," the government enterprise may not be intent on pursuing profits, but rather on gaining political objectives and as a consequence may be willing to sell at a loss for an extended period in order to gain what it wishes. This competition seems to be growing rather than declining, and is likely to have further adverse effects on American business.

Foreign Expropriation of American Business

The shadow of expropriation continually hangs over business operations in foreign countries. In many cases, after American businessmen have acquired and developed business properties abroad, the government of the country has taken this property away, frequently without compensation. Under the U.S. Constitution, neither state nor federal government may take the property of persons (including corporations) without "due process of law" or without adequate compensation. These constitutional restrictions, of course, do not apply to the activities of foreign governments and frequently revolutionary governments—especially in Latin America—have seized American business property. Other than securing action of some sort from the U.S. government (usually too little, too late, or both), there is little that can be done by American businessmen under such circumstances, which condition explains their caution in making investments in countries in which the political situation is unstable.

Purchases and Sales by Foreign Governments

Since in many foreign nations the national government plays such a large role in economic activity, American businessmen are frequently involved in selling to agencies of foreign governments. The Soviet Union, for example, has a trading agency called Amtorg in New York City, which handles over half of the total U.S.-Soviet trade volume. In its buying activities, this agency conducts itself in no unusual way and apparently is in no position to bring any influence to bear on American firms other than that which any large buyer is able to employ. Sales by foreign governments to American business are not very important in total amount, although some raw materials—such as crude petroleum—are sold to American manufacturers.

INTERNATIONAL GOVERNMENT AND BUSINESS

The problems confronting businessmen engaged in business abroad when there is no world government to turn to for help have been reduced somewhat by the establishment of government agencies to perform functions that tend to promote international business. Various international agencies affecting business exist in the United Nations, and others independent of that body have been established. Many nations, including the United States, are parties to international agreements seeking to provide greater stability and, therefore, certainty in the conditions under which world trade is concerned. Some of these agreements cover tariffs and commodities and therefore have important influences on the prices at which goods will be sold and the quantities that will be purchased.

International government is not the same as world government. If world government existed (which it does not), a diagrammatic presentation of it might be as shown in Figure 28–1. The world government

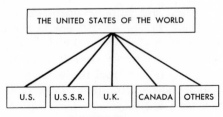

FIGURE 28–1.

would be supreme and would be the only sovereign government. It would have the power to force its decisions upon its member states. International government—that is, the agreements made and agencies created by groups of nations—would, diagrammatically, be just the reverse, as shown in Figure 28–2. The national governments establishing an

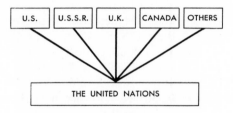

FIGURE 28–2.

international agency (such as the United Nations) are superior to it and retain their sovereignty. The international government has no authority over the citizens (including businessmen) of its member nations, whereas a world government has such authority. An international agency makes recommendations that it hopes its member nations will adopt and will use their governmental powers to enforce; if, however, its member nations refuse to do so, there is little that the international agency can do about it. So when the United States enters into tentative agreements with other nations, such agreements have no power to affect American businessmen directly unless the federal government acts.

United Nations Agencies

The General Assembly of the United Nations affects American business indirectly, operating through the Economic and Social Council. The Council, consisting of eighteen members elected by the General Assembly, coordinates the economic activities of the permanent commissions and the specialized agencies of the United Nations. There are more than a score of these agencies, and a few are worthy of mention here.

INTERNATIONAL LABOR ORGANIZATION. The International Labor Organization was established during World War I, and was a part of the League of Nations until 1946, but has since come under the UN. Since the United States was not a member of the League, the operations of the ILO have had an impact on the U.S. only since World War II. The purpose of this international group is to promote uniform labor legislation throughout the world—laws to improve wages, hours, and working conditions of labor. Although the ILO has adopted a number of conventions dealing with labor law, only a small minority of nations have ratified them. The United States has ratified only a few of them, although other American legislation has achieved the goals of the ILO recommendations. Businessmen in America would likely benefit from the widespread adoption of the ILO conventions, since they would tend to bring up foreign labor standards and costs to the level prevailing in the United States.

FOOD AND AGRICULTURE ORGANIZATION. The Food and Agriculture took over some of the functions of a League committee and of the International Institute of Agriculture. Its purposes are, in part:

securing improvements in the efficiency of the production and distribution of all food and agricultural products,

bettering the condition of rural populations, and thus contributing toward an expanding world economy.

In addition to its functions of collecting and disseminating information, and furnishing technical assistance and "missions," the FAO promotes and recommends national and international action concerning production, processing, marketing, and distribution of food and agricultural products. Agricultural credit, agricultural commodity arrangements, and conservation of natural resources are also a concern of the FAO. The impact of FAO activities on American business is a mixed one: To the extent that agricultural production is improved in foreign countries (where FAO activities are concentrated), it may reduce markets for American agricultural commodities; on the other hand, some of U.S. export industries might be the beneficiaries of increased income of rural populations in foreign nations.

THE WORLD BANK. Another important UN agency is the International Bank for Reconstruction and Development. Organized at the end of

World War II, the World Bank (as it is also called) aims at facilitating the investment of capital for productive purposes in various countries in the world. It promotes private foreign investment in less developed countries and elsewhere by guaranteeing or participating in loans made by private investors. In cases in which it feels that private capital is not available on reasonable terms, it may engage in such financing out of its own resources. The net effect of the operations of the Bank on American business is probably beneficial: American lenders have been encouraged to make profitable loans they might otherwise not have made; the funds made available to governments and private concerns abroad have been used to purchase capital equipment and other necessities from American business; and the competition of the Bank with American financial institutions has not been great because the World Bank is run on quite conservative banking principles.

INTERNATIONAL MONETARY FUND. Closely associated with the International Bank is the International Monetary Fund. Among its central objectives is the facilitation of an expanded and balanced international trade. This is accomplished by international monetary cooperation in the establishment of stability in foreign exchange rates, the promotion of orderly exchange arrangements among members, and the avoidance of competitive exchange depreciation. The fund uses the gold and currency provided by members to achieve these ends; here, again, the net effect is favorable for American business.

European Economic Community

The European Economic Community (or "Common Market" as it is commonly referred to) came into being January 1, 1958, under the Treaty of Rome. The movement for a European common market without barriers to trade had been initiated shortly after World War II by Belgium, the Netherlands, and Luxembourg; these countries were joined in the 1957 treaty by Italy, France, and West Germany. Although most of the activities of the organization have been aimed at reducing tariffs among the member nations, it has done other things as well. To expand trade, it has drafted uniform antimonopoly and patent laws for the six nations. The original treaty outlawed business practices likely to restrain competition among member states and this policy has been implemented by regulations that extend to American firms doing business in EEC countries. For example, the franchise agreements of Coca-Cola, Chrysler, Westinghouse, DuPont and others have been examined to determine whether or not they restrain trade. This is in accordance with the policy of the EEC—to eliminate not only governmental restrictions but also those obstructions to free trade created by private companies.

The creation of a common market and European "super-state" by the six countries has other significance for American business as well. It is the fastest-growing market in the world and the world's biggest trading unit. With the addition of England, the EEC may surpass the United States as the biggest producer in the world. As it gains in economic and political strength, it will create vastly different conditions from those prevailing at the end of World War II, when Europe was divided and weak. By 1970, for example, the EEC hopes to set up a common external tariff. Already, the United States has felt the impact of joint tariff action by the EEC. In 1962, under pressure from U.S. glass and carpet producers, the Kennedy Administration raised tariffs on imports of such products. Both of these increases hit Belgium hard and the EEC came to Belgium's aid. It threatened to retaliate by raising tariffs on petrochemicals and tobacco products imported from the U.S. When action from the American government was not speedily forthcoming, the EEC did increase import taxes about 20 per cent on certain chemical products sold by U.S. companies in Western Europe. For the producers involved, this action meant almost total exclusion from the Common Market.

Also, the expansion of the domestic market for manufacturers in the six countries will probably result in increased size and productive efficiency of many of them. This will not only enable them to compete more effectively with American manufacturers in the European market but in other markets as well, including the American market. Since the EEC external tariff policy is aimed at the reduction of trade barriers throughout the world, Common Market action will likely result in competition from Europe such as has not been seen since before World War I. However, this policy will also open European markets to American products and the removal of trade barriers will have good as well as bad effects on American business, depending on the products and industries involved. Proponents of free international trade contend that all nations benefit, but it should be pointed out that not all industries benefit. Although more industries may gain than may lose, this is little consolation for those firms in industries that will be adversely affected.

Other "Common Markets"

Other "blocs" of trading nations have existed for some time before the creation of the EEC and some have been created since. England has long been involved in a preferential trade arrangement with the Commonwealth countries (former colonies in the British Empire). However, it has recently chosen to sever its exclusive trading ties with the Commonwealth and to attempt to enter the EEC. In addition, England has been a member of the European Free Trade Association, an organization similar to the EEC composed of six other nations: Sweden, Norway,

Denmark, Switzerland, Austria, and Portugal. If England is successful in being admitted to the "Inner Six," it is likely that the rest of the "Outer Seven" will also be admitted and hence expand the Common Market countries from six to thirteen.

The Communist countries under the leadership of the Soviet Union also constitute a trading bloc. To the extent that the economic policies adopted by this group of nations succeed in creating a strong, integrated economic organization, it may mean the loss of Eastern European markets to some American producers as well as greater competition in world markets.

Some trading blocs have been established in the Western Hemisphere. A Latin American Free Trade Association (LAFTA) has been created to eliminate most of the tariff barriers among its nine member nations— Mexico and the South American nations of Argentina, Brazil, Chile, Columbia, Ecuador, Paraguay, Peru, and Uruguay. By creating a broad market that will encourage the construction of new manufacturing plants, LAFTA hopes to speed industrial development of Latin America. In addition, a Central American Common Market—composed of Guatemala, El Salvador, Honduras, and Nicaragua—has eliminated most trade barriers among those nations. Both LAFTA and the Central American Common Market are the outcome of plans made before World War II to stimulate trade among Latin American countries that were formalized by treaties signed in late 1960 and early 1961. Latin America's trade has been essentially an exchange of agricultural and mineral products for the manufactured goods of the U.S. and Europe. By expanding the size of their domestic markets, the two groups hope to enable efficient manufacturing industries to develop in their own nations. Many American manufacturing companies already have branches in Latin America and will be helped or hindered by these developments, depending on whether the actions of the free trade associations expand markets or create competition.

Organization for Economic Cooperation and Development

In September, 1961, a new international agency was created to continue the work of the Organization for European Economic Cooperation, a body that had been administering U.S. Marshall Plan aid to Europe. Although regarded by some as little more than a bureaucratic device to keep alive its predecessor, others have seen in it the possibility of having an impact on world economic affairs greater than that of a dozen United Nations.

OECD is composed of the fifteen members of the North Atlantic Treaty Organization (which includes the U.S. and Canada) and the "neutral" nations of Austria, Switzerland, Sweden, Spain, and Ireland. It includes, in other words, all of Western Europe and most of the world's non-Communist industrial countries.

As a legacy from its predecessor, foreign aid is a major concern of OECD. However, it is also concerned with other matters of somewhat greater importance to American business. In the field of national economic policy, it has urged expansionist programs on its members, including the U.S. If the U.S. government adopts fiscal measures aimed at producing a strong expansion of the American economy—including, if necessary, substantial budgetary deficits—business will boom. Also, consultation among members of the organization has reassured others about the U.S. balance-of-payments situation and has encouraged some European nations to take steps to help protect the stability of the dollar. Since business is promoted when confidence exists in the soundness of American currency, these actions have been valuable. Yet another area of concern dealt with by the OECD is restraints on trade among members. It has aided in eliminating trade barriers other than tariffs in more than 300 nonagricultural products and has also brought about the lowering of exchange restrictions and other obstacles to the free movement of capital among its members, particularly in France and Italy.

The restrictions on trade attacked are, among other things, import quotas and unequal administration of tariffs and laws that inhibit the importation of foreign products, although supposedly aimed at some other objective. One such law of importance to American business is the levying of license fees on autos owned by the French. Owners of cars with powerful engines—such as American producers make—are assessed almost prohibitively high license fees (which are based on horsepower) and U.S. auto manufacturers complain that such fees deny them the opportunity of selling in French markets even when they can surmount tariff barriers. OECD has worked to have such fees cut, although as is true with all international agencies, it must try to persuade France to do so since it has no power to order this fee cut nor, for that matter, to give any orders to its member nations. Also, OECD does not concern itself with discussions aimed at lowering tariff barriers, leaving such attempts to promote world trade to another international organization.

General Agreement on Tariffs and Trade

After World War II, some members of the United Nations hoped to establish an agency dealing with tariffs and trade—the International Trade Organization—to complement the activities of the World Bank and the International Monetary Fund. While the charter for the organization of ITO was being worked out, governments comprising the preparatory committee agreed to sponsor negotiations aimed at lowering customs tariffs and at reducing other trade restrictions among themselves, without waiting for the International Trade Organization to come into being. The tariff concessions resulting from these negotiations were embodied in a multilateral contract called the General Agreement on Tariffs and Trade, or GATT. When it became evident that the Congress of the United States was unwilling to include the U.S. in ITO membership, the attempt to establish that organization was abandoned, but GATT has survived.

There are presently thirty-seven "contracting parties" to the General Agreement, including the U.S. The stated objectives of the agreement are to help raise standards of living; to achieve full employment; to develop the world's resources; to expand production and exchange of goods; and to promote economic development. The member countries, which account for over 80 per cent of the world's trade, are pledged to work toward reducing existing barriers to trade. In particular, they have attacked tariff barriers. By 1963, five tariff bargaining conferences had been held and customs duties on tens of thousands of products had been reduced. Such products accounted for more than half of the world's international trade. Other import taxes have been "frozen" so that they could not be raised quickly.

In addition, GATT has worked with the International Monetary Fund to break down governmental restrictions on conversion of currency and other barriers to the natural flow of imports and exports. Under GATT rules, countries that have no foreign exchange shortages or other legitimate justifications must eliminate their quantitative restrictions on imports.

GATT has established a code of fair practices in international trade, and deals with complaints arising from alleged breaches of that code. As a consequence, complaints are settled that in earlier days might have resulted in more trade restrictions or other forms of economic warfare. The agreement also provides for reduction of "paper barriers" to trade—the unnecessary filling out of forms and other formalities some governments used to insist on.

Each member country is to give all the other members fair and equal treatment in trade and not discriminate among them. The only exceptions made from the GATT rules are for less-developed nations; these are governed by special trade rules that permit them to encourage the development of new industries by temporarily restricting imports in ways not normally permitted.

International Commodity Agreements and Organizations

For a number of years, governments of producing and consuming nations of certain agricultural and mineral commodities have engaged in activities influencing the prices of those commodities, the quantities sold in certain markets and, on occasion, the quantities produced in the producing countries. A recent count of agreements embodying policies affecting prices, sales, and production revealed that no less than seven such agreements exist, covering wheat, sugar, coffee, cotton, wool, rubber, and tin. The United States is not a party to all of these agreements, although it has studied them with an eye to possible participation. It has been involved in varying degree in those dealing with wheat, coffee, and sugar.

Commodity agreements usually aim at keeping commodity prices stable and at preventing the dumping of surplus products on world markets for whatever price can be secured. Normally, a price range is set within which wholesale commodity prices are permitted to fluctuate. Keeping price changes from exceeding the limits set is supposed to be achieved through the allocation of quotas to export nations that will keep the supply coming into the market in balance with world demand at that price. Any production in an exporting nation in excess of its export quota (and in excess of domestic consumption) is to be held off the market until increased demand permits it to be sold without upsetting prices.

The International Wheat Agreement has been one of the few successful commodity agreements. This has been fortunate for the U.S. government, which is thus able to solve some of its surplus wheat problems. It has also enabled American wheat producers to sell in markets that might otherwise have been closed to them, or at least might have been quite chaotic. However, to the extent that U.S. processors of wheat are forced to pay prices considerably in excess of world prices for their raw material as a result of such pacts, it should be concluded that not all American business benefits from their existence.

In some cases, international organizations are established to administer international commodity agreements. The International Tin Council has six tin-producing countries and fourteen consuming nations as members. As set up in 1956, it has built up a "buffer stock" of the metal and sells from its stockpile when prices go over a certain figure and buys for the stockpile when prices fall below a somewhat lower figure. In addition, it has set quotas for exporting nations. There is also an International Sugar Council and an International Wheat Council.

Not many of the international commodity agreements have met with success; the International Wheat Agreement is the major exception. This success is perhaps owing to the fact that international trade in wheat is dominated by the U.S. and Canada and that both of these countries are engaged in extensive programs to control the production and marketing of wheat and have sufficient funds to enable them to stockpile surplus output and thereby prevent great fluctuations on grain exchanges.

Even if all of the commodity agreements did work, it is not certain that all business would benefit thereby. Producers want stable high prices whereas consumers (that is, firms that process these primary commodities) would prefer stable low prices. Too, commission firms that buy and sell for others on commodity exchanges would like to see fluctuating prices because the bulk of business done on such exchanges is by speculators who hope to make profits from substantial increases or from reductions in prices.

However, the outlook is for an increased number of such agreements and agencies. Aluminum producers in the U.S., hurt by imports, have proposed an international agreement to regulate imports into the U.S. International copper, lead, and zinc agreements have been proposed; some sentiment exists to make the U.S. a member of certain existing agreements. Whether or not the U.S. is a member of any international commodity agreement, the number of agreements is great and growing, and American businessmen will inevitably be affected by them, for better or worse.

CONCLUSIONS

What is true of international commodity agreements is also true of foreign and international government generally. All of it is growing in its importance to American business. The United States seems to be involved in a new movement in international business, which is seeing the emergence of new producing and consuming areas, the expansion of previously existing foreign production and markets—partly by national growth, but more importantly as a consequence of the development of common markets—and the greater use of the powers of government—American, foreign, and international—to promote free trade and the interests of producers and consumers.

This development is a reversal of a long trend. Early in the history of American business, international trade was of major importance. After the War of 1812, the development of domestic markets and domestic manufacturing grew increasingly more important. The United States and other nations—under pressure from manufacturing interests and with an eye to the national strength which came from industrialization—increasingly raised barriers to imports of manufactured goods from other countries. This international development reached a peak during the 1930's; some contend that the restrictive policies adopted led to World War II. At any rate, since that war we have seen the growth of a number of international agencies acting to break down economic barriers among nations and to promote economic growth throughout the world so that there will be little economic basis for future international conflict. Although these agencies have not yet fully realized their goals, they are growing in power and they, along with foreign governments, will be of much greater importance in the near future than they were in the not-so-distant past.

READING: Europe Super-State: The Common Market's Government-like Acts Push into Varied Fields *
by Ray Vicker

. . . .

It Readies Uniform Patent, Monopoly Laws, Retrains Those Idled by Tariff Cuts

. . . .

For the Staff, an Income Tax

. . . .

BRUSSELS—While world attention focuses on the European Common Market's progress in lowering tariffs among its member nations, these other developments have been taking place with considerably less fanfare at the organization's Brussels headquarters:

A single anti-monopoly law has been drafted for the six member states—France, West Germany, Italy, Belgium, Holland and Luxembourg.

Uniform patent and bankruptcy laws, a unified transportation investment policy, and a uniform policy for the use of various fuels are being prepared.

A job-retraining program has been started for workers in industries hurt by Common Market tariff cuts, and other social welfare measures, including one to standardize a 40-hour work week in most Common Market industry, are under study.

In the non-European world, policies such as these usually are shaped only by national governments. And even in the European Economic Community, as the Common Market is formally named, such measures must be approved by authorities of six fully sovereign nations.

Court, Parliament and Diplomats. But to plan the unification of their economies, and to administer some of the necessary measures, the six nations have created a central organization that increasingly is taking on the look of a European super-government. [See Figure 28–3.] Already the EEC has its own executive branch, its own Court of Justice, its own European Parliament with advisory powers. It has its own budget—some $58.1 million this year—and collects its own income taxes from its staff. It even has independent diplomatic contacts with the U.S. and 29 other nations, which have accredited diplomatic missions directly to the EEC.

How this apparatus works to mesh the tariff and other economic policies of six diverse countries is little understood outside Europe. Yet perhaps nothing

* Reprinted by permission from *The Wall Street Journal* (March 7, 1962).

will do more to determine the strength of some of the U.S.'s most important military allies and industrial rivals. So it may be profitable to examine the structure of the EEC, and meet some of the men who are running this "European government."

The EEC came into being Jan. 1, 1958, under the Treaty of Rome. In this document, the six nations pledged to lower tariff barriers among themselves, free

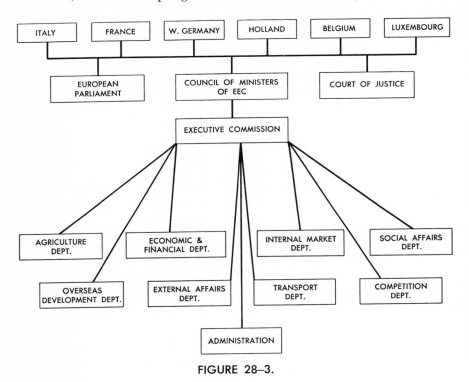

FIGURE 28–3.

the movement of goods, capital and labor across their frontiers, and take other steps to unify their economies. Today, any EEC staff member questioned about his organization's powers probably will reply: "Well, the treaty says . . ." and reel off a section verbatim in one of the EEC's four official languages—French, German, Dutch and Italian.

Treaty Is General. What "the treaty says," however, usually is a generality. A typical example: "The objectives of this treaty shall, with regard to transport, be pursued by the member states within the framework of a common transport policy." Translating these generalities into specifics is primarily the task of the Commission of the European Economic Community, the executive branch of the EEC "government."

The Commission is by far the biggest EEC body. It employs some 2,000 international civil servants in three widely scattered Brussels buildings. It drafts the common tariff and transport policies, the uniform patent and anti-monopoly laws. When and if these policies are accepted by the EEC member nations, it turns watchdog to see that they are enforced. If necessary, it can hail into the EEC Court of Justice any companies, industries or even governments it suspects of disobeying its regulations.

The Commission is divided into nine departments, each headed by a commissioner. Together, these men make up the Executive Commission, a group that might be likened to a company management.

Heading the Commission as president is Professor Walter Hallstein, a scholarly ex-aide to West German Chancellor Adenauer. His top aides are three vice presidents: Sicco Mansholt, an ex-farmer and former Dutch minister of agriculture, who heads the agriculture department; Robert Marjolin, who heads the economic and financial department; and Giuseppe Caron, who heads the internal market department. The other departments are for social affairs, transport, external affairs, overseas development, competition and administration.

To staff the departments, the Commission tries to maintain a hiring ratio of 25% Germans, 25% Italians, 25% Frenchmen, 10% Hollanders, 10% Belgians, and 5% Luxembourgers. Most of its employees speak at least two languages. They take no orders from their native countries, only from the Commission. Their independence is signified by the blue license plates on their cars, which bear six stars and the letters EUR.

Many of these men are young; Jacques Denniau, a lanky French intellectual who heads the Commission's representatives in current negotiations to admit Britain to the Common Market, is 33. Jacques Vandamme, a Belgian lawyer in charge of EEC anti-monopoly investigations, is 38.

Most of the staff men display a deep devotion to European unity. Dr. Winfried Hauschild, a West German lawyer who lost an arm in World War II, joined the EEC competition department in 1958, he says, because "I wanted to work for this organization even if it had to be at a lower salary. After three and a half years with the Commission, I am convinced more than ever that national cooperation is the answer to some of the problems of Europe."

How a Transport Policy Grows.   To get an idea of how these staff men formulate policy, visit Gunter Krauss, a husky West German, who was chief of the Hamburg Port Railroad before coming to EEC three years ago. As head of the general affairs section of the EEC transportation department, Mr. Krauss has been meeting for months with transportation experts from all the EEC countries to give form to the Treaty of Rome mandate to work out "a common transport policy." So far, the group has agreed the EEC member states should require common carriers to publish freight rates publicly to let shippers know true charges; consult regularly with each other to work out a "certain measure" of coordination in transportation investments; and make any necessary changes in their laws to eliminate double taxation on any form of transport.

In similar fashion, Dr. Hauschild heads a group in the EEC competition department which is trying to determine how the six countries could eliminate conflicts in laws affecting public contracts. Another EEC group is trying to frame a common bankruptcy law for the six countries which, among other things, would allow creditors of a bankrupt person or firm to attach their possessions no matter where in the Common Market area they are located. A third among the dozens of groups is framing a common policy to determine how much of the area's anticipated energy needs should be met by using coal, how much by oil, how much by atomic energy.

Once a policy is formulated, it goes to the EEC Council of Ministers for approval. This group is composed of top government officials of the six member nations, chosen according to the topic under discussion. At times, the Council has been composed of government ministers of agriculture; this month it probably will be made up of financial officials. That's because the next meeting is scheduled to take up tax changes that might be necessary in each country to eliminate discrimination against outside business—so that a West German company doing business in Italy, say, would not be taxed more heavily than its Italian competitors.

The Council's Powers.   The Council is the final voice in EEC matters. If it votes against a proposal, the proposal dies. If it eventually votes to approve the proposed uniform patent law, each EEC government will be bound to present the bill to its national parliament, and do its utmost to secure passage. If the Council votes for a proposal that can be carried out by executive action of the member governments, its action creates an obligation in international law under the Treaty of Rome.

When a policy is approved, the EEC wherever possible relies on established agencies of member governments to carry it out. Thus, although the EEC Commission is supervising the erection of the common tariff wall around the Common Market countries, actual duties on foreign goods entering the area will be collected by customs officials of each of the EEC governments.

The EEC Commission does have some enforcement authority, though. In the anti-monopoly field, each EEC government will continue to prosecute cartels operating only within its boundaries. But Jacques Vandamme, chief investigator of cartels for the EEC competition department, will probe the activities of cartels suspected of hampering free competition in international trade. M. Vandamme says he will try to use "persuasion" to get them to change their ways. If persuasion doesn't work, an EEC-drafted law going into effect next August will empower him to start proceedings to fine violators up to $1 million each.

EEC Court Cases.   To aid its enforcement work, the EEC Commission has a legal staff which can file complaints with the EEC Court of Justice against companies, industries or even governments it believes are disobeying EEC policies. Companies or individuals can file complaints, too. So can the EEC competition department.

The Court already has proved its power. Most of its cases so far have involved complaints against companies or industries. But in one recent case Dutch farmers accused the government of Italy of violating EEC policy by continuing to ban pig meat imports from other EEC nations after the EEC Council had voted to free agricultural imports. The Court ordered the Italians to drop the ban. The

Italian government, perhaps anticipating the ruling, reversed its policy before the verdict came down.

The EEC possesses no true legislative branch in the sense of a body actually empowered to pass laws. The European Parliament, which meets periodically in Strasbourg, France, does act in some ways like a legislature. Members voice their views on EEC policy in floor debates much as Senators do in the U.S., and committees study EEC tax proposals, say, in a manner similar to the U.S. House Ways and Means Committee. But the Parliament has power only to submit advisory reports to the EEC Commission and Council of Ministers.

EEC-Parliament Link. The European Parliament is composed of members of the national legislature of the EEC countries, however, and so serves as a link between these bodies and the EEC executive branch. Such liaison is important, since measures like EEC anti-monopoly laws must be passed by each national legislature to become effective. The West German Bundestag, the French Chamber of Deputies, or any of the other four national parliaments could vote down an EEC measure, and throw the EEC machinery into chaos.

In practice, this is unlikely. The painstaking process of consultation among representatives of all six member states at each step of the policy-making process assures that objections likely to be raised by national parliaments will be faced before a bill gets to them. Moreover, European public opinion to date has favored the Common Market and its workings so heavily that European political experts believe any national government or parliament defying a major EEC proposal would risk its own downfall.

Another check on the possibility of a member state revolting against an EEC policy existed until last Dec. 31, because up to then EEC proposals could be readied for action only by a unanimous vote of the Council of Ministers. As of Jan. 1, however, the Council switched to a new voting system under which Germany, France and Italy have four votes each, Belgium and Holland two votes each, and Luxembourg one vote. Many decisions, though not all, can be carried by a majority of 12 of these 17 votes. So it is now possible for an EEC state to be bound to a policy decision it voted against on the Council.

This year's $58.1 million budget for the EEC Commission is up from $44.2 million last year. France, West Germany and Italy each contribute 28% of the budget; Belgium and Holland 7.9% each, and Luxembourg 0.2%.

Starting Jan. 1 the Commission began levying an income tax of 8% to 45% on its 2,000 employees, who are excused from paying income taxes to their national governments.

SUGGESTED READINGS

Watkins, James T., and J. William Robinson, *General International Organization* (Princeton, N.J.: Van Nostrand, 1956). A selection of documents on international organizations, with some being of special importance to business.

Woytinsky, W. S., and E. S. Woytinsky, *World Commerce and Governments* (New York: Twentieth Century Fund, 1955). Discusses those international governments of especial significance to American businessmen.

CHAPTER 29

THE
ADMINISTRATIVE
PROCESS AND
BUSINESS

Administrative agencies and officials of the various levels of American government cannot proceed arbitrarily in their dealings with the business-man. At least, they must not give the appearance of doing so. The decisions they make and the actions they take must be in accordance with some uniform procedure established, usually, by the law setting up the agency or by some general law governing administrative procedures. Failure to follow proper procedures by the administrative agency can lead to the reversal of its decision or action by the courts on the ground that "due process of law" has not been observed. Administrative decisions are preceded by investigations that are required to be in conformity with rules established by the administrative body. Since many such decisions are made by subordinate officials in an agency, opportunities for review by top officials of such decisions frequently exist. Finally, judicial review of administrative decisions is frequently provided for, and even where no specific provision is made the acts of administrative agencies have been held to be subject to review in the courts. In all of these steps—rule-making, investigation, administrative review and judicial review—opportunities exist for the businessman and other interested parties to influence the final decision of the administrative agency. An examination of these procedural steps and the ways in which those affected by administrative decisions can influence them provides some clues as to what businessmen can do to secure decisions favorable to them.

ADMINISTRATIVE RULE–MAKING

The statutes that assign certain administrative duties to government agencies rarely spell out in detail the rules under which the agencies must operate. Rather, a general policy is declared, along with the objectives of the legislation, and the agencies make rules to implement that policy and those objectives. The result has been a great output of administrative rules that have the force of law. A noted educator and judge has declared:

> The outstanding development of the law in the present century has, beyond any doubt, been the growth of innumerable administrative agencies. They have flourished in both the national government and in the states in peace and time of war alike. The volume of subordinate legislation promulgated by them exceeds by many times the corresponding additions to the statute books and the number of their decisions is so vast as to dwarf, in comparison, the output of the traditional courts.

The ways in which rules are made by administrative agencies vary among agencies, although greater uniformity has recently been secured by general legislation governing administrative procedures. In 1946, Congress passed the Administrative Procedure Act governing federal agencies. The American Bar Association and the National Conference of Commissioners on Uniform State Laws have taken steps that have led to the development of a Model State Administrative Procedure Act that many states have adopted or have used as a basis for whatever legislation governing administrative procedures they have enacted. The following discussion rests heavily on an analysis of the processes established in this federal and state legislation.

A definition of "rule" is necessary to understand clearly what is under discussion when administrative agencies make rules. The Model Act states:

"Rule" includes every regulation, standard, or statement of policy or interpretation of general application and future effect, including the amendment or repeal thereof, adopted by an agency, whether with or without prior hearing, to implement or make specific the law enforced or administered by it or to govern its organization or procedure, but does not include regulations concerning only the internal management of the agency and not directly affecting the rights of or procedures available to the public.

Rules, no less than statutes, lay down standards of conduct for all to whom their terms apply. In addition to substantive rules, which have statutory effect, agencies also issue interpretative rules, which have persuasive authority in the construction of statutory language, and procedural rules, which guide the conduct of all administrative action.

The federal government normally provides for public participation in the making of rules. There are some cases in which the public interest requires secrecy in the rule-making process, but the exemption of certain rules from provisions for public participation lessens the opportunity of businessmen and other interested parties to influence the rules. For example, the 1946 federal statute exempted rules relating to agency management or personnel, interpretative rules, general statements of policy, or rules of agency organization, procedure, or practice. Also, the federal government exempts many rules of interest to, and vitally affecting, private parties because they relate to military, naval, or foreign affairs functions. Many rules governing "public property"—such as procedures respecting such property, loans, benefits and contracts, which often have a direct bearing on private interests—are declared, by some agencies, to be exempt from the rule-making procedures of the Administrative Procedure Act. The Post Office Department asserted at one time that its rule-making is exempt from the act because the property interest the Government has in the mails makes it subject to exemptions relating to "public property." Such exemptions were disapproved of by the Task Force on Legal Services and Procedure in its report to the Commission on Organization of the Executive Branch of the Government in 1955 in one of its conclusions:

> The task force concludes that the existing exemption of military, naval and foreign affairs may be repealed without endangering the activities of the departments and agencies which promulgate such rules. And the task force believes that proprietary functions may likewise be effectively executed by agencies with public participation in the rule-making process. The exemption under Section 4(a) of the Administrative Procedure Act with respect to interpretative rules, general statements of policy and rules of agency organizations, procedure, or practice also should be repealed.

The requirement of public participation does not subject departments and agencies to an unreasonable procedural burden, nor does it in any way affect the authority of the agency or its discretion. All that is required is the giving of notice and an opportunity to interested persons to present their views concerning the proposed rule. The department or agency may give such consideration to the views presented as it deems warranted under the facts.

Those states that have adopted the essence of the Model Act have made provisions for public participation in rule-making. No specific procedure is required by the Act; it states only that "in addition to other rule-making requirements imposed by law" the agency shall "so far as practicable, publish or otherwise circulate notice of its intended action and afford interested persons opportunity to submit data or views orally or in writing." California's law goes beyond the requirement of the Model Act by requiring an opportunity to interested parties to present their views through giving notice of a proposed rule at least 30 days in advance of its adoption. At the time and place indicated in the notice, interested persons have the opportunity to present statements, arguments, or contentions in writing, although the agency is not required to permit oral testimony. Other states, such as Indiana and Ohio, require a public hearing with an opportunity to present oral testimony.

The initiative in changing administrative rules is not left solely to government agencies. Most of the state statutes that have been adopted prescribing certain administrative procedures permit interested parties to file petitions for the issuance of new rules and for the amendment or repeal of existing ones. Thus the role of the businessman in the making of rules can be one in which he initiates new rules or rule changes as well as presents his views at formal proceedings in which such matters are discussed. Of course, even when no formal arrangements are made for hearings or other proceedings during which administrative rules are made, businessmen can still communicate with the agencies establishing rules and attempt to influence rules through persuasion, or they may work indirectly through legislators or other elected officials to have rules made that are favorable to them.

ADMINISTRATIVE INVESTIGATION AND
DECISION–MAKING

Since the rules made by administrative agencies do not enforce themselves, steps need to be taken to secure behavior in accordance with public policy. Some of these aim at gaining observance of the rules through voluntary action by the individuals and groups affected. For example, government officials may declare certain policies to be in the public interest and hope that citizens will refrain from taking action contrary to that policy. Sometimes this is effective. The Department of State has on occasion disapproved the shipment of war materials to certain countries or has disapproved the participation of American financial institutions in loans to certain countries: these declarations usually have had the desired effect on policies adopted by the firms involved. On the other hand, in recent years we saw an incident in which President Kennedy declared inflationary wage increases as being contrary to public policy, and some firms in the steel industry raised prices regardless of the fact that the President viewed the wage increase granted by the industry as noninflationary. The price increase was later rescinded, but not until President Kennedy brought powerful pressures to bear. Sometimes laws have been passed that have declared certain public policies, but where there have been no sanctions that administrators could bring to bear on violators such legislation has generally been ineffective.

Some kinds of administrative action seek to gain compliance with public policy through voluntary agreements on the part of those affected. Many commercial standards—such as grades of cotton and grain—have been established by government agencies and voluntarily adopted by those in the industries concerned. Mediation and conciliation activities by the federal and state governments aim at securing industrial peace by persuading the employers and unions to agree to resolve their differences without disruption of business. Conferences are held by government agencies in which interested parties can agree to certain actions in the public interest; the trade practices conferences sponsored by the Federal Trade Commission are examples.

There are a number of other ways in which administrative agencies attempt to secure compliance with public policy without bringing the coercive power of government to bear on individuals and groups investigated. The government may try to set an ideal example for others to follow—that is, it may attempt to act as an "ideal employer" and hope that other employers adopt the ideal. Also, government agencies have demonstrated ideal methods of agriculture and have gone into the operation of some electricity-generating facilities with the objective of establishing a "yardstick" against which the operations of privately owned electric utilities might be judged. However, business firms in the electric power industry sometimes regard this as employing the coercive power of government competition to keep electric rates down. Publicity of nonobservance of public policy is also said to be "noncoercive," but those firms that experience social and economic pressure as a consequence probably regard this publicity as being as coercive as is legal action.

The more important actions taken against individual businessmen and firms usually have the coercive power of government behind them. Except in extreme instances, such power cannot be brought to bear on business until after some investigation has been made to determine whether or not the businessman or firm has been engaging in conduct according to the rules.

Administrative Investigation

It should be pointed out at the beginning that not all investigations are initiated by government agencies. An aggrieved employee or union may complain to a body such as the National Labor Relations Board that a certain firm is engaging in unfair labor practices. A competitor may feel that unfair trade practices are being engaged in and make a complaint to some official agency. Stockholders may feel that a corporation is not filing truthful financial reports and ask that an investigation be made. Government agencies are, however, interested in achieving their objectives, and sometimes initiate investigations that will enable them to do so even though requests or complaints from outsiders are not forthcoming.

Investigations preceding the issuance of orders by administrative bodies are conducted in a number of ways. Some are fairly simple and routine, as in the case of meat inspection. If a particular carcass does not meet the standards of the inspector, he refuses to pass it (in effect, ordering its disposal in some other fashion). On the other hand, some investigations by administrative bodies are very complex, and highly formal procedures have been developed for conducting them. These processes are very similar to those conducted in the courts and, consequently, such administrative action has been called "administrative adjudication." There are some distinctions between procedures before such administrative tribunals and the courts. Legal counsel need not be employed, nor are the rules of evidence as formal in administrative investigations. These relatively informal proceedings before subject-matter experts rather than before judges can yield (although they do not always do so) speedy decisions.

Normally, in these more complex administrative investigations, the initial hearing of the issues is before a referee, examiner, arbitrator, or individual member of the administrative agency. He gives notice to the affected parties of the hearing date along with a statement of the facts asserted to be true and that are the cause of action and also makes reference to the pertinent laws and administrative rules. The parties involved then have an opportunity to submit facts, arguments, offers of settlement, or proposals of adjustment. On the basis of the facts and arguments presented, as well as on the laws and rules involved, the hearing officer makes an initial decision. In order to preserve the "judicial integrity" of the officer hearing the case, he is normally made independent of the government agents prosecuting the case and the latter are prohibited from entering into the making of his decision. This decision is not final, however, and in due course is reviewed by the senior members of the administrative agency.

Administrative Review

Administrative procedures normally provide for a review of a decision made by a hearing officer before a board of several persons, or at least before an officer superior to the one who held the original hearing. Usually such reviews permit the parties to submit additional evidence and arguments either to support the original decision or to reverse it. After the matter has been reviewed at the highest level of an administrative agency and a final decision is reached, an order is issued (although an earlier order might have been given by the hearing officer).

The issuance of binding orders by administrative agencies is a relatively recent development. Originally, only certain courts in the United States could issue orders to compel individual action. Although there had been a few earlier instances in which legislatures had granted the power to give orders to administrative agencies and officials, it was not until Congress passed the Interstate Commerce Act in 1887 that the "modern era" in the use of directing power by administrators began. The Interstate Commerce Commission was empowered by the original legislation to order railroads to "cease-and-desist" from certain violations of the law and of rules made by the Commission. In 1906, this agency was given the power to determine what were just and reasonable railroad rates. Since then, this agency and others have been given considerable administrative power to issue orders to individuals. Perhaps we should note that some of the states had engaged in railroad regulation before the Interstate Commerce Commission was created, and had established administrative agencies having similar powers (although some legislatures sought to engage in railroad regulation through direct legislation rather than establish a body to conduct investigations, make decisions, and issue binding orders).

The more important orders issued by administrative agencies to businessmen are "corrective." That is, individual firms are directed to do something or to refrain from certain action. Railroads and other common carriers coming under the jurisdiction of the Interstate Commerce Commission may be directed to charge certain rates or to provide certain services. In a recent case, some eastern railroads were directed to refrain from making special rates to certain firms when the shippers, in exchange for the special rates, agreed to ship the bulk of their freight over the lines of the railroads making the special concessions. Radio and television stations are directed to operate on certain wave-lengths or channels and are directed to refrain from operating on others.

Not all orders issued by government agencies or officials direct individuals to comply with public policy as stated in the law or administrative rulings. On occasion, "orders of exemption" may be issued exempting certain individuals from general rules. Very frequently, planning commissions are asked by businessmen for exemptions from the application of zoning laws that would prohibit their conducting a certain kind of business (or any business) in a certain location. Sometimes "variances" are granted by the administrative bodies involved.

Before leaving the matter of administrative decision-making, we might note that sometimes the decisions of agencies shape new rules. It may be that there is no clear rule of law or administrative rule to guide the administrator(s) making the decision. Having made a certain decision under a certain set of circumstances, this decision becomes a precedent for aiding the making of future decisions under the same or similar circumstances. Thus individual decisions and orders may establish a new rule for the guidance of the agency and of those affected by the work of the administrative body or official.

ADMINISTRATIVE SANCTIONS

In order to secure compliance with their decisions and orders, administrative agencies have certain sanctions they can employ. Such powers are not always necessary because some of the parties adversely affected by administrative action would accept the situation and carry out the letter, if not the spirit, of the decision or order. Earlier, we mentioned the fear of adverse publicity as being a reason that some orders would be implemented by businessmen even though no coercive powers were available to agencies and officials. There are other reasons as well why some decisions and orders are obeyed voluntarily. However, since there will always be some cases in which individuals and groups will refuse to obey unless forced to do so, administrators have sanctions they may employ to compel obedience.

A sanction is "a conditional evil annexed to a law to produce obedience to that law." In the past, such sanctions were imposed by courts, and the most important of them still are. However, considerable power has been given government administrators over the years to impose sanctions in order to secure compliance with their decisions and orders. Such power has been granted by legislatures, which have also in many instances set the penalties for refusal to comply with the law when directed to do so by the executive branch of government; although, in some cases, a certain degree of discretion is left to the administrator in applying the penalties.

The more important sanctions available to administrative agencies or officials involve refusal or withdrawal of benefits conferred by the government. Since government provides a number of valuable services, refusing individuals or groups those services may compel them to obey the law. For example, the Post Office Department provides valuable services to business. However, if business firms employ the mails to defraud customers or if they mail obscene or otherwise objectionable matter, the withdrawal of the privilege of using the mails has tremendous adverse influence on their operations. Unless firms are willing to comply with employment practices specified in certain laws, they are refused the right to bid on, and secure, public contracts. Farmers who do not comply with acreage restrictions under certain crop control plans may be denied the payments the federal government would otherwise make. The refusal to grant a business or professional license, or the suspension or revocation of such a license, is yet another example of the importance of the refusal or withdrawal of governmental benefits that gives administrators substantial coercive powers in cases in which such benefits are important to the affected party.

Also, some officials possess "summary powers" to compel obedience to laws and rules. A summary power is "administrative power to apply compulsion or force against person or property to effectuate a legal purpose, without a judicial warrant to authorize such action." The collection of taxes, including those on business, provides an illustration. Property of the person who has not paid his taxes can be seized and sold by the tax collector without a court order permitting such action. If, for example, customs duties (import taxes) are not paid on certain imports, customs officers seize the goods and sell them at a public sale. Under the Federal Meat Inspection Act, inspectors can compel the destruction of condemned carcasses in their presence without first obtaining a court order. In New York, the superintendent of banking may take possession of banks that he has decided are unsafely conducted or have not complied with his orders. In short, there are a number of situations in which administrative officers may seize the property of businessmen to compel obedience to their decisions and orders without relying on judicial power. On the other hand, there are only rare cases in which the person of a businessman is affected by administrative powers. In California, the Railroad Commission has the same power as do courts to administer oaths, to take testimony, and to punish for contempt as do courts of record, which might mean that if railroad companies refused to produce certain records, or were otherwise in contempt, officers of the railroad might be fined or even given a jail sentence. However, such strong powers are usually left in the hands of the courts.

COURTS AND THE ADMINISTRATIVE PROCESS

Normally only the courts of the country have the power to compel certain behavior. Although we have noted some instances in which administrators may take summary action, that is, action not requiring judicial warrant, their role as wielders of governmental sanctions is distinctly secondary to that of the courts. When individuals or groups refuse to obey the decisions or orders of administrators, such government officials are frequently unable to compel action without securing the assistance of the courts. In asking the aid of the judiciary, the bureaucracy finds its decisions being called into question and sometimes being reversed or otherwise modified by the courts. That is, the courts engage in a review of administrative decisions and sometimes make different and more binding ones.

Judicial Enforcement

The courts, when administrators are successful in securing judicial enforcement of their orders, adopt one or the other of two alternatives: they either apply the sanctions stated in the statutes under which administrative action was taken or they issue their own orders that may be enforced through the sanctions possessed by the courts. Legislation assigning certain duties to administrative agencies normally states certain penalties in terms of fines or prison terms to be imposed on those not obeying the law. When the courts are convinced by administrative officials that the law has been violated, they impose the fine and/or imprisonment provided for by statute. In addition to whatever statutory penalties they might impose, the courts may issue another order to the party refusing to obey the order of the administrator—such an order frequently being a repetition or modification of the administrative order. However, since it is now a court order, disobedience becomes contempt of court, and additional penalties of fines and/or imprisonment might be levied.

Judicial Review

However, the courts need not always support the administrative agency and enforce its orders. The courts of the United States are not intended to be part of the enforcement machinery of the administrative branches of government. Instead, they occupy (at least in theory) a position in which they assess the claims of those appearing before the courts and attempt to do justice under the law. As far as the courts are concerned, administrative agencies and officials are just another class of individuals and groups that may make certain representations before judges who will then decide what to do. There are, in practice, very few decisions of administrators that cannot be reviewed before the courts.

Some judicial review of administrative orders is quite limited. In the case of orders of the independent regulatory commissions—such as the National Labor Relations Board—the extent to which the courts can review decisions is limited. The congressional laws creating that Board and assigning it certain responsibilities—such as determining whether or not a firm is guilty of engaging in unfair labor practices—limit the extent to which the courts can review such determinations. After some complaint has been made attributing an unfair labor practice to some employer, a hearing is conducted and an order to "cease and desist" might be issued by the Board. If the employer refuses to obey the order, the Board may petition a federal Circuit Court of Appeals to enforce the order. The appeals court then reviews the evidence on which the order was issued, but it is limited to examining the evidence the Board considered, and the findings of fact (based on that evidence) made by the Board are regarded as conclusive if the evidence considered as a whole supports such findings. However, although the court accepts the findings of fact, it may conclude that those facts should have been interpreted differently so as to yield a different decision. Therefore, even being limited as to what evidence it may consider, a court may still arrive at a different decision from that arrived at by the administrative agency, and it is the judicial decision that takes precedence.

In other cases, judicial review is broader. Those who have received adverse decisions from administrative agencies may present new and additional evidence before the courts that is also considered before any judicial decision is arrived at. In such cases, the administrative agency may be found by the courts to have made errors in findings of fact, and the administrative decision will therefore be held to be in error. There are other grounds on which administrative decisions may be invalidated by the courts. It may be found that the administrator has abused his discretionary power to gain personal or political objectives. Also, it might be discovered that the administrator lacks jurisdiction, either over persons and property in a certain area or under his lawful responsibilities. That is, administrative officials have only a certain geographical area under their jurisdiction and they cannot act against persons or property outside this area. Too, the law only gives them limited authority to act and they may not legally exceed those powers in carrying out their duties. Administrators may misinterpret the law—at least the judges are presumed to be "learned in the law" and their declaration that an official has misconstrued the law is final. Finally, the courts may find errors in the procedures employed by the administrators. The Fifth and Fourteenth Amendments to the United States Constitution prohibit both federal and state governments from depriving persons (which has been construed to include corporations) of life, liberty, and property without due process of law. Where administrative agencies and officials do not follow what the courts regard as "due process" (or where legislation prescribing procedures to be followed by administrators does not meet judicial standards of "due process"), the decisions of the administrators may be invalidated on constitutional grounds.

BUSINESS AND THE ADMINISTRATIVE PROCESS

Businessmen frequently complain about the "bureaucrats" and question whether all of the steps in the administrative process are necessary or desirable. True, there is a considerable amount of disutility to business in the administrative process. Not only do administrators sometimes restrain businessmen from taking action they would like to take (although this complaint might more properly be aimed at legislators), but presenting evidence and securing hearings before administrative bodies and the courts also are burdensome, consuming the time and money of businessmen. Since no decision on which the businessman can really rely is handed down until judicial review has taken place at the highest level possible (with state supreme courts and the U.S. Supreme Court being the final courts of appeal for judicial review of administrative decisions), securing a reliable decision *is* expensive and time consuming. However, there is considerable value to the businessman in the administrative process, and the benefits appear to outweigh the disadvantages.

First, the administrative process protects the businessman from hasty and arbitrary government action. Through its provisions for review, final action will be delayed until all pertinent evidence can be presented and considered by a number of relatively impartial judges. (There are some cases, as we have mentioned, in which delay in the execution of an administrative order might be contrary to public policy. In such cases there is no provision for review, although if an individual is wronged by such action, he can recover through bringing some kind of action against the administrator.) Thus, no change need be made in business operations until there is no doubt about the legality of the decision.

Also, the existence of such a governmental process enables the businessman to bring the power of government to bear on other private parties who may be acting in an illegal or unruly fashion. For example, a union may be engaging in an unfair labor practice. The firm adversely affected by this practice may appeal to the National Labor Relations Board (if it has jurisdiction), which may, after investigation, issue an order to the union to "cease and desist." Not only may unions be proceeded against in this fashion, but so may unfair competitors, suppliers discriminating against the firm, and so on.

Another important reason why the administrative process has value to businessmen is that its complexity permits them to prevent or delay adverse administrative action. Administrators have a certain amount of discretion in enforcing laws and securing compliance with rules, partly because administrative agencies rarely have large enough staffs to secure universal compliance. Therefore, a businessman whose practices have come into question may be able to convince the investigator from the agency having jurisdiction over a certain matter that it would not be a good use of the agency's resources to proceed against him. (We might also mention that there have been cases in which businessmen have been able to "buy" favorable decisions from government officials.) If the businessman is unable to persuade the official making the initial investigation to discontinue it, then he might be able to present such strong evidence on his side of the case before a hearing officer or those reviewing the initial decision that he is able to secure a favorable decision. Finally, by appealing the decision to the courts, he enters an arena in which administrative decisions are frequently reversed. In short, the administrative process seems to provide considerable room for maneuver on the part of those businessmen who wish to avoid being adversely affected by the decision of a "bureaucrat" (the reading at the end of this chapter shows how some businessmen have done so), and businessmen need not take an unfavorable view of it.

READING: The Not-So-Long Arm of the Law *
by Consumers Union

[*The following reading, as is apparent, is a critical commentary on the administrative practices of certain federal agencies as well as on certain business practices. Also illustrated is the fact that administrative procedures leave considerable room for maneuver on the part of those businessmen who do not want to obey the "spirit" of rules, regulations, or laws. Only a portion of the original article has been excerpted and reproduced here.*]

* Reprinted with permission from the October 1958 issue of *Consumer Reports*, Vol. 23, No. 10. Copyright by Consumers Union, a nonprofit organization.

A critical examination of the way our Federal regulatory agencies are exercising their mandate affecting consumers:

The degree to which consumer welfare is dependent on the effective functioning of several Federal regulatory agencies all too often is forgotten. During this past year, however, a number of events have dramatized once again how much the health and pocketbook of every citizen can be affected by the vigor or laxity with which the Federal Trade Commission, the Federal Food and Drug Administration and the U.S. Post Office—to name an important three—carry out their mandates from Congress to guard the public against unfair economic exploitation, false advertising, health hazards, and frauds. One of the most recent of these events was the publication in August of the long delayed Federal Trade Commission's "Economic Report on Antibiotics Manufacture." This report charged six leading drug manufacturers with conspiracy to fix prices of the new "wonder drugs." (Consumer Reports will report on details of this study, and on the general subject of why drug prices are so high, in an early issue.)

About the same time that the antibiotics report was released by the FTC, Congressman John A. Blatnik (D., Minn.), chairman of a subcommittee of the House Government Operations Committee, took another segment of the drug industry apart in a report of his group's findings on the sale of fraudulent weight-reducing medicines and devices. Significantly, however, Congressman Blatnik hurled words at the FTC ("atrophy," "indifference," "apathy," and "weak and tardy") which were almost as strong as those the subcommittee used to condemn the weight reducers which, it said, "bilk the American consumer out of $100 million annually."

The U.S. Post Office, in the same report, came in for praise for the relative speed and directness with which it handles frauds sold by mail. At the hearings upon which the report had been based, a representative of the Post Office had testified that "medical frauds are more lucrative than at any other time in history." It takes the Post Office an average of about four months from hearings on complaints to final decisions for action in these matters. But, as the Post Office General Counsel Abe McGregor Goff commented: "The quacks with their nostrums, the miracle makers who can bring new sexual vigor to old men, grow hair or make it 'permanently' vanish, develop the bust, cure every ill from cancer to hemorrhoids, produce pills to make skinny people fat or fat people skinny, persist in their efforts. . . ."

One of the ways they persist in escaping the full effect of the Post Office order is by shifting to other sales methods—they place ads in the newspapers or over radio and TV and sell their products through retail outlets or by house-to-house men instead of by mail. So procedures to stop them must start all over, through the FTC and the FDA.

And the new start must be made from the bottom up. On the basis of present law, the FTC cannot use the Post Office findings of fact but must dig up its own. It takes the FTC, according to Congressman Blatnik, an average of *two years* before it can issue a cease-and-desist order. For this reason, the Blatnik subcommittee report recommended that control over advertising of foods and drugs be shifted from the FTC to the FDA.

But, as the record shows, the FDA, under present circumstances at least, is far from an answer to this urgent need of the times. As the law now stands, the FDA comes into the picture when a food, drug, cosmetic or medical device is adulterated, hazardous to health, or fraudulently labeled. Under these circumstances, it has the power to seize the products of law violators and hail such manufacturers into court for judgment and fines. The question is, how well does it use the power? For some evidence on this point, see the following pages.

Who's to Blame?   In presenting the following four case histories, which illustrate some of the ways in which the spirit of the law seems all but lost in the letter of ineffectual action, *Consumer Reports* does not condemn the Federal agencies. They are forced to operate on grossly inadequate appropriations and the lack of funds makes the mandate of Congress a legislative mislabeling of actual practice. They are understaffed. They are sometimes denied cooperation from other Government agencies (and the press certainly gives little space to the actions they do take). There is little general awareness of the size of the task they face. In order to function effectively they need an aroused public opinion. Without public pressure to counter private stratagems, they are weakened. Informed and indignant demand for improvement by consumers can bolster their position and, CU hopes, stiffen their spines. It is to this end that we present the case histories from official files on the pages following.

Drugs and Deception.   (When you take a prescription to be filled at your local pharmacy, it is chiefly the U.S. Food and Drug Administration which is responsible for seeing that the drugs dispensed by the pharmacist meet standards for purity, quality, and strength. The same is true of proprietary medicines, which you buy over-the-counter without a prescription. How fully are these responsibilities of the FDA being carried out? Three case histories from official files, each covering a period of years, suggest that the level of enforcement leaves much to be desired.)

The Bonded Laboratories Case.   In January 1952, Bonded Laboratories, Inc. of Brooklyn, New York, sent to East Orange, New Jersey, a shipment of phenobarbital tablets, each tablet supposed to contain 1½ grains of the prescription drug phenobarbital. A month or so later, an alert FDA inspector picked up some of the tablets for testing, and the FDA laboratory reported that they contained less than the proper amount. Accordingly, 13,000 of the tablets were seized by the U.S. Marshal.

Proceeding under Section 304 of the Food, Drug, and Cosmetic Act, the FDA next asked the court to order the substandard tablets destroyed. When no one appeared to claim or defend the tablets, their destruction was ordered. The FDA also could have sought criminal penalties under Section 303 of the Act—"imprisonment for not more than one year, or a fine of not more than $1000, or both such imprisonment and fine" for a first offense; and up to three years' imprisonment or $10,000 fine, or both, for subsequent violations. But the FDA did not seek criminal prosecution under Section 303. As a result, the only penalty suffered was loss of the tablets.

Was this "tap on the wrist" sufficient to deter further violations? Hardly. Here is the subsequent record of official actions against substandard Bonded Laboratories drugs shipped to New Jersey:

August, 1953: 165,200 *Visnico* tablets seized on the ground that they contained less than the proper amounts of two ingredients—potassium nitrate and sodium nitrite.

September 1953: Two 50,000-tablets drums of aspirin seized on the grounds that ". . . when shipped, its quality and purity fell below the standard . . . in that the article had a strong odor of acetic acid, many of the tablets were discolored, and a portion of the tablets contained less than 5 grains of acetylsalicylic acid."

November 1953: 1700 sulfadiazine tablets seized on the ground that they contained less than 78.3 per cent of the labeled amount of sulfadiazine.

November 1953: 3300 diethylstilbestrol tablets seized on the ground that they contained not more than 76.4 per cent of the labeled amount of diethylstilbestrol.

In yet another instance there was a switch on the usual charge against Bonded Laboratories' drugs. The FDA New Jersey inspector secured the seizure of 140,000 *Natrico* tablets on the ground that they contained *too much* sodium nitrite—79.5 milligrams instead of 60. Too much of a drug in a tablet, of course, can in some instances be even more dangerous than too little.

In all of these cases, no one appeared to defend against the FDA action, and the tablets were ordered destroyed.

Bonded Laboratories ships to many other states besides New Jersey. The FDA inspector in Miami, Florida, initiated five seizure actions against Bonded Laboratories products during 1953 and 1954. Two FDA records serve to illustrate the pattern:

In November 1953, Bonded Laboratories sent to Miami a shipment of *Dietabs,* each supposed to contain 1/12th grain of amphetamine sulfate. Some 80,000 of these tablets were seized in March 1954, on the ground that they contained less than that amount of the drug. Just a few weeks later, according to the FDA, Bonded Laboratories made a second shipment of the same tablets to the same city. Some 201,500 tablets of the second shipment were also seized, and for the same reason.

The other seizures in Miami were of estradiol tablets known as *Estorals,* and of vitamin products known as *Bever Miamivites* and *Zilifer-B's.* In all five instances, the charge was substrength tablets. In all five, the owner failed to appear and the tablets were ordered destroyed.

All of the actions already described were peripheral, aimed at shipments received in other states rather than at Bonded Laboratories itself, back in Brooklyn. The FDA also, however, served Bonded Laboratories directly with a "Notice of Hearing" on charges (1) that some of its diethylstilbestrol tablets contained only 80 per cent of the proper amount, and (2) that some of its phenobarbital tablets were so compounded that they failed to dissolve in the stomach or intestinal tract and were therefore useless for therapeutic purposes. Counsel for the company thereupon assured the FDA that Bonded Laboratories' factory procedures had been revised, so that it would be "practically impossible for the concern to err again." Accordingly, no further action was taken on these charges.

Not until April 1954 did the FDA file a complaint in court against the company itself. This complaint listed some striking violations—for example:

> *Visnico pulviods* containing only 68 per cent of the proper amount of potassium nitrate and not more than 77 per cent of the proper amount of sodium nitrite.
>
> *Siccoid* hematinic tablets containing not more than 66 per cent of the proper amount of vitamin C.
>
> *Siccoid* Special Supplement containing 50 per cent of the proper amount of vitamin D. Another lot of this product contained 10 per cent of the proper amount of vitamin A and 5 per cent of the proper amount of vitamin C.
>
> *Sulfadiazine* tablets containing from 20 to 21.2 per cent of the proper amount of sulfadiazine. These tablets "were also of a different composition from that declared on their labels by reason of the substitution in part of a large amount of sulfathiazole for the sulfadiazone ingredient. . . ."

How could such errors continue to be made, month after month and even year after year? The FDA complaint supplied part of the answer. FDA inspectors had visited Bonded Laboratories' plant in Brooklyn, the complaint declared, in 1950, 1951, 1953, and 1954—"at which times the defendants were informed of certain inadequacies in their control system. . . ." These "inadequacies" were then listed:

> Failure to assay (test for strength) the raw materials used. Lack of care in identifying containers of raw materials.
>
> Lack of care in identifying finished products. Lack of an adequate checking system to insure that the proper amounts of the various chemicals used were put into the batches.
>
> The making of only a "very few" quantitative tests of the finished products.

"At every inspection," the FDA told the court, "defendants have been warned that their procedures were such that inaccuracies in the composition of their products would likely occur. . . . Nor, despite repeated warnings, have the defendants attempted to rectify the situation." Indeed, on the last of the four FDA inspections visits, "defendants' prodecures were found to be substantially unchanged."

On the basis of this record, the FDA asked for and procured a temporary order, restraining Bonded Laboratories from further violations of the law. In December 1955, with the consent of Bonded Laboratories, a permanent injunction was issued. But still no criminal prosecution against Bonded Laboratories was initiated. Despite the FDA's declaration to the court that "the protection of the public health is too vital to permit continued negligent conduct, backed by unfulfilled promises of improvement," the upshot was one more tap-on-the-wrist for Bonded Laboratories.

The Parkinson Case. What happens when the FDA does file criminal charges? For a revealing answer, let's consider next the record of Allen Parkinson, president of the Sleep-Eze Company, Inc., of Long Beach, California.

At least as early as February 1948, according to FDA records, Allen Parkinson (as head of a corporation then called Hudson Products Company †) was selling Hudson brand male and female "sex hormone tablets." The male hormone tablets contained a synthetic sex hormone, methyl testosterone, deemed harmful because of its profound and sometimes dangerous effects on the body metabolism and glandular functions. Leaflets accompanying the Hudson male tablets alleged —according to a subsequent criminal complaint—that the tablets "would stimulate growth and development of the sex organs and the male sex characteristics, such as distribution of hair, muscular development, and depth of voice," would "correct lack of sexual power and impotence," and would, in addition, be effective for "flushes, sweats, chills, impaired memory . . . nervousness, depression, general weakness," and so on.

The Food and Drug Administration investigated, and in April 1949, after the tablets had been on the market at least 14 months, the U.S. Attorney's Office, on behalf of the FDA, filed a criminal information against Parkinson. Claims made for these hormones, the Government alleged, were false—as were claims made for Hudson female sex hormone tablets. Moreover, according to the Government, the statements accompanying the female tablets failed to warn purchasers that use of the pills "in the dosage and with the duration of administration recommended on its labeling may result in uterine bleeding and damage to the ovaries."

Parkinson pleaded not guilty; the case came to trial quite promptly, and he was found guilty in July 1949. The judge, when pronouncing sentence, said he was convinced beyond a reasonable doubt that these hormone tablets constituted not merely a potential danger but also an actual danger to health when used indiscriminately by layman. The maximum penalty provided by law was $1000 fine and one-year imprisonment on each of four counts. Yet, in consideration of the fact that this was Parkinson's first food-and-drug offense, the judge let him off with a $400 fine.

Less than a month after this modest deterrent, according to a subsequent Government complaint, Allen Parkinson "again embarked upon a widespread mailorder promotion of drugs containing methyl testosterone." In addition, he circularized druggists to tell them about "an intensive national advertising campaign" he was launching, which would remind "every man and woman that they can buy *Hudson Hormones* at their favorite drugstore. Twenty-five million match books will be circulated in California alone."

This time the FDA and U.S. Attorney's office acted with promptness. In September 1949, a "Complaint for Injunction" was filed in court.

"While the composition of said drugs was altered by the addition of vitamin B_1 and the labeling of said drugs was modified," the Government declared, "said

† Not to be confused with Hudson Vitamin Products, Inc., of New York City.

Allen H. Parkinson continued to make substantially the same rejuvenation claims. . . ."

This case took longer to close, since Parkinson defended himself by pointing out that his labels *told* people to consult their physicians before taking the tablets. The case went from the District Court to the Circuit Court of Appeals and then back to the District Court. Ultimately, in July 1951, a permanent injunction was issued prohibiting Parkinson from further sales of misbranded drugs.

Now Parkinson went on to market three products called *Vita-Glan, Bio-Glan* and *Adler's Compound.*

All three of these preparations were offered in both "single strength" and "double strength" or "super strength." The difference? The tablets were identical; but those labeled "double strength" or "super strength" were accompanied by instructions directing users to take twice as many tablets each day.

More or less similar claims were made for *Vita-Glan, Bio-Glan,* and *Adler's Compound*—that they would overcome "male sexual weakness, nervousness, loss of muscle tone, aches and pains, fatigue, irritability," and so on. One product, *Bio-Glan,* was alleged to contain "the gland substance of whole bull testicles, vacuum dried," as well as pancreatin, U.S.P., made from the pancreas gland," plus "prostate gland substances," and other ingredients. But unlike the potent methyl testosterone included in the original *Hudson Hormones,* according to medical witnesses, the so-called glandular substances in *Vita-Glan, Bio-Glan,* and *Adler's Compound* were "inert"—that is, lacking any medicinal effect.

Nor did *Bio-Glan* seek to conceal the fact. Apparently relying on some public confusion concerning the meaning of the word *inert,* one advertisement openly boasted that the gland substances in the tablets "are inert and perfectly safe to use." This statement was not challenged in any of the subsequent litigation.

The most interesting of these three promotions was for *Adler's Compound.* A 30-day supply containing 60 "single strength" tablets was priced at $10; the price of these tablets in the wholesale market was 25 cents for all 60.

In marketing *Adler's Compound,* according to the record, the promoters found a German printer in California and had him print a letterhead with the name "Konrad Adler & Company" in German script. Main offices, according to the letterhead, were at Frankfurt-am-Main, Germany; sales offices were in Paris and Rome; plus a sales and advertising office in London. On this letterhead, letters were run off which opened:

Dear Sir:
    "From out of post-war Germany a new and amazing medical miracle for all males suffering from psychogenic sexual weakness has been developed to relieve this most common of all masculine complaints. . . ."

A photograph of a stern, dignified-looking gentleman appeared on the order form, accompanied by this assurance:

> "I certify that ADLER'S COMPOUND
> is absolutely safe for home use.
>   (signed) Konrad Adler"

FDA investigators subsequently were able to show that the photo of the mythical "Konrad Adler" actually was a likeness made 10 years earlier of a Hollywood bit actor named James Carlisle; it had been taken by a commercial photographer who maintained a file of such "stock shots," which he sold for $10 apiece.

SUGGESTED READINGS

Heady, Ferrel, *Administrative Procedure Legislation in the States* (Ann Arbor, Mich.: U. of Mich., 1952). A valuable aid in understanding administrative procedure at the state level. According to the author, administrative procedure must strike a balance between the objective of protecting individuals from arbitrary action by administrative agencies and the equally important goal of expeditious execution of public policy.

White, Leonard D., *Introduction to the Study of Public Administration,* 4th ed. (New York: Macmillan, 1955). A study of the general field of government administration, including administrative powers and procedures.

CHAPTER 30

BUSINESS
AND THE
COURTS

American courts affect American business in a variety of ways. In the preceding chapter we noted that they reviewed the decisions of administrative agencies of government and issued orders that could be enforced by law-enforcement officers. The work of the courts extends beyond reviewing, and possibly enforcing, the decisions of government administrators. Sometimes, businessmen are involved in court proceedings because some private party—competitor, creditor, stockholder, union, and so on—brings some complaint against a firm. On other occasions, business firms attempt to promote their interests by initiating court action against individuals and groups, both public and private. The importance of such action is testified to by the existence of legal departments in corporations to defend the firm from attacks in the courts as well as to take court action against others when the interests of the corporation seem best served by such a strategy. Whether attacked or attacking, businessmen require (in addition to some knowledge of the law) some understanding of the nature of the courts and court procedures in order to protect and promote their interests. The system of courts and judicial procedures in the United States is quite complex, but there are a few aspects of considerable importance. These we shall examine in order to gain some basic knowledge of this important class of individuals and groups in the political environment of business and an idea of how they proceed.

AMERICAN COURTS

It is sometimes asserted that we have a "dual system" of courts. That is, each state has a system of courts and the federal government has its own separate system (*see* Figure 30–1). We find, on closer examination, that

COURT SYSTEM OF THE UNITED STATES

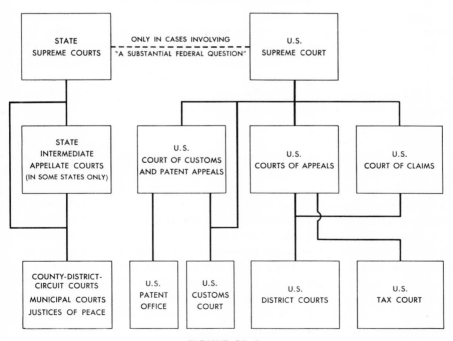

FIGURE 30–1.

there tends to be some overlapping in the jurisdiction of state and federal courts—that is, in any state, there may be some legal issue that might be brought before either a state or federal court. However, they normally have jurisdictions over different matters. Courts may also be classified according to whether they are "courts of original jurisdiction" or "appeals courts." In the following discussion, we shall examine the nature of these different kinds of courts.

State Courts

In order of their establishment, state courts preceded federal courts. During the colonial period, each colony had its own system of courts. When the thirteen colonies declared their independence in 1776, each "free and independent" state had a state court system, unlinked either to the courts of England or to those of other states. As additional states were admitted to the Union, they also developed similar systems. There are now thousands of state courts, in which the great bulk of judicial proceedings take place. These courts, fortunately for the purpose of analysis, fall into roughly five different classifications. There are in each state justice of peace courts, city or municipal courts, county courts, the superior or appellate court (only in some states), and the state supreme court. Although by far the largest number of cases are handled by justice of peace courts, we shall not accord them any substantial consideration. They deal essentially with petty cases: in suits where money damages are sought, for example, they may not award more than fifty dollars, one hundred dollars or—in only a few states—five hundred dollars. Also, justice of peace courts tend to be located in rural areas or small towns, whereas most business is conducted in larger urban communities.

The cities have their counterpart of the justice of peace court in magistrates' courts. These have jurisdiction over both civil and criminal matters and, since the presiding officers have not been required in most cases to be "learned in the law," they have dispensed injustice along with justice. However, there is a movement away from both justice of peace and magistrates' courts. In some cases, special courts have been established to deal with juveniles, domestic relations, traffic violations, small claims, and so on. These courts are presided over by persons with higher qualifications than are possessed by justices of the peace or magistrates. Another development has been that of the unified municipal court, which has jurisdiction over all matters arising under municipal or state law within the limits of the city. Although specialized branches exist for dealing with small claims, domestic relations, and so on, responsibility is centered in a chief justice, and qualified judges are assigned to various branches.

The small claims courts are perhaps the most important of municipal courts to businessmen. In them, businessmen might prosecute claims against others (or may be proceeded against by others) in cases in which the sums involved are not large. Court costs are nominal and justice is speedy, with considerable formality being dispensed with (along with the services of lawyers, who may be used, but whose presence is not required). However, since the jurisdiction of such courts is limited to cases involving quite modest sums, businessmen are frequently involved in other courts as well.

From the English, we inherited the county as a political unit. Consequently, courts were established having general jurisdiction over legal issues arising within a county. In some states, there is one such court for each county and they are called county courts. However, in most of the states, two or more counties have been combined into a single judicial district, and the courts are called district courts or circuit courts. In addition to handling criminal cases, civil suits without restriction as to amount are commenced in such courts (and appeals from decisions rendered in justice of peace courts, magistrate courts, and small claims courts are also heard in such courts). Sometimes these courts have been involved in administrative activities as well as judicial—that is, sometimes the county court might be properly conceived of as an administrative body—but the present tendency is to assign the task of administration to others and maintain the county, district, and circuit courts as judicial organizations.

There would seem to be no need for any additional courts. However, state governments wish to administer justice uniformly throughout the state. Therefore, a state supreme court usually performs this function as well as permits parties to litigation to secure high-level judicial review of the decisions of lower courts. In some states, such a large volume of appeals had been made to state supreme courts that intermediate courts of appeal have been established in the state court systems. These have been given a variety of names—courts of appeal, district courts of appeal, superior courts, appellate divisions (in the case of New York, the intermediate court of appeals is called the supreme court, and the highest court in the state is known as the court of appeals).

State supreme courts (the highest courts in the states) render final decisions involving the constitutions and laws of the states. Some decisions of state supreme courts may be appealed to the United States Supreme Court, but only when a "federal question" is involved—that is, only when there is involved some interpretation of the U.S. Constitution, a federal law, or a treaty to which the federal government is a party. A distinguishing characteristic of appeals courts is that they normally have more than one judge, ranging anywhere from three to nine justices in composition. A result of this is that quite frequently such courts render decisions that are not unanimous.

Federal Courts

Congress has put into effect the provisions of the U.S. Constitution dealing with the establishment of a federal judiciary. Article III of that instrument states, in part: "The judicial power of the United States, shall be vested in one supreme Court, and in such inferior Courts as the Congress may from time to time ordain and establish." After the Constitution was ratified by a sufficient number of states, the Congress met and created a system of federal courts. The Judiciary Act of 1789 established the Supreme Court, three circuit courts, and thirteen district courts. The circuit courts tried the more important cases and heard appeals from decisions of the district courts, which initially had jurisdiction over relatively minor matters. These circuit courts had three judges as members; two Supreme Court justices, and the district court judge from the district. Eventually this created too great a workload for the justices of the Supreme Court and a change was made. In 1911, the circuit courts were abolished and the circuit courts of appeal (which had been created twenty years earlier) took over completely the task of hearing appeals from decisions of district courts. Also in 1911, Congress increased the status and importance of district courts by giving them jurisdiction over major matters as well as those of minor importance. Now there are more than ninety federal district courts, and eleven circuit courts of appeals.

The jurisdiction of lower federal courts is somewhat limited. In the Constitution, it is stated:

> Section 2. The judicial Power shall extend to all Cases, in Law and Equity, arising under this Constitution, the Laws of the United States, and Treaties made, or which shall be made, under their Authority;—to all Cases affecting Ambassadors, other public Ministers and Consuls;—to all Cases of admiralty and maritime Jurisdiction;—to Controversies to which the United States shall be a Party;—to Controversies between two or more States;—between a State and Citizen of another State;—between Citizens of different States;—between Citizens of the same State claiming Lands under Grants of different States, and between a State, or the Citizens thereof, and foreign States, Citizens or Subjects.

From an examination of this statement, it would seem that federal courts have substantial jurisdiction. However, despite the phrase "shall extend," the Congress—in its creation of the federal court system—did not give federal district courts, circuit courts, or circuit courts of appeal jurisdiction over all eight of these classes of cases. The Constitution itself provides that the Supreme Court shall have original jurisdiction in" . . . all Cases affecting Ambassadors, other public Ministers and Consuls and those in which a State shall be Party. . . ." Furthermore, Congress was slow in giving the lower federal courts jurisdiction over matters the Constitution permitted them to consider. On the other hand, Congress has extended the jurisdiction of federal courts—through legislation—over matters that at one time were the sole province of state courts. Even so, some state courts may handle cases involving only federal law or cases in which there are questions of federal law. The resulting situation is quite complex and confusing, but in general we might conclude that the jurisdiction of federal courts is somewhat less than that of state courts.

In addition to the federal courts created under Article III of the Constitution, Congress has created other courts. These have been called "legislative courts"; they decide certain issues arising out of the activities of the federal government authorized by Congress. At the present the following legislative courts exist: the Court of Claims, the United States Customs Court, the United States Court of Customs and Patent Appeals, the Tax Court of the United States, and some other federal courts in Washington, D.C. All of them are stated by Congress to be courts, their members are normally called judges, and they adjudicate issues arising between individuals and the United States. For example, the Tax Court can be turned to by either individuals or collectors of certain internal revenue taxes for a decision. Such decisions can be reviewed by the "constitutional courts" established under Article III, but there is no denying these legislative courts perform judicial functions. As their titles indicate, some hear issues of considerable importance to businessmen, involving patents, import taxes, and internal revenue taxes (which include many business taxes). The Court of Claims is also of significance, since it considers financial claims arising out of contracts which the federal government has with business firms, among other matters.

Courts have jurisdiction over two kinds of cases—civil and criminal. Civil suits involve an alleged wrong by one individual (or group) against another individual (or group). Government agencies and officials may be parties to such cases, either as plaintiffs or defendants, or only private parties may be involved. The court decides in favor of one party or the other and orders the losing party to give something of value to the individual or group winning the case (sometimes the "something" is an award of money damages, but there are other kinds of court orders of value, as we shall see later). In criminal cases, the government is always a party, prosecuting some individual or group for some wrong against the "public." Only rarely are businessmen involved in criminal suits— although executives of some of the electrical equipment companies judged guilty of conspiring to fix prices were fined and sent to jail. Since criminal suits against business are rare, the following discussion will deal only with civil proceedings before federal and state courts.

Courts of Original and Appellate Jurisdiction

Sometimes courts are classified according to whether their work consists of hearing and deciding original issues or whether they review the findings of fact and law of lower courts. Unfortunately, only very few courts perform only one or the other function. Justices of peace, magistrates, and some other judges having jurisdiction over only relatively minor matters usually have original and no appellate jurisdiction. However, almost every court above this level—including supreme courts—has some original jurisdiction in addition to appellate jurisdiction. In the more important classes of courts in the United States, district courts have original jurisdiction over major law suits; appeals courts and supreme courts engage mainly in hearing appeals from lower courts. State and federal laws and constitutions determine which court will have what kind of jurisdiction, and since legislatures have some control over this matter, the division of judicial labor changes from time to time.

POWERS OF THE COURTS

The more obvious powers of the courts consist of their authority to make binding decisions on cases over which they have jurisdiction and to issue orders enforcing those decisions. Not quite so obvious is the courts' power to legislate. Not only to judicial decisions establish certain rules of law, but courts in the United States have assumed the power to examine acts of legislative bodies and to declare them invalid. For example, although the United States Supreme Court is not given the explicit constitutional power to invalidate legislation passed by Congress and approved by the President, on a number of occasions the Court has declared such law to be in violation of the Constitution and has refused to uphold it. State supreme courts have acted in similar fashion, and this judicial review of legislative enactments has become one of the more important powers of the government. Before examining this power, we shall look at some of the more usual powers that courts possess.

Power to Make Binding Decisions

Only some appellate courts make binding decisions. Although courts of original jurisdiction make a decision in the cases they hear, their decisions can be appealed to higher state or federal courts. Some intermediate courts of appeal are also the last courts to which parties may appeal who have lost in lower courts, but it is the state supreme courts and the

U.S. Supreme Court that are regarded as the final courts of appeal. Their decisions are binding. Such decisions involve two matters: findings of fact and interpretation of law. Not all appeals courts will review findings of fact, proceeding on the assumption that the decision of the lower courts on what the facts of the matter are is correct. Since the decision as to what the true facts are determines, along with rules of law, the outcome of court cases, some appellants contend that the lower courts have not made a proper determination of the true facts and sometimes secure a hearing from higher courts. In all cases, the appeals courts decide whether or not the rules of law were properly applied to the facts of the situation. That is, an appellant might allege that the law was improperly interpreted in a particular case and secure support for this contention from a higher court. When a binding decision on matters of fact or law has been secured from the highest appeals court, orders to enforce the decision are issued. The appellate courts do not themselves issue orders directly to the parties at the bar; instead, they issue instructions to the courts of original jurisdiction. Sometimes these instructions require the court having original jurisdiction to conduct an additional investigation, but more often the decision of the appellate court results in the lower court issuing an order.

Power to Issue Orders

There is a great variety of court orders, not all of them relevant to our discussion. In the chapter on the administrative process, we discussed some of the ways in which courts become involved in reviewing administrative procedures and the orders they sometimes issue as a consequence. After a final decision is reached in a civil suit, there are certain orders the courts might issue that differ from those issued after judicially reviewing administrative actions. Some such orders involve payment of money to the individual or group in whose favor the decision is made; others require certain other kinds of performance on the part of the person(s) against whom the decision goes.

ORDERS TO PAY MONEY. The great majority of civil actions are commenced by plaintiffs who seek to obtain money from the defendants. Plaintiffs claim either that the money is due from the defendant in payment of a just debt or that money damages should be awarded the plaintiff as compensation for damage inflicted upon him by a wrongful act of the defendant. If, after the proper procedure has been carried out, the court decides that money should be paid the plaintiff, a certain sum to be paid is fixed by the court at the end of the proceeding. This determination by a court that a certain sum of money is due usually results in a money judgment. This is *not* a court order requiring the defendant to pay that sum to the plaintiff. However, if the defendant refuses to pay the sum, other court orders can be issued (if the plaintiff takes the required action) that will result in payment.

INJUNCTIONS. In some cases, money is not sought by the plaintiff. Rather, the court is requested to issue an order terminating existing wrongs or preventing threatened wrongful actions by the defendant. Such an order is called an injunction. It directs the wrongdoer to desist or the potential wrongdoer to refrain from engaging in certain activities. This is sometimes a superior alternative to waiting until after the wrong has been committed and then suing for money damages. For example, some actions by labor unions have been held to be "conspiracies" that will have a damaging effect on a business. Businessmen in the past were frequently able to secure writs of injunction forbidding unions to carry out their "illegal conspiracy" rather than to have to wait to sue after the damage was done. Legislative changes have made it more difficult for businessmen to secure such injunctions, but it still is possible in a number of jurisdictions. A court order similar to the injunction, but aimed at government officials, is called *quo warranto*. When a businessman feels that a zealous agent of government is exceeding his legal authority in his dealings with that businessman, a court may issue an order asking what authority (or warrant) the official has for his actions. Such an order will be issued only if the court decides that there is no legal warrant for such behavior, and the result is the same as achieved by an injunction—wrongful action is either terminated or prevented.

Power to Compel Specific Performance

Sometimes those seeking court orders want to compel action rather than prevent it. If the failure of another party to fulfill a contractual obligation is willful and if money damages are not a satisfactory remedy for such breach of contract, the court will sometimes issue orders of "specific performance" requiring the defendant to perform certain actions. A similar order called a writ of *mandamus* is available to compel officials to discharge their legal duty. For example, if a businessman has a contract with a government agency but cannot secure payment as contracted, he has two options. He may sue the government agency for money damages stemming from such breach of contract, or he may secure a court order requiring the agency to pay the amount legally due under the contract.

The foregoing discussion illustrates the two different kinds of civil jurisdictions of American courts. Some cases heard by courts are law suits and others are suits in equity. Sometimes law suits are inadequate to protect the interests of a person wronged by another, and he may then sue in a court of equity. In England (from which many of our laws and legal procedures are inherited), separate equity courts existed at one time to supplement and remedy the incompleteness of the existing law. The practice in America has been to permit courts to deal with both law and equity pleas by plaintiffs. However, the orders by courts to prevent action or to require action are issued by them sitting as courts of equity. As courts of law, they are limited to waiting until after a wrongful act has occurred and then determining the sum of money due the wronged person.

Power to Revise Administrative Decisions

The federal legislative courts previously referred to have some special powers not held by other courts. Normally, an appeals court reviews the decision of a lower court and either agrees or disagrees with it. In the event of disagreement, the matter is sent back to the court of original jurisdiction for further processing in accordance with the instructions of the appellate court. However, the legislative courts sometimes review *and revise* administrative decisions of certain administrative agencies. A businessman feeling that the action of a federal agency coming under the jurisdiction of one of the legislative courts was contrary to the law would have two courses of action open to him. He might appeal to a court created under the Constitution—a Circuit Court of Appeals—to secure an order preventing the agency or official from violating the law by exceeding or misusing his powers. However, this court could not change the administrative agency's decision, but would have to return the matter to the agency in question. As an alternative, the businessman might turn to a legislative court to secure some modification of the administrative order. The Supreme Court has upheld the power of legislative courts to make administrative decisions, although Constitutional courts may not do so.

Power to Invalidate Legislation

In Chapter 25, we dealt with the power of judges to make laws. Here we shall examine a peculiar aspect of this power: the power that courts have assumed to invalidate laws passed by legislatures. What the courts are doing here is to make statute law conform to the law as the courts think it ought to be (and thus we might conceive of this behavior as being law-making activity on the part of the courts, even though it involves striking down laws passed by other law-making bodies). The courts do not state the matter as bluntly as we have here; instead, they say that certain legislation is contrary to the highest law of the land (as embodied in the federal and state constitutions). However, since constitutions are what the courts say they are (and since the interpretation of constitutional provisions have varied considerably as courts have changed in their membership), the end result is that legislation passed by other bodies is sometimes invalidated by courts because the laws disagree with the way in which the courts would like to interpret constitutions.

Almost any court trying a case under a statute can declare the legislative act repugnant to constitutional provisions; however, the matter of the validity of statutes is not finally settled until either a state supreme court or the Supreme Court of the United States rules on the question. This power of judicial review of legislation goes back prior to the adoption of the Constitution. In 1786, a law was passed in Rhode Island requiring merchants to accept paper money issued by the state as legal tender in payment for goods. The justices of the state supreme court declared this law to be "repugnant and unconstitutional." As this incident indicates, judicial review of state legislation frequently has been employed to protect the interests of businessmen against laws passed that worked against those interests. When Congress passed the first Judiciary Act in 1789, it indicated that it expected that courts would hold acts of Congress unconstitutional and gave the Supreme Court the authority to hear appeals in cases in which state supreme courts had raised some question concerning the constitutionality of federal legislation. Shortly after the adoption of the new Constitution, U.S. circuit courts held some state laws enacted to ease the burdens of debtors unconstitutional on the grounds that they impaired the obligation of contracts. State courts too declared state laws invalid and federal courts began to question the constitutionality of acts of Congress. In 1803, the Supreme Court declared that since Congress had passed a law imposing duties upon the Court contrary to constitutional provisions, it was obliged to enforce the Constitution. Thus, the federal courts acquired a power not expressly conferred upon them by the Constitution—the power to declare acts of Congress invalid when the courts interpreted the Constitution to be in conflict with the statutes.

CIVIL COURT PROCEDURES

Unlike administrative agencies, the courts do not actively attempt to enforce the law. Instead, they wait for issues to be brought to them for their decision. Rather than being partisan participants, the judges sit above the conflict among the adversaries appearing before them. Attorneys on each side of the issue present the best possible case for their clients, employing "stratagem, artifice, appeal to prejudice, and even false pretense." The judge is the umpire whose main task during the conduct of a case is to see that rules governing such conflicts are observed. It is up to the attorneys to develop the facts rather than for the judge to conduct an investigation into the situation and make some decision on the merits of the case. Considerable criticism has been raised against such proceedings because they frequently result in injustice. But businessmen must adjust to court procedures as they exist, which fact warrants their further examination.

Civil proceedings begin when a plaintiff charges that some individual or group has wronged him in some fashion. Usually he is required to set forth his grievances in a formal complaint to the court, stating the facts that constitute the cause of action, along with the remedy he wishes the court to secure for him. The defendant against this action has an opportunity to answer this complaint, stating the facts of the matter as *he* sees them frequently accompanied by denials of facts alleged to be true by the plaintiff. If there is a disagreement between plaintiff and defendant as to the facts of the matter, then "issues of fact" exist to be resolved in the proceedings. Sometimes both parties agree on the facts but disagree on how the law applies to that particular set of facts; in such cases, "issues of law" are involved and the judicial process aims at resolving such issues. At this stage of the proceedings, attorneys for either side might ask the presiding judge for a "summary judgment" in favor of their client; if the court is unwilling to grant such a judgment, the case will go to trial.

If the case is going to trial, there may be some other pretrial proceedings taken by the plaintiff. He may attempt to secure one or more of a variety of "conservatory" orders from the presiding judge in order to protect his position during the conduct of the trial. For example, if the plaintiff seeks money, he may want the court to prevent the defendant from disposing of his property in such a way as to make meaningless any award of money made by the court. Also a temporary injunction might be sought to cause the defendant to discontinue or refrain from wrongful actions that work an injury upon the plaintiff. Usually the defendant has an opportunity to show why he should not be obliged to "cease and desist" from the action complained of by the plaintiff, but there are circumstances under which the court will issue a temporary restraining order until a decision on a temporary injunction can be reached.

Not all civil cases are conducted before juries because the Constitution requires jury trial only in criminal cases. Juries decide only issues of fact, and in cases in which there are only issues of law, juries are not necessary. In civil cases, even in those in which there are issues of fact, juries are not necessarily employed to resolve factual questions. In the vast majority of cases involving issues of fact, either party may request and receive a jury trial in order to determine the true facts. In other cases, a judge may decide such issues even though one of the parties wishes a jury trial. If neither party requests a jury trial, the trial judge decides issues of fact as well as issues of law.

Whether issues of fact are tried before a jury or a judge, the plaintiff normally bears the burden of proving that certain facts are true. If the court does not feel that the plaintiff has proved the facts he had alleged to be true in the complaint, the judge may direct a verdict for the defendant. On the other hand, if the court feels that the plaintiff has proved his facts and that the facts proved by the defendant do not constitute a legal defense against the complaint, the judge may direct a verdict for the plaintiff. When a jury decides issues of fact, a judge may conclude that its decision is so contrary to the weight of evidence (as he see it) that he sets aside the jury's verdict and directs a contrary verdict. Such developments are rare, however, and in the normal course of events anyone wishing to secure the reversal of decisions reached in a court of original jurisdiction must avail himself of the appeals procedure.

A plaintiff or defendant in a civil action who is dissatisfied with the judgment of the court is almost always entitled to have the judgment reviewed by an appellate court. Appeals are quite expensive, with the appellant being obliged to provide the court of appeals with a transcript of the proceedings before the court of original jurisdiction, together with a "brief" stating why the decision of the lower court should be overturned. If the appellate court agrees with the appellant, it has the power to set aside the verdict of the jury and order a new trial to be held. Also if the court of appeals finds that the judge of the lower court should have directed a verdict contrary to the one which the jury arrived at, the appellate court may itself direct such a verdict. Where the judgment in the court of original jurisdiction is reached by a judge rather than a jury, the higher court may modify that judgment or send the matter back to the lower court for further action under instruction of the court of appeals.

In our discussion of courts of appeal, we pointed out that the federal courts and some state court systems have intermediate appellate courts in addition to supreme courts (which are the highest courts to which appeals might be taken). Very few appeals are taken from the intermediate courts to the supreme courts, since there are a number of restrictions on the matters which can be so appealed. Too, supreme courts may decline to hear appeals unless there is very good reason for them to do so, which means in most cases that the appeal to the intermediate appeals court (where these courts exist) is the final appeal that can be made of the decision rendered in a court of original jurisdiction.

THE BUSINESSMAN AND THE COURTS

In the preceding discussion, we have noted the nature of American courts and how civil actions proceed before judicial tribunals. This part of the political environment and the way in which various parties in it act have some significance for business behavior. Businessmen who wish to gain certain objectives can employ the court system and judicial procedures to assist them in gaining their goals. One obvious implication of the discussion is that having a good attorney or legal staff is essential to a firm. Since the proceedings are essentially contests among adversaries, having the best gladiator in the arena will frequently bring victory regardless of the merits of the case. Also, since ultimate victory sometimes goes to that party financially able to appeal the decisions of lower courts, a firm that is financially strong is sometimes able to outlast a weaker opponent or to gain some concessions from the adversary in exchange for discontinuing the legal struggle. Too, the appeals procedure makes it possible to delay the implementation of decisions of courts of original jurisdiction long enough so that adverse judgments, even if upheld, will have little adverse impact on the firm.

Not so obvious is the fact that political action may be taken to influence court decisions. Judges are either elected or appointed by some elected official. Those disliking the decisions made by those occupying judicial positions may work for their removal, normally through defeating the incumbent judges in elections or by electing officials who will appoint the "right kind" of judges. (There is another means, that of impeachment, but it is rarely effective—although some have urged the impeachment of Chief Justice Warren of the United States Supreme Court in the perhaps mistaken notion that if this could be accomplished, the decisions of the Court would be different.) Some groups—although businessmen are rarely among them—have urged recall of judicial decisions by popular vote, but this means does not exist and if it did, it is unlikely that it would be of much value to business.

Political action to influence legislation might also enable businessmen to gain their objectives. After all, the very existence of most courts depends upon legislative action. Too, legislatures make many of the legal rules that bind the decisions of courts, and statutory law takes precedence over common (or judge-made) law. The procedures governing the actions of courts are in most cases determined by legislative bodies, and if businessmen can have some influence on laws governing such proceedings they can create a more friendly political environment.

Perhaps we should inject a sobering observation. The changes that have been made in American courts and in judicial procedures have generally worked contrary to the interests of the businessman. Other groups—including farm and labor organizations—have gained political power and influenced the election or appointment of judges favorable to them (and sometimes unfriendly to businessmen) as well as secured legislation that has made the rules of law different from what many businessmen would like them to be. Although this is true, we still see many instances in which businessmen have been able to influence favorably this aspect of their political environment, thereby promoting their interests.

READING: Enforcement of Fair Trade Contracts *
by Edward M. Brecker

[*Many firms avail themselves of the judicial system to gain their objectives. The following reading demonstrates how one firm proceeded through court action to try to secure the desired retail price for its product. Of special interest is the substantial expenditure of money and effort apparently necessary to gain desired judicial decisions and court orders even when the law is on the side of the complaining firm. Although this excerpt is from an article written in 1949, "fair trade" laws still are on the statute books and the burden of their enforcement is still upon those private parties seeking to maintain certain retail prices. General Electric has become disenchanted with "fair trade," partly because the results were not worth the costs involved in attempting to secure compliance with the laws.*]

As shown by CU's nationwide survey of discount houses, retailers all over the United States are selling leading brands of merchandise at substantial discounts —10%, 20%, or even more—below the prices fixed by the manufacturers of the products. They are selling $59.50 Bulova watches for $47.50; $329.75 Frigidaire refrigerators for $269; $39.95 Zenith radios for $32; and a long list of other branded, price-fixed articles at similar price reductions (Consumer Reports, August). Yet 45 states have so-called "fair-trade" laws, which permit a manufacturer to fix a minimum retail price on his product, and which require retailers to maintain such minimum prices. Why are these laws ineffective in preventing the price-cutting of discount houses?

* *From:* Edward M. Brecker, "Buying at a Discount." Reprinted with permission from the September 1949 issue of *Consumer Reports*, Vol. 14. No. 9. Copyright by Consumers Union, a nonprofit organization.

In some lines, notably drugstore items, the price-fixing laws have had the desired effect; it is very nearly impossible in most cities to buy a tube of Pepsodent tooth paste for less than the 43¢ fixed price, or a large box of Kotex for less than $1.29. But on items like refrigerators, automatic washing machines, or television receivers, the situation is very different. Here a 20% discount may mean a saving of $50 or more, which makes it worth the consumer's while to hunt up a discount house and perhaps undergo some inconvenience; and the retailer's margin, even after the discount, still is high enough to make the sale worthwhile to him.

Outside the drug trade, moreover, manufacturers are often not sufficiently enthusiastic about retail price maintenance to make an all-out enforcement effort. And even when a manufacturer outside the drug trade does try to enforce minimum prices, he is likely to find that the price-fixing laws, like the Prohibition laws of an earlier decade and other statutes backed by no particular popular support, are difficult to police effectively.

Consider, for example, one of the most intensive drives to enforce price maintenance through court action in the history of "fair trade"—the series of cases brought against New York City retailers by the General Electric Company.

The GE story began back in February 1948, when GE apparently resolved to appeal to the courts to eliminate price-cutting of GE products. It turned to the celebrated Wall Street law firm of White & Case for legal counsel, and it employed the famous Pinkerton National Detective Agency to collect evidence of violations.

During the week of February 6, 1948, five Pinkerton detectives made the rounds of New York City "discount houses" for GE. With apparently no difficulty at all they purchased from ten dealers a total of 28 GE automatic electric blankets at an average of $6.84 below the minimum retail prices designated by the company. This represented an average discount of 17%. All 28 blankets purchased, according to the affidavits of the Pinkerton detectives, were genuine GE products, brand new.

Acting on the Pinkerton evidence, GE brought suit in the New York courts. The ten retailers charged with selling GE goods below the price fixed by GE entered various defenses. One company pointed out, for example, that the market for electric blankets was pretty well over by February, and that the discount he gave was a sort of "end-of-season" sale. Another told the judge: "A rather curious situation has been created by the plaintiff (GE) and its management. Mr. Charles E. Wilson, the president of the corporation, recognizing the necessity to combat the inflation, has announced a 5% reduction of the price of some GE products. . . . He calls upon all business to cooperate by combating high prices and states that the General Electric price cuts are 'the best contributions we can make toward strengthening the economy of our country. . . .' By asking this Court to restrain the defendant and other dealers, General Electric is insisting on maintaining high prices on GE products at a time when everybody . . . is making every effort to stem the rising cost of living."

The most ingenious defense, however, was put in by one of the largest of the ten defendants, Monarch-Saphin. When papers were served on Mr. Saphin by the GE attorneys, based on the Pinkerton work, he did some counter-detecting of his own. He had people he knew call people they knew, to ask about getting GE blankets at wholesale. The answer, in two cases, was "Sure." All you had to do, it appeared, was to know somebody who purchased from the General Electric Supply Corp., a wholly-owned subsidiary of GE. A phone call to the right man there, and you could buy a blanket for less than the list price, in fact, for less than you paid at a discount house. GE, in short, was undercutting the price-cutters.

Neither this nor the other defenses urged by the ten retailers impressed the New York courts, however. Injunctions were granted in all ten cases. GE emerged victorious.

The following winter, in December, 1948, GE again sent out detectives to see how "fair trade" was progressing. The result must have been quite discouraging. Going to the same stores once again, the detectives were able to purchase General Electric blankets, and other General Electric merchandise, at discounts averaging 19%.

General Electric again went to court, this time charging eight of the stores with contempt of court for having violated the injunctions. Monarch-Saphin, which had put in the most vigorous defense the first time around, and another retailer who had threatened to appeal the original injunction, were left alone in GE's second round of litigation.

Again GE won the round. Six of the eight defendants were fined $100 each, the seventh was fined $50, and the eighth got a suspended sentence.

Here was a concrete example of a complete victory for "fair trade." Yet CU's shoppers report that it is still possible to buy GE merchandise at a discount (though some discount houses may try to sell you a competing brand instead). The net effect of two years of detective work and legal action was $650 in fines and a general resolve on the part of discount houses to be more careful about selling GE goods to Pinkerton men in the future. One of the original ten defendants, Monarch-Saphin, is currently accused by GE of continuing to sell GE appliances at a discount as late as June 1949.

The available evidence suggests that other efforts to enforce the "fair trade" laws among retailers who make a practice of selling at a discount have been equally unsuccessful. Of course, the discount houses don't go in much for the lower-priced impulse items—notably drugs—on which fixed prices are quite well maintained. Liquor is seldom sold at a discount, for a retail liquor store may lose its license if it repeatedly sells below the "fair trade" price.

Price-Cutting Is Not A Crime. Even where all the legal preliminaries are carried through, moreover, the "fair trade" laws are not self-enforcing. It is not a criminal offense to sell goods below the fixed price. The police departments, the county and state prosecuting attorneys, and other public officials have no mandate to enforce price-fixing laws. Rather, selling below the fixed price resembles what the law calls a "tort," or private injury. It gives the manufacturer a right to sue for damages, or in most states to get an injunction prohibiting further sales below the fixed price. But the policing of the retail trade, and the burden of bringing suit, is on the manufacturer or distributor who fixes prices, not on the state.

Retailers are the manufacturers' customers. Often the "discount house" is a very good customer indeed; it pays cash and no one really likes to shoot Santa Claus. So even where a manufacturer price-fixes his merchandise, he has many reasons for not enforcing those prices.

Are the "Fair Trade" Laws Effective? Despite enforcement difficulties, there can be no doubt that the "fair trade" laws have had considerable effect on the distribution of some kinds of goods.

The greatest effectiveness has been in the drug trade, where the "pine board" cut-rate drug stores of the depression years have been reduced to negligible proportions or eliminated altogether, and price-cutting by drug chains and others has been sharply curtailed. "Fair trade" has also been fairly effective in the book trade, with the one very important exception of "book clubs."

Large department stores like Macy's, and mail-order houses like Sears, Roebuck and Montgomery Wards, have been forced to maintain "fair trade" prices on national brands; but they have met the problem by price-cutting on their own "private brands".

In the grocery trade, price-fixing is practically unknown, except for a few items (Pablum, Ovaltine, some soap brands, Airwick, etc.) sold in both drug and grocery stores.

So far as discount houses are concerned, the "fair trade" laws have had comparatively little effect. In one respect, retail price maintenance by other retailers may even have benefited the discount houses; for where other retailers are restrained from cutting prices, the relative advantages of the discount house are enhanced. On the other hand, the discount house in a "fair trade" state must risk the occasional harassment of defending a court suit, and may perhaps have to pay an occasional fine. Its advertising is likely to be rejected by the newspapers, for most "fair trade" laws forbid the advertising of products below fixed prices as well as actual sales at a discount. But newspapers were not very hospitable to discount house advertising even before the "fair trade" laws. Finally, the discount house in a "fair trade" state must be on the alert to avoid, as much as possible, sales to detectives and spotters—no doubt a minor annoyance.

The evidence seems clear that discount houses survive, and even prosper, despite depression, war, inflation, and "fair trade." Back in 1937, Retailing Daily published a survey of discount houses in the New York area, and found them to be flourishing despite the New York "fair trade" statute, relatively new at the time. It published a list of 26 discount houses then firmly established, and noted that two of these had already been in business for 15 years—since 1922.

A recheck by CU in August 1949 showed at least 19 of the 26 still in business under the same names, at or near the same address, as in 1937. Among the 19 survivors were the two established back in 1922. In view of the high mortality of retail stores generally, the longevity of discount houses under "fair trade" seems quite impressive.

SUGGESTED READINGS

Mayers, Lewis, *The Machinery of Justice* (Englewood Cliffs, N.J.: Prentice-Hall, 1963). An introduction to legal structure and process, this work concerns itself with how legal rules are made, the dual court structure, civil proceedings, criminal proceedings, administrative justice, and the courts as a check on the executive and legislatures.

Westin, Alan F., *The Anatomy of a Constitutional Law Case* (New York: Macmillan, 1961). This history and analysis of *Youngstown Sheet & Tube Co.* v. *Sawyer* (the Steel Seizure Case) illustrate the American judicial process in its entirety.

Ziegler, Benjamin M., *The Supreme Court and American Economic Life* (New York: Harper & Row, 1962). An annotated collection of 37 landmark Supreme Court cases pertaining to the American economy, reflecting the attitude of the Court toward fundamental changes in our social and economic life.

CHAPTER 31

LEGISLATURES AND THE LEGISLATIVE PROCESS

The importance of knowledge of the nature of legislatures and the legislative process to businessmen should be apparent. Not only does this lead to greater understanding of the political environment, but it may also contain clues for action. That is, business can and does play a role in legislation, and to the extent that it is effective it helps create a "favorable political climate."

Although some rules are made by judges and administrators, many laws of importance are the products of legislation. Not all legislation, however, stems from legislatures. There has been a growth in the use of the initiative and referendum as means of direct legislation. However, since the federal government does not employ this method of legislation and since less than one-half of the states have constitutions providing for such law-making, we shall not give further consideration to the procedures involved in getting laws passed through direct legislation by the electorate. The bulk of legislation is the result of actions taken by legislative bodies—Congress, state legislatures, county boards, city councils, and so on. Although some of these bodies establish constitutional or charter provisions, their ordinary legislative business consists of introducing bills, investigating and debating their provisions, and making some determination of the kind of legal rules (whether called statute, ordinance, or law) to be legislated. Since some proposed statutes, after passage by a legislature, require the signature of the President, a governor, or other chief executive, it is obvious that the legislative process includes action by other than members of the legislative body. Also obvious is the fact that other members of the administrative branches of government have some hand in the shaping of legislation and that some private or nonofficial groups also play a role in the legislative process. Before examining that process, we shall take a look at the kinds of legislatures that exist in the political environment of the businessman and at those official and nonofficial individuals and groups attempting to influence legislation, although they are not part of the legislative body.

AMERICAN LEGISLATURES

There are some similarities among the various kinds of American legislatures. Nowadays, except in the relatively rare cases where a member of a legislative body dies, resigns, or is impeached, all legislators are elected. This was not always true: we have already noted that until the second decade of this century U.S. Senators were appointed by state legislatures. At present, appointments are made to legislative bodies only in the circumstances mentioned. Although legislators are elected by those whom they represent, it is a rare legislature in which each representative of the electorate represents approximately the same number of constituents as do his fellows. Perhaps legislative bodies should not contain members representing roughly the same number of constituents, but there is no doubt that rural areas and agricultural states have greater representation than do urban areas and industrial states. In some instances this nonproportional representation has worked against businessmen because most of them are located in urban areas and industrial states. On the other hand, there have been occasions on which representatives from rural regions and agricultural states have taken conservative positions on legislative matters and have thereby protected businessmen from the passage of legislation by liberal and labor representatives who tend to come from urban areas or industrial states. We have discussed in Chapter 23 the significance for business behavior of the fact that legislative representatives are elected because business participation in the elective process concerns the election of administrators and judges in addition to legislators. In the discussion that follows we shall look at specific legislatures because each has some unique characteristics of importance.

Congress

The general outlines of the nature of the Congress of the United States are well known. Each state has two Senators and a number of Representatives based on the population of the state. The Senators are elected "at large" by the whole electorate of the state, but the Representatives represent certain districts of a state; sometimes these districts may have constituencies with quite different interests and hence Representatives from the same state may take opposing positions in the Congress. Perhaps we should also point out that a Senator's main support may come from one area of a state, but he usually is obliged to secure as wide support as possible (that is, a Senator may find his main support in labor and liberal groups of the major metropolitan area(s) of his state, but he normally looks for support in the rural areas as well).

Less well known are the workings of Congress. The Senators and Representatives do not meet in their respective chambers to introduce bills and pass laws in an unorganized fashion. About 90 per cent of all of the work of the Congress on legislative matters is carried on through committees. Even after reorganization in 1946, which resulted in a substantial reduction in the number of congressional committees, there still remained nineteen standing committees in the House of Representatives and fifteen in the Senate. Also, there are some permanent joint committees having members from both houses of Congress. In addition to these, there are special committees and conference committees. Committees frequently have subcommittees which play important roles in the legislative process. Although special committees do not normally introduce legislation, the other committees do and they have been quite aptly called "little legislatures." Unless committees favorably act upon a bill which has been introduced, that proposal rarely becomes law.

The most powerful positions in Congress—with the exception of that of the Speaker of the House of Representatives—are the chairmanships of the various committees. A committee chairman can call meetings when he wishes, is consulted and courted by parties interested in the passage of a particular bill, and has considerable control over the agenda of his committee—that is, he determines which bills will be considered and when. The Rules Committee of the House is especially powerful. Even though another committee recommends that a particular bill be passed, it will not be voted upon by the House unless and until the Rules Committee permits it to be considered. Under its power, it can delay and sometimes prevent bills from being considered unless they are amended to meet the wishes of the Rules Committee (especially its chairman). This committee is even able to substitute a wholly new bill for one that has been drafted and approved by another committee. Also, by adopting certain procedural rules governing the handling of bills on the floor of the House, the Rules Committee may influence the chances of passing the bill in unamended form. We shall, in our discussion of the legislative process, note the way in which the committee structure of Congress plays a large role in determining the kind of statutes enacted.

In addition to committee chairmen, there are a number of other powerful members of Congress. Their power does not come from control over a committee, but from their position in the ranks of the major political parties. The Speaker of the House of Representatives has great power—partly because his position has considerable authority attached to it, but partly because he is the leader of members of the majority party in the House. In his official capacity, he directs the conduct of debate on the floor of the House and appoints members of select and conference committees. In his capacity as the party leader in the House, he attempts to secure legislation desired by the party leadership. There is also a majority floor leader and a minority floor leader in the House, and both are concerned with securing legislation and other congressional action in line with the policies of the political parties they represent. The Senate has similar party leaders, but the Vice President is not always a member of the majority party in the Senate and has considerably fewer formal and informal powers than does the Speaker of the House.

An incident occurring in the early days of the first Eisenhower administration amply demonstrates the importance of the Speaker of the House and of committee chairmen. Although the Administration favored eventual elimination of the excess profits tax, it sought to secure an extension of that tax until the end of 1953. However, Chairman Reed of the House Ways and Means Committee wanted the tax to expire on June 30, 1953, as earlier tax legislation had scheduled it to end. Initially Chairman Reed was able to thwart any attempts to secure a 6-months' extension of the tax by refusing to call a meeting of his committee. Apparently, a majority of the committee favored the Administration's proposal, but were helpless to act in the face of their chairman's refusal to do so. Even personal urgings by President Eisenhower were of no influence with Representative Reed.

The Speaker of the House then brought his enormous power into play. Speaker Joseph W. Martin supported the Administration, of course, and both cajoled and threatened Chairman Reed in an attempt to get him to go along with the extension. When this had no effect, he turned to the Rules Committee. Since that committee has the power to introduce its own measures on the floor of the House, if a majority could be induced to approve such legislation, a tax-extension bill could come up for a vote despite the opposition of the chairman of the committee, which normally had jurisdiction over tax laws. Not only was the Speaker able to get the Rules Committee to go along with such a proposition, through using persuasion and patronage, but he also was able to get a majority of the members of the Ways and Means Committee to support a "discharge petition" which would bring the tax-extension bill out of that committee even though the committee chairman was unwilling to consider it. Upon hearing this, Chairman Reed realized he had lost his fight. He called a meeting of his committee, which then proceeded to approve the Administration's bill, but only after the members of the committee overruled a ruling by the chairman that consideration of the bill was not in order.

State Legislatures

State legislatures are very similar in their organization and operation to the Congress. All states except Nebraska have bicameral (two-chambered) legislatures normally called the house and the senate. Committees do the basic legislative work, thereby making committee chairmen powerful figures, as in Congress. The lieutenant-governor (a counterpart of the Vice President of the U.S.) presides over the state senate while a speaker is elected by the membership of the house (and is a representative of the majority party). If anything, the speaker of a state house of representatives has relatively greater power than the Speaker in Congress because in the state legislatures, members of *all* house committees are appointed by the speaker. Of course, as the spokesman for the majority party in the state legislature, the speaker must concern himself with the wishes of the party leadership and does not have a free hand.

There is less proportionate representation in state legislatures than in Congress. Persons in rural areas are relatively overrepresented as compared to those in urban areas. For example, in the state of New York more than one half of both houses of the state legislature come from outside of New York City, although that metropolis has more than one half of the population of the entire state. This is true of almost every state having one or more large metropolitan areas. Recent decisions by the U.S. Supreme Court may bring about greater equality of representation, but it will apparently be some time before this is achieved. Whether this will be a boon or a bane to businessmen is not yet known, and a matter in which there is some difference of opinion because rural representatives have tended to support some legislative measures desired by urban businessmen.

The sessions held by state legislatures are shorter and less frequent than those of Congress. Over forty states provide for a legislative session every other year rather than each year. In addition to relatively infrequent sessions, most states limit the length of sessions to a specific number of days. Sixty-day sessions are the most common, with the range being from forty days in Wyoming to one hundred and fifty in Connecticut. Various subterfuges are employed by legislatures to continue proceedings until the necessary work is done even though the legal limit has been exceeded; the Minnesota legislature "covers the clock" before midnight on the last legal day it may convene and continues in operation for days and weeks, because no one in the legislature has officially seen the final day come to an end. It may be supposed that state legislatures are behind the times and are not willing to pass legislation providing for more frequent and longer meetings. This is not the case. At one time state legislatures met annually and stayed in session until their work was finished. However, about 1800, Tennessee began a movement toward the biennial session. A cynicial interpretation of this movement is that there was sufficient popular feeling against the unwise and unnecessary laws passed that it was decided that state legislatures could do only half as much harm if they met only half as often. It is perhaps true that state legislators pass a considerable amount of legislation that appears to be "bad law" to some observers. What this may reflect, however, is the fact that state legislatures are more susceptible to pressure by various special interests and less inclined to pass the program of the dominant political party than is Congress. In any event, reducing the frequency and length of legislative sessions does not seem to have resulted in better legislation, and may have had the opposite effect.

The power of state legislatures is apparently declining somewhat. This is due, in part, to the expanded role of the federal government in matters of importance to business. When Congress passes legislation under its constitutional powers, it has precedence over that of the states. Not only has Congress been active in passing laws affecting business, but decisions of the U.S. Supreme Court have expanded the power of federal government in relation to that of the states. However, the power of state legislatures to affect businessmen or any other citizens has been diminished also by the inclusion of restrictions on legislative powers in state constitutions.

Almost all state constitutions are quite long and readily amended, and their many provisions have the effect of reducing the authority of state legislatures, intentionally and unintentionally.

Other Legislatures

In addition to legislative bodies of federal and state governments, those of local governments are of some importance—especially to small business. Legislative councils of foreign and international governments are of consequence to business firms engaged in foreign and international operations, but because of their variety and relative unimportance we shall consider them no further.

Local governments in the United States normally have unicameral legislatures. The city council is such a one-chambered legislative body, as are the boards drafting laws governing the operations of counties, towns, villages, and special districts. Committees seem to be of major importance in the case of city councils, with the boards of other local governments normally being small enough in number, so that the entire group considers the proposals for new legislation.

All units of local government in a state are in some measure agents of the state. State legislatures grant charters to cities, and state laws govern what city officials may and may not do. Within their charters and existing state legislation, cities have some freedom to adopt ordinances they deem desirable, and these can have some impact on business. Less freedom is had by county, town, village, and special district boards, whose scope of operations is quite narrowly circumscribed by state law. As a consequence, those who wish to influence legislation governing the activities of local government are obliged to work at the state level as well as at the local level.

Since state and federal legislatures are of greatest importance to businessmen, in the following discussion we shall deal with their operations. Also, since both Congress and state legislatures have essentially the same organizational structure and methods of operation, our discussion of the legislative process applies to both even though we shall employ congressional procedure as an example. Before examining that process in some detail, we should note the presence of individuals and groups other than legislators who play a considerable role in legislation.

LOBBYING AND LOBBYISTS

The "lobby" has been referred to as the "third chamber" of bicameral legislatures. At one time the lobbies outside the legislative chambers were the scenes of activity in which members of the legislatures were sought out by those who hoped to influence legislative action on certain bills. Members of Congress (and of state legislatures) still are sought out in their offices, in their homes, in the corridors, and on the floor of the legislative chamber. However, lobbying has taken on expanded meaning with the development of new lobbying techniques. Letters, telegrams and phone calls are employed to make known the views of interested individuals and groups. Sometimes a march on the Capitol is organized, as are other forms of mass demonstration. Attempts are made to arouse public opinion for or against a particular legislative proposal. In short, a variety of techniques are employed by those not in the legislatures to influence legislative action, and lobbying has come to embrace all such devices.

Those who engage in lobbying occupy both official and nonofficial capacities in government. Although the Chief Executive of the nation and the governor of a state have a constitutional role in the legislative process (in that they have the power to veto legislation unacceptable to them), Presidents and governors have been unwilling to limit their legislative activities to employing the veto power. Instead, they have developed their own legislative programs and employed a number of techniques, including lobbying, to secure legislative approval of those programs. Sometimes, the administration may not have any established view on a bill and agencies and officials within the administrative branch may engage in lobbying activities in opposition to one another. In our earlier discussion, we pointed out the variety of nonofficial groups—labor unions, consumer organizations, trade associations, general business organizations, farm groups, and so on—that sometimes take political action. Part of that action is lobbying, and in our examination of the legislative process we shall see them in action as well as note the activities of individuals and groups in the administrative branches of government.

THE LEGISLATIVE PROCESS

Before a proposal becomes law as a consequence of the action of a legislature, a number of steps must be taken. A bill is introduced; it is referred to a committee; if the committee decides to act on the bill it holds hearings (if the bill involves a major change in the law); the committee makes some disposition of the bill; if the bill is approved by the committee, it may be scheduled for debate on the floor of the legislative chamber; if that chamber approves the measure, the bill goes to the other chamber where the process may be repeated; if both chambers approve the same measure, the bill goes to the chief executive for his approval; if the two chambers disagree, a conference committee is appointed to draft a bill acceptable to both chambers; if the conference committee is able to do so, and if both chambers approve the bill, the measure then goes to the chief executive; if the chief executive vetos the bill, the legislature may pass it over his veto or attempt to draft a bill acceptable to him.

These are the bare bones of the legislative process. The established method of fleshing out the skeleton is to trace the progress of a bill through the various steps so that the activities of the various parties involved may be noted. Recently, Professor Earl Latham wrote an exceedingly illuminating study of the legislative progress of a bill of considerable importance to businessmen (*The Group Basis of Politics: A Study in Basing-Point Legislation*). The book is a study of the struggle in the Eightieth and Eighty-first Congresses to enact legislation dealing with the basing-point system of quoting delivered prices. The Supreme Court, in the Cement Case of 1948, had thrown the legality of basing-point systems into doubt, and those individuals and groups adversely affected then attempted to remedy the situation by getting Congress to pass remedial legislation. The account of the struggle to enact such legislation provides one of the best illustrations of the legislative process available.

Introduction of a Bill

Shortly after the decision in the Cement Case was announced by the Supreme Court, bills were introduced in Congress to modify the impact of that decision. Although the Court's action directly affected only the Cement Institute and its members, it appeared likely that other industries employing basing-point systems of pricing might also have their systems condemned as illegal. Senator Capehart of Indiana introduced a resolution in 1948 to investigate the impact of the cement decision on consumers and business. Other bills of importance were introduced later. Since Pennsylvania is an important steel state, and since the steel industry had been employing a basing-point system of pricing (abandoned by U.S. Steel shortly after the decision in the Cement Case), 1949 saw the introduction of two bills by congressional representatives from Pennsylvania—one by Representative Walters and the other by Senator Myers—providing for a legislative moratorium on further administrative proceedings against business under the decision in the Cement Case pending an investigation of that decision's effects. However, since the Capehart bill had been introduced first, early legislative action concerned that proposal.

Referral to a Committee

The Capehart resolution was referred to the Senate Committee on Interstate and Foreign Commerce because it concerned subject matter under the jurisdiction of that body. After making amendments, that committee then referred it to the Committee on Rules and Administration (a body similar to the House Rules Committee with jurisdiction over the conduct of the business of the Senate), which brought the bill onto the floor of the Senate, where it was passed as amended. The resolution called for an investigation by the Senate into the legislation underlying the Supreme Court decision and the impact of such laws, as interpreted by the Court, "with particular relation to the basing-point or freight-equalization system of pricing." Senator Capehart was then made chairman of the Subcommittee of the Senate Committee on Interstate and Foreign Commerce on S. Res. 241 and proceeded to conduct hearings on his resolution.

Committee Hearings

Although the Capehart Committee did not commence hearings until after the elections in November, 1948, it did take some preliminary action to secure some opinions on the Court decision and its effects. An advisory council was appointed in August, 1948, composed of forty-five representatives from the cement, sugar, steel, and railroad industries (all of which were involved in basing-point pricing systems); from labor unions especially interested in the measure (such as the Cement Workers Union); and from three major farm organizations—the American Farm Bureau Federation, the National Grange and the National Farmers Union. This council issued a majority report favorable to basing-point pricing, although the farm organizations did not sign it (two of them—the Grange and Farmers Union—wrote minority reports). However, the Capehart Committee did not rely solely on the opinions expressed by representatives from interested organizations and held hearings in November and December in which other individuals and groups made presentations.

According to Latham:

> The witnesses before the Committee represented a great congeries of group interests: steel customers; cane and beet sugar growers and refiners whose products were sold on a delivered price basis; candy and glucose manufacturers, including some under complaint by the Federal Trade Commission; cement customers; building materials manufacturers and dealers; cement producers; steel producers; railroad traffic spokesmen; pulp and paper producers; some officials of the Department of Justice and the Federal Trade Commission; spokesmen for trade associations in lumber, groceries and other commodities; small-business-association representatives; and representatives of the Army, Navy, and other federal agencies. A scattered representation from other assorted enterprises appeared, and some minor public officials. Three unions were represented, one of which was a small

union in the cement industry and another in the railroads. All three were from industries representing basing-point interests or benefiting from basing-point systems. None of the major unions appeared, although telegrams and statements were sent by several locals. None of the principal farm organizations appeared. Big steel and cement producers were notably absent.[1]

Most of the witnesses before the Capehart Committee were against "f.o.b. pricing," which, Senator Capehart asserted, the Supreme Court decision seemed to require. A few witnesses—an economist from the University of Washington, and representatives from the Department of Justice, the Federal Trade Commission, and a small-business group—stated that either the decision did not seem to require f.o.b. pricing or that such a requirement was a good idea. These unfavorable witnesses were the only ones cross-examined.

The subcommittee under the chairmanship of Senator Capehart did not issue a report or propose new legislation as a result of the investigation it conducted. In the elections of 1948, the Democrats were victorious and the committees of Congress were reorganized with Republicans being removed from their positions as committee chairmen. Senator Johnson of Colorado replaced Senator Capehart as the head of the subcommittee, but there was no apparent difference in the policies of the two men. In fact, even before a report was made to the Senate of the investigation under the original resolution, Senators Johnson and Capehart introduced a bill to amend the law so as to permit basing-point pricing, except when it was the result of a price-fixing conspiracy. This bill was referred, through the Senate Committee on Foreign and Interstate Commerce, to the subcommittee, now headed by Johnson rather than Capehart.

Brief hearings were held by the subcommittee on the new bill. The United States Chamber of Commerce, local and state chambers, industrial associations, and the American Bar Association were represented, together with spokesmen for a number of trade associations—the National Canners Association, the National Retail Lumber Dealers Association, food associations, and truck owners' associations. Also heard were a representative from United Steel Workers of America (who said that the feared results of abandoning basing-point pricing had not materialized in the steel industry) and some government witnesses. The chairman of the Interstate Commerce Commission felt that some of the phraseology of the bill might alter the jurisdiction of the ICC and that this would be undesirable. Witnesses from the Federal Trade Commission gave some conflicting testimony, since the policy of the FTC was to permit differences of opinion to exist among its staff even though they might be contrary

[1] Earl Latham, *The Group Basis of Politics* (Ithaca, N.Y.: Cornell U. P., 1952) pp. 104–105.

to the majority opinion in the commission. Although some amendments were made in the bill introduced by Senators Johnson and Capehart as a result of the hearings, attempts to pass that bill were abandoned since another senate bill appeared which supporters of modification of the Supreme Court decision through legislation felt would better serve their purpose. This was the Myers bill, previously mentioned, which would have the effect of providing a "legislative moratorium" on new administrative proceedings against pricing practices outlawed by the Supreme Court decision.

Although the bill introduced by Senator Myers had originally been referred to the Interstate and Foreign Commerce Committee, Senator Johnson made the unusual move of recommending that jurisdiction of the Myers bill *and* of the bill that he (Johnson) and Senator Capehart had jointly introduced be transferred to the Committee on the Judiciary. The subcommittee of which Senator Johnson was chairman completed its work by issuing an interim report on the investigations conducted by the Capehart-Johnson Committee on the 1948 resolution and on the 1949 Johnson-Capehart proposal. Although this report recommended no permanent changes in legislation to counteract the Supreme Court decision, it did propose that the Senate and Congress immediately pass a temporary legislative moratorium (as called for by the Myers bill) while further consideration was being given to what permanent changes should be made in the law concerning basing-point pricing.

The Judiciary Committee now provided a new arena in which those individuals and groups interested in basing-point legislation struggled to gain their goals, with the bill introduced by Senator Myers as the center of attention. The Myers bill provided for a temporary legislative moratorium and also indicated that it was not the intent of Congress to deprive individual companies of the right to use delivered-price systems or to absorb freight costs, provided that it was not the result of a combination or conspiracy or other agreement in restraint of trade.

Only brief hearings were held by the Senate Judiciary Committee on the Myers bill. In three days, a subcommittee heard a spokesman for the Congress of Industrial Organizations (CIO), an Associate General Counsel of the Federal Trade Commission (FTC), members of Congress, and spokesmen for the National Federation of Small Business, National Farmers Union, American Steel Warehouse Association, and the Order of Railway Conductors. The CIO spokesman (the research director for the Steelworkers' union) opposed the bill, although he pointed out that steel companies were soliciting support for the measure from local steel unions. Senators Myers and Johnson spoke for the measure, as did Representative Walter of Pennsylvania, who had introduced a similar bill in the House. The witness from the FTC presented the view that the proposed legislation would increase confusion as to the application of the Federal Trade Commission Act and other laws administered by the Commission rather than reduce it.

The Committee Report to the Senate

After an amendment had been made to the Myers bill, the Judiciary Committee favorably reported the bill to the Senate, recommending that it be passed by the entire upper house. There was a minority report by Senator Langer, who felt that passage of the bill would weaken the antitrust laws. About one month after the committee's report, Senator Myers moved that the Senate consider the approved bill. However, just before debate was scheduled to begin, Senator O'Mahoney discussed with Myers and other senators the possibility of introducing a substitute bill for the Myers measure. Although debate on the Myers bill had already begun, O'Mahoney submitted his substitute bill. This was referred to the Committee on the Judiciary, which examined it the next day and reported the substitute measure out on the floor of the Senate, without having held hearings on it.

Senate Debate on the Bills

The Judiciary Committee selected Senator O'Conor of Maryland to speak for the Myers bill, as amended. Senators Langer of North Dakota and Morse of Oregon—staunch antimonopolists—spoke against it at length and other senators also opposed the measure. However, the debate was not very extensive since the O'Mahoney bill was substituted for the Myers bill and the Senate, after first accepting it as a substitute, proceeded to pass the O'Mahoney bill with little debate and on a voice vote (that is, individual senators did not go on record as being for or against). The essential difference between the two bills was that O'Mahoney's measure provided that the legislative moratorium be permanent, rather than for only two years, as the Myers proposal provided.

Since O'Mahoney had earned a reputation as an ardent antimonopolist in the Senate, his support of a permanent moratorium was somewhat confusing to the opponents of such legislation. However, in the hearings before the Capehart Committee, Senator O'Mahoney had accompanied the spokesman for a chemical company interested in developing some of the mineral resources of Wyoming, who stated that it might be difficult for his firm to do so unless it could absorb extra transportation costs so as to be able to compete with other firms in the U.S. As a representative of his state, Senator O'Mahoney was desirous of seeing the law changed in order to encourage business development in Wyoming.

O'Mahoney's bill did not pass unamended. Senator Kefauver of Tennessee—a member of the antimonopoly forces in the Senate—got O'Mahoney to accept an amendment making illegal any freight absorption that would substantially lessen competition. Although a motion was made to reconsider the bill after its initial passage, this move failed and the amended O'Mahoney bill was referred to the House of Representatives.

Consideration of the Bill by the House

In the House of Representatives, the measure that had been passed by the Senate was referred to the Judiciary Committee. This committee held a one-day hearing on the measure. Most of the witnesses were from the government, with one of the most influential being Senator O'Mahoney, who urged the House Judiciary Committee to delete the Kefauver amendment, which O'Mahoney had accepted on the floor of the Senate. The subcommittee conducting the hearing agreed to the proposal of Senator O'Mahoney to drop the amendment and then favorably reported the bill to the full House Judiciary Committee. Although opponents of the bill attacked it in this committee, it was decided to report the bill favorably to the entire House. The Rules Committee granted a rule providing for three hours of debate on the bill. Representative Wright Patman of Texas was the chief opponent of the measure in the House, arguing against it before the Judiciary Committee, opposing the granting of a rule permitting debate, and attempting, unsuccessfully, to get such debate delayed. Moreover, as Chairman of the House Select Committee on Small Business, he held hearings on the bill even though it had not been referred to his committee. Protests were recorded against the measure by economists, small business organizations, wholesale and retail distributors, the Farmers Union, the American Trucking Association, and Federal Trade Commission spokesmen. The only effect these opponents had was to incorporate an amendment to the House bill similar to the Kefauver amendment of the Senate bill. This amended bill passed the House, but since the House bill and the Senate bill were different, the differences had to be resolved in some fashion.

Action in the Conference Committee

The Senate was unwilling to agree to accept the amendment made by the House, and voted to submit the differences to a conference. Senate conferees were appointed, and the House was asked to name members of a conference committee. The conferees appointed to represent the Senate were not satisfactory to the opponents of the bill, and they attempted to get the Senate to reconsider its vote to send the bill to conference. This move failed, and a conference committee considered the bill in order to iron out the differences between the House and Senate versions.

The conference committee issued its report in the closing days of the first session of the Eighty-first Congress. Although the compromise bill arrived at in that committee was unacceptable to the chairman of the House Judiciary Committee and other Representatives, it passed the House by a vote of about 2 to 1. The compromise bill, however, had more difficulty in securing Senate passage. Senator Douglas objected to the conference report in its entirety, and moved that further consideration of it be postponed until the beginning of the second session in January 1950. Senator O'Mahoney also objected to the conference committee report, since the language of the original Senate bill had been changed in a manner unacceptable to him. Without O'Mahoney's support of the conference committee bill, its proponents were unable to prevent a vote favoring postponement of consideration of the conference report until the next session.

In January 1950, the Senate again considered the report of the conference committee. After considerable debate, this body rejected the conference report and the bill was returned to the conference committee for further changes. The recommended changes were quickly made and the modified bill reported out of conference was quickly passed by the House. The Senate did not consider the report until almost two months after it was issued. Once having taken up discussion of the bill, the Senate consumed two weeks in debating the measure. Opponents attempted to delay a final vote through employing certain parliamentary manuevers, but were unsuccessful (if the Senate had not passed the measure as a result of such delays during the second session of the Eighty-first Congress, the entire procedure would have had to be repeated in the Eighty-second Congress in order to get a bill through the national legislature). With the passage of the conference committee bill by both House and Senate, the measure now went to the President for his approval.

The President's Veto

The President of the United States is given, by the Constitution, a period of ten days in which to make some disposition of bills passed by Congress and submitted to him. He may sign the bill (which makes it law), he may refuse to sign the bill (which will also result in the bill becoming law *unless* Congress has adjourned during the ten-day period, in which case an unsigned bill does *not* become law), or he may veto the bill (which will prevent the bill from becoming law unless two thirds of each house of Congress votes to override the veto). In the case of the basing-point bill, after consulting party leaders and other interested parties, President Truman vetoed the measure. Since there were not sufficient votes in Congress to pass the bill over his veto, there the matter rested.

BUSINESS AND THE LEGISLATIVE PROCESS

The role that businessmen and business organizations can and do play in the legislative process should be apparent. Although it was not evident in the basing-point bill, entire bills or important phrases to be incorporated into bills are sometimes drafted by business lobbyists and introduced by friendly legislators. Such elected representatives may be able to have a bill sent to a friendly committee. Businessmen and business groups are able to present their views before legislative committees as well as to make attempts to influence others to support certain measures. After Congress has passed a measure, business representatives make their views known to the President either directly or indirectly and attempt to get him either to approve or veto a bill passed by Congress, depending on whether the bill is felt to promote or injure certain business interests. We should point out that all of business will not be affected the same way by a certain piece of proposed legislation, and frequently some firms, industries, and general business organizations support a bill, but others oppose it (in the case of the basing-point bill, generally speaking, "big business" supported it, but "small business" opposed it).

Although business *can* influence legislation, this begs the question of whether it *should* do so. The question of what the political responsibilities of business are embraces something more than the role it plays in influencing the legislative process. Public policy, as we have seen, stems initially from the activities of legislatures, administrators, and the courts. However, since legislators, administrative officials, and judges are put in positions where they can determine public policy as a consequence of the elective process (since they are either elected or appointed by elected officials), the question of the political responsibilities of business involves issues concerning the participation of businessmen in elections, in administrative and judicial processes, and in the legislative process. In the next chapter, we shall examine some views on what are the responsibilities of business in the political arena.

READING: Report of the House Select Committee on Lobbying Activities,* by the Buchanan Committee

Lobbying is as natural to our kind of government as breathing is to the human organism, and it is almost equally complex. Part of this complexity springs from the fact that there are no significant interests in our society—economic, social, or ideological—which do not in one way or another seek something from government. With so many conflicting voices clamoring to be heard, the only means of securing a full hearing has been to constantly find new techniques by which your views can be presented more effectively than your competitor's. The demands of vigorous competition have thus made lobbying an exacting and an ever-evolving profession. The encyclopedia of lobbying practices needs frequent supplements to keep it up to date.

And they had best be cumulative supplements; for while lobbying techniques are continually being streamlined, the old standbys of pressure tactics are only slowly relinquished. New methods are added but old ones are not dropped. For example, direct contacting of legislators, the critical component of any traditional definition of lobbying, is still a common practice. Individuals and groups very properly seek to apprise legislators directly of their views on public issues. The variations on this old practice are, of course, endless.

Some groups make their views known by letters, telegrams, and phone calls. Others depend largely on personal contact with Members of Congress, and still others think that they can best serve their cause by organizing delegations for marches on the Capitol. The Civil Rights Congress has often used this last approach and has on numerous occasions sponsored mass train trips to Washington for the purpose of what its officers call "speaking on . . . legislation."

Members of Congress are used to being sought out in their offices, in their homes, in the corridors of the office buildings and of the Capitol, in the cloakrooms and restaurants, on the floor of the Chamber itself. They expect and welcome letters, telegrams, and telephone calls from constituents and from those outside their districts as well. In an age where the actions of Congress directly affect the lives of so many, legislators depend on these communications in a very real and immediate way. They are both the pipelines and the lifelines of our kind of representative government.

But such statements and comments are not always as spontaneous, original, or genuine as they appear. Some tend to degrade the right of petition into a solemn-cynical game of blind man's bluff, a test of wits between the lobbyist and the legislator. Representative Clarence Brown remarked jocularly during an early hearing that he could smell such inspired pressure letters without opening the

---

* [*The House Select Committee on Lobbying Activities (Congressman Buchanan, Chairman) was created by a resolution of the 81st Congress (elected in 1948) to investigate all lobbying activities "intended to influence, encourage, promote, or retard legislation." Only selected portions of the report are reproduced here.*]

envelopes; but it is not always easy to separate the real expression of opinion from the contrived one.

The National Association of Real Estate Boards, however, has systematized all means of direct contact between its members and legislators more completely than any other group appearing before this committee. This group conducts letter and telegram campaigns. It also prepares, sometimes on request, specific letters which local members transmit to their Senators and Representatives. The association has developed through its local member boards remarkably extensive lists of congressional "contacts," persons who are expected to wield particular influence with the Representative or Senator from the district or State concerned. There is, among others, a list of "special contacts" for the House Banking and Currency Committee; another for the Senate Banking and Currency Committee; a third for the House Rules Committee; and a fourth which is labeled "Key Senate Phone Contacts." When a pressure campaign reaches the critical stage, when a final ounce of effort may be the margin between success or failure, the "contact" swings into action. The expectation is, of course, that the "contact's" political, business, or personal acquaintance with the Member of Congress—and it is on this basis that he is selected as contact—will enable him to make a decisive impression of the Member's thinking. Six to seven hundred of these contacts make up the membership of what the National Association of Real Estate Boards calls the enlarged committee of the Realtors' Washington Committee, which handles and directs much of the lobbying for the association. Herbert U. Nelson, National Association of Real Estate Boards executive vice president, describes the work of the enlarged committee as follows:

> The specific objective and activity of the enlarged committee, when called upon, is to wire or write their Senators or Representatives regarding any critical matters which may arise from time to time that seriously affect the real estate industry and where quick action is required. Only those who have shown a willingness or desire to render support in this manner, or who are closely acquainted or have personal contact with Members of Congress, have been appointed on the enlarged committee.

There is, of course, nothing essentially new in this approach except the degree of careful organization and planning which the National Association of Real Estate Boards applies to it. Every pressure group worthy of the name has recognized since at least 1910 that the sheer volume of letters and wires from home is apt to have some influence on congressional decisions. They have also recognized, however, that volume alone is apt to raise congressional suspicion. Hence, the National Association of Real Estate Board's careful selection of contacts, usually men of substance within their communities, men whose views are likely to command maximum respect. . . .

In the days when lobbying meant little more than unabashed bribery, committees of Congress were the favorite focus of the old lobby barons. Then as now, crucial decisions were made in committee, and men having entree to them could quietly make the necessary arrangements. The committees are even more important in the modern legislative process, but with the institution in 1911 of open hearings on all major legislation the possibilities of easy influence diminished. The lobbyist who appears formally before committees today is generally obliged to argue on the merits. Despite public scrutiny and the watchfulness of competitors, however, some misrepresentation is still possible. . . .

Although the techniques of direct contact with Members and committees are as old as lobbying itself, they can still be of service to the modern pressure group in the presentation of its point of view. New twists have to be added to keep the old methods useful, but they continue to be of importance in the overall lobbying picture. Not only do these techniques allow groups and individuals to present their views but they also provide the means by which valuable and perhaps otherwise unavailable information can be brought to the Congress' attention. This intelligence function of lobbying is likewise not new, but it does assume special importance in an era of complex and wide-ranging legislation. The pressure group is, of course, quite likely to exaggerate its research and informational activities. The National Association of Manufacturers typically maintains, for instance, that at least 80 per cent of its operations are of this character. Although such claims bear close scrutiny, it is nevertheless true that most well-established pressure bodies take their informational work quite seriously.

Facts are seldom presented for their own sake, or without having been carefully selected for maximum impact. But where a full hearing is available for all interested groups, we can rely on competitive watchfulness and public scrutiny as partial safeguards against misrepresentation of the facts by any one group.

The service function in lobbying takes many forms. When representatives of organized groups appear before committees of Congress, for example, they are not only presenting their own case but they are also providing Members of Congress with one of the essential raw materials of legislative action. By the same token, the drafting of bills and amendments to bills, the preparation of speeches and other materials for Members, the submission to Members of detailed memoranda on bill-handling tactics—all of these are means by which lobby groups service the legislative process and at the same time further their own ends.

In addition to these services rendered to Members of Congress in their official capacities, lobbying organizations often perform favors of a more personal sort. Three generations ago, when standards of congressional morality were less exacting than they are today, the lobbyist could favor the Member in ways which strike the modern mind as crude. The lobbyist of the 1880's was a bountiful host, a social guide, a financial confidant, and a free-handed companion at the gaming table. But times change, and, while the theme of personal attentiveness still runs through modern pressure tactics, the forms which it takes have changed. Formal dinners for Members of Congress and, in addition to these, more casual and intimate gatherings, remain part of the lobby group's stock in trade. But apart from these vestiges of the old "social lobby," the personal service aspects of lobbying have been considerably revamped. Today, the resourceful pressure group may seek to serve themselves as well as Members of Congress by arranging remunerative speaking or writing engagements for them or by such friendly acts as helping the new Member to secure housing in Washington.

The relationships between Members of Congress and groups interested in legislation are infinitely varied. Many Members have spoken before such groups, frequently for no remuneration whatsoever. In other cases, Members have arranged for groups to reproduce their writings on public issues. One Member, for example, has regularly written a weekly Washington column which has been distributed by a group filing reports under the Lobbying Act. He has received no pay for this writing, but he has received "research expenses" which have ranged from $250 to $500 per month. Obviously, those groups which cannot work on equally close terms with Members are left at a considerable disadvantage.

There is a final long-standing lobbying technique which, without any modernization at all, has become increasingly prevalent during the past 40 years. We refer to the use of the franking privilege for mass mailings of printed matter.

. . . .

If lobbying consisted of nothing more than the well-established methods of direct contact, there would have been relatively little need for our investigation. These methods may lack finesse, but they generally have the virtue of directness. At least the effort to influence runs straight-line from the individual or group to the Member of Congress. Although the process may be sleeked up occasionally, it is essentially uncomplicated and straightforward.

Ever since President Wilson's first administration, however, the ever-growing army of pressure groups has recognized that the power of government ultimately rests on the power of public opinion. This simple discovery lies at the root of the evolution of lobbying techniques since 1913. The extensive use of franked releases antagonistic to the chief items of the Underwood tariff bill of that year was probably the first large-scale effort to bring public opinion to bear on legislation. In this sense, the use of highly charged franked releases as an instrument of pressure was the bridge between the old lobbying and the new. It opened the way to the development of entirely new dimensions in the theory and practice of lobbying. Today, the long-run objective of every significant pressure group in the country is and must inevitably be the creation and control of public opinion; for, without the support of an articulate public, the most carefully planned direct lobbying is likely to be ineffective, except on small or narrow issues.

If a descriptive label is needed, this new emphasis in pressure tactics might best be called "lobbying at the grass roots." What it amounts to is this: Rather than attempt to influence legislation directly, the pressure group seeks to create an appearance of broad public support for its aims, support which can be mobilized when the legislative situation demands it. The general premise underlying this effort is that if people are made to feel deeply enough about an issue they will translate their feelings into action which will affect that issue's resolution by the Congress. This expression of public opinion may be genuine in the sense that the views expressed are expressed spontaneously and with conviction. . . . Or, on the other hand, such expression may be artificial and contrived. In either case, the process is one which has been deliberately and specifically instigated by one group or another having a particular stake in legislative issues. This process may bear little resemblance to the lobbying of 1880, but the intent behind it and the end results are unquestionably the same; namely to influence the determination of legislative policy. As Representative Halleck succinctly observed:

The committee has pretty well discovered, I think, that one of the very effective ways to influence legislation is to operate out at the grass roots and possibly to deal in public opinion.

The suggestion that efforts to influence public opinion might, under certain circumstances, be classified as "lobbying" met with considerable resistance from numerous witnesses appearing before us. They usually described themselves as "educators" or "publishers" or, in one case, "educator-publisher." As such, a number of them claimed that they had never lobbied in their lives. Although we have reason to suspect these protestations of injured innocence, they do raise important questions of policy. Where, for example, is the line to be drawn between "lobbying at the grass roots" and publishing or education, which may also be concerned with the creation of opinion? So far as stimulating people to exert pressure on their Congressmen is concerned, is it not true that "every idea is an incitement," as Justice Holmes once said?

The answers to these questions are closer at hand than the protestors care to admit. Those who are reticent to make public disclosure of their activities and sources of financial support enjoy their self-made confusion. The all-pervading purpose and intent of the Lobbying Act was to bring into the open activities intended to influence legislation, directly and indirectly, and to provide full public disclosure of the financing and expenditures involved in these activities. Lobbying at the grass roots is no hazy myth; it is a basic reality of modern efforts to influence legislation. We have already stated our position on the question of full disclosure: A group's own allegations that is exempt from the Lobbying Act are plainly self-serving. Where doubt exists, sound public policy calls for full disclosure of the facts.

Unfortunately, many people attach sinister significance to the word "lobbying." The present statute on the subject does not contain the word "lobbying" anywhere in its substantive provisions. Except in the title, the statute speaks only of attempts to influence legislation, directly and indirectly.

. . . .

Mass distribution of books and pamphlets is only one of the means by which the pressure groups have sought to influence legislation through the creation and exploitation of a charged public opinion. Wherever public opinion is made, the pressure group is likely to be found. The variations are endless, but a few examples will serve to indicate the general outlines of this approach.

Many pressure groups recognize the importance of educational institutions as molders of public opinion, and a particular effort is made to reach and to utilize these institutions and their personnel to the fullest extent. There are many different approaches. The National Association of Real Estate Boards, for example, has induced colleges and universities to set up special courses in which its general point of view was taught. It has also stimulated the writing of textbooks on real estate, home building and management, and real estate economics, which it estimates are currently used by 127 colleges and universities. Other groups like the Foundation for Economic Education include prominent educators among their officers. This is particularly useful in selling the group's activities as nonpartisan and educational. The foundation also operates a "college-business exchange program," under which college teachers spend the summer months with industrial and financial organizations, which finance the "fellowships." In countless other ways the pressure groups have recognized the importance of the educational process. They do not necessarily pervert this process, but they make every effort to exploit it.

The pressure groups have long been aware of the power of the press and have sought to harness this power for their ends. One of the prime conditions of successful public relations is anonymity of the source; thus it is not surprising that the effort to use the Nation's newspapers and periodicals as instruments of pressure politics has been concentrated on gaining access to editorial and news columns. . . .

The pressure group cannot be satisfied. If it fails to achieve its aim at once, it keeps fighting to achieve it. If it gets what it wants, then with very few exceptions it wants something more. This is part of what was meant by the earlier reference to lobbying as inherently expansive. One-shot organizations, groups which fight for specific objectives and fold up shop when they have won them, are relatively few in number. There is an institutional momentum which tends to limit pressure group mortality.

But lobbying is inherently expansive in an even more significant sense. We refer to the fact that modern pressure politics is not and cannot be confined to legislative policy alone. One of the oldest textbook truisms about lobbying is that it is non-political in the sense that pressure groups are interested only in issues and not in men. We think, however, that our investigation provides evidence to the contrary; a majority of the groups which we investigated were in some degree engaged in influencing the outcome of elections. This is not said in condemnation, express or implied, but simply as a statement of the facts.

SUGGESTED READINGS

Bailey, Stephen K., *Congress Makes a Law* (New York: Random, 1950). A study of the realities of the legislative process, investigating the social forces and individual contributions that went toward the formulation, introduction, amendment and passage of the Employment Act of 1946. Professor Bailey concludes that the will of the people, as expressed in elections, is thwarted by our lawmakers in the conflict of interests.

Harris, Richard, *The Real Voice* (New York: Macmillan, 1964). An "inside story" of Congress at work: specifically, with the investigation of the drug industry by Senator Kefauver's Senate Subcommittee on Antitrust and Monopoly, the emergent bill, and the battle to get it passed.

Jewell, Malcolm E., *The State Legislature* (New York: Random, 1962). A short, but comprehensive study of the realities of party politics and legislative behavior at the state level.

CHAPTER 32

THE POLITICAL RESPONSIBILITIES OF BUSINESS

Throughout the history of the United States, businessmen have been active in attempting to influence public policy. Such action has not always had the desired effect, nor has it always been regarded as responsible behavior. Although businessmen continue to play a prominent political role, they are urged—somewhat surprisingly—to become more active in politics in addition to being told what their political responsibilities are. As in our previous examination of statements urging certain responsibilities upon business, we note that they come from a number of sources and frequently give conflicting advice. Before examining what various individuals and groups see as the political responsibilities of business, perhaps we should take note of the political actions that have been taken by businessmen.

POLITICAL ACTIVITY OF BUSINESS

Since the beginning of our national existence, American businessmen have been politically active. Indeed, the American Revolution was brought about in part by actions taken by colonial businessmen. John Hancock, for example, was a Boston merchant who had been engaged in a number of anti-British activities in concert with other colonial businessmen aggrieved by the restrictions Parliament placed on colonial business. Although it is unlikely that many of them saw revolution as the solution to the problems confronting them, the actions taken by them to force the English to liberalize their regulation of colonial trade eventually led the British government to declare the colonies to be in a state of rebellion and the colonies to declare themselves to be "free and independent states."

The Constitution, adopted in 1789, and the new federal government stemming from the adoption of the new governmental charter reflected the political influence of businessmen, as we have already noted. In the dozen years prior to the election of Jefferson as President, business influence was strong in the nation's capital and was evident in the actions of Congress and the Administration. Although from 1801 to 1861 the national government was in the hands of those with whom the influence of business was not very strong, the actions of state governments in promoting the interests of business reflected political action by businessmen on that level during this period.

With the formation of the new Republican party in the 1850's—roughly a coalition of eastern businessmen and northern farmers—business again gained a strong voice in national affairs. The Republicans (despite defections of agrarians from their ranks) virtually dominated national politics from the beginning of the Civil War until the beginning of World War I —a period of more than fifty years, with Grover Cleveland (a conservative Democrat from New York) being the only President elected from another party. It was only because of dissension within the Republican party—the split between the Roosevelt progressives and the Taft conservatives—that Woodrow Wilson was elected in 1912 (receiving only a minority of the popular votes cast). Although Wilson was re-elected in 1916, the Republicans again gained control of national government in 1920 and asserted that "the business of America is business."

Businessmen continued to be successful in state politics at the same time the Republicans were gaining ascendancy in national political affairs. This was not uniformly true, of course, since agrarians, dissatisfied with their partnership with business in the Republican party, formed third parties in some of the northern states, gained control of state government, and passed legislation adverse to certain business interests. In the South, some states controlled by Democrats also took antibusiness measures. However, such adverse action occurred only in a minority of the states and for the most part state governments were friendly to business. Although they were a minority group, businessmen had sufficient political resources to enable them to overcome the challenges of third parties—some of which bore the title of "Anti-Monopoly Party"—and to maintain a favorable political environment through securing the election of those who were friendly to business. There were, of course, some exceptions. Theodore Roosevelt unexpectedly became President and gained some notoriety through his prosecution of "bad trusts." Federal and state regulatory legislation was passed in increasing volume, but for the most part it was administered in a friendly fashion.

Indeed, in the eyes of some observers, the political success of business in the years following the Civil War was a cause for alarm. It was asserted that the nation faced a crisis and that a choice would have to be made between "social democracy" and "plutocracy." Charges (frequently true) were made against businessmen for bribing public officials and making the United States Senate into a "rich man's club." Socialists, progressives, and liberals—all voiced concern over the dominant role of the businessman in politics and proposed certain solutions.

Some changes were made. Senators now are elected directly by the people of a state rather than by state legislatures. Corrupt practices acts have been passed by Congress and most states. Extension of the suffrage to women and others formerly not possessing the franchise has occurred. Reapportionment of legislative districts has increased popular control over legislatures. All of these measures reduced the political influence of business.

One of the most dramatic changes has been the decline of the Republican party to a position where it has difficulty in commanding a majority of the popular votes in national elections. Although it was able to secure the election of a popular general after World War II, for the largest part of his administration President Eisenhower had to work with a Congress controlled by the Democrats. To the extent that the Republican party is the party of the businessman (which considerably exaggerates the nature of that organization), this may seem to be a cause for some concern on the part of business.

Although the political changes that have taken place may tend to reduce the influence of businessmen in politics, businessmen continue to be politically active. The nature of their activity has changed somewhat, but they take action in a number of "political arenas" to attain their objectives, and with considerable success.

Business and the Elective Process

In the preceding chapters, we noted that the kinds of laws, legislators, administrators, and judges confronting businessmen ultimately depended on what happened in elections. Although opportunities still exist for interested parties to influence government officials directly, greater emphasis has been placed on influencing elections as a means of securing the "right" decisions from agencies and officers in various levels of government. There seems to be considerable opportunity for businessmen to influence elections because there is a very close relationship between the amount of money spent by a candidate in promoting his candidacy and his chances of election. Since most candidates are not personally wealthy, this means that they must secure contributions from various sources in order to wage an effective campaign. Although corporations are prohibited from making campaign contributions, individual businessmen are not. Candidates for public office might like to disclaim having any obligation to those contributing to their election campaign, but there is no doubt that either consciously or unconsciously such an obligation is felt and when the successful candidate is asked for a favor by those making substantial contributions, it is difficult for him to refuse it.

Business participation in election campaigns is not limited to making contributions. Some businessmen enter politics and run for public office. Senator Goldwater operated a department store in Phoenix before entering politics; Senator Kerr of Oklahoma made a fortune from his business activities; on the state and local political scenes, we see businessmen occupying public office after making successful election campaigns. Some firms urge their employees to run for public office and to "get out and vote." In some cases, managers make it quite clear whom their employees should vote for. Businessmen have served as campaign managers for certain candidates and on voluntary committees to promote the election of particular candidates, even to the extent of "ringing doorbells."

Many businessmen become involved in party politics. Through their influence in a political party, they may be able to secure the nomination of friendly candidates. Frequently, this is an easier way of getting the "right people" elected than engaging in the final election campaign because in some areas the nominee of a certain party is normally elected.

Business and the Legislative Process

Earlier we noted that businessmen participate in various ways in getting legislatures to pass desired laws or to defeat undesired legislation. Although in the nineteenth century it was not unusual to see wholesale bribery of a legislature, or at least the bribery of a few key figures, that day is apparently past (though some see little difference between campaign contributions and old-fashioned bribery). By getting friendly legislators to introduce desired legislation, to block the passage of unfavorable bills, and to vote "right," some desired effect can be secured. Normally businessmen do not engage in such activity themselves, but generally work through lobbyists for a firm, industry, or business. Through publicity and public relations, attempts are made to crystallize public opinion and secure its expression in an influential way. Presenting the views of a firm, industry, or "business" at hearings on legislation may also have some effect. Thus, despite the passage of corrupt practices legislation, legal means have been found to influence legislative bodies, with some apparent effect.

Business and the Administrative Process

In our examination of the administrative process, we pointed out the opportunities existing to influence administrative decisions by interested parties. Businessmen have attempted to secure favorable decisions by a variety of means. When hearings have been conducted on rules changes or when those interested in the application of certain rules have been given an opportunity to express their views, firms and industries have made strong presentations (even employing college professors as "expert witnesses") in order to gain a decision regarded as favorable. If initial decisions are adverse, appeals are made to reviewing agencies or officials. Although these may be unsuccessful, they frequently have the merit of delaying the implementation of the adverse decision. Some of the measures adopted by businessmen to gain desired decisions are not as "socially acceptable" as the foregoing means: they have had key legislative officials exert pressure on administrative officers to make the "right" decisions, and there have been a number of instances in which bribery of officials has taken place—not always with money, but with gifts of mink coats, freezers, and certain services.

Business and the Judicial Process

Court decisions are susceptible to business influence. Although there is less evidence of bribery and other corrupt influence in this political arena, businessmen still have resources they can employ to gain the "right" decision or to delay the implementation of a "wrong" one. Basically, their resource is money. They are able to hire legal representatives capable of putting up strong defenses against legal attack and of conducting a powerful offense. Even though success may not reward efforts in courts of original jurisdiction, the appeals procedure may bring reversal of the decision of a lower court or at least a delay in the implementation of that decision. The existence of the appeals procedure also appears to reward those who have the money needed to employ this means of gaining certain ends, thereby favoring those with substantial financial resources, including businessmen.

THE POLITICAL RESPONSIBILITY OF BUSINESS

Thus a cursory examination of the history of political activity undertaken by businessmen and of the actions currently taken by them to influence public policy and its administration in various political arenas reveals that businessmen have been politically active. This does not answer the question of what their responsibilities should be. As in the case of all issues concerning the responsibilities of business, a variety of voices are heard, giving conflicting advice. Political philosophers vary in their views as to what role, if any, business and other "special interests" should play in the formulation and administration of public policy. Politicians and government officials generally urge political activity upon businessmen, but have some strong opinions on the proper conduct of such action. Trade associations and general business organizations are firm believers in political action, although their recommendations to businessmen differ somewhat. Some businessmen and firms have also gone on record as to what their political responsibilities are. In examining these various views, we shall cover the more important statements of what business responsibilities are in the realm of politics.

Political Philosophers on the
Political Responsibilities of Business

As is true about almost all philosophies, there is one highly individual philosophy for each political philosopher; all we can do is look at some of these and classify them. In Chapter 23, we adopted a classification scheme that put each political thinker in the category of being an "idealist," a "rationalist," or a "realist." Idealists believe in "the public" and feel that political parties and interest groups (such as business organizations taking political action) operate in ways inimical to the "public interest." That is, they urge businessmen to discharge their political responsibilities as ordinary citizens and not to take part in partisan politics or to act as a "special interest" group. Rationalists take a somewhat different line, although they are also against special interest groups. According to the rationalists, businessmen ought to support those political parties that best articulate the "public will" and should subordinate their special interests to the general good. The realists do not recognize the existence of a public good or a public will, but see society as being made up of a number of "publics" having rather special interests. Therefore they have no objection to political parties representing certain special interests, nor to the existence of special interest groups, regarding both as performing useful political functions. However, they frequently object that business interest groups have excessive political power as compared to other groups and recommend that businessmen use their great power more responsibly—that is, they suggest that the interests of those without as much political influence be taken into account.

Although a number of individual political philosophers exist in the U.S. and periodically prescribe proper political behavior for businessmen, an interesting collection of philosophers has been brought together in the Center for the Study of Democratic Institutions. The Center is the main activity of the Fund for the Republic (initially established by the Ford Foundation), which conducts a number of studies of the "great issues" confronting America and publishes pamphlets, occasional papers, reports, interviews, conversations, bulletins, books, discussions, and dialogues on such issues. The titles of some of these publications indicate the nature of the Center's interests and of its prescriptions for business behavior. A pamphlet, *The Economy under Law,* has been issued; it is "a call for bringing the economic order under the political order." Another pamphlet, *Politics and Ethics,* discusses "the need to change our present-day concept of an amoral politics and an unpolitical ethics and bring politics and ethics into harmony." That is, certain ethical principles are urged upon those involved in politics. An occasional paper, "Government and Business in International Trade," is "a call for standards in U.S. foreign trade policies and for corporations to be the responsible party in trade with other nations." In a major book published by the Center (*The Corporation in Modern Society*), the modern corporation is charged with responsibility for the "quality and tone of American life," including "the level of political morality." Although the writers differ somewhat in their opinions, throughout their discourses there is evident a central theme that business (or that creature which exists only in the eye of the law, "the corporation") has not properly discharged its political responsibilities. A variety of courses of action are then prescribed for those agreeing with the diagnoses. Since these philosophers (and others) apparently have little power to compel or persuade businessmen to accept their views, perhaps we may write off their statements as being of little consequence, however well-thought-out and well-articulated they may be.

The Views of Politicians and Government Officials

Since political power is largely in the hands of those occupying governmental positions and posts of prominence in political parties, their views on the nature of the political responsibilities of businessmen are of greater importance. However, only rarely do we see a candid expression of those views: for the most part, the public expressions of politicians and government officials seem to be concerned with "creating a favorable image" rather than with candidly pointing out what is really felt to be politically responsible behavior on the part of businessmen. However, in the absence of knowledge of what goes on in secret, the only alternative available to us is to examine such public statements.

Before the presidential campaign of 1960, the chairmen of the Democratic and Republican national committees spoke to a meeting of the American Management Association attended mainly by business managers. Although Paul Butler, Chairman of the Democratic National Committee, and Senator Thruston B. Morton, Chairman of the Republican National Committee, urged businessmen to support both political parties, it is difficult to believe that each would not prefer to have stronger business support for his own party. Both of these politicians encouraged businessmen to support the party of their choice, not only through contributions and voting but also by playing an active role in partisan politics. Also, both urged businessmen to encourage their employees to be more active politically to the point of seeking appointive or elective office.

Some advice given businessmen concerning their political responsibilities by the national chairmen of the two major parties was different, but not conflicting. Paul Butler, the Democrat, stated that those businessmen who enter the political arena only to secure special advantage create suspicion of the business community. The right way, according to Butler, was for each businessman to recognize that he was a citizen first and a businessman second. Butler's comments seemed to reflect the fact that northern businessmen tend to be Republicans, since he urged that employees be assured that they would not be penalized if they did not hold the same political views as the boss and suggested that the practice of ostracizing certain employees (presumably Democrats) who showed certain political leanings was still quite prevalent. Apparently, through generally proposing that businessmen permit and encourage political action by their employees, the chairman of the Democratic national committee felt that his party would gain relative to the Republicans.

The chairman of the Republican national committee emphasized political participation by businessmen. Men of the business community, he stated, should not hesitate to undertake political chores such as "doorbell ringing, poll-watching and even soap-box orating." Further, he suggested that they "not shirk the sometimes painful duty of contributing to the party" of their choice. Anticipating a question that might be of some concern to businessmen, he declared it "a myth that the businessman who engages in politics automatically harms his own business interests." Despite this declaration, some businessmen feel (apparently with good cause) that too close an association with a certain political party may prove to be a liability rather than an asset, especially when government contracts are handed out or if their business is subject to a considerable amount of government regulation.

What government officials say about the political responsibilities of the businessman deals more with the role of business in the legislative and administrative processes than its role in partisan politics. Although a variety of opinions have been expressed by officials, one of the more comprehensive statements was made in 1963 by Secretary of Commerce Luther Hodges in a book entitled *The Business Conscience*. Having been in business as well as in government, Hodges was well aware of the political activities of businessmen and did not regard all of them as being responsible. He took businessmen to task for the "careless thinking and careless talk" they engaged in concerning such things as "government encroachment on the business community, centralization of power, and a trend toward socialism." He pointed out that what government does reflects the actions of business as well as of other groups and that businessmen have been responsible for much governmental activity, either through political action or through irresponsible economic action. Also, he scored businessmen for looking to government to solve their problems instead of tackling them without governmental assistance. Too, he suggested that too many businessmen engaged in "beating the government," "legal brinksmanship" (violating the spirit of the law while barely observing the letter of the law), deliberate violations of the law, and corruption of government officials. In conclusion, he urged businessmen to recognize that "playing fair" with the government was an important part of their total responsibility.

The Views of Business

Businessmen, firms, trade associations, and general business organizations—all have made public statements on the nature of the political responsibilities of businessmen in addition to taking action to influence elections, legislation, administration, and court decisions. In the reading at the end of this chapter the political activities of corporations are discussed, including explicitly and implicitly the views of certain businessmen and firms on what are the political responsibilities of business. Trade associations generally represent the interests of members of an industry in various political arenas, and they tend to view the responsibilities of their members as consisting of support of the association in various ways, including letter-writing and appearing as witnesses before various tribunals. However, it seems to be the general business organization that has the greatest concern with the political responsibilities of businessmen and that urges political action of quite specific sorts on them.

The two major general business organizations on the national scene are the U.S. Chamber of Commerce and the National Association of Manufacturers. Both are involved in developing policy statements that they hope to see translated into public policy. Both the NAM and the National Chamber are involved in lobbying activities in order to gain legislation and administration in accordance with their policies. However, the National Chamber possesses a considerably larger membership (almost 3 million individuals) and seems to give greater stress to political action by them. For example, it has a "Congressional Action Program" designed to equip businessmen and others to be able to express "personal, persuasive views to Congress" on issues of concern to business. Too, it has a "Political Participation Program" to equip businessmen to be more influential and effective in politics. More specifically, the program is aimed at getting businessmen involved in partisan politics in order that the "right" people might be nominated and elected to public office. This program has been quite effective, and business-supported candidates have triumphed over the candidates supported by labor organizations in a number of localities. Generally speaking, the general business organizations urge greater political activity on businessmen in order to promote business interests.

WHAT *ARE* THE POLITICAL RESPONSIBILITIES OF BUSINESS?

Certainly, one should hesitate to add another voice to the great multitude already engaged in instructing the businessman in his political responsibilities, but some words of caution are in order. In their political actions, businessmen might do well to adopt a principle previously stated: "Take into account the interests of all parties concerned in proportion to some measure of those interests." Business—whether regarded as consisting of businessmen, firms, trade associations, or general business organizations—has some understanding of what are the interests of business, but it should not equate the business interest with the public interest. This is not to say that the two are incompatible, nor that they are not the same in some cases. However, we might properly conceive of the public interest as being promoted by action that harmonizes the interests of the various

publics that make up a society—and business is only one of those publics. There are occasions when the interests of business conflict with those of other publics and it would be unwise to ignore such conflicts, to say that only the interests of business are the same as the public interest or to ride rough-shod over others when the political resources of business happen to be greater than those of other interested parties. The history of governmental relations with business contains considerable evidence that none of these policies has worked in the long-term interest of business. Ignoring the interests of others and the winning of political battles against other interested individuals and groups have resulted in the rise of "countervailing power" and relegation of business to a relatively weak role in the formulation of public policy. Business cannot conceivably "win the war" in the political arena (although it may win some battles) and should abandon that objective.

Instead, businessmen should concern themselves with the structuring of political institutions that will give a proper voice in the formulation of public policy to all interested parties. This means encouraging the development of representative institutions that include procedures for securing the expression of opinions from all interested parties and that are able to develop policies that attempt to harmonize those interests rather than to declare one party the victor over the other or others. This means abandoning the pretense that the business interest is the same as the public interest, although it does not mean foregoing the attempt to discover what the nature of the business interest is and articulating it. Business should continue to do the latter, but should recognize that in the long run no permanent success can be gained from the establishment of public policies that attach too great weight to the interests of business and too little importance to the interests of others. Since public policy is influenced by the political resources possessed by the various interested parties and by the way in which those resources are managed, this may mean that business should be somewhat cautious in how it employs its resources because their irresponsible employment may mean that limitations may be placed on the political power of business or that other parties may increase their relative strength. Corrupt practices legislation followed exposures of bribery of public officials by businessmen, and new exposures of irresponsible political behavior will lead to new legal limits on what business may do in the political arena.

We should not conclude this chapter without pointing out the problems confronting the businessman who does or who would like to act responsibly in the realm of politics. Other interested parties do not always act responsibly—certainly labor unions have in recent years used their great political power to frustrate the attainment by business of some of its legitimate objectives. Also the organization and procedures of American governments assume that the interests of all persons are essentially the same: since this is not true in fact, and since businessmen feel that their interests are underrepresented, we can perhaps sympathize with the plight of the businessman, although we may not necessarily condone the measures he employs to gain the goals he could properly attain if our political institutions were structured in such a way as to give all interested parties political influence in proportion to their interest in a given matter. Too, the majority of businessmen have conducted themselves tolerably well in their political activities, but the irresponsible behavior of a minority has resulted in the arousing of suspicion of all political activity of business as well as in the placing of limitations on actions of all businessmen. Since responsibility and guilt are individual, it is unreasonable and unfair to charge all businessmen for the actions of a few when the majority have no authority over the actions of the minority, although this seems to happen. Finally, as we noted in earlier discussions of business responsibilities, when there are a number of different and frequent conflicting prescriptions for responsible behavior, it is impossible to meet all of the standards set. Whatever businessmen might do in the political arena, there will always be those who will regard such behavior as "irresponsible." However, the outlook for business is not as gloomy as this conclusion may suggest; in our concluding chapter on the future environment of business we shall note the existence of a number of bright spots on the political horizon.

READING: Corporations Make Politics Their Business *

The hottest extracurricular activity of many corporate managements today is not golf but a more complex game—politics. These managements are surging back into what they sense as a breach in their security. They are marshaling executives in training courses for practical politics and issuing ready-made arguments for the fray. If this intense effort becomes just another blind bid for power, business-in-politics will again be engulfed by the big battalions against which it flings itself. But, simultaneously, another trend is at work: many businessmen are rediscovering political ideas that dominated the U.S. long before it became "a business country." They are deepening their understanding of the relation between democratic political principles and free enterprise. If enough of them act upon what they find, the unnatural antagonism between business and politics will abate. Businessmen will discover that the primary aim of their present intense political program is the defense of a system in which other and more numerous segments of the society also have a stake.

The two new business trends—vastly intensified interest in practical politics and a strenuous reaching for political principle—are destined to be bound

* Reprinted by permission from the December 1959 issue of *Fortune.*

together or to fizzle out separately. But each trend has an interesting, separate history of its own.

Within recent years a few pioneers—notably General Electric, Ford Motor, and Johnson & Johnson—boldly began to experiment with frankly labeled "political action" programs involving (1) the direct encouragement of employees to engage in political activities, and (2) the open declaration of corporate positions with respect to controversial political issues. Today General Electric and Ford have fairly elaborate departments that are exclusively concerned with government and political affairs, and are headed by executives of standing who have the full confidence and backing of top management. In recent months both G.E. and Ford have been besieged by visiting delegations and inquiries from companies that are contemplating similar programs. Among the larger companies that have already undertaken fairly comprehensive political-action efforts are Gulf Oil, American Can, Monsanto, Republic Steel, and Borg-Warner. Hundreds of other companies, large and small, have sponsored bipartisan training courses in the art of practical politics for their middle-management people.

The "practical politics" seminar is certainly not very weighty in intellectual content, but it has pulled thousands of young businessmen into the picture, created an enormous amount of publicity and talk, and given the whole business-in-politics movement an exciting grass-fire effect. The typical program works this way: In groups of twelve to twenty, supervisors and junior executives spend a couple of hours a week for ten weeks or so (sometimes on company time, more often after office hours) studying such subjects as political precincts, political clubs, campaigns, party financing, patronage, etc. Often politicians from both parties are brought in as guest lecturers, and usually students supplement the study periods with a certain amount of field work: they are detailed to make door-to-door registration canvasses, write letters to their Congressmen, etc.

The U.S. Chamber of Commerce brought out a practical-politics course early this year, which has been used by 162 individual firms and 479 local chambers; over 20,000 people have taken it. The N.A.M. has a course that has been purchased by around 100 companies and taken by some 5,000 people. The Effective Citizens Organization (E.C.O.), a corporation-sponsored group, has presented a special seminar at universities around the country to over 1,000 executives from the top-level managements of more than 500 companies since 1956, and reports that it can no longer keep up with requests for the presentation.

When it comes to the more ticklish phase of declaring corporate stands on issues, there is a wide variety of approaches. Quite a few managements feel that a company should speak out only on those issues that affect its operations directly and visibly. Others, notably General Electric under the leadership of Ralph J. Cordiner, speak out boldly on issues ranging from labor laws to foreign policy.

Action and Passion. What generated these programs for practical politics? Not, certainly, pure cerebration about the relation between economic and political principles in a free society. To most Americans, life, as Mr. Justice Holmes once put it, is "action and passion." There was plenty of passion in the conception of the present wave of corporate political action. The elemental emotion most prominent was fear of the political power of organized labor. When businessmen saw labor strength persisting through a Republican Administration, when they saw in 1958 a Democratic victory that they attributed to labor, they became more than ever convinced that they had to organize a countervailing movement.

The limitations of merely passionate action become apparent. Assume that labor is as well organized for politics and as skillful as many businessmen think it is. Then, obviously, it will be a long time before management matches labor in political savvy. And what happens when management does become equal in political skill? It will confront an opponent several hundred times as numerous in a contest where numbers are decisive. Indeed, for twenty-five years this is the way the battle lines, if such they are, have been drawn. Every effort to mobilize business for politics has been instantly seized upon by political opponents of business as the most effective way of defining their own position and increasing their own ranks. Franklin Roosevelt was a past master of the political judo by which the political exertions of business were made to land business on its face.

Some of the wiser business leaders who are committed to the principle of corporate political action recognize the peril. Vice President James Worthy of Sears, Roebuck says: "There is serious danger that enthusiastic amateurs will make mistakes that will give the whole idea of businessmen in politics a bad name. What has started out as a trend of great intrinsic value may sputter out as a short-lived fad or—much worse—seriously alienate business from the community at large."

If elemental fear and frustration, if a simple struggle for power through competing group organizations, were all that lay behind the present activity, Worthy's warning could serve as an epitaph written in advance. The suspense in the present situation derives from the presence of some factors other than interest and passion—some factors of rationality that make up the second trend. On the labor front, for example, businessmen began to note that the framework of debate had been altered against them. They looked up from the annual or biennial or permanent collective-bargaining crisis to discover that labor was appealing successfully to public assumptions within which the management case could not be made. They were like ballplayers stumbling after elusive balls who suddenly discovered that the diamond was no longer the one prescribed by the rule book; hurdles had been erected at points inconvenient for the defense. They saw that the management-labor contest had to change, in part, from a players' competition for the most runs to a debate over the changes in the playing field and in the rule book.

Nor did all the influences leading to the present corporate political activity have the high emotional charge of the labor contest. The case of Johnson & Johnson illustrates how practical business problems can lead toward corporate participation in politics. Back in 1951, Chairman Robert Wood Johnson called a meeting of his principal executives to make a general assay of the company's situation. They agreed that production was well ordered, sales splendid, and research extremely promising. What's more, Johnson & Johnson did not, in its opinion, have a labor problem. "We have," summarized General Johnson, "only three major problems: (1) inflation; (2) taxes; and (3) our inability to set aside sufficient funds for the capital expansion we calculate we'll need." But there was very little that Johnson & Johnson itself could do about any one of these problems—they were all posed by government, and the solutions lay in politics. It was at that point that Johnson & Johnson started a movement to prepare some of its people for political action.

What happened at Republic Steel illustrates the next step—the step that took corporations into the study of political principle. Republic, about to set up a political-action training course, decided to run in advance a survey of its managerial brains. It found that 87 per cent of supervisors had no clear idea of what kind of government the U.S. Constitution sets up; 55 per cent didn't know how federal laws are passed; and 49 per cent couldn't explain why balanced federal budgets are important. The men surveyed could not have said what business wanted in politics or why it wanted it or how its objectives related to the society as a whole. In the face of such ignorance, apathy, and disconnection, any program of practical political action by business was doomed—even if the roster of American management had contained all the great political organizers from Julius Caesar to Sidney Hillman.

After pondering the survey, Republic turned for help not to practical politicians but to academic authorities on fundamental political ideas and institutions. A team of professors and others designed for Republic a course spanning the entire spectrum of political science and emphasizing such subjects as the federal constitutional system and the role of the Supreme Court. A group selected from Republic's staff, now taking special training, will in turn conduct the course for other employees.

In Mark Hanna's Golden Days. The question arises: How come business now has to squeeze its knees under the desks of the political first grade? For American businessmen were not always as threatened and bewildered lambs in the political arena. In Mark Hanna's golden days, business in politics spoke with confidence and, often, command. "The business interest," candidly so called, could be effectively and even ravenously pursued without much thought for the rules of the game. What changed? The briefest survey of the historic shift will explain why business is today developing an intense interest in the principles of political economy.

In its political heyday business overstepped boundaries deeply posted in public morality. Such conservatives as Theodore Roosevelt and Woodrow Wilson vigorously expressed reservations about the political activities of favor-seeking businessmen. The great depression exposed a long-growing weakness in business' public position. Businessmen had taken too much for granted the political and economic system in which they operated. They did not know enough or care enough about it, and they did not understand the extent to which it had been undermined by their enemies and by themselves. This accounts for the apparently incredible suddenness of the businessman's fall from public favor. To be sure, up to the New Deal, both major parties were glad to have business leaders publicly arrayed at their sides; as late as 1932, John Raskob, of du Pont and General Motors, was at home and welcome in Democratic politics. But within a few years the name of Pennsylvania's Joe Grundy, an honest and intelligent reactionary, had become a recognized liability to Republicans. In 1934, Walter Lippmann soberly wrote, "In the past five years the industrial and financial leaders of America have fallen from one of the highest positions of influence and power that they have ever occupied in our history, to one of the lowest." Under the circumstances, there was little wonder that young men entering business were thoroughly indoctrinated with the idea that "business and politics do not mix." And most of the subsequent efforts to mix them have turned out badly for business because it continued to underestimate the damage that had been done, in public opinion, to "the system."

Support of the principles of a free political economy had been so weakened that there was little resistance to a long series of "practical" expedients, which had the effect of altering the essential rules of the game. Farm subsidies were not proposals of doctrinaire Socialism; they merely seemed like a good idea at the time, a way of dealing with an enormous and urgent practical problem. But farm subsidies, as we now begin to see clearly, have deep and dangerous consequences in a free-market economy. It may be to the immediate interest of a given corporation that its farmer-customers have pockets full of government cash. The long-range effect on business of farm subsidies, however, is to undermine the free market and the economic-political complex of institutions bound up with it.

U.S. labor, the main emotional stimulus of business-in-politics, is not consciously against the system or even committed to a class struggle with management. Labor, nonetheless, manages to define its aims and establish its values to the extent it needs to do so. For labor is neither defending a system nor explicitly engaged in trying to establish an alternative. It is pursuing particular expedients, some of which may be and some of which may not be compatible with the needed ground rules of a free society. Should business follow suit and fight each issue on its narrow front? If it continues to do so, it will lose.

Foremost in realizing this has been General Electric's Cordiner. All the elements—passionate, practical, and rational—stimulated General Electric to its present position of leadership in the political resurgence of business. Labor pressure became so intense that G.E. saw that it touched fundamental aspects of the political economy. But G.E. spokesmen did not stop with dire warnings. They began to work on public problems, some not directly connected with General Electric. Testifying this year before a Senate committee, Cordiner opposed farm subsidies. His main reason throws much light on the new attitude of business. As a manufacturer, he could have adopted the classic stand that artificially high food prices raise labor costs and thereby hurt his competitive position in foreign markets. As a heavy corporate taxpayer, he could have argued that farm subsidies were unfair. He by-passed both these positions and attacked farm subsidies on the general ground that *all* peacetime subsidies are contrary "to the ideal of a free society" because they interfere with the proper working of a free market.

General Electric has shown that it continues to respect such principles even when they hurt. A recent corporate bulletin looks askance at too heavy federal expenditures for airports. The chief beneficiaries of such subsidies are the airlines—important customers of G.E. Cordiner understands that in the highly dangerous political climate of this generation the deeper long-range interests of any corporation may run counter to that corporation's immediate pocketbook interest.

A corporate self-denial of immediate interests, however, is not the way to resolve such a conflict. Cordiner and others in the van of the present movement seek a solution by connecting immediate, practical problems to their long-range concern for the health of the free society. . . .

Learning by Doing.   In terms of vote getting, all these practical political programs are probably not worth the effort that corporations are putting into them. Necessarily, many of the newly trained political missionaries are "preaching to the converted" in their own neighborhoods and country clubs. But the chief value of the programs is indirect. The clue to this value lies in the changes that have occurred in American management over the last two generations.

"Management" in the year 1900 was likely to mean the town's millowner, who was one of the four or five "leading citizens" of his community. In the normal course of his business and social life he knew the other leading citizens well, and was in contact with most of the twenty or thirty other influential men of the community's second echelon. Politics was part of the built-in agenda of his contacts. No problem of doorbell-ringing arose. Moreover, our millowner's business brought him into frequent touch with local, state, and national political issues and personalities.

Today the function of the millowner has been broken into ten, a hundred, a thousand parts. Most of these human atoms, who now form management, never come across a political problem in the normal course of their corporate work. The top executives, the corporate counsel, and the public-relations men, who have a regular contact with political problems, do not ordinarily transmit the results of their experiences to the engineers, accountants, and sales managers. The contrast with management in 1900 is twofold: (1) modern management does not usually form political convictions of depth and sophistication; (2) when it does, its channels of communicating these convictions to the rest of the community are not effective.

The present programs are an effort to compensate for these political disadvantages. New-style management now learns in seminars a part of what old-style management used to learn in bar and barbershop, at dinner tables of lawyers and editors, and on trips to Columbus or Harrisburg or Washington. Given the intensely pragmatic character of U.S. business, there was never any chance that training programs would stop with books and panel discussions. There had to be an effort to translate knowledge into action through calls on committeemen, fund raising, and candidacies for office. No doubt these activities can be readily satirized, but they are not essentially funny. Business is relearning politics in the way business generally learns—by doing.

Above the Power Struggle.   Similarly, the true value of public corporate pronouncements on political issues is more indirect than immediate. G.E.'s plant letters arguing against the union shop as an infringement of the freedom of workers probably do not convert any hard-bitten unionists. But consider the implications of the opposite course—refraining from an argument over the principles involved in a union shop. A management that refuses to grant a union shop appears to withhold something that "costs the corporation nothing." If it concedes a union shop, as many corporations did under government and public pressure during World War II, the corporation may find that it has contributed to the establishment of a climate of labor relations which can have quite serious practical consequences for business and for the whole society. Arguing the issue seriously in terms of principle, while it may make few immediate converts, does lift the question out of the context of a pure labor-management power struggle. Only by trying to associate such an issue with the logic of a free society can management hope to affect both the climate and—ultimately—the practicalities.

To date, the outstanding success of the new business interest in politics is its contribution to the present intense public awareness of how dangerous chronic inflation can be. Business opposition to inflation is as old as the Republic— indeed, it had a good deal to do with the birth of the Constitution. But anti-inflation sentiment among businessmen has not always been intense or whole-hearted. Debts, high inventories, and many another business situation can make a management yearn for inflationary deliverance. In the postwar years, manage-ments generally gave in to labor wage pressure and let prices rise accordingly. They accepted inflationary levels of government spending. In the past five years, however, this sloppy acquiescence has been replaced by a much firmer manage-ment realization that in the long run inflation is bad for business. The change did not come about by a series of practical demonstrations that inflation had hurt first corporation A, then B, then C. Businessmen were persuaded because they had been paying closer attention to the *general* consequences of inflation in a free society, with property as one of its essential pillars.

Pay-envelope Principles.   In such changes of climate, the work of the Com-mittee for Economic Development has been effective. Hundreds of influential businessmen were drawn into serious paper work and panel discussions. They produced reports and recommendations. Who was convinced? First of all, the business participants themselves. Men who had formerly paid careless lip service to such concepts as federal balanced budgets began to think of safeguards against inflation as being of great importance to their own business futures. This intensifi-cation of business emotion and extension of business knowledge about inflation was a major factor in a great shift in the public attitude toward the subject. President Eisenhower and his Secretaries of the Treasury would have been help-less in their efforts to hold the price line had it not been for the changed public climate. Steel management's public position in the 1959 strike would be quite impossible if the conflict had been seen as a simple power struggle. Millions of people understand now, as they did not a decade ago, that rapidly rising wages can hurt them by hurting the system in which they live.

For instance, David L. Harrington, board chairman of Reuben H. Donnelley Corp. and former president of the Illinois Chamber of Commerce, thinks he "has a responsibility to acquaint our (8,500) employees with the political-economic facts of life." A pay envelope in his company may contain a slip reading: "This paycheck can be used for the yearly premium on your life-insurance policy, which will cover the education of your children and the support of your widow. If inflation continues, in ten years you may need half again as many dollars to accomplish the same things."

Arguments such as this work because they are not based on the company's narrow interest against the individual interests of the workers. William T. Gossett, legal vice president of Ford Motor, has said: "The measure of (the corporation's) effectiveness in public affairs is the degree to which its policies reflect the values, objectives, aspirations, and reservations of society as a whole. If a corporation's policies are at odds with these, or seem to be, then no amount of money, technique, or protestation is likely to have the slightest public influence."

Banana Peels. To point out what a reawakened business interest in politics has done and to suggest the more important goals it may achieve is not to predict success for the present movement. The path before it is bright with banana peels.

Objections and warnings against the new approach come from many business-men. The lowest criticism is that of one unreconstructed Pittsburgher who, deploring ideology, says he still favors "the buy-partisan approach"—buy any politician who can be approached. At the other end of the scale, the highest line of criticism is exemplified by President George Romney of American Motors, who holds that "if we are to have a free society, the citizen must exercise his political rights directly, and not through his economic affiliation or interest—whether business or labor."

Such arguments as Romney's against a larger political role for corporations may stem from a mistaken belief that corporations play a less important role in American society than they do. To most Americans the corporation is a presence filling a large part of the social horizon. Because it looms so large, the corpora-tion, whether it is active or passive, will be assumed to be playing a political role. Political motives will be ascribed to it, and politicians will rise to power by interpreting or attacking those assumed motives, whether true or false. No corpo-ration can, in fact, today stay wholly detached from all-pervasive politics. If it is hurt directly by politics, it will intervene in self-defense—and such desperate intervention is likely to be clumsy, ineffective, and too late. The question really is whether corporate managements can learn to explain with their own voices their political motives and to argue about the terms and standards that will decide specific political issues.

The present movement is attracting some of the best management types, senior and junior. It is also attracting some "promoter" types, the parasites who think they can "sell free enterprise" like, say, lipstick. This is too bad because if these fleas on the program become too numerous, business may then feel it has to kill the dog.

The cry of "coercion" has already been raised against the new programs—and they will have to be guarded against this. Realistically, however, the chance that management today could politically coerce factory or clerical workers is exceedingly dim. In middle management the danger is not to the rights of individuals, but rather that political activity presents a specially attractive field of opportunity to yes-men who encumber the ranks of management.

In short, the possibilities are real and numerous that the new business interest in politics will do more harm than good. But it need not.

· ·

In a democratic society an election campaign can be either a circus, or a contest of personalities, or an educational institution to impart political fact and philosophy.

If a changed public climate requires candidates to argue immediate issues in terms of fundamental principle, then business will have advanced to a point where it can expect to win a much higher proportion of the practical political decisions than has been the case in the past. With luck and good management, the new interest of business in politics could help bring further into the light such issues as inflation, subsidies, the relation of free enterprise to foreign policy, and other current questions that cluster around the American conception of strong but limited government.

SUGGESTED READINGS

Bradford, R. F., "Politics, Pressure Groups and the Businessman," *Harvard Business Review* (November 1953). Former Governor of Massachusetts, the author speaks of the need for businesmen to be well versed in political maneuvering in order to avoid the "Government's Rolling Pin." Urges businessmen to learn to recognize and live with our American political institutions, such as pressure groups, the party system, lobbies, and so on.

Williams, G. Mennen, "Can Businessmen Be Democrats?" *Harvard Business Review* (March 1958). A businessman and one-time Democratic Governor of Michigan states that the Democratic party is not antibusiness and that businessmen should support it because it serves business better than does the Republican party.

PART IV

Business and
Its Environment
in the Future

CHAPTER 33

THE FUTURE

What will be the future shape of American business and its environment? "Past is prologue," says the historian, and by looking at the past and extending trends we may gain some reasonable estimate of the near future. History, however, never repeats itself exactly and trends have a habit of reversing themselves. Some forecasts do not depend on the examination of past trends but are made on the basis of current data. In the following discussion, we shall make use of both the past and the present in attempting to foretell the future.

BUSINESS IN THE FUTURE

We can safely say that there will be no dramatic changes in the nature of American business in the near future. There seems to be considerable stability in the present proportions of big, middle-sized, and small business. Although the manufacturing and distributive industries have experienced substantial changes in the past—developing from aggregations of many small firms to domination by a few large firms—this has not been so true of the extractive and service industries. Also, we should note that even though large firms dominate most fields of manufacturing and distribution, there seems to be considerable room in these industries for small and middle-sized firms. For example, in the automobile industry a number of niches are occupied by specialized firms supplying parts and services to the major manufacturers; too, some firms producing vehicles (such as the Jeep) in quantities not suited for mass production by major producers have found places on the fringe of the industry. If there is no substantial change in the relative proportions of firms of various sizes, then we may also expect to see little change in the relative proportions of corporations, partnerships, and proprietorships—in which case proprietorships would continue to far outnumber the other two forms that business firms normally take.

American corporations will continue to dominate the business scene. Although less than 10 per cent of firms take this form, the bulk of business done (as measured in sales) is accounted for by corporations and this proportion, though increasing very slowly, may be regarded as essentially constant. Salaried managers will increasingly be the chief executives of most corporations, but the fears of some of those concerned about the "managerial revolution" are unlikely to be realized. At one time, when it became quite obvious that paid managers were replacing owner-managers, some observers declared that salaried managers would concern themselves only with their own interests and neglect the interests of the shareholders. Although there have been some instances of this, for the most part "professional" managers have been quite sensitive to the continuing need for advancing the interests of owners of corporate stock and have been more sensitive to the needs of other parties with interests in corporate affairs than were the owner-managers of old. In 1941, when James P. Burnham wrote *The Managerial Revolution*,[1] he foresaw the development of a situation in which managers would move for government ownership of corporations on the grounds that only then would the

[1] (New York: John Day, 1941)

management be safe from uprisings of stockholders. No such movement
has taken place, possibly because managers realize that they would be
subject to greater control by a seemingly omnipresent bureaucracy than
they are by absentee shareholders. In any case, "managerialism" seems
to have worked well for stockholders and for others with legitimate interests in the affairs of corporate enterprises.

One recent trend in business that may continue into the near future is
the "merger movement." It has been under way since shortly after World
War II and seems to have enough momentum to continue for some time
into the future. In some cases, mergers have taken place between firms in
the same industry. This has been especially evident in banking and in the
railroad industry. However, a more important development has been the
acquisition by one corporation of a majority of the voting stock of another corporation in a different industry. This may be the result of recent
legislation prohibiting acquisition of corporations through stock purchases
or exchanges when the result would substantially lessen competition
(which inhibits mergers of major firms in the same industry), but it may
also suggest that some operating companies are gradually turning into
investment firms holding the stock of a number of diverse operating companies. However, this is really not a new development. Since the time of
John Jacob Astor, American businessmen and firms—after acquiring
wealth through operations in a single industry—have become investing
capitalists and investment companies with diverse holdings.

There will be some slight change in the industrial structure of America.
Productive resources (especially labor) will continue to be shifted out
of agriculture and some of the other extractive industries, such as coal-
mining. The service industries will continue to account for an increasing
proportion of the gross national product. Generally speaking, there are no
large unfilled gaps in the industrial structure and consequently there are
no great opportunities in business as there existed in the years before the
U.S. became a mature industrial nation. However, science, technology,
invention, and innovation will continue to create new business opportunities and industries. Perhaps they will not make such dramatic changes
in business as when television came along (years after U.S. economy was
declared "mature"), but there is no doubt that they will come—especially
from industries devoting substantial sums to research such as the aerospace, electronics, and chemicals industries.

Businessmen, too, are changing. For a number of years large and
middle-sized corporations have been hiring college graduates for various
positions, and the result has been the increasing "professionalization" of
business administration. Executive development programs have "re-
treaded" those without collegiate education in business administration,

thus reinforcing the effect of employing college men and women. As a professional attitude permeates business, we may expect to see business-men being more responsive and responsible, more effective and efficient.

THE FUTURE ECONOMIC ENVIRONMENT

There will be, of course, no end to economic change (barring a war or other catastrophe wiping out mankind). American businessmen will see new developments in product and resource markets, and will themselves adopt technological innovations having substantial economic impact. Some of the more important changes will take place in foreign and world markets as the nations of the world emerge from a period of protectionism and embrace policies providing for freer trade and greater international investment. One of the most perplexing economic problems of the future will be how to keep product markets expanding as rapidly as the pro-ductive capacity of America so as to provide relatively full employment of our productive resources—including labor.

Recently, the Twentieth Century Fund published a study in which it attempted to forecast economic change between 1962 and 1975. The con-clusions reached by this research organization were fairly optimistic. Gross national product in 1972 will be about 75 per cent more than in 1962 and will amount to approximately one trillion dollars. The rate of growth in real value of national output needed to attain that figure will be about 4.5 per cent per year (on the average) and although this is a higher rate than the growth rate of the recent past, it is not very much higher and cannot be labeled unrealistic. Thus the Fund does not see any substantial unemployment problem in the future; although both the labor force and labor productivity (as measured in terms of output per man-hour) will see substantial expansion, increases in total spending and a slight reduction in the workweek will keep unemployment down below 5 per cent of the labor force, and probably around 4 per cent.

Some interesting forecasts of spending by consumers, business buyers, governments, and foreigners were made in the study. Total expenditures for personal consumption will rise by a smaller proportion than GNP (about 65 per cent as compared to 75 per cent). Although per capita personal consumption spending is expected to increase at about the same dollar amount per year as it has since World War II, this really means that the rate of increase (in percentage terms) is decreasing. This, plus forecasts of changes in the number of consumers, leads to the con-clusion that consumer spending will not increase as rapidly as national output.

The nature of consumer spending will also change. We normally expect that as consumer incomes increase, a higher proportion will be spent on "luxuries" and a smaller percentage on "necessities." To some degree, this is true. Expenditures for food, liquor, and tobacco have been a declining percentage of total consumption expenditures for some years, and this tendency is expected to continue. Spending on clothing, accessories, and personal care has also been a decreasing share of total consumer spending. However, when we take a look at the third member of "food, clothing and shelter," we note an interesting development. Although spending on housing and utilities (as a percentage of total consumption expenditures) had been declining since early this century, in recent years there has been an upturn in such expenditures as well as in spending for household equipment and operation. Too, though it may be difficult to separate the part of transportation expense that is necessary from the part that is for pleasure, it is apparent that a higher proportion of consumer spending has been going into transporting persons and this trend, although leveling off somewhat, may be expected to continue for some time. Medical care and insurance ought, perhaps, to be regarded as necessities; they have accounted for expenditure of larger parts of the consumer's dollar in the recent past. Other expenditures have remained surprisingly constant, which means that changes in consumer spending have in large part taken place in categories that are to a large degree made up of necessities. Within these broad classes of consumer spending, important changes are taking place; limited space, however, does not permit detailed consideration of these changes.

If consumption expenditures will not increase as rapidly as gross national product, then at least one other kind of spending must be expected to increase at even a higher rate than will national output. In an earlier discussion of the major kinds of spending, we noted that in addition to spending on consumption, private domestic investment (including business spending on capital goods), government expenditures, and purchases by foreigners accounted for major shares of the total sales of the final products of the American economy. Although exports are expected to increase at a higher rate than in the past, the forecast is that the increase will be at about the same percentage rate as the increase in GNP. Thus only two categories of spending are left—private investment and government expenditures—both of which are expected to increase more rapidly than will the growth in national product. By the end of 1975, the Fund estimates that both kinds of spending will be about double what they were in 1962 (assuming no price changes).

Perhaps businessmen will regard the increase in investment more favorably than they will the projected growth in government spending, which to some is wasteful and an adverse reflection on the ability of a private economy to be self-sustaining. Private investment in plant and equipment is expected to be about 104 per cent more than the 1962 figure of $49 billion (that is, approximately $100 billion), and it is anticipated that government spending will increase to $225 billion, just about double the 1962 amount. The accuracy of the forecasted level of GNP depends rather heavily on the accuracy of the estimate of business investment spending; the economists of the Fund have said that such spending will be at an appreciably higher rate between 1962 and 1975 than it was during the fifties and the early part of this decade. However, data on purchases of plant and equipment since 1962 suggest that the forecast of increased levels of expenditure may be quite realistic.

There will be some changes in resource markets as well as in product markets. One of the most noteworthy will be the change taking place in raw materials markets. For many years, many American business firms have benefited from the generous natural endowments of the U.S. Although we have lacked some important natural resources, in large part the nation has been self-sufficient. This is now changing. Business demands for raw materials are continuing to expand as gross national product expands, with the result that some extractive inputs are more difficult to secure from domestic sources. Although we shall continue to rely mainly on supplies of raw materials found in the U.S., there will be an expansion of imports from other countries having a relative abundance of natural resources. Actually such a movement has been under way for some time, with crude oil and iron ore being imported in ever-larger quantities to satisfy the demand of domestic manufacturers for high-grade, low-cost raw materials. As might be expected, such imports have come, and will continue to come, from those nations that have not developed substantial manufacturing industries of their own—that is, from the "underdeveloped" countries in South America, Asia, and Africa.

The "population explosion" since World War II will result in a great increase in the number of "sellers" in labor markets. Presently, the labor force is about 75 million, and it is expected to be over 90 million in 1975 —an increase of more than 20 per cent. How much of the labor force will be employed and what kinds of workers will be hired will depend, of course, on the demands of the employers. Some forecasters doubt the ability of business to absorb such a substantial growth in the numbers of those looking for employment, and expect that government—especially the federal government—will be embarking on programs to alleviate unemployment problems. Concern with possible substantial unemployment stems in part from technological changes that have enabled extractive and manufacturing industries to substitute equipment for labor and that have in many cases made certain production processes almost wholly automatic. The increased pace of automation has led to a situation in which there has been an absolute as well as a relative reduction in the number of blue-collar workers. Business will continue to demand more and more highly skilled, technically trained persons (who will apparently be in ample supply because of changes in education and of the increase in population). Wages will continue to rise, although perhaps at a lower rate. With international competition among industrial nations becoming more important, relatively high wage rates in the U.S. have put American producers at a disadvantage. Greater attempts will be made to keep wage increases tied to increases in productivity, and may have greater success as the power of labor unions declines.

In the money markets, there seem to be no prospects for great change. If anything, there will be more money available in such markets, which may reduce the cost (that is, a lower interest rate might prevail) or make it possible to secure money more readily. There are some observers who feel that credit will be too easy to secure by everyone and that competition among the lenders will lead to an unhealthy financial situation in the money markets. At any rate, there seems to be no prospective shortage of money.

Another basic assumption of the Twentieth Century Fund forecast is that there will be no major depression between 1962 and 1975. This may not have much meaning for present-day college students, for the last great downturn in output, employment, and income took place in the 1930's. Since World War II, we have had brief periods of recession. However, the magnitude of the recent dips in production and employment has been much less than that of the Great Depression—for example, strong concern is expressed whenever unemployment is more than 5 per cent of the labor force; in the 1930's, more than 25 per cent of those willing and able to work were unable to secure employment. Employment opportunities were not available because business firms suffered drastic decreases in sales and cut back their output and payroll accordingly. Business failures were very common and a financial panic existed in the early part of the "depression decade" when it was evident that a large number of banks were not going to be able to meet the demands of their depositors. Although banks still fail, the failure rate is at its lowest level in U.S. national history.

Why do forecasters generally discount the probability of another great depression occurring? Mainly because both government and business take measures to prevent its occurrence, or at least to "dampen" extreme fluctuations in economic activity. Beginning in the New Deal period, the national government has employed fiscal policy (in addition to the monetary measures that had been previously used) in order to maintain a sufficiently high level of total spending—that is, the federal government deliberately spent more than it received in revenues so that the total of consumer, business, and government spending would be high enough to maintain a satisfactory level of output and employment. Both major political parties are now committed to such a policy, and this militates against a long and deep depression such as occurred in the 1930's. Laws have been adopted—such as those providing for unemployment insurance—which act as "automatic stabilizers" by helping to maintain the level of consumer spending. A host of other federal statutes also aim at the prevention of depression. Businessmen themselves have been concerned with business policies that might be adopted to stabilize the economy. To the extent that businessmen have adopted counterdepression policies, and they have done so to an appreciable and growing degree, this reinforces government action. Actually, the policies adopted by both government and business are countercyclical rather than just counterdepression. There are some reasonable grounds for believing that periods of booming business activity lead to economic decline; thus policies are aimed at discouraging "booms" as well as preventing "busts."

The major problem confronting the American economy, according to a number of economists, is how to maintain economic growth without inflation. Makers of public and business policy do not lack for good advice on how to solve this problem, but their ability or their willingness to follow such advice is not certain. In terms of priorities, both government and business put growth ahead of stabilization of prices. In recent years, prices have been increasing on an average of about 1½ per cent per annum, and there is little likelihood that this rate will be reduced substantially or that inflation will be eliminated. With business accounting practices being what they are, price increases create illusory profits, which perhaps encourage businessmen to make decisions not warranted by the true state of affairs (although it has been pointed out that this effect might not be undesirable because it leads to business expansion). The federal government's ability to prevent inflation without inhibiting economic growth is not very great, although spokesmen for the national government urge business, labor, and other economic classes to refrain from raising prices or from taking action (such as demanding excessive wage increases) that will lead to higher prices. In 1962, the Kennedy administration took strong action against the steel industry when it raised prices after a noninflationary wage agreement was signed with the steel union, but the effects of such unusual action were apparently only temporary. The problem of inflation (although perhaps not as great as that of depression) will continue to exist, and businessmen will have to continue making adjustments to upward-creeping prices in the foreseeable future.

FUTURE AMERICAN SOCIETY

It is not our purpose here to examine all prospective changes in American society. Throughout this volume, we have concerned ourselves essentially with society as it confronts the business firm—that is, with those classes of individuals and groups having some relationship with and influence upon business. The firm has important relations with customers, suppliers of various resources, competitors, trade associations, general business organizations, community organizations, and government. It would be difficult to forecast accurately how all of these will act in the future, but there seem to be discernible outlines of the prospective nature of consumer activity, unions, farm groups, and government.

The consumers' movement continues to grow. Legislation on both state and national levels testifies to the consumer interest in "truth-in-lending" and "truth-in-packaging" laws. States are continuing to establish special agencies to protect the interests of the consumer, although the federal government has not yet created a Department of the Consumer; however, pressure for a Department of Urban Affairs may soon result in a cabinet department having jurisdiction over federal agencies presently concerned with protection of the interests of the domestic consumer). Consumer political influence will probably increase as a consequence of the formation of new alliances. In the past, farmers have tried to secure higher prices for farm products by a variety of group efforts and workers have joined unions to gain increased wages. Both of these classes are losing their power to secure higher prices and wages and will likely become even more involved in the consumer movement than they have been in the past. Although consumer political action will be important, there will continue to be some growth in consumer cooperatives as a means of keeping prices relatively low. In some countries, such organizations account for a much larger part of economic activity than they do in the United States, and it is reasonable to expect some growth in our future.

Unions, as we have suggested, might be expected to lose some of their present influence. This conclusion rests on something more than the fact that in recent years the total number of union members has not increased appreciably, and even appears to have declined somewhat. Throughout the history of American labor, there have been a number of stages of union decline that preceded substantial gains in union membership. However, this time there does not seem to be much prospect of great increases in the ranks of organized labor. The blue-collar worker has been easiest to organize, and he is rapidly becoming of minor importance in the labor force. White-collar workers are more difficult to organize into unions, as are women (who are also becoming a larger part of the work force). Some observers see few, if any, new fields for labor organizations to bring under their jurisdiction and conclude, therefore, that labor unions may have hit their peak in membership.

In addition to losing numerical strength, unions are losing the favor of the public, and perhaps as a consequence, are losing struggles in the political arena. Recent public opinion polls have shown that the public generally feels that "big labor" is a bigger problem than "big business" or "big government." Revelations of wrongdoing by union leaders, unrealistic demands by unions, and the tying up of the economy over issues that strike no responsive chord in the public generally have caused unions to lose public favor. Since World War II, both Congress and state legislatures have passed laws restricting the legitimate activities of unions. Although such legislation may reflect the political power of farmers and other businessmen rather than that of the general public, there is no denying that the effect of such statutes has been to reduce the kinds of actions that unions may legally take. Even Democratic national administrations— friendly toward unions since Woodrow Wilson—have taken action that some unions have regarded as unfriendly (as in the case of the Teamsters' Union and those railroad unions engaged in "featherbedding" practices). As a result of their decline in power, unions can be expected to be more "reasonable" in the future.

Farmers, too, will not have the influence in the future they have had in the past. In part, this is due to the fact that the number of farmers is also decreasing. Technological innovations have made it possible for fewer farmers to grow more food, feed, and fibers. Although cooperative economic activity by agricultural producers will continue to be of importance and may keep the prices of some farm products high, the political power of the farmer is declining. As the number of farmers declines, the "farm vote" will be less important and fewer political concessions will be made to the agriculturalists. In the past, although declining in numbers, farmers were able to maintain considerable political strength by maintaining systems of representation in Congress and in state legislatures that gave those in rural areas a more-than-proportionate voice in determining who went to the state or national legislature. Ironically, farm groups pressed for direct election of U.S. senators as a means of increasing their political influence, but found that taking the appointment of senators out of the hands of state legislatures resulted in greater urban influence in the Senate than would be true if farmer-dominated legislatures named representatives of the states in Congress. Periodic redistricting of the House of Representatives also has reduced farmer influence. Recent Supreme Court decisions have invalidated the systems that a number of states have been using to give greater representation to farmers in state legislatures, and it appears that eventually state legislative districts will be established primarily on the basis of population. With the decline in political power of the farmer may come the fall of price-support systems, abolition of exemption of farm groups from some of the antimonopoly laws, and the repeal of other legislation that has helped to keep farm prices high and to keep low the prices of the products that farmers buy.

The heyday of the radical farm group, strongly "antimonoply," seems to be past. Both the National Grange and the Farm Bureau Federation are now quite conservative; the Farmers' Union is not, but occupies a relatively minor position among farm organizations (and even it is "mellowing" somewhat). As these groups have become more aware of the interdependence between agriculture and other business enterprise, they have been less hostile in their actions.

FUTURE POLITICAL ENVIRONMENT

Government, as it confronts the American businessman, will be increasingly complex but more benign. As we have noted, American government—conceived of as laws, agencies, and officials—reflects the political influence of various individuals and groups in society. In the past, those in both labor and agriculture have taken hostile political action toward certain industries and business generally. As these two major classes lose political power, their ability to influence business adversely will decline. It is doubtful that any new antibusiness class will replace them. There are, of course, the occupants of official regulatory positions created in the days when there was greater suspicion of business by politically powerful groups. However, their power to influence legislation is limited and it is likely that the bureaucracy will be unable to swim against the political tide. That tide seems to be running in favor of business, not so much because businessmen have greatly expanded their political activity (although they have) as because others with political influence have seen their dependence on the successful operation of American business. Perhaps the celebrated statement "What is good for General Motors is good for the country!" has considerable merit, at least for those employees, suppliers, dealers, communities, stockholders, and others having some interdependent relationship with G.M.

There is considerable evidence that American governments are attempting to create a more favorable environment for business firms. Revisions in tax laws have been made recently to increase the profitability of business, and such changes are likely to continue. Although considerable regulatory legislation is on the statute books, those in regulatory agencies have become (to the distress of some of their critics) more aware of the problems of business and have on a number of occasions acted as though their mission is to aid business rather than to regulate it. Government competition with business is declining in many industries and governments are stepping up their purchases from private business enterprise. Various measures for the direct promotion of business continue to be taken by the agencies and officials of national, state, and local government. Almost nowhere is hostility to be noted.

The only dark clouds on the political horizon are in the area of foreign and international government. As the United States increasingly finds itself in the position of the other major industrial nations of the world of not having sufficient raw materials for its economic machine nor large enough markets to absorb all of its production, it must go abroad for resources and markets. However, the day of colonialism by capitalistic countries is about over and the governments of the nations that were formerly colonies are frequently immature, unstable, or both. Consequently, their actions are often contrary to the interests of American firms doing business abroad (and possibly contrary to the best long-run interests of the nation whose officials are taking such action). It is likely that maturity and stability will eventually develop, but in the meantime those firms engaged in business in other countries must expect occasional disruptions of their activity by agencies and officials of foreign governments.

International government poses somewhat different problems than do foreign governments. World government is unlikely, and thus American businessmen will be governed only by those international agreements and agencies the federal government is willing to support. Only those will be supported that seem to be in the "national interest," including, normally, the interest of our nation's business firms. Since it seems to be the attitude of the federal government to support international agreements and agencies that are engaging in promoting international trade, some American industries will prosper and some will suffer (although, on balance, more gain than loss should be had). The United Nations is likely—so long as it retains its present form—to be increasingly uninfluential. Its General Assembly is badly in need of "redistricting according to population," and the industrial nations do not have influence proportionate to their importance and will consequently not accede in economic matters to those numerous small nations that now dominate the General Assembly. However, other agencies of international government will become of increasing importance as the U.S. enters into additional international agreements.

THE FAVORABLE FUTURE

In short, the future for American business looks good. This too is a conclusion to which the study of history leads. Consider the environment of the businessman in the early colonial period: abundant natural resources, but scarcities of capital and labor; no well-developed money, labor, or commodity markets; lack of adequate current knowledge of overseas markets, and domestic markets not large enough to support any but small-sized business; poor transportation along with poor communication; poor government, including the lack of adequate currency of stable value; no banking system providing checks as a medium of exchange—the list is long. Since the beginning of business in what is now the United States the environment of business has improved, mainly because of the economic, social, and political activities of businessmen themselves. Businesses still fail, of course, but not so much because the environment is unfavorable. Rather, it is because of poor management, which in large part means not understanding the nature of the environment and not taking the proper measures to come to terms with it. Collegiate education in business administration aims at providing future businessmen with the necessary understandings and with the means for coming to successful terms with the economic, social, and political environment of the business firm. This volume aims at establishing the nature of that environment and leaves to other studies the acquisition of those skills and attitudes necessary for effective adaptation to or influencing of those forces external to the firm that shape it and determine its future.

SUGGESTED READINGS

Anshen, Melvin, and George L. Bach, eds., *Management and Corporations, 1985* (New York: McGraw-Hill, 1960). Fifteen leaders from business, government, universities, law, and religion discuss the problems that will face the modern corporation before 1985.

Barach, Arnold R., *U.S.A. and Its Economic Future* (New York: Macmillan, 1964). An updated Twentieth Century Fund survey based on *America's Needs and Resources: A New Survey* written in 1955 by J. Frederic Dewhurst and associates. Past economic developments are traced and projected up to 1975.

Gainsburgh, Martin R., *American Enterprise: The Next Ten Years* (New York: Macmillan, 1961). The edited proceedings of the 44th annual meeting of the National Industrial Conference Board dealing with the international outlook for business, domestic markets, technological change and its potential impact, and on the prospects of financing continuing economic growth.

Safire, William, *The Relations Explosion* (New York: Macmillan, 1963). Building upon some empirical findings, the author describes the corporation of tomorrow and its public relations.

Index

Administrative decision-making, 553–56
Administrative investigation, 553–55
Administrative law, 476
Administrative officials, and business, 440–41
Administrative process, and business, 615
Administrative rule, defined, 552
Administrative rule-making, 551–53
Administrative sanctions, 557–59
African markets, 169–70
Agricultural price-supports, 307–308
Agricultural products, suppliers of, 305–308

Agriculture Department, and business, 498–99
American business
development of, 23–31
nature of, 9–11
American business system, 91–92
American capitalism, ideologies of, 95–100
American courts, 571–76
American economic system, 84–91
American economy, structure of, 92–95
American Federation of Labor (AFL), 272–73, 276–78, 282

647

American Federation if Labor–Congress of Industrial Organizations (AFL-CIO), 272–74, 278, 281–82
American industries
classifications of, 67–76
development of, 66–67
Standard Industrial Classification, 76–78
American legislatures, 590–95
American national character, nature of, 235
American products, development of overseas markets for, 158–59
American society
class nature of, 223–25
group nature of, 225–26
national character, 223
nature of, 222–26
views of some philosophers, 222–23
American unions
future of, 278–82
history of, 274–78
Analytical framework, as a determinant of opinion, 381–82
Appellate jurisdiction, courts of, 576
Articles of Confederation, 491
Asian markets, 169
Attitudes
cultural determinants of, 383–84
defined, 382
determinants of, 383–86
personal determinants of, 385–86
social determinants of, 384–85

Better Business Bureaus, 348–49
Big business, *Look* poll on, 378–79
Bourgeois and proletarians, 114–17
Business
and the administrative process, 561–69
and the courts, 583–87
as an activity, 9
as a system of firms, 91–92
as a system of industries, 92
development of, 20–23
in colonial America, 24–25
in the future, 634–36
in the new nation, 26–27
purchases by, 125–26
since 1930, 30–31
Business behavior
business historian's view, 6
businessman's view, 8–9
economist's view, 5–6
popular view, 4
views of, 4–9
views of administrative scientists, 8
views of behavioral scientists, 7

views of other social scientists, 7
Business buyers
behavior of, 250–52
motives of, 249–50
Business credit, development of, 90–91
Business customers, 248–52
Business environment, defined, 11–12
Business establishment, 10
Business ethics, 413–19
Business Ethics Advisory Council, 418–19
Business image
and business professors, 400–401
and cartoonists, 404–405
and college education, 398–401
and economists, 399–400
and government, 405–406
and historians, 399
and novelists, 403
and playwrights, 403–404
and public education, 398
and religious education, 401–402
and unions, 405
and writers, 402–404
and writers of fiction, 403–404
and writers of nonfiction, 404
business as a creator of, 406
cultural heritage and the, 407–11
defined, 377
Business institutions, development of American, 88–91
Business responsibilities
any beyond profits? 423–30
effect of others on discharge of, 420–21
lack of authority to discharge, 420
lack of power to discharge, 419–20
Business sector, defined, 93
Business system, 11
Business unionism, 266–67
Business units, kinds of, 10–11

Cabinet departments, development of, 493–94
Canadian market, 167–68
Capital goods, defined, 149
Capital goods markets, 149–50
Capitalism
classical ideology of, 96
export ideology of, 99–100
ideology of countervailing power, 97–98
ideology of people's, 98–99
managerial ideology of, 96–97
Central American Common Market, 540
Chambers of commerce
in general, 340–46

local, 341–44
state, 344
Christian ethics, and business, 413–14
Churches, and business, 364–65
City government, 518–19
Class struggle, 235–37
Collectional economy, 19–20
College professors, and business, 362
Colleges, and business, 361–62
Commerce Department, and business, 499
Commercial law, 480–81
Committee for Economic Development (CED), 96, 347–48, 353–54
Committee for Industrial Organization, 277
Commodity exchanges, 147–49
Common law, 476–77
Common markets, 538–40
Communist Manifesto, 113–19
Communist Party, in relation to other opposition parties, 119
Community
defined, 355
development of, 355–56
group nature of, 357–58
nature of, 356–58
social classes in, 356–57
Community action, businessman's role in, 367–76
Community chests, and business, 359–60
Community groups
educational organizations, 360–63
religious and moral organizations, 363–66
Community organizations
civic, health, and welfare, 358–60
service clubs, 358–59
Community wants, 356
Competition, nature of, 326–28
Competition with business
by cooperatives, 322–23
by foreign governments, 534
by local government, 521–22
by states, 517
Competitive markets, defined, 129
Competitors
classes of, 320–21
cooperation among, 322, 328–32
defined, 319–20
foreign, 325–26
governments as, 323–24
private business firms as, 320–22
Conflict
undesirability of, 227
ways of avoiding, 227–28
Congress, 591–93

Congressional powers; *see* U.S. Constitution, powers of Congress
Congress of Industrial Organizations (CIO), 272–73, 277–78, 282
Consumer boycotts, 246
Consumer motivation, 243–44
Consumer organizations
consumer cooperatives, 245
information and education groups, 245–46
in general, 244–48
Consumer political action, 246–48
Consumers' goods industry, defined, 75
Consumers, purchases by, 125
Consumers' Union, 245–46, 254–61, 562
Contract law, 479
Cooperative marketing, by farmers, 305–307
Cooperatives
consumer-owned, 323
producer-owned, 323
Cooperativism
in England, 110
in general, 110–11
in Sweden, 111
"Corporate Democracy," 291–93
Corporations, 52–54, 89
County government, 518
Court power
in general, 576–80
to compel specific performance, 578
to invalidate legislation, 579–80
to issue injunctions, 578
to issue orders, 577–78
to issue orders to pay money, 577–78
to make binding decisions, 576–77
to revise administrative decisions, 579
Court procedures, 580–83
Courts, and the administrative process, 559–61
Creditors
activities of, 286–88
in general, 285–88
objectives of, 286
resources of, 286–88
Crude oil, controlling the flood of, 80–81
Crude oil market, Standard Oil and the, 152–56
Cultural nomadic economy, 20
Currency, business-issue, 90
Currency and credit, development of, 89–91

Defense Department, and business, 494
Department of Health, Education and Welfare, and business, 500
Domestic consumers, 243–48

Durable goods, sales of, 123–24

Economic action, 230–31
Economic environment
   coming to terms with changing, 189–90
   in the future, 636–40
   of business, 12–13
Economic growth
   defined, 212
   factors affecting, 214–15
   importance of, 215
   in America, 211–18
   recent record of, 214
Economic institutions
   American, 84–87
   development of American, 87–88
Economic motivation, institution of, 86
Economic organizations
   cooperative associations, 41
   families, clans and tribes, 40–41
   governmental enterprises, 41–42
   modern business firms, 42–57
Economic responsibilities of business
   beating the Communists, 208–209
   making profits, 202
   preserving economic stability, 205–206
   preserving free market institutions, 205
   preserving growing economy, 207–208
   preserving high output and employment, 206–207
   solving the balance-of-payments problem, 209–10
   toward others in markets, 202–205
   what _are_ they? 210–11
Educational action, 232
Educators, and business, 398–402
Elective process, and business, 614
Employee organizations, 265–74
Employers' associations, 331–32, 346
English colonies, founding of, 31–37
Entrepreneur, 10
Environment, defined, 11
Environment of business
   coming to terms with, 15–16
   favorable future, 644–45
   nature of, 11–15
Ethical codes
   adopted by business, 416–17
   established by government, 417–18
European Common Market, 538–39, 545–49
European Economic Community; _see_ European Common Market
European Free Trade Association, 539–40
European markets, 166–67
Exchange, development of, 19–20

Expropriation of business, by foreign governments, 534–35
Extractive products suppliers, other than farmers, 308

Fascism, 112–13
Federal bureaucracy, development of, 492–503
Federal courts, 574–75
Federal government
   development of power of, 491–92
   independent agencies of, 501–503
   independent regulatory commissions of, 503–506
Federation of Organized Trades and Labor Unions, 276
"Fierce Competitors," 320–22
Financial capitalism, 285, 294
Financial capitalist, 22–23
Firm
   essential nature of, 42
   theory of, 45–51
Firms
   forms of, 51–54
   functions of, 54–57
   goal attainment by, 45
   objectives of, 43–45
Food and Agriculture Organization, 537
Foreign and world markets, present importance of, 160–61
Foreign buyers, purchases by, 127
Foreign government, and American business, 532–35
Foreign markets
   importance of, 165–70
   in general, 163–64
Foreign productive resources, historical importance of, 159–60
Free markets, institution of, 86–87

General Agreement on Tariffs and Trade, 541–42
Giant business, growth of, 27–30
Government
   commercial relations with business, 438
   competition with business, 438–39
   promotion of business, 436–37
   purchases from business, 126–27
   regulation of business, 437–38
   relations with business, 436–39
   taxation of business, 437
Government customers, 252–54
Government officials, 439–42
Governmental laws
   classified according to who writes the laws, 475–78
   in general, 475–86

Granger movement, 314
"Group mind," 387–88

High school students, poll of, 389–93
Household enterprises, 40
Human needs, 264
Human wants
  nature of, 18
  satisfaction of, 18–19

Idealist political theory, 445–46
Individual freedom, institution of, 87
Individual opinion, bases of, 380–86
Individualistic ethic, and business, 414–
  15
Industrial capitalist, 22
Industrial Workers of the World, 277
Industries; *see also* American industries
  classified by number of firms, 73–75
  classified by type of utility created, 73
  economists' classifications of, 70–75
  government classifications of, 70
  other classifications of, 75–76
  Standard Industrial Classification of,
    76–78
Industry, as a business unit, 10
Information, as a basis of opinion, 381–82
Information campaigns, 386–87
Institutional advertising, 387
Institution, defined, 11
Intellectuals
  and business, 395–97
  defined, 395
Interindustry relationships, 71
Interior Department, and business, 497–
  98
International Bank for Reconstruction
  and Development, 537–38
International Chamber of Commerce,
  345–46
International commodity agreements,
  542–44
International government
  and American business, 535–44
  defined, 536
International Industrial Assembly of
  North America, 275
International Labor Organization, 537
International Monetary Fund, 538
International Trade Organization, 541–42
International treaties, 477–78
Investors League, 295
Invisible imports, 173–74

Joint-stock company, defined, 52
Judicial enforcement, 559
Judicial officials, and business, 442

Judicial process, and business, 615–16
Judicial review, 559–61
Justice Department, and business, 495–96

Knights of Labor, 276

Labor
  classes of, 263
  defined, 144
Labor Department, and business, 499–
  500
Labor markets, 144–47
Latin American Free Trade Association,
  540
Latin American markets, 168–69
Law, defined, 472
Laws
  classified, 473–75
  classified according to influence on
    business, 481
Legal action, 231
Legislative officials, and business, 441
Legislative process
  and business, 604, 614–15
  committee hearings, 598–601
  committee reporting of bill, 601
  conference committee action, 602–603
  consideration of bill by House, 602
  debate by Senate, 601–602
  in general, 441, 596–604
  introduction of a bill, 597
  President's veto, 603–604
  referral of bills to committee, 597–98
Loanable funds, markets for, 143–44
Lobbying, 595–96, 605–10
Lobbyists, 595–96
Local government, and business, 517–22
Local legislative bodies, 595
Local markets, defined, 121

Managerial capitalism, 285
Managerial class, 23
Managerial motivation, 43–44
Manufacturers' associations, 346–47
Market, defined, 121
Market changes
  capital goods markets, 186–87
  causes of, 187–89
  cyclical, 182
  erratic, 183
  historical charts of, 184, 190–200
  labor markets, 185–86
  length of, 182–83
  money markets, 186
  nature of, 180–87
  product markets, 183–85
  raw materials markets, 187

Market changes (*Cont.*)
   resulting from changes in those influ-
     encing markets, 189
   resulting from changing income and
     tastes, 188–89
   resulting from changing technology,
     188
   seasonal variations, 182
   secular trends, 182
Marketing, defined, 54–55
Markets
   general theory of, 129–30
   in general, 121–22
   tendencies in, 183–87
   theories of, 127–30
   traditional economic theory of, 127
Maxims of equity, 478–79
Mechanics' Union of Trade Associations,
   274
Mercantile capitalist, 22
Money, defined, 140
Money markets, 140–44
Monopoly markets, defined, 129
Moral groups, and business, 365–66
Moral laws, 473
Munn v. Illinois (1877), 522–24

National Association of Manufacturers
   (NAM), 96, 332, 347–48, 352–53,
   401, 417
National Board of Trade, 341
National capitalism, 285
National Chamber of Commerce; *see* U.S.
   Chamber of Commerce
National character, and the historians,
   233–34
National Labor Union, 275–76
National markets, defined, 122
National Trades' Union, 275
Natural law, 473–74
Nebbia v. New York (1934), 524–29
Nondurable goods, sales of, 124

Oil industry, continuing problems of, 79–
   81
Organization for Economic Cooperation
   and Development, 540–41
Original jurisdiction, courts of, 576
Other economic systems, significance of,
   113
Over-the-counter market, 142–43
Owners
   in general, 288–95
   objectives of, 289–90

Partnership, defined, 52
Partnerships, 41

Parts suppliers, 309
People's Party, political platform of, 314–
   18
Petroleum industry
   in general, 78–82
   technological developments in, 81–82
Petroleum, in the U.S. economy, 78–79
Petroleum products, markets for, 132–37
Petty capitalists, 21
Plymouth Plantation, Articles of Agreement of, 37
Political action, 231
Political activity of business
   history of, 612–13
   in general, 612–16, 622–30
Political environment
   in general, 14–15
   in the future, 643–44
Political parties, 443
Political process, 442–43, 447–51
Political responsibilities of business
   in general, 616–22
   views of business, 619–20
   views of government officials, 619
   views of political philosophers, 616–
     17
   views of politicians, 618–19
   what *are* they? 620–22
Political theories, 443–46
Political unionism, 267
Populists, 314
Positive law, 474
Post Office Department, and business,
   496–97
Pre-industrial economies, 103–104
Private enterprise, 40–41
Private law, 479–81
Private property, institution of, 85–86
Producers' goods industries, defined, 75
Product markets, 122–27
   buyers in, 124–27
   history of, 130–32
Production, defined, 54
Productive resources, defined, 140
Professional manager, 10
Profit motive, 43
Profits, *Fortune* poll on, 378
Proletarians and Communists, 117–19
Promotion of business
   by foreign governments, 532–33
   by local governments, 520–21
   by states, 514–16
Proprietorship, defined, 51
Public law, 479
Public opinion
   changing unfavorable, 386–89
   of business, 378–79

Public opinion polling, problems in, 379–80

Public relations
defined, 421
history of, 421–23

Public relations movement, 421–23
Public schools, and business, 361
Purchases from business
by foreign governments, 535
by states, 516

Quo warranto, defined, 578

Rationalist political theory, 445
Raw materials, defined, 147
Raw materials markets, 147–49
Raw materials suppliers, 304–309
extractive producers, 305–308
other than extractive producers, 308–309

Realist political theory, 443–45
Reciprocity, 250–51
Recreational groups, and business, 366
Reform unionism, 267
Regional markets, defined, 121–22
Regulation of business
by foreign governments, 533
by local governments, 519–20
by states, 511–14

Regulatory laws, 481–86
and classes of "legal law," 485–86
common-law regulations, 481–83
statutory regulations, 483–85

Resources, defined, 140
Responsible business behavior, difficulty of, 419–21
Rules of law, 478–79

Sales to business
by foreign governments, 535
by states, 516

Sanction, defined, 557
Scholars, and business, 398–402
Securities exchanges, 141–42
Self-serving ethics, 416
Services, sales of, 124
Settled village economy, 20, 103–104
Social action, kinds of, 230–32
Social class
in America, 237–40
Marxist view of, 223–24
sociologists' view of, 224–25

Social environment
coming to terms with, 228–30
individuals and groups in, 226–27
of business, 13–14
in the future, 640–43

Social ethic, and business, 415–16
Socialism, 104–110
in Great Britain, 108–10
in the Soviet Union, 106–108

Society, firm's relations with, 227–28
Special districts, 519
Standard Oil Company (New Jersey)
annual meeting of, 295–301
early history and environment of, 57–63

Standard Oil Company (New Jersey), *et al.* v. the United States (1911), 486–89

Standard Oil Trust, 79–80
State agencies and officials, 510–17
State courts, 572–73
State Department, and business, 495
State legislatures, 593–95
State powers, 508–10
development of, 508
police power, 510
power to incorporate, 509–10
tax power, 510

Stockholders
activities of, 290–95
big individual, 290–91
representatives of, 293–95
resources of, 290–95
small but docile, 293
small but vocal, 291–93

Summary powers, 558–59
Suppliers
of goods for resale, 309–14
manufacturers, 310–12
wholesalers, 313
of labor and services, classes of, 263
of parts, 309
of raw materials, 304–19

Supporting functions, defined, 55–56

Taxation of business
by foreign governments, 534
by local governments, 521
by states, 516

Torts, 479–80
Total sales by business, changes in, 178–80
Trade associations, 328–30
activities of, 332–37
Treasury Department, and business, 494–95

Union-management cooperation, 269–70
Unions
actions of, 268–70
city central labor, 272
classified by objectives, 266–68

Unions (*Cont.*)
  craft, 270
  economic activities of, 268–69
  educational activities of, 269
  federations of, 272–74
  industrial, 270
  joint boards of, 270–72
  jurisdictional disputes of, 269
  local, 270–72
  national, 270–72
  political activities of, 269
  resources of, 268
  structure of, 270–74
United Nations
  and American business, 536–38
  Economic and Social Council, 536–37
United Shareholders of America, 295
U.S. Chamber of Commerce, 96, 341,
    344–45, 347–48, 350–52
  poll of high-school students, 389–93
U.S. Constitution
  development of, 466
  development of federal government's
    power under, 491–92
  excerpts from, 467–70
  implementation of, 465–66
  important amendments to, 463–65
    "Bill of Rights," 463–64
    Eighteenth Amendment, 465
    Seventeenth Amendment, 464–65
  origin of, 454–55
  powers of Congress under, 455–61
    tax power, 455–56
    to borrow money, 456
    to coin money and regulate its value,
      457–58
    to establish post offices and post
      roads, 459

    to establish uniform laws on bank-
      ruptcies, 457
    to fix the standard of weights and
      measures, 459
    to grant patents and copyrights, 459–
      60
    to provide for the "common de-
      fence," 460–61
    to regulate commerce, 456–57
  prohibitions on state action, 462–63
  provisions important to business, 455–
    65
  restrictions on Congressional power
    on power to prohibit slave trade, 461
    on tax power, 461–62
    on the commerce power, 462
    restrictions on state powers, 522–29
U.S. imports, 171–74
U.S. investment abroad, 174–75

Virginia
  First Charter of, 32–34
  Second Charter of, 35–36

Wage determination, 263–64
"Walton's Law," 420–21, 472
  statement of, 45
"Walton's Moral Law," 415–16, 420–21
Women Shareholders in Business, Amer-
    ican Federation of, 292, 294
Worker wants, 264–65
World Bank, 537–38
World economy, recent role of U.S. in,
    170–76
World markets, 164–65
Written law, 474–75